GENTLE SHEPHERD MINISTRIES DISCIPLESHIP AND SUPPLEMENTATIONS COURSES

By

Rayola Kelley
Jeannette Haley

Hidden Manna Publications

GENTLE SHEPHERD MINISTRIES DISCIPLESHIP AND SUPPLEMENTATIONS COURSES

ISBN: 978-1-7347503-9-3

Cover artwork
"Follow Me"
Jeannette Haley

Except where otherwise indicated, all Scripture quotations in this book are taken from the King James Version of the Bible.

Hidden **M**anna **P**ublications
P.O. Box 3572
Oldtown, ID 83822
www.gentleshepherd.com

Facebook:
https://www.facebook.com/HiddenMannaPublications/

CONTENTS

Course One:
Gentle Shepherd Ministries Discipleship Course

Course Two:

Gentle Shepherd Ministries Supplementations

Gentle Shepherd Ministries Discipleship Course

Course One

By
Rayola Kelley

Gentle Shepherd Ministries Discipleship Course

How to use this material:

Supplementary materials and books have been provided to intensify the study of this course. In each of the boxes that are found in each chapter of the course, material or books about the subject being considered are identified that will elaborate, challenge, clarify, or edify. The various books have been put into volumes according to themes. The volume number along with the position of the book within the volume will be given to expedite locating it. Most of the information in the boxes is self-explanatory.

Books and studies are clearly identified. However, "sup" or "supplement" in the boxes points to the manual titled, *Gentle Shepherd Ministries Supplementation,* the second course in this book.

Certificate:

A certificate of completion of the discipleship course will be offered to anyone who presents the necessary proof that the study was completed. Proof will include a written summary of each chapter of the discipleship course as well as the answers to both the questions and tests of each book or manual. These questions and tests are not only located in the *Supplementations* of this book, but they are also located in the *Reference Study Guide* that has been made available on our website. This proof can be sent to the address provided on the website (www.gentleshepherd.com).

PREFACE

This Discipleship Course was originally prepared in January of 1992, and has been re-typed four times. The information in this course initially represented 15 years of study involving the most precious book, the Word of God. The first draft consisted of over 1,000 hours of preparation and typing, which involved a team effort.

This material has been adapted for overseas missionaries who disciple those who have not had the privilege of being exposed to the Word of God. It is simple in its presentation, yet profound enough to challenge those who hear it to live a committed and holy life. Thus far, this course has been sent to Africa, Pakistan, Cuba, the Philippines, and India.

The Discipleship Course was prepared for the purpose of laying a strong foundation by which others could be established in a sound faith upon the Immovable Rock of Ages, Jesus Christ. The goal behind this material is to keep the presentation of the basic tenets of the Christian faith simple. Simplicity ensures balance and spiritual growth.

I want to thank my precious Lord for giving me the opportunity to serve Him in this capacity. Appreciation also goes to my co-laborers in the Gospel, Jeannette Haley for ensuring the correctness of this material. I also want to thank Kitty Miller for her hard work in re-typing this present course, and to Carrie Seaney, and Donna Spencer for their support in making this material available to others.

Finally, I want to dedicate this information to all the servants of God who have a vision for the lost and dare to do something about it. God be with each of you.

April 29, 2003
Rayola Kelley

Section I

TENETS OF FAITH

Chapter 1

THE GODHEAD

Supplements:
(Before chapter 1)
What Must I Do To Be Saved? **Sup: 2**
Foundation of Our Faith, **Sup: 1, Lesson 1**
Discipleship Bible Study, **Sup: 1**
(During chapter 1)
Volume 1, Book 5
Study: *Unmasking The Cult Mentality*
Section 2
(After chapter 1)
Foundation of Our Faith, **Sup: 1**
Lesson 2

Genesis 1:1 declares,
"In the beginning God created the heaven and the earth."

Obviously, a person's life must begin and end with God. There will be no order or meaning to life outside of God. But, who is God? The word <u>God</u> means deity or divine. We know He created heaven and earth. All we see and enjoy is His handiwork. Most people sense there is something greater than themselves. Upbringing, culture, and religious encounters often determine their idea of who they perceive God to be.

Isaiah 45:21-22 make this declaration about the Creator of the world,"...there is no God else beside me; a just God and a Saviour; there is none beside me. Look unto me, and be ye saved all the ends of the earth; for I am God, and there is none else."

First, we see this God is <u>righteous</u>. Righteous is a word, which is used for just and perfect. Secondly, we read how He is <u>Savior</u>. This word implies He <u>delivers</u> us. This deliverance has something to do with saving us from something we have no control over. Three times this scripture shows us there is only one God.

In **1 Corinthians 8:4-6** we read,
"As concerning therefore the eating of those things that are offered in sacrifice unto idols, we know that an idol is nothing in the world, and that there is none other God but one. For though there be that are called gods, whether in heaven or in earth (as there be gods many, and lords many.) But to us there is but one God, the Father, of whom are all things, and we in him; and one Lord Jesus Christ, by whom are all things and we by him."

When the term "God" is used in relationship to Jesus or the Holy Ghost in the New Testament it means the Father. (See **2 Corinthians 13:14**, and refer to **1 John 3:1**.) The first three commandments deal with the issue of Jehovah God being our only God and having a proper attitude towards Him. If anything, or anyone is more important to us than God, it is an idol or 'god'. The Bible clearly tells us there is only one true God.

The key to identifying the true God is found in **Galatians 4:8**,
"Howbeit then, when ye knew not God, ye did service unto them which by nature are not gods."

The main word to note in this Scripture verse is nature. When it comes to the makeup of God it is not 1+1+1 = 3; rather, it is 1x1x1=1. One will always equal itself and God will always equal who He is. You compare Him to anything else, He will always equal deity. He will never cease to be who He is and that is why we must believe He is. (See **Hebrews 11:6**.) Nature means unchangeable characteristics that identify something. In short God is distinguished by His attributes. These characteristics of His nature include the following:

Faithful: Deuteronomy 7:9; 1 Corinthians 1:9
Immutable (unchanging): Hebrews 6:18; 13:8; James 1:17
Gentle: Psalm 18:35; 2 Corinthians 10:1
Good: Psalm 25:8; Romans 2:4
Holy: Psalm 99:9; Revelation 15:4
Great: Psalm 77:13; Isaiah 12:6
Impartial: Matthew 5:45; Acts 10:34
Jealous: Joshua 24:19-20; 1 Corinthians 10:22
Light: Psalm 27:1; Revelation 22:5
Love: Ephesians 2:4; 1 John 4:8
Omnipotent (all powerful): Psalm 115:3; Luke 1:37
Omnipresence (everywhere present): Psalm 139:8; Proverbs 15:3
Omniscience (all knowing): John 2:24; 16:30
Truth: Deuteronomy 32:4; John 14:16

(The above partial list was taken from the concise concordance found in The New Scofield Reference King James Bible; l967.)

The names of God give us insight into His nature. Here are examples of His names.

Jehovah-Elohim – The Eternal Creator (Genesis 2:4-25)
Adoni-Jehovah – The Lord our Sovereign & Master Jehovah (Exodus 15:2, 18)
Jehovah-Jireh – The Lord will see or our Provider (Genesis 22:8-14)
Jehovah-Nissi – The Lord our banner (Exodus 17:15)
Jehovah-Ropheka – The Lord our healer (Exodus 15:26)
Jehovah-Shalom – The Lord our peace (Judges 6:24)
Jehovah-Tsidkeenu – The Lord our righteousness (Jeremiah 23:6; 3:16)
Jehovah-Mekaddishkem – The Lord our sanctifer (Exodus 3l:13)
Jehovah-Saboath – The Lord of hosts (1 Samuel 1:3)
Jehovah-Shammah – The Lord is present (Ezekiel 48:35)
Jehovah-Elyon – The Lord most high (Psalm 7:17)
Jehovah-Rohi – The Lord my Shepherd (Psalm 23:1)
Jehovah-Hoseenu – The Lord our Maker (Psalm 95:6)
Jehovah-Eloheenu – the Lord our God (Psalm 99:5)

(The names of God were acquired from Dake's Annotated King James Reference Bible; l963; page 52.)

The writer of Acts makes this statement about God in **Acts 17:29**,
"...we ought not to think that the Godhead is like unto gold, or silver, or stone, graven by art and man's device."

Creation's Declaration

The Word of God shows us there are three persons who are referred to as God.

1 Corinthians 8:6 tells us,
"But to us there is but one God, the Father..."

John 1:1 says this about Jesus, the Son of God,
"In the beginning was the Word, and the Word was with God, and the Word was God."

In **Acts 5:1-4**, Peter, one of Jesus' apostles rebuked a couple because they lied about the money they promised for God's work.

This statement was made in **Acts 5:4** about The Holy Spirit,
"...thou hast not lied unto men, but unto God."

According to Biblical teachers, the name of God used in **Genesis 1:1** (God-Elohim) implies plurality. We see plurality in reference to God in the following scriptures:

Genesis 3:22 reads,
"And the Lord God said, Behold, the man is become as one of <u>us</u>, to know good and evil:..." (Emphasis added.)

Genesis 11:7 states,
"Go to, let <u>us</u> go down, and there confound their language, that they may not understand one another's speech." (Emphasis added.) See also **Genesis 1:26** and **Isaiah 6:8**.

Adonai and El Shaddai (God Almighty) denotes plurality as well. Elohim is used 2,500 times; Adonai 90 times, and El Shaddai, 48 times. (Information obtained from *Jewish Faith and the New Covenant*, Ruth Specter Lascelle, pages 62-63; I980.) There are three persons within the essence or makeup of God—the Father, and the Son and the Holy Spirit. These three are co-eternal and co-equal. They are distinct in subsistence, but have the same characteristics or substance; therefore, they equal one God in nature, status, and importance. This belief of God is known as the Doctrine of the Trinity. The King James Version of the Bible refers to this concept as the <u>"Godhead."</u>

The writer of Romans made this statement about the Godhead in **Romans 1:20**,
"For the invisible things of him from the creation of the world are clearly seen, being understood by the things that are made, even his eternal power and <u>Godhead</u>; so that they are without excuse." (Emphasis added.)

This verse in **Romans,** tells us the unseen things of God's very creation confirms the truth of the Godhead. For instance, everything is made up of unseen things such as atoms, molecules, protons, neutrons and etc. That which is seen, such as water, comes in different forms: liquid, ice, and fog depending on the environment. Although the appearance of water may vary, it is still water by nature. Although unseen, like water, the nature or attributes of God are also being fully expressed in three different persons. They manifest themselves in different ways, but each one is God by nature. Another example of the Godhead is an egg because it has three ingredients, the shell, the white, and the yoke. Each part of the egg has a distinct purpose and taste, yet all three sections are necessary to make an egg. Like the egg, each person of the Godhead has different responsibilities or functions. **John 3:17** tells us God sent His Son, Jesus Christ.

John 8:16 identifies the person of the Godhead who sent the Son,
"(God, the Son is speaking) 'And yet if I judge, my judgment is true: for I am not alone, but I and the Father that sent me."

Genesis 1:1 tells us God created the heavens and earth.

Colossians 1:15-17 gives us insight into the identity of our Creator,
(Speaking of God, the Son) "Who is the image of the invisible God, the firstborn of every creature: For by him were all things created, that are in heaven, and that are in earth, visible and invisible, whether they be thrones, or dominions, or principalities, or power: all things were created by him, and for him. And he is before all things, and by him all things consist."

1 Thessalonians 4:3 and **5:23** tells us how God sanctifies or sets man apart from evil influences to serve Him.

1 Peter 1:2 tells us what person of the Godhead sanctifies man,
"...through sanctification of the Spirit..."

Genesis 1:27 gives us another example of God's creation which speaks of the Godhead,
"So God created man in his own image, in the image of God created he him; male and female created he them."

Man is an example of the Godhead.

1 Thessalonians 5:23 gives us this insight into the makeup of man,
"And the very God of peace sanctify you wholly; and I pray God your whole spirit and soul and body be preserved blameless unto the coming of our Lord Jesus Christ."

Like his Creator, man is made up of three different parts in which he expresses his very person or personality—spirit, soul, and body. His mind is made up of the intellect, the sensibility, and the will. However, it takes child-like faith to trust in what we can't see or understand. We must approach God's Word as being true and by faith believe it is true. If God said it, I choose to believe it is so.

Personal Notes:____

____

God in Bodily Form

Colossians 2:9 makes this statement,
"For in him dwelleth all the fulness of the Godhead bodily."

Christ made this statement to Philip, one of His followers in **John 14:9**,
"...he that hath seen me hath seen the Father;..."

Why did God become flesh and come to earth?

The answer can be found in **John 3:16**,
"For God so loved the world, that he gave his only begotten Son, that whosoever believeth in him should not perish, but have everlasting life."

God loves each of us so much He sent His Son on your behalf. Jesus became a substitute for each of us. However, for the second person of the Godhead to become a substitute, Jesus had to take on the form of a man to become an acceptable sacrifice to suffice the judgment of God's Law upon all sin. (See **Hebrews 10:5**.)

The writer of Romans tells us why the Son had to come to earth for each of us in **Romans 3:10**: "...There is none righteous, no, not one."

God is a righteous God. Man's righteousness or best attempts are unacceptable to our Creator.

Isaiah 64:6 tells us how God views our best attempts to please Him,
"But we are all as an unclean thing, and all our righteousness are as filthy rags;..."

Man's unrighteous condition separates him from his Creator, and God desires to have a relationship with man. He, therefore, sent His Son to take care of our hopeless situation. This unrighteous state is referred to as sin. Sin which is known as offense to God because of transgressing His Law is due to the fact we have been born in an ungodly state of iniquity which is best described as a God-resisting disposition, which is anarchy.

2 Corinthians 5:21 tells us how the Son of God dealt with this condition,
"For he hath made him (Jesus) to be sin for us, who knew no sin; that we might be made the righteousness *of* God in him."

God's main concern is to have a relationship with each of us. This relationship results in the salvation of our souls. This is why God's focus is directed at Jesus Christ, the Son of God. The Bible tells us that both the Father and the Holy Spirit point man to Jesus Christ.

John 6:45 tells us,
"It is written in the prophets, And they shall be all taught of God. Every man therefore that hath heard, and hath learned of the Father, cometh unto me."

John 15:26 says this about the Holy Spirit,
"But when the Comforter is come, whom I will send unto you from the Father, even the Spirit of truth, which proceedeth from the Father, he shall testify of me."

Do you know God? Do you desire to know Him? He loves you and wants a relationship with you. You must recognize you are separated from Him. You must acknowledge that Christ is the only way to this relationship **(John 14:6)**.

Remember what **Isaiah 45:22** says,
"Look unto me, and be ye saved, all the ends of the earth; for I am God, and there is none else."

Personal Notes: ____

Chapter 2

THE NATURE OF SIN

Supplements: *(Before Chapter 2)* Foundation of our Faith **Sup. 1, Lessons 3 & 8** *(During Study)* **Volume 1** **Book 2:** *The Anatomy of Sin* **Book 5:** ***Study: Unmasking the*** *Cult Mentality* **Section 3:** Sin

Sin is independence, rebellion, and disobedience towards God. It is a spiritual disease of man's soul. It is man doing it his way rather than God's way. Sin came through the disobedience of the first man, Adam. Adam lived in a perfect place: the Garden of Eden. God asked him to not eat of the fruit of one tree in the garden. Adam disobeyed and ate the fruit. The result was the sinful state being passed down through all mankind.

Romans 5:12 makes this statement,
"Wherefore, as by one man sin entered into the world, and death by sin; and so death passed upon all men, for that all have sinned."

Because of Adam's rebellion in the garden, all men operate under the dictates of sin **(Romans 6:18-20).** Sin works within the *disposition* of man, and results in death. Death means separation. Physical death means our spirit and soul become separated from our body. Spiritual death is when our spirit and soul are separated from God.

I John 1:8 & 10 says this about sin,
"If we say that we have no sin, we deceive ourselves, and the truth is not in us. If we say that we have not sinned, we make him a liar, and his word is not in us."

By denying our condition of sin, we show we lack truth and are calling God a liar.

The truth is defined in **John 14:6**,
"Jesus saith unto him, I am the way, the truth, and the life: no man cometh unto the Father, but by me."

Jesus Christ is the summary of all truth. If the truth is not in you, then eternal life is not in you.

Personal Notes: ____

____

The Progression of Sin

It is important to understand how sin works. It is independent and selfish; therefore, it has no heart inclination towards God. It justifies sin and makes it right in a person's mind. The writer of Romans gives us this insight into our sinful disposition.

Consider how sin affects our motivation and activities according to **Romans 7:18**,
"For I know that in me (that is, in my flesh) dwelleth no good thing: for to will is present with me; but how to perform that which is good I find not."

Romans 1:24, 26, and **28** explains how sin starts and finishes in man. These Scriptures show that judgment simply means God turns a person over to his or her desires to pay the consequences.

Romans 1:24 tells us,
"Wherefore God also gave them up to uncleanness through the lusts of their own hearts, to dishonour their own bodies between themselves."

All sin begins in the heart. (See **Proverbs 4:23.**) Both the prophet Jeremiah and the Lord Jesus Christ confirmed this fact.

Jeremiah 17:9 says,
"The heart is deceitful above all things, and desperately wicked: who can know it?"

Jesus said this in **Matthew 15:17-19** to the religious leaders of His day,
"Do not ye yet understand, that whatsoever entereth in at the mouth goeth into the belly, and is cast out into the draught? But those things which proceed out of the mouth come forth from the heart; and they defile the man. For out of the heart proceed evil thoughts, murders, adulteries, fornications, thefts, false witness, blasphemies:"

Romans 1:26 tells us the next stage of sin,
"For this cause God gave them up unto vile affections *(their perversion): for* even their women did change the natural use into that which is against nature." *(Emphasis added.)*

This verse shows us that after sin takes root in our heart, it will manifest in outward bodily actions. This is when the consequences will follow.

Galatians 6:7-8 talks about reaping the outcome for our actions,
"Be not deceived; God is not mocked: for whatsoever a man soweth, that shall he also reap. For he that soweth to his flesh shall of the flesh reap corruption; but he that soweth to the Spirit shall of the Spirit reap life everlasting."

<u>Lust</u> means strong craving or desire.

The book of James gives us an insight into how a man's lust works in **James 1:13-15**:
"Let no man say when he is tempted, I am tempted of God: for God cannot be tempted with evil, neither tempteth he any man: But every man is tempted, when he is drawn away of his own lust, and enticed. Then when lust hath conceived, it bringeth forth sin: and sin, when it is finished, bringeth forth death.

<u>Temptation</u> in this text means to attract someone to do evil. God does not do this, but man's self-centered disposition will. It serves as an open door to the attractions of the world and the snares of Satan.

Romans 1:26 gives us the final result of sin,
"And even as they did not like to retain God in their knowledge, God gave them over to a reprobate mind, to do those things which are not convenient."

In order for sin to reign in our hearts, we must become deceived about it being in our lives.

The writer of Hebrews makes this statement in **Hebrews 3:12-13**,
"Take heed, brethren, lest there be in any of you an evil heart of unbelief, in departing from the living God. But exhort one another daily, while it is called to day; lest any of you be hardened through the deceitfulness of sin."

A corrupt mind with its vain imaginations deludes the individual about his or her sinful condition. (See **2 Corinthians 10:3-5; Ephesians 4:17-19; 2 Thessalonians 2:9-12.)**

The final result and attitude of man can be found in **Isaiah 5:20**,
"Woe unto them that call evil good, and good evil; that put darkness for light, and light for darkness; that put bitter for sweet, and sweet for bitter!"

A perverted mind will call evil good and good evil. This implies delusion. Great disaster will come to such a person.

The Root of Sin

The root of sin can be found in the temptation of Jesus in **Matthew 4:1-11**. We must first lay a foundation and explain the temptation of Jesus.

Hebrews 4:15 tells us,
"For we have not an high priest which cannot be touched with the feeling of our infirmities; but was in all points tempted like as we are, yet without sin."

This Scripture verse shows us Jesus was tempted in every way we are tempted.

John summarizes sin in **1 John 2:16**,
"For all that is in the world, the lust of the flesh, and the lust of the eyes, and the pride of life, is not of the Father, but is of the world."

The lust of the flesh includes such sins as sexual immorality, witchcraft, hatred, jealousy, anger, selfish ambition, envy, drunkenness, and drug abuse. (See **Proverbs 6:16-19; Romans 1:28-32; Galatians 5:19-21** and **Revelation 21:8**.) The lust of the eyes includes adultery and a strong desire to gain or possess that which is off limits or hold our affections captive. The pride of life involves the exaltation of self.

Personal Notes: ____

____

Satan tempted Jesus in all three areas: The word <u>Satan</u> means enemy of God.

Jesus made this comment about Satan in **John 14:30**,
"Hereafter I will not talk much with you: for the prince of this world cometh, and hath nothing in me."

Note the first part of **1 John 2:16**,
"For all that is in the world..."

Jesus tells us in **John 14:30** that Satan is the prince of this world. Prince means ruler. The writer of **2 Corinthians 4:4** confirms this by referring to Satan as the god of this world. In **Matthew 4:1-11** we see the ruler of this world tempting Jesus in the wilderness. The first temptation involved bread. Christ was hungry after being in the wilderness without food for 40 days.

Matthew 4:3-4 gives us this account,
"And when the tempter came to him, he said, If thou be the Son of God, command that these stones be made bread. But he answered and said, It is written, Man shall not live by bread alone, but by every word that proceedeth out of the mouth of God." (Refer to **Deuteronomy 8:3.)**

Satan tempted Jesus' flesh. But Jesus knew there was something far greater weighing in the balance than His physical hunger. He knew that souls were more important to the Father.

In **John 6:32-33, 35,** Jesus gives us this insight,
"...but my Father giveth you the true bread from heaven. For the bread of God is he which cometh down from heaven, and giveth life unto the world. And Jesus said unto them, I am the bread of life: he that cometh to me shall never hunger; and he that believeth on me shall never thirst." (Refer to **Exodus 16:4, 14-15.)**

Matthew 4:6-7 tells us about the second test,
"...If thou be the Son of God, cast thyself down: for it is written, He shall give his angels charge concerning thee: and in their hands they shall bear thee up, lest at any time thou dash thy foot against a stone. Jesus said unto him, It is written again, Thou shalt not tempt the Lord thy God." (Refer to **Psalm 91:11-12** and **Deuteronomy 6:16.)**

This temptation involved the pride of life. Jesus is the Son of God. What would it have hurt if Jesus proved it? Satan knew who Jesus was. The enemy of God wanted Him to submit Himself to a foolish game. Signs followed Jesus that identified Him as the Promised One. He even brought this out when John the Baptist questioned Him about being the Messiah, but He was not here to prove His identity to the unbelieving with performances. He is who He is. It was clear that His face was set towards the cross where He would give His life for each of us. (See **Luke 9:51**.*)*

Philippians 2:8 says,
"And being found in fashion as a man, he humbled himself, and became obedient unto death, even the death of the cross."

This third test involved the lust of the eyes.

We read this account in **Matthew 4:8-10**,
"Again, the devil taketh him up into an exceeding high mountain, and sheweth him all the kingdoms of the world, and the glory of them; And saith unto him, All these things will I give thee, if thou wilt fall down and worship me. Then saith Jesus unto him, Get thee hence, Satan: for it is written, Thou shalt worship the Lord thy God, and him only shalt thou serve." (Refer to **Deuteronomy 6:13**.)

Satan offered Jesus all of his kingdoms. He appealed to His physical sight. In Jesus' final reply we sense Satan's real temptations. It was more than just the test of the flesh, pride of life, or lust of the eyes. He was tempting Jesus, who was his Creator, to worship or become subject to him. Satan desires worship. Is this any different than man who tries to get God to bow down to his whims by giving him his way regardless of whether it is right or wrong or according to His perfect will? It is vital to keep in mind every time people submit to the sins of the world they submit to Satan. Satan is the god or ruler of this world. Subjection to or worship of the devil can be summarized in one sin. This sin is idolatry. Idolatry is to worship or exalt something above God.

We read this statement in **1 Corinthians 10:13-14**,
"There hath no temptation taken you but such as is common to man: but God is faithful, who will not suffer you to be tempted above that ye are able; but will with the temptation also make a way to escape, that ye may be able to bear it. Wherefore, my dearly beloved, flee from idolatry."

We will be tempted to submit to the god of this world, but God will provide a way out. We need to be like our Lord and resist temptation with the Word of God. We need to flee from our circumstances and submit to God. (Refer to **2 Timothy 2:22**.)

James 4:7 instructs us in this way,
"Submit yourselves therefore to God. Resist the devil, and he will flee from you."

The Bible emphasizes that Jesus was without sin. The salvation of souls hung in the balance when Satan tempted Jesus. The Lord came to set each of us free from Satan in order to serve God. Sin must no longer reign in our lives. Only God's grace must abound.

Grace is God's undeserved favor extended to man. It serves as the limitation to sin, not the permission to commit it. We do not deserve God's salvation, but because of His grace He freely offers it to each of us. If Christ had submitted to Satan's temptation, we would not have the hope of eternal life. Who are you submitting to? Are you serving God or Satan? (Refer to **Joshua 24:15.)**

Romans 5:21 tells us,
"That as sin hath reigned unto death, even so might grace reign through righteousness unto eternal life by Jesus Christ our Lord."

We will conclude this subject with **Romans 6:1-2**,
"What shall we say then? Shall we continue in sin, that grace may abound? God forbid. How shall we, that are dead to sin, live any longer therein?"

These Scripture verses show us the type of attitude we must have towards sin. (Refer to **1 John 3:5-10**.)

Personal Notes:____

____

____

Chapter 3

THE GOSPEL

Supplements:
Volume 2
Book 2:
Revelation of the Cross
Volume 1 Book 5:
Study: *Unmasking The Cult Mentality*
Section 3

The word gospel means good news. The good news which is extended from God to man is the hope of eternal life.

The writer of Romans explains the power of the Gospel in **Romans 1:16-17**,
"For I am not ashamed of the gospel of Christ: for it is the power of God unto salvation to every one that believeth; to the Jew first, and also to the Greek. For therein is the righteousness of God revealed from faith to faith: as it is written, The just shall live by faith."

In **1 Corinthians 15:1-4** the writer, the Apostle Paul, tells us what the message of the Gospel is,
"Moreover, brethren, I declare unto you the gospel which I preached unto you, which also ye have received, and wherein ye stand; By which also ye are saved, if ye keep in memory what I preached unto you, unless you have believed in vain. For I delivered unto you first of all that which I also received, how that Christ died for our sins according to the scriptures; And that he was buried, and that he rose again the third day according to the scriptures."

There are four points to the gospel message. The first one is Christ died for man's sins.

Romans 5:6 tells us,
"For when we were yet without strength, in due time Christ died for the ungodly."

In the day of Jesus, the Jewish nation made sacrifices for their sins. This sacrifice was a way of atoning for their sins. They used animals. The one animal they used especially for their religious celebrations was the lamb. This was especially true for the Passover celebration, which marked Israel's deliverance from Egypt. (See **Exodus 11-12**.)

John 1:29 gives us this insight about Jesus Christ, the Son of God,
"The next day John seeth Jesus coming unto him, and saith, Behold the Lamb of God, which taketh away the sin of the world." *(See also **Revelation 5:6.**)*

Jesus' death came by way of the cross. The Roman soldiers used this method of a torturous death on those who were not Roman citizens. Christ became a sacrifice from God for our sins. The Bible tells us Jesus was beaten and His body broken. Isaiah gives us a descriptive picture of the final result of His physical sufferings. (Refer also to **Psalm 22:1, 6-7, 11-18; Zechariah 12:10 & 13:6**.)

Isaiah 52:14 gives us this picture,
"As many were astonied at thee; his visage was so marred more than any man, and his form more than the sons of men."

Isaiah 53:4-5 gives us a detail description how Jesus paid the complete price for our redemption,
"Surely he hath borne our griefs, and carried our sorrows: yet we did esteem him stricken, smitten of God, and afflicted. But he was wounded for our transgressions, he was bruised for our iniquities: the chastisement of our peace was upon him; and with his stripes we are healed."

Jesus took upon Himself our sins, guilt, and condemnation. By doing this He provided a way in which man could be reconciled back to his Creator, producing peace in the soul.

Colossians 1:19-20 declares this about Jesus Christ,
"For it pleased the Father that in him should all fulness dwell; And, having made peace through the blood of his cross, by him to reconcile all things unto himself; by him, I say whether they be things in earth, or things in heaven." (See also **Ephesians 2:12-17**.)

The word, reconcile means to restore to a close relationship.

Personal Notes: ____

____

The Death

The second point of the Gospel is the death of Christ. Although we mentioned this in showing He died for sinners, we still must understand the full meaning of His death.

Romans 4:25 tell us,
"Who was delivered for our offences, and was raised again for our justification."

Jesus had to first die for sin in order to bring justification to man. Justification means to set right. The writer of Corinthians, the Apostle Paul, gives us a clear picture of the effects of death.

I Corinthians 15:56 says,
"The sting of death is sin; and the strength of sin is the law."

There is a curse or power, which comes with death. Christ destroyed its power with His death. (See **Galatians 3:13**.)

Hebrews 2:14-15 confirms this thought:
"Forasmuch then as the children are partakers of flesh and blood, he also himself likewise took part of the same; that through death he might destroy him that had the power of death that is, the devil; And deliver them who through fear of death were all their lifetime subject to bondage."

We do have victory over death through Christ. We therefore, can rejoice.

1 Corinthians 15:57 makes this comment,
"But thanks be to God, which giveth us the victory through our Lord Jesus Christ."

Personal Notes: ____

____

The Burial

The third meaning to the message of the Gospel is Christ's burial.

Colossians 2:12-13 makes this declaration,
"Buried with him in baptism, wherein also ye are risen with him through the faith of the operation of God, who hath raised him from the dead. And you, being dead in your sins and the uncircumcision of your flesh, hath he quickened together with him, having forgiven you all trespasses."

Christ's burial implies all the power and consequences of sin were taken to the grave. Sin no longer has any power or right to our lives. Believers can relate Christ's burial to the death and burial of the "old life" or the reign of sin. As we know, if something is dead, we must bury it. Therefore, our former life of sin must be buried in order for a new life to come forth. (Refer also to **Romans 6:3-12.)**

Ephesians 4:22-24 says this in regard to the "old life",
"That ye put off concerning the former conversation the old man, which is corrupt according to the deceitful lusts; And be renewed in the spirit of your mind; And that ye put on the new man, which after God is created in righteousness and true holiness."

The Apostle Paul told how he dealt with his "old life" in **1 Corinthians 15:31**,
"...I die daily."

Paul also tells us what it means to put to death this "old life" in **Colossians 3:5-6, 8-9**,
"Mortify therefore your members which are upon the earth; fornication, uncleanness, inordinate affection, evil concupiscence, and covetousness, which is idolatry: For which things' sake the wrath of God cometh on the children of disobedience: But now ye also put off all these; anger, wrath, malice, blasphemy, filthy communication out of your mouth. Lie not one to another, seeing that ye have put off the old man with his deeds."

Here we see we must put to death our "old life". This means we must separate ourselves from our former lifestyles. We then must die to self by taking our "old way" and burying it. Like Jesus who took the power of sin to the grave to silence its tormenting ways, we must make sure it never reigns in our lives. (See **Matthew 9:16-17** and **Titus 3:5-7**.)

1 John 3:5-6 tells us,
"And ye know that he was manifested to take away our sins; and in him is no sin. Whosoever abideth in him sinneth not; whosoever sinneth hath not seen him, neither known him."

Personal Notes: ____

____

The Resurrection

The last and final part of the Gospel message is Christ's resurrection. The word resurrection means to return to life after death has occurred. The resurrection of Christ is the heart of the Gospel.

The Apostle Paul made this statement about the importance of the resurrection of Christ in **1 Corinthians 15:14**,
"And if Christ be not risen, then is our preaching vain, and your faith is also vain."

If Christ had not been raised from the grave, man would still be dead in his sins awaiting God's wrath.

1 Corinthians 15:17 confirms this thought,
"And if Christ be not raised, your faith is vain; ye are yet in your sins."

Our hope of being delivered from sin and death rests totally in the empty grave of Christ.

Christ made this statement concerning his resurrection power in **John 11:25-26**,
"Jesus said unto her, I am the resurrection, and the life: he that believeth in me, though he were dead, yet shall he live: And whosoever liveth and believeth in me shall never die. Believeth thou this?"

By believing in Christ, we are assured of being raised up with Him.

Ephesians 2:6 tells us,
"And hath raised us up together, and made us sit together in heavenly places in Christ Jesus."

Colossians 3:1-3 gives us this instruction,
"If ye then be risen with Christ, seek those things which are above, where Christ sitteth on the right hand of God. Set your affection on things above, not on things on the earth. For ye are dead, and your life is hid with Christ in God."

The Apostle Paul in **Romans 6:4** informs us what being raised with Christ implies,
"...that like as Christ was raised up from the dead by the glory of the Father, even so we also should walk in newness of life."

Paul describes this new life in **Colossians 3:10, 12-13**,
"And have put on the new man, which is renewed in knowledge after the image of him that created him: Put on therefore, as the elect of God, holy and beloved, bowels of mercies, kindness, humbleness of mind, meekness, longsuffering; Forbearing one another, and forgiving one another, if any man have a quarrel against any: even as Christ forgave you, so also do ye."

Personal Notes: ______________________________

____

Beware of Another Gospel

Supplement:
Volume 5
Book 2: *Presentation of the Gospel*

The Gospel is the death, burial, and resurrection of Jesus Christ. This message brings the hope of salvation to all who will believe it.

The Apostle Paul made this statement in **1 Corinthians 2:2**,
"For I determined not to know any thing among you, save Jesus Christ, and him crucified."

The Apostle Paul committed his whole life to sharing the Gospel message.

In **Galatians 1:8-9** he tells us to beware of any other Gospel,
"But though we, or an angel from heaven, preach any other gospel unto you than that which we have preached unto you, let him be accursed. As we said before, so say I now again, If any man preach any other gospel unto you than that ye have received, let him be accursed."

2 Corinthians 11:3-4 says,
"But I fear, lest by any means, as the serpent beguiled Eve through his subtility, so your minds should be corrupted from the simplicity that is in Christ. For if he that cometh preacheth another Jesus, whom we have not preached, or if ye receive another spirit, which ye have not received, or another gospel, which ye have not accepted, ye might well bear with him."

There are other gospels and other Christ's. We must beware of what we accept as truth.

Matthew 7:13-14 makes this statement,
"Enter ye in at the strait gate: for wide is the gate, and broad is the way, that leadeth to destruction, and many there be which go in thereat: Because strait is the gate, and narrow is the way, which leadeth unto life, and few there be that find it."

The way to heaven is narrow. Only through believing in the true Christ will we live eternally with God. Do you know Jesus Christ? If you died today, would you wake up in the arms of Jesus? If your answers are no to each question, you need to know the Gospel message is for you.

Acts 4:12 tells us,
"Neither is there salvation in any other: for there is none other name under heaven given among men, whereby we must be saved."

Personal Notes: ______________________________

____

____

Chapter 4

FOUNDATION FOR BELIEF

> **Supplements:**
> *(Before Chapter 4)*
> Foundation of Our Faith, **Sup. 1, Lesson 4**
> **Volume 2**
> **Book 1:** *He Actually Thought it Not Robbery*

Scripture compares the Christian life to a building. Buildings are comprised of the foundation and the structure. God has designed the foundation and He desires to make man the acceptable structure in which to reside.

Ephesians 2:22 confirms this thought,
"In whom ye also are builded together for an habitation of God through the Spirit."

1 Corinthians 3:9 concurs with this concept as well:
"For we are labourers together with God: ye are God's husbandry, ye are God's building."

Before a healthy structure can be prepared, a foundation must first be laid. In the secular world there are different foundations. The area determines the foundation used. Elements such as soil condition play a part in the support laid. In the spiritual life there is only one correct foundation to build upon.

Personal Notes: ____

____

The Apostle Paul established the correct foundation for the Christian's life in **1 Corinthians 3:11**,
"For other foundation can no man lay than that is laid, which is Jesus Christ."

When it comes to true faith or eternal purposes, Christ is the only correct foundation. He serves as our example in all spiritual matters. (Refer to **John 13:13-15** and **1 Peter 2:21**.) It means spiritual ruin to those who lack Him as their spiritual foundation

Isaiah 28:16 tells us,
"Therefore thus saith the Lord GOD, Behold, I lay in Zion for a foundation a stone, a tried stone, a precious corner stone, a sure foundation; he that believeth shall not make haste."

Jesus is also our spiritual cornerstone.

The letter of Peter, in compliance with the prophet Isaiah, says this in **1 Peter 2:6**,
"...Behold, I lay in Sion, a chief corner stone, elect, precious: and he that believeth on him shall not be confounded."

Structures were built to conform to the cornerstone. Our beliefs, motivations, and lifestyles must line up with our spiritual cornerstone, Jesus Christ. The goal of Jesus Christ is to build a church. This church would be comprised of people who would believe Him for His salvation.

Jesus confirmed this to one of his followers, in **Matthew 16:18**,
"And I say also unto thee, That thou art Peter, and upon this rock *(the rock is Jesus)* I will build my church; and the gates of hell shall not prevail against it." *(*Emphasis added.) (Refer also to **Colossians 1:15-19.***)*

Peter means little stone or pebble. In Acts 2 we see the fulfillment of this Scripture. Peter shared the message of Christ with multitudes of people.

Acts 2:41 tells us,
"Then they that gladly received his word were baptized: and the same day there were added unto them about three thousand souls."

Acts 2:47 concludes with this statement,
"...And the Lord added to the church daily such as should be saved."

Peter confirms this thought in **1 Peter 2:5** with these words,
"Ye also, as lively stones, are built up a spiritual house, an holy priesthood, to offer up spiritual sacrifices, acceptable to God by Jesus Christ." (See **Hebrews 13:15-16** and **1 Peter 2:5** for what constitute acceptable sacrifices.)

Personal Notes: ____

____

____

Who Do You Say I Am?

Supplements:
Biggest Little Word
Sup. 3
(After Chapter 4)
What Are You Doing With Jesus?
Sup. 2

We must know Jesus in a personal way to insure a right foundation.

In Jesus' confrontation with Peter in **Matthew 16:13 & 16**, He asked him an important question,
"...Whom do men say that I the Son of man am? And Simon Peter answered and said, Thou art the Christ, the Son of the Living God."

Peter acknowledged the identity of Christ. The word Christ means "the Messiah" or "the Anointed one." To be anointed means you have been entrusted with the power and authority to carry out a specific duty.

Luke 4:18-19 tells us what Christ's purpose was as the Messiah,
"The Spirit of the Lord is upon me, because he hath anointed me to preach the gospel to the poor; he hath sent me to heal the brokenhearted, to preach deliverance to the captives, and recovering of sight to the blind, to set at liberty them that are bruised, To preach the acceptable year of the Lord." *(*Refer to **Isaiah 61:1-2**.)

Jesus came to set people free from the affects and consequences of sin.

Matthew 9:10-13 tells us,
"And it came to pass, as Jesus sat at meat in the house, behold, many publicans and sinners came and sat down with him and his disciples. And when the Pharisees saw it, they said unto his disciples, 'Why eateth your Master with publicans and sinners?' But when

Jesus heard that he said unto them, They that be whole need not a physician, but they that are sick. But go ye and learn what that meaneth, I will have mercy, and not sacrifice: for I am not come to call the righteous, but sinners to repentance." *(See also* **Hosea 6:6**.*)*

Isaiah 53:5 states,
"...and with his stripes we are healed."

Jesus came to set people free from the dictates of sin. He came to heal mankind spiritually and physically.

John 21:25 gives this insight into the affect Christ had on this earth,
"And there are also many other things which Jesus did, the which, if they should be written every one, I suppose that even the world itself could not contain the books that should be written. Amen."

We are once again reminded of God's motivation in sending Christ in **Romans 5:8**,
"But God commendeth his love toward us, in that, while we were yet sinners, Christ died for us."

Jesus Christ is the Son of God. This means He is the sole revealer of God's love, grace, and truth to mankind. He came to earth to set man free by offering Himself as a sacrifice.

1 Peter 3:18 gives us this insight,
"For Christ also hath once suffered for sins, the just for the unjust, that he might bring us to God, being put to death in the flesh, but quickened by the Spirit."

John 3:18 declares,
"He that believeth on him is not condemned: but he that believeth not is condemned already, because he hath not believed in the name of the only begotten Son of God."

1 John 5:11-12 states,
"And this is the record, that God hath given to us eternal life, and this life is in his Son. He that hath the Son hath life; and he that hath not the Son of God hath not life."

The Jesus Christ of the Bible is the only sure foundation upon which to build our spiritual lives. Check out your foundation. Is it established on religion rather than a relationship with God through Jesus Christ?

Maybe you have based your life on "good works" rather than what God has accomplished through the death of His Son. Your spiritual well-being for now and eternity rests on this one issue.

Personal Notes: ____

____

____

Chapter 5

BUILDING ON GOD'S FOUNDATION

Supplement: Volume 5 Book 1: *The Issues of Life*

We have established the spiritual foundation. Christianity is a life that must be walked out. It is not a matter of who you think you are in God that counts, rather it is about who He becomes in you. Now we must construct the believer's spiritual life according to God's plan.

The first clue of this building process is found in **Matthew 7:24-27**
"Therefore whosoever heareth these sayings of mine, and doeth them, I will liken him unto a wise man, which built his house upon a rock. And the rain descended, and the floods came, and the winds blew, and beat upon that house; and it fell not: for it was founded upon a rock. And every one that heareth these sayings of mine, and doeth them not, shall be likened unto a foolish man, which built his house upon the sand: And the rain descended, and the floods came, and the winds blew, and beat upon that house; and it fell: and great was the fall of it."

To endure the storms of life we must obey the commandments of God. These commandments are found in the Bible. (Refer to **James 1:21-25**.)

The Apostle Paul said this concerning the purpose of the Word of God in **2 Timothy 3:16-17**,
"All scripture is given by inspiration of God, and is profitable for doctrine, for reproof, for correction, for instruction in righteousness: That the man of God may be perfect, thoroughly furnished unto all good works."

Many people use the Bible for personal vainglory. They glory in their knowledge of it and their ability to argue all points of doctrine. Clearly, the instructions of the Bible are not designed for such purposes. They are to bring Jesus' followers to spiritual maturity **(Hebrews 5:11-6:2)**. This maturity will produce a life of service for the glory of God. Spiritual growth takes place as believers allow the Word to align them to the revelation of Jesus Christ. Revelation means to uncover. The truth concerning the Person of Jesus Christ and His plan for mankind must unfold throughout scripture. (See also **2 Peter 1:19-21**.)

1 Peter 1:13-14 gives us insight into this matter,
"Wherefore gird up the loins of your mind, be sober, and hope to the end for the grace that is to be brought unto you at the revelation of Jesus Christ; As obedient children, not fashioning yourselves according to the former lusts in your ignorance."

Jesus is the Living Word **(John 1:1)**. If we do not come to a revelation of Jesus Christ through His written Word, it will become a dead letter to us. If it is dead-letter, it will not be able to penetrate our hearts.

Paul warns of this condition in **Romans 7:6**:
"But now we are delivered from the law, that being dead wherein we were held; that we should serve in newness of spirit, and not in the oldness of the letter."

Personal Notes: ____

____

Proof of Discipleship

Supplements: Progression 1 & 2 Sup. 3

The relationship Jesus calls believers to is that of a teacher to a student. Jesus was called Rabbi which means master, teacher, or doctor, (specifically teacher of the law). He referred to His followers as disciples or students, (followers of His teachings). There were distinct responsibilities of the disciples of Christ. They are summarized in these categories:

***The Cross** ***Love** ***Obedience**

Jesus made this statement in **Luke 14:26-27**,
"If any man come to me, and hate not his father, and mother, and wife, and children, and brethren, and sisters, yea, and his own life also, he cannot be my disciple. And whosoever doth not bear his cross, and come after me, cannot be my disciple."

The cross is symbolic of death to the self-life. Denial of self entails both suffering and discipline. This type of suffering is the means of learning acceptable obedience to God. Jesus confirmed this by leaving us with an example of suffering. (See **2 Timothy 3:12; Hebrews 5:8-9** and **1 Peter 2:21**.)

Self includes attitudes, lifestyles, personal rights, and priorities. This type of self-denial includes a willingness to forsake (hate) everything including families, homes, and life to follow the Master. It is a sold-out, consecrated life for the glory of God that is being consumed by His love that makes all other loyalties and allegiances pale in comparison to it.

The Apostle Paul made this statement about the work of the cross in **Galatians 2:20**,
"I am crucified with Christ: nevertheless I live; yet not I, but Christ liveth in me: and the life which I now live in the flesh I live by the faith of the Son of God, who loved me, and gave himself for me."

The purpose of the cross is to conform us to the image of Christ. (Refer to **John 12:32**.)

Romans 8:29 shows us this is the plan of God,
"For whom he did foreknow, he also did predestinate to be conformed to the image of his Son, that he might be the firstborn among many brethren."

Personal Notes: ____

____

Jesus tells us in **John 13:34-35**,
"A new commandment I give unto you, That ye love one another; as I have loved you, that ye also love one another. By this shall all men know that ye are my disciples, if ye have love one to another." (Refer to **1 Peter 4:8** and **1 John 4:16-19**.)

Love proves Christ is in our life.

John brought this out in **1 John 4:7-8**,
"Beloved, let us love one another: for love is of God; and everyone that loveth is born of God, and knoweth God. He that loveth not knoweth not God; for God is love."

God's love must be the motivation behind the disciple's life of service. (Refer to **Romans 5:5** and **2 Corinthians 5:14-15**.) Without this love his or her service to God will become an unattractive noise that offers nothing, and will be void of heavenly rewards **(1 Corinthians 13:1-3).**

Personal Notes: ____

____

Jesus made this declaration in **John 8:31-32**,
"Then Jesus said to those Jews which believed on him, If ye continue in my word, then are ye my disciples indeed; And ye shall know the truth, and the truth shall make you free."

Obedience to our Lord's instructions is necessary! But some Christians who have the Word of God available to them see the Word as a burden rather than a privilege. It is the very milk, bread, and meat that sustains believers in their lives **(John 6:35; 63; Hebrews 5:12-13)**. Sadly, improper attitudes towards the Word of God will cause a spiritual famine in the land **(Amos 8:11)**.

1 Samuel 15:22 puts obedience in this perspective
"...Behold, to obey is better than sacrifice,..."

To obey our Master's teachings will insure liberty. We will have freedom from guilt, condemnation, and delusion. We will know joy as we see a greater revelation of Jesus Christ, the summary of all truth. We must fight for this freedom. The Bible warns us to beware of teachers and teachings which will lead us away from the truth of Jesus Christ.

Jesus gave us a warning in **Matthew 24:24**,
"For there shall arise false Christs, and false prophets, and shall shew great signs and wonders; insomuch that, if it were possible, they shall deceive the very elect." (Refer to **2 Corinthians 11:3-4** and **13-15**.)

The Apostle Paul gives us this warning in **1 Timothy 4:1**,
"Now the Spirit speaketh expressly, that in the latter times some shall depart from the faith, giving heed to seducing spirits, and doctrines of devils."

Ephesians 4:13-14 gives us the key to recognizing false doctrine,
"Till we all come in the unity of the faith, and of the knowledge of the Son of God, unto a perfect man, unto the measure of the stature of the fullness of Christ: That we henceforth be no more children, tossed to and fro, and carried about with every wind of doctrine, by the sleight of men, and cunning craftiness, whereby they lie in wait to deceive"

Maturing in the knowledge of Christ will protect us from deception.

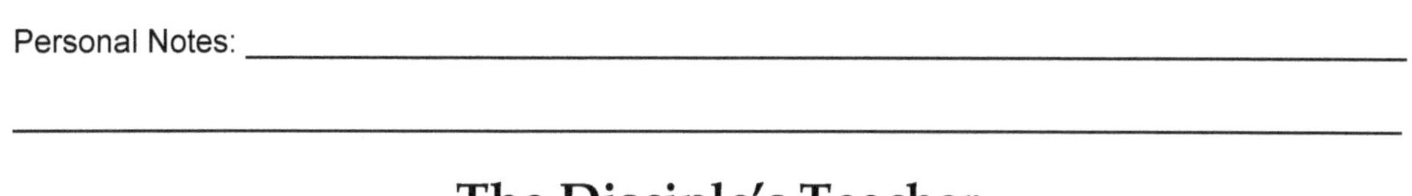
Personal Notes: ______________________________

____

The Disciple's Teacher

We must keep in mind the Bible is a spiritual book. It is a diary and expression of God's love, mercy, and grace being freely extended to man. It reveals His will, desire, and purpose for man in the spiritual kingdom that He is building. To understand this spiritual Book, we must allow the spiritual teacher to lead us into all truth. (See **Ephesians 1:17**.)

The Gospel of John identifies our spiritual teacher in **John 14:26**,
"But the Comforter, which is the Holy Ghost, whom the Father will send in my name, he shall teach you all things, and bring all things to your remembrance, whatsoever I have said unto you." (Refer also to **John 16:13**.)

The Holy Spirit will ensure a right foundation. He will bring life to dead-letter doctrine, a greater revelation of Christ, and maturity to our life. He will give us purpose and direction. (See also **Mark 13:11**.)

The Apostle Paul makes this statement about the work of the Holy Spirit in **Philippians 1:6**,
"Being confident of this very thing, that he which hath begun a good work in you will perform it until the day of Jesus Christ."

Do you desire to have a beautiful life? Accept the challenge of the cross. Ask the Lord to give you His love. Determine in your heart to obey Him. Give the Holy Spirit permission to lead you into all truth about Jesus. Allow Him to bring the necessary changes to your life for the glory of God.

Personal Notes: ______________________________

____

Chapter 6

THE INFLUENCE AND POWER OF GOD'S WORD

Supplements:
(For chapters 6-9)
Volume 1
Book 1: *My Words are Spirit and Life*
Volume 1, Book 5
Study: *Unmasking The Cult Mentality*

In order to be obedient to God, we must know His Word. If you do not know His Word, you will not know how to conduct your life. This lack of knowledge will mean destruction.

The prophet Hosea confirms this fact in **Hosea 4:6a**,
"My people are destroyed for lack of knowledge:"

There is much said about the Word of God. We know it is eternal.

This declaration was made in **Psalm 119:89**,
"For ever, O Lord, thy word is settled in heaven."

Jesus tells us in **Matthew 5:18** that all prophecies will be fulfilled:
"For verily I say unto you, Till heaven and earth pass, one jot or one tittle shall in no wise pass from the law, till all be fulfilled."

The word fulfilled implies completion. The word prophecy means to foretell events uttered by divine inspiration. It also means teaching the revelation of the will of God. The Bible is God's infallible Word written to man. Infallible means without error. Therefore, there is nothing lacking in His Word. It contains everything man needs to know to embrace the reality of God and the salvation He freely offers. In **Psalm 119** we get a clear picture of this valuable Book. The Bible is referred to as the following:

His ways (testimonies) – **119:3**	His precepts – **119:4**
His statutes – **119:2**	His commandments – **119:6**
His righteous laws (judgment) – **119:7**	His word – **119:9**
His law – **119:34**	Our Counselors – **119:24**

The combination of all these words gives us a complete picture of the Bible. For instance, as our law, it gives us direction, teaching, and instruction. As God's testimonies (ways) it establishes a witness that testifies of the holy attributes of God. As our Lord's precepts, statues, and commandments they represent His doctrines, ordinances, rules, and regulations. As His word, each believer will be exposed to His expression and thought. In the context of His judgments (righteous law), discernment is produced. Serving in the position of our counselors it will serve as our capable spiritual advisors.

Jesus adds the word "scripture" to complete the description of the Bible in **John 10:34-36**. The word Scripture means the written Word.

The goal of the written Word can be summarized in **John 5:39**,
"Search the scriptures; for in them ye think ye have eternal life: and they are they which testify of me.

The main purpose of the written Word is to lead man to Jesus Christ and His salvation. This goal is the main theme found in the Word of God.

Personal Notes: ______________________________

____

The Author of the Bible

We have been considering the power and purpose of the Bible. The power of it is found in the revelation of Jesus Christ. The purpose of God's word is to lead man into eternal life. The authority of His Word is found in the fact it was inspired by our God. Inspiration means inbreathed by God.

We are reminded of Paul's words in **2 Timothy 3:16**,
"All scripture is given by inspiration of God,..."

2 Peter 1:20-21 gives us this assurance about the Word,
"Knowing this first, that no prophecy of the scripture is of any private interpretation. For the prophecy came not in old time by the will of man: but holy men of God spake as they were moved by the Holy Ghost."

Godly men wrote the Bible as the Holy Spirit moved on them. Therefore, we have a sure word to stand on. The validity and authority of the Bible is constantly being reaffirmed throughout Scripture. Today, there is much controversy about the validity of the Bible due to man's involvement with it. But, the issue of its validity does not rest with man, but God. The question is can God maintain the spirit or intent of His Word? If a person understands the character of God, he or she will be able to answer the question in confidence. **Psalm 119** makes the following declarations abut the inspired Word. It is:

Righteous (perfect) – **119:172**	Good – **119:39**
Sweet – **119:103**	Wonderful – **119:129**
Tested (pure) – **119:140**	Truth – **119:142**

It is destructive to consider the Bible as fallible. To lack regard for its authority is to denounce the existence of the true God. In short this is calling God a liar.

The Apostle Paul makes this statement in **Romans 3:4**:
"...let God be true, but every man a liar;..."

Personal Notes: ______________________________

____

Man has proved the validity of the Bible. This proof comes in three areas:

***Historical-archaeological** ***Prophetical** ***Scientific-discoveries**

Historically, we have records of Jesus' life. Scripturally, we can observe the fulfillment of prophecies. For instance, some Bible Scholars have calculated that Christ fulfilled 300 prophecies while on earth. In the first four chapters of Matthew, seven prophecies were fulfilled surrounding the birth of Christ and His ministry. (See **Matthew 1:22-23; 2:5-6, 15, 17-18, 23; 3:1-4; 4:14-16.**) The fulfillment of these Scriptures has been backed up by numerous archaeological discoveries. By combining the historical facts with the scientific discoveries, one can only conclude the existence of a God who has supernaturally intervened in the history and lives of men. We must also reckon with the truth that all prophecies will come to pass.

This is why King David made this observation in **Psalm 14:1** and **53:1**,
"The fool hath said in his heart, There is no God."

The Word of God is simple and pure in spirit. Its truths are not complicated. In fact, when Scripture is made confusing or complicated, this is the first indication that either man or Satan is mishandling it. Obviously, it is understandable, sufficient for our needs and problems, and a complete spiritual instruction for us. By adhering to it, we will find the fullness of salvation at the end of the road.

Psalm 119:155 says,
"Salvation is far from the wicked: for they seek not thy statutes."

Examine your attitude about the Word of God. Do you believe it is God's Word? Do you believe it is without error? Is it your final authority concerning all spiritual matters to test the real state of your doctrine, disposition, attitude, and conduct?

Personal Notes: ____

____

____

Chapter 7

THE OUTCOME OF GOD'S WORD

Obedience to the Word builds our lives before God. This building begins as the Word is allowed to make our spiritual foundation sound.

Isaiah 28:10 confirms this thought,
"For precept must be upon precept, precept upon precept; line upon line, line upon line; here a little, and there a little."

The building of our spiritual lives is not a matter of technically getting Scripture right, but one of Jesus being unveiled in Scripture by the Holy Spirit. As we allow God's doctrines to be laid upon one another in obedience, revelation of Jesus will come with each line of truth. These precepts and lines will emerge into various pictures. Each picture will unveil the glory of Christ in greater ways.

Personal Notes: ______________________________

____

The Word serves as a complete spiritual map. This map will guide us in the perfect ways of God. Are you looking to God's Word for direction?

Psalm 119:105 tells us,
"Thy word is a lamp unto my feet, and a light unto my path."

Personal Notes: ______________________________

____

The Word is God's surgical knife. The Lord as the great physician effectively uses this knife to reveal the hearts of men.

Hebrews 4:12 gives us this insight,
"For the word of God is quick, and powerful, and sharper than any twoedged sword, piercing even to the dividing asunder of soul and spirit, and of the joints and marrow, and is a discerner of the thoughts and intents of the heart."

God's Word is living and active. It reveals the spirit motivating us by exposing our thoughts and attitudes. The response we have to the Word will be evident. For instance, a right reaction will produce a changed life.

Personal Notes: ______________________________

____

The Word serves as our food. It is sustaining and brings maturity to our spiritual life.

1 Peter 2:1-2 says,
"Wherefore laying aside all malice, and all guile, and hypocrisies, and envies, and all evil speakings, As newborn babes, desire the sincere milk of the word, that ye may grow thereby."

Response to the Word of God will bring maturity. This maturity will result in discernment of good from evil. Discernment in the life of a Christian serves as a means of protection. The writer of Hebrews reproved those believers who refused to allow the Word to bring them to spiritual maturity.

We read this reproof in **Hebrews 5:11-14,**
"Of whom we have many things to say, and hard to be uttered, seeing ye are dull of hearing. For when for the time ye ought to be teachers, ye have need that one teach you again which be the first principles of the oracles of God; and are become such as have need of milk, and not of strong meat. For every one that useth milk is unskillful in the word of righteousness: for he is a babe. But strong meat belongeth to them that are of full age, even those who by reason of use have their senses exercised to discern both good and evil."

The Word will serve as our milk and meat. Spiritual milk is for new believers. It represents the pure doctrine of Jesus Christ. (See **Hebrews 6:1-2.**) The meat is for those who are mature in Christ. It represents the life of Christ manifesting itself according to the will of God in obedience, attitudes, lifestyles, and ministry, (service). Would you be considered spiritually retarded because you have not matured?

Personal Notes: ____

____

The Word of God inspires our belief (faith) in God. You must take Him at His Word. Your life and fruits will reveal whether you believe Satan or God.

Romans 10:17 tells us,
"So then faith cometh by hearing, and hearing by the word of God."

Personal Notes: ____

____

Overcoming With the Word

As we have observed, there is both power and life in the Word of God.

The writer **of Psalm 119:11** summarized the power of the Word,
"Thy word have I hid in mine heart, that I might not sin against thee."

You might wonder why the Word would keep you from sinning. The answer is found in learning the ways of God. God's ways are revealed throughout His Word.

Isaiah 55:8-9 makes this declaration about God's ways,
"For my thoughts are not your thoughts, neither are your ways my ways, saith the Lord. For as the heavens are higher than the earth, so are my ways higher than your ways, and my thoughts than your thoughts."

Psalm 18:30 gives us this insight into God's ways,
"As for God, his way is perfect:..."

Psalm 145:17 tells us this about God's ways,
"The Lord is righteous in all his ways, and holy in all his works."

By knowing God's way, we can gain a clear perspective of man's ways.

We find this warning in **Proverbs 21:2**,
"Every way of a man is right in his own eyes: but the Lord pondereth the hearts."

Proverbs gives us the following overview of man's ways when not in compliance to God's ways:

Proverbs 21:8 states,
"The way of man is froward and strange: but as for the pure, his work is right."

Proverbs 21:12-15 says,
"The righteous man wisely considereth the house of the wicked: but God overthroweth the wicked for their wickedness. Whoso stoppeth his ears at the cry of the poor, he also shall cry himself, but shall not be heard. A gift in secret pacifieth anger: and a reward in the bosom strong wrath. It is joy to the just to do judgment: but destruction shall be to the workers of iniquity."

Again, we see the characteristics of sin. Man's ways are sinful and deceptive no matter how right they may seem because his motive, agenda, and priorities may be very selfish and worldly.

The result of man going his own way is summarized in **Proverbs 14:12**,
"There is a way which seemeth right unto a man, but the end thereof are the ways of death."

The Word hidden in your heart will establish righteous boundaries based on God's ways. An upright life will be pleasing and acceptable to God.

Psalm 119:138 tells us,
"Thy testimonies that thou hast commanded are righteous and very faithful."

Personal Notes: ____

____

The Believer's Sword

Ephesians 6:12 tells us we are in a wrestling match with an unseen enemy. We read,
"For we wrestle not against flesh and blood, but against principalities, against powers, against the rulers of the darkness of this world, against spiritual wickedness in high places.

We already have mentioned the enemy of God. His name is Satan. He is referred to as the prince and god of this world (**John 14:30** and **2 Corinthians 4:4**). See also **Isaiah 14:12-16**.

Revelation 12:12 reveals Him in another light,
"...Woe to the inhabiters of the earth and of the sea! For the devil is come down unto you, having great wrath, because he knoweth that he hath but a short time."

Devil means accuser. In **Revelation 12:10** we are told he accuses the believers in the courts of heaven.

Jesus gives us this insight about our accuser in **John 8:44**,
"Ye are of your father the devil, and the lusts of your father ye will do. He was a murderer from the beginning and abode not in the truth, because there is no truth in him. When he speaketh a lie, he speaketh of his own: for he is a liar, and the father of it."

Satan is a master of deception. When he tempted Jesus in the wilderness he used Scripture out of context **(Matthew 4:1-11)**.

This is why we read this warning in **2 Corinthians 11:13-15**,
"For such are false apostles, deceitful workers, transforming themselves into the apostles of Christ. And no marvel; for Satan himself is transformed into an angel of light. Therefore it is no great thing if his ministers also be transformed as the ministers of righteousness; whose end shall be according to their works."

Satan works through religious avenues. He has established churches with false doctrines. He uses religious figures to destroy the work God has done or desires to do through His servants and in man.

Peter in his first letter described Satan in this manner in **1 Peter 5:8**,
"Be sober, be vigilant; because your adversary the devil, as a roaring lion, walketh about, seeking whom he may devour."

We are basically in the lion's den by being in the world. The devil desires to destroy our lives in God. But, praise God, our Lord has given us a weapon to put him on the run.

We find this weapon in **Ephesians 6:17**,
"And take the helmet of salvation, and the sword of the Spirit, which is the word of God."

The Word of God is our weapon. We must learn how to use this weapon effectively.

2 Timothy 2:15 instructs us on this subject,
"Study to shew thyself approved unto God, a workman that needeth not to be ashamed, rightly dividing the word of truth."

We must study the Word. To study means to meditate, examine, and ponder in order to gain knowledge. Knowledge gained through studying will come out in practical use.

In **Psalm 119:15** we read,
"I will meditate in thy precepts, and have respect unto thy ways."

Psalm 119:59 says,
"I thought on my ways, and turned my feet unto thy testimonies."

Satan took the Word out of context; Jesus quoted it according to its real intent and purpose. It is easy to use the Word in the wrong way. It is also a serious offence to God, worthy of His wrath. (See **Romans 1:18**.)

2 Peter 3:15-16 says,
"And account that the long suffering of our Lord is salvation; even as our beloved brother Paul also according to the wisdom given unto him hath written unto you; As also in all his epistles speaking in them of these things; in which are some things hard to be understood, which they that are unlearned and unstable wrest, as they do also the other scriptures, unto their own destruction."

Revelation 22:18-19 gives us this warning,
"For I testify unto every man that heareth the words of the prophecy of this book, If any man shall add unto these things, God shall add unto him the plagues that are written in this book: And if any man shall take away from the words of the book of this prophecy, God shall take away his part out of the book of life, and out of the holy city, and from the things which are written in this book." (Refer also to **Deuteronomy 4:2** and **12:32**.)

We must be careful not to use the Word of God for our personal causes. If we use the Word as a means to unfairly judge our brother, we will be judged in like manner. If we use Scripture to serve our own purposes and justify wrong actions, we will be held accountable. If we add our own doctrines and ideas, we will experience God's wrath. If we take away from the Word of God, we will be separated from God for eternity. Jesus defeated Satan with the whole Bible. We can defeat him in the same manner. Do you have a love for God's Word? Does it serve as the final authority for your beliefs? Take time to study it. Allow your spiritual teacher (the Holy Spirit) to reveal Christ to you in every scripture. Let the Lord's Word penetrate every area of your heart.

Personal Notes ____

____

Chapter 8

GOD'S MEANS OF PURIFICATION

Supplement: *(Enlarge perspective about the church)* **Volume 5 Book 4:** *Whatever Happen to The Church?*

The Apostle Paul made this statement in **Ephesians 5:25-26**,
"...even as Christ loved the church, and gave himself for it; That he might sanctify and cleanse it with the washing of water by the word."

The word <u>sanctification</u> means holy or to be set apart. It is the opposite of sin. A Christian must be set apart in heart, attitude, and lifestyle for the glory of God.

2 Timothy 2:21 tells us,
"If a man therefore purge himself from these, he shall be a vessel unto honour, sanctified and meet for the master's use, and prepared unto every good work."

Sanctification involves a process. It includes cleansing and purification. Cleansing is associated with water and purification with fire. Both will separate the holy from the unholy. One of the tools used for the process of sanctification is the Word of God.

Jesus in **John 17:17** made this plea to the Father in prayer:
"Sanctify them through thy truth: thy word is truth."

Jesus made this claim in **John 15:3**,
"Now ye are clean through the word which I have spoken unto you."

In **Jeremiah 23:29** we read,
"Is not my word like as a fire?..."

Psalm 119:9 says,
"Wherewithal shall a young man cleanse his way? By taking heed thereto according to thy word."

The Word of God has the ability to clean with water and purify with fire. In order for the Word to accomplish this, we must obey it. Obedience will cause a separation from that which is unholy, unto that which is holy and acceptable to God.

1 Peter 1:22 confirms this cleansing,
"Seeing you have purified your souls in obeying the truth through the Spirit unto unfeigned love of the brethren, see that ye love one another with a pure heart fervently:"

Personal Notes: ______________________________

____

The Blood

Supplements:
God's Offering, Parts 1 & 2
Sup. 3

Another instrument used for cleansing is the blood of Jesus.

1 John 1:7 says,
"But if we walk in the light, as he is in the light, we have fellowship one with another, and the blood of Jesus Christ his Son cleanseth us from all sin."

In **Revelation 1:5** we read,
"And from Jesus Christ, who is the faithful witness, and the first begotten of the dead, and the prince of the kings of the earth, Unto him that loved us, and washed us from our sins in his own blood."

There is a cleansing ability in the precious blood of Jesus for it was God's way of redeeming us. Redeem means to purchase. (Refer to **Isaiah 1:18-19**.)

Hebrews 9:12 states,
"Neither by the blood of goats and calves, but by his own blood he entered in once into the holy place, having obtained eternal redemption for us."

Once a year the High Priest of the Jewish Nation entered the Holy of Holies. God's presence and the ark made up this inner holy room. Included as part of the ark was the Mercy Seat. This is where both God's judgment of sin and His unending mercy came together. The High Priest would offer a sacrifice on the Mercy Seat for the sins of the nation of Israel. (See **Exodus 25:9-22** and **Leviticus 16**.) Hebrews tells us Jesus entered this place by His own blood after obtaining an eternal redemption for man. His death brought God's judgment and mercy together. When judgment and mercy come together at a point of love, it produces grace. Today, Jesus serves as the believer's High Priest who is sitting at the place of mercy, ever making intercession for His people. (Refer to **Ephesians 2:8-9** and **Hebrews 7:24-28**.)

Hebrews 4:16 adds this insight on the subject,
"Let us therefore come boldly unto the throne of grace, that we may obtain mercy, and find grace to help in time of need."

The common man was never allowed into the Most Holy Place (the Holy of Holies). In fact, the only individual who could ever enter this room was the High Priest. He only did this once a year. When Christ purchased the souls of men on the cross, much happened.

Jesus made this declaration while he was on the cross in **John 19:30**,
"...It is finished:..."

Jesus' blood sufficed God's judgment of sin. The payment was complete.

Hebrews 9:28 confirms this:
"So Christ was once offered to bear the sins of many;..."

In **Luke 23:45** we read this important information surrounding Christ's crucifixion:
"And the sun was darkened, and the veil of the temple was rent in the midst."

There was a curtain, which separated the Most Holy Place from the Holy Place. Bible teachers tell us this curtain was estimated to be 60 feet long, 30 feet high and the thickness of a palm in the temple constructed by Herod. Once man's eternal redemption was secured by Christ, the curtain was ripped by the very hand of God. Man now has access to come into the Most Holy Place with boldness.

1 John 1:7 tells us how we can experience the cleansing effect of the blood,
"But if we walk in the light, as he is in the light, we have fellowship one with another, and the blood of Jesus Christ his Son cleanseth us from all sin."

Light exposes sin. If one is walking in the light it is because the individual acknowledges and deals with sin in his or her life.

Hebrews 9:14 says,
"How much more shall the blood of Christ, who through the eternal Spirit offered himself without spot to God, purge your conscience from dead works to serve the living God?"

To have a clear conscience implies we are silencing the devil by faith knowing with surety that the redemption of Jesus took care of our sins. This points us to the forgiveness of God which allows us to walk in liberty.

1 John 1:9 tells us how this is accomplished,
"If we confess our sins, he is faithful and just to forgive us our sins, and to cleanse us from all unrighteousness."

Confession means to acknowledge. By acknowledging our sins, we show we are in agreement with God about our situation. This agreement allows God to cleanse us from all of the effects of sin.

Personal Notes: ____

____

The Holy Spirit

Supplement:
Foundation of Our Faith
Sup. 1, Lesson 5

Another means of sanctification in the believer's life is the Holy Spirit.

The Apostle Paul made this statement about his ministry to the Gentiles in **Romans 15:16**,
"That I should be the minister of Jesus Christ to the Gentiles, ministering the gospel of God, that the offering up of the Gentiles might be acceptable, being sanctified by the Holy Ghost."

Sanctification makes us an acceptable sacrifice to God. It must be noted that what has not been sanctified by God does not belong to Him. Our God is holy; therefore, those who follow Him must be holy. (See **Hebrews 12:14** and **1 Peter 1:15-16**.)

Exodus 29:43-44 gives us insight on how sanctification takes place,
"And there I will meet with the children of Israel, and the tabernacle shall be sanctified by my glory. And I will sanctify the tabernacle of the congregation, and the altar: I will sanctify also both Aaron and his sons, to minister to me in the priest's office."

The presence of God is what sets something apart.

1 Corinthians 6:19 gives us this insight,
"What? Know ye not that your body is the temple of the Holy Ghost which is in you, which ye have of God, and ye are not your own?"

We do not belong to ourselves for we are the temples of God. God is in us through the indwelling presence of the Holy Spirit.

In **1 Thessalonians 5:23** we read one of Paul's desires for God's people,
"And the very God of peace sanctify you wholly; and I pray God your whole spirit and soul and body be preserved blameless unto the coming of our Lord Jesus Christ."

The Apostle Paul wanted to see the work of separation take place in our spirit, soul, and body.

Titus 3:5 tells us how the Holy Spirit sanctifies us,
"Not by works of righteousness which we have done, but according to his mercy he saved us, by the washing of regeneration, and renewing of the Holy Ghost."

The Holy Spirit is the person who does the work of regeneration. Regeneration means new life being brought forth.

Romans 12:2 tells us how the Spirit of God accomplishes this process,
"And be not conformed to this world: but be ye transformed by the renewing of your mind, that ye may prove what is that good, and acceptable, and perfect, will of God."

The reason for the transforming of the mind can be summarized in **Philippians 2:5**,
"Let this mind be in you, which was also in Christ Jesus:'

Jesus' attitude was to please God. He took on the role of an obedient servant. This attitude reveals the purpose of sanctification.

Hebrews 9:14 shows us why this work is necessary,
"...to serve the living God."

2 Timothy 2:21 confirms the work of sanctification,
"If a man therefore purge himself from these, he shall be a vessel unto honour, sanctified, and meet for the master's use, and prepared unto every good work."

1 Peter 2:9 says,
"But ye are a chosen generation, a royal priesthood, an holy nation, a peculiar people; that ye should shew forth the praises of him who hath called you out of darkness into his marvelous light."

We do belong to God. We have been set apart for service. Our life should bring glory to our Holy God. Sanctification is done by the Holy Spirit, but we must desire and allow it to happen. This desire and openness to holiness comes from commitment. Commitment results in taking the necessary steps to separate ourselves from the unholy, which is a form of consecration or abandonment.

2 Corinthians 6:14-17 gives us the main clue to spiritual separation,
"Be ye not unequally yoked together with unbelievers: for what fellowship hath righteousness with unrighteousness? And what communion hath light with darkness? And what concord hath Christ with Belial? Or what part hath he that believeth with an infidel? And what agreement hath the temple of God with idols? For ye are the temple of the living God as God hath said, I will dwell in them, and walk in them; and I will be their God, and they shall be my people."

We must set ourselves apart from those things which are not acceptable to God. Believers are referred to as saints. The word saint means a holy person. Saints have been saved unto good works to bring glory to God. It takes the Word, the blood of Jesus, and the Holy Spirit to do the work of sanctification.

Ephesians 5:27 tells us the final result of this work,
"That he might present it to himself a glorious church, not having spot, or wrinkle, or any such thing; but that it should be holy and without blemish."

Do you want God to receive you? Do you want to serve Him? If you answer yes to both questions, you need to get serious about submitting to the work of sanctification. God wants you to be a holy person capable of representing Him in this dark world. (See **Matthew 5:13-16**.)

Personal Notes: ____

____

____

____

Chapter 9

THE MIRROR OF GOD

The Word of God is powerful and living! We have observed how it leads to eternal life and sanctifies us. It inspires belief, sustains our spiritual life, and gives us victory over sin and Satan. The Word of God is also our mirror. It reveals our spiritual condition in light of Jesus Christ. But, for it to serve as a reliable mirror, obedience must be worked into every fiber of our spiritual lives.

James 1:22 gives us this instruction,
"But be ye doers of the word, and not hearers only deceiving your own selves."

If all you do is hear the Word, but do not obey it, you will not come to a clearer understanding of Jesus. This will create a deception about your own spiritual condition.

The Apostle Paul makes this comment in **2 Timothy 3:7**,
"Ever learning, and never able to come to the knowledge of the truth."

Wisdom is knowledge put into practice. (Refer to **1 Corinthians 8:1-3**.)

James 3:13-17 says this about wisdom,
"Who is a wise man and endued with knowledge among you? let him shew out of a good conversation his works with meekness of wisdom. But if ye have bitter envying and strife in your hearts, glory not, and lie not against the truth. This wisdom descendeth not from above, but is earthly, sensual, devilish."

In **Luke 12:42-44** we see a description of a wise servant,
"And the Lord said, Who then is that faithful and wise steward, whom his lord shall make ruler over his household to give them their portion of meat in due season? Blessed is that servant, whom his lord when he cometh shall find so doing. Of a truth I say unto you, that he will make him ruler over all that he hath."

A wise servant is a faithful and obedient servant.

Luke 12:47 tells us what will happen to the unwise servant,
"And that servant, which knew his lord's will, and prepared not himself, neither did according to his will, shall be beaten with many stripes."

Proverbs 4:5-7 tells us what our response to wisdom should be,
"Get wisdom, get understanding: forget it not; neither decline from the words of my mouth. Forsake her not, and she shall preserve thee: love her, and she shall keep thee. Wisdom is the principal thing; therefore get wisdom: and with all thy getting get understanding."

Personal Notes: ____

____

____

Obedience must be the consistent reply of the Christian life. It produces action.

For instance, in the area of belief (faith), **James 2:14-17** says,
"What doth it profit, my brethren, though a man say he hath faith, and have not works? can faith save him? If a brother or sister be naked, and destitute of daily food, And one of you say unto them, Depart in peace, be ye warned and filled; notwithstanding ye give them not those things which are needful to the body; what doth it profit? Even so faith, if it hath not works, is dead, being alone."

James 2:18 concludes this thought with this statement,
"Yea, a man may say, Thou hast faith, and I have works: shew me thy faith without works, and I will shew thee my faith by my works."

Personal Notes: ____

____

____

Love is the heartbeat of true Christian faith.

1 John 3:16-18 tells us love will result in action,
"Hereby perceive we the love of God, because he laid down his life for us: and we ought to lay down our lives for the brethren. But whoso hath this world's good, and seeth his brother have need, and shutteth up his bowels of compassion from him, how dwelleth the love of God in him? My little children, let us not love in word, neither in tongue; but in deed and in truth."

Personal Notes: ____

____

James brings these thoughts together in **James 1:27**,
"Pure religion and undefiled before God and the Father is this, To visit the fatherless and widows in their affliction, and to keep himself unspotted from the world."

Belief, which expresses itself in action, serves as a testimony to others. It is also an example of commitment that will glorify God. We clearly see this in the redemption wrought by Jesus on the cross.

Matthew 5:16 gives this instruction,
"Let your light so shine before men, that they may see your good works, and glorify your Father which is in heaven."

Paul tells us why we will serve as a visible example to the world in **2 Corinthians 3:2-3**,
"Ye are our epistle written in our hearts, known and read of all men: Forasmuch as ye are manifestly declared to be the epistle of Christ ministered by us, written not with ink, but with

the Spirit of the living God; not in tables of stone, but in fleshy tables of the heart." (See also **Romans 7:6**.)

Obedience to the Word of God establishes it in our hearts. Once it is instituted in our lives it will manifest itself in our outward appearance.

The final product is summarized in **1 Corinthians 15:49**,
"And as we have borne the image of the earthly, we shall also bear the image of the heavenly."

If Christ is not being reflected in our lives, then we must assume we are not being obedient to His Word.

This is why when James instructed us to be doers of the Word, he related complacency (indifference) to it in this manner in **James 1:23-24**,
"For if any be a hearer of the word, and not a doer, he is like unto a man beholding his natural face in a glass: For he beholdeth himself, and goeth his way, and straightway forgetteth what manner of man he was."

Complacency toward the things of God is unacceptable. We read Christ's reaction towards complacency (indifference) found in the church of Laodicea.

Revelation 3:15-16 says,
"I know thy works, that thou art neither cold nor hot: I would thou wert cold or hot. So then because thou art lukewarm, and neither cold nor hot, I will spue thee out of my mouth."

James 1:25 gives us a promise if we are doers of the Word,
"But whoso looketh into the perfect law of liberty, and continueth therein, he being not a forgetful hearer, but a doer of the work, this man shall be blessed in his deed."

The Bible lifts Christ up in His glory. As we submit to its instruction, our Lord's glory will be uncovered in our lives.

2 Corinthians 3:18 says,
"But we all, with open face beholding as in a glass the glory of the Lord, are changed into the same image from glory to glory, even as by the Spirit of the Lord."

Personal Notes: ______________________________

____

____

The Judge

Jeremiah 23:29 makes this statement about the Word,
"Is not my word like as a fire? Saith the Lord; and like a hammer that breaketh the rock in pieces?"

Isaiah 55:11 declares,
"So shall my word be that goeth forth out of my mouth: it shall not return unto me void, but it shall accomplish that which I please, and it shall prosper in the thing whereto I sent it."

We have been learning how the main purpose of the Word is to lead us to eternal life. We know it serves as our mirror to our spiritual life. But in Jeremiah, we are told about the ability of the Word to break us. This breaking implies judgment.

John 12:48 confirms this thought,
"He that rejecteth me, and receiveth not my words, hath one that judgeth him: the word that I have spoken, the same shall judge him in the last day."

Isaiah 55:11 tells us God's Word will not return empty. It will either bring eternal life to us, or it will judge us. Judgment means separation. Remember, the Word of God will cause a separation in our life. This judgment of the Word has a two-fold purpose to it. If we respond to it in obedience, it will set us apart from the things that are not holy and acceptable to God to set us apart for His use. The second judgment is a separation of the children of disobedience from Jesus Christ. This separation makes those who are disobedient subject to God's wrath. Wrath means anger.

Romans 5:9 makes this statement,
"Much more then, being now justified by his blood, we shall be saved from wrath through him."

Colossians 3:5-6 gives us this instruction,
"Mortify therefore your members which are upon the earth; fornication, uncleanness, inordinate affection, evil concupiscence, and covetousness, which is idolatry: For which things' sake the wrath of God cometh of the children of disobedience."

Personal Notes: ____

____

____

As we know, Jesus is the Living Word. The Bible shows us He will have a similar effect on us as the written Word.

Jesus tells us He will be our judge on judgment day in **John 5:22**,
"For the Father judgeth no man, but hath committed all judgment unto the Son."

Jesus made this statement about Himself in **Matthew 21:44**,
"And whosoever shall fall on this stone shall be broken: but on whomsoever it shall fall, it will grind him to powder."

Once again, we see separation being done in both ways. We will come face to face with Jesus Christ. As the stone He will break us which produces repentance and eternal life, or He will crush us resulting in spiritual death. This particular judgment means hell or eternal separation from God.

Matthew 10:28 says this about hell,
"And fear not them which kill the body, but are not able to kill the soul: but rather fear him which is able to destroy both soul and body in hell."

I must note, according to *Vine's Expository Dictionary*, the word destroy in this scripture does not mean to extinguish from existence. It actually means destruction or ruin of an inner well-being.

2 Peter 3:9 tells us what God's will is for man,
"The Lord is not slack concerning his promise, as some men count slackness; but is longsuffering to us-ward, not willing that any should perish, but that all should come to repentance."

God does not want us to perish. His will is that we all come to repentance. Repentance means you have a strong desire to change once convicted of sin. This desire will cause a person to turn from sin to do right before God. This decision will lead to eternal life. Our eternal destination will be determined by our attitude and response to Jesus Christ and His Word. We must choose Christ to have eternal life and see heaven. A lack of response or rejection towards Him will mean eternal separation and hell.

Personal Notes: ____

____

The correct attitude and response to the Living Word (Jesus) and the Written Word (the Bible) is godly fear.

Ecclesiastes 12:13-14 makes this statement,
"Let us hear the conclusion of the whole matter: Fear God, and keep his commandments: for this is the whole duty of man. For God shall bring every work into judgment, with every secret thing, whether it be good, or whether it be evil."

Psalm 119:120 says,
"My flesh trembleth for fear of thee; and I am afraid of thy judgments."

The fear of the Lord is a healthy fear towards our holy God. It is an awesome respect for God, which produces obedience to His commands. It is a dread of displeasing the Lord that avoids evil and results in an upright heart. It is an attitude of reverence that is motivated by love.

Paul gives us this instruction in **Philippians 2:12**,
"...work out your own salvation with fear and trembling."

We must fear the Lord to keep a right attitude towards our God. This attitude will keep us upright in our heart and deeds. (Refer also to **Ephesians 5:21**.)

Personal Notes: ____

____

____

The way we can avoid the awesome judgment of our Lord is to first judge (examine) ourselves.

1 Corinthians 11:31 says,
"For if we would judge ourselves, we should not be judged."

We must be careful how we judge ourselves. Never examine yourself based on religious affiliation or works. Remember that good works are a product of salvation—they are not necessarily the sole evidence of it. Jesus made it quite clear there is a means in which we can judge ourselves.

We read these words in **Matthew 7:16**,
"Ye shall know them by their fruits. Do men gather grapes of thorns, or figs of thistles?"

We need to judge the fruit of our life. This fruit will tell us if we are right before God.

The Apostle Paul tells us what this fruit consists of in **Galatians 5:22-23**,
"But the fruit of the Spirit is love, joy, peace, longsuffering, gentleness, goodness, faith, meekness, temperance: against such there is no law."

Always examine your life in light of the fruit coming from it and by the complete Word of God. If you find you are not living right, determine in your heart to do it God's way. Ask His forgiveness and power to overcome. Totally submit your life to Him. Not only will Satan flee, but also the sin, which keeps you from being effective, will fall to the wayside.

Personal Notes: ____

____

____

____

Chapter 10

REPENTENCE!

Supplements:
(For Review)
Volume 1
Book 2: *The Anatomy of Sin,*
Chapter 13
(To Edify)
Volume 4
Book 1:
Hidden Manna Revised
Chapter 8

Repentance is a necessity to ensure salvation. Jesus brought this point out in **Luke 13:3** and **5**. Without repentance, people will perish in their sins. We have already mentioned this subject in the last chapter.

We are once again reminded of Peter's words in **2 Peter 3:9**,
"The Lord is not slack concerning his promise, as some men count slackness; but is longsuffering to us-ward, not willing that any should perish, but that <u>all</u> should come to repentance." (Emphasis added.)

Repentance is the initial response of the convicted sinner towards the message of the cross. It is the believer's first response towards conviction of sin by the Holy Spirit. It is a turning away from sin. To turn away from sin involves a change in attitude about sin, which produces a changed heart condition.

This change involves:

- a decision,
- a determination and
- a deviation or change in direction.
- Walking in the right way.

True repentance requires us to change our minds or make a correct decision about sin in our life. This change results in an acknowledgement and confession of sin. This means a person agrees with God's evaluation of his or her attitude or action in a matter. (Refer also to **1 John 1:9**.)

Proverbs 28:13 makes this statement,
"He that covereth his sins shall not prosper: but whoso confesseth and forsaketh them shall have mercy."

The next step in repentance is determination. We must determine in our heart to do it God's way. Daniel is a good example of an individual who made a heart determination to be obedient to God.

Daniel 1:8 makes this distinction,
"But Daniel purposed (determined) in his heart that he would not defile himself..." (Parenthesis added.)

Daniel made this determination as a young slave in the courts of his enemy.

We see the results of this resolution in his later years in **Daniel 6:4**,
"...but they could find none occasion nor fault; forasmuch as he was faithful, neither was there any error or fault found in him."

Daniel's enemies could not find anything wrong with his conduct. He was a man representative of his Holy God. Once the change has occurred in the mind and heart, it will produce a change in direction.

Isaiah 55:7 declares,
"Let the wicked forsake his way, and the unrighteous man his thoughts: and let him return unto the Lord, and he will have mercy upon him; and to our God, for he will abundantly pardon."

Repentance is simply an about face. Man will cease from doing it his way to doing it according to the Word of God. (Consider man's ways in light of **Proverbs 14:12; 16:2** and **21:8**.) A good example of real repentance is found in the story of the prodigal son in **Luke 15:11-32**. Verses **11-14** show the prodigal son's wicked ways. In **Luke 15:17-19**, we see him acknowledging his sin and determining to go a different way. In verse **20** we see him changing his direction and going home.

In the last part of verse **20**, we see a beautiful picture of the heart of his father in **Luke 15:20**,
"And he rose, and came to his father. But when he was yet a great way off, his father saw him, and had compassion, and ran, and fell on his neck, and kissed him.

This is the picture of God's heart, which is extended towards mankind. He desires to see his children come to Him in repentance. He is long-suffering in His waiting. Due to His incredible love, He is quick to forgive.

We see His love being summarized in the statement of the father in **Luke 15:32**,
"It was meet that we should make merry, and be glad: for this thy brother was dead, and is alive again; and was lost, and is found." (For another example of true repentance, see the Apostle Paul's conversion in **Acts 9:1-29**.)

God's love for us shows the highest form of commitment. (See **John 3:16-19**.)

Jesus confirms this commitment of love in **Luke 15:4-6**,
"What man of you, having an hundred sheep, if he lose one of them, doth not leave the ninety and nine in the wilderness, and go after that which is lost, until he find it? And when he hath found it, he layeth it on his shoulders, rejoicing. And when he cometh home, he calleth together his friends and neighbors, saying unto them, Rejoice with me; for I have found my sheep which was lost."

In **Isaiah 53:6**, we read these descriptive words,
"All we like sheep have gone astray; we have turned every one to his own way:..."

Man is compared to sheep. He needs a shepherd to lead him. But, he must hear and follow his Shepherd when He calls him.

John 10:14-16 gives us this insight about Jesus,
"I am the good shepherd, and know my sheep, and am known of mine. As the Father knoweth me, even so know I the Father: and I lay down my life for the sheep. And other sheep I have, which are not of this fold: them also I must bring, and they shall hear my voice; and there shall be one fold, and one shepherd."

To follow our Shepherd implies repentance. We are changing our master and our direction to follow Him.

We read the results of repentance in **Luke 15:7**,
"I say unto you, that likewise joy shall be in heaven over one sinner that repenteth, more than over ninety and nine just persons, which need no repentance."

Personal Notes: ____

____

____

The Humble Beginnings of Repentance

Repentance implies a brokenness and humility before God.

Psalm 51:17 says,
"The sacrifices of God are a broken sprit: a broken and a contrite (repentive) heart..." (Parenthesis added.)

Psalm 34:18 reads,
"The Lord is nigh unto them that are of a broken heart; and saveth such as be of a contrite spirit."

Real repentance involves brokenness in heart and humbleness in spirit. These characteristics are motivated by a hatred for sin. Both will occur when sin is identified in a heart that desires God above all else. Such people will be spurred on by the idea that any sin displeases God and breaks valuable fellowship with Him. This type of repentance will end with the salvation of one's soul.

The last part of **Psalm 51:17** tells us God's response to brokenness and humility,
"...O God, thou wilt not despise."

James 4:6 & 10 adds this insight,
"But he giveth more grace. Wherefore he saith, God resisteth the proud, but giveth grace unto the humble. Humble yourselves in the sight of the Lord, and he shall lift you up."

Jesus made this statement in **Matthew 5:3** about those who acknowledge and come to terms with their true spiritual condition.

Matthew 5:3 stated,
"Blessed are the poor in spirit: for theirs is the kingdom of heaven."

Personal Notes: ____

____

Worldly Remorse

The Apostle Paul tells us there are different types of repentance in **2 Corinthians 7:10**, "For godly sorrow worketh repentance to salvation not to be repented of: but the sorrow of the world worketh death."

> There is a worldly sorrow that has the appearance of repentance. It is simply a disguise for self-pity. Self-pity sees itself as having rights. Rights allow the person to become a victim in a situation, rather than a responsible, repentant soul who loves the truth and above all else desires a relationship with God. This type of sorrow can show great remorse with emotional outbursts. We see this worldly sorrow in the case of Judas Iscariot. Judas was the one who betrayed Jesus.

Matthew 27:3-5 gives us this account of Judas' response to his betrayal of Christ, "Then Judas, which had betrayed him, when he saw that he was condemned, repented himself, and brought again the thirty pieces of silver to the chief priests and elders, Saying I have sinned in that I have betrayed the innocent blood. And they said, What is that to us? See thou to that. And he cast down the pieces of silver in the temple, and departed, and went and hanged himself."

> Godly repentance will always lead an individual to Jesus in search of forgiveness and restoration. Judas never really acknowledged that he had betrayed the Son of God, the Messiah. He referred to Jesus as an innocent man, which shows he failed to comprehend the extent of his evil deeds. The fact Judas hung himself shows us it was his attempt of making himself right. Man's attempts to right his wrongs may look noble, but it is a false repentance, usually based on fake nobility. Fake nobility is a disguise for pride. It will ultimately lead man to his destruction.

We see this worldly repentance in Esau, Abraham's grandson, in **Hebrews 12:16-17**, "Lest there be any fornicator, or profane person, as Esau, who for one morsel of meat sold his birthright. For ye know how that afterward, when he would have inherited the blessing, he was rejected: for he found no place of repentance, though he sought it carefully with tears."

> Esau sold his birthright for food. The birthright involved preserving the lineage of the Messiah. Esau was an earthly man who only cared about this present world. Because of his attitude, he was considered a fornicator or profane, unholy person. As a result, he lost the blessing. He blamed this all on his brother, Jacob. If you study the life of Esau, you will find hatred towards his brother, Jacob. Although, he viewed Jacob as robbing him of his inheritance, a right heart would have accepted the consequences and rejected a godless attitude. (See **Genesis 25:23-34** and **27**.)

Genesis 27:41 gives us this information about Esau's heart, "And Esau hated Jacob because of the blessing wherewith his father blessed him: and Esau said in his heart, the days of mourning for my father are at hand; then will I slay my brother Jacob."

Esau transposed his failures onto his brother. He made a determination to kill him for the consequences that were a result of his personal moral deviations. True repentance will ultimately lead to reconciliation of relationships. Remember that reconciliation is a restoration of relationships. This restoration implies forgiveness and healing.

2 Corinthians 5:18 says,
"And all things are of God, who hath reconciled us to himself by Jesus Christ, and hath given to us the ministry of reconciliation."

Jesus gave us this instruction in **Matthew 5:22-24**,
"But I say unto you, That whosoever is angry with his brother without a cause shall be in danger of the judgment: and whosoever shall say to his brother, Raca, shall be in danger of the council: but whosoever shall say, Thou fool, shall be in danger of hell fire. Therefore if thou bring thy gift to the altar, and there rememberest that thy brother hath ought against thee; Leave there thy gift before the altar, and go thy way; first be reconciled to thy brother, and then come and offer thy gift."

1 John 3:15 gives us this insight,
"Whosoever hateth his brother is a murderer: and ye know that no murderer hath eternal life abiding in him."

Beware of "repentance" which falls short of seeking out Christ for forgiveness. Forgiveness results in reconciliation of relationships. Never mistake worldly remorse of emotional tears of self-pity or pleading for true repentance. All show and no change in direction is simply surface and will lead to destruction.

Personal Notes:____

____

The Only Way to True Faith

Faith will follow true repentance, but it will never precede it.

John the Baptist enters the scene preaching repentance. We read these words in **Matthew 3:1-2**:
"In those days came John the Baptist, preaching in the wilderness of Judea. And saying, Repent ye: for the kingdom of heaven is at hand."

Mark 1:14-15 shows Jesus preaching a similar message,
"...Jesus came into Galilee, preaching the gospel of the kingdom of God, And saying, The time is fulfilled, and the kingdom of God is at hand: repent ye, and believe the gospel."

In this scripture we see the command to repent first, then to believe the good news.

Acts 2:38 & 41 tells us Peter preached this same order,
"Then Peter said unto them, Repent, and be baptized every one of you in the name of Jesus Christ for the remission of sins, and ye shall receive the gift of the Holy Ghost. Then they that gladly received his word were baptized: and the same day there were added unto them about three thousand souls."

There must be a change in heart and mind about sin before there can be saving faith. Without first recognizing and acknowledging sin there will be no need to receive the gift of eternal life. Saving faith comes from the foundation of godly repentance. Without this repentance, there is only destruction to look forward to.

Jesus confirms this **in Luke 13:3 & 5**,
"I tell you, Nay: but, except ye repent, ye shall all likewise perish."

Is your Shepherd looking for you right now? Is He calling you? Do you need to be reconciled to someone? In summary do you need to repent? If the Holy Spirit is convicting you, heed to it right now. The heavenly host is waiting to rejoice upon your return (**Luke 15:7 & 10**).

Personal Notes: ____

____

____

Chapter 11

TRUE FAITH

Supplement:
(For the next two chapters)
Volume 2
Book 3: *In Search of Real Faith*

We have learned from past studies that the Word of God inspires faith.

Apostle Paul gives us an indication of how important faith is to our Christian life in **2 Corinthians 5:7**,
("For we walk by faith, not by sight.")

Ephesians 4:4-6 tells us,
"There is one body, and one Spirit, even as ye are called in one hope of your calling; One Lord, one faith, one baptism. One God and Father of all, who is above all, and through all, and is you all."

There is only one true faith. It is important we come to a clear understanding of faith based on the Word of God. (See **2 Corinthians 13:5**.)

Hebrews 11:1 gives us a decisive definition of faith,
"Now faith is the substance of things hoped for, the evidence of things not seen."

Faith is not hope, but it is the solid or essential part of hope. Hope is having a confident expectation based on faith. Faith is for now. It is based on the nature of God. Basically, faith is your perception of God. You either believe God is who He is or you do not. You believe His Word about Him or you will go into utter unbelief. Therefore, the substance of our hope is based on God and our expectation is according to His promises.

Sadly, many people put faith in their faith. This means faith is conjured up in the imagination as people try to fake their life before God. They put confidence in the promises, things, or abilities of God, rather then in Who He is. As a result, these individuals try to wrestle God into their way of thinking by using His Word or promises against Him.

1 Peter 1:21 tells us,
"Who by him do believe in God, that raised him up from the dead, and gave him glory; that your faith and hope might be in God."

Hebrews 11:6 makes this statement,
"But without faith it is impossible to please him: for he that cometh to God must believe that he is, and that he is a rewarder of them that diligently seek him."

Faith involves belief, truth, and confidence. Believing exercises faith. This belief must come from the heart as being true.

Romans 10:10 says,
"For with the heart man believeth unto righteousness; and with the mouth confession is made unto salvation."

<u>Trust</u> implies a child-like response to God.

Matthew 18:2-4 states,
"And Jesus called a little child unto him, and set him in the midst of them, And said, Verily I say unto you, except ye be converted, and become as little children, ye shall not enter into the kingdom of heaven. Whoso- ever therefore shall humble himself as this little child, the same is greatest in the kingdom of heaven."

A child-like response includes purity, sincerity, and simplicity. These three qualities are opposite of pride and hypocrisy.

Paul makes this statement in **1 Timothy 1:5,**
"Now the end of the commandment is charity out of a pure heart, and of a good conscience, and of faith unfeigned."

Confidence produces hope.

Proverbs 3:26 summarizes our confidence,
"For the LORD shall be thy confidence..."

1 John 2:28 tells us,
"And now, little children, abide in him; that, when he shall appear, we may have confidence, and not be ashamed before him at his coming."

This confidence is maintained in our life as long as we abide in Christ.

Jesus made these statements in **John 15:7 & 10,**
"If ye abide in me, and my words abide in you, ye shall ask what ye will, and it shall be done unto you. If ye keep my commandments, ye shall abide in my love; even as I have kept my Father's commandments, and abide in his love."

We cannot see God, but we believe in our heart He exists. We cannot touch God, but we respond in sincerity in order to be touched by His glory. We cannot comprehend His salvation, but we have confidence in receiving it because of His faithfulness.

Personal Notes: ____

____

____

Based on God's Word

Supplement: Volume 3 Book 3: *Don't Touch That Dial*

Faith is based solely on the Word of God. It is believing God and His Word.

Hebrews 11:7 tells us,
"By faith Noah, being warned of God of things not seen as yet, moved with fear, prepared an ark to the saving of his house; by the which he condemned the world, and became heir of the righteousness which is by faith."

Noah by his faith condemned the world. A walk of faith brings a contrast to those who walk according to the flesh and the influences of the world. In the previous scripture we see four different qualities involved in Noah's faith.

They are:

* Communication
* Obedience
* Believing
* Fear of the Lord

The first quality of Noah's faith was communication. God had to have warned Noah about pending judgment. Communication involves sensitivity to God's voice.

In **1 Kings 19:11-12** we read how God chose to speak to His prophet, Elijah,
"And he said, go forth, and stand upon the mount before the LORD. And, behold, the LORD passed by, and a great and strong wind rent the mountains, and brake in pieces the rocks before the LORD; but the LORD was not in the wind: and after the wind an earthquake; but the LORD was not in the earthquake: And after the earthquake a fire; but the LORD was not in the fire: and after the fire a still small voice."

1 Kings 19:12 tells us God chose the gentle whisper to speak to Elijah. Although Elijah had witnessed powerful elements, it was the still small voice that cause this great prophet to cover his face (**1 Kings 19:13**).

In **John 10:3-4,** Jesus said this about His sheep,
"To him the porter openenth; and the sheep hear his voice: and he calleth his own sheep by name, and leadeth them out. And when he putteth for this own sheep, he goeth before them, and the sheep follow him: for they know his voice."

The second characteristic of faith was Noah believed God. Although Noah had not seen the upcoming of rain and the flood, he responded to God's direction.

Hebrews 3:10-11 talks about the reason and consequences for a lack of faith,
"Wherefore I was grieved with that generation, and said, They do always err in their heart; and they have not known my ways. So I sware in my wrath, They shall not enter into my rest."

The lack of faith implies unbelief. Unbelief kept the Nation of Israel from entering into the Promised Land. The Hebrew people possessed this unbelief because they did not know the ways of their God. The third trait was obedience. **Hebrews 11** tells us about great people who walked in obedience because of their faith.

Hebrews 11:8 says,
"By faith Abraham, when he was called to go out into a place which he should after receive for an inheritance, obeyed; and he went out, not knowing whither he went."

Hebrews 11:24-25 says,
"By faith Moses, when he was come to years, refused to be called the son of Pharaoh's daughter; choosing rather to suffer affliction with the people of God, than to enjoy the pleasures of sin for a season."

Hebrews 11:29-31 says,
"By faith they passed through the Red Sea as by dry land: which the Egyptians assaying to do were drowned. By faith the walls of Jericho fell down, after they were compassed about seven days. By faith the harlot Rahab perished not with them that believed not, when she had received the spies with peace."

Because of the obedient walk of faith, people obtained promises, avoided sin, and were spared of judgment.

For this reason, Paul makes this statement about faith in **Romans 14:23**,
"And he that doubteth is damned if he eat, because he eateth not of faith: for whatsoever is not of faith is sin."

The fourth quality was the fear of the Lord. Noah moved in awe of His God.

Hebrews 12:28-29 tells us why we need the fear of the Lord,
"Wherefore we receiving a kingdom which cannot be moved, let us have grace, whereby we may serve God acceptably with reverence and godly fear: For our God is a consuming fire."

God is a consuming fire. Fire implies judgment. We, therefore, need to respond to our holy God with godly fear to avoid His judgment. (See **Philippians 2:12**.)

Personal Notes: ____

____

____

Confession of Our Faith

We must consider all of Paul's words in **Romans 10:9-10**,
"That if thou shalt confess with thy mouth the Lord Jesus, and shalt believe in thine heart that God hath raised him from the dead, thou shalt be saved. For with the heart man believeth unto righteousness; and with the mouth confession is made unto salvation."

Supplement: Servant Or Slave **Sup. 3**

We have been studying how saving faith begins in the heart. These scriptures show us how this faith ends, with the verbal confession of Jesus Christ being Lord. The Word Lord implies owner. If Jesus is Lord of our life, we have no personal rights. We belong to Him and must be obedient in service to Him. The Bible has much to say about this term in relation to Jesus.

Ephesians 4:4-5 tells us,
"There is one body, and one Spirit, even as ye are called in one hope of your calling; One Lord, one faith, one baptism."

Isaiah 45:21 makes this declaration about the Lord,
"Tell ye, and bring them near; yea, let them take counsel together: who hath declared this from ancient time? who hath told it from that time? Have not I the Lord? And there is no God else beside me; a just God and a Savior; there is none beside me."

Isaiah shows us our Lord is both God and Savior. We know **John 1:1** declares Jesus is God.

1 John 4:14 shows us Jesus is our Savior,
"And we have seen and do testify that the Father sent the Son to be the Saviour of the World."

Our Lord is the Christ or "the Anointed One."

1 John 4:15 gives us the last piece of the picture concerning the identity of our Lord,
"Whosoever shall confess that Jesus is the Son of God, God dwelleth in him, and he in God."

Jesus is the "Son of God." But before you can understand Him as the Son of God, you must know Him as God, Savior, and the Christ. In these titles we recognize He is divine by nature, and He came as the Christ in order to die for our sins. The identity of our Lord is of utmost importance to saving faith. True faith rests in the nature, purpose, work, and salvation of our Lord.

Revelation 3:20 says,
"Behold, I stand at the door, and knock: if any man hear my voice, and open the door, I will come in to him, and will sup with him, and he with me."

Jesus stands at the door of our heart. He is a gentleman. He is not a bully who will knock the door down and demand His own way. He is not a thief who will steal our hearts away while we are not looking. He is knocking, calling, and waiting for those who are heirs to His salvation to open the door. Remember what Jesus said in **John 10:4** and **16**, His sheep will know His voice. When one allows Jesus in, they will do so in light of His position as Lord. He will reign. They will only hear His voice and serve Him in love and total commitment. The problem with many people is that they want Jesus to save them, but they do not want Him to reign. Jesus comes in one package. A person cannot have His salvation without recognizing His Lordship.

Paul made this statement abut Jesus in **1 Timothy 6:15**,
"Which in his times he shall shew, who is the blessed and only Potentate, the King of kings, and Lord of Lord."

In Christ, we have deity, royalty, and eternal inheritance. Paul said in **Romans 10:9**, we must confess Jesus is Lord. This shows our agreement with God and serves as a testimony to man. We see this public confession taking place in the Scripture.

In **Matthew 14:33** we read this declaration made by our Lord's disciples,
"...Of a truth thou art the Son of God."

Martha made this proclamation about Jesus in **John 11:27**,
"...I believe that thou art the Christ, the Son of God, which should come into the world."

Thomas, a disciple of Christ made this declaration about Jesus in **John 20:28**,
"...My Lord and my God."

Hebrews 3:1 tells us,
"Wherefore, holy brethren, partakers of the heavenly calling, consider the Apostle and High Priest of our profession, Christ Jesus;"

Matthew 10:32-33 gives us an insight behind the importance of confessing Jesus before men,
"Whosoever therefore shall confess me before men, him will I confess also before my Father which is in heaven. But whosoever shall deny me before men, him will I also deny before my Father which is in heaven."

Jesus is our high priest. He intercedes for us.

The Apostle Paul confirms this in **Romans 8:34**,
"Who is he that condemneth? It is Christ that died, ye rather, that is risen again, who is even at the right hand of God, who also maketh intercession for us."

If we do not confess Christ before men, He will not acknowledge us before the Father. We need our High Priest to make intercession for us.

1 John 2:1-2 tells us why,
"My little children, these things write I unto you, that ye sin not. And if any man sin, we have an advocate with the Father, Jesus Christ the righteous: And he is the propitiation for our sins: and not for ours only, but also for the sins of the whole world."

In closing, do you have saving faith? Is your faith based on God? Do you believe in your heart that Christ was raised from the dead? Have you confessed that He is Lord? Have you heard His voice and opened the door of your heart to Him?

The answer to these questions will determine your eternal destination.

Personal Notes: ____

____

____

Chapter 12

FAITH IN ACTION

We know the level of our faith will be based on our perception of God. We know it must be inspired and established by the Word of God. It is eternal in nature **(1 Corinthians 13:13)**. Now, we need to grasp the purpose of faith in our spiritual lives.

Hebrews 11:6 tells us the importance of faith in our life,
"But without faith it is impossible to please him:..."

The key of having a faith which is pleasing to God is found in **Romans 1:17**,
"For therein is the righteousness of God revealed from faith to faith: as it is written, The just shall live by faith."

A walk of faith is motivated by having right standing before the Lord as a means to please Him. This righteousness is only obtained through a relationship with Jesus Christ.

1 Corinthians 1:30 confirms this,
"But of him (God) are ye in Christ Jesus, who of God is made unto us wisdom, and righteousness, and sanctification, and redemption." (Parenthesis added.)

Jesus is the believer's righteousness. Righteousness means being in right standing or being upright before God. By having faith in Christ, we have His righteousness imparted in our lives. This faith results in a right relationship between God and man. This life avoids walking in sin.

1 John 3:7-8 says,
"...he that doeth righteousness is righteous, even as he is righteous. He that committeth sin is of the devil;..."

Proverbs 20:7 tells us,
"The just man walketh in his integrity:..." (Also see **Psalm 51**.)

An upright life will display characteristics that are representative of the God we serve. These qualities will be evident in every area of an individual's life. The following scriptures confirm this.

Matthew 25:37-40 says,
"Then shall the righteous answer him, saying, Lord, when saw we thee an hungred, and fed thee? or thirsty, and gave thee drink? When saw we thee a stranger, and took thee in? or naked, and clothed thee? Or when saw we thee sick, or in prison, and came unto thee? And the King (Jesus) shall answer and say unto them, Verily I say unto you, Inasmuch as ye have done it unto one of the least of these my brethren, ye have done It unto me." (Parenthesis added.)

Psalm 37:21 declares,
"The wicked borroweth, and payeth not again: but the righteous sheweth mercy, and giveth."

Psalm 37:30 states,
"The mouth of the righteous speaketh wisdom, and his tongue talketh of judgement."

Proverbs 29:7 makes this statement,
"The righteous considereth the cause of the poor: but the wicked regardeth not to know it."

Our attitudes, consideration for others, and our tongue are just a few areas in which righteousness should be displayed.

Religion Versus Righteousness

Supplement: Volume 6 Book 1: *The Many Faces of Christianity*

Jesus gave us a test to determine if our righteousness is real in **Matthew 5:20**,
"For I say unto you, That except your righteousness shall exceed the righteousness of the scribes and Pharisees, ye shall in no case enter into the kingdom of heaven.

The Pharisees were the religious leaders of Jesus' day. Jesus gave these instructions in **Matthew 6:2, 5** and **16** to expose the "acts of righteousness" done by these leaders. These acts were surface. They were done for the purpose of bringing recognition to them and not to God.

Matthew 6:2, 5 & 16 says,
"Therefore when thou doest thine alms, do not sound a trumpet before thee, as the hypocrites do in the synagogues and in the streets, that they may have glory of men. Verily I say unto you, They have their reward...And when thou prayest, thou shalt not be as the hypocrites are: for they love to pray standing in the synagogues and in the corners of the streets, that they may be seen of men. Verily I say unto you, they have their reward. ...Moreover when ye fast, be not, as the hypocrites, of a sad countenance, for they disfigure their faces, that they may appear unto men to fast, Verily I say unto you, they have their reward.

Jesus made this statement about these religious leaders in **Matthew 15:6-9**,
"...Thus have ye made the commandment of God of none effect by your tradition. Ye hypocrites, well did Esaias prophesy of you saying, This people draweth nigh unto me with their mouth, and honoureth me with their lips; but their heart is far from me. But in vain they do worship me, teaching for doctrines the commandments of men.

The Pharisees and teachers of the Law took pride in their "appearance of righteousness." They not only taught the rigid Law, but they added their own traditions. Therefore, they destroyed the purpose of the Law.

Jesus summarized the effect on the people who would follow their example and rules in **Matthew 23:13**,
"But woe unto you, scribes and Pharisees, hypocrites! for ye shut up the kingdom of heaven against men: for ye neither go in yourselves, neither suffer ye them that are entering to go in."

Man is saved by grace not by works.

The Apostle Paul confirmed this in **Ephesians 2:8-9**,
"For by grace are ye saved through faith; and that not of yourselves: it is the gift of God: Not of works, lest any man should boast."

James 2:10 gives us this insight about obeying the Law,
"For whosoever shall keep the whole law, and yet offend in one point, he is guilty of all."

We cannot keep the full intent of the Law.

The purpose of the Law can be summarized by **Romans 5:20**,
"Moreover the law entered, that the offence might abound. But where sin abounded, grace did much more abound."

The Law cannot justify, it can only condemn. The Law was given to show man that he is a sinner. This truth is designed to lead man to Jesus Christ.

Paul confirms this in **Galatians 3:24**,
"Wherefore the law was our schoolmaster to bring us unto Christ, that we might be justified by faith."

Christ satisfied the Law by fulfilling the requirements of the Law with His sacrifice. This means He maintained the intent or spirit of the Law. Likewise, we are to fulfill the Law by loving God and others. The love of God will ensure the spirit of the Law. This will produce obedience to Him. (Refer to **Mark 12:29-31; John 13:34-35; 14:14:15;** and **Romans 13:8-10**.)

Romans 10:4 says,
"For Christ is the end of the law for righteousness to every one that believeth."

The Apostle Paul explained how Christ fulfilled the law in **Galatians 3:13**,
"Christ hath redeemed us from the curse of the law, being made a curse for us: for it is written, Cursed is every one that hangeth on a tree."

Our inability to obey the full intent of the Law makes us aware of our need for the salvation of Jesus Christ. This salvation is based on the grace of God and comes through faith in Christ.

Romans 5:1-2 states,
"Therefore being justified by faith, we have peace with God through our Lord Jesus Christ: By whom also we have access by faith into this grace wherein we stand, and rejoice in hope of the glory of God."

The Pharisees traded a relationship with God for a religion of dead works. They preferred the bondage of the Law to the liberty of Jesus Christ. Sadly, most people do prefer some type of religious bondage to the liberty that puts a person's spiritual condition and relationship with God in his or her hands.

Galatians 5:1 says,
"Stand fast therefore in the liberty wherewith Christ hath made us free, and be not entangled again with the yoke of bondage."

We have been set free from the bondage of the Law. We have been justified by faith in Christ. We are now partakers of His righteousness. Why would we want to exchange this powerful relationship with a religion that destroys the effectiveness of the Word of God?

Personal Notes: ____

____

____

Mountain Moving Faith

In **Mark 9:23,** we read Jesus' words,
"...If thou canst believe, all things are possible to him that believeth."

We have examined how a walk of faith is a product of righteousness. Now we are going to consider what faith is capable of doing in our relationship with God.

Jesus made this statement to His disciples about faith in **Matthew 17:20**,
"Because of your unbelief: for verily I say unto you, If ye have faith as a grain of mustard seed, ye shall say unto this mountain, Remove hence to yonder place; and it shall remove: and nothing shall be impossible unto you."

It is not our faith which moves the mountain, but rather our faith in a powerful God. It is believing God and allowing Him to be God that results in much being done, including the impossible.

Jesus confirms this in **Matthew 19:26,**
"...With men that is impossible; but with God all things are possible."

BEWARE! Never put your faith in faith. There can be a fine line between having faith in God and having faith in faith. By having faith in faith, you are making faith a god. In the end, you will actually be exalting self in some fashion, form or works.

In God's Word there are many promises. These promises often involve the impossible where man is concerned.

2 Peter 1:3-4 tells us,
"According as his divine power hath given unto us all things that pertain unto life and godliness, through the knowledge of him that hath called us to glory and virtue: Whereby are given unto us exceeding great and precious promises: that by these ye might be partakers of the divine nature, having escaped the corruption that is in the world through lust."

These promises involve every area of our life.

For instance, **Philippians 4:19** gives us this guarantee about our physical needs,
"But my God shall supply all your need according to his riches in glory by Christ Jesus."

Note God will supply our needs, not necessarily our wants.

For our spiritual well-being we read this in **James 1:17**,
"Every good gift and every perfect gift is from above, and cometh down from the Father of lights, with whom is no variableness neither shadow of turning.

Our God does not change. His promises remain the same. Each promise of God is conditional. Obedience to God's way is the requirement necessary to receive the fullness of God's promises. For instance, you must believe the gospel to receive eternal life.

Here are other examples of promises found in **Psalm 37:4-6**,
"Delight thyself also in the LORD; and he shall give thee the desires of thine heart. Commit thy way unto the LORD; trust also in him; and he shall bring it to pass."

We need to delight ourselves in the Lord. Once we respond in this way, He will give us the desires of our heart. If we commit our way to the Lord and trust in Him, He will bring forth righteousness that shines in our life. Faith is taking God at His Word. It is trusting God with every area of our lives. It is having confidence in knowing that no matter what happens, God is still in control and He is allowing it for our benefit and His glory.

Another popular way of spelling faith is **r..i..s..k:** One must risk what he or she knows or his or her comfort zones in order to discover the hidden treasures of God.

Another popular way of spelling out faith gives a picture of it in action:

Forsaking
All
I
Take
Him

Peter summarized true faith in **1 Peter 1:8**,
"Whom having not seen, ye love; in whom, though now ye see him not, yet believing, ye rejoice with joy unspeakable and full of glory: Receiving the end of your faith, even the salvation of your souls."

Do you have saving faith?

Personal Notes: ______________________________

____

____

____

Chapter 13

BAPTISM

Christ gave His followers two ordinances. An ordinance is an established rule, religious rite, or ceremony. The first ordinance was instituted at the beginning of His ministry. It is known as water baptism.

These are Jesus' words to John the Baptist at His water baptism in **Matthew 3:15**, "Suffer it to be so now: for thus it becometh us to fulfill all righteousness."

The second ordinance is communion **(1 Corinthians 11:23-34)**. Communion means fellowship, sharing, or agreement. This religious rite took place on the night Jesus was betrayed, (at the end of his earthy mission). This ceremony is done in recognition of the price Jesus paid on the cross for our sins. It serves as a memorial or reminder of His broken body and shed blood.

It can be summarized in Jesus' statement in **Luke 22:19**,
"...this do in remembrance of me."

Each ceremony is representative of our Christian life. Water baptism identifies us with Christ. Communion maintains our life by keeping us focused on Christ's work on the cross. The religious ceremony we will be presently considering is water baptism.

Jesus gave His disciples this instruction in **Mark 16:15-16**,
"Go ye into all the world, and preach the gospel to every creature. He that believeth and is baptized shall be saved; but he that believeth not shall be damned."

Salvation should lead to water baptism. Note, water baptism is commanded, but will not ensure salvation. The word baptism comes from a word that means to cause something to be dipped or immersed into fluid and taken back out. This immersion is complete. There are four kinds of baptism mentioned in Scripture.

They are:

* A Baptism of Repentance
* The Believer's Baptism
* A Baptism of Suffering
* The Baptism of the Holy Spirit

Each baptism is representative of the different stages of the Christian walk. Each identifies the believer with Christ in His life and ministry. For instance, *baptism of repentance* implies our acknowledgement of sin and our need of forgiveness. *Baptism of suffering* represents the believer's preparation for the cross. The *believer's baptism* is symbolic of the believer becoming identified with Christ in His death, burial, and resurrection. The *baptism of the Holy Spirit* associates the believer with Christ in power and authority, resulting in a fruitful life and an effective ministry. We must consider each of these baptisms in light of Christ and His plan for man.

Personal Notes: ____

____

____

The Baptism of Repentance

In **Matthew 3**, we see John the Baptist entering the scene. John was the cousin of Jesus and the one who would prepare the way for Him.

Mark 1:2-3 makes this reference to John the Baptist,
"As it is written in the prophets, Behold, I send my messenger before thy face, which shall prepare thy way before thee. The voice of one crying in the wilderness, Prepare ye the way of the Lord, make his paths straight."

Mark 1: 4-5 tells us what John was proclaiming,
"John did baptize in the wilderness, and preach the baptism of repentance for the remission of sins. And there went out unto him all the land of Judaea, and they of Jerusalem, and were all baptized of him in the river Jordan, confessing their sins."

Matthew 3:6 shows us the people's response to John's preaching,
"And were baptized of him in Jordan, confessing their sins."

The goal of John's baptism was simple. It was designed to turn people toward Jesus Christ. In order for people to be receptive to Christ's salvation, they had to first acknowledge their sinful condition and their need for forgiveness. He also stated that it was necessary to bring forth fruits fit for repentance **(Matthew 3:8)**. Fruits of repentance come in the form of change that is evident to others.

Personal Notes: ____

____

____

Baptism of Suffering

Jesus made this statement in **Luke 12:50**,
"But I have a baptism to be baptized with; and how am I straitened till it be accomplished!"

In **Matthew 20:22** we see Jesus once again referring to this baptism while talking to his disciples,
"...Are ye able to drink of the cup that I shall drink of,..."

The cup Jesus talked about involved His sufferings surrounding the cross. Scripture gives us a picture of His sufferings. Jesus knew what was going to happen as well.

We see Him trying to prepare His followers for the upcoming events in **Matthew 20:18-19**, "Behold, we go up to Jerusalem; and the Son of man shall be betrayed unto the chief priests and unto the scribes, and they shall condemn him to death, And shall deliver him to the Gentiles to mock, and to scourge, and to crucify him: and the third day he shall rise again."

Isaiah 50:6 gives us this insight about Jesus' sufferings,
"I (Jesus) gave my back to the smiters, and my cheeks to them that plucked off the hair: I hid not my face from shame and spitting." (Parenthesis added.)

Psalm 22:7, 14-18 gives us this clear picture of Christ's sufferings,
"All they that see me laugh me to scorn: they shoot out the lip, they shake the head, ...I am poured out like water, and all my bones are out of joint: ...My strength is dried up like a potsherd; and my tongue cleaveth to my jaws...they pierced my hands and my feet. I may tell all my bones: they look and stare upon me. They part my garments among them, and cast lots upon my vesture."

This sober picture reminds me of the words found in **Isaiah 53:2-3**,
"...he (Jesus) hath no form nor comeliness; and when we shall see him, there is no beauty that we should desire him. He is despised and rejected of men; a man of sorrows, and acquainted with grief:..." (Parenthesis added.)

We catch a glimpse of Jesus' agony before the cross.

We read this in **Luke 22:41-44,**
"...and kneeled down, and prayed. Saying Father, if thou be willing, remove this cup from me: nevertheless not my will but thine, be done. And there appeared an angel unto him from heaven, strengthening him. And being in agony he prayed more earnestly: and his sweat was as it were great drops of blood falling down to the ground."

What was Jesus' real agony? Was it the physical suffering? He knew the flesh was weak. Was it the fact all of His followers would desert Him for He predicted as much because He knew He had to go the way of Calvary alone to pay the price of redemption? Or, was it the ordeal of the cross? Some Bible teachers feel His agony had nothing to do with his physical suffering. They believe that when Jesus became sin for us, God turned His back on Him for that moment. (See **2 Corinthians 5:21**and **Isaiah 53:5**.)

Isaiah 59:2 may shed some light on this concept,
"But your iniquities have separated between you and your God, and your sins have hid his face from you, that he will not hear."

God cannot look upon iniquity. The presence of sin breaks fellowship with Him. Keep in mind, Jesus had never been separated from His Father.

Many conclude as a result of this separation, Christ said these words from the cross **Matthew 27:46**,
"...My God, my God, why hast thou forsaken me?"

If God had turned His back on Jesus for that moment it would explain the real cup of suffering Jesus wanted to avoid. Briefly, we can gain some insight into the terrible agony Christ must have experienced on the cross. But the truth is all that believers will fully experience is the ultimate victory which was secured on the cross.

This victory can be summarized in Christ's final statement made on the cross in **John 19:30**:
"...It is finished:..."

Jesus paid the complete price for our sins. He became broken so we could be made whole. He became separated from the Father so we could have an intimate fellowship with our Creator. He died so we could have life. He rose again so that we might know victory over death.

Personal Notes: ____

____

The Apostle Paul made this statement in **Philippians 3:10**,
"That I may know him, and the power of his resurrection, and the fellowship of his sufferings, being made conformable unto his death."

If anyone understood the meaning of Christ's sufferings it would have been Paul.

He gives us this account about his life in **2 Corinthians 11:24-25 & 27**,
"Of the Jews five times received I forty stripes save one. Thrice was I beaten with rods, once was I stoned, thrice I suffered shipwreck, a night and a day I have been in the deep...In weariness and painfulness, in watchings often, in hunger and thirst, in fastings often, in cold and nakedness."

Paul rejoiced in his sufferings.

He explained why in **2 Corinthians 12:9-10**,
"And he (Jesus) said unto me, My grace is sufficient for thee: for my strength is made perfect in weakness. Most gladly therefore will I rather glory in my infirmities, that the power of Christ may rest upon me. Therefore I take pleasure in infirmities, in reproaches, in necessities, in persecutions, in distresses for Christ's sake: for when I am weak, then am I strong." *(Parenthesis added.)*

Paul made this statement in **2 Corinthians 4:7-10**,
"But we have this treasure in earthen vessels, that the excellency of the power may be of God, and not of us. We are troubled on every side, yet not distressed; we are perplexed, but not in despair; Persecuted, but not forsaken, cast down, but not destroyed; Always bearing about in the body the dying of the Lord Jesus, that the life also of Jesus might be made manifest in our body."

Sufferings are part of our dying-out process. The purpose for these sufferings is to work the life of Jesus in us.

James 1:2-4 tells us,
"My brethren, count it all joy when ye fall into divers temptations; Knowing this, that the trying of your faith worketh patience. But let patience have her perfect work, that ye may be perfect and entire, wanting nothing."

It is hard to consider sufferings in terms of pure joy. But the key to suffering is that it serves as a type of door in which you enter into fellowship with Jesus. This fellowship cannot be measured in light of worldly importance, only in consideration of eternal value.

1 Peter 1:6-7 says,
"Wherein ye greatly rejoice, though now for a season, if need be, ye are in heaviness through manifold temptations: That the trial of your faith, being much more precious than of gold that perisheth, though it be tried with fire, might be found unto praise and honour and glory at the appearing of Jesus Christ:"

There is no shortcut to this intimate fellowship, for this reason, Paul made this statement about the difficult process Christians find themselves in **2 Corinthians 4:15**,
For all things are for your sakes, that the abundant grace might through the thanksgiving of many redound to the glory of God."

2 Corinthians 1:3-6 gives us this insight about how such suffering brings glory to God,
"Blessed be God, even the Father of our Lord Jesus Christ, the Father of mercies, and the God of all comfort; Who comforteth us in all our tribulation, that we may be able to comfort them which are in any trouble, by the comfort wherewith we ourselves are comforted of God. For as the sufferings of Christ abound in us, so our consolation also aboundeth by Christ. And whether we be afflicted, it is for your consolation and salvation, which is effectual in the enduring of the same sufferings, which we also suffer: or whether we be comforted, it is for your consolation and salvation."

In order to effectively minister the life of Christ to others we must enter into His sufferings. This life of suffering should be considered an honor.

In conclusion, Paul gives us this promise in **2 Timothy 2:12**,
"If we suffer, we shall also reign with him: if we deny him, he also will deny us."

Personal Notes: ____

____

____

Chapter 14

THE BELIEVER'S BAPTISM

Supplement:
Volume 1
Book 5
Study:
Unmasking The Cult Mentality
Section 4:
Ordinances
Of the Church

The believer's baptism signifies an outward sign of total commitment. It identifies the believer to Jesus Christ.

We must consider Jesus' command in **Matthew 28:18-19**,
"...All power is given unto me in heaven and in earth. Go ye therefore, and teach all nations, baptizing them in the name of the Father, and of the Son and of the Holy Ghost."

We see two commands in these scriptures. We must make disciples of all nations. This means we teach people to observe or obey the things of God.

Matthew 28:20 confirms this,
"Teaching them to observe all things whatsoever I have commanded you: and, lo, I am with you always, even unto the end of the world."

Matthew 5:19 gives us this insight about the somber responsibility of teaching people to obey the commandments of God,
"Whosoever therefore shall break one of these least commandments, and shall teach men so, he shall be called the least in the kingdom of heaven: but whosoever shall do and teach them, the same shall be called great in the kingdom of heaven."

To be effective in disciplining, one must teach by example more than with words. The second command is to baptize in the name of the Father, the Son, and the Holy Spirit. Here we are being identified with the Godhead. It must be pointed out that all three Persons of the Godhead were present at Jesus' baptism in **Matthew 3**. The Father spoke, the Son was revealed in human form, and the Holy Spirit came down in the form of a dove. Each Person of the Godhead has a vital part in our salvation; therefore, it is only proper that we become identified with each of them at our baptism. It is also a reminder that our life must clearly be established in God.

Colossians 3:3 tells us,
"For ye are dead, and your life is hid with Christ in God."

It is important to once again note baptism is not a requirement of salvation, but rather an act of obedience.

Remember, Jesus' words about His baptism in **Matthew 3:15**,
"...Suffer it to be so now: for thus it becometh us to fulfil all righteousness...."

The only requirement to salvation is to believe on the Lord Jesus.

Mark 16:16 confirms this,
"He that believeth and is baptized shall be saved; but he that believeth not shall be damned."

Note condemnation will only come to those who do not believe. The real emphasis of the message of salvation is the Gospel and not baptism.

Paul wrote these words in **1 Corinthians 1:17**,
"For Christ sent me not to baptize, but to preach the gospel: not with wisdom of words, lest the cross of Christ should be made of none effect."

Paul was concerned about taking away from the powerful message of the Gospel. Beware of people who tell you baptism is part of the Gospel message. The death, burial, and resurrection of Christ is the only message which leads to salvation. Baptism is simply the obedient response of those who are saved.

Personal Notes: ____

____

What This Baptism Symbolizes

Christian baptism identifies the believer with the death, burial, and resurrection of Jesus Christ.

Romans 6:3 tells us,
"Know ye not, that so many of us as were baptized into Jesus Christ were baptized into his death?"

Hebrews 10:22 puts this light on what it means to be clean spiritually,
"Let us draw near with a true heart in full assurance of faith, having our hearts sprinkled from an evil conscience, and our bodies washed with pure water."

The real cleansing comes when we draw near to God, knowing with confidence we can find forgiveness because of what Christ did on the cross. (See **Psalm 103:12**.) The act of submerging the person into the water is symbolic of the grave where the old life must remain.

Romans 6:4 says,
"Therefore we are buried with him by baptism into death: that like as Christ was raised up from the dead by the glory of the Father, even so we also should walk in newness of life."

Coming up out of the water symbolizes the new spiritual life being brought forth.

Paul made this statement about the new life in **2 Corinthians 4:16**,
"For which cause we faint not; but though our outward man perish, yet the inward man is renewed day by day."

The importance of being identified with the death of Christ is found in **2 Timothy 2:11**,
"...For if we be dead with him, we shall also live with him:"

Galatians 3:27 gives us this complete picture of baptism,
"For as many of you as have been baptized into Christ have put on Christ."

The new life is summarized by the righteousness of Christ becoming evident in our lives.

Personal Notes: ____

____

The Picture of Salvation

Water baptism identifies us with Christ's death, burial, and resurrection. This identification with the Gospel is what leads to salvation. But it also symbolizes the work of salvation being worked out in our lives.

The Apostle Peter summarized this picture of salvation in **1 Peter 3:20-21**,
"Which sometime were disobedient, when once the longsuffering of God waited in the days of Noah, while the ark was a preparing, wherein few, that is, eight souls were saved by water. The like figure whereunto even baptism doth also now save us (not the putting away of the filth of the flesh, but the answer of a good conscience toward God,) by the resurrection of Jesus Christ."

Salvation means deliverance. God delivered Noah and his family through the flood.

Note the sentence in **1 Peter 3:20**,
"...were saved by water."

Water represents two spiritual sources. It symbolizes God's Word.

Ephesians 5:26 states,
"That he might sanctify and cleanse it (the church) with the washing of water by the word." (Parenthesis added.) Also refer to **Hebrews 4:12**.

The Holy Spirit is represented by water in the scriptures.

Jesus said this in **John 7:38-39a**,
"...If any man thirst, let him come unto me, and drink. He that believeth on me, as the scripture hath said, out of his belly shall flow rivers of living water. (But this spoke he of the Sprit...)"

These two spiritual sources of water can be associated with three distinct acts, which must take place in a person's life to ensure true salvation.

Jesus gives us an insight into the first work of deliverance in **John 3:5-6**,
"...Verily, verily, I say unto thee, Except a man be born of water and of the Spirit, he cannot enter the kingdom of God. That which is born of the flesh is flesh: and that which is born of the Spirit is spirit."

1 Peter 1:23 gives us this insight,
"Being born again, not of corruptible seed, but of incorruptible, by the word of God, which liveth and abideth for ever."

Man must experience a spiritual birth. This birth is a result of believing the Word and allowing the Holy Spirit access to his life. The second act is spiritual cleansing or sanctification. Scripture reminds us how the Church will be cleansed by the Word in **Ephesians 5:26**.

Paul made this statement about believers in **Romans 15:16**,
"...being sanctified by the Holy Ghost."

The Holy Spirit is setting believers apart from the unholy.

Paul makes this statement about sanctification in **2 Timothy 2:19-20**,
"...And, Let every one that nameth the name of Christ depart from iniquity. But in a great house there are not only vessels of gold and of silver, but also of wood and of earth; and some to honour, and some to dishonour."

The third spiritual application of water is regeneration. Regeneration is new life coming forth. It is related to the activities surrounding springtime.

Titus 3:5 tells us,
"...he (God) saved us, by the washing of regeneration, and renewing of the Holy Ghost." (Parenthesis added.)

The spiritual birth, sanctification, and regeneration describe the work of salvation. True salvation will result in an upright life. A righteous life implies a good conscience towards God.

This brings us back to the words of Christ in **Matthew 3:15**,
"And Jesus answering said unto him, Suffer it to be so now: for thus it becometh us to fulfil all righteousness..."

Fulfill means complete. An individual who becomes identified with Christ in both His death and in His work of salvation will have a complete life in Him. Let us examine both representations of baptism:

Identified with Christ		**Work of Salvation**
Death	equals	Spiritual Birth
Burial	equals	Sanctification
Resurrection	equals	Regeneration

Would you not say this is a complete picture of our life in Jesus Christ?

Personal Notes: ____

____

____

____

Chapter 15

THE BAPTISM OF THE HOLY SPIRIT

In the last chapter, we learned how we must be born again.

John 3:3 confirms this,
"…Except a man be born again, he cannot see the kingdom of God."

This experience is known as the spiritual birth. This birth occurs when we receive Jesus as Lord and Savior. The Holy Spirit is then given to man as a gift from the Father. He will take up residence in a person's spirit. This reminds me of the saying, "Born twice, die once, born once, die twice." Man must be born twice (physically and spiritually) to avoid the second death. (See **Revelation 21:8**.)

Jesus made this comment about the Holy Spirit in **John 14:17,**
"Even the Spirit of truth; whom the world cannot receive, because it seeth him not, neither knoweth him: but ye know him; for he dwelleth with you, and shall be in you."

John 16:7 adds this insight about the Holy Spirit,
"Nevertheless I (Jesus) tell you the truth; It is expedient for you that I go away: for it I go not away, the Comforter will not come unto you; but if I depart, I will send him unto you." (Parenthesis added.)

Jesus had to go to the Father before the Holy Spirit could be sent.

Before His ascension to heaven, He gave this instruction to His disciples in **Luke 24:49,**
And, behold, I send the promise of my Father upon you: but tarry ye in the city of Jerusalem until ye be endued with power from on high."

The Bible tells us much about the third person of the Godhead.

John 16:8-11 states,
"And when he comes, he will reprove the world of sin, and of righteousness, and of judgment: Of sin, because they believe not on me; of righteousness, because I go to my Father, and ye see me no more; of judgment, because the prince of this world is judged."

The Holy Spirit convicts man of his need for salvation. He lifts Jesus up as the only standard of righteousness. He ultimately brings a person to a place of decision where he or she will commit all things to judgment or separation for the purpose of following Jesus. If a person fails to choose Jesus, then he or she can be assured of coming under the judgment that has been allotted to Satan and his world.

Ephesians 1:13-14 says this about the Holy Spirit,
"In whom ye also trusted, after that ye heard the word of truth, the gospel of your salvation in whom also, after that ye believed, ye were sealed with that Holy Spirit of promise, Which is

the earnest of our inheritance until the redemption of the purchased possession, unto the praise of his glory."

The Holy Spirit is the believer's seal. His presence in our life associates us to the salvation of Christ. He serves as our guarantee on earth to an eternal inheritance.

John the Baptist gives us another insight concerning the Holy Spirit in **Matthew 3:11**,
I indeed baptize you with water unto repentance: but he that cometh after me is mightier than I, whose shoes I am not worthy to bear: he shall baptize you with the Holy Ghost, and with fire."

This is the baptism of the Holy Spirit. Jesus referred to the Holy Spirit as the believer's Living Water. For this baptism to take place we must be totally immersed by the Holy Spirit.

Jesus makes a reference to this baptism in **Acts 1:5**,
"For John truly baptized with water; but ye shall be baptized with the Holy Ghost not many days hence."

We see the fulfillment of these scriptures in **Acts 2:1-4**,
And when the day of Pentecost was fully come, they were all with one accord in one place. And suddenly there came a sound from heaven as of a rushing mighty wind, and it filled all the house where they were sitting. And there appeared unto them cloven tongues like as of fire, and it sat upon each of them. And they were all filled with the Holy Ghost, and began to speak with other tongues, as the Spirit gave them utterance."

Can you imagine the excitement on the day of Pentecost? There were people in Jerusalem from different parts of the country who heard uneducated fishermen speak in their own language.

Acts 2:11-12 tells us their reaction,
"...we do hear them speak in our tongues the wonderful works of God. And they were all amazed, and were in doubt, saying one to another, What meaneth this?"

The reason for the baptism of the Holy Spirit can be found in Jesus' words in **Acts 1:8**,
"But ye shall receive power, after that the Holy Ghost is come upon you: and ye shall be witnesses unto me...."

We have begun our Christian life with *repentance*. We have entered into *suffering* for the purpose of preparation for our death. We come into the death, burial, and resurrection of Jesus in order for a *new life* to come forth. **Acts 1:8** shows us that our new life will have power and authority behind it. This power is necessary to be effective witnesses for Jesus Christ.

Personal Notes: ____

____

____

Avoiding Confusion

Baptism of the Holy Spirit is often confused with the spiritual birth. These acts are separate. Jesus distinguished these two events. In **John 14:17**, Jesus tells His disciples that the Holy Spirit was with them, but not in them. The born-again experience takes place when the Spirit of God comes and resides in the person. We can actually see where Jesus gave His followers the Holy Spirit. It happened after His resurrection and before His ascension.

John 20:22 records this event,
"And when he had said this, he breathed on them, and saith unto them, Receive ye the Holy Ghost."

Jesus instructs His disciples to wait in Jerusalem for the power of the Holy Spirit to be imparted upon them. (Refer to **Luke 24:49** and **Acts 1:8**.) We know this impartation to be the baptism of the Holy Spirit.

In **Acts 19:2-6** we read this conversation between Paul and some followers of Jesus,
(Paul is speaking) "He said unto them, Have ye received the Holy Ghost since ye believed? And they said unto him, We have not so much as heard whether there be any Holy Ghost. And he said unto them, Unto what then were ye baptized? And they said, Unto John's baptism. Then said Paul, John verily baptized with the baptism of repentance, saying unto the people, that they should believe on him which should come after him, that is, on Christ Jesus. When they heard this, they were baptized in the name of the Lord Jesus. And when Paul had laid his hands upon them, the Holy Ghost came on them; and they spake with tongues, and prophesied."

John the Baptist already had baptized these men. They believed in Christ and were baptized in His name. Remember the only requirement for salvation is to believe on the Lord Jesus Christ. The Holy Spirit is a gift to any believer as a seal of eternal redemption. Although these individuals were not aware of His presence in their inner being, He was still there. When Paul placed his hands on them, the Holy Spirit came on them signifying baptism. A similar incident occurred in **Acts 8:9-17**. In **Acts 9**, we read about the Apostle Paul's' conversion. Paul met Christ in a powerful way while traveling to persecute believers. **Acts 9:1-5** tell us how God sent a man to Paul to lay hands on him.

Acts 9:17 explains why God sent this man to Paul,
"...Brother Saul, the Lord, even Jesus, that appeared unto thee in the way as thou camest, hath sent me, that thou mightest receive thy sight, and be filled with the Holy Ghost."

Personal Notes: ____

____

____

The Evidence

Supplement:
Prayer Bible Study
Sup. 1

Once the baptism of the Holy Spirit occurs, there is evidence which follows. We read about this evidence in the following incidents.

Acts 2:4 states,
"And they were all filled with the Holy Ghost, and began to speak with other tongues..."

While Peter was still speaking these words, the Holy Spirit came on all who heard the message. The circumcised believers who had come with Peter were astonished that the gift of the Holy Spirit had been poured out even on the Gentiles.

Acts 10:44-46 tells about the Holy Spirit coming on Gentiles. **Acts 10:46** reveals the end results,
"For they heard them speak with tongues, and magnify God..."

Acts 19:6 says,
"...the Holy Ghost came on them, and they spake with tongues and prophesied."

Although it is controversial it appears that the consistent, visible evidence of this baptism was speaking in other tongues. But I personally believe it is only one of the evidences of this baptism. In **Acts 19:6**, prophecy was also a manifestation of this baptism. The purpose for this immersion from above is not to speak in unknown tongues, but to become powerful witnesses for Jesus **(Acts 1:8)**. I believe this power will be evident not only in the use of gifts such as tongues and prophecy, but in living the Christian life and understanding the deep things of God's Word. Therefore, a person should never seek the evidence of this baptism, but rather he or she should come to Jesus to receive all that He has for him or her.

There are two types of tongues in use.

The Apostle Paul makes this distinction in **1 Corinthians 14:13-15**,
"Wherefore let him that speaketh in an unknown tongue pray that he may interpret. For if I pray in an unknown tongue, my spirit prayeth, but my understanding is unfruitful. What is it then? I will pray with the spirit, and I will pray with the understanding also: I will sing with the spirit, and I will sing with the understanding also."

Paul made a distinction between the gift of tongues (speaking) that is used for the edification of the church, and also praying in tongues. When you speak in a tongue for the benefit of the congregation, it must be interpreted.

Paul confirms this in **1 Corinthians 14:27**,
"If any man speak in an unknown tongue, let it be by two, or at the most by three, and that by course; and let one interpret."

Paul adds this insight into the gift of tongues in **1 Corinthians 14:6**,
"Now, brethren, if I come unto you speaking with tongues, what shall I profit you, except I shall speak to you either by revelation, or by knowledge, or by prophecy, or by doctrine?"

Paul puts the subject of tongues in this perspective in **1 Corinthians 14:2**,
"For he that speaketh in an unknown tongue speaketh not unto men, but unto God: for no man understandeth him; howbeit in the spirit he speaketh mysteries."

A tongue not used for the edification of the church serves as a prayer language. This language is between God and the individual. It is the Holy Spirit in them uttering mysteries through prayer for the glory of God.

In **Ephesians 5:18-19** we read these words,
"And be not drunk with wine, wherein is excess; but be filled with the Spirit. Speaking to yourselves in psalms and hymns and spiritual songs, singing and making melody in your heart to the Lord."

Ephesians 6:18 gives us this instruction,
"Praying always with all prayer and supplication in the Spirit, and watching thereunto with all perseverance and supplication for all saints."

1 Thessalonians 5:17 tells us,
"Pray without ceasing."

Prayer is communication with God. There is power in prayer if we are continually being filled up with the Spirit as we seek more of God and His will. We need to pray in the Spirit. Therefore, we need this filling daily to keep our lines of communication open at all times.

Do you want the power of the Holy Spirit? If you do, you need to ask Jesus to baptize you with the Living Water.

Personal Notes: ____

____

____

____

Chapter 16

RECEIVING THE BAPTISM OF THE HOLY SPIRIT

Supplement: Volume 5 Book 3: *For the Purpose of Edification* **Chapter 2**

Acts 1:4 makes this statement about the Holy Spirit,
"...but wait for the promise of the Father, which, saith he, ye have heard of me."

We first of all see the Holy Spirit is a gift. A gift is something you cannot earn or buy, only receive. Simon the Sorcerer is a good example to consider. He offered the apostles money for this powerful gift.

Peter said these words to him in **Acts 8:20,**
"...Thy money perish with thee, because thou hast thought that the gift of God may be purchased with money."

The second truth we must note is the Holy Spirit is a promise from God. A promise from God is something you can be assured of; however, a promise involves the sovereign move of God and often has some kind of conditions that must be met. Conditions entail preparing a person to properly handle or receive the promise. In summary, God will choose the time, means, and place to fulfill His promise based on the environment that is present. In **John 21**, we see Jesus putting God's sovereign rights in perspective. Peter had just received insight about his destiny. He turned to Jesus and asked Him about the Apostle John's future.

We read Jesus' reply in **John 21:22**,
"...If I will that he tarry till I come, what is that to thee? follow thou me."

Once again, God's choice in fulfilling a promise will often be based on man's spiritual condition, desire, calling, and openness to receive it. We see this is true concerning the promise of the Holy Spirit.

Acts 1:14 & 2:1 gives us this insight about the people who were together on the day of Pentecost,
"These all continued with one accord in prayer and supplication, with the women, and Mary the mother of Jesus, and with his brethren...they were all with one accord in one place."

We must first keep in mind that the crucifixion of Christ and His ascension were still clear in these people's minds. They had come by way of the cross.

They were in constant prayer and they were being obedient to Jesus' instruction in **Luke 24:49**,
"...but tarry ye in the city of Jerusalem, until ye be endued with power from on high."

Obviously, obedience plays an important part. These people were waiting because of Christ's instruction. Sometimes a person is blessed enough to be saved and baptized with the Holy Spirit all at once. Other times people find themselves waiting for this promise. The key in waiting is obedience to what you know God wants you to do.

Luke 16:10 says,
"He that is faithful in that which is least is faithful also in much:..."

Being faithful to what is before us is a valuable lesson each believer must strive to master. Much of a believer's life seems to consist of waiting for God to move. Being faithful during these times will lead to greater experiences and responsibilities in the kingdom of God. Keep in mind, God desires to give all of us the power from on high to carry out our commission as a living witness.

We find this promise and instruction in **Psalm 27:13-14**,
"I had fainted, unless I had believed to see the goodness of the Lord in the land of the living. Wait on the LORD: be of good courage, and he shall strengthen thine heart: wait, I say, on the LORD."

Personal Notes: ____

____

Seeking God

Supplement: Volume 3 Book 2: *Prayer and Worship*

In **Acts 10**, we see the baptism of the Holy Spirit occurring in the lives of a Gentile man and his family. The man's name was Cornelius.

Acts 10:2 gives us this information about Cornelius and his family,
"A devout man, and one that feared God with all his house, which gave much alms to the people, and prayed to God alway."

Here we see a Gentile who was a devout believer. He feared God and gave generously to those in need."

2 Corinthians 9:7 says this about a cheerful giver,
"Every man according as he purposeth in his heart, so let him give; not grudgingly, or of necessity: for God loveth a cheerful giver."

Hebrews 13:16 tells us,
"But to do good and to communicate forget not: for with such sacrifices God is well pleased."

Finally, we see Cornelius was a man of prayer. It is in prayer that we seek God. There are great blessings which come with seeking God.

Jeremiah 29:13 tells us,
"And ye shall seek me, and find me, when ye shall search for me with all your heart."

If we are seeking God with all of our heart, we will find Him. Cornelius' dedication, service, and prayer life set him apart. As a result, he was the first Gentile to receive the power from on high.

A successful prayer life is summarized in **James 5:16**,
"...The effectual fervent prayer of a righteous man availeth much."

Successful prayer begins with the motivation to see God and to know His will. It must include seeking forgiveness for any sin.

Jesus said in **Matthew 6:12** to ask God,
"And forgive us our debts, as we forgive our debtors."

Effective prayers entail the sacrifice of praise.

Hebrews 13:15 instructs us,
"By him therefore let us offer the sacrifice of praise to God continually, that is, the fruit of our lips giving thanks to his name."

Praise is recognizing and honoring God for who He is. It is during a time of praise that many have been baptized with the Holy Spirit.

Psalm 22:3 says,
"But thou are holy, O thou that inhabitest the praises of Israel."

Thankfulness must be present in effectual prayer.

1 Thessalonians 5:18 tells us,
"In everything give thanks: for this is the will of God in Christ Jesus concerning you."

The Apostle Paul made this statement in **Philippians 4:6-7**,
"Be careful for nothing; but in every thing by prayer and supplication with thanksgiving let your requests be made known unto God. And the peace of God, which passeth all understanding, shall keep your hearts and minds through Christ Jesus."

A thankful heart will bring contentment to our lives. The Apostle Paul talked about people who lacked contentment in **1Timothy 6:3-8**. He told how they had wrong doctrine. They were interested in arguing and causing trouble. They had a corrupt mind for they had been robbed of the truth.

He then made these statements in **1Timothy 6:5-8**,
"...supposing that gain is godliness: from such withdraw thyself. But godliness with contentment is great gain. For we brought nothing into this world, and it is certain we can carry nothing out. And having food and raiment let us be therewith content."

Hebrews 13:5 tells us,
"Let your conversation be with out covetousness; and be content with such things as ye have: for he hath said, I will never leave thee, nor forsake thee."

Powerful prayer includes intercession for other believers.

Paul gave this instruction in **Ephesians 6:18**,
"Praying always with all prayer and supplication in the Spirit, and watching thereunto with all perseverance and supplication for all saints."

We need to pray in the name of Jesus. This means praying in line with His character, examples, and ways.

Jesus said this in **John 14:13-14**,
"And whatsoever ye shall ask in my name, that will I do, that the Father may be glorified in the Son. If ye shall ask any thing in my name, I will do it."

The final requirement to effective prayer is found in **1 John 5:14**,
"And this is the confidence that we have in him, that, if we ask anything according to his will, he heareth us."

God's will must be our main concern. We know God desires to give us this power from on high. We, therefore, need to seek His face to receive all that He has for us. We need to have the confidence. He alone will give it to us to enable us to serve Him in an effective way.

Personal Notes: ____

____

____

Laying On of Hands

Another means by which people have received the baptism of the Holy Spirit can be found in **Acts 19:6**,
"And when Paul had laid his hands upon them, the Holy Ghost came on them; and they spake with tongues, and prophesied.

The men involved in this incident received the baptism of the Holy Spirit when Paul placed his hands on them.

We see a similar incident in **Acts 8:14-17**. **Acts 8:17** says,
"Then laid they their hands on them, and they received the Holy Ghost."

Scripture shows us the Apostle Paul received the baptism of the Holy Spirit with the laying on of hands.

We read this in **Acts 9:17**,
"And Ananias went his way, and entered into the house; and putting his hands on him said, Brother Saul, the Lord, even Jesus, that appeared unto thee in the way as thou camest, hath sent me, that thou mightest receive thy sight, and be filled with the Holy Ghost."

The Apostle Paul also gives this warning about the laying on of hands in **1 Timothy 5:22**,
"Lay hands suddenly on no man, neither be partaker of other men's sins: keep thyself pure."

Witches and New Agers lay hands on others to impart spirits. This is why Paul is warning others to not lay hands on people until they are assured of their spirit **(1 John 4:1)**. This concept applies towards those who you allow to lay hands on you as well. You must be sensitive to the spirit in operation in a person's life. Do not subject yourself to a wrong spirit because it will make you a partaker of that person's wrong spirit, ultimately defiling you.

When we consider these incidents, we must acknowledge the attitudes found in these people towards this subject. The people in **Acts 8** and **19** were open to the baptism of the Holy Spirit. They submitted to the laying on of hands in order to receive it. In the case of Paul, we see a man in need of a touch from God.

But, we also read these words about him in **Acts 9:15-16**,
"...Go thy way: for he (Paul) is a chosen vessel unto me, to bear my name before the Gentiles, and kings, and the children of Israel: For I will shew him how great things he must suffer for my name's sake." *(Parenthesis added.)*

The motivation behind our desire for the baptism of the Holy Spirit must be considered as well. Jesus does not baptize us so we can show off or feel superior to others. The baptism of the Holy Spirit is to empower us to be powerful witnesses and to live a fruitful life. This powerful life will be lived out for the glory of God.

Paul made this statement in **1 Corinthians 1:31**,
"...He that glorieth, let him glory in the Lord."

God deserves all honor or praise for a believer's accomplishments. The promise of the Holy Spirit is to ultimately bring deserved honor to our God. Are you baptized with the Holy Spirit? If not ask the Lord to baptize you with the Living Water. Seek God's face in confidence. Be open to His promise. Allow true servants of God to lay hands on you. If you have to wait for the baptism, be prayerful, faithful, obedient, and confident. God will not withhold His promise from you. (See **Luke 11:13**.)

Personal Notes: ____

____

Chapter 17

BECOMING WITNESSES

Jesus made this statement in **Acts 1:8,**
"But ye shall receive power, after that the Holy Ghost is come upon you: and ye shall be witnesses unto me both in Jerusalem, and in all Judea, and in Samaria, and unto the uttermost part of the earth."

It is important to understand why God sent the power from on high down to common man. As I mentioned in the last chapter, it was not for show.

It was not to give preference to anyone, for as **Romans 2:11** says,
"For there is no respect of persons with God."

The purpose for sending the Holy Spirit down was to make the followers of Christ powerful witnesses. The word witness has two meanings. The first meaning of witness is to testify or tell what one has seen, heard, or experienced. Christ's disciples went about the country telling others what they had seen and experienced.

In **1 Peter 5:1** we read these words of Peter,
"The elders which are among you I exhort, who am also an elder, and a witness of the sufferings of Christ, and also a partaker of the glory that shall be revealed."

Peter made these proclamations in **Acts 10:39-41** about Jesus,
"And we are witnesses of all things which he did both in the land of the Jews, and in Jerusalem; whom they slew and hanged on a tree: Him God raised up the third day, and shewed him openly; Not to all the people, but unto *witnesses* chosen before of God, even to us, who did eat and drink with him after he rose from the dead."

In **Acts 2:32** we read these words,
"This Jesus hath God raised up, whereof we all are witnesses."

Acts 5:31-32 gives us this glorious testimony,
"Him hath God exalted with his right hand to be a Prince and a Saviour, for to give repentance to Israel, and forgiveness of sins. And we are his witnesses of these things; and so is also the Holy Ghost, whom God hath given to them that obey him." *(Refer to* **1 John 5:6-12***.)*

The combination of all these testimonies gives us the picture of the death, burial, and resurrection of Jesus Christ. We not only hear about Christ in the light of the cross from these witnesses, but we see Him in His glory through their eyes. These witnesses of Christ carried authority according to the Old Testament Law.

Jesus gives us this insight in **Matthew 18:15-16**,
"Moreover if thy brother shall trespass against thee, go and tell him his fault between these and him alone: if he shall hear thee, thou hast gained thy brother. But he will not hear thee,

then take with thee one or two more, that in the mouth of two or three witnesses every word may be established."

An incident is declared truth when there are two or more witnesses verifying it. Christ's death, burial, and resurrection were established by hundreds of witnesses who testified of it.

Paul gives us this testimony in **1 Corinthians 15:5-8**,
"And that he *(Jesus)* was seen of Cephas, then of the twelve: After that, he was seen of above five hundred brethren at once; of whom the greater part remain unto this present, but some are fallen asleep. After that, he was seen of James; then of all the apostles. And last of all he was seen of me also, as of one born out of due time." (Parenthesis added.)

In **Acts 1**, we see the disciples gathering to choose someone to replace Judas Iscariot. (Judas betrayed Jesus and hung himself. See **Matthew 27:3-5**.)

We read the main requirement for choosing this disciple in **Acts 1:21-22**,
"Wherefore of these men which have companied with us all the time that the Lord Jesus went in and out among us. Beginning from the baptism of John, unto that same day that he was taken us from us, must one be ordained to be a witness with us of his resurrection."

The followers of Jesus testified of what they had seen, heard, and experienced. As the Holy Spirit moved upon individuals, the message became real. Today, those who encounter Jesus as Lord and Savior have kept the Gospel alive. What we proclaim is the same message of hope the disciples shared over 2,000 years ago. The good news about Jesus' death, burial, and resurrection is timeless, and still is the most treasured event in all history.

Personal Notes: ____

____

Becoming Martyrs

Supplement: Volume 3 Book 1: *Godly Discipline*

The second meaning of witness is martyr. Martyr means one who constantly suffers. Suffering often produces godly discipline (**1 Peter 4:1-6**). Ultimately, a martyr's uncompromising beliefs will result in death. The idea of death is not attractive. But, to be an effective witness for Christ, a person must become identified with the Lord in His suffering and death.

John 12:23-26 says,
"And Jesus answered them, saying, The hour is come, that the Son of man should be glorified. Verily, verily, I say unto you, Except a corn of wheat fall into the ground and die, it abideth alone: bit if it die, it bringeth forth much fruit. He that loveth his life shall lose it; and he that hateth his life in this world shall keep it unto life eternal. If any man serve me, let him follow me; and where I am, there shall also my servant be: if any man serve me, him will my Father honour."

All followers of Christ must adhere to this principle of dying to self. Jesus left His disciples with this example. He would die first in order that those following in His steps would become heirs to eternal life.

Colossians 1:18 says,
"And he *(Jesus)* is the head of the body, the church: who is the beginning, the firstborn from the dead; that in all things he might have the preeminence." (Parenthesis added.)

Like Christ, His followers must die in order to be effective witnesses for Him. As witnesses for Christ they will be instruments used by the Holy Spirit to add to the kingdom of heaven.

Paul said this in **Galatians 6:14**,
"But God forbid that I should glory, save in the cross of our Lord Jesus Christ, by whom the world is crucified unto me, and I unto the world."

To be powerful witnesses we must allow the Holy Spirit to set us apart for God's service. This will mean becoming identified with Christ in His sufferings and death.

Paul gives us this instruction in **Romans 12:1**,
"I beseech you therefore, brethren, by the mercies of God, that ye present your bodies a living sacrifice, holy, acceptable unto God, which is your reasonable service."

We must become a "perpetual" (ongoing) living sacrifice. This means selling out for the glory of God. It implies giving up all of your rights. In light of God's mercy, this is the least we could do for Him.

1 Corinthians 3:9 tells us what our relationship in this life of service will be with God,
"For we are labourers, together with God:..."

We are co-laborers with God in sharing the Gospel with those of the world. As Christians the death, burial, and resurrection of Christ is our message; therefore, it must be real and personal to us. We were first saved because we heard the Gospel. Our personal experiences of answered prayer, and being aware of His intervention in our lives makes our testimony grow. Walking with Him through trails, problems, crises, and uncertainty brings forth His glory in our lives so others can see Him in us.

2 Corinthians 3:17-18 tells us,
"Now the Lord is that Spirit: and where the Spirit of the Lord is, there is liberty. But we all, with open face beholding as in a glass the glory of the Lord, are changed into the same image from glory to glory, even as by the Spirit of the Lord."

If the Holy Spirit has freedom in our lives, He will bring the glory of our Lord forth. It is the visible evidence of Christ in us which verifies and gives authority to our claims concerning Him. To be like Christ, we must live uprightly.

Ephesians 4:22-24 says,
"That ye put off concerning the former conversation the old man, which is corrupt according to the deceitful lusts; And be renewed in the spirit of your mind; And that ye put on the new man, which after God is created in righteousness and true holiness."

We cannot live an upright life in our own power. It is the Holy Spirit in us who enables us to live this life.

Galatians 5:16 says,
"This I say then, Walk in the Spirit, and ye shall not fulfil the lust of the flesh."

The Christian life is a disciplined life. Every area of our lives must come under the control of the Holy Spirit. This not only includes our lifestyles but our conversation as well.

James 1:26 says this about the tongue,
"If any man among you seem to be religious, and bridleth not his tongue, but deceiveth his own heart, this man's religion is vain."

There is much in the Word about our conversation.

Ephesians 4:25 tells us,
"Wherefore putting away lying, speak every man truth with his neighbour: for we are members one of another."

Ephesians 4:29 gives us this instruction,
"Let no corrupt communication proceed out of your mouth, but that which is good to the use of edifying, that it may minister grace unto the hearers."

Ephesians 5:4 says,
"Neither filthiness, nor foolish talking, nor jesting, which are not convenient: but rather giving of thanks."

Proverbs 25:28 gives us this insight,
"He that hath no rule over his own spirit is like a city that is broken down, and without walls."

Jesus summarized what the extent of our conversation should be in **Matthew 5:36-37**,
"Neither shall thou swear by thy head, because thou canst not make one hair white or black. But let your communication be, Yea, yea: Nay, nay: for whatsoever is more than these cometh of evil."

Our conversation must be pure, truthful, and reliable. If the credibility of our word is not important to us, it will not have any influence with others. We must bring our minds under the control of the Holy Spirit.

Romans 12:2 instructs us,
"And be not conformed to this world: but be ye transformed by the renewing of your mind, that ye may prove what is that good, and acceptable, and perfect will of God."

We read these words in **2 Corinthians 10:5**,
"...and bringing into captivity every thought to the obedience of Christ."

Philippians 4:8 tells us what we need to be thinking to ensure a right attitude,
"Finally brethren, whatsoever things are true, whatsoever things are honest, whatsoever things are just, whatsoever things are pure, whatsoever things are lovely, whatsoever things are of good report; it there be any virtue, and if there be any praise, think on these things."

In order to ensure our lifestyles are upright and under the control of the Spirit, we must obey the following instructions:

- ...flee from idolatry **(1 Corinthians 10:14)**.
- Flee the evil desires of youth as you pursue righteousness, faith, love, and peace along with those who call on the Lord out of a pure heart **(2 Timothy 2:22)**.
- Abstain from all appearance of evil **(1 Thessalonians 5:22)**.
- Humble yourselves under God's mighty hand, that in due time He may exalt you. Cast all of your anxiety on Him because He cares for you **(1 Peter 5:6-7)**.

If we totally submit to the separation of the Holy Spirit, He will reveal Christ to us in greater ways. As we grow in the knowledge of Christ, our testimony grows. As our testimony grows, we will have more impact on people.

A testimony that never grows shows that an individual is not growing in the revelation of Jesus Christ. If we lack growth in this area, our witnessing will lack heart and authority. If we express the Gospel without the glory of Christ evident, we will simply display a religion without life. If we treat the proclamation of the Gospel as a religious duty, we show a lack of love for the One we are representing.

Is your life a living testimony of the One you have been called to serve? Is your relationship with the Lord so personal that those around you can see His influence? If you are failing in this area, keep in mind a powerful witness of Jesus Christ will be confirmed by the evidence of Jesus' glory shining through your life.

Personal Notes: ____

____

____

Chapter 18

COMMISSIONED

Supplement:
Evangelism
Bible Study
Sup. 2

The Holy Spirit is also represented by oil. Oil was used as a means of anointing. people.

1 John 2:20 says,
"But ye have an unction from the Holy One, and ye know all things."

An "anointing" sets an individual apart for a specific duty. In the Old Testament they anointed the kings and prophets with oil. Anointing implies commission. Commission means an act of entrusting someone with a responsibility. When someone is commissioned, he or she is given the authority to carry out his or her duty. Men of God were often commissioned by the laying on of hands. Then, they were sent out with authority.

Acts 13:2-3 tells us,
"As they ministered to the Lord, and fasted, the Holy Ghost said, separate me Barnabas and Saul (Paul) for the work where unto I have called them. And when they had fasted and prayed, and laid their hands on them, they sent them away." *(Parenthesis added.)*

When the Holy Spirit comes upon us we receive the power to carry out the commission.

The commission Christians have been given by the King of kings can be found in **Mark 16:15**,
"And he said unto them, Go ye into all the world, and preach the gospel to every creature."

This commission also includes the commands found in **Matthew 28:19-20**,
"Go ye therefore, and teach all nations, baptizing them in the name of the Father, and of the Son, and of the Holy Ghost. Teaching them to observe all things whatsoever I have commanded you:..."

Our commission is two-fold. We are commissioned to preach the Gospel and to make disciples of all nations. It is not enough to bring people into the kingdom if we fail to teach them how to properly live the Christian life.

Jesus made this statement in **Matthew 28:18**,
"...All power is given unto me in heaven and in earth."

We are sent out in the authority of the King of the universe. This authority gives us the right to carry out the King's commission.

Paul said in **2 Corinthians 5:20**,
"Now then we are ambassadors for Christ, as though God did beseech you by us: we pray you in Christ's stead, be ye reconciled to God."

We have an official title of ambassador in the kingdom of heaven. An ambassador is the highest diplomatic position in a government. The baptism of the Holy Spirit is symbolic of anointing. We have been anointed with power to carry out our duty. This power makes us effective witnesses for the kingdom of God.

Personal Notes: ____

____

Led By the Spirit

Studying the lives of the Apostle Paul and the Apostle Peter gives the perspective of what it means to be sold out to God for service. The truth is believers need to sell out to God to receive His power and to reap His promises. The key to the success of these men can be found in the fact that the Spirit led them.

In **Acts 10:19-20** we read these words about Peter,
"While Peter thought on the vision, the Spirit said unto him, Behold, three men seek thee. Arise therefore, and get thee down, and go with them, doubting nothing: for I have sent them."

We read this information about Paul in **Acts 16:6**,
"Now when they had gone throughout Phrygia and the region of Galatia, and were forbidden of the Holy Ghost to preach the word in Asia."

In **Acts 8:26-40** we read about Philip, another disciple of Christ. An angel of the Lord sent Philip to Gaza. The Holy Spirit then instructed him to walk along side a chariot belonging to a eunuch from Ethiopia. Philip witnessed to this man. The eunuch received Christ and was baptized in water.

Acts 8:39 shows us what happened after Philip baptized the Ethiopian,
"And when they were come up out of the water, the Spirit of the Lord caught away Philip, that the eunuch saw him no more: and he went on his way rejoicing."

The world is a vast harvest field. We have been commissioned to share the good news and teach others to follow Christ in this harvest field.

In spite of the fact that all believers are called, we still read these words of Jesus in **Matthew 22:14**,
"For many are called, but few are chosen."

Jesus gives us this insight to what it means to be chosen in **John 15:15-17**,
"Henceforth I call you not servants; for the servant knoweth not what his lord doeth: but I have called you friends; for all things that I have heard of my Father I have made known unto you. Ye have not chosen me, but I have chosen you, and ordained you, that ye should go and bring forth fruit, and that your fruit should remain: that whatsoever ye shall ask of the

Father in my name, he may give it you. These things I command you, that ye love one another."

Jesus made this statement in regard to His Father's business in **Matthew 9:36-38**,
"But when he saw the multitudes, he was moved with compassion on them because they fainted, and were scattered abroad, as sheep having no shepherd. Then saith he unto his disciples. The harvest truly is plenteous, but the labourers are few; Pray ye therefore the Lord of the harvest, that he will send forth labourers into his harvest."

> The laborers are few in the harvest field. People's souls are lost for eternity because many believers lack a vision for their real purpose on this earth. Today, some believers need a vision of the devastation caused by their unwillingness to obey their commission. They need to realize this destruction will eventually come back on them. (See **Ezekiel 3:16-22** and **Joel 3:14**.)

Proverbs 29:18 says,
"Where there is no vision, the people perish:..."

> The key to becoming a laborer in the harvest field is the willingness to follow the Lord of the harvest. Many believers will follow the Lord as long as it serves their purpose. But, when the reality of the cross becomes evident, many will fall along the wayside. (Refer to **Isaiah 6**.)

We catch a glimpse of why many fail to follow the Lord all of the way in **Luke 9:62**,
"And Jesus said unto him, No man, having put his hand to the plough, and looking back, is fit for the kingdom of God."

> As servants of God, we must not look back to our former life, dreams, or goals. We must become crucified to all of these influences. We see the consequences of looking back in the situation of Lot's wife **(Genesis 19).** Lot was the nephew of Abraham. He and his family lived in the wicked city of Sodom. God was about to destroy this city. Two angels were sent to take Lot and his family out before God's destruction came upon it. These messengers of God told Lot to escape with his wife and daughters and not to look back **(Genesis 19:17).**

In **Genesis 19:26** we read,
"But his (Lot's) wife looked back from behind him, and she became a pillar of salt." (Parenthesis added.)

In **Matthew 5:13** we read Jesus' words,
"Ye are the salt of the earth:..."

> There is a vast difference between becoming a pillar of salt, which reminds people of God's judgment, and salt which makes a difference in people's lives. As a believer you will either be a pillar of salt representing God's judgment or you will be salt which is exemplary of God's love, truth, and greatness. It is your decision. This decision must not be based on emotion. It must not come from an intellectual consideration. But rather it must be a heart determination to finish the course set before you for the glory of God.

Paul made this statement in **Philippians 3:14**,
"I press toward the mark for the prize of the high calling of God in Christ Jesus."

Maybe right now you are saying I want to make a commitment but I am afraid of sharing the good news with others.

We have this promise in **2 Timothy 1:7**,
"For God hath not given us the spirit of fear; but of power, and of love, and of a sound mind."

Jesus gives us this promise in **Matthew 10:18-20**,
"And ye shall be brought before governors and kings for my sake, for a testimony against them and the Gentiles. But when they deliver you up, take no thought how of what ye shall speak: for it shall be given you in that same hour what ye shall speak. For it is not ye that speak, but the Spirit of your Father which speaketh in you."

Maybe you have a physical handicap that you feel keeps you from serving God. Moses claimed he had a speech problem in **Exodus 4:10**.

In **Exodus 4:12** we read God's reply to him,
"Now therefore go, and I will be with thy mouth, and teach thee what thou shalt say."

In **2 Corinthians 10:10**, Paul tells how some accused him of being unimpressive in appearance and his speech amounted to nothing.

Remember what Jesus said to Paul in **2 Corinthians 12:9**,
"My grace is sufficient for thee: for my strength is made perfect in weakness...."

Supplement: *(Challenge the attitude.)* **Volume 5 Book 5** *Exposition: Women's Place in the Kingdom of God.*

Some of you may be thinking God cannot use you because of your gender or age.

Paul tells us in **Galatians 3:28**,
"There is neither Jew nor Greek, there is neither bond nor free, there is neither male nor female: for ye are all one in Christ Jesus."

God used all types of vessels. He has used men like Peter and Paul. He used women like Deborah and the three Mary's. Deborah was a judge and prophetess for Israel. She led Israel to victory in a battle against a cruel king who had oppressed the Israelites **(Judges 4-5)**. Mary (the sister of Lazarus) was the first one to anoint Jesus for His burial **(John 12:3-9)**. The other Mary's (Mary Magdalene and Mary, the mother of James along with other women) were the first ones to tell others about the resurrection of Christ **(Matthew 28:1-10** & **Luke 24:10)**. He has used young men and women. For instance, the prophet Jeremiah considered himself a youth when he was called by God **(Jeremiah 1:6-10)**. God used a young maiden to direct the great soldier Naaman to the prophet Elisha for healing **(2 Kings 5:2-4)**. Finally, God used a donkey to warned the prophet Balaam, of God's displeasure with him **(Numbers 22:21-34)**.

Finally, we read this statement made by Jesus in **Luke 19:37-40**,
"...the whole multitude of the disciples began to rejoice and praise God with a loud voice for all the mighty works that they had seen; Saying, Blessed be the King that cometh in the name of the Lord: peace in heaven, and glory in the highest. And some of the Pharisees from among the multitude said unto him, Master, rebuke thy disciples. And he answered

and said unto them, I tell you that, if these should hold their peace, the stones would immediately cry out."

Note, the stones would have cried out. Our God is sovereign. His ways and thoughts are not like ours. His Word will go forth! His message will be preached with or without us! He will use any available vessel. God does not look at a person's gender or age. He looks at the individual's heart. (Refer to **Isaiah 55:8-9** and **11**.)

1 Samuel 16:7 confirms this,
"But the Lord said unto Samuel, look not on his countenance, or on the height of his stature; because I have refused him: for the Lord seeth not as man seeth; for man looketh on the outward appearance, but the Lord looketh on the heart."

Personal Notes: ____

____

Maybe you feel you have responsibilities which would prevent you from fulfilling your commission. God understands your situation. Your mission field could be right where you live. Jesus sent the man He had delivered from the legion of devils back to his community to be His witness **(Mark 5:19-20)**. Dorcus, a disciple of Christ, was known as a woman who always did good and helped the poor. She made such an impression that when she died, the people who knew her urged Peter to pray over her. As a result, she was raised up to continue her valuable service to others **(Acts 9:36-41)**. God desires to use each of us. We limit God when we allow our fears and excuses to hinder us from making ourselves available to Him. The Holy Ghost is the one who readies us to work in the harvest. He goes before us to prepare those in the harvest field to hear and receive the message. Therefore, we must become sensitive to His leading and direction. We must allow Him to set us apart for service.

Hebrews 12:1 says,
"Wherefore seeing we also are compassed about with so great a cloud of witnesses, let us lay aside every weight, and the sin which doth so easily beset us, and let us run with patience the race that is set before us."

This sensitivity towards the Holy Spirit will lead to an intimate relationship with God.

Romans 8:13-17 tells us,
"For if ye live after the flesh, ye shall die: but if ye through the Spirit do mortify the deeds of the body, ye shall live. For as many as are led by the Spirit of God, they are the sons of God. For ye have not received the spirit of bondage again to fear; but ye have received the Spirit of adoption, whereby we cry, Abba, Father. The Spirit itself beareth witness with our spirit, that we are the children of God: And if children, then heirs; heirs of God, and joint-heirs with Christ; if so be that we suffer with him, that we may be also glorified together."

Jesus made this statement to His parents in **Luke 2:49**,
"...How is it that ye sought me? wist ye not that I must be about my Father's business?"

If you have received Christ into your heart, are you about your Father's business? If He has called you, you must choose to follow Him.

Chapter 19

POWERFUL WITNESSES

Supplement: Volume 6 Book 4: *The Power of Our Testimonies*

When the king or leader of a country sends representatives out in his name, they are sent with credentials. For instance, the Egyptian Pharaoh gave Joseph his signet ring to verify the authority he had given him **(Genesis 41:42)**. Nehemiah was sent out with letters from the king to oversee the building of the wall around Jerusalem **(Nehemiah 2:7-10)**. In the case of Esther, a decree was issued by the king for the Israelites to protect themselves. To make it irreversible, he sealed it with his signet ring **(Esther 8:7-17)**. As witnesses of the Most High God we have been sent out with evidence to verify our commission.

We find these credentials in **Mark 16:17-18**,
"And these signs shall follow them that believe; In my name shall they cast out devils; they shall speak with new tongues; They shall take up serpents; and if they drink any deadly thing, it shall not hurt them: they shall lay hands on the sick, and they shall recover."

Hebrews 2:3-4 confirms these credentials,
"How shall we escape, if we neglect so great salvation; which at the first began to be spoken by the Lord, and was confirmed unto us by them that heard him; God also bearing them witness, both with signs and wonders, and with divers miracles, and gifts of the Holy Ghost, according to his own will?"

Matthew 4:24 summarizes much of what Jesus did during His time on earth,
"And his fame went throughout all Syria: and they brought unto him all sick people that were taken with divers diseases and torments, and those which were possessed with devils, and those which were lunatick, and those that had the palsy; and he healed them."

We also know Christ raised the dead. He raised Lazarus in **John 11** and Jairus' daughter **(Matthew 9:18-26)**. Christ did many miracles.

John made this statement in **John 21:25**,
"And there are also many other things which Jesus did, the which, if they should be written every one, I suppose that even the world itself could not contain the books that should be written. Amen."

Jesus said this in **John 14:12**,
"Verily, verily, I say unto you, He that believeth on me, the works that I do shall he do also; and greater works than these shall he do; because I go unto my Father."

Jesus said His disciples would not only do the same works, but they would do many more. Remember, first He had to go to the Father in order to send the Holy Spirit down to empower His followers to do these works. In Scripture, we see Jesus' disciples doing the same works.

Luke 10:17 gives us this information about the seventy-two who Christ first sent out,
"And the seventy returned again with joy, saying Lord, even the devils are subject unto us through thy name."

Acts 5:15-16 gives us this information about Peter,
"Insomuch that they brought forth the sick into the streets, and laid them on beds and couches, that at the least the shadow of Peter passing by might overshadow some of them. There came also a multitude out of the cities round about unto Jerusalem, bringing sick folks, and them which were vexed with unclean spirits: and they were healed every one."

Acts 20:10 & 12 says this about Paul in regards to the death of Eutychus,
"And Paul went down, and fell on him, and embracing him said, Trouble not yourselves; for his life is in him... And they brought the young man alive, and were not a little comforted."

In **Acts 28:3 & 5** we read this about Paul,
"And when Paul had gathered a bundle of sticks, and laid them on the fire, there came a viper out of the heat, and fastened on his hand... And he shook off the beast into the fire, and felt no harm."

The Gospel was confirmed because of the miracles that followed these men.

We read the final results in **Acts 5:14**,
"And believers were the more added to the Lord, multitudes both of men and women."

Personal Notes: ____

____

Beware of Unbelief and Fear

We see a disagreement between different religious groups over the issue of miracles. Some feel the miracles ceased after the Church was established. To confront this division, we must consider our God's nature.

Hebrews 13:8 tells us this about Jesus Christ,
"Jesus Christ the same yesterday, and to day, and for ever."

James 1:17 says this about God,
"Every good gift and every perfect gift is from above, and cometh down from the Father of lights, with whom is no variableness, neither shadow of turning."

God does not change according to the times, people, or social trends. God has always been and will be in the business of miracles. Miracles may be extraordinary and supernatural to us but they are normal to God. He desires to show Himself mighty to those who love Him. He desires to make Himself known to others through His people. Why would He change now? Such a change would go against His very nature.

Mark 6:5-6 gives us insight as to why people do not see God move in miraculous ways,
"And he could there do no mighty work, save that he laid his hands upon a few sick folk, and healed them. And he marvelled because of their unbelief. And he went round about the villages, teaching."

Jesus was at His hometown of Nazareth in the following incident. **Luke 4:16-20** shows Him proclaiming His mission in His hometown synagogue. These people became insulted with His claims because the miracles that a couple of Gentiles had received in the past by faith, were now passing them by because of unbelief. His hometown people refused to accept Him in any other way except as being the son of Joseph **(Luke 4:22)**. When challenged in their unbelief, they became so angry they tried to throw Him off a cliff **(Luke 4:29)**.

Luke 4:30 tells us Christ's final response to their attempt,
"But he passing through the midst of them went his way."

Christ is walking through the midst of people today without touching their lives. Like those at Nazareth, much of what Christ desires to do in the lives of people will only be fulfilled in their ears and not in their lives **(Luke 4:21)**. The reason is because they refuse to believe and receive Christ in His full capacity. They may be comfortable with Him as Savior, but they refuse to accept Him as Lord and God who desires to do the impossible in and through each of us. This unwillingness to recognize Christ in His fullness is a form of unbelief.

This unbelief is a product of skepticism and fear. Skepticism is a product of earthly knowledge. This knowledge makes miracles seem foolish or beneath logical reasoning.

Paul gives us this perspective about this type of approach or attitude in **1 Corinthians 1:27-28**,
"But God hath chosen the foolish things of the world to confound the wise; and God hath chosen the weak things of the world to confound the things which are mighty; And base things of the world, and things which are despised, hath God chosen, yea, and things which are not, to bring to naught things that are:"

Personal Notes: ____

____

Fear can keep us from believing and accepting God's power in our life. We see this fear in the Gadarenes in **Matthew 8:28-34**. They saw the deliverance of two men from demon possession. These demons had been sent into a herd of pigs. The pigs ended up running into the lake and drowned."

Although the Gadarenes saw the two men set free, we see this response from them in **Matthew 8:34**,
"And behold, the whole city came out to meet Jesus: and when they saw him, they besought him that he would depart out of their coasts."

These people displayed fear towards Jesus. They did not really understand what was going on. They had possibly lost their livelihood because of the destruction of the pigs. The idea of losing control of a situation or losing something we value can bring fear into anyone's heart. As a result, these people asked Jesus to depart from them. We must not become so comfortable with Jesus, we put Him in a box. We must not be so afraid of His move or intervention in our lives that we ask Him to depart from our midst. We need to stand on His truth.

James 1:16-17 says,
"Do not err, my beloved brethren. Every good gift and every perfect gift is from above, ..."

We have this promise in **Matthew 7:9-11**,
"Or what man is there of you, whom if his son ask bread, will he give him a stone? Or if he ask a fish, will he give him a serpent? If ye then, being evil, know how to give good gifts unto your children, how much more shall your Father which is in heaven give good things to them that ask him?"

Everything that comes from God is good and perfect. He will not give us something that will destroy us or go against our potential. However, what we need to understand is God will not give us gifts unless we first ask Him. He will not force any of His gifts on us. In conclusion, much of receiving what God has for us comes down to simply trusting Him. God desires to move in our lives in greater ways. Once He is allowed to, He will move though us in a miraculous way to touch others.

Personal Notes: ____

____

Keeping Miracles in Perspective

We must be careful not to abuse signs and wonders. It is important to keep in mind that miracles are to verify our commission and the message of the Gospel.

Mark 16:20 confirms this,
"And they went forth, and preached every where, the Lord working with them, and confirming the word with signs following. Amen."

Signs and wonders are not to bring the messenger recognition. They are designed to point unbelievers to a merciful God and bring Him His deserved glory.

Jesus made mention of this in the raising of Lazarus in **John 11:4**,
"...This sickness is not unto death, but for the glory of God, that the Son of God might be glorified thereby."

We must keep in mind the person who was considered the greatest in the kingdom of God did not perform one miracle **(John 10:41)**. That person was John the Baptist.

Jesus said this about John in **Matthew 11:11**,
"Verily I say unto you, Among them that are born of women there hath not risen a greater than John the Baptist: notwithstanding he that is least in the kingdom of heaven is greater than he."

Christians must beware of how much emphasis they put on signs and wonders. Some believers have a tendency to chase after signs and wonders for their own benefit.

Jesus made this statement in **Matthew 16:4** to the Jewish leaders who were always requiring a sign from Him,
"A wicked and adulterous generation seeketh after a sign; and there shall no sign be given unto it, but the sign of the prophet Jonas."

The greatest miracle ever to take place was the resurrection of Christ. Signs and wonders are to confirm this message to unbelievers. Therefore, Christians should not be chasing after them. Believers are to walk by faith and not by sight.

Jesus said this to His disciple, Thomas, in **John 20:29** after he refused to believe His resurrection unless He saw Him,
"...because thou hast seen me, thou hast believed: blessed are they that have not seen, and yet have believed."

If we as believers are busy seeking a sign, we will be deceived.

Jesus gives us this warning in **Matthew 24:24**,
"For there shall arise false Christs, and false prophets, and shall shew great signs and wonders; insomuch that, if it were possible, they shall deceive the very elect."

Believers should be a part of God's miracles and not bystanders to them. As His witnesses God wants to show Himself real though us, not to us.

1 John 4:1 gives us this instruction,
"Beloved, believe not every spirit, but try the sprits whether they are of God: because many false prophets are gone out into the world."

Today there are many people running around performing miracles in the name of Christ. Miracles do not confirm the individual, only the message. The ultimate result of all signs should be for the glorification of God, and not for the recognition of any person. All those claiming to be servants of God must be tested according to their doctrinal stands and fruit.

What kind of witness you will be for the Lord depends on your openness to be used by Him. Maybe right now you desire to be known as a powerful witness for God. But, to ensure this position, why don't you first seek after the reputation of greatness like the one Jesus accredited to John the Baptist? John simply was faithful to do God's will. He prepared the way for the Lord with his message of repentance. He then decreased in his ministry in order for Christ to increase in His work of salvation **(John 3:30)**.

Would you be willing to decrease? This principle is the true secret behind greatness in the kingdom of heaven. (Refer to **Matthew 18:2-4** and **20:25-28**.)

Personal Notes: ______________________________

____

____

____

Chapter 20

THE HEARTBEAT OF CHRISTIANITY

Supplements:
(For the next two chapters.)
Christian Conduct Bible Study
Sup. 2
Volume 2
Book 4:
Think on These Things

There are two distinct motivations behind man. One type of motivation is pride. The following scriptures give us this information about pride.

Psalm 10:2 says,
"The wicked in his pride doth persecute the poor: let them be taken in the devices that they have imagined."

Proverbs 13:10 tells us,
"Only by pride cometh contention:..."

Proverbs 14:3 says,
"In the mouth of the foolish is a rod of pride:..."

Proverbs 21:24 gives us this insight about pride,
"Proud and haughty scorner is his name, who dealeth in proud wrath."

2 Timothy 3:2-4 gives us this picture concerning man in the last days,
"For men shall be lovers of their own selves, covetous, boasters, proud, blasphemers, disobedient to parents, unthankful, unholy, Without natural affection, trucebreakers, false accusers, incontinent, fierce, despisers of those that are good."

The unregenerate man is motivated by pride for it is the essence of the selfish disposition of man. It is usually the main idol that not only reigns unhindered in man, but also inspires greater idolatry. In these last days we will see pride at its worst **(2 Timothy 3:1-7)**. Pride is a preoccupation with self. It prefers self over others. It strives to get is own way, and demands recognition and honor from those who come under its seductive covering or rigid demands.

Jeremiah 49:16 gives us this insight about pride,
"Thy terribleness hath deceived thee, and the pride of thine heart,..."

Pride will deceive you about your true spiritual condition. It will justify or make right any wrongs to preserve its position of importance. It judges and walks according to vain imaginations. Fear also walks hand in hand with pride. People who allow pride to motivate them will either be driven or paralyzed by fear. This fear could include fear of failure, fear of rejection, or fear of being wrong, or even fear of losing control of a situation. The outward product of both pride and fear is confusion. Confusion occurs when an individual fails to live up to his or her idea of self.

Proverbs 8:13 tells us God's attitude towards pride,
"The fear of the Lord is to hate evil: pride, and arrogancy, and the evil way, and the froward mouth, do I hate."

James 4:6 tells us God's reaction towards pride,
"...God resisteth the proud, but giveth grace unto the humble."

Personal Notes: ____

____

The other motivation people have is God's love.

Paul made this statement in **2 Corinthians 5:14,**
"For the love of Christ constraineth us;..."

This love is totally opposite of pride. In **1 Corinthians 13** we are given a clear picture of the love of God. While pride breeds contention, God's unfailing love is a commitment to respond to others in an honorable way.

1 Corinthians 13:5 & 7 says,
"Doth not behave itself unseeemly, seeketh not her own, is not easily provoked, thinketh no evil... Beareth all things, believeth all things, hopeth all things, endureth all things."

Boasting is the product of the proud and foolish.

1 Corinthians 13:4 reveals love's contrary response to pride,
"...charity *(love)* vaunteth not itself, is not puffed up." *(Parenthesis added.)*

1 Corinthians 13:6 tells us how it will not regard or overlook iniquity,
""Rejoiceth not in iniquity, but rejoiceth in the truth."

While pride is reinforced by fear, **1 John 4:18** tells us this about God's love,
"There is no fear in love; but perfect love casteth out fear: because fear hath torment. He that feareth is not made perfect in love."

Love will not overlook iniquity, but it will cover personal discrepancies or irritations of others. It is God's desire we become consumed with His love. For it is His love that maintains our confidence in Him.

Romans 5:5 tells us,
"And hope maketh not ashamed; because the love of God is shed abroad in our hearts by the Holy Ghost which is given unto us."

Paul puts love in this perspective in **1 Corinthians 13:1-3**. We can speak in tongues but if we do not have love, we become as,

"...as sounding brass, or a tinkling cymbal."

We can have profound knowledge and great faith, but without love,

"...I am nothing."

We can give all of our possessions and our life for our beliefs, but without love,

"...it profiteth me nothing."

Love is the heartbeat of Christianity. It is the essential part of our spiritual life. It must motivate us in all we do for God.

A lack of this love is summarized in **1 John 4:8**,
"He that loveth not knoweth not God; for God is love."

If we have Christ in our hearts, God's love will be motivating us.

Personal Notes: ____

____

The Power of God's Love

In **Matthew 22:37-40** we read Jesus' reply to a religious teacher's question about what commandment was the greatest.
"...Thou shalt love the Lord thy God with all thy heart, and with all thy soul, and with all thy mind. This is the first and great commandment. And the second is like unto it. Thou shalt love thy neighbour as thyself. On these two commandments hang all the law and the prophets."

The Apostle Paul made this statement in **Romans 13:8**,
"Owe no man any thing, but to love one another: for he that loveth another hath fulfilled the law."

Love fulfills the law. It results in obeying as well as maintaining the intent or spirit of God's commandments.

1 John 2:5 states,
"But whoso keepeth his word, in him verily is the love of God perfected: hereby know we that we are in him."

God's love will be evident in our reaction towards others. In fact, I have a saying; if you want to know what people are doing with God behind closed doors, watch how they are treating others. Our attitude and reactions towards others will expose the real condition of our relationship with God.

1 John 3:16-17 confirms this,
"Hereby perceive we the love of God, because he laid down his life for us: and we ought to lay down our lives for the brethren. But whoso hath this world's good, and seeth his brother have need, and shutteth up his bowels of compassion from him, how dwelleth the love of God in him?"

The love of God reigning in our heart will knock down all human barriers. It destroys such walls as hate.

1 John 2:9-10 tells us,
"He that saith he is in the light, and hateth his brother, is in darkness even until now. He that loveth his brother abideth in the light, and there is none occasion of stumbling in him."

God's love produces forgiveness in our hearts.

This forgiveness enables us to comply to Jesus' command in **Matthew 5:44**,
"But I say unto you, Love your enemies, bless them that curse you, do good to them that hate you, and pray for them which despitefully use you, and persecute you."

The reason we can love our enemy is found in **1 Peter 4:8**,
"And above all things have fervent charity among yourselves; for charity shall cover the multitude of sins."

This perfect love shows no partiality. Therefore, it dissolves any walls of prejudice.

James 2:1, 8-9 states,
"My brethren, have not the faith of our Lord Jesus Christ, the Lord of glory, with respect of persons... If ye fulfil the royal law according to the scripture. Thou shalt love thy neighbour as thyself, ye do well. But if ye have respect to persons, ye commit sin, and are convinced of the law as transgressors."

Standards based on ignorance or prejudices inspire unmerciful judgments toward those who fall short of them.

James 2:13 says this about these types of judgment,
"For he shall have judgment without mercy, that hath shewed no mercy; and mercy rejoiceth against judgment."

Because of the love of God we will show both mercy and commitment in going the extra mile for someone.

Jesus gives us these instructions in **Matthew 5:39-42**,
"But I say unto you, That ye resist not evil: but whosoever shall smite thee on thy right cheek, turn to him the other also. And if any man will sue thee at the law, and take away thy coat, let him have thy cloke also. And whosoever shall compel thee to go a mile, go with him twain. Give to him that asketh thee, and from him that would borrow of thee turn not thou away."

Personal Notes: ____

____

The Most Excellent Way

In **1 Corinthians 12**, we read about how the body of believers must function. As we know, this body is also referred to as the Church. In **1 Corinthians 14**, we are given instructions concerning the operations of the gifts of the Spirit.

In the midst of God's instructions about the body and the gifts, we read these words from Paul in **1 Corinthians 12:31**,
"But covet earnestly, the best gifts: and yet shew I unto you a more excellent way."

The most excellent way is the love of God. Gifts will cease when we finally meet that which is perfect in our lives and in heaven, Jesus Christ. But God's love is eternal **(1 Corinthians 13:8-12)**.

The Apostle Paul made this statement about love in **1 Corinthians 13:13**,
"And now abideth faith, hope, charity (love), these three; but the greatest of these is charity." (Parenthesis added.)

God's love will bind believers together. His love is sincere; therefore, producing qualities that display exemplary actions.

Paul gives us an insight into this pure love in action in **Romans 12:9-10, 13, 15-16**,
"Let love be without dissimulation (hypocrisy)...Be kindly affectioned one to another with brotherly love; in honour preferring one another...Distributing to the necessity of saints; given to hospitality...Rejoice with them that do rejoice, and weep with them that weep. Be of the same mind one toward another. Mind not high things, but condescend to men of low estate. Be not wise in your own conceits." (Parenthesis added.)

In **Ephesians 4:2** we read this instruction,
"With all lowliness and meekness, with longsuffering, forbearing one another in love."

Love is the most excellent way of the Christian way of life. It is greater than gifts because it binds the believers together by putting self down and preferring the other person's well-being. It expresses a commitment that reaches beyond the greatest obstacles of selfishness.

This is why Jesus said these words in **John 13:35**,
"By this shall all men know that ye are my disciples, if ye have love one to another."

We can't make it to heaven without God's love. You can have all the religious activities and appearances, but without God's love, it is all in vain and only a mask or cloak. The presence of godly love is the only true test to our Christianity.

This is why Paul expressed this desire for believers in **Ephesians 3:17-19**,
"That Christ may dwell in your hearts by faith; that ye, being rooted and grounded in love, May be able to comprehend with all saints what is the breadth, and length, and depth, and height; And to know the love of Christ, which passeth knowledge, that ye might be filled with all the fulness of God."

We find this promise in **Romans 8:35, 38-39**,
"Who shall separate us from the love of Christ? Shall tribulation, or distress, or persecution, or famine, or nakedness, or peril, or sword?... For I am persuaded, that neither death, nor life, nor angels, nor principalities, nor powers, nor things present, nor things to come, Nor height, nor depth, nor any other creature, shall be able to separate us from the love of God, which is in Christ Jesus our Lord."

Are you passing the test of Christianity by allowing the love of God to compel you? Maybe you are motivated by pride? The attitudes and reactions you have towards others will expose your motivations.

Personal Notes: ______________________________

____

____

Chapter 21

THE ABUNDANT LIFE

Supplement: Volume 3 Book 4: *The Face of Thankfulness*

Jesus promised us two types of lives: An eternal life and an abundant life.

Jesus talked about the abundant life in **John 10:10**,
"The thief (Satan) cometh not, but for to steal, and to kill, and to destroy: I am come that they might have life, and that they might have it more abundantly." (Parenthesis added.)

Eternal life is our present hope to experience the fullness of eternity with God when we pass through the physical door of death, but the abundant life is for now. We can experience a full life in the midst of crises and problems. Such a life should produce a thankful attitude in God's people. The key to an abundant life is to possess the life Christ has made available to us. This life displays the attitude of Christ, and will produce godly fruit.

Galatians 5:22-23 shows us the virtues that will be present in this life,
"But the fruit of the Spirit is love, joy, peace, longsuffering, gentleness, goodness, faith, meekness, temperance (self-control): against such there is no law." (Parenthesis added.)

By studying the picture of God's love in **1 Corinthians 13**, you will see all nine of these characteristics described within this text. Let's examine this picture.

Love - is not self-seeking **(13:5)**
Joy - does not delight in evil, but rejoices in the truth. **(13:6)**
Peace - is not easily angered. **(13:5)**
Patient (long-suffering) – is patient, always perseveres**, (13: 4** & **7)**
Kindness - does not envy nor keep records of wrong. **(13:4-5)**
Goodness-is kind. **(13:4)**
Faithfulness-always trusts, always hopes. **(13:7)**
Gentleness (meekness) – is not proud. **(13:4)**
Self-control (temperance) – does not boast nor is it rude. **(13:4-5)**

(The above concept was obtained from "A Gardener Looks at the Fruits" by W. Phillip Keller; © l986.)

The commitment of God's love is the root, which produces these nine characteristics. What we must keep in mind in **1 Corinthians 13** is a description of Jesus Christ. Christ possesses all of these characteristics. He was God's visible expression of love to all men. As these qualities come forth in our lives, we become God's expression of love to those around us. This life will be attractive to those who desire to find solutions to their unproductive lives. However, to obtain a fruitful life we must abide in the only source of true love, Jesus Christ.

Supplement: Volume 1 Book 3: *The Principles of the Abundant Life*

Jesus confirms this in **John 15:5**,
"I am the vine, ye are the branches. He that abideth in me, and I in him, the same bringeth forth much fruit: for without me ye can do nothing."

To abide in something means to dwell or actually live in something. Words such as continue, remain, and endure are a few of the words that add to the description of abiding. Jesus shows us we are simply the branches. Outside of the vine, the branches are nothing.

Jesus describes a branch which is no longer in the vine in **John 15:6**,
"If a man abide not in me, he is cast forth as a branch, and is withered; and men gather them, and cast them into the fire, and they are burned."

Fruit growers will tell you that occasionally a limb is partially separated from the trunk of the tree. This partial separation is discovered when the fruit formed on the branch falls short of its required quality. Christians must ensure their fruit by remaining in the Vine as well.

John 15:9 shows us how we remain in the vine,
"As the Father hath loved me, so have I loved you: continue ye in my love."

John 15:1-2 tells us,
"I am the true vine, and my Father is the husbandman. Every branch in me that beareth not fruit he taketh away: and every branch that beareth fruit, he purgeth it, that it may bring forth more fruit."

In this scripture we see bearing fruit is not an option. If we do not bear fruit, we will experience separation as a form of God's judgment. If we are bearing fruit, we need to realize God will separate us unto Himself in greater ways by pruning us. This separation is designed to bring forth more fruit, and is the work of sanctification, which is done by the Holy Spirit.

Jesus said these words in **John 15:16**,
"Ye have not chosen me, but I have chosen you, and ordained you, that ye should go and bring forth fruit, and that your fruit should remain: that whatsoever ye shall ask of the Father in my name, he may give it you."

Fruit takes on two meanings: the first is the life of Christ manifested in us and through us. The second is your investment in souls.

Jesus made this statement in **John 12:32**,
"And I, if I be lifted up from the earth, will draw all men unto me."

Jesus was referring to His death on the cross in the above Scripture verse. But as His believers there is an example here for us to consider. If we die to self, Christ will be lifted up in our lives. If people see Christ in us, they will be drawn to His salvation. Salvation of souls is the fruit God desires to see. But, in order for this to happen the life of Christ must be worked out in us on a continual basis.

It is obvious that we do not display godly characteristics one day, and have contrary responses the next day. Although we will occasionally fall short in this area, our fruit will remain constant if we are abiding in Christ.

Are you abiding in Christ?

Personal Notes: ______________________________

____

Understanding the Fruit

We already have discussed how love works in our Christian life. Now we must consider the other eight characteristics that make up the fruit of the Spirit. Joy means to delight in or to be glad in.

Jesus said this about joy in **John 15:11**,
"These things I have spoken unto you, that my joy might remain in you, and that your joy might be full."

Joy is based on our confidence or hope in God. **Psalm 37:4** says,
"Delight thyself also in the LORD; and he shall give thee the desires of thine heart."

Our joy becomes full as we allow our life to rest in God. We begin to experience His love, grace, and power.

Peter made this statement about joy in **1 Peter 1:8**,
"Whom having not seen, ye love; in whom, though now ye see him not, yet believing, ye rejoice with joy unspeakable and full of glory."

Joy comes as we become acquainted with our God. Each new revelation of Him results in a joy, which could never be expressed by words.

Personal Notes: ______________________________

Peace implies wholeness. This wholeness comes about when man is reconciled to God.

Ephesians 2:16-17 tells us about Jesus' work on the cross,
"And that he might reconcile both unto God in one body by the cross, having slain the enmity thereby: And came and preached peace to you which were afar off, and to them that were nigh."

Jesus made this statement in **John 14:27**,
"Peace I leave with you, my peace I give unto you: not as the world giveth, give I unto you. Let not your heart be troubled, neither let it be afraid."

Peace stipulates a right relationship with God.

James 3:18 states,
"And the fruit of righteousness is sown in peace of them that make peace."

Philippians 4:6-7 tells us how to maintain this peace in our life,
"Be careful for nothing; but in every thing by prayer and supplication with thanksgiving let your requests be made known unto God. And the peace of God, which passeth all understanding, shall keep your hearts and minds through Christ Jesus."

We must trust every area of our lives to Christ. Such trust will result in a peace, which passes all human understanding.

Personal Notes: ____

Patience or longsuffering is to bear, endure, and suffer. This patience is a product of suffering.

Romans 5:3-4 says this about patience,
"And not only so, but we glory in tribulations also: knowing that tribulation worketh patience; And patience, experience; and experience, hope."

The characteristic patience produces is described in **James 1:4**,
"But let patience have her perfect work, that ye may be perfect and entire, wanting nothing."

Patience will bring character or maturity. Maturity is necessary for effective ministry. It can take much long-suffering to bring people into the kingdom of God. (See **Acts 14:22**.)

Personal Notes:____

Kindness or gentleness means to be easy or gracious. It implies sweet reasonableness.

Jesus made this statement in **Matthew 11:29**,
"Take my yoke upon you, and learn of me; for I am meek and lowly in heart: and ye shall find rest unto your souls."

Christ was the example of gentleness. His yoke is easy. It only requires us to submit to His love. This submission was inspired by His love for us and made possible by His Spirit in us. He never lays unreasonable burdens on us. He actually volunteers to take our burdens on Himself **(1 Peter 5:7)**.

In **2 Timothy 2:24-25** we read this instruction,
"And the servant of the Lord must not strive; but be gentle unto all men, apt to teach, patient, In meekness instructing those that oppose themselves; if God peradventure will give them repentance to the acknowledging of the truth."

As servants of God, we must respond to others in the same way as Christ responded. Kindness will make us available to lead or instruct, but never to put unreasonable demands on people.

Personal Notes: ____

Goodness means to have moral qualities. Such goodness can only come from God. It involves a desire for what is good or pleasing to God.

In **1 Thessalonians 5:21** we read this instruction,
"Prove all things; hold fast that which is good,"

1 Corinthians 15:33 says,
"Be not deceived: evil communications corrupt good manners."

We must strive for goodness if we are going to have it in our life.

Personal Notes: ____

Faithfulness means trustworthy or reliable. This is the main quality God is looking for in his servants. God will trust a servant with more if he or she proves faithful in small ways.

Paul said this in **1 Corinthians 4:1-2**,
"Let a man so account of us, as of the ministers of Christ, and stewards of the mysteries of God. Moreover it is required in stewards, that a man be found faithful."

The desire of a servant of God should be to hear these words from his Master found in **Matthew 25:21**,
"His lord said unto him, Well done, thou good and faithful servant: thou hast been faithful over a few things, I will make thee ruler over many things: enter thou into the joy of the lord."

Personal Notes: ____

Gentleness or meekness means mild. Meekness has also been referred to as controlled strength or rage. It means all of our pursuits, strengths, and weaknesses are under the control of the Holy Spirit.

Jesus said this about meekness in **Matthew 5:5**,
"Blessed are the meek: for they shall inherit the earth."

To be under the control of the Spirit implies a strength that will not submit to other influences. This controlled strength denotes a power that will overcome the world and possess what God has for the believer.

Personal Notes: ____

Self-control or temperance means exercising control or discipline. Before we can exercise godly control in our lives we must be under the control of the Spirit (meekness). We find **Acts 24:25** and **2 Peter 1:6** referring to how self-control works in our lives.

Acts 24:25 says,
"And as he (Paul) reasoned of righteousness, temperance, and judgment to come, Felix trembled." (Parenthesis added.)

2 Peter 1:5-6 states,
"And besides this, giving all diligence, add to your faith virtue; and to virtue knowledge; And to knowledge temperance;..."

In **Acts 24:25** we see self-control following righteousness. This implies godly exercise is a product of righteousness. In **2 Peter 1:5-6** we see self-control added to knowledge. This means we exercise what we know as being right. As we consider each of these godly qualities, we can see how they signify an abundant life. Each characteristic leads us back to a confident relationship with God. They inspire a right relationship with others resulting in a life which overflows with God's Living Water.

Personal Notes: ____

(Note: The meaning of the virtues found in the Fruit of the Spirit was obtained from Scripture, *Strong's Exhaustive Concordance of the Bible*, and *Webster's New Collegiate Dictionary*.)

Testing the Fruit

Jesus made this statement in **Matthew 7:18-20**,
"A good tree cannot bring forth evil fruit, neither can a corrupt tree bring forth good fruit. Every tree that bringeth not forth good fruit is hewn down, and cast into the fire. Wherefore by their fruits ye shall know them.

Jesus made this statement in reference to false prophets or teachers. The person's fruit will give him or her away. To test any spirit involves a doctrinal test and a fruit test. A person can have a right doctrine, but a wrong spirit. An individual can say all the right things, but still promote a wrong doctrine. Therefore, both tests are needed to make a sound judgment. The fruit test is also a good way to examine our own lives. (See **1 Corinthians 11:28, 31-32** and **2 Corinthians 13:5**.)

The reason for this type of examination can be found in **Luke 18:11**
"The Pharisee stood and prayed thus with himself, God, I thank thee, that I am not as other men are, extortioners, unjust, adulterers, or even as this publican."

The Pharisee fit Paul's description in **2 Timothy 3:5**,
"Having a form of godliness, but denying the power thereof: from such turn away."

Our hearts will deceive us about our spiritual condition. Rigid religious lifestyles may give us an appearance of righteousness, but they can be based on pride. The fruit test is the only sound way of determining what is really going on in our hearts. Godly characteristics produce right attitudes and responses to not only God, but to those around us. We must consider the attitudes and responses we have towards our spouses, children, neighbors, friends, co-workers, and other believers. This examination is the only reliable test as to whether we are abiding in the Vine.

Right now, examine your attitudes and interactions with others. Do they display the fruit of the Spirit?

Personal Notes: ____

____

____

Chapter 22

THE BLESSED HOPE

Supplement: Volume 6 Book 2: *Possessing Our Souls*

In **Acts 1:10-11** we read this promise to the disciples,
"And while they looked steadfastly toward heaven as he went up, behold, two men stood by them in white apparel; Which also said, Ye men of Galilee, why stand ye gazing up into heaven? this same Jesus, which is taken up from you into heaven, shall so come in like manner as ye have seen him go into heaven."

History is winding down to a climatic event. This event involves Christ coming back for His Church. The blessed expectation is mentioned prophetically throughout Scriptures. Christians from the beginning of the church age have been looking upward and forward to this moment.

2 Timothy 4:8 tells us what our attitude needs to be towards this happening,
"Henceforth there is laid up for me a crown of righteousness, which the Lord, the righteous judge, shall give me at that day: and not to me only, but unto all them also that love his appearing."

Hebrews 9:28 offers this insight,
"So Christ was once offered to bear the sins of many; and unto them that look for him shall he appear the second time without sin unto salvation."

1 Thessalonians 4:16-17 gives us this descriptive information about this event:
"For the Lord himself shall descend from heaven with a shout, with the voice of the archangel, and with the trump of God: and the dead in Christ shall rise first: Then we which are alive and remain shall be caught up together with them in the clouds, to meet the Lord in the air: and so shall we ever be with the Lord."

1 Corinthians 15:50-53 adds this insight,
"Now this I say, brethren, that flesh and blood cannot inherit the kingdom of God; neither doth corruption inherit incorruption. Behold, I shew you a mystery; we shall not all sleep, but we shall all be changed. In a moment, in the twinkling of any eye, at the last trumpet: for the trumpet shall sound and the dead shall be raised incorruptible, and we shall be changed. For this corruptible must put on incorruption, and this mortal must put on immortality."

Every believer will receive a new body in the twinkling of an eye **(1 Corinthians 15:52)**. Saints who have preceded those who are alive in physical death, will be the first to raise in a new imperishable body. Those who are still alive will also receive an immortal body. Together they will meet the Lord in the air.

Colossians 3:4 summarized this event,
When Christ, who is our life, shall appear, then shall ye also appear with him in glory."

What a blessed hope indeed! The Church will be summoned by the last trumpet to meet her Savior and Lord in the air. The blowing of this trumpet not only signifies her Lord's coming, but a summons to a special celebration.

We read about this celebration in **Revelation 19:6-7**,
"And I heard as it were the voice of a great multitude, and as the voice of many waters, and as the voice of mighty thunderings saying, Alleluia: for the Lord God omnipotent reigneth. Let us be glad and

rejoice, and give honour to him: for the marriage of the Lamb is come, and his wife hath made herself ready."

The Church, the bride of Christ is being summoned to the wedding super by the bridegroom. There will be a celebration!

Personal Notes: ____

____

Recognizing The Times

Jesus gave this parable in **Luke 21:29-33**,
"And he spake to them a parable; Behold the fig tree, and all the trees: When they now shoot forth ye see and know of your own selves that summer is now nigh at hand. So likewise ye when ye see these things come to pass, know ye that the kingdom of God is nigh at hand. Verily I say unto you, This generation shall not pass away, till all be fulfilled. Heaven and earth shall pass away: but my words shall not pass away."

Supplement:
Strange Fire and False Anointing
Sup. 3

Matthew 24:1-14 gives us a summary of the events leading up to Christ's coming:

A. There will be much deception inspired by the appearance of false Christ's and prophets **(Matthew 24:4-5, 22-24)**. This deception will create the great falling away or the apostasy in the church. **2 Thessalonians 2:3** confirms this condition: "Let no man deceive you by any means: for that day shall not come, except there come a falling away first, ..."
B. You shall hear of wars and rumors of wars. For nation will rise against nation and kingdom against kingdom **(Matthew 24:6-7)**.
C. There will be famines (starvation) **(Matthew 24:7)**.
D. There will be pestilence (diseases) **(Matthew 24:7)**.
E. There will be earthquakes in many places **(Matthew 24:7)**.

Jesus made this reference in **Matthew 24:8** to these events,
"All these are the beginning of sorrows."

The list continues with precautions, betrayals, and the Gospel being preached in the entire world **(Matthew 24:9-10 & 14)**. Jesus tells us these sorrows will affect everyone in the world.

In **Luke 21:35** we read,
"For as a snare shall it come on all them that dwell on the face of the whole earth."

Jesus gave this description of mankind in **Matthew 24:12**,
"And because iniquity shall abound, the love of many shall wax cold."

We read the description of the future wicked kingdom in **Daniel 7:19-21**,
"Then I would know the truth of the fourth beast, which was diverse from all the others, exceeding dreadful, whose teeth were of iron and his nails of brass; which devoured, brake in pieces and stamped the residue with his feet; And of the ten horns that were in his head, and of the other which came up, and before whom there fell: even of that horn that had eyes, and a mouth that spake very great things, whose look was more stout than his fellows. I beheld, and the same horn made war with the saints, and prevailed against them:"

This means a one-world leader will come into power. He will be referred to as the anti-Christ (substitution for the real Christ). He will come on the scene offering peace and solutions to the world's problems. This individual will eventually replace God in man's heart. He will rule over all governments, economic, and religious systems. Right now, we are watching the events described in **Matthew 24** coming true. All political walls and economic barriers are coming down to bring about globalism. We are witnessing the move to bring all religious systems under one leader. If you are a believer you need to know you are living in exciting times. Prophetically, we sense the nearness of Christ coming for His bride.

Jesus made this statement in **Luke 21:28**,
"And when these things begin to come to pass, then look up, and lift up your heads; for your redemption draweth nigh."

Today there is much discussion and speculation as to the time of Christ's coming. In fact, some have made belief systems and causes around it.

Jesus said this in **Matthew 24:36**,
"But of that day and hour knoweth no man, no, not the angels of heaven, but my Father only."

Personal Notes: ____

____

Being Prepared

Supplement: Superstition and the Supernatural **Sup. 3**

Jesus made this statement in **Matthew 24:42-44**,
"Watch therefore; for ye know not what hour your Lord doth come. But know this, that if the goodman of the house had known in what watch the thief would come, he would have watched, and would not have suffered his house to be broken up. Therefore be ye also ready: for in such an hour as ye think not the Son of man cometh."

1 Thessalonians 5:1-2 says,
"But of the times and the seasons, brethren, ye have no need that I write unto you. For yourselves know perfectly that the day of the Lord so cometh as a thief in the night."

Christ will come like a thief in the night to those who are not expecting Him. For this reason, we are instructed to watch!

Jesus said in **Matthew 24:37**,
"But as the days of Noe (Noah) were, so shall also the coming of the Son of man be." (Parenthesis added.)

People in the days of Noah lived their lives without consideration of God. Noah warned them about God's pending judgment. They simply disregarded it.

2 Peter 3:3-4 tells us,
"Knowing this first, that there shall come in the last days scoffers, walking after their own lusts, And saying, where is the promise of his coming? for since the fathers fell asleep, all things continue as they were from the beginning of the creation."

<u>Scoffing</u> is cynicism. <u>Cynicism</u> comes from unbelief and a lack of respect for God. These mockers will use these terrible times as an excuse to make fun of the Christians' "blessed hope."

Jesus said in **Luke 18:8**,
"...Nevertheless when the Son of man cometh, shall he find faith on the earth?

> If people look at the events, they will lose hope. Our confidence does not rest in what type of circumstances we see coming or find ourselves in, but in Christ and His promises.

Paul confirms this in **2 Timothy 1:12**,
"...for I know whom I have believed, and am persuaded that he is able to keep that which I have committed unto him against that day."

> Believers need to be watchmen. This requires them to be on guard against all that would exploit what is holy, true, and godly. Each believer needs to be aware of what is gong on around them. Faith is under attack, truth is being adjusted, and Christianity redefined as emphasis is made on the heretical or supernatural. These are all signs that we are living in the end days. As believers, we must be on guard against all counterfeits, while we remember that our real duty is to watch for our Lord's return. Therefore, we must be ready for His return at all times.

Jesus gave this warning in **Matthew 24:48-51**,
"But and if that evil servant shall say in his heart, My lord delalyeth his coming; and shall being to smite the fellow-servants, and to eat and drink with the drunken; The Lord of that servant shall come in a day when he looketh not for him, and in an hour that he is not aware of, And shall cut him asunder, and appoint him his portion with the hypocrites: there shall be weeping and gnashing of teeth."

> As His Church and Body, believers must be ready to meet their bridegroom.

Ephesians 5:26-27 says this about the Church**,**
"That he might sanctify and cleanse it with the washing of water by the word, That he might present it to himself a glorious church, not having spot, or wrinkle, or any such thing; but that it should be holy and without blemish."

In **Revelation 19:7-8** we read these words,
"Let us be glad and rejoice, and give honour to him: for the marriage of the Lamb is come, and his wife hath made herself ready. And to her was granted that she should be arrayed in fine linen, clean and white: for the fine linen is the righteousness of saints."

> The Apostle Paul tells us how to be ready for our bridegroom in the following Scripture verses.

1 Timothy 6:11 & 14 states,
"But thou, O man of God, flee these things; and follow after righteousness, godliness, faith, love, patience, meekness... That thou keep this commandment without spot, unrebukeable, until the appearing of our Lord Jesus Christ:"

Titus 2:11-13 declares,
"For the grace of God that bringeth salvation hath appeared to all men. Teaching us that denying ungodliness and worldly lusts, we should live soberly, righteously, and godly, in this present world; Looking for that blessed hope, and the glorious appearing of the great God and our Saviour Jesus Christ."

Jesus adds this warning in **Luke 21:36**,
"Watch ye therefore, and pray always, that ye may be accounted worthy to escape all these things that shall come to pass, and to stand before the Son of man."

We need to be praying. God needs to prepare our hearts and minds for whatever confronts us.

Matthew 24:13 gives us this promise,
"But he that shall endure unto the end, the same shall be saved."

Let us stand firm in Christ Jesus. We need to trust Him with every area of our lives. We need to believe no matter what is happening He is still sitting on the throne.

If Christ came today for His Church, would you be ready? Consider your relationship with God. Maybe you need to repent and rededicate yourself? Maybe you need to receive Jesus Christ into your life as Lord and Savior?

Personal Notes: ____

____

____

Chapter 23

THE MILLENNIUM

> **Supplements:**
> Kingdom Theology
> **Sup. 3**
> *(Interesting reading for the next couple of chapters)*
> **Volume 7**
> **Books 1 & 2:**
> *Interview in Hell & Interview on Earth*

In **Matthew 24:29-31** we read these words,
"Immediately after the tribulation of those days...And then shall appear the sign of the Son of man in heaven: and then shall all the tribes of the earth mourn, and they shall see the Son of man coming in the clouds of heaven with power and great glory. And he shall send his angels with a great sound of a trumpet, and they shall gather together his elect from the four winds, from one end of heaven to the other."

Jesus first came as a baby in a manager. He was humble servant in His ministry. Here we see Him coming back in power and glory as the King of kings and the Lord of lords **(Revelation 19:16)**! The whole world will see Him. This magnificent event is known as the Second Coming of Christ. (See also **Revelation 1:7**.)

The Apostle John gives us this description of Jesus in His glory and power in **Revelation 19:11-13; 15**,
"And I saw heaven opened, and behold a white horse; and he that sat upon him was called Faithful and True, and in righteousness he doth judge and make war. His eyes were as a flame of fire, and on his head were many crowns; and he had a name written, that no man knew, but he himself. And he was clothed with a vesture dipped in blood: and his name is called The Word of God. And out of his mouth goeth a sharp sword, that with it he should smite the nations: and he shall rule them with a rod of iron: and he treadeth the winepress of the fierceness and wrath of Almighty God."

> **Zechariah 14** tells us Jesus is coming to fight for Jerusalem. Clearly Jesus will be setting up His kingdom. However, scriptural truth is under attack. There are those who believe that Christians will set up Jesus' kingdom to usher in His Second Advent.

Zechariah 14:4 says,
"And his feet shall stand in that day upon the Mount of Olives, which is before Jerusalem on the east, and the mount of Olives shall cleave in the midst thereof toward the east and toward the west, and there shall be a very great valley; and half of the mountain shall remove toward the north, and half of it toward the south."

John tells us the makeup of the army opposing Christ in **Revelation 19:19**,
"And I saw the beast, and the kings of the earth, and their armies, gathered together to make war against him that sat on the horse, and against his army."

> The beast could represent a godless system and a one-world leader. He along with the false prophet will require all the people of the earth to take a number in order to buy and sell. If any individual receives this number, it will seal his or her doom.

Revelation 14:9-10 confirms this,
"...If any man worship the beast and his image, and receive this mark in his forehead, or in his hand, the same shall drink of the wine of the wrath of God, which is poured out without

mixture into the cup of his indignation; and he shall be tormented with fire and brimstone in the presence of the holy angels, and in the presence of the Lamb."

Zechariah 14:6-7 tells us about the day of our Lord's wrath,
"And it shall come to pass in that day, that the light shall not be clear, nor dark: But it shall be one day which shall be known to the Lord, not day, nor night: but it shall come to pass, that at evening time it shall be light."

Revelation 19:20 tells us the outcome of this war,
"And the beast was taken, and with him the false prophet that wrought miracles before him, with which he deceived them that had received the mark of the beast, and them that worshipped his image. These both were cast alive into a lake of fire burning with brimstone."

Revelation 6:15-17 tells us what the final response of the kings and their armies will be,
"And the kings of the earth, and the great men, and the rich men, and the chief captains, and the mighty men, and every bondman, and every free man, hid themselves in the dens and in the rocks of the mountains; And said to the mountains and rocks, Fall on us, and hide us from the face of him that sitteth on the throne, and from the wrath of the Lamb: For the great day of his wrath is come; and who shall be able to stand?"

We read this concerning the fate of those who followed the beast in **Revelation 19:21**,
"And the remnant were slain with the sword..."

Romans 5:9 gives the believers this assurance,
"Much more then, being now justified by his blood, we shall be saved from wrath through him."

Christians can be confident that they are not appointed to God's wrath. God delivers His people. For instance, He delivered Noah through the flood, which destroyed the whole world. He delivered Lot out of Sodom before He rained fire on it.

The question you must answer now is, are you appointed to God's wrath?

Personal Notes: ____

____

The Reign of Christ

Supplements:
Foundation of Our Faith
Sup. 1
Lesson 6
Has He Taken His Rightful Place?
Sup. 3

Revelation 20:1-2 gives us this information,
"And I saw an angel come down from heaven, having the key of the bottomless pit and a great chain in his hand. And he laid hold on the dragon, that old serpent, which is the Devil, and Satan, and bound him a thousand years."

Zechariah 14:9 tells us,
"And the LORD shall be king over all the earth: in that day shall there be one LORD, and his name one."

In **Revelation**, we see Satan, the adversary of God, being locked up for a thousand years. This event marks the end of a period of history identified by God's grace as the church age. We then see Christ taking His rightful place as King of kings and ruling the whole earth.

Revelation 20:4 gives us this insight about Christ's reign,
"And I saw thrones, and they sat upon them, and judgement was given unto them: and I saw the souls of them that were beheaded for the witness of Jesus, and for the word of God, and which had not worshiped the beast neither his image, neither had received his mark upon their foreheads, or in their hands; and they lived and reigned with Christ a thousand years." (See also **2 Timothy 2:12**.)

We now see what the believers will be doing during the Lord's reign. They will be ruling with the Lord in this kingdom. This kingdom will last a thousand years. Christ will govern totally different than Satan, the ruler of this present world. (Refer to **John 16:11; 2 Corinthians 4:3-6** and **Ephesians 2:2-3**.)

Isaiah 9:7 tells us,
"…upon the throne of David, and upon his kingdom, to order it, and to establish it with judgment and with justice from henceforth even forever. The zeal of the Lord of hosts will perform this."

To ensure justice and righteousness, all rebellion must be put down.

Revelation 19:15 says,
"…and he shall rule with a rod of iron:…"

Isaiah 11:4 confirms this,
"…and he shall smite the earth with the rod of his mouth,…"

This righteousness and justice will produce lasting peace. (See also **John 14:27**.)

Isaiah 9:6-7 states this about Jesus Christ,
"…and his name shall be called Wonderful, Counsellor, The mighty God, the Everlasting Father, The Prince of Peace. Of the increase of his government and peace there shall be no end,…"

Scriptures in **Isaiah** give us this picture of His perfect peace.

Isaiah 2:4 states,
"And he shall judge among the nations, and shall rebuke many people: and they shall beat their swords into plow-shares, and their spears into pruning hooks: nation shall not lift up sword against nation, neither shall they learn war any more."

Isaiah 11:6 tells us,
"The wolf also shall dwell with the lamb, and the leopard shall lie down with the kid; and the calf and the young lion and the fatling together; and a little child shall lead them."

In **Isaiah 11:9** we read these words,
"…for the earth shall be full of the knowledge of the Lord, as the waters cover the sea."

Zechariah 14:16 says,
"And it shall come to pass, that every one that is left of all the nations which came against Jerusalem shall even go up from year to year to worship the King, the LORD of hosts, and to keep the feasts of tabernacles."

These scriptures show us the earth will be full of the knowledge of the Lord. He will be the center of everyone's adoration. The Feast of Tabernacles was the last celebration prescribed by the Jewish Law. It lasted eight days and commemorated the entrance into the Promised Land after wandering in the wilderness. This feast could also represent the difference between being under the harsh rule of Satan and coming into abundance under God's reign. It is hard to believe people would prefer any other ruler than the Prince of Peace.

Personal Notes: ____

____

The Last Rebellion

Revelation 20:7-9 tells us the events after the thousand year reign of Christ,
"And when the thousand years are expired, Satan shall be loosed out of his prison. And he shall go out to deceive the nations which are in the four quarters of the earth, Gog, and Magog, to gather them together to battle; the number of whom is as the sand of the sea. And they went up on the breadth of the earth, and compassed the camp of the saints about, and the beloved city: and fire came down from God out of heaven, and devoured them."

How could people choose Satan after knowing God's greatness and peace? (Refer to **John 8:44** and **10:10**.)

The answer to the previous question can be found in **2 Thessalonians 2:10**,
"And with all deceivableness of unrighteousness in them that perish; because they received not the love of the truth, that they might be saved."

Jesus is the summary of all truth **(John 14:6)**. If man does not love the truth, he does not love Christ. We must love the Christ of the Bible to ensure we do not become deceived. This deception comes through two avenues: False doctrine and pride. The means used to inspire man to rebel openly against God is pride. Pride will tell man he does not need God. In fact, he can be his own god and control his own destiny. This is the example of ultimate rebellion. After the thousand year reign of the Lord Jesus, Satan once again deceives many to believe they can come up against God Almighty and win.

We read their fate in **Revelation 20:9-10**,
"...and fire came down from God out of heaven and devoured them. And the devil that deceived them was cast into the lake of fire and brimstone, where the beast and the false prophet are, and shall be tormented day and night for ever and ever."

God will be the final victor in all battles. Right now, you need to determine what side you are on. Maybe you are convinced you can put off making a decision for Jesus Christ? Maybe you think it will be worth paying the consequences? Maybe you think in the end you will win?

My Bible tells me in **John 3:16**,
"...that whosoever believeth in him should not perish, but have eternal life."

The rich man in the story found in **Luke 16:20-31** tripped over one man and found himself in hell. The man was simply a beggar, but he served as a test to the rich man. Many people are tripping over Jesus. He may seem unrealistic, too harsh, or unacceptable, but He serves as a test, and those who trip over Him in unbelief will find themselves in hell.

Personal Notes: ____

____

Chapter 24

THE GREAT WHITE THRONE JUDGEMENT

Supplement: Foundation of Our Faith **Sup. 1 Lesson 7**

John 5:22 tells us,
"For the Father judgeth no man, but hath committed all judgment unto the

Romans 14:10 says,
"...for we shall all stand before the judgment seat of Christ."

Jesus is the judge over all. He has been given the authority to execute all judgment by the Father. (See **John 5:26-27**.)

John 5:30 tells us this about Christ's judgment,
"I can of my own self doing nothing: as I hear, I judge: and my judgment is just; because I seek not mine own will, but the will of the Father which hath sent me."

As I have stated previously, judgment means separation. There are two distinct separations when it comes to God and His kingdom.

Matthew 25:31-33 & 46 defines these judgments,
"When the Son of man shall come in his glory, and all the holy angels with him, then shall he sit upon the throne of his glory: And before him shall be gathered all nations: and he shall separate them one from another, as a shepherd divideth his sheep from the goats. And he shall set the sheep on his right hand, but the goats on the left.... And these shall go away into everlasting punishment: but the righteous into life eternal."

One type of judgment involves God setting His followers apart for Himself. In the other judgment God separates the wicked from Himself.

Personal Notes: ____

____

The Believer and Judgment

The Bible mentions three main judgments. The first one we will be considering is the judgment of the believers.

1 Peter 4:17 tells us,
"For the time is come that judgment must begin at the house of God: and if it first begins at us, what shall the end be of them that obey not the gospel of God?"

Judgment will begin with the believers.

1 Corinthians 3:12-15 gives us this insight about the judgment involving the Christians, "Now if any man build upon this foundation gold, silver, precious stones, wood, hay, stubble; Every man's work shall be made manifest: for the day shall declare it, because it shall be revealed by fire; and the fire shall try every man's work of what sort it is. If any man's work shall be burned, he shall suffer loss: but he himself shall be saved; yet so as by fire. Know ye not that ye are the temple of God, and that the Spirit of God dwelleth in you?"

Our life must be built on Jesus Christ. A life established on the right foundation will secure the deeds of the Christian on judgment day.

The Apostle Paul made this mention about believers appearing before the judgment seat of Christ in **2 Corinthians 5: 9-10**,
"Wherefore we labour, that, whether present or absent, we may be accepted of him. For we must all appear before the judgment seat of Christ; that every one may receive the things done in his body, according to that he that done, whether it be good or bad."

Paul is talking about the Christian receiving rewards.

In **Colossians 3:23-24**, we get an insight into our real reward,
"And whatsoever ye do, do it heartily, as to the Lord, and not unto men: Knowing that of the Lord ye shall receive the reward of the inheritance: for ye serve the Lord Christ."

Our greatest reward is the inheritance of eternal life. (See **Ephesians 1:11-14**.)

Paul gives us this promise in **2 Corinthians 5:8,**
"We are confident, I say, and willing rather to be absent from the body, and to be present with the Lord."

Jesus said in **John 14:1-2**,
"Let not your heart be troubled: ye believe in God, believe also in me. In my Father's house are many mansions: if it were not so, I would have told you, I go to prepare a place for you."

Once we are separated from our physical bodies, we have the promise of being in the presence of our Lord. Peter referred to Christians as strangers in this world **(1 Peter 2:11)**.

Like Abraham, we need to be looking for, "a city which hath foundations, whose builder and maker is God") **(Hebrews 11:10)**.

This world offers nothing to the Christian. We are simply passing through. Therefore, our whole manner of living should express a detachment from the world.

Personal Notes: ____

____

Supplement:
(For Review)
Volume 1
Book 2: *The Anatomy of Sin*
Chapter 12

A Temporary Holding Place

Matthew 5:29-30 tells us about a second type of judgment,
"And if thy right eye offend thee, pluck it out, and cast it from thee: for it is profitable for thee that one of thy members should perish, and not that thy whole body should be cast into hell. And if they right hand offend thee, cut it

off, and cast it from thee: for it is profitable for thee that one of thy members should perish, and not that thy whole body should be cast into hell."

Hell is a place for unredeemed man and encompasses different areas from a temporary holding place to a lake of everlasting fire, where, as we will see, along with death it will be cast into it. The one thing that distinguishes hell is that God's presence is absent. If God is not present, then what remains is the tormenting reality of a lifeless existence that is void of any life, goodness, hope, or salvation. It is an existence that is plagued by unrelenting torment that has no end to its despair and devastation. **Luke 16:19-31** gives us a description of it as a place of utter torment.

Luke 16:23 says,
"And in hell he lift up his eyes, being in torments,..."

Luke 16:24 tells us,
"...for I am tormented in this flame."

Hell is clearly a place of fire, torment, and agony.

2 Peter 2:4 says,
"For if God spared not the angels that sinned, but cast them down to hell, and delivered them into chains of darkness, to be reserved unto judgment."

God did not create hell for man; rather, it was made as a holding place for the fallen angels until judgment. Right now, it is also serving as a holding place of punishment for unredeemed man until the final judgment.

Isaiah 5:14-15 gives us this insight into hell,
"Therefore hell hath enlarged herself, and opened her mouth without measure: and their glory, and their multitude, and their pomp, and he that rejoiceth, shall descend into it. And the mean man shall be brought down, and the mighty man shall be humbled, and the eyes of the lofty shall be humbled."

I must stress hell is not a holding place to give man a second chance to reconsider his decision about Jesus Christ and His redemption.

Hebrews 9:27 states,
"And it is appointed unto men once to die, but after this the judgment."

Those in hell are facing the ultimate judgment. There is no hope of deliverance or salvation once man dies in his sins.

Revelation 20:14 tells us the fate of hell,
"And death and hell were cast into the lake of fire. This was the second death"

Personal Notes: ____

____

____

The Final Judgment

There is a final judgment for the wicked.

Revelation 20:11-12 tells us about this judgment,
"And I saw a great white throne, and him that sat on it, from whose face the earth and the heaven fled away; and there was found no place for them. And I saw the dead, small and great, stand before God; and the books were opened: and another book was opened, which is the book of life: and the dead were judged out of those things which were written in the books, according to their works."

Here we see the great white throne judgment.

Revelation 20:13 gives us this insight,
"And the sea gave up the dead which were in it; and death and hell delivered up the dead which were in them: and they were judged every man according to their works.'

Christians will be judged according to their life of service to their Lord. The wicked will be considered in light of the Law of God which declares them guilty, as well as the only standard of righteousness available since the beginning of creation, Jesus Christ.

Romans 1:20 says,
"For the invisible things of him from the creation of the world are clearly seen, being understood by the things that are made, even his eternal power and Godhead; so that they are without excuse."

Romans 3:23 reminds us of the condition of man,
"For all have sinned, and come short of the glory of God."

God has intervened by sending his Son, Jesus Christ. The Creator even promised Him to Adam and Eve in the garden after they had sinned in **Genesis 3:15**. It is interesting to note every pagan culture has a story built into it about a deliverer coming one day to save them from their plight. Therefore, there will be no excuse on judgment day.

Hebrews 2:3 puts God's salvation in this perspective,
"How shall we escape, if we neglect so great salvation;..."

Revelation 20:15 tells us the final outcome for those standing in their own righteousness,
"And whosoever was not found written in the book of life was cast into the lake of fire."

Revelation 14:10-11 gives us this description of the lake of fire,
"...and he shall be tormented with fire and brimstone in the presence of the holy angels, and in the presence of the Lamb: And the smoke of their torment ascendeth up for ever and ever: and they have no rest day nor night, who worship the beast and his image, and whosoever receiveth the mark of his name."

This last judgment of everlasting punishment represents the ultimate harsh reality of hell. It is referred to as the second death. It also could be considered as the second separation from God. Remember that the first separation was the temporary holding place of hell. This everlasting punishment is something we cannot comprehend. God did not choose this for man. It is man who makes this choice when he rejects the salvation of God. When man denies his need for God, he has simply made a choice not to spend eternity with his Creator. God will honor his decision. The only place God's presence will not be is in the lake of fire.

Personal Notes: ____

____

A New Heaven and A New Earth

Revelation 21:1-2 says,
"And I saw a new heaven and a new earth: for the first heaven and the first earth were passed away; and there was no more sea. And I John saw the holy city, new Jerusalem, coming down from God out of heaven, prepared as a bride adorned for her husband."

2 Peter 3:12-13 tells us,
"Looking for and hasting unto the coming of the day of God, wherein the heavens being on fire shall be dissolved, and the elements shall melt with fervent heat? Nevertheless we, according to his promise, look for new heavens and a new earth, wherein dwelleth righteousness."

What a beautiful home the new heaven and earth will be.

Revelation 21 & 22 gives us the following description of the new city we will reside in.

A. God's glory serves as the light for the new city **(21:11, 25-26)**.
B. It will have pearl gates **(21:21)**.
C. It will have 12 foundations made of every kind of precious stone **(21:19-20)**.
D. The wall will be made of jasper **(21:18).**
E. The city will be made of pure gold **(21:21)**.
F. There will be a street of gold **(21:21)**.
G. Nothing impure will enter the city **(21:27)**.
H. River of the water of life will run through the middle of the city **(22:1-2)**.
I. There will be the tree of life on each side of the river to bring healing **(*22:2*)**.

Revelation 21:3-4 gives us this promise,
"And I heard a great voice out of heaven saying, Behold, the tabernacle of God is with men, and he will dwell with them, and they shall be his people, and God himself shall be with them, and be their God. And God shall wipe away all tears from their eyes; and there shall be no more death, neither sorrow, nor crying, neither shall there be any more pain: for the former things are passed away."

Personal Notes: ____

____

Decision Time

You might be at a crossroad in your life right now.
Maybe you do not know Jesus Christ.
By not choosing Christ you are making a choice of eternal punishment.

You need to respond to the message found in **2 Corinthians 6:2**,
"(For he saith, I have heard thee in a time accepted, and in the day of salvation have I succoured thee: behold, now is the accepted time; behold, now is the day of salvation.)"

If you are a Christian who has turned an indifferent ear to God's call to holiness, you need to adhere to these warnings.

2 Peter 3:10-11, & 14 says,
"But the day of the Lord will come as a thief in the night; in the which the heavens shall pass away with a great noise, and the elements shall melt with fervent heat, the earth also and the works that therein shall be burned up. Seeing then that all these things shall be dissolved, what manner of persons ought ye to be in all holy conversation and godliness... Wherefore, beloved, seeing that ye look for such things, be diligent that ye may be found of him in peace, without spot and blameless."

Jesus said these words in **Matthew 7:21**,
"Not every one that saith unto me, Lord, Lord, shall enter into the kingdom of heaven; but he that doeth the will of my Father which is in heaven."

Revelation 21:7 gives us this summary of what it takes to be a part of this new eternal city,
"He that overcometh shall inherit all things; and I will be his God, and he shall be my son."

Scripturally speaking we must overcome the flesh, the world, and Satan. *This is not an option!* If your life is falling short of this holy walk, you need to repent and submit to God. Avoid repentance that only involves the emotions and does not require you to seek forgiveness. Never allow yourself to be released from your responsibility to live this upright life and to serve your Lord. Submit daily to allow the Holy Spirit to work the life of Christ in you. Keep in mind what you do with Jesus and His life is your decision.

Personal Notes: ____

____

Supplement:
Volume 4
Book 1:
Hidden Manna Revised

For review and edification: The following book, *Hidden Manna Revised,* will give greater insight into human nature and a person's potential in the kingdom of God. It will bring into focus how sin, pride, and repentance work within the selfish disposition. This book is also important to read before you read, *Bring Down the Sacred Cows.*

Section II

MARRIAGE AND FAMILY

Chapter 25

INSTITUTION OF MARRIAGE

Supplement:
(For the next three chapters.)
Volume 4
Book 2:
Bring Down the Sacred Cows

Strong families are the strength of churches, communities, and nations. The breakdown of the family ultimately means destruction of any society. Healthy families begin with a stable marriage. The stability of a marriage is determined by whether or not God is its foundation and source.

Jesus said these words to the Pharisees about marriage in **Matthew 19:4-5**,
"And he answered and said unto them, Have ye not read, that he which made them at the beginning made them male and female, And said, For this cause shall a man leave father and mother, and shall cleave to his wife: and they twain shall be one flesh.?"

God must be the foundation of marriage because He established it. His rules and attitude towards it must be instituted in our approach and attitude about it.

We find one of the reasons God created marriage in **Genesis 2:18**,
"And the LORD God said, It is not good that the man should be alone; I will make him an help meet for him."

In all of God's creation the only thing not considered good was man being alone. Good in this sense implies the best of something, pleasant, or delightful.

In **Genesis 2:19-20** we read this information,
"...and (God) brought them unto Adam to see what he would call them: and whatsoever Adam called every living creature, that was the name thereof. ...but for Adam there was not found an help meet for him." (Parenthesis added.)

It is interesting to point out God brought all living creatures to Adam to show him none of creation could fill this place of a helper.

Genesis 2:21-22 tells us the rest of the story,
"And the LORD God caused a deep sleep to fall upon Adam, and he slept: and he took one of his ribs, and closed up the flesh instead thereof. And the rib, which the LORD God had taken from man, made he a woman, and brought her unto the man."

God made woman to share in man's life. He did not make another man or beast to be Adam's helper. Because God established this relationship, it is to serve as a holy bond.

For something to be <u>holy</u> implies it has been set apart for the purpose and glory of God. The New Testament marriage also represents the union found among the Father and the Son.

Jesus made this statement about His followers on the night He was betrayed in John **John 17:11**,
"And now I am no more in the world, but these are in the world, and I come to thee. Holy Father, keep through thine own name those whom thou hast given me, that they may be one, as we are"

The ultimate goal of marriage is for two to become one. To be one represents agreement in purpose, direction, and goal. (See **Amos 3:3**.) The Father and Son were one in all of their functions. They had total agreement in unity of the Spirit.

This agreement is the same as fellowship. Therefore, marriage is symbolic of the type of relationship which exists between the Father and the Son. Another relationship represented by marriage is the one established between Christ and His Church.

Ephesians 5:30-32 says,
"For we are members of his body, of his flesh, and of his bones. For this cause shall a man leave his father and mother, and shall be joined unto his wife, and they two shall be one flesh. This is a great mystery: but I speak concerning Christ and the church.

<u>Oneness</u> also implies equality. This brings us to the subject of the wife being a helper. The King James Version uses the term "helpmeet". <u>Helpmeet</u> denotes a helper fit for the man. This position does not mean servitude. In fact, wherever there is a lesser vessel in God's kingdom, it must be honored or exalted. (See **1 Corinthians 12:19-24** and **1 Peter 3:7**.) Some Bible teachers agree God created woman to point man back to Him.

This belief runs consistent with the whole purpose of God's creation as stated in **Romans 1:20**:
"For the invisible things of him from the creation of the world are clearly seen, being understood by the things that are made, even his eternal power and Godhead; so that they are without excuse."

Marriage is an honorable institution as long as God's instructions govern it. These instructions must be complemented and reinforced by the right attitudes.

Attitudes

Attitudes surrounding marriage are mainly determined by culture and religious upbringing. These ideas have often encouraged attitudes that have degraded the purpose and holiness of marriage rather than enhance it. Therefore, each of us must consider our attitudes in line with scriptural emphasis. God's instructions are for the purpose of challenging and establishing godly attitudes toward this holy bond.

The Apostle Paul made this statement in **1 Corinthians 7:4**,
"The wife hath not power of her own body, but the husband: and likewise also the husband hath not power of his own body, but the wife."

Once again, we see a picture of oneness. A wife's body belongs to her husband. A husband's body belongs to his wife. In order for this type of union to work, personal identities and rights must be set aside by both parties. Consideration of the other's needs must become a matter of importance because each one is responsible for the other. Since both people have this responsibility and right over the other, we once again see equality.

The positions and responsibilities of husbands and wives have been established for the sake of harmony and well-being in the family. These positions were never meant to determine the importance of men over women. In God's eyes men and women have been and are equally important to the family and His kingdom. Attitudes of superiority and feelings of inferiority have caused resentment, frustration, and bitterness in marriage. These feelings have made marriage a battleground. This must cease! The solution is only found in allowing scriptural principles to govern and challenge us in this area. The main key to godly marriage is denial of self. Such denial results in preferring another over self. This preference results in submission.

The Apostle Paul made this statement regarding all Christians in **Ephesians 5:21**,
"Submitting yourselves one to another in the fear of God."

Romans 12:10 says,
"Be kindly affectioned one to another with brotherly love, in honour preferring one another."

Christian qualities and responses are not limited to the body of believers. They must be evident in godly marriages as well. What do your attitudes say about this area? Do they display the attitudes of Christ or the attitudes of culture and religious beliefs? Allow them to be examined. The family is a vital harvest field to God. The awesome responsibility of this field lies with the type of relationship the husband and wife develop with each other.

Personal Notes: ____

The Issue of Divorce

The divorce rate serves as an indicator of the massive spiritual breakdown that exists everywhere.

Jesus said this about divorce in **Mark 10:2-5**,
"And the Pharisees came to him, and asked him, Is it lawful for a man to put away his wife? tempting him. And he answered and said unto them, What did Moses command you? And they said Moses suffered to write a bill of divorcement, and to put her away. And Jesus answered, and said unto them, For the hardness of your heart he wrote you this precept."

A hard heart points to unbelief **(Hebrews 3:8-14)**. Therefore, divorce is a product of the sin of unbelief towards God. Sin breaks fellowship. A lack of fellowship indicates separation. <u>Separation</u> means a lack of communication. A lack of communication establishes and reinforces walls of rebellion, fear, and hurt. Eventually you have a vicious cycle, which ends in the death of a marriage. God did not make marriage to fail.

Jesus said this in **Matthew 19:6**,
"...What therefore God hath joined together, let not man put asunder."

The key here is that God puts the marriage together. Few consider Him in this area. What God puts together He is able to honor. God intended marriage to bring Him glory and last a lifetime. There are two scriptural reasons for a divorce.

Matthew 5:32 tells us the first acceptable reason for this procedure,
"But I say unto you, That whosoever shall put away his wife, saving for the cause of fornication, causeth her to commit adultery: and whosoever shall marry her that is divorced committeth adultery."

Fornication includes all illicit sex, while adultery addresses sex outside of marriage. Adultery is the worse type of betrayal in the marriage relationship because it not only breaks a vow an covenant established before God, but it breaks trust that is vital to the marriage relationship.

Proverbs 6:32 gives us this insight about adultery,
"But whoso committeth adultery with a woman lacketh understanding: he that doeth it destroyeth his own soul."

Adultery destroys a man's soul because it brings a person into agreement with the unholy. (See also **1 Corinthians 6:15-20**.)

The Apostle Paul tells us why in **1 Corinthians 6:9-10**,
"Know ye not that the unrighteous shall not inherit the kingdom of God? Be not deceived: neither fornicators, nor idolaters, nor adulterers, nor effeminate, nor abusers of themselves with mankind, Nor thieves, nor covetous, nor drunkards, nor revilers, nor extortioners, shall inherit the kingdom of God."

Jesus gives us this insight on adultery in **Matthew 5:27-28**,
"Ye have heard that it was said by them of old time, Thou shalt not commit adultery: But I say unto you, that whoso-ever looketh on a woman to lust after her hath committed adultery with her already in his heart."

The act of adultery is not excluded to an outward act. It actually begins in the heart and can be committed with the eyes. The righteous man Job even made a covenant with his eyes to not look upon a handmaiden in a wrong, lustful way (**Job 31:1**).

Hebrews 13:4 tells us,
"Marriage is honourable in all, and the bed undefiled: but whoremongers and adulterers God will judge."

Adultery is the most blatant disrespect towards marriage. It will be judged!

Personal Notes: ____

____

The second reason for divorce can be found in **1 Corinthians 7:12-13, & 15**,
"But to the rest speak I, not the Lord: If any brother hath a wife that believeth not, and she be pleased to dwell with him, let him not put her away. And the woman which hath an husband that believeth not, and if he be pleased to dwell with her; let her not leave him.

...But if the unbelieving depart, let him depart. A brother or a sister is not under bondage in such cases: but God hath called us to peace."

> If an unbelieving partner wants a divorce, a Christian can honor his or her request. There can be another reason for divorce. If there is abuse, honor is lacking; therefore, the covenant is being broken. This dishonoring of marriage brings us to the consideration about a person's real spiritual condition: A godly man or woman would not be a part of such abuse. Legal separation or divorce may be necessary to preserve emotional and physical health. After all, God does not require people to become sacrifices on the altars of man's selfishness.

Jesus gives us this insight into divorce in **Matthew 5:32**,
"But I say unto you, That whosoever shall put away his wife, saving for the cause of fornication, causeth her to commit adultery: and whosoever shall marry her that is divorced committeth adultery."

> Remarriage outside of the acceptable reasons for divorce is considered adultery. Remarriage is a controversial issue in the Church. Many respected Christians maintain all remarriages among believers is the sin of adultery. Others believe God can sanction remarriage as long as the divorce was within scriptural bounds, and God ordains the present marriage. The Apostle Paul in **1 Corinthians 7** points out that such a matter requires a wise judgment call that is both discerning and in line with God's will.
>
> What Christians must keep in mind is the real issue is not divorce but sin. Sin produces bad attitudes. As these attitudes are adopted towards this holy bond, they give birth to the real problems facing this institution. The biggest problem is that people are not willing to put down selfishness and allow the mind of Christ to motivate them.

Jesus made this statement in **Matthew 24:37-39**,
"But as the days of Noe (Noah) were, so shall also the coming of the Son of man be. For as in the days that were before the flood they were eating and drinking, marrying and giving in marriage, until the day that Noah entered into the ark. And knew not until the flood came, and took them all away; so shall also the coming of the Son of man be." (Parenthesis added.)

> Attitudes toward marriage reveal the true attitude people have about the Creator of marriage. There are many issues surrounding marriage. But, all of these issues must be put to the side and attitudes examined. If you are married and your marriage is falling short of scriptural instructions, begin to examine yourself. Repent, and ask God to deal with any unacceptable attitudes or responses.

Personal Notes: ____

____

____

Chapter 26

HUSBANDS AND WIVES

The Apostle Paul made this statement in **1 Corinthians 7:3**,
"Let the husband render unto the wife due benevolence: and likewise also the wife unto the husband."

There are decisive scriptural responsibilities which the husband and wife must fulfill towards one another. (Benevolence in this Scripture implies owing one good will or kindness.) We find these marriage responsibilities outlined in **Ephesians 5:22-33** and **Colossians 3:18-23**. These instructions also inspire correct attitudes and godly responses in this relationship.

In **Ephesians 5:22**, we read this instruction,
"Wives submit yourselves unto your own husbands, as unto the Lord."

Wives must submit to their husbands, but the boundary of this submission must line up to Jesus Christ. His Lordship will serve as a guideline in righteousness and a point of protection and integrity to the woman. It will govern the motive and actions of her submission. This will always ensure that the Lord will be glorified in the woman's life as well as the marriage. The truest form of acceptable submission comes in the position of a servant.

Philippians 2:7-8 says this about Jesus Christ,
"But made himself of no reputation, and took upon him the form of a servant, and was made in the likeness of men: And being found in fashion as a man, he humbled himself, and became obedient unto death, even the death of the cross."

Matthew 20:26-27 states,
"...but whosoever will be great among you, let him be your minister; And whosoever will be chief among you, let him be your servant."

The greatest example in the kingdom is a servant. Submission is the response of a servant but such submission is always in light of that which is worthy of consideration and respect. A submissive servant has no personal rights. A servant must be ready to present his or her life as a perpetual living sacrifice as his or her Lord desires.

1 Corinthians 7:22-23 confirms this level of commitment,
"For he that is called in the Lord, being a servant, is the Lord's freeman: likewise also he that is called, being free, is Christ's servant. Ye are bought with a price; be not ye the servants of men."

These Scriptures show that women must not become a servant to their husbands, but must be a servant of Jesus in their marriages. They will serve as His perpetual or living sacrifice, ready to be offered up for His purpose and glory for the benefit of the family. (See **Romans 12:1-2**.)

We gain an insight into an example of a perpetual living sacrifice in **2 Samuel 23:14-16**. These scriptures show us King David was in a stronghold while in battle. David desired some water. Three men broke through the opposing army. They brought him back a cup of water.

2 Samuel 23:16 tells us David's reaction to their sacrifice,
"...nevertheless he would not drink thereof, but he poured it out unto the Lord."

Three men willingly sacrificed their lives for David. Sacrifice for the benefit of others is the truest means of glorifying God. A woman who becomes a perpetual living sacrifice for the benefit of her family will bring glory to God. She will serve as the example of greatness in His kingdom. Everything a wife does must be for the glory of God. Husbands are the head of the family, but Jesus must be reigning in the hearts of both godly husbands and wives to ensure their purity and integrity in this godly institution. Jesus must be their final authority.

Acts 5:29 states,
"...We ought to obey God, rather than men."

1 Samuel 25:2-40 confirms this in the story of Abigail and Nabal.

1 Samuel 25:3 tells us about the character of Nabal,
"...but the man was churlish and evil in his doings;..."

We read about Abigail's qualities in **1 Samuel 25:3**,
"...she was a woman of good understanding; and of a beautiful countenance:..."

King David and his army had protected Nabal's household. When David's men asked Nabal for needed supplies, he mocked and insulted them. David's reaction was to destroy Nabal and his household. Abigail heard about her husband's wicked deeds. She gathered the supplies and met David on his way to destroy Nabal's household. She presented the supplies and asked David to forgive her husband.

We read David's reply to Abigail in **1 Samuel 25:32-34**,
"And David said to Abigail, Blessed be the Lord God of Israel, which sent thee this day to meet me: And blessed be thy advice, and blessed be thou, which hast kept me this day from coming to shed blood, and from avenging myself with mine own hand. For in very deed, as the Lord God of Israel liveth, which hath kept me back from hurting thee, except thou hadst hasted and come to meet me, surely there had not been left unto Nabal by the morning light any that pisseth against the wall."

If Abigail had obeyed her husband's wishes, her whole household would have been destroyed. We see destructive results with Ananias and Sapphira **(Acts 5:1-11)**. Together they kept back money promised for God's work. Ananias was struck dead when he lied about it. When Sapphira was confronted, she also lied to Peter about withholding the money.

Acts 5:10 tells us about her consequence,
"Then fell she down straightway at his feet, and yielded up the ghost: and the young men came in, and found her dead, and carrying her forth, buried her by the husband."

Wives will be held accountable for their own actions. Therefore, they must obey the Lord at all times.

Proverbs 31:30 gives us this insight into a godly woman,
"...but a woman that feareth the LORD, she shall be praised."

1 Peter 3:3-4 tells us this about a woman of God,
"Whose adorning let it not be that outward adorning of plaiting the hair, and of wearing of gold, or of putting on of apparel. But let it be the hidden man of the heart, in that which is not corruptible, even the ornament of a meek and quiet spirit, which is in the sight of God of great price."

The real beauty will only come forth in a woman when her hope rests in God.

1 Peter 3:5 adds this thought,
"For after this manner in the old time the holy women also, who trusted in God, adorned themselves, being in subjection unto their own husbands."

Titus 2:3-4 gives women these instructions,
"The aged women likewise, that they be in behavior as becometh holiness, not false accusers, not given to much wine, teachers of good things; That they may teach the young women to be sober, to love their husbands, to love their children."

It is interesting to note younger women were taught how to love their husbands and children. True love is not an emotion, but a commitment. It expresses itself in outward submission. This submission comes through examples of kindness and purity. It is motivated by obedience and reverence towards God.

In **1 Peter 3:1-2,** we read this,
"Likewise, ye wives, be in subjection to your own husbands; that if any obey not the word, they also may without the word be won by the conversation of the wives; While they behold your chaste conversation coupled with fear."

Many women go to the extreme in the area of submission. Some women hide a lack of commitment to God behind a mask of submission to their husbands. They compromise what they know would not be pleasing to God in the name of so-called "scriptural submission" to their husbands. Some women hide a lack of love for their husbands behind religious disguises. In the name of God or religion they refuse to submit to their husband in ways they should. Neither reaction is acceptable to God. The acceptable response involves a fine line, which takes fear, wisdom, love, and scriptural obedience. It must produce a desire to please God. When all factors are in place, wives can be assured of a right response towards their mates.

Personal Notes: ____

____

Husbands

Ephesians 5:23 gives this insight about a husband's position,
"For the husband is the head of the wife, even as Christ is the head of the church: and he is the saviour of the body."

This scripture defines the position of the husband in light of Jesus' relationship and commitment to the Church. He is to be the 'head' of the family. To be a "head" of something can have two meanings according to *Vine's Expository Dictionary of Biblical Words*. The first meaning denotes authority. However, true authority simply influences in the right way, it never dictates, demands, or provokes.

The second implication means leadership or direction through example. In order for the husband to understand his authority, he must first understand the type of leadership he has been entrusted with. Positions of authority require subjection. Subjection comes in two forms. First, we see people obeying authority in an outward manner because it is required of them. The other form of subjection comes through trust. This trust is the product of persuasion that greatly influences a person in his or her way of thinking. Persuasion is the result of trust earned because of consistent example. Although Christ has the authority to demand worship and dedication from his followers, He first earned their love and obedience through example.

1 John 4:10 states,
"Herein is love, not that we loved God, but that he loved us, and sent his Son to be the propitiation for our sins."

God first loved us, therefore ensuring our love. As we can see, Christ's "headship" was one based on example, and not on the exaltation of His authority. His example served as a means of giving direction to others.

Jesus made this statement in **John 13:15**,
"For I have given you an example, that ye should do as I have done to you."

1 Peter 2:21 says,
"For even hereunto were ye called: because Christ also suffered for us, leaving us an example, that ye should follow his steps."

The Bible clearly states Christ is our example. When it comes to the headship of a husband, Christ is his only example as to the acceptable attitude and real responsibility that governs his position.

This responsibility is stated in **Ephesians 5:25**,
"Husbands love your wives, even as Christ also loved the church,..."

Husbands, headship is defined by your duty to love your wife. By loving their wife as Christ loved the Church, they will persuade her to submit to their position of leadership.

The last part of **Ephesians 5:25** reads,
"...and gave himself for it."

Christ's ultimate show of love for the Church was becoming a sacrifice. This sacrifice prepared the way for man to have a relationship with God. Husbands must become the sacrifice on the altar in order to persuade their families to follow them into the kingdom of God. They must strive to put their "rights" aside in order to verify their spiritual leadership to their wives and children.

Ephesians 5:28 says,
"So ought men to love their wives as their own bodies. He that loveth his wife loveth himself."

Husbands, you must take care of your wives in the same way you would care for your own bodies. You must be sensitive to the needs of your wife in the same manner you are aware of the needs of your own body.

1 Peter 3:7 instructs husbands in this manner,
"Likewise, ye husbands, dwell with them according to knowledge, giving honour unto the wife, as unto to the weaker vessel, and as being heirs together of the grace of life; that your prayers be not hindered."

Many interpret this scripture to mean women are weaker because of their physical makeup. This may be true in a sense, but I feel there is a deeper meaning here. Women are also the weaker partner because of their position of submission. Women are at the mercy of their husbands because of their place in the marriage. Therefore, husbands are instructed to treat them with respect by honoring them.

Colossians 3:19 says,
"Husbands love your wives, and be not bitter against them."

This harshness includes a husband's manner of speech. Verbal abuse is the most common means of destruction in marriage. Both men and women are guilty of this abuse, and it is unacceptable conduct to God.

Ephesians 4:29 reminds us of what manner of speech is acceptable to God,
"Let no corrupt communication proceed out of your mouth, but that which is good to the use of edifying, that it may minister grace unto the hearers."

All manner of speech from Christians should edify, not tear down.

Ephesians 5:29 adds this insight,
"For no man ever yet hated his own flesh: but nourisheth and cherisheth it,..."

Husbands, you have the responsibility of providing for your family. This provision includes physical, emotional, and spiritual needs.

1 Timothy 5:8 says,
"But if any provide not for his own, and specially for those of his own house, he hath denied the faith, and is worse than an infidel."

The Apostle Paul gave this instruction in **2 Thessalonians 3:7-10**,
"...but to make ourselves an ensample unto you to follow us. For even when we were with you, this we commanded you, that if any would not work, neither should he eat."

Husbands, you are to be a model to your family. Do not put unfair burdens on them. Never allow yourself to be idle in your Scriptural responsibilities. Keep in mind you must give way to the heart and mind of Jesus to become a sacrifice for the benefit of your whole family. As a sacrifice you will ensure your family has the necessary example and provisions to meet their needs. As "head" of the family you must live an upright and responsible life. This is an awesome responsibility and must not be taken lightly.

1 Peter 3:7 tells us what the consequences will be for a husband who does not treat his wife in a godly manner.
"...that your prayers be not hindered."

Men if your prayers are not being answered, perhaps you are not treating your wife right in the sight of God. In conclusion, Christian couples need to consider if they are upholding their scriptural positions in this godly bond. If you are not fulfilling your obligation you need to repent. Ask the Lord to make you the godly, upright partner your spouse needs. Consider your responsibility as a sacrificial love offering to Jesus, rather than a burden too great to bear.

Personal Notes: ____

____

Chapter 27

CHILDREN

Supplement: Volume 4 Book 4: *Parents are People Too*

Psalm 127:3 states,
"Lo, children are an heritage of the LORD: and the fruit of the womb is his reward."

Children make up the family. They are a heritage of the Lord. This implies children are inherited from the Lord and one day they will be presented back to Him. They are a reward. The issue of children is a precious subject to God.

Matthew 19:13-14 says,
"Then were there brought unto him little children, that he should put his hands on them, and pray: and the disciples rebuked them. But Jesus said, Suffer little children and forbid them not, to come unto me: for of such is the kingdom of heaven."

In **Matthew 18:5-7** we read these words of Jesus,
"And whoso shall receive one such little child in my name receiveth me. But whoso shall offend one of these little ones which believe in me, it were better for him that a millstone were hanged about his neck, and that he were drowned in the depth of the sea. Woe unto the world because of offences! for it must needs be that offences come; but woe to that man by whom the offence cometh!"

Children are an awesome responsibility from God. As parents we must be sober in the raising of our children. Today children are the major victims of immorality and divorce. They are being sacrificed for the god of self and convenience. The biggest means of sacrifice is abortion. There are many debates about this subject. Many people logic life does not begin at conception. Opinions of this subject change according to the philosophy of the individual. But, the only one who can determine this issue is the one who created life. God's Word gives us insight about this matter. In the end, His Word will ultimately silence all debates on this subject.

Psalm 139:13-16 gives us this insight,
"For thou hast possessed my reins: thou hast covered me in my mother's womb. I will praise thee; for I am fearfully and wonderfully made: marvellous are thy works; and that my soul knoweth right well. My substance was not hid from thee, when I was made in secret, and curiously wrought in the lowest parts of the earth. Thine eyes did see my substance, yet being unperfect; and in thy book all my members were written, which in continuance were fashioned, when as yet there was none of them."

We read these words in **Jeremiah 1:4-5**,
"Then the word of the LORD came unto me, saying, Before I formed thee in the belly I knew thee; and before thou camest forth out of the womb I sanctified thee, and I ordained thee a prophet unto the nations."

Luke 1:14-15 gives us this information about John the Baptist,
"...and many shall rejoice at his birth. For he shall be great in the sight of the Lord, and he shall drink neither wine nor strong drink; and he shall be filled with the Holy Ghost, even from his mother's womb."

David told how God formed and knitted him together in his mother's womb. Jeremiah was told he was ordained to be a prophet before he was born. John the Baptist was actually baptized by the Holy Spirit while in the womb of his mother. These scriptures show the life and purpose of children are ordered by the Creator of all life. The idea that the lives of children in the womb can be disposed of because they are not yet considered human is a lie from the pit of hell. When man plays God in this type of issue, he will eventually consider it his right to take life as he chooses. This can be observed throughout history. Different races, people who are handicapped, and the elderly have been targeted by this philosophy in the past. In many countries, abortion is a form of legalized murder. It is a sin, but not an unforgivable one. God desires to heal the heart and take away the sin of any individual who has believed this lie and submitted to it.

Isaiah 1:18 says,
"Come now, and let us reason together, saith the LORD: though your sins be as scarlet, they shall be as white as snow; though they be red like crimson, they shall be as wool."

Personal Notes: ____

____

____

Training Children

Proverbs 22:6 states,
"Train up a child in the way he should go: and when he is old, he will not depart from it."

Parents must train their children in the ways of God. God gave these instructions to the nation of Israel about the training of their children.

Deuteronomy 6:6-7 says,
"And these words, which I command thee this day, shall be in thine heart: And thou shalt teach them diligently unto thy children, and shalt talk of them when thou sittest in thine house, and when thou walkest by the way, and when thou liest down, and when thou risest up."

In order for parents to teach their children about God, communication must be present in their relationship. Verbally instructing children, reading God's Word to them, and sharing God's greatness are effective ways of training a child. Training comes though example. If a parent is living inconsistent with their Christian claims, children will often adopt a hypocritical view of God.

Proverbs 14:26 states,
"In the fear of the LORD is strong confidence: and his children shall have a place of refuge."

Proverbs 20:7 tells us,
"The just man walketh in his integrity: his children are blessed after him."

Remember the fear of the Lord results in obedience to God. The righteous man walks upright before the Lord. Part of training a child involves nurturing them. Nurturing can be related to cultivating. This part of a child's training involves loving and fair discipline.

Proverbs 13:24 says,
"He that spareth his rod hateth his son: but he that loveth him chasteneth him betimes."

Children need to feel loved, accepted, and have a sense of belonging. The feeling of love to a child is associated with loving discipline. Children who are not disciplined feel they do not belong because they perceive that their parents do not really care for them.

Hebrews 12:5-10 brings this truth out concerning a believer's relationship with his or her Father in heaven,
"...My son, despise not thou the chastening of the Lord, nor faint when thou art rebuked of him: For whom the Lord loveth he chasteneth, and scourgeth every son whom he receiveth. If ye endure chastening, God dealeth with you as with sons; for what son is he whom the father chasteneth not? But if ye be without chastisement, whereof all are partakers, then are ye bastards, and not sons. Furthermore we have had fathers of our flesh which corrected us, and we gave them reverence: shall we not much rather be in subjection unto the Father of spirits, and live? For they verily for a few days chastened us after their own pleasure; but he for our profit, that we might be partakers of his holiness."

God shows His love for us when He disciplines us. If He does not discipline us, we do not belong to Him. This principle applies to the relationship of the parent and child. Discipline must be done wisely and according to the child. It is to show a child what is acceptable attitude and behavior, but it must never break his spirit.

The Apostle Paul gives us this instruction in **Ephesians 6:4**,
"And ye fathers, provoke not your children to wrath: but bring them up in the nurture and admonition of the Lord."

Unfair demands and rules on your children will cause bitterness and discouragement rather than establish sound direction in their life.

Colossians 3:21 says,
"Fathers, provoke not your children to anger, lest they be discouraged."

The goal of training a child is to direct them towards God and eternity.

Proverbs 19:18 confirms this,
"Chasten thy son while there is hope, and let not thy soul spare for his crying."

Parents, by disciplining your children you will teach them to respect authority. This respect is necessary if they are going to respect God's authority.

There are awards for parents who discipline their children according to **Proverbs 29:17**,
"Correct thy son, and he shall give thee rest; yea, he shall give delight unto thy soul."

Personal Notes: ____

____

The Promise of Obedience

Children, there is a promise which follows obedience to parents.

Ephesians 6:1-3 tells you,
"Children, obey your parents in the Lord: for this is right. Honour thy father and mother; which is the first commandment with promise; That it may be well with thee, and thou mayest live long on the earth."

Children, parents have been put over you by God. They are to watch over your well-being, and will be held accountable to God if they abuse this position. But you must honor or respect their position as your parents.

We see God's attitude about stubborn and rebellious children in **Deuteronomy 21:18-21**,
"If a man have a stubborn and rebellious son, which will not obey the voice of his father, or the voice of his mother, and that, when they have chastened him, will not hearken unto them: Then shall his father and his mother lay hold on him, and bring him out unto the elders of his city, and unto the gate of his place. And they shall say unto the elders of his city, This our son is stubborn and rebellious, he will not obey our voice; he is a glutton, and a drunkard. And all the men of his city shall stone him with stones, that he die: so shalt thou put evil away from among you; and all Israel shall hear, and fear."

Although presently parents do not have a right to kill disobedient children, God has not changed His attitude about unacceptable conduct. God's instruction to swiftly take care of disobedience was designed to bring constructive fear into the hearts of His people. This was an effective means of ensuring obedience to His laws. Note this action was taken only when the rebellious son did not respond to discipline. Parents' position requires the child to be in subjection to them, but personal respect will come because of persuasion through godly example and fair discipline. Disrespect injures communication and a healthy relationship between you and your children.

Proverbs 17:21 says,
"He that begetteth a fool doeth it to his sorrow: and the father of a fool hath no joy."

Proverbs 10:1 tells us,
"...A wise son maketh a glad father: but a foolish son is the heaviness of his mother."

We see how children can bring grief or joy to their parents.

Proverbs 10:17 gives us insight about the different consequences based on the responses to discipline,
"He is in the way of life that keepeth instruction: but he that refuseth reproof erreth.

There is leadership in both righteousness and rebellion. Adults and children alike must make a choice as to the type of leadership they submit to.

Proverbs 13:1 says,
"A wise son heareth his father's instruction: but a scorner heareth not rebuke."

> Young people are you displaying wisdom in your response to your parents or are you a mocker? If you are wise you need to know you will enjoy the promise of God which is a long life.

Personal Notes: ____

____

Chapter 28

THE SINGLE CHRISTIAN VS. MARRIAGE

Supplement: Volume 4 Book 3: *Manual For the Single Christian Life*

An important issue facing young Christian adults is the subject of marriage. This is one area Satan can effectively work in to destroy both the call and testimony of young believers. For this reason, young Christian adults must soberly consider this subject in light of God's Word and will for their lives.

The Apostle Paul made this statement in **1 Corinthians 7:1-2**,
"Now concerning the things whereof ye wrote unto me: It is good for a man not to touch a woman. Nevertheless, to avoid fornication, let every man have his own wife, and let every woman have her own husband."

Paul remained single. He recognized that a servant of God could best serve his Lord by remaining unmarried.

We read these words of Paul in **1 Corinthians 7:32-34**,
"But I would have you without carefulness. He that is unmarried careth for the things that belong to the Lord, how he may please the Lord: But he that is married careth for the things that are of the world, how he may please his wife. There is difference also between a wife and a virgin. The unmarried woman careth for the things of the Lord, that she may be holy both in body and in spirit: but she that is married careth for the things of the world, how she may please her husband."

When a servant of God is married there is a division of loyalties. Paul recognized that people have passions. In the case of fleshly passions that cannot be brought under control, marriage is necessary and acceptable to God.

1 Corinthians 7:8-9 says,
"I say therefore to the unmarried and widows, It is good for them if they abide even as I. But if they cannot contain, let them marry: for it is better to marry than to burn."

Often the major motivation behind the decision of marriage is unabated lust. This is why young adults must consider God's will in this matter. Decisions concerning marriage must be taken out of the carnal or fleshly realm and considered in light of eternal significance.

Paul made this statement in reference to marriage in **1 Corinthians 7:31**,
"And they that use this world, as not abusing it: for the fashion of this world passeth away."

Marriage is part of the world. It will pass away with the world.

Jesus confirmed this in **Matthew 22:29-30**,
"Jesus answered and said unto them, Ye do err, not knowing the scriptures, nor the power of God. For in the resurrection they neither marry, nor are given in marriage, but are as the angels of God in heaven."

Marriage should be examined in light of eternity to ensure a correct perspective. Each young adult must earnestly seek the mind of God in this matter.

Personal Notes: ____

____

____

Finding the Right Partner

The Apostle Paul said this in **1 Corinthians 7:7**,
"For I would that all men were even as I myself. But every man hath his proper gift of God, one after this manner, and another after that."

Paul is telling us that being single or married is a gift. Paul does not look down on those who do desire the gift of marriage. But there are some strict scriptural considerations in choosing a partner.

The first one is found in **2 Corinthians 6:14**,
"Be ye not unequally yoked together with unbelievers: for what fellowship hath righteousness with unrighteousness? and what communion hath light with darkness?"

When a Christian marries an unbeliever, he or she is courting disaster. Many Christians have deceived themselves into believing they can change their partner once they are married. This is a fallacy of the devil.

Judges 2:3 gives us an insight into the destructive implications of a mixed relationship,
"...but they shall be as thorns in your sides, and their gods shall be a snare unto you."

You may be a totally dedicated Christian, but marriage to an unbeliever will become a snare to you. For the sake of peace, you may eventually find yourself submitting to another god. God is calling all of His people to live a separated life. This life involves choosing a godly partner.

In **Ezra** we read an account of the Jewish people being called to separation. This separation to holiness required the men of Israel to give up their foreign wives and children.

We read this in **Ezra 10:3, 10-11**,
"Now therefore let us make a covenant with our God to put away all the wives, and such as are born of them, according to the counsel of my lord, and of those that tremble at the commandment of our God; and let it be done according to the law... And Ezra the priest stood up, and said unto them, Ye have transgressed, and have taken strange wives, to increase the trespass of Israel. Now therefore make confession unto the LORD God of your fathers, and do his pleasure: and separate yourselves from the people of the land, and from the strange wives."

Ezra 10:17 shows us the final results,
"And they made an end with all the men that had taken strange wives by the first day of the first month."

To maintain a right life before God you must marry someone who is evenly matched in spiritual matters.

The Apostle Paul made this statement in **Philippians 2:1-2**,
"If there be therefore any consolation in Christ, if any comfort of love, if any fellowship of the Spirit, if any bowels and mercies, Fulfil ye my joy, that ye be likeminded, having the same love, being of one accord, of one mind."

To be evenly matched involves more than going to the same church. One must be likeminded having Christ's love, and being one in spirit and purpose. If a marriage partner does not have the same goal in ministry, the same spirit, and the same doctrine, Satan will use these differences to bring division. For the Christian marriage to be effective and powerful in God, both individuals must share a common agreement and vision. Never look for a partner. Allow God to have his way in your life by bringing you the right mate.

Genesis 2:22 states,
"And the rib, which the LORD God had taken from man, made he a woman, and brought her unto the man."

Young people, avoid choosing a perspective spouse according to their looks or your personal standards. God is the only one who can look at the heart and make a perfect choice for you. Get rid of cultural beliefs that would serve as burdensome demands and requirements to a spouse. Remember you are marrying a person who has feelings, needs, and personal opinions, and not an image. If you cannot love and accept the individual as he or she is, do not marry him or her. Do not allow lust, expectations, and self-serving attitudes blind you to the real purpose behind marriage.

Never go into a marriage for your own selfish reasons. Keep in mind how you can best serve the needs of the individual you are marrying in order to properly challenge, compliment, and encourage him or her in their life in Christ. This is the beginning of the sacrificial life that must be maintained throughout a successful marriage.

Personal Notes: ____

____

____

Overcoming The Flesh

Sexual immorality is the greatest temptation for young people. But if marriage is to be holy between a Christian couple, they must refrain from pre-martial relationships. In God's eyes sexual immorality is known as fornication. Fornication involves all illicit sex. Illicit sex is described in **Leviticus 18:6-23**. Included in these abominable acts are the following: Adultery, homosexuality, incest, and bestiality.

Leviticus 18:27-29 tells the consequences of immoral actions,
"(For all these abominations have the men of the land done, which were before you, and the land is defiled;) That the land spue not you out also, when ye defile it, as it spued out the

nations that were before you. For whosoever shall commit any of these abominations,even the souls that commit them shall be cut off from among their people."

Paul tells us this about the judgment against fornicators in **Ephesians 5:3 & 5**,
"But fornication, and all uncleanness, or covetousness, let it not be once named among you, as becometh saints... For this ye know, that no whoremonger, nor unclean person, nor covetous man, who is an idolater, hath any inheritance in the kingdom of Christ and of God."

God's Word is consistent regarding one's response towards any sexual temptation.

1 Corinthians 6:18-20 states,
"Flee fornication. Every sin that a man doeth is without the body; but he that committeth fornication sinneth against his own body. What? Know ye not that your body is the temple of the Holy Ghost which is in you, which ye have of God, and ye are not your own? For ye are bought with a price: therefore glorify God in your body, and in your spirit, which are God's."

2 Timothy 2:22 tells us,
"Flee also youthful lusts: but follow righteousness, faith, charity, peace, with them that call on the Lord out of a pure heart."

To flee means to run away from something. Young people must run from situations, influences, or places that would tempt them. Another place where this battle must be won is in the mind. If you allow your mind to think about this subject it will reinforce lust.

2 Corinthians 10:5 gives us this instruction,
"...and bringing into captivity every thought to the obedience of Christ."

Philippians 4:8 tells us how to keep our thoughts under control,
"Finally brethren, whatsoever things are true, whatsoever things are honest, whatsoever things are just, whatsoever things are pure, whatsoever things are lovely, whatsoever things are of good report; it there be any virtue, and if there be any praise, think on these things."

We must take control over every thought. Although sexual fantasy may seem normal, it must be avoided as it will produce lust.

What are your plans? Do you have a call in your life to serve God? Do you want to get married? Are you living a pure life before God? Right now, seek the face of God. Desire His will above earthly desires and possessions. Determine in your heart to be holy in your conduct. Let Him be God in every area of your life.

Personal Notes: ____

____

____

Section III

SANCTIFICATION

Chapter 29

SEPARATION

Supplement: The Call to Holiness **Sup. 2**

1 Peter 1:15-16 says,
"But as he which hath called you is holy, so be ye holy in all manner of conversation; Because it is written, Be ye holy; for I am holy."

Our God is holy. Holy in reference to God means righteousness. Holiness to the Christian means separation. It is a state that ensures a place of humility, an attitude of righteousness, and godly conduct. Separation entails sanctification and consecration. Sanctification is the actual **work** of setting something apart. Consecration involves an **act** of setting something apart. Good examples of consecration are the anointing of a prophet or circumcision. These acts are considered holy because God ordained them as a means of distinguishing His servants and His people. Sanctification and consecration have been used interchangeably in Scripture. There are two extreme points of view about the work of holiness. One idea is that because of our disposition of sin, we cannot be holy. This is partially true. We cannot be holy in our own power, but man does not do the real work of holiness.

1 Peter 1:2 tells us who does the work of holiness in the life of the believer,
"Elect according to the foreknowledge of God the Father, through sanctification of the Spirit, unto obedience and sprinkling of the blood of Jesus Christ: Grace unto you, and peace, be multiplied."

The Holy Spirit sanctifies the believer. He causes separation from the inside out. Man's relationships, beliefs, and priorities will become subject to change. This change creates an outward appearance that will express itself in godly characteristics. The other belief is that man can be holy through his own attempts. Scripture clearly refutes this.The Apostle Paul said there is no good thing in the flesh, and we know man's best is as filthy rags to God **(Isaiah 64:6**; **Romans 7:18)**.

The Apostle Paul defined the believer's righteousness in **2 Corinthians 5:21**,
"For he hath made him to be sin for us, who knew no sin; that we might be made righteousness of God in him."

Christ in us is our true righteousness. He is the only acceptable righteousness to God. If a person can become holy by his or her own attempts, why have the Holy Spirit? It is the presence of God in an individual that always sets him or her apart from the world.

When people feel they are living a holy life by their own power, they have replaced God's work of sanctification with their own pathetic, unacceptable righteousness. The Pharisees were guilty of having this type of righteousness that is referred to as self-righteousness.

Jesus said this about their holy living in **Matthew 23:27-28**,
"Woe unto you, scribes and Pharisees, hypocrites! for ye are like unto whited sepulchers, which indeed appear beautiful outward, but are within full of dead men's bones, and of all uncleanness. Even so ye also outwardly appear righteous unto men, but within ye are full of hypocrisy and iniquity."

You may have a very disciplined lifestyle, but this does not constitute holiness to God. Uprightness always begins in the heart and will eventually manifest itself in attitudes and manner of living. The work of holiness involves both sanctification and consecration. <u>Sanctification</u> is God's work done by the Holy Spirit and <u>consecration</u> is man's part. The act of consecration on man's part is a separation from those things that are not pleasing to God and come from submission to the Holy Spirit. This separation is not an act of nobility on our part, but one of necessity and obedience. It is necessary if we are to be holy before our righteous God and pleasing to Him.

Personal Notes: ____

____

____

The Cross

One of the acts of consecration on man's part is submission to his personal cross.

Jesus made this statement to His disciples in **Matthew 16:24**:,"...If any man will come after me, let him deny himself, and take up his cross, and follow me."

The cross represents total separation. It is symbolic of suffering, humiliation, and death.

Hebrews 13:10-13 states,
"We have an altar, whereof they have no right to eat which serve the tabernacle. For the bodies of those beasts, whose blood is brought into the sanctuary by the high priest for sin, are burned without the camp. Wherefore Jesus also, that he might sanctify the people with his own blood suffered without the gate. Let us go forth therefore unto him without the camp, bearing his reproach."

The Living Bible in **Hebrews 13:10** refers to the Christian altar as the cross. On this altar the sacrifice of Jesus Christ was offered up for all sins. The altar was an important part of the religious life of the Jewish nation. It was at their altars where the people of Israel met with God, and paid homage to Him. There were three types of altars. One type of altar was for sacrifices. Another type of altar served as a memorial. The third altar represented prayer. At the first altar mentioned, one must come to terms with is the altar for sacrifice. Christ became a sacrifice for our sins on the altar of the cross.

But **Romans 12:1** tells us about another sacrifice,
"I beseech you therefore, brethren, by the mercies of God, that ye present your bodies a living sacrifice, holy, acceptable unto God, which is your reasonable service."

To offer our lives to God in this manner is a type of consecration and a form of paying homage to Him.

Psalm 51:17 gives us insight into this subject,
"The sacrifices of God are a broken spirit: a broken and a contrite heart, O God, thou wilt not despise."

A sacrifice on the altar will result in brokenness. Brokenness implies repentance.

In **Exodus 17:15** we read this about Moses' altar,
"And Moses built an altar, and called the name of it Jehovah-nissi: (The LORD is my Banner)."

Moses' altar served as a memorial or reminder of his great God. If a Christian becomes and serves as a living sacrifice, he or she will also serve as a living memorial of God.

Ephesians 5:1-2 tells us how believers serve as a memorial,
"Be ye therefore followers of God, as dear children; And walk in love, as Christ also hath loved us, and hath given himself for us an offering and a sacrifice to God for a sweet-smelling savour."

Our lives need to serve as a reminder of our great loving God. The Jewish people had an altar of incense in their tabernacle. This altar represented perpetual prayer before God. One of the ingredients used in the incense was a substance that served as a fragrance called frankincense. \This substance was used on certain sacrifices as well. As the sacrifice for sin was consumed in the fire, the fragrance was released. The sacrifice was for the benefit of covering man's sin, but the fragrance was for God. Frankincense is symbolic of perfection. In **Ephesians 5:2** we read how Christ serves as the fragrance to God. It is in the perfection of Christ in us that we stand acceptable in our presentation of our lives to God for His glory and in our prayers. (Refer also to **2 Corinthians 2:15-16**.)

John 14:13-14 says,
"And whatsoever ye shall ask in my name, that will I do, that the Father may be glorified in the Son. If ye shall ask any thing in my name, I will do it."

A Christian's life of prayer and ministry must begin and end with Jesus Christ. Christians must go to the altar (the cross) provided for them. There, they must present their lives as a sacrifice. In doing so, they will find cleansing through Jesus' blood. In their brokenness, their sins will be consumed by the life of Christ being worked in them by the Holy Ghost. The ultimate result will be Christ's life coming forth as a continual sweet fragrance before God.

Personal Notes: ____

____

The Cost

Many new Christians are excited about their newfound life. This excitement can be short lived as they begin to realize there is a cost.

Jesus said this in **Luke 14:28-30**,
"For which of you, intending to build a tower, sitteth not down first, and counteth the cost, whether he have sufficient to finish it? Lest haply, after he hath laid the foundation, and is not able to finish it, all that behold it began to mock him. Saying, This man began to build, and was not able to finish."

It costs you something to be a Christian. Salvation is free, but the work of holiness is a lifetime process and will eventually cost us the old life with its identification with the world, along with its many associations. Jesus is saying in **Luke**, first count the cost of this spiritual life. King David recognized the need to pay a price for a piece of property on which to build an altar. This altar was for the purpose of satisfying God's judgment on the people of Israel. This judgment was a result of David counting the people without first requiring them to pay ransom for their souls **(Exodus 30:12-16)**. The owner of the property was willing to give the land to David without cost.

We read David's reply in **2 Samuel 24:24**,
"...Nay, but I will surely buy it of thee at a price: neither will I offer burnt offerings unto the LORD my God of that which doth cost me nothing. So David bought the threshingfloor and the oxen for fifty shekels of silver."

It is inconceivable for Christians to think their Christian life will cost them nothing when it cost God His best—His only begotten Son. And, it cost Jesus His all—His life. The cost can be summarized into one word for the believers—*separation*. What God may require in ways of separation will never destroy us, but rather set us free to love and serve Him. The question you may be asking yourself is what will it cost me to know God and possess Jesus, the treasure of heaven **(Colossians 2:1-4)**.

Jesus tells us the cost in **Luke 14:33**,
"So likewise, whosoever he be of you that forsaketh not all that he hath, he cannot be my disciple."

Personal Notes: ______________________________

____

The Ultimate Price

God will not ask us to give up anything unless it will keep us from knowing and following Him. Jesus confronted a rich young man who claimed he was ready to follow Him. Jesus outlined the price for becoming His disciple.

Matthew 19:21 says,
"...If thou wilt be perfect, go and sell that thou hast, and give to the poor, and thou shall have treasure in heaven: and come and follow me."

Matthew 19:22 tells us the response of the young man,
"But when the young man heard that saying, he went away sorrowful: for he had great possessions."

We may feel we are willing to pay the price, but the price required of us will be the very thing we are holding tightly to. Nothing must stand in the way of us following Jesus. If there is, we are exalting another god. We must hold all things of this world lightly. This is necessary to ensure a willingness to lay it on the altar if requested to do so. One of the things we must hold lightly are relationships.

Luke 14:26 confirms this,
"If any man come to me, and hate not his father, and mother, and wife, and children, and brethren, and sisters, yea, and his own life also, he cannot be my disciple."

All relationships must pale in light of our devotion, love, and service to Jesus Christ. So many times, relationships define us as a person, and our type of service to God. If any person or relationship is more important than loving, following, and serving Jesus, it is idolatrous, perverted, and unacceptable to God.

Another area we must lightly hold on to is our position in Christ. This position includes ministry, promises, and gifts given to us by God. In **Genesis 22**, we see where God actually required a servant to lay his most precious promise on the altar as a sacrifice. This promise was his son, Isaac. The man's name was Abraham.

We read what happened just as Abraham was ready to sacrifice his son in **Genesis 22:11-12**,
"And the angel of the LORD called unto him out of heaven, and said, Abraham, Abraham: and he said, Here am I. And he said, Lay not thine hand upon the lad, neither do thou any thing unto him: for now I know that thou fearest God, seeing thou hast not withheld thy son, thine only son from me. *(*Refer to **Hebrews 11:17-19**.*)*

Isaac was a promise from God. God tested Abraham by requiring him to give his son back to Him. God will test his servants in this area. He will expose any divided loyalties or idolatry. Christians need to remember our greatest reward is not ministry, God's promises, or His gifts, but God Himself. (Refer to **Genesis 15:1** and **Philippians 3:7-8**.) If anything takes importance over possessing God, He will require us to lay it on the altar. The harder we are holding on to it, the more devastating it will be when we finally have to release it. Are you willing to pay the price to know and possess the God of the Bible? If you are not, you will never gain the greatest prize of all.

Paul tells us what the prize is in **Philippians 3:14**,
"I press toward the mark for the prize of the high calling of God in Christ Jesus."

Personal Notes: ______________________________

____

____

Chapter 30

BECOMING A HOLY TEMPLE

Supplements:
(For Review)
Volume 1
Book 2:
The Anatomy of Sin
Chapters 11 & 15
(For the next three chapters.)
Volume 2
Book 5:
Follow That Pattern

Exodus 29:43 says,
"...and the tabernacle shall be sanctified by my glory."

The tabernacle and the temple were the centers of the religious life of the Jewish nation. The tabernacle was simply a tent with three compartments. The temple was a building designed in the same way as the tabernacle, but it was built on a larger scale. Both the temple and tabernacle served as a place for God to dwell among His people.

Paul made this statement in **Acts 17:24**,
"God that made the world and all things therein, seeing that he is Lord of heaven and earth, dwelleth not in temples made with hands."

God used to dwell in structures made with men's hands. Now He resides in man, making him a temple.

1 Corinthians 3:16-17 confirms this.
"Know ye not that ye are the temple of God, and that the Spirit of God dwelleth in you? If any man defile the temple of God, him shall God destroy; for the temple of God is holy, which temple ye are."

Christians are to be sacred temples. <u>Sacred</u> implies consecrated to God. This consecration started for the Christian when they receive Christ as Lord and Savior, and were sealed by the Holy Spirit **(Ephesians 1:13)**. But there needs to be an ongoing work of separation from self, sin, and the world. Although Christians are consecrated to God, it does not necessarily mean they are sanctified by the Spirit. Sanctification occurs inwardly, and results in a person being separated unto God for His work and glory **(1 Thessalonians 5:23)**.

Personal Notes: ______________________________

____

Opening the Doors

During the reign of King Hezekiah there was a great spiritual reformation. The spiritual life of the nation of Israel was at its lowest and it needed to be revived. <u>Revived</u> means to bring back to life or health. Hezekiah's father, King Ahaz's actions symbolized the need for revival when he actually closed the doors of the temple.

2 Chronicles 29:3 tells us what Hezekiah did in the first month of his reign,
"...(he) opened the doors of the house of the LORD, and repaired them." (Parenthesis added.)

As temples of God, we must open up our hearts for examination. This examination is necessary in case we need to repair our relationship with God.

2 Corinthians 13:5 says,
"Examine yourselves, whether ye be in the faith; prove your own selves. Know ye not your own selves, how that Jesus Christ is in you, except ye be reprobates?"

We need to ensure God is reigning in the inner chambers of our heart.

Ezekiel 8:12 tells us about the most prevalent sin found in the inner chambers of the temple,
"Then said he unto me, Son of man, hast thou seen what the ancients of the house of Israel do in the dark, every man in the chambers of his imagery? for they say, The LORD seeth us not; the LORD hath forsaken the earth."

Ezekiel 14:3 states,
"Son of man, these men have set up their idols in their heart, and put the stumblingblock of their iniquity before their face: should I be enquired of at all by them?

Idolatry is the major sin taking place in the inner chambers of men's hearts and in the high places of their minds.

2 Corinthians 6:16-17 states,
"And what agreement hath the temple of God with idols? for ye are the temple of the living God; as God hath said, I will dwell in them, and walk in them; and I will be their God, and they shall be my people. Wherefore come out from among them, and be ye separate, saith the Lord, and touch not the unclean thing: and I will receive you."

The biggest god reigning in man's heart is pride. It often goes unchallenged and unhindered. Very few recognize it in their own lives, and become repulsed with its attitudes and ways in others. This is the sin that causes the most breakdowns in relationships. Pride simply is an image, concept, or idea of self. It insists on reigning; therefore, exalting itself over God, and often lording itself over others. It will sacrifice righteousness and crucify truth. This is why the Word has some tough things to say about it.

Proverbs 16:5 states,
"Every one that is proud in heart is an abomination to the LORD: though hand join in hand, he shall not be unpunished."

To deal with pride, we must allow our heart to be circumcised. Circumcision of the heart implies cutting away the dictates of sin.

Deuteronomy 30:6 tells us,
"And the LORD thy God will circumcise thine heart, and the heart of thy seed, to love the LORD thy God with all thine heart, and with all thy soul, that thou mayest live."

This Scripture verse tells us that a person's heart must be circumcised in order to love God with his or her whole heart. This Scripture was directed to the nation of Israel, but we see the same principle being set forth to the Christians in **Romans 2:28-29**.

Romans 2:28-29 says,
"For he is not a Jew, which is one outwardly; neither is that circumcision, which is outward in the flesh. But he is a Jew, which is one inwardly; and circumcision is that of the heart, in the spirit, and not in the letter; whose praise is not of men, but of God."

Once we allow the Spirit to circumcise our hearts, we can then sanctify or set Christ apart in the inner chambers of our heart.

1 Peter 3:15 says,
"But sanctify the Lord God in your hearts..."

Once self is out of the way, Christ can reign in our hearts. Putting pride down will be an ongoing battle. It must be recognized, and its demands, desires, and ways unheeded and neglected.

Jesus describes this battle in **Luke 9:23**,
"...If any man will come after me, let him deny himself, and take up his cross daily, and follow me."

Dealing with self is a daily struggle. Who is reigning in the inner chambers of your heart? Throw open the door of your heart. Allow the Holy Spirit to expose any idolatry. If you find another god, repent! Allow your heart to be broken and circumcised. Ask Christ to reign as Lord in your life, no matter the cost.

Personal Notes: ______________________________

____

____

Purifying the Temple

King Hezekiah gave this order to the priest about the temple in **2 Chronicles 29:5**,
"...sanctify now yourselves, and sanctify the house of the LORD God of your fathers, and carry forth the filthiness out of the holy place."

1 Corinthians 5:6-8 states,
"Your glorying is not good. Know ye not that a little leaven leaveneth the whole lump? Purge out therefore the old leaven, that ye may be a new lump as ye are unleavened. For even Christ our passover is sacrificed for us: Therefore let us keep the feast, not with old leaven, neither with the leaven of malice and wickedness; but with the unleavened bread of sincerity and truth."

<u>Yeast</u> can represent sin. We must get rid of all the dictates and residue of sin in our temple.

2 Chronicles 29:16 tells us,
"And the priests went into the inner part of the house of the LORD to cleanse it, and brought out all the uncleanness that they found in the temple of the LORD into the court of the house of the LORD, And the Levites took it, to carry it out abroad into the brook Kidron."

The Apostle Paul gives us this instruction in **Colossians 3:5**,
"Mortify therefore your members which are upon the earth; fornication, uncleanness, inordinate affection, evil concupiscence, and covetousness, which is idolatry."

We must put to death all influences of self.

2 Chronicles 29:18-19 tells us what the priest did next in the consecration of the temple,
"Then they went in to Hezekiah the king, and said, We have cleansed all the house of the LORD, and the altar of burnt offering, with all the vessels thereof, and the shewbread table, with all the vessels thereof. Moreover all the vessels which king Ahaz in his reign did cast away in his transgression..."

There were certain articles prepared and designated for use in the temple.

2 Timothy 2:19-21 gives us this insight about the Christian,
"...And let every one that nameth the name of Christ depart from iniquity. If a man therefore purge himself from these, he shall be a vessel unto honour, sanctified, and meet for the master's use and prepared unto every good work."

Christians are not only the temples of God, they are the instruments used for His kingdom. We must become holy vessels for Him to use in His work.

2 Chronicles 29:19 tells us the final destination of all the articles of the temple,
"...and, behold, they are before the altar of the LORD."

Up to this point man had consecrated the temple and instruments, but now they had to be sanctified by God. <u>Sanctification</u> involves purging. The only place this can be done for the Christian is at the foot of the cross. The next step is the offering of sacrifices.

2 Chronicles 29:22-23 gives us this account,
"So they killed the bullocks, and priests received the blood, and sprinkled it on the altar: likewise, when they had killed the rams, they sprinkled the blood upon the altar: they killed also the lambs, and they sprinkled the blood upon the altar. And they brought forth the he goats for the sin offering before the king and the congregation: and they laid their hands upon them."

<u>Atoning</u> means to cover in the Old Testament, but in the New Testament it points to reconciliation. The reason the meaning of atonement was changed is because the ultimate sacrifice was made on the cross **(Hebrews 9:11-15)**. As a result, the door of reconciliation between God and man was opened **(2 Corinthians 5:18-19)**. Christians now have access into the very throne room of God **(Hebrews 4:14-16)**. Before we enter the throne room, we must come by the way of the altar (cross) and the sacrifice (Christ) provided for each of us.

1 John 1:9 gives us this assurance,
"If we confess our sins, he is faithful and just to forgive us our sins, and to cleanse us from all unrighteousness."

Hebrews 9:13-14 gives us this insight,
"For if the blood of bulls and of goats, and the ashes of an heifer sprinkling the unclean, sanctifieth to the purifying of the flesh: How much more shall the blood of Christ, who through the eternal Spirit offered himself without spot to God, purge your conscience from dead works to serve the living God?"

A Christian's main goal must be to serve the living God. Acceptable service can only result after separation.

2 Chronicles 29:35 confirms this,
"And also the burnt offerings were in abundance, with the fat of the peace offerings, and the drink offerings for every burnt offering. So the service of the house of the LORD was set in order."

The real motivating factor behind holiness is the fear of the Lord. Have you confessed the name of the Lord? If you have, are you serving as His holy temple and vessel? Has your life been established for the sole purpose of service to God? It is important to take time to examine yourself.

The reason behind this examination can be found in **2 Peter 3:12 & 14**,
"Looking for and hasting unto the coming of the day of God,... Wherefore, beloved, seeing that ye look for such things, be diligent that ye may be found of him in peace, without spot, and blameless."

Personal Notes: ____

____

____

Chapter 31

BEING PRIESTS

1 Peter 2:9 tells us,
"But ye are a chosen generation, a royal priesthood, an holy nation, a peculiar people; that ye should shew forth the praises of him who hath called you out of darkness into his marvellous light."

God has always had a people. He first chose the Jewish nation to be His people.

Deuteronomy 14:2 states this about the nation of Israel,
"For thou art an holy people unto the Lord thy God, and the Lord hath chosen thee to be a peculiar people unto him-self, above all the nations that are upon the earth."

Deuteronomy 4:20 tells us why He chose a nation,
"But the LORD hath taken you, and brought you forth out of the iron furnace, even out of Egypt, to be unto him a people of inheritance, as ye are this day."

Jeremiah 13:11 gives us this information,
"For as the girdle cleaveth to the loins of a man, so have I caused to cleave unto me the whole house of Israel and the whole house of Judah, saith the LORD; that they might be unto me for a people, and for a name, and for a praise, and for a glory: but they would not hear."

God has a people who He desires to give an inheritance to. These people in turn will bring Him glory in the midst of the rest of the world.

Titus 2:14 tells us this about the Christian,
"Who gave himself for us, that he might redeem us from all iniquity, and purify unto himself a peculiar people, zealous of good works."

Hebrews 9:15 tells us what our inheritance is,
"...they which are called might receive the promise of eternal inheritance."

Matthew 5:16 gives us this insight into our purpose as Christians in the world,
"Let your light so shine before men, that they may see your good works, and glorify your Father which is in heaven."

Christians have an eternal inheritance. We need to represent God in this world in such a manner as to bring Him honor. In order to bring honor to God we need to become lights in this dark world.

Matthew 5:14 states,
"Ye are the light of the world. A city that is set on a hill cannot be hid."

In order to be a light, you must be in fellowship with God.

1 John 1:5-7 confirms this,
"This then is the message which we have heard of him, and declare unto you, that God is light, and in him is no darkness at all. If we say that we have fellowship with him, and walk in darkness, we lie, and do not the truth: But if we walk in the light, as he is in the light, we have fellowship one with another, and the blood of Jesus Christ his Son cleanseth us from all sin."

There is purification obtained when you have fellowship with God. This cleansing comes as light exposes sin. The Christian who desires to have an intimate fellowship with God will quickly deal with sin. The individual who had the greatest access to God in the Old Testament were the priests.

Hebrews 9:6 gives us this information about the priests,
"Now when these things were thus ordained, the priests went always into the first tabernacle, accomplishing the service of God."

The priest stood between God and Israel. They ministered to God and took care of the duties of the temple. These priests came out of a particular family group known as the Levites. Unlike the nation of Israel, all Christians are called to take their rightful position as a priest in the New Testament priesthood and His kingdom.

Revelation 1:5-6 confirms this information,
"And from Jesus Christ, who is the faithful witness, and the first begotten of the dead, and the prince of the kings of the earth. Unto him that loved us, and washed us from our sins in his own blood, And hath made us kings and priests unto God and his Father; to him be glory and dominion forever and ever. Amen."

Priests are to be holy people. They stand between God and a lost world. They must represent their God in a way that brings Him praise and glory. They are to be separated unto God in order to minister to Him. The first separation that takes place in the lives of the priest is to be set apart from the world.

Personal Notes: ____

____

Setting Us Apart From the World

God delivered the Jewish nation out of Egypt. Egypt is symbolic of the world. This deliverance was necessary if God was going to separate the people to Himself.

1 John 2:15 gives us this instruction,
"Love not the world, neither the things that are in the world. If any man love the world, the love of the Father is not in him."

James 4:4 tells us why loving the world signifies we do not love God,
"Ye adulterers and adulteresses, know ye not that the friendship of the world is enmity with God? whosoever there-fore will be a friend of the world is the enemy of God."

Jesus talked about the world's reaction towards Him in **John 7:7**,
"The world cannot hate you; but me it hateth, because I testify of it, that the works thereof are evil."

The world hates Christ because He exposes its evilness. Therefore, Christians must become separated from the evil influences of the world. Interestingly, the crowds who followed Jesus were led away from the activities of the world.

Matthew 4:25-5:2 confirms this,
"And there followed him great multitudes of people... And seeing the multitudes, he went up into a mountain...."

In **John 6:1-3** we read,
"After these things Jesus went over the Sea of Galilee, which is the sea of Tiberias. And a great multitude followed him, because they saw his miracles which he did on them that were diseased. And Jesus went up into a mountain, and there he sat with his disciples."

Matthew 8:1 says,
"When he came down from the mountain, great multitudes followed him."

Matthew 15:29-30 tells us,
"And Jesus departed from thence, and came nigh unto the Sea of Galilee; and went up into a mountain, and sat down there. And great multitudes came unto him..."

Matthew 19:1-2 says,
"...that when Jesus had finished these sayings, he departed from Galilee, and came into the coasts of Judea beyond Jordan; And great multitudes followed him; and he healed them there."

If we are following Christ, we will find Him leading us away from the world. This is necessary if He is going to lead us into intimate places in God.

Psalm 23:3 tells us where He leads us,
"...he leadeth me in the paths of righteousness for his name's sake."

Are you willing to follow Christ away from the world into the unknown? The world's attitude towards you will eventually tell what kind of association you have with it.

In **John 15:18-19** Jesus said these words,
"If the world hate you, ye know that it hated me before it hated you. If ye were of the world, the world would love his own: but because ye are not of the world, but I have chosen you out of the world, therefore the world hateth you."

Does the world hate you?

Personal Notes: ____

____

Consecration

In reference to the revival during King Hezekiah's reign, we read this in **2 Chronicles 29:4-5**,
"And he brought in the priests and the Levites, and gathered them together unto the east street, And said unto them, hear me, ye Levites, sanctify now yourselves, and sanctify the house of the LORD God of your fathers,..."

2 Timothy 1:9 says,
"Who hath saved us, and called us with an holy calling, not according to our works, but according to his own purpose and grace, which was given us in Christ Jesus before the world began."

Like the priests of the Old Testament, believers are called to a life of holiness.

Exodus 28:3 tells us the priest had special garments made, distinguishing them from the rest of the people,
"And thou shalt speak unto all that are wise hearted, whom I have filled with the spirit of wisdom, that they may make Aaron's garment to consecrate him, that he may minister unto me in the priest's office."

Christians have a special clothing as well.

Colossians 3:12 says,
"Put on therefore, as the elect of God, holy and beloved, bowels of mercies, kindness, humbleness of mind, meekness, longsuffering."

As priests we must allow ourselves to be brought down to a low estate in order to minister to God by ministering to others.

Exodus 29:4 tells us the next step of consecrating the priests,
"And Aaron and his sons (the priests) thou shalt bring unto the door of the tabernacle of the congregation, and shalt wash them with water." (Parenthesis added.)

1 Corinthians 6:11 tells us how the believer is washed,
"...but ye are washed, but ye are sanctified, but ye are justified in the name of the Lord Jesus and by the Spirit of our God."

We see how God sanctifies us through the salvation of Jesus Christ and the indwelling presence of the Holy Spirit. But we need to understand our part as priests: that of faith.

Acts 15:9 tells us,
"And put no difference between us and them, purifying their hearts by faith."

The Apostle Paul stated the commission he was given by Jesus in **Acts 26:17-18**,
"...unto whom now I send thee, To open their eyes, and to turn them from darkness to light, and from the powers of Satan unto God, that they may receive forgiveness of sins, and inheritance among them which are sanctified by faith that is in me."

Romans 5:1 says,
"Therefore being justified by faith, we have peace with God through our Lord Jesus Christ."

A walk of faith will cleanse, sanctify, and justify our life before God. It will set us apart from an unbelieving world where fear reigns in darkness and hopelessness.

Hebrews 10:22 gives us this instruction,
"Let us draw near with a true heart in full assurance of faith, having our hearts sprinkled from an evil conscience, and our bodies washed with pure water."

Exodus 29:7 tells us the final step of consecration,
"Then thou shalt take the anointing oil, and pour it upon his head, and anoint him."

Keep in mind if someone is anointed, he or she is being set apart for something special.

2 Corinthians 1:21-22 tells us,
"Now he which stablisheth us with you in Christ, and hath anointed us, is God; Who hath also sealed us, and given the earnest of the Spirit in our hearts."

We know the Holy Spirit has anointed us.

Ephesians 1:4-6 tells us what we have been set apart for,
"According as he hath chosen us in him before the foundation of the world, that we should be holy and without blame before him in love: Having predestinated us unto the adoption of children by Jesus Christ to himself, according to the good pleasure of his will, To the praise of the glory of his grace, wherein he hath made us accepted in the beloved."

John 15:16 gives us this information,
"Ye have not chosen me, but I have chosen you, and ordained you, that ye should go and bring forth fruit, and that your fruit shall remain:..."

We are chosen by God to do His will. His will is to bring Him glory, and to bear heavenly fruit.

Exodus 29:21 tells us the final step of consecration,
"And thou shalt take of the blood that is upon the altar, and of the anointing oil, and sprinkle it upon Aaron, and upon his garments, and upon his sons, and upon the garments of his sons with him: and he shall be hallowed..."

Hebrews 13:20-21 states a similar form of consecration taking place with the believer,
"Now the God of peace, that brought again from the dead our Lord Jesus, that great shepherd of the sheep, through the blood of the everlasting covenant. Make you perfect in every good work to do his will, working in you that which is well pleasing in his sight, through Jesus Christ; to whom be glory forever and ever. Amen."

Supplement: Volume 1 Book 4: *The Place of Covenant*

Because of the blood of Christ, we are now a part of a covenant. A covenant is an agreement between two parties. This agreement can be nullified if one party does not fulfill his or her part. God's part of the agreement is eternal life. Our part is doing his will. The beauty about keeping our end of the agreement is God has given us the power through the Holy Spirit to be obedient.

Leviticus 2:13 gives us this information about a substance which served as a covenant in the Old Testament,
"And every oblation of thy meat offering shalt thou season with salt; neither shalt thou suffer the salt of the covenant of thy God to be lacking from thy meat offering: with all thine offerings thou shalt offer salt."

Salt served as a covenant. It was used with the meal offering.

Matthew 5:13 states,
Ye are the salt of the earth: but if the salt have lost his savour, wherewith shall it be salted? It is thenceforth good for nothing, but to be cast out, and to be trodden under foot of men."

Our part in the kingdom of God is to be the salt. Salt was used to preserve and add flavor. We must give way to and preserve the work of sanctification in our lives through obedience to the will of God. In doing so, we will make a difference in the world. The difference will set us apart, bringing glory to God.

Personal Notes: ____

____

____

Chapter 32

SANCTIFIED!

We have been talking about sanctification in the last three chapters. Hopefully you have an idea of what the work of holiness means.

First, it means being set apart from:
Self, sin, and the world.

We know it involves a cost, which includes:
An Altar, a sacrifice, brokenness, and death.

For holiness to take place, we must be:
Motivated by fear of the Lord and walking by faith.

We must become a:
Place of residence for God, the light of the world, and the salt of the earth.

The final result will produce a life that brings glory to God.

Paul made this statement in **1 Thessalonians 5:23**,
"And the very God of peace sanctify you wholly; and I pray God your whole spirit and soul and body be preserved blameless unto the coming of our Lord Jesus Christ."

The work of sanctification must take place in our spirit, soul, and body. As stated before, it is an on-going process.

Jesus said these words in **John 10:36**,
"Say ye of him, whom the Father hath sanctified, and sent into the world, Thou blasphemest; because I said, I the Son of God?"

This verse shows us the Father sanctified Jesus.

In **John 17:19,** Jesus made this statement,
"And for their sakes I sanctify myself, that they also might be sanctified, through the truth."

Although divine by nature, set apart by the Father, we now see in **John 17:19**, Jesus sanctifying Himself. This meant He was submitting everything on behalf of mankind in order to comply with the will of the Father to bring Him glory. (See **Philippians 2:6-11**.) The work of sanctification is not being solely done on behalf of man, but for God's purpose as well. He is holy, and can only accept and use that which is set apart for His glory. Although Christians have already been set apart by the presence of the Holy Spirit, they must begin the process of submitting everything to Him for the purpose of sanctification.

Paul tells us in **Philippians 2:5**,
"Let this mind be in you, which was also in Christ Jesus."

The attitude of Jesus Christ was to be in total obedience to the will of the Father. Christians can only gain this attitude when God's point of view becomes an obsession with them. This means earthly interests must fade and the emphasis of God becomes a major concern and pursuit.

Hebrews 11:6 states,
"...for he that cometh to God must believe that he is, and that he is a rewarder of them that diligently seek him."

People need to be seeking God for who He is and not what He can give. This search will bring them into the very glory of God.

Moses made this request to God in **Exodus 33:18** after being in the presence of God for days,
"And he said, I beseech thee, shew me thy glory."

Moses was anointed by God. He had seen God in His greatness through various miracles. He had been in His presence, and now He wanted to see His glory. The Bible is constantly talking about God's glory. To experience His glory a person is required to enter into suffering.

Romans 8:17 states,
"...if so be that we suffer with him, that we may be also glorified together."

Sanctification brings glory to God. It will identify us to Him.

Exodus 34:29-30 tells us this about Moses after he was in the presence of God and saw His glory,
"And it came to pass, when Moses came down from mount Sinai with the two tables of testimony in Moses' hand, when he came down from the mount, that Moses wist not that the skin of his face shone while he talked with him. And when Aaron and all the children of Israel saw Moses, behold, the skin of his face shone; and they were afraid to come nigh him."

The Israelites had seen Moses in the midst of miracles. They had followed him through various situations where they had witnessed God's deliverance, but when they saw his face radiant after being in the presence of God, they feared him. We want people to recognize our spiritual lives. Therefore, we desire anointing and power. But our motives make such spiritual things a matter of our glory and confirmation instead of God's glory. Real association with God will only come when self is out of the way. This allows the glory of God to shine forth through us. (Refer to **2 Corinthians 3:13-18**.)

This glory will only be present after we have been in the Lord's presence, experiencing sweet fellowship with Him. The problem found in some Christians is that they fear coming into God's presence. They want His power, but they are afraid of Him. This reluctance to know God for ourselves can lead to idolatry in high places. To the Christian idolatry in high places simply means worshipping the things of God rather than God. This type of idolatry is hard to detect.

Personal Notes: ____

____

God's Peace

1 Thessalonians 5:23 states,
"And the very God of peace sanctify you wholly;..."

> Christians who allow the work of holiness in their lives experience peace. Sanctification brings peace to lives because self is being put down on a regular basis. With self under control, believers will cease from warring with God and become submissive to the Holy Spirit.

The Apostle Paul talked about the battle of the flesh and the spirit in **Galatians 5:17**:
"For the flesh lusteth against the Spirit, and the Spirit against the flesh: and these are contrary the one to the other: so that ye cannot do the things that ye would."

> The devil is the one who brings accusation, confusion, fear, guilt, and condemnation into our lives.

If you are resisting evil and submitting yourself to God, **James 4:7** tells us the devil,
"...will flee from you."

> The work of holiness means cleansing is taking place. This purging occurs because of our obedience to the Word.

1 Peter 1:22 says,
"Seeing ye have purified your souls in obeying the truth through the Spirit unto unfeigned love of the brethren, see that ye love one another with a pure heart fervently."

> Obedience, which comes because of fear of God, produces godly love in our hearts. Obedience and love will put us in the center of God's will. (See **1 John 3:23-24**.)

1 Peter 4:1-2 tells us,
"Forasmuch then as Christ hath suffered for us in the flesh, arm yourselves likewise with the same mind: for he that hath suffered in the flesh hath ceased from sin; That he no longer should live the rest of his time in the flesh to the lusts of men, but to the will of God."

1 Thessalonians 4:3-4 states,
"For this is the will of God, even your sanctification, that ye should abstain from fornication. That every one of you should know how to possess his vessel in sanctification and honour."

> By being in God's will we live separated lives for His glory. God's will also includes the following: Believing on Jesus **(John 6:38-40)**, repentance **(2 Peter 3:9)**, doing good **(1 Peter 2:15-17)**, and giving thanks in all circumstances **(1 Thessalonians 5:18)**. It is in the will of God that we find assurance and refuge.

Psalm 27:5 gives us this promise,
"For in the time of trouble he shall hide me in his pavilion: in the secret of his tabernacle shall he hide me; he shall set me up upon a rock."

We can see why the peace of God reigns in a life sanctified by Him. Do you have God's peace? If you do not, examine whether or not you have submitted to the work of holiness.

Personal Notes: ____

____

Realizing the Cost

The decision of holiness is not an emotional or intellectual decision. It is a heart determination. This determination comes from the pure desire to know God and to serve Him. If your spiritual desires and priorities fall short of knowing God in an intimate way, you will fall to the wayside during the work of holiness. For holiness is not intended for man's benefit, but for God's glory. Man, of course, will ultimately reap spiritual and eternal rewards from sanctification, but not without first paying the price. You must always count the cost of holiness in light of eternity.

1 Peter 1:7 says,
"...though it be tried with fire,..."

Like the children of Israel, it means you will spiritually go through fiery trials.

Deuteronomy 1:19 says this about Israel's experience,
"...we went through all that great and terrible wilderness,..."

These deserts can involve the wilderness of uncertainty and harshness. These wilderness experiences are necessary if a Christian is ever going to enter into the Promised Land.

You might find yourself relating to **Psalm 23:4**,
"...I walk through the valley of the shadow of death,..."

Matthew 13:44-46 confirms this,
"Again, the kingdom of heaven is like unto treasure hid in a field; the which when a man hath found, he hideth, and for joy thereof goeth and selleth all that he hath, and buyeth that field. Again, the kingdom of heaven is like unto a merchant man, seeking goodly pearls: Who, when he had found one pearl of great price, went and sold all that he had, and bought it."

1 John 2:17 tells us our final reward,
"And the world passeth away, and the lust thereof: but he that doeth the will of God abideth forever."

Personal Notes: ____

____

Giving God Permission

2 Peter 1:4 says,
"Whereby are given unto us exceeding great and precious promises: that by these ye might be partakers of the divine nature, having escaped the corruption that is in the world through lust."

The work of holiness will make us partakers of Jesus' divine nature. It will bring the very image of Christ out in us. This truly identifies us with the on-going work of sanctification.

Matthew 7:7-8 tells us,
"Ask, and it shall be given you; seek, and ye shall find; knock, and it shall be opened unto you: For every one that asketh receiveth; and he that seeketh findeth; and to him that knocketh it shall be opened."

The work of holiness will begin when you ask God in sincerity to do it. This on-going separation will only take place as you earnestly seek God. Your search will lead you to places of commitment, where the doors of your heart must be opened to allow the life of Christ to come forth in glory. Do you want the work of holiness to take place in you? Ask God now to begin this work. Earnestly seek His face to know His will, and to reaffirm what separation needs to take place in your life. Let the doors of your heart be thrown wide open for all the light and glory of Christ to shine through you.

Personal Notes: ____

____

____

Section IV

THE GIFTS OF THE SPIRIT

Chapter 33

INTRODUCTION TO THE GIFTS

Supplements:
(For Review)
What is the Church?
Sup. 1
Volume 1
Book 5:
Study: *Unmasking the Cult Mentality*
Section 4
The Makeup of the True Church?
(For the next five chapters.)
Volume 5
Book 3:
For the Purpose of Edification

The Apostle Paul made this statement in **1 Corinthians 12:1**,
"Now concerning spiritual gifts, brethren, I would not have you ignorant."

The Church has been given spiritual gifts.

Paul tells us the purpose of these spiritual gifts in **1 Corinthians 12:7**,
"But the manifestations of the Spirit is given to every man to profit withal."

These gifts are a manifestation of the Holy Ghost. In other words, these gifts in operation reveal that the Holy Ghost is present and working in the Body. The gifts of the Spirit are for the profit, edification, or common good of the Body of believers.

Paul gives us this insight about the gifts in **1 Corinthians 12:4-6**,
"Now there are diversities of gifts, but the same Spirit. And there are differences of administrations, but the same Lord. And there are diversities of operations, but it is the same God which worketh all in all."

There are different gifts. These Scripture verses show us that the three Persons of the Godhead are involved in the edification of the Body. Each Person of the Godhead has different functions and responsibilities in the Body. But, the common source of these gifts is the one who gives them: The Holy Spirit.

Ephesians 4:4 confirms this about the Holy Spirit,
"There is one body, and one Spirit, even as ye are called in one hope of your calling."

1 Corinthians 12:11 states this about the gifts of the Spirit,
"But all these worketh that one and the selfsame Spirit, dividing to every man severally as he will."

Hebrews 2:4 states,
"God also bearing them witness, both with signs and wonders, and with divers miracles, and gifts of the Holy Ghost, according to his own will?

These scriptures show us the sovereign right of God in the area of gifts. The Scripture verse in **1 Corinthians 12** tells us which Person of the Godhead determines who receives these gifts. It is the Holy Spirit who distributes these gifts as He so desires. One must keep in mind it is God working His will and eternal plan within the lives of believers and the Church or Body of Christ, but it is up to man to give way to His will, work, and grace by faith. Anything God does in regard to man is an act of grace. Man's part is simple—believing and receiving His work by faith.

Romans 12:6 tells us,
"Having then gifts differing according to the grace that is given to us, whether prophecy, let us prophesy according to the proportion of faith."

These gifts are a product of the baptism of the Holy Spirit.

1 Corinthians 12:13 tells us,
"For by one Spirit are we all baptized into one body, whether we be Jews or Gentiles, whether we be bond or free; and have been all made to drink into one Spirit."

The gifts of the Spirit are a manifestation of God's miraculous power in action through man.

Jesus confirms this in **Luke 24:49** when He told His disciples to tarry in Jerusalem,
"...until ye be endued with power from on high."

1 Corinthians 12:31 gives us this instruction about gifts,
"But covet earnestly the best gifts..."

We are instructed to desire these gifts. To not desire them is to be disobedient to God. God uses this power to confirm His existence and to minister to the body of believers. These gifts are for the Christian's benefit and the Church's edification or growth.

Once again we are reminded of what **James 1:17** says,
"Every good gift and every perfect gift is from above, and cometh down from the Father of lights..."

The key word is "gift." We can't do anything to earn gifts nor can we determine the gifts that are given to us. We may hint about the gifts we desire, but the gifts we receive will be according to the discretion of the one who gives it to us. Therefore, believers have no control over what gifts come their way. What believers do with such gifts is a matter of choice on their part. For example, they can receive or reject gifts. They can abuse or wisely use gifts. But the Word is clear, God gives gifts according to His will, His eternal plan, and because He is a loving Father who wants to bless His children as well as nurture them.

Personal Notes: ____

____

Ephesians 4:4 says,
"There is one body..."

Colossians 1:18 tells us what the Body is,
"And he (Jesus) is the head of the body, the church: who is the beginning, the firstborn from the dead; that in all things he might have the preeminence." (Parenthesis added.)

The body of believers is the Church. The word church comes from a Geek word which means assembly or called out. The real Church is not made up of denominations or buildings, but of people who love and serve the Lord Jesus Christ.

Romans 12:4-5 gives us this insight about the body,
"For as we have many members in one body, and all members have not the same office: So we being many, are one body in Christ, and every one members one of another."

First of all, the members of the Body must work according to one purpose: the function of the whole Body. In order for the Body to do this, it must be in compliance with the head, Jesus Christ. If this Body functions properly, it will in turn bring glory to its head, Redeemer, and Creator, Jesus Christ.

Paul confirms this in **1 Corinthians 12:14-17**,
"For the body is not one member, but many. If the foot shall say, Because I am not the hand, I am not of the body; is it therefore not of the body? And if the ear shall say, Because I am not the eye, I am not of the body; is it therefore not of the body? If the whole body were an eye, where were the hearing? If the whole were hearing, where were the smelling?"

Each member of the body of Christ is equally important to the function of the whole body.

1 Corinthians 12:22-24 gives us this information,
"Nay, much more those members of the body, which seem to be more feeble, are necessary: And those members of the body, which we think to be less honourable, upon these we bestow more abundant honour; and our uncomely parts have more abundant comeliness. For our comely parts have no need: but God hath tempered the body together, having given more abundant honour to that part which lacked."

God honors the parts that seem less important.

1 Corinthians 12:25 tells us why God operates in this way,
"That there should be no schism in the body; but that the members should have the same care one for another."

Christians have a way of bringing worldly standards into the Church, which promote superiority over others. This superiority has been enhanced in the Church by exalting titles and responsibilities over others in the Body. This exaltation has resulted in pride, fear, jealously, and division among Christians. These sins will put the things of God into a realm of competition.

James 3:16 confirms this,
"For where envying and strife is, there is confusion and every evil work."

Believers need to get serious about dealing with worldly attitudes and standards. These must not be operating within the body. Such practices will be exposed through division.

1 Corinthians 14:33 states,
"For God is not the author of confusion, but of peace, as in all churches of the saints."

The Bible is clear as to the type of attitudes we should have towards one another in the Body. To ensure the healthy function of the Body, we must deny selfish rights. We must strive to develop the mind of Christ towards one another. Remember, it is our love for one another which will identify us as true disciples of Christ **(John 13:35)**.

Personal Notes: ____

____

Avoiding Divisions

1 Corinthians 12:26 tells us,
"And whether one member suffer, all the members suffer with it; or one member be honoured, all the members rejoice with it."

Each Christian must realize they cannot function properly when they are working independent of the needs of the whole Body. So many times we want members of the Body to do it our way. This shows a lack of love and understanding as to how the Body is to function.

As we know according to **1 Corinthians 13:5** God's love,
"...seeketh not her own,..."

Christians often try to direct or become a conscience as to how each member should function in the Body. When an individual does this, he or she is playing the Holy Spirit.

1 Corinthians 12:18 tells us,
"But now hath God set the members every one of them in the body, as it hath pleased him."

We must become sensitive to each member of the Body. This sensitivity must be evident in our attitudes and actions toward one another.

Ephesians 5:21 commands us to,
"Submitting yourselves one to another in the fear of God."

Romans 12:3, 10, 13-16 summarizes our responsibility to one another,
"...not to think of himself more highly than he ought to think; but to think soberly, according as God hath dealt to every man the measure of faith... Be kindly affectioned one to another with brotherly love; in honour preferring one another;... Distributing to the necessity of saints; given to hospitality. Bless them, which persecute you: bless, and curse not. Rejoice with them that do rejoice, and weep with them that weep. Be of the same mind one toward another. Mind not high things, but condescend to men of low estate. Be not wise in your own conceits."

Galatians 6:2-4 gives us this instruction,
"Bear ye one another's burdens, and so fulfil the law of Christ. For if a man think himself to be something, when he is nothing, he deceiveth himself. But let every man prove his own work, and then shall he have rejoicing in himself alone, and not in another."

Colossians 3:12-15 says,
"Put on therefore, as the elect of God, holy and beloved, bowels of mercies, kindness, humbleness of mind, meekness, longsuffering; Forbearing one another, and forgiving one another, if any man have a quarrel against any: even as Christ forgave you, so also do ye. And above all these things put on charity, which is the bond of perfectness. And let the peace of God rule in your hearts, to the which also ye are called in one body; and be ye thankful."

Keep in mind at all times what Jesus said in **Matthew 20:25-27**,
"...Ye know that the princes of the Gentiles exercise dominion over them, and they that are great exercise authority upon them. But it shall not be so among you: but whosoever will be great among you, let him be your minister; And whosoever will be chief among you, let him be your servant."

Christians are responsible to put down all high opinions of self. They must hate pride, jealousy, and fear because these sins produce a competitive attitude towards God's kingdom. Their desire should be to become a servant to all for the glory of God.

Personal Notes: ____

____

Introduction To The Gifts

A gift is something that is freely given to you. It cannot be earned. There are nine gifts of the Spirit. They fall into three classifications. Here is a list of the gifts in light of how they are classified:

1. Gifts of Revelation: A. Word of Wisdom B. Word of Knowledge C. Discerning of Spirits
2. Gifts of Power: A. Faith B. Miracles C. Healing
3. Gifts of Inspiration (vocal gifts): A. Prophecy B. Different kinds of tongues C. Interpretation of tongues

(Note, the breakdown in regard to the classifications of gifts and some of the following information and examples in the next four chapters were inspired by Harold Horton's book, "The Gifts of the Spirit"; 1934.)

Remember these gifts are for the common good of the Church. They are the evidence that God is still moving in a miraculous way among His believers.

Personal Notes: ____

____

____

Chapter 34

GIFTS OF REVELATION

Revelation means to uncover. The gifts, which fall into this classification, are used in a couple of ways. The first is to reveal the heart and mind of God to His people, while the second is to reveal that which is unseen that is in operation in regard to others. They are used as a means of rebuking, warning, encouraging, protecting, and giving insight into the future.

The Word of Knowledge

1 Corinthians 12:8 tells us the Holy Spirit imparts some with,
"...the word of knowledge by the same Spirit;..."

The word of knowledge is the supernatural uncovering of facts concerning the mind of God and the present status of man.

Proverbs 15:3 says,
"The eyes of the Lord are in every place, beholding the evil and the good."

God knows everything that is going on in heaven and earth. His knowledge is not the same as man's.

The Lord said this in **Isaiah 55:9**,
"For as the heavens are higher than the earth, so are my ways higher than your ways, and my thoughts than your thoughts."

The Apostle Paul made this statement in **1 Corinthians 13:9 & 12**,
"For we know in part,...now I know in part..."

1 Corinthians 8:1 says this about the final result produced by man's knowledge,
"...we know that we all have knowledge. Knowledge puffeth up, but charity edifieth."

Man has a very high opinion of what he thinks he knows, but he only knows in part. (Refer to **1 Corinthians 8:2; 10:13** and **Galatians 6:3**.) If this knowledge is not kept in godly perspective, it will end in pride. The word of knowledge is based on God's infinite knowledge and not man. This gift can reveal facts such as man's present spiritual condition and activities as well as his thoughts, motives, and heart intent. We see the word of knowledge in operation in the lives of the prophet Samuel in the Old Testament and Nathaniel, the disciple of Jesus.

In **1 Samuel 3:11-14** we read about an incident, which involved the priest, Eli and his sons,
"And the LORD said to Samuel, behold, I will do a thing in Israel, at which both the ears of every one that heareth it shall tingle. In that day I will perform against Eli all things which I have spoken concerning his house: when I begin I will also make an end. For I have told him that I will judge his house forever for the iniquity, which he knoweth; because his sons

made themselves vile, and he restrained them not. And therefore I have sworn unto the house of Eli that the iniquity of Eli's house shall not be purged with sacrifice nor offering forever."

John 1:47-48 tells us,
"Jesus saw Nathanael coming to him, and saith of him, Behold an Israelite indeed in whom, is no guile. Nathanael saith unto him, Whence knowest thou me? Jesus answered and said unto him, Before that Philip called thee, when thou wast under the fig tree, I saw thee.

In one situation the word of knowledge revealed present sin and pending judgment. In the other incident it involved a revelation about sincerity on the part of Nathanael. Here are other examples where the word of knowledge was used or can be used:

A. Warning of pending destruction because of present actions. (See **2 Kings 6:9-12**.)
B. To enlighten and encourage a servant of God. (See **1 Kings 19:14-18**.)
C. Exposing a hypocrite. (See **2 Kings 5:20-27**.)
D. To show a sinner he needs a Savior. (See **John 4:18-19, & 29**.)
E. To show an individual is in need.
F. To reveal corruption in the church.
G. To uncover facts about private lives for spiritual correction.

God is the one who holds the future events in His hands. He is the one who looks at the mind and heart of man in terms of eternity. He is the one who reveals secrets to expose sins in order to bring about repentance, reconciliation, and salvation.

Psalm 7:9 makes this declaration,
"...for the righteous God trieth the hearts and reins."

Every gift carries an awesome responsibility. You must, therefore seek God concerning your responsibility towards His supernatural gift of knowledge. God has a timing and a place for sharing any revelation. Since this gift may bring a warning, reproof, or serve as a means of encouragement, motives must be examined and sensitivity must be in operation. Sometimes God reveals certain facts and the only required response is that of prayer. Scriptures show us there are procedures and responsibilities that go with each gift. One must keep in mind that they are only the tool, while God is the source behind the gift. Man's duty is to be sensitive to the leading of the Holy Spirit to ensure proper presentation or application of the gift in the Body.

Personal Notes: ____

____

The Word of Wisdom

1 Corinthians 12:8 says,
"For to one is given by the Spirit the word of wisdom;..."

Wisdom is often termed as knowledge put into practice. Knowledge is part of wisdom, but wisdom can be absent in knowledge. This is why the word of wisdom is considered the chief of the two gifts in this category. The word of wisdom is the revelation of facts, which only the divine mind of God can know. It always has a point of instruction.

James 3:17 tells us what God's wisdom is like,
"But the wisdom that is from above is first pure, then peaceable, gentle, and easy to be intreated, full of mercy and good fruits, without partiality, and without hypocrisy."

Every Christian should display God's wisdom. But the word of wisdom goes farther than godly wisdom imparted to man through scriptures and godly instruction. It is a combination of the past and the present coming together in regard to the future. This supernatural wisdom shows God's infinite understanding of everything that will happen throughout the eternal ages. It includes His judgment motivated by the past that will come to be in another generation. It entails instruction of how this knowledge can be applied to the present to change the course of man's life for today and the future. We see the word of wisdom in operation in the situation involving a wicked king of Israel and his wife. The king's name was Ahab and his wife's name was Jezebel. Ahab wanted to possess a certain vineyard. The owner refused to sell it to him. Ahab became so upset by the man's refusal that he laid on his bed and began to sulk and refused to eat. His evil wife discovered he wanted the vineyard. She instructed the elders of the city to falsely accuse the owner, Naboth. They obeyed and the poor man was put to death.

In **1 Kings 21:17-19**, we read these words of God directed to Ahab,
"And the word of the LORD came to Elijah the Tishbite, saying. Arise, go down to meet Ahab king of Israel, which is in Samaria: behold, he is in the vineyard of Naboth, whither he is gone down to possess it. And thou shalt speak unto him, saying, Thus saith the LORD, hast thou killed, and also taken possession? And thou shalt speak unto him, saying, thus saith the LORD, in the place where dogs licked thy blood of Naboth shall dogs lick they blood, even thine."

The word of knowledge came into action when the prophet confronted the king over a present sin due to a past event. The king's action brought a pronouncement of future judgment. Then in **1 Kings 21:27-29**, we see the exposure of the sins producing repentance. In turn the future was adjusted according to the king's wise response.

1 Kings 21:27-29 says,
"And it came to pass when Ahab heard those words, that he rent his clothes, and put sackcloth upon his flesh, and fasted, and lay in sackcloth, and went softly. And the word of the LORD came to Elijah the Tishbite, saying. Seest thou how Ahab humbleth himself before me? because he humbleth himself before me, I will not bring the evil in his days: but in his son's days will I bring the evil upon his house."

God is quick to show mercy, but He is not a liar and all that He declares must come to pass. Because He is all-powerful, He will simply adjust the timing of future events according to His purpose and will. Christians confuse the word of knowledge with the word of wisdom. Let's summarize the difference between these two gifts:

Word of knowledge reveals past dealings and/or present spiritual condition, while *word of wisdom* tells of the future in regards to the past and present. It reveals the mind of God toward evil deeds. The mercy of God is always available for the present to those who are repentant. He can, therefore, adjust His purpose and will concerning the future according to man's response to His warning and instruction.

Here are some other examples of the word of wisdom:

A. Warn or guide people concerning future judgment.
B. Revealing God's plans to His servants.
C. Confirmation of a servant of God's commission.
D. To assure of coming deliverance in times of trouble.
E. Revealing God's will and His future acts to change present direction and conduct.

Personal Notes: ____

____

Discernment of Spirits

1 Corinthians 12:10 states,
"...to another discerning of spirits;..."

All Christians need to learn how to discern.

Hebrews 5:14 gives us this insight about discernment,
"But strong meat belongeth to them that are of full age, even those who by reason of use have their senses exercised to discern both good and evil."

1 John 4:1 gives this command to every Christian,
"Beloved, believe not every spirit, but try the spirits whether they are of God: because many false prophets are gone out into the world."

God's people need to know how to discern between good and evil. They must test the spirit. This type of discernment involves two steps of spiritual evaluation: testing and judging. Christians must examine all things according to the Word of God. To test implies a critical examination of something. The second evaluation is judging the fruits. To judge is to make a determination after gathering evidence. In the case of Christianity, it comes down to the type of fruit an individual displays. (See **Matthew 7:15-19**.)

The gift of discerning spirits is a supernatural ability to see into the spiritual realm to determine if a spirit behind an individual, religious organization, or miraculous act is from the kingdom of darkness or from the kingdom of God. It is the most limited among the gifts of revelation, but a vital part of protecting the flock of Jesus. A good example of discernment of spirits can be seen in the incidents that took place between Jesus, James, and John and between Jesus and Peter.

Jesus had set his face towards Jerusalem—towards the cross. He and His disciples were going by way of Samaria. When the Samaritans failed to properly respond to Jesus, James and John wanted to call the fire of judgment down from heaven.

This was Jesus' response to them in **Luke 9:55**,
"Ye know not what manner of spirit ye are of."

In the incident with Peter, he had just declared Jesus was the Christ. Jesus began to tell His disciples about His crucifixion.

Matthew 16:22-23 gives us this account,
"Then Peter took him, and began to rebuke him, saying Be it far from thee, Lord: this shall not be unto thee. But he turned, and said unto Peter, Get thee behind me, Satan: thou art an offence unto me: for thou savourest not the things that be of God, but those that be of men."

Jesus was discerning the spirit behind Peter. He recognized and separated the influence of Satan from the man. Here is a list of other ways the discernment of spirits is used in the body.

A. Helping in the deliverance of the afflicted, oppressed, and tormented.
B. To discover a servant of the kingdom of darkness in the midst of God's servants.
C. To help in checking the plans of Satan.
D. To expose error.
E. To discern miracles inspired by demons.

Sometimes Satan's power resembles God's. We need this supernatural gift to unmask him. Discernment of spirits is necessary for the protection of the Church. For the enemy's tactics are to come in to the Church, counterfeit the things of God, and bring the Church down from within through division **(Matthew 12:22-30)**.

The gifts of revelation are for the purpose of the Church knowing God's concern, mind, and will about a matter. It enables the Church to see into the spiritual realm in a supernatural way. Gifts are an honor to have, but they must never be abused by man using them for his own glory or purpose. Those who claim they have such gifts must be tested in light of scriptural truths, practices, and by the type of spirit that motivates them along with the fruit that is being produced.

Personal Notes: ____

____

Chapter 35

GIFTS OF POWER

The gifts of power work within two boundaries: Man's faith and God's sovereign will.

Romans 12:3 says,
"For I say, through the grace given unto me, to every man that is among you, not to think of himself more highly than he ought to think; but to think soberly according as God hath dealt to every man the measure of faith."

God has given us all a measure of faith. This faith inspires us to move towards Him in whatever direction we need to go, be it salvation, ministry, or gifts. This faith will allow God to move freely in and through our lives. In **Mark 9:17-26** we read about an incident involving a young boy who was subject to a demon. This demon kept throwing the boy on the ground in a fit of seizures.

In **Mark 9:21-24,** we read this conversation,
"And he (Jesus) asked his father, How long is it ago since this came unto him? And he said, Of a child. And ofttimes it hath cast him into the fire, and into the waters, to destroy him: but if thou canst do any thing, have compassion on us, and help us. Jesus said unto him, if thou canst believe, all things are possible to him that believeth. And straightway the father of the child cried out, and said with tears, Lord, I believe; help thou mine unbelief." (Parenthesis added.)

It takes faith to simply receive from God. Sometimes in our desire to receive from God, we lack the expectation to simply believe He wants to do something for us. This type of attitude comes from one of two attitudes. First attitude occurs because the person's heart is sick because hope has been deferred **(Proverbs 13:12)**. The second attitude is that man recognizes he is unworthy to receive from a holy God. Each individual must keep in mind there is healing of wounded hearts made available through Christ, and that there is no condemnation to those who are in Him **(Luke 4:18; Romans 8:1)**. However, the gifts of power must also be considered in light of God's will.

Romans 9:18-21 tells us,
"Therefore hath he mercy on whom he will have mercy, and whom he will he hardeneth. Thou wilt say then unto me, why doth he yet find fault? For who hath resisted his will? Nay but, O man, who art thou that repliest against God? Shall the thing formed say to him that formed it, Why hast thou made me thus? Hath not the potter power over the clay, of the same lump to make one vessel unto honour, and another unto dishonour?"

God is in control of events. Christians who do not understand the ways of God have unmercifully told people that the reason they have not been healed is because they lack faith or they have some hidden sin. Sometimes this is true, but in other cases it is not. False accusations of these types have not only turned people off to the gifts of the Spirit, but they have turned many away from God. Once again, we must be careful in the handling of gifts.

Jesus made this statement in **John 9:1-3**,
"And as Jesus passed by, he saw a man which was blind from his birth. And his disciples asked him, saying, Master, who did sin, this man or his parents, that he was born blind? Jesus answered, Neither hath this man sinned, nor his parents: but that the works of God should be made manifest in him."

The gifts of power are designed to bring glory to God.

John 11:4 confirms this in the raising of Lazarus,
"When Jesus heard that, he said, This sickness is not unto death, but for the glory of God, that the Son of God might be glorified thereby."

These gifts are also for the purpose of confirmation.

In **John 10:38**, Jesus said this about the miracles He performed,
"But if I do, though ye believe not me, believe the works: that ye may know, and believe, that the Father is in me, and I in him."

Gifts of power confirm the message being preached.

Mark 16:20 states,
"And they went forth, and preached every where, the Lord working with them, and confirming the word with signs following."

We must keep the gifts of power in a correct perspective to ensure we do not abuse them or take credit for them.

Personal Notes: ____

____

Gift of Healing

1 Corinthians 12:9 says,
"...to another the gifts of healing by the same Spirit."

The gift of healing is supernatural. It does not depend on the means of man's medical intelligence or procedures to bring it forth. It is healing which comes from God above. We see this supernatural healing done in the following scriptures.

Matthew 9:27-30 says,
"And when Jesus departed thence, two blind men followed him, crying, and saying, Thou Son of David, have mercy on us. And when he was come into the house, the blind men came to him: and Jesus saith unto them, Believe ye that I am able to do this? They said unto him, Yea, Lord. Then touched he their eyes, saying, according to your faith be it unto you. And their eyes were opened; and Jesus straitly charged them, saying, see that no man know it."

Mark 2:10-12 gives us this account of a miraculous healing,
"But that ye may know that the Son of man hath power on earth to forgive sins, (he saith to the sick of the palsy,) I say unto thee, Arise, and take up thy bed, and go thy way into thine house. And immediately he arose, took up the bed, and went forth before them all; insomuch that they were all amazed, and glorified God,..."

Luke 17:12-14 tells us,
"And as he (Jesus) entered into a certain village, there met him ten men that were lepers, which stood afar off. And they lifted up their voices, and said, Jesus, Master, have mercy on us. And when he saw them, he said unto them, go shew yourselves unto the priests. And it came to pass, that, as they went, they were cleansed." (Parenthesis added.)

Acts 3:1-9 gives us this account about a lame man at the temple's gate begging for money to help him in his plight. Peter and John's attention is drawn to him.

Acts 3:6-7 tells us what Peter said to this man and the final results,
"Then Peter said, Silver and gold have I none; but such as I have give I thee: in the name of Jesus Christ of Nazareth rise up and walk."

All of these healings were miraculous, but we must keep these healings in perspective.

Jesus made this statement in **Matthew 9:12-13**,
"But when Jesus heard that, he said unto them, they that be whole need not a physician, but they that are sick. But go ye and learn what that meaneth, I will have mercy, and not sacrifice: for I am not come to call the righteous, but sinners to repentance."

Sin is the terminal disease of the soul. Christ is more concerned about the spiritual healing of man's eternal soul than the healing of his physical body. God's salvation is the only eternal lifesaving medicine to remedy the problem of eternal separation from God, and it has been made available to all mankind. People have a habit of taking the spiritual application and applying it to the physical. Although God would like us to be healed physically, but the real significance of being healed by His stripes in **Isaiah 53:5** is that of spiritual healing. The gift of healing includes the following:

A. Deliverance of the sick and destruction of the works of Satan in the human body.
B. To confirm God's existence and salvation.
C. To confirm faith and inspire courage in believers.

Personal Notes: ____

____

The Gifts of Miracles

1 Corinthians 12:10 states,
"...to another the working of miracles;..."

The gift of miracles are supernatural acts outside of the natural function of this world.

One example of such an act is found in **Exodus 14:21-22**,
"And Moses stretched out his hand over the sea; and the LORD caused the sea to go back by a strong east wind all that night, and made the sea dry land, and the waters were divided. And the children of Israel went into the midst of the sea upon the dry ground: and the waters were a wall unto them on their right hand, and on their left."

The parting of the Red Sea is an example of a miraculous act. This act went against natural laws and elements that govern the activities of the earth, and were witnessed by the physical eye.

The incident found in **Joshua 10:12-14** is another example of the miraculous happening,
"Then spake Joshua to the LORD in the day when the LORD delivered up the Amorites before the children of Israel, and he said in the sight of Israel, Sun, stand thou still upon Gibeon; and thou Moon, in the valley of Ajalon. And the sun stood still, and the moon stayed, until the people had avenged themselves upon their enemies. Is not this written? in the book of Jasher? So the sun stood still in the midst of heaven, and hasted not to go down about a whole day. And there was no day like that before it or after it, that the LORD hearkened unto the voice of a man: for the LORD fought for Israel."

We read this about Jesus in **Mark 4:37-39**,
"And there arose a great storm of wind, and the waves beat into the ship, so that it was now full. And he was in the hinder part of the ship, asleep on a pillow: and they awake him, and say unto him, Master, carest thou not that we perish? And he arose, and rebuked the wind, and said unto the sea, Peace be still. And the wind ceased, and there was a great calm."

Hebrews 11:3 states,
"Through faith we understand that the worlds were framed by the word of God, so that things which are seen were not made of things which do appear."

God created the world. Man is bound by the world's laws and elements, but God is not. Although man does his best to explain away these miracles according to his understanding, they stand as a witness to God's incredible power. Other examples of the gift of miracles are the following:

A. Provision for those in need.
B. Means of carrying out divine judgment.
C. The raising of the dead.

Miracles have been one of the main means of confirming the Word. It is God's way of showing His existence to an unbelieving and hopeless world. However, it is important to point out that miracles were done in proportion to the need or situation. For example, God would not part the Red Sea for one man (Peter) than He would have caused all the children of Israel to walk on water to cross over the Red Sea. God is not a show-off.

Personal Notes: ____

____

The Gift of Faith

1 Corinthians 12:9 says,
"To another faith by the same Spirit;..."

The gift of faith is considered the greatest of the three power gifts. Faith is the only virtue mentioned as both a fruit of the Spirit and a gift. For instance, the righteous shall live by faith. This righteousness is the fruit of the Spirit. It implies character. The servant of God shall walk by faith. A life, which involves a walk of faith, displays authority and power. This power comes from having an assurance in God. This assurance can move mountains.

Matthew 21:22 confirms this thought,
"And all things, whatsoever ye shall ask in prayer, believing, ye shall receive."

The gift of faith is a supernatural assurance of God's intervention. This faith can result in supernatural healing.

We read these words in **Matthew 9:20-22**,
"And, behold, a woman, which was diseased with an issue of blood twelve years, came behind him, and touched the hem of his garment: For she said within herself, If I may but touch his garment, I shall be whole. But Jesus turned him about, and when he saw her, he said, Daughter, be of good comfort; thy faith hath made thee whole. And the woman was made whole from that hour."

This gift of faith can result in miracles.

Matthew 14:25-29 gives this account,
"And in the fourth watch of the night Jesus went unto them, walking on the sea. And when the disciples saw him walking on the sea, they were troubled, saying, It is a spirit; and they cried out for fear. But straightway Jesus spake unto them, saying, Be of good cheer; it is I; be not afraid. And Peter answered him and said, Lord, if it be thou, bid me come unto thee on the water. And he said, Come. And when Peter was come down out of the ship, he walked on the water, to go to Jesus."

Although the gift of faith can result in miraculous acts, its greatest quality is the display of supernatural trust in God during the greatest crises. Christians often associate God's greatness to miracles, when in fact they need to simply trust God according to His character and greatness. This trust does not require a sign from Him in order for the individual to believe in His power or deliverance. This faith brings a knowing in an individual's spirit that allows him or her to enter into rest no matter what is going on. It actually can be related to being in the eye of the storm. This type of faith serves as a greater witness to people of God's greatness.

If an individual shows this abiding trust during crises, his or her testimony of God gives direction and confidence to those who are seeking a place of rest. Christians limit God's power. They feel people would believe God if He would only show Himself through miracles. This is not true. God's greatest witness comes through those who have an abiding faith in Him. This is why Jesus made this statement to Thomas in **John 20:29** after Thomas declared he would only believe Jesus' resurrection when he could put his hands in Jesus' nail prints:

John 20:29 states,
"Jesus said unto him, Thomas, because thou hast seen me, thou hast believed: blessed are they that have not seen, and yet have believed."

Abiding faith has more far-reaching power than the gifts of healing and miracles. However, these two gifts appeal to the fleshly senses of man, while the gift of faith is a sustaining power within the spirit of man. Remember, the things which attract the flesh will pass away, but those things which are of the Spirit are eternal **(1 John 2:17)**.

This is why Paul made this statement in **1 Corinthians 13:13**,
"And now abideth faith, hope, charity, these three; but the greatest of these is charity."

Faith is eternal. Our assurance in God will keep us going through this life, and will be present with us in eternity. In eternity our confidence will be made complete as we abide in the presence of the One in whom our faith firmly stands upon.

Colossians 1:22-23 says,
"In the body of his flesh through death, to present you holy and unblameable and unreproveable in his sight: If ye continue in the faith grounded and settled, and be not moved away from the hope of the gospel, which ye have heard, and which was preached to every creature which is under heaven; whereof I Paul am made a minister."

Other examples of the gift of faith include the following:

A. Personal protection in crises.
B. Being sustained during fasting and famine.
C. Receiving the promises of God.
D. Being able to experience supernatural victory.
E. Raising the dead and casting out demons.

Personal Notes: ____

____

____

Chapter 36

THE GIFTS OF INSPIRATION

The final three gifts are the gifts of inspiration. These are the vocal gifts that are used as a means of inspiration during worship. These three gifts are the only gifts of the Spirit where man must come into total subjection. For instance, the Holy Spirit inspires the individual with one of these gifts during worship, but man must submit as the vocal instrument to utter the inspired message.

The Gift of Tongues

1 Corinthians 12:10 states,
"...to another divers kinds of tongues;..."

The most discussed gift is the gift of tongues. We read the following scriptures about the gift of tongues.

Mark 16:17 states,
"And these signs shall follow them that believe; In my name shall they cast out devils; they shall speak with new tongues."

1 Corinthians 14:4-5 says,
"He that speaketh in an unknown tongue edifieth himself; but he that prophesieth edifieth the church. I would that ye all spake with tongues, but rather that ye prophesied: for greater is he that prophesieth than he that speaketh with tongues, except he interpret, that the church may receive edifying."

First of all, tongues are promised to those who believe. Paul desired that all would speak in tongues, but he also put it in perspective by calling it the lesser of the gifts. The reason it is the least of the gifts is because it only edifies the individual unless it is interpreted. The gift of tongues is the most controversial subject among the Christian denominations. The reason for this reaction is because it creates the most fear and confusion. s a result, it is the most visible, abused, and misunderstood gift. Paul talked much about this gift in **1 Corinthians 14** in order to put it in perspective.

1 Corinthians 14:40 gives us this boundary,
"Let all things be done decently and in order."

The correct procedure for the gift of tongues is found in **1 Corinthians 14:27-28**,
"If any man speak in an unknown tongue, let it be by two, or at the most by three, and that by course; and let one interpret. But if there be no interpreter, let him keep silence in the church; and let him speak to himself, and to God."

There must not be more than three messages in tongues in any one meeting. All tongues must be interpreted when they are verbally spoken in the Body. Disregard for these instructions will signify the service is out of order and that the flesh or another spirit is in operation.

1 Corinthians 14:22 gives us this insight about the use of tongues in the congregation, "Wherefore tongues are for a sign, not to them that believe, but to them that believe not..."

Tongues are to serve as sign to unbelievers. But, in order to serve in this capacity, they must be understood. Therefore, interpretation is a requirement if the message is not being spoken in their native tongue.

Paul gives us this insight in **1 Corinthians 14:23**,
"If therefore the whole church be come together into one place, and all speak with tongues, and there come in those that are unlearned, or unbelievers, will they not say that ye are mad?"

1 Corinthians 14:6 tells us this about tongues,
"Now, brethren, if I come unto you speaking with tongues, what shall I profit you, except I shall speak to you either by revelation, or by knowledge or by prophesying or by doctrine?"

Tongues are used to edify believers through messages of knowledge, prophecy, and instruction. This points to prophecy, the word of knowledge, and the word of wisdom often being imparted to individuals or believers through the gift of tongues. But, once again it must be interpreted. (See **Ephesians 1:17**.)

Paul makes this statement in **1 Corinthians 14:7-9**,
"And even things without life giving sound, whether pipe or harp, except they give a distinction in the sounds, how shall it be known what is piped or harped? For if the trumpet give an uncertain sound, who shall prepare himself to the battle? So likewise ye, except ye utter by the tongue words easy to be understood, how shall it be known what is spoken? for ye shall speak into the air."

Tongues are useless to others unless they are interpreted for the purpose of ministering to them. This once again reminds us that gifts are about what God wants to accomplish in others. Le's face it, our language becomes commonplace to us and it takes something out of the ordinary to get our attention. Another tongue accomplishes such a feat. It is the Lord's way of reaching out to people in a supernatural way to confirm it is from Him.

Paul made this statement in **1 Corinthians 14:26**,
"...Let all things be done unto edifying."

The Apostle Paul made this statement in **1 Corinthians 14:18-19**,
"I thank my God, I speak with tongues more than ye all: Yet in the church I had rather speak five words with my understanding, that by my voice I might teach others also, than ten thousand words in an unknown tongue."

The building up of the Body is the main reason for the gifts. We need to desire the gift that will minister and encourage the whole Body. Tongues without interpretation will build up the individual, but will confuse instead of encourage others in spiritual growth.

Paul ends with this instruction in **1 Corinthians 14:39**,
"Wherefore, brethren, covet to prophesy, and forbid not to speak with tongues."

Churches, who forbid the use of the gifts in the Body, tongues included, are being disobedient to the Word of God. They are stifling the Holy Spirit from ministering to God's people through the Body.

1 Thessalonians 5:19 says,
"Quench not the spirit."

We need to sense God's moving today as much as they did in the days of the early apostles. The idea God has changed His ways is not scriptural. God desires to show Himself to His Church, but it will be on His terms and not ours.

This is why we read these words in **1 Corinthians 1:19-20**,
"For it is written, I will destroy the wisdom of the wise, and will bring to nothing the understanding of the prudent. Where is the wise? where is the scribe? where is the disputer of this world? hath not God made foolish the wisdom of this world?"

The gifts especially that of tongues, seem foolish to much of the Church. Lack of understanding closes Christians' minds to scriptural instruction. Thus, they reject the gifts, especially tongues, by relying on their own understanding rather than the clear Word of God and the work, character, and moving of the Holy Ghost.

Personal Notes: ____

____

Gift of Interpretation

1 Corinthians 12:10 states,
"...to another the interpretation of tongues."

The gifts of tongues and interpretation are supernatural utterance. These gifts do not come from man's intellectual understanding. Both come from the Holy Spirit who gives the unknown tongue and the understanding of it. Interpretation is not the same as translation. The individual who is interpreting tongues has no understanding of the language. He or she is simply repeating what the Holy Spirit is revealing to him or her. Scripture once again gives us decisive instructions on this subject.

1 Corinthians 14:10-11 says,
"There are, it may be, so many kinds of voices in the world, and none of them is without signification. Therefore if I know not the meaning of the voice, I shall be unto him that speaketh a barbarian, and he that speaketh shall be a barbarian unto me."

1 Corinthians 14:27 tells us,
"If any man speak in an unknown tongue, let it be by two, or at the most by three, and that by course; and let one interpret."

1 Corinthians 14:8 states,
"For if the trumpet give an uncertain sound, who shall prepare himself to the battle?

The gift of tongues must be followed up by interpretation. If there is no interpretation the tongues are out of order. Tongues, which are out of order, usually come from an individual who is operating in the flesh. People do make mistakes in distinguishing the difference between the prompting of the Holy Spirit and their own carnal influences. People who step outside of scriptural boundaries must be taken aside and gently instructed. The Body as a whole should be scripturally instructed in this area as well. Any deviance from the rules set up in the Bible is to be tested and put back within biblical boundaries. This is vital if Christians are to avoid abusing the gifts of the Holy Spirit.

Personal Notes: ____

____

The Gift of Prophesy

1 Corinthians 12:10 says,
"...to another prophecy;..."

Prophecy means to foretell or forthtell. It implies one is speaking on behalf of someone else. The gift of prophecy denotes someone is speaking forth the things of God in compliance with the Word of God. Once again, this revelation of God's truth is supernatural and is considered the greatest of the three inspirational gifts. It is used in the capacity of warning, rebuking, encouraging, and instructing the Church. This gift is strictly for the edification of the Body.

The Apostle Paul made this statement in **1 Corinthians 14:3-5**,
But he that prophesieth speaketh unto men to edification, and exhortation, and comfort. He that speaketh in an unknown tongue edifieth himself; but he that prophesieth edifieth the church. I would that ye all spake with tongues, but rather that ye prophesied: for greater is he that prophesieth than he that speaketh with tongues,..."

The gift of prophecy is different than the office of a prophet. An individual who is a prophet in position cannot be separated from his office. The gift of prophecy is given to an individual as the Holy Spirit desires. We need to be seeking after the gift of prophecy, but not after the office of a prophet. The office of the prophet is subject to different scriptures. A prophet is an individual who often foretells. He or she must line up to such instructions as found in **Deuteronomy 18:20-22**.

Deuteronomy 18:20-22 states,
"But the prophet, which shall presume to speak a word in my name, which I have not commanded him to speak, or that shall speak in the name of other gods, even that prophet shall die. And if thou say in thine heart, how shall we know the word which the LORD hath not spoken? When a prophet speaketh in the name of the LORD, if the thing follow not, nor come to pass, that is the thing which the LORD hath not spoken, but the prophet hath spoken it presumptuously: thou shalt not be afraid of him."

Everything a prophet foretells must come true or he or she is not a true prophet of God. The gift of prophecy has different scriptural boundaries. Forthtelling implies the speaker is inspired by the Holy Spirit, but will be using scriptural instruction. John the Baptist was a prophet who warned and contended with people, and prepared the people for Jesus.

1 Corinthians 14:29-32 gives us this instruction,
"Let the prophet speak two or three, and let the other judge. If any thing be revealed to another that sitteth by, let the first hold his peace. For ye may all prophesy one by one that all may learn, and all may be comforted. And the spirits of the prophets are subject to the prophets."

Once again there should be no more than three messages of prophecy. More than three indicates influences of the flesh or of familiar spirits. Familiar spirits counterfeit the Holy Spirit in this area. Each message must line up with the Word of God; therefore, it must be tested by those who have been used in the same capacity. There has been a lot of abuse of this gift. Many people are running around with a prophecy for every occasion. These people usually prove to be full of pride and rarely correct. They exalt themselves as prophets of the Church, totally ignorant of the strict stipulations governing both the office and gift. It is an awesome responsibility to be entrusted with any of these gifts. Use of them must be done within scriptural instructions, and must be tested. Any abuse or misrepresentation of these gifts must be dealt with quickly by those who are in leadership position.

1 Thessalonians 5:20 gives us this instruction,
"Despise not prophesying."

Prophesies from God are for our benefit. We need to test if they are of God, and if so, we must submit to them and allow them to instruct and guide us.

We are reminded of Paul's words in **1 Corinthians 12:29-31**,
"Are all apostles? are all prophets? are all teachers? are all workers of miracles? Have all the gifts of healing? do all speak with tongues? do all interpret? But covet earnestly the best gifts: and yet shew I unto you a more excellent way."

Most people want to determine how God should use them. Each believer needs to submit to the move of the Holy Spirit for the edification of the whole Body. In order to see perfect results, Christians must take the things of God out of the fleshly realm. Once they do this, they can accept the greatest of gifts. These are the gifts that do the deepest work within. They are the ones that cannot be measured by the naked eye, but will result in God's greatness being manifested in its fullness by building up the Church of Jesus Christ.

Personal Notes: ____

____

Chapter 37

PUTTING GIFTS IN PERSPECTIVE

The Apostle Paul made this statement in **1 Corinthians 12:31**,
"..and yet shew I unto you a more excellent way."

The only boundary to ensure the correct use and attitude towards the operation of the gifts in the Church is love. The Apostle Paul clearly makes this point by showing how each classification of gifts is useless without the motivation of love.

Paul made this statement in reference to the gift of tongues in **1 Corinthians 13:1**,
"Though I speak with the tongues of men and of angels, and have not charity, I am become as sounding brass, or a tinkling cymbal."

1 Corinthians 13:2 puts the gifts of inspiration, revelation, and power into this perspective:
"And though I have the gift of prophecy, and understand all mysteries, and all knowledge; and though I have all faith, so that I could remove mountains, and have not charity, I am nothing."

Interestingly, the Apostle Paul is referring to knowledge along with the main gifts of prophecy, wisdom, and faith. He is saying he could have all of these gifts, but they would mean nothing if he had no love. Again, we see the emphasis on having the right motivation instead of outward manifestations.

The Apostle Paul tells us this about love in **Romans 12:9**,
"Let love be without dissimulation."

God's pure love will inspire the needed unity in the Body, enabling it to function properly.

Ephesians 4:3 says,
"Endeavouring to keep the unity of the Spirit in the bond of peace."

I must stress there cannot be unity without agreement in spirit and in truth. If there is a disagreement in either area, we must separate ourselves **(John 4:24; 2 Corinthians 6:14-18)**. Divisions can also be a product of sin. Sin must be overcome if unity is to be present.

Jesus made this prayer request in **John 17:22-23**,
"And the glory which thou gavest me I have given them; that they may be one, even as we are one: I in them, and thou in me, that they may be made perfect in one; and that the world may know that thou hast sent me, and has loved them, as thou hast love me.

Personal Notes: ____

____

The Freedom of the Spirit

2 Corinthians 3:17 says,
"Now the Lord is that Spirit: and where the Spirit of the Lord is, there is liberty."

There is liberty where the Holy Spirit has free reign. Keep in mind, the Holy Spirit is a gentleman. We have already scripturally shown the sensitivity of the Holy Spirit. He can be easily grieved by that which is profane.

Ephesians 4:30 gives this instruction,
"And grieve not the Holy Spirit of God, whereby ye are sealed unto the day of redemption."

Isaiah 63:10 tells us we can vex the Holy Spirit,
But they rebelled, and vexed his Holy Spirit: therefore he was turned to be their enemy, and he fought against them."

The Holy Ghost can be insulted.

Hebrews 10:29 states,
"Of how much sorer punishment, suppose ye, shall he be though worthy, who hath trodden under foot the Son of God, and hath counted the blood of the covenant, wherewith he was sanctified, an unholy thing, and hath done despite unto the Spirit of grace?"

The Spirit of God can be resisted.

Acts 7:51 says,
"Ye stiffnecked and uncircumcised in heart and ears, ye do always resist the Holy Ghost: as your fathers did, so do ye."

Man can blaspheme the Holy Spirit. We are told this is the only unforgivable sin. The reason is because the Holy Spirit is the one who convicts of sin, reproves of righteousness, and of judgment to bring about salvation **(John 16:7-11)**. He is, in essence, the last defense against judgment and wrath upon disobedience.

Mark 3:29 tells us,
"But he that shall blaspheme against the Holy Ghost hath never forgiveness, but is in danger of eternal damnation!"

Blaspheme means to show irreverence towards something regarded as sacred. It is giving credit to the wrong source. In other words, accusing the Holy Spirit of being behind the profane and crediting Satan with being behind that which is holy. This is why we have to be careful to discern the spirit behind a matter to make sure we do not accredit the Holy Spirit with something that is unholy, or declaring His work is of the devil.

1 Corinthians 2:12-14 gives us this insight into the function of the Spirit,
"Now we have received, not the spirit of the world, but the spirit which is of God; that we might know the things that are freely given to us of God. Which things also we speak, not in the words which man's wisdom teacheth, but which the Holy Ghost teacheth; comparing spiritual things with spiritual. But the natural man receiveth not the things of the Spirit of

God: for they are foolishness unto him: neither can he know them, because they are spiritually discerned."

A man who lives by fleshly appetites cannot receive the things of God. Therefore, the fullness of God will elude him. One of the problems Christians must be aware of is the tendency to focus on the gifts, rather than the Giver of the gifts. Some Christians strive hard to receive the things of God without first seeking God and His truths. This will cause abuse, insensitivity, and an incorrect perspective of God's gifts and promises. This insensitivity will stifle or quench the Holy Spirit from moving in lives.

We read this instruction in **Matthew 6:33**,
"But seek ye first the kingdom of God, and his righteousness; and all these things shall be added unto you."

We need to seek after God first, then all else will fall into place. It is when God's people operate improperly that the Spirit can be easily quenched, and His work resisted.

This is why we read this prayer request from King David in **Psalm 51:11**,
"Cast me not away from thy presence; and take not thy holy spirit from me."

There is freedom where the Spirit's presence is evident. Therefore, we must major in learning to be sensitive to Him and minor in emphasizing His gifts. By focusing on the Person of the Holy Spirit, we can be assured of having His work manifest itself in a powerful way in our lives.

Personal Notes: ____

____

Inherent Gifts

Romans 12:6-8 says,
"Having then gifts differing according to the grace that is given to us, whether prophecy, let us prophesy according to the proportion of faith; Or ministry, let us wait on our ministering: for he that teacheth, on teaching; Or he that exhorteth, on exhortation: he that giveth, let him do it with simplicity; he that ruleth, with diligence; he that sheweth mercy, with cheerfulness."

Christians are given inherent gifts that are part of their makeup. These gifts grow as they are properly exercised. They can be used in both the secular world and in the edification of the Church.

Colossian 3:23-24 gives us this instruction,
"And whatsoever ye do, do it heartily, as to the Lord, and not unto men; Knowing that of the Lord ye shall receive the reward of the inheritance: for ye serve the Lord Christ."

As servants of Christ, we owe nothing. Everything we have belongs to Him and must bring Him honor. In **Matthew 25:14-30** we read the parable about the talents. The Lord gave talents to three of His servants. Two of the servants invested their talents. The third one buried his talent. When the Lord came back, he settled the accounts with them. The one who buried the talent lost it all, while the other two inherited more.

We read this account of the irresponsible servant in **Matthew 25:26-30**:
"His lord answered and said unto him, Thou wicked and slothful servant, thou knewest that I reap where I sowed not, and gather where I have not strawed: Thou oughtest therefore to have put my money to the exchangers, and then at my coming I should have received mine own with usury. Take therefore the talent from him, and give it unto him which hath ten talents. For unto every one that hath shall be given, and he shall have abundance: but from him that hath not shall be taken away even that which he hath. And cast ye the unprofitable servant into outer darkness: there shall be weeping and gnashing of teeth."

Faithfulness is the test for all of God's servants. This virtue allows God to bless those who obey even in small, insignificant ways. Faithfulness can result in weariness if one does not see any results right away, but each faithful servant has this promise in **Galatians 6:9**.

Galatians 6:9 states,
"And let us not be weary in well doing: for in due season we shall reap, if we faint not."

1 Peter 5:6 gives us this instruction,
"Humble yourselves therefore under the mighty hand of God, that he may exalt you in due time."

Personal Notes: ____

____

Positions

In **1 Corinthians 12:28** we read,
"And God hath set some in the church, first apostles, secondarily prophets, thirdly teachers, after that miracles, then gifts of healings, helps, governments, diversities of tongues."

Supplement:
Volume 1
Book 5:
Study:
Unmasking the Cult Mentality
Section 4
True Leadership

I have already alluded that there is a difference between positions in the Church and the gifts of the Holy Spirit. People designated and prepared by God will fill the positions in the Church. These offices carry strict scriptural responsibilities. The difference between positions and gifts is clear. Individuals who are in these positions in the Church have the responsibility of *building* a Church, while the gifts are used to build *up* the Body. For instance, apostles are sent out to start churches. Prophets are sent forth to scripturally line up churches to the Cornerstone, Jesus Christ. Teachers are necessary to establish the Church firmly on the foundation of Jesus Christ.

Ephesians 4:11 adds two more positions to the list in **1 Corinthians 12**,
"And he gave some, apostles; and some, prophets; and some, evangelists; and some, pastors and teachers."

Evangelists are sent in to stir up and awaken the Church. This stirring up is for the purpose of bringing revival to the Body by renewing its vision and calling. True revival will produce fruit, a heart of servitude, and a vision for the lost. Pastors are shepherds or overseers of God's people. They must love Jesus' sheep in the same way He does, sacrificially and in servitude. They must lead by example, and not as a harsh lord or dictator.

Ephesians 4:12-13 tells us the purpose of these positions in the Church,
"For the perfecting of the saints, for the work of the ministry, for the edifying of the body of Christ: Till we all come in the unity of the faith, and of the knowledge of the Son of God, unto a perfect man, unto the measure of the stature of the fulness of Christ."

The goal of these positions is to bring the followers of God to maturity, enabling them to serve their God. In America we see a lot of emphasis put on these positions. People are running around bragging about being an apostle or prophet. True apostles and prophets are not braggarts. Instead, they are recognized because they are obedient doers of the Word of God. Their only goal is to see the Church reach its maturity in Christ.

Personal Notes: ____

____

In Conclusion

Much more could have been said about the gifts. This is a simple overview. It is not intended to put the Holy Spirit or His gifts in a small compartment for each individual to analyze. Christians need to realize the gifts of the Holy Spirit can overlap. This can cause difficulty in distinguishing between them. The main focus Christians must maintain is on the Giver of these gifts.

Keep in mind to always strive to be obedient to **1 Corinthians 12:31**,
"But covet earnestly the best gifts:.."

Right now, you need to consider your availability to the Holy Spirit. Are you willing to be used in the capacity of establishing or building up the Body of believers? Submit your life to God. Open yourself up to the gifts of the Holy Spirit. Put all of your talents on the altar. Stand back and watch as He brings you forth as a sanctified vessel, ready for use in ministering to the Body of believers.

Personal Notes: ____

____

____

Section V

SPIRITUAL WARFARE

Chapter 38

BECOMING SOLDIERS

Supplement:
Volume 6
Book 5:
The Victorious Journey

2 Timothy 2:3 says,
"Thou therefore endure hardness, as a good soldier of Jesus Christ."

Christians are involved in different battles. Therefore, they are called to a life of military duty.

Romans 7:23 gives us insight into one of our battles,
"But I see another law in my members, warring against the law of my mind, and bringing me into captivity to the law of sin which is in my members."

We have an on-going battle with self and sin. We must overcome both to ensure victory.

Ephesians 6:12 tells us about the enemy who opposes us,
"For we wrestle not against flesh and blood, but against principalities, against powers, against the rulers of the darkness of this world, against spiritual wickedness in high places."

1 Timothy 6:12 gives us this information as to the type of battlefield these battles will be fought on,
"Fight the good fight of faith, lay hold on eternal life, whereunto thou art also called, and hast professed a good profession before many witnesses."

The battlefield concerns our faith and the faith of others. In other words, the enemy desires to undermine our faith in God; therefore, tripping us up in our walk with Him.

Personal Notes: ____

____

Boot Camp

Supplement:
(For Review)
Volume 3
Book 1: *Godly Discipline*
Chapters: 4-6

Every soldier's training begins with boot camp. Boot camp is for the purpose of changing the way an individual thinks, acts, and dresses.

2 Timothy 2:4 states,
"No man that warreth entangleth himself with the affairs of this life; that he may please him who hath chosen him to be a soldier."

First of all we read that a soldier's life is contrary to his former life. Part of the process a soldier goes through is obtaining his uniform. This uniform identifies him to his type of duty and rank.

Ephesians 4:22-24 tells us,
"That ye put off concerning the former conversation the old man, which is corrupt according to the deceitful lusts; And be renewed in the spirit of your mind; And that ye put on the new man, which after God is created in righteousness and true holiness."

A true soldier will walk contrary to his civilian life. He no longer belongs to himself. His attitudes and thoughts must line up to his military duty.

2 Corinthians 10:5 states,
"...and bringing into captivity every thought to the obedience of Christ."

A soldier must become subject to his commander's orders. This is necessary if his life will serve as an example of the kingdom he represents. In boot camp, soldiers learn how to march together according to the orders of their leaders.

Romans 8:4 tells us who our leader is,
"...who walk not after the flesh, but after the Spirit."

The one who guides us through our military life is the Holy Spirit.

Ephesians 4:1 tells us what kind of (walk or) life we must be living,
"I therefore, the prisoner of the Lord, beseech you that ye walk worthy of the vocation wherewith ye are called."

Ephesians 5:15-17 gives us these instructions,
"See then that ye walk circumspectly, not as fools, but as wise, Redeeming the time, because the days are evil. Wherefore be ye not unwise, but understanding what the will of the Lord is."

1 John 2:6 summarizes the Christian soldier's life in this way,
"He that saith he abideth in him ought himself also so to walk, even as he walked."

A Christian soldier must separate himself from his former life. He must walk the walk of a soldier in compliance with his commander's orders and will.

2 John 6 adds this insight,
"And this is love, that we walk after his commandments. This is the commandment, That, as ye have heard from the beginning, ye should walk in it."

Walking this upright life shows our love for our commander. In the military there is a term used when soldiers are not wearing their uniform properly. They are considered as being "out of uniform." This occurs when military uniform is mixed with civilian clothes or different uniforms are interchanged incorrectly. Being out of uniform shows a disregard for one's position and for the country he or she represents. This act brings retribution. Christians are "out of uniform" when they walk contrary to their holy calling.

Titus 1:16 talks about a hypocritical walk,
"They profess that they know God; but in works they deny him, being abominable, and disobedient, and unto every good work reprobate."

2 Timothy 2:4 states,
"No man that warreth entangleth himself with the affairs of this life;..."

Personal Notes: ____

____

The Armor of God

Soldiers have the responsibility of protecting their country. This is an awesome obligation. Therefore, boot camp is used as the means to train and equip soldiers to go into battle. Soldiers are trained how to use their equipment and what to do in battle. The Christian soldier is no different. Like the secular military, the Christian's Commander has issued the necessary armor to fight a good fight.

Ephesians 6:13 gives us this instruction,
"Wherefore take unto you the whole armor of God, that ye may be able to withstand in the evil day, and having done all, to stand."

We can find a description of this armor in **Ephesians 6:14-17**.

Ephesians 6:14 gives us the description of the first article in the armor,
"Stand therefore, having your loins girt about with truth,..."

A belt in the military is used to hold the uniform firmly in place. Truth is necessary for the whole armor to fit correctly on the soldier.

2 Corinthians 13:7-8 says this about the truth,
"Now I pray to God that ye do no evil; not that we should appear approved, but that ye should do that which is honest, though we be as reprobates. For we can do nothing against the truth, but for the truth."

Armor that does not fit firmly leaves room for defeat. As soldiers, we must line up to Scriptural truth so any gap in our spiritual life is closed against Satan's attack.

The Christian's truth is summarized by **John 14:6**,
"Jesus saith unto him, I am the way, the truth, and the life:..."

Jesus is the truth. Our life should portray His characteristics. There is a standing rule in the secular military that can serve as a valuable example to us. During inspection, the officer had to be able to see his reflection in the belt buckle of the soldier. The inspection of our spiritual lives holds a similar rule. A Christian's test rests in whether or not others can see the reflection of Jesus Christ in his or her life.

Personal Notes: ____

____

Ephesians 6:14 tells us what the next article of our armor is,
"...and having on the breastplate of righteousness."

The breastplate protects the heart. The heart of Christianity is the relationship we have with our Commander. As long as we live obedient before Him, we can be assured of right standing with God and protection from our enemy. We read these promises surrounding the righteous.

Proverbs 2:7 gives us this insight,
"He layeth up sound wisdom for the righteous: he is a buckler to them that walk uprightly.

Psalm 34:15 says,
"The eyes of the LORD are upon the righteous, and his ears are open unto their cry."

Psalm 92:12 states,
"The righteous shall flourish like the palm tree:..."

Matthew 13:43 tells us,
"Then shall the righteous shine forth as the sun in the kingdom of their Father..."

Righteous people have clout with God. They will stand no matter what comes at them in times of battle.

Personal Notes: ____

____

Ephesians 6:15 tells us what our next piece of armor is,
"And your feet shod with the preparation of the gospel of peace."

Soldiers must have correct shoes. They are on call 24 hours a day to carry out any marching orders. Christians already have their marching orders.

Mark 16:15 gives us the first part of our orders,
"And he (Jesus) said unto them, Go ye into all the world, and preach the gospel to every creature." (Parenthesis added.)

Matthew 28:19-20 gives us the final part of our instruction,
"Go ye therefore, and teach all nations, baptizing them in the name of the Father, and of the Son, and of the Holy Ghost. Teaching them to observe all things, whatsoever I have commanded you: and, lo, I am with you always, even unto the end of the world."

Christian soldiers must be willing to preach the gospel to every creature. They must then, be available to disciple all nations to follow Christ into a life of holiness and service. The Gospel of Christ and His commandments are what sets people free and brings peace to the downtrodden.

Isaiah 52:7 gives us this beautiful promise in relationship to the Christian's marching orders:
"How beautiful upon the mountains are the feet of him that bringeth good tidings, that publisheth peace; that bringeth good tidings of good, that publisheth salvation; that saith unto Zion, Thy God reigneth!"

Personal Notes: ____

____

Ephesians 6:16 tells us,
"Above all, taking the shield of faith, wherewith ye shall be able to quench all the fiery darts of the wicked."

According to information on the days of Jesus, there were certain shields that were large enough for a man to hide behind. They not only served as protection, but they also enabled him to advance forward.

1 John 5:4-5 tells us,
"For whatsoever is born of God overcometh the world: and this is the victory that overcometh the world, even our faith. Who is he that overcometh the world, but he that believeth that Jesus is the Son of God?"

Faith in our great God enables us to overcome our enemies, reclaim territory, and move forward in victory.

Jude 20 gives us this instruction,
"But ye, beloved, building up yourselves on your most holy faith, praying in the Holy Ghost."

Personal Notes: ____

____

Ephesians 6:17 tells us what the next article of our armor is,
"And take the helmet of salvation, and the sword of the Spirit, which is the word of God."

A helmet protects the head. All functions of our body begin and are maintained by our brain. Our spiritual life operates in the same manner. It begins and ends with salvation. The efficiency of our spiritual life is dependent on the work of salvation taking place in our lives on a daily basis.

1 Thessalonians 5:8-9 gives us this insight,
"But let us, who are of the day, be sober, putting on the breastplate of faith and love, and for an helmet, the hope of salvation. For God hath not appointed us to wrath, but to obtain salvation by our Lord Jesus Christ."

Matthew 10:22 gives us, the Christian soldier, this promise,
"And ye shall be hated of all men for my name's sake, but he that endureth to the end shall be saved."

We know that the belt, breastplate, the shield, and the helmet of our armor protect us in battle, while the shoes advance us forward but the Word of God is our only defensive weapon. It will put Satan on the run and keep us standing in every attack. It is a double-edge sword that will destroy any advancement of the enemy, and we have the assurance that in the end, it will be the only weapon left standing in victory for it is eternal (**Hebrews 4:12; 1 Peter 1:25**).

This concludes our spiritual armor. There is a simple way of summarizing the essence of this armor. Here is a graphic illustration of our spiritual protection:

Jesus is our truth **(John 14:6)**. He is also our righteousness **(1 Corinthians 1:30)**. Jesus' death burial, and resurrection makes up the gospel of peace **(1 Corinthians 15:1-4, Colossians 1:19-27)**. Jesus is the author and finisher of our faith **(Hebrews 12:2)**. He is also the author of our salvation and the Living and Eternal Word **(John 1:1-3; Hebrews 5:9)**.

This picture shows us that Christ reigning in our life serves as our spiritual armor.

In **John 16:33**, we read this promise from Jesus,
"These things I have spoken unto you, that in me ye might have peace. In the world ye shall have tribulation: but be of good cheer; I have overcome the world."

Are you now protected by the spiritual armor provided?

Personal Notes: ____

____

Chapter 39

THE ENEMY

Supplements:
(For the next three chapters)
Book & Workbook
BATTLE FOR THE SOUL

In boot camp, soldiers are taught how to recognize their enemies. This training is necessary if a soldier is going to effectively fight those who oppose the kingdom he is representing.

Ephesians 6:12 tells us what we are not fighting against,
"For we wrestle not against flesh and blood, but against principalities, against powers, against the rulers of the darkness of this world, against spiritual wickedness in high places."

Like our armor; our enemy is spiritual and unseen. We know him as Satan. We have already discussed Satan in previous chapters. Here is a list of his many names:

Lucifer-Morning Star	**(Isaiah 14:12)**
The Devil	**(Matthew 4:1)**
Liar-murderer	**(John 8:44)**
Prince of this world	**(John 14:30)**
God of this world	**(2 Corinthians 4:4)**
Abaddon (destroyer)	**(Revelations 9:11)**
Belial (evil-wicked)	**(2 Corinthians 6:15)**
Accuser	**(Revelation 12:10)**
Beelzebub (lord of dung)	**(Matthew 12:24)**
Evil (wicked) one	**(1 John 2:13)**
Tempter	**(Matthew 4:3)**
Serpent/Dragon	**(Revelation 20:2)**
Angel of light	**(2 Corinthians 11:14)**

Satan has many disguises, but few tactics.

The Apostle Paul made this statement in **2 Corinthians 2:11**,
"Lest Satan should get an advantage of us: for we are not ignorant of his devices."

Isaiah 14:12-15 gives us this introduction to Satan,
"How art thou fallen from heaven, O Lucifer, son of the morning! how art thou cut down to the ground, which didst weaken the nations! For thou hast said in thine heart, I will ascend into heaven, I will exalt my throne above the stars of God: I will sit also upon the mount of the congregation in the sides of the north: I will ascend above the heights of the clouds; I will be like the most High. Yet thou shalt be brought down to hell, to the sides of the pit."

Ezekiel 28:17 tells us this about Satan,
"Thine heart was lifted up because of thy beauty, thou hast corrupted thy wisdom by reason of thy brightness: I will cast thee to the ground, I will lay thee before kings, that they may behold thee."

The world has presented Satan as a grotesque creature. This is not true. He was the most beautiful angel before he rebelled. He can present himself as a very beautiful creature as he did in the Garden of Eden. Some Christians believe Satan is in hell. This is also untrue. He was cast down to earth, and we can find him presenting himself in heaven with the other angels in Job **(Job 1:6; 2:1)**. When Adam chose to submit to Satan in the Garden of Eden, Satan gained dominion over the earth, earning him the title of god of this world. Man now lives in Satan's domain.

Ephesians 2:2 says,
"Wherein in times past ye walked according to the course of this world, according to the prince of the power of the air, the spirit that now worketh in the children of disobedience."

Satan is a ruler of a kingdom. It is known as the kingdom of darkness. This kingdom operates in and through this world.

According to **Matthew 12:24 & 29** there are ranks within the kingdom,
"But when the Pharisees head it, they said, This fellow doth not cast out devils, but by Beelzebub the prince of the devils.... Or else how can one enter into a strong man's house, and spoil his goods, except he first bind the strong man? and then he will spoil his house."

Satan is a ruler over demons and spirits. These two words are interchangeable, but due to the ranks of demons, they hold certain positions and responsibilities. For example, demons are associated with entities who inspire idolatry and seek out men or animals to reside in. A spirit is associated to a ghost. Spirits often push and prod people. These entities are used to substitute, defile, or pervert God's work in a person's life or in the Church. There are many references to the activities of these beings. Here are some names they have been referred by:

Unclean or evil spirits	**(Matthew 10:1)**
Familiar spirits-mediums	**(Leviticus 19:31)**
Spirit of divination	**(Acts 16:16)**
Spirit of dumbness	**(Mark 9:17)**
Spirit of fear	**(2 Timothy 1:7)**
Spirit of infirmity	**(Luke 13:10-11)**
Spirit of slumber (spiritual slumber)	**(Romans 11:8)**
Lying spirits	**(1 Kings 22:22)**

Scripturally, one can see how these entities serve as the very expression of their leader, Satan.

Personal Notes: ______________________________

____

The Kingdom of Darkness

Jesus made this statement in **John 8:44**,
"...for he is a liar, and the father of it."

Satan is the arch deceiver; therefore his greatest tool is deception. Scripturally, we can see how this deception works.

In **1 Kings 22:22** we read this account,
"...I will go forth, and I will be a lying spirit in the mouth of all his prophets,...."

In **1 Timothy 4:1** we are given this insight about Satan's methods:
"Now the Spirit speaketh expressly, that in the latter times some shall depart from the faith, giving heed to seducing spirits, and doctrines of devils."

Matthew 4:5-7 gives us this account,
"Then the devil taketh him up into the holy city, and setteth him on a pinnacle of the temple, And saith unto him. If thou be the Son of God, cast thyself down: for it is written, He shall give his angels charge concerning thee: and in their hands they shall bear thee up, lest at any time thou dash thy foot against a stone. Jesus said unto him, It is written again, Thou shalt not temp the Lord thy God."

2 Corinthians 11:14 gives us this information about Satan,
"And no marvel; for Satan himself is transformed into an angel of light."

Supplement: Volume 1, Book 5:
Study: *Unmasking the Cult Mentality*
Section 5: *Confronting the Cult Mentality*

Satan disguises himself in such a way that even the elect could be deceived if it were possible.

John warned Christians about a religious spirit referred to as the anti-Christ spirit in **1 John 4:3**,
"And every spirit that confesseth not that Jesus Christ is come in the flesh is God; and this is that spirit of antichrist, whereof ye have heard that it should and even now already is it in the world."

The anti-Christ spirit serves as a substitute for Christ. This spirit is behind the following:

- All Cults
- New Age Movement-New World Order
- Hinduism-Reincarnation/Yoga/TM/Karma
- Visualization-Positive Imaging
- Psychology
- Spirit Guides
- Extraterrestrial intelligence (Spirits)
- Secret Orders
- Mind Science Techniques (Positive & Negative)
- Humanism (includes evolution)
- Freemasonry

The goal behind the antichrist spirit is to unite the religions, governments, and economic systems into one governed by one individual. This individual will be known as the antichrist. The antichrist spirit can be distinguished by its denial that there is only one true God and one way to heaven. It teaches that man can be a god. This is the original lie of Satan to Eve in the Garden of Eden **(Genesis 3:5)**. Satan disguises himself through miracles.

2 Thessalonians 2:9-10 gives us this information,
"Even him, whose coming is after the working of Satan with all power and signs and lying wonders, And with all deceivableness of unrighteousness in them that perish; because they received not the love of the truth, that they might be saved."

Satan is a capable foe in deceiving people. Christians need to adopt sobriety towards God's Word in order to recognize the enemy. One way we can test Satan is by the fruits. If an individual senses the following, he or she can be assured it is from the enemy of God.

*	fear	*	confusion
*	depression	*	guilt-condemnation
*	hopelessness	*	lack of love

It is through these types of feelings Satan is able to put individuals in bondage. This spirit of bondage keeps a person from trusting God and seeking Him out for forgiveness and deliverance.

Romans 8:15 talks about this spirit,
"For ye have not received the spirit of bondage again to fear; but ye have received the Spirit of adoption whereby we cry, Abba, Father."

Another successful method Satan uses, is to push Christians into extremes. For instance, when a Christian displays complacency or religious fanaticism his or her testimony will be rendered ineffective. Attitudes about Satan range in the extremes. Either people do not recognize him as a real foe to be reckoned with, or they give him too much credit and recognition. Balance in either area will only come as Christians seek to understand their position in Christ and makes the Word of God their only authority. Extremes imply perversion. Perversion can include lust, which appeals to fleshly appetites and pride. The final result is evilness. This evilness is the expression of the spirit who operates in this world.

1 Corinthians 2:12 tells us,
"Now we have received, not the spirit of the world, but the spirit which is of God; that we might know the things that are freely given to us of God."

What spirit is motivating you? Check out the fruit from your life. Consider if you are operating in any extreme. If you find any influence of Satan you must recognize you have allowed him access.

1 Samuel 15:23 tells us what two open doors will give Satan entrance into our lives,
"For rebellion is as the sin of witchcraft, and stubbornness is as iniquity and idolatry."

Personal Notes: ____

____

Witchcraft

There are two sources of power in this world: God's and Satan's. Today many people want supernatural power. The tragedy is many are seeking or settling for the power of

Satan. There is a very fine line between God's power and Satan's. It can be hard to distinguish where some power is coming from; therefore, unsuspecting Christians have opened themselves up to Satan's power while in pursuit of God's power. It takes a great deal of integrity to resist, using, or tapping into Satan's power. Keep in mind rebellion and pride are the two openings, or doors, in our lives which give access to Satan. This is not a surprise, for these are the two characteristics that resulted in Satan being thrown out of heaven.

Satan's presence in a life will either create an oppression (bondage) or possession (control). Satan's power is often referred to as the occult or witchcraft.

In **Deuteronomy 18:10-12**, we are given a list of the avenues Satan uses to administer his power through,
"There shall not be found among you any one that maketh his son or his daughter to pass through the fire, or that useth divination, or an observer of times, or an enchanter, or a witch. Or a charmer, or a consulter with familiar spirits, or a wizard, or a necromancer. For all that do these things are an abomination unto the LORD: and because of these abominations the LORD thy God doth drive them out from before thee."

Leviticus 20:27 tells us what the required judgment was for those who practiced witchcraft in the Old Testament,
"A man also or woman that hath a familiar spirit, or that is a wizard, shall surely be put to death: they shall stone them with stones: their blood shall be upon them."

Witchcraft is on the rise. People are seeking answers thought supernatural means other than God. Such practices are leading them to hell. Here is a list of practices, which are related to modern day witchcraft:

*Superstition
*Tarot cards
*Astrology
*Praying to the dead
*Magic
*Fortune telling
*Automatic writing
*Palm reading
*Séances
*Crystals/crystals balls

Any practice which alters the mind serves as an open door for possession. Those things which alter the mind include the following:

*Drugs & alcohol
*Yoga
*Trances
*Transcendental meditation
*Hypnosis
*Music

Revelation 9:21 states,
"Neither repented they of their murders, nor of their sorceries, nor of their fornication, nor of their thefts."

Study of this scripture reveals that the word "sorcery" **in Revelation 9:21** refers to drugs. Drugs have been one of Satan's major avenues to usher in paganism and the practices of witchcraft.

Revelation 21:8 tells us the final consequences of those who do not repent of witchcraft, "But the fearful, and unbelieving, and the abominable, and murderers, and whoremongers, and sorcerers, and idolaters, and all liars, shall have their part in the lake which burneth with fire and brimstone: which is the second death."

If you are involved in any of these practices, you need to repent and renounce all association with them. Jesus is waiting for you. He desires to forgive you and set you free from their bondage.

Personal Notes: ____

____

Deliverance?

1 John 4:4 says,
"Ye are of God, little children, and have overcome them: because greater is he that is in you, than he that is in the world."

Supplement: Volume 6, Book 3: *Experiencing The Christian Life*

The Spirit in Christians is greater than the one in the world. We do have deliverance and victory available to us in Jesus Christ. Deliverance is another subject one must pray about and study Scriptures to gain a balanced perspective. Jesus is our greatest example. Examine His attitudes and dealings with the kingdom of darkness. First of all, Jesus was not a demon-chaser. Many who needed deliverance were brought to Him or demons manifested in His presence.

We read these two accounts. **Matthew 12:22** says,
"Then was brought unto him one possessed with a devil, blind and dumb: and he healed him, insomuch that the blind and dumb both spake and saw."

Mark 1:23-24 says,
"And there was in their synagogue a man with an unclean spirit; and he cried out, Saying, Let us alone; what have we to do with thee, thou Jesus of Nazareth? art thou come to destroy us? I know thee who thou art, the Holy One of God."

Jesus did not cast out every demonic entity He encountered.

Mark 3:11-12 says,
"And the unclean spirits, when they saw him, fell down before him, and cried, saying, Thou art the Son of God. And he straitly charged them that they should not make him known."

Casting out demons is not our commission. For instance, Paul did not cast the spirit of divination out of the damsel until it had harassed him for many days **(Acts 16:16-18)**. As Christians, we must be willing and ready to take authority over the powers of darkness if the situation demands it. We must be sensitive to the Holy Spirit's leading in this area as to whether the person desires to be set free through Jesus Christ.

Matthew 12:43-45 gives us insight to the danger of deliverance,
"When the unclean spirit is gone out of a man, he walketh through dry places, seeking rest, and findeth none. Then he saith, I will return into my house from whence I came out; and when he is come, he findeth it empty, swept, and garnished. Then goeth he, and taketh with himself seven other spirits, more wicked than himself, and they enter in and dwell there: and the last state of that man is worse than the first..."

People must desire to repent and fill their lives up with the Holy Spirit to ensure real spiritual deliverance. Man can try to live right, but unless he fills up his life with God, he will end up being worse off. Another thing Christians must be aware of is seeing a spirit behind every illness and every sin of man. Many people have been turned off to God when they have been falsely accused of having demons. Illness is part of the curse man received in the Garden of Eden. God sometimes allow sickness in our lives to work a greater depth of spiritual maturity. The majority of man's sinful actions are brought on by his own rebellion and not by demonic influences. Although rebellion is a door for spiritual oppression, the individual must first close it in order to overcome any demonic influence. A good way to determine the source behind man's actions is through observation and sensitivity to the Spirit. If the individual fluctuates back and forth in his or her emotions and anger, you are most likely dealing with rebellion. If you feel yourself running into an unseen wall, it is most likely demonic oppression.

Christians do have authority over the power of darkness, but they must be careful how they exercise it. Believers must be Spirit led to avoid abuse and to ensure effectiveness.

Jesus put authority over Satan in this perspective in **Luke 10:19-20**,
"Behold, I give unto you power to tread on serpents and scorpions, and over all the power of the enemy: and nothing shall be any means hurt you. Notwithstanding in this rejoice not, that the spirits are subject unto you; but rather rejoice, because your names are written in heaven."

Personal Notes: ____

____

____

Chapter 40

SPIRITUAL WEAPONS

Like all soldiers, Christians have their weapons as well.

2 Corinthians 10:3-4 states,
"For though we walk in the flesh, we do not war after the flesh. (For the weapons of our warfare are not carnal, but mighty through God to the pulling down of strong holds)."

Our weapons are divine. They are capable of bringing down any stronghold. Part of the training done in boot camp involves the correct use of weapons. If a soldier does not know how to use his weapons, he can cause great harm to those who are his comrades. In boot camp, a soldier must be able to take his weapon apart and put it together. He must maintain it at all times. He is trained how to use it correctly.

Ephesians 6:17 identifies one of the Christian's weapons,
"And take the helmet of salvation, and the sword of the Spirit, which is the word of God."

As already mentioned, the Word of God is an effective weapon against Satan. We must understand how it works in order to use it. A Christian soldier must; therefore, study the Word.

2 Timothy 2:15 tells us why we must study the Word,
"...shew thyself approved unto God, a workman that needeth not to be ashamed."

Christians need to maintain their weapon through obedience to it.

John 15:7 states,
"If ye abide in me, and my words abide in you, ye shall ask what ye will, and it shall be done unto you."

By maintaining the weapon, it will not let you down during any battle. It will give you the necessary clout, liberty, and power to ensure victory.

2 Timothy 2:15 instructs Christians to learn to,
"...rightly (divide or handle) the word of truth." (Emphasis added.)

Christians who do not know how to handle the Word correctly are already defeated. They cannot fight back properly. Misuse of the weapon will also destroy the lives of others. For instance, other Christians who have used the Word of God in the wrong way have wounded believers.

The Word is a very powerful weapon and it is available. It not only protects the soldier, but it will put the enemy on the run. If you are not acquainted with this weapon, you need to make the commitment to learn it.

Jesus made this statement about this subject in **Matthew 4:4**,
"But he answered and said, It is written, Man shall not live by bread alone, but by every word that proceedeth out of the mouth of God."

Personal Notes: ____

____

The Name of Jesus

Jesus made this statement in **Matthew 18:18**,
"Verily I say unto you, whatsoever ye shall bind on earth shall be bound in heaven: and whatsoever ye shall loose on earth shall be loosed in heaven."

> Christians have authority to do God's bidding according to the will, word, work, and plan of God. Loosing in the previous Scripture means a matter is permitted, where binding implies that a matter is prohibited according to what God has set forth in His Word. This Scripture has been taken out of context when it comes to authority in relationship to Satan's kingdom, but all authority comes from God, and is realized within what is acceptable to Him.

Luke 10:17 reveals the weapon which gives us this authority,
"And the seventy returned again with joy, saying, Lord, even the devils are subject unto us through thy name."

> The name of Jesus is the weapon used in this type of battle. Name is associated with Jesus' character. It is because Jesus is who He is that there is authority and power in His name.

Jesus made these statements about His name in **John 14:13-14**,
"And whatsoever ye shall ask in my name, that will I do, that the Father may be glorified in the Son. If ye shall ask any thing in my name, I will do it."

Philippians 2:8-11 gives us this insight behind the power found in the name of Jesus,
"And being found in fashion as a man, he humbled himself, and became obedient unto death, even the death of the cross. Wherefore God also hath highly exalted him, and given him a name, which is above every name: That at the name of Jesus every knee should bow, of things in heaven, and things in earth, and things under the earth; And that every tongue should confess that Jesus Christ is Lord, to the glory of God the Father."

> It cost Jesus Christ his life to provide us with the power we have in His name. One problem is some people use the name of Jesus like a magic wand. It is not the name of Jesus that establishes our authority over Satan, but the relationship we have with the Person of Jesus Christ.

Acts 19:13-16 confirms this,
"Then certain of the vagabond Jews, exorcists, took upon them to call over them which had evil spirits the name of the Lord Jesus, saying, We adjure you by Jesus whom Paul preacheth. And there were seven sons of one Sceva, a Jew, and chief of the priests, which did so. And the evil spirit answered and said, Jesus I know, and Paul I know; but who are

ye? And the man in whom the evil spirit was leaped on them, and overcame them, and prevailed against them, so that they fled out of that house naked and wounded."

Using the name of Jesus without knowing Jesus is using His precious name in a flippant manner. Usage of the Lord's name without recognition of who He is, is using His name in vain.

This goes against the commandment of the Lord found in **Exodus 20:7**,
"Thou shalt not take the name of the LORD thy God in vain; for the LORD will not hold him guiltless that taketh his name in vain."

The name of Jesus should bring humility and respect to our spirits. It should create in us a sense of praise and worship. Therefore, use of His name must be done with sobriety and in recognition that He is God. It is because of Jesus' deity there is power in His name. In the name of Jesus, miracles of healing and deliverance occur.

Acts 4:10 gives us this account,
"Be it known unto you all, and to all the people of Israel, that by the name of Jesus Christ of Nazareth, whom ye crucified, whom God raised from the dead, even by him doth this man stand here before you whole."

Acts 16:18 says,
"...But Paul being grieved, turned and said to the spirit, I command thee in the name of Jesus Christ to come out of her. And he came out the same hour."

The greatest miracle, which occurs in the name of Jesus, is and always will be the salvation of man.

Act 4:12 states,
"Neither is their salvation in any other: for there is none other name under heaven given among men, whereby we must be saved."

Before you use the name of Jesus in an authoritative manner, make sure you are establishing a sound relationship with Him. Keep in mind the cost behind the power of Jesus' name. Strive to maintain a right attitude toward this most precious name of the Son of God.

Personal Notes: ____

____

The Blood of Jesus

Revelation 12:11 says,
"And they overcame him (Satan) by the blood of the Lamb, and by the word of their testimony; and they loved not their lives unto the death." (Parenthesis added.)

The blood of Jesus plays an important part in the salvation of man. We know from past lessons it is the means of both reconciliation between God and man, and purification of man's sins **(Colossians 1:20; 1 John 1:7)**. **Revelation 12:11** tells us the blood of Jesus is a weapon, which enables us to overcome Satan.

1 Corinthians 11:25 lays a foundation to its significance in the area of spiritual warfare, "After the same manner also he took the cup, when he had supped, saying, This cup is the New Testament in my blood: this do ye, as oft as ye drink it, in remembrance of me."

The blood of Jesus serves as the covenant between Him and those who love Him. Once again, we must remember that covenant means testament or agreement.

Hebrews 9:15-17 gives us insight into this new agreement,
"And for this cause he is the mediator of the new testament, that by means of death, for the redemption of the transgression that were under the first testament, they which are called might receive the promise of eternal inheritance. For where a testament is, there must also of necessity be the death of the testator. For a testament is of force after men are dead: otherwise it is of no strength at all while the testator liveth."

The covenant Christians enjoy involves an eternal inheritance. This inheritance gives us the right to partake of the benefits of this covenant.

John 1:12 tells us what our right is,
"But as many as received him, to them gave he power to become the sons of God, even to them that believe on his name."

We have a right to enter into an intimate relationship with God. This relationship allows us to enjoy God's promises, protection, and heavenly possessions. The other part of this covenant means we belong to God.

1 Corinthians 7:23-24 confirms this,
"Ye are bought with a price; be not ye the servants of men. Brethren, let every man, wherein he is called, therein abide with God."

By belonging to God, Satan has no rights or power over the Christian's life unless God gives him permission. We see this in the case of Job. God gave Satan permission to afflict Job, but Satan could not cross the boundaries ordained by God. (See **Job 1:6-12** and **2:1-7**.) Since Christians belong to God, they must love and obey Him to keep their part of this agreement. As long as they do their part, they can be assured of His protection, partake of His promises, and trust Him with their lives regardless of the circumstances.

Romans 8:28 gives us this promise,
"And we know that all things work together for good to them that love God, to them who are the called according to his purpose."

There is power in the blood of Jesus. But, like His name some people use His blood as if it is a magic formula for every ailment. The blood of Jesus must be sacred to the Christian. It serves as the lifeline to an eternal promise and inheritance. To the powers of darkness, it serves as a notification they have no power or right over the Christian, unless God so ordains.

Ephesians 2:13 tells us,
"But now in Christ Jesus ye who sometimes were far off are made nigh by the blood of Christ."

We come to a clear understanding of the power and importance of being able to draw near to God in **James 4:7-10**,
"Submit yourselves therefore to God. Resist the devil, and he will flee from you. Draw nigh to God, and he will draw nigh to you. Cleanse your hands, ye sinners; and purify your hearts, ye double minded. Be afflicted, and mourn, and weep: let your laughter be turned to mourning, and your joy to heaviness. Humble yourselves in the sight of the Lord, and he shall life you up."

Personal Notes: ____

____

Your Testimony

Revelation 12:11 gives us insight into another weapon,
"And they overcame him by the blood of the Lamb, and by the word of their testimony; and they loved not their lives unto the death."

> A very important weapon is a Christian's testimony of Jesus Christ. A testimony is an individual's belief and proclamation of who Jesus Christ is, and what He has done for him or her. The key to a powerful testimony rests in it growing. Growth takes place as one seeks to know Jesus in greater ways.

Paul made this desire known to the Ephesians in **Ephesians 1:17**,
"That the God of our Lord Jesus Christ, the Father of glory, may give unto you the spirit of wisdom and revelation in the knowledge of him."

Paul made his statement in **Philippians 3:8**,
"Yea doubtless, and I count all things but loss for the excellency of the knowledge of Christ Jesus my Lord: for whom I have suffered the loss of all things, and do count them but dung, that I may win Christ."

> Paul had a testimony of his precious Lord that sustained him through many tribulations. His testimony grew as he searched and succeeded to know his Lord better.

In the end he was able to make this powerful declaration in **2 Timothy 1:12**,
"For the which cause I also suffer these things: nevertheless I am not ashamed: for I know whom I have believed, and am persuaded that he is able to keep that which I have committed unto him against that day."

> Paul knew Jesus. He stood firmly on the foundation of his faith in the One he had grown to love and trust. He had an immovable assurance because Jesus had become his God, Lord, and friend. What kind of testimony do you have of Jesus? Is it growing or has it become stagnant? A growing testimony is not an option. It is a must if you are to overcome Satan and endure to the end.

Note the last part of **Revelation 12:11**,
"...and they loved not their lives unto the death."

This death points to the death to the dictates of self and the influences of the world. If you are dead at these points, you can actually choose to live unto God. Satan finds inroads into people's lives through these two avenues. Application of the cross to both gives one such great liberty to live unto and for God. (See **Galatians 2:10** and **6:14**.)

Personal Notes: ____

____

Prayer & Fasting

In **Mark 9:20-29** we read an incident about a demon-possessed boy. The disciples had previously tried to deliver the young boy from the demon without success. The father brought the boy to Jesus. Jesus delivered him.

We read this conversation between Jesus and his disciples in **Mark 9:28-29**,
"And when he was come into the house, his disciples asked him privately, Why could not we cast him out? And he said unto them, this kind can come forth by nothing, but by prayer and fasting."

Prayer is an important part of the Christian life. It is our means of communicating with God. This communication is for our benefit. It is during times of fellowship that we are prepared by God. He reveals His will to us and gives us direction, assurance, and comfort.

The Apostle Paul showed the importance of prayer by ending the description of the spiritual armor with this instruction in **Ephesians 6:18**,
"Praying always with all prayer and supplication in the Spirit, and watching thereunto with all perseverance and supplication for all saints."

I refer to prayer as the "big guns" of Christianity. There is nothing more confusing to the enemy than a Christian on his or her knees. In fact, the enemy tries to keep each of us from pressing into God through prayer.

James 5:16 tells us the one necessary ingredient for prayers to be effective,
"Confess your faults one to another, and pray one for another, that ye may be healed. The effectual fervent prayer of a righteous man availeth much."

Being upright before God will make us sensitive to His will. It will allow Him to answer our prayers because we are lined up with His nature and ways. (Refer to **1 John 5:14-15**).

Romans 12:12 gives us this instruction,
"...continuing instant in prayer."

Luke 18:1 confirms Paul's instruction about prayer,
"And he spake a parable unto them to this end, that men ought always to pray, and not to faint.'

Endurance is necessary for effective prayer.

Luke 18:7-8 reads,
"And shall not God avenge his own elect, which cry day and night unto him, though he bear long with them? I tell you that he will avenge them speedily. Nevertheless when the Son of man cometh, shall he find faith on the earth?"

Fasting is another subject, which can be taken to the extreme. The Pharisees used it as a means to appear righteous before others **(Matthew 6:16-18)**. Some people use it as an avenue to get their way with God or to have a mystical experience. BEWARE! The real test behind anything in the kingdom of God is motivation. Our motivation in prayer or fasting must be to see God's will being done in order to ensure He receives the deserved glory. Men such as Moses and Jesus prayed and fasted for the purpose of preparation for service to God and to experience His glory. This type of preparation can only be done in private times of fellowship with the Lord. Fellowship must take place on a daily basis through prayer and the study of the Word of God. (By the way, there is a difference between simply reading the Word and studying it. Both are necessary. (See **Ecclesiastes 12:12**.)

Preparation is necessary to obey Paul's instruction found in **2 Timothy 4:2**,
"Preach the word; be instant in season, out of season; reprove, rebuke, exhort with all longsuffering and doctrine."

Check out your motivation and use of God's gifts and weapons. Make sure you are using them to bring glory to His name.

Personal Notes: ____

____

____

Chapter 41

LEARNING TO TEST

Supplement: *(For summation of Christianity)* **Volume 3, Book 5:** *ABC's for the Christian Life*

We learned in the first two chapters about our opposition from the flesh and Satan. In our last chapter we examined our weapons. Now we must understand our battlefield. In the military, strategic points are located. These locations are determined by whether they can benefit the army in winning the war. As a result, these locations become the real battlefields. The Christian soldier has a very important strategic point. This is where his greatest battles will be fought.

2 Corinthians 10:5 gives us an introduction to our battlefield,
"Casting down imaginations, and every high thing that exalteth itself against the knowledge of God, and bringing into captivity every thought to the obedience of Christ."

The greatest battle begins in our mind. This battle involves our perception, or knowledge, of God. The ultimate target can be summarized in two words, "our faith."

Jude 3 gives us this instruction,
"Beloved, when I gave all diligence to write unto you of the common salvation, it was needful for me to write unto you, and exhort you that ye should earnestly contend for the faith which was once delivered unto the saints."

Satan will use pride, fear, doubt, worldly knowledge, and false religious beliefs and practices to destroy our hearts and minds. If Satan defeats us here, we will lose the war! It is important to know how to maintain our home front.

1 Corinthians 11:31 says,
"For if we would judge ourselves, we should not be judged."

2 Corinthians 13:5 states,
"Examine yourselves, whether ye be in the faith; prove your own selves. Know ye not your own selves, how that Jesus Christ is in you, except ye be reprobate?

We must test ourselves to see if we are winning the war. There is a test Christians can take to see where they are in their spiritual life. It is found in the first letter of John. In **1 John** the word "truth" is used many times. But we see the following terms being used throughout the letter:

* We know
* We have known
* How to know

John is telling us in his letter that we can know the truth about our spiritual condition. If we do not know the truth about our life before God, we should strive to know for our spiritual well-being. If we have decided we do not need to know our condition (because we think we are okay) we better choose to know for our spiritual survival. I have broken the **1 John** test down into three parts. They are:

- Doctrinal Test
- Relationship Test
- The Fruit Test

Each of these tests establishes and confirms the others. For instance, if you do not have the right doctrine, your relationship with God will not be right. If your relationship with God is not right, the fruit of your life will tell on you.

Personal Notes: ____

____

The Foundational Test

There are two foundational tests found in **1 John**. These two issues make up the base of the Christian faith.

The first test is found in **1 John 1:8 & 10**,
"If we say that we have no sin, we deceive ourselves, and the truth is not in us... If we say that we have not sinned, we make him a liar, and his word is not in us."

We need to recognize our sinful condition in order to keep our relationship with Christ in perspective. The truth of our condition will keep us humble and in need of God's intervention.

Matthew 5:3 tells us,
"Blessed are the poor in spirit: for theirs is the kingdom of heaven."

As long as we recognize we are spiritually bankrupt without Christ, we will be assured of being a part of the kingdom of heaven. (Beware of people who believe they don't have to contend with sin in their lives!) Although we may have a sinful disposition, we must not allow it to reign. Knowledge of our God and His Word will keep us from sinning.

1 John 2:1 confirms this,
"My little children, these things write I unto you, that ye sin not..."

John goes on to add this promise if we do sin in the rest of **1 John 2:1**,
"...And if any man sin, we have an advocate with the Father, Jesus Christ the righteous."

Jesus Christ is the only mediator between man and God.

1 Timothy 2:5 confirms this,
"For there is one God, and one mediator between God and men, the man Christ Jesus."

The second test involves the identity of Jesus Christ. **1 Corinthians 3:11** declares that there is only one foundation in which a person can build his or her spiritual life upon. Jesus warned us in **Matthew 24:23-24** that there would be many claiming to be Christ.

There is only one Jesus Christ. He is described in the Word of God. The real test is whether an individual believes in the true Jesus. We see Jesus making reference to this in **Matthew 16:15**. Jesus asks Peter this question, "Who do you say I am?"

Jesus did not ask Peter if he believed in Him. He asked him who he believed Him to be. John establishes the identity of Jesus in both his Gospel and his first letter. According to John's epistle, a believer must be able to make four declarations about Christ.

1 John 2:22 gives us the first insight into the identity of Jesus Christ,
"Who is a liar but he that denieth that Jesus is the Christ? He is antichrist, that denieth the Father and the Son."

There is only one Christ the Messiah, the Anointed One. A believer must believe the Jesus of the Bible is the only Christ.

1 John 4:2 gives us the next test to Christ's identity,
"Hereby know ye the Spirit of God: every spirit that confesseth that Jesus Christ is come in the flesh is of God.

One must believe and claim Jesus is God come in the flesh. This aspect of Jesus' nature is where the majority of cults differ from mainline Christianity.

1 John 4:14 gives us the next test to Christ's identity,
"And we have seen and do testify that the Father sent the Son to be the Saviour of the world."

Jesus is not one of the Saviors of the world; He is the only Savior of the world. He must be your personal Savior, and the one you run to for salvation, solutions, direction, and purpose.

1 John 4:15 tells us the final examination,
"Whosoever shall confess that Jesus is the Son of God, God dwelleth in him, and he in God."

As the Son of God, Jesus is sole revealer of His Father's love, grace, and mercy. He is the expression of His Father in human form. He came as the Anointed One to reveal the Father's love to a dying world. Since He was divine by nature and perfected in His humanity through suffering, He could become the acceptable sacrifice, giving access to man to be reconciled back to his God (**Hebrew 5:8-9**). As Savior, He is man's only hope for deliverance from self, sin, and the world. Without understanding Jesus as the Christ, God in the flesh and Savior, you cannot correctly grasp Him as the Son of God. The fullness of Christ exists in all four of His identities, and to acknowledge Him in a lesser light is to reveal you do not know the Jesus of the Bible.

1 John 5:10-11 says,
" He that believeth on the Son of God hath the witness in himself: he that believeth not God hath made him a liar; because he believeth not the record that God gave of his Son. And this is the record, that God hath given to us eternal life, and this life is in his Son."

Do you have a testimony of the Jesus of the Bible? If you do not, you need to know to establish assurance. Right now, He could very well be standing at the door of your heart, knocking and waiting to be let in.

Personal Notes: ____

____

The Relationship Test

There are four parts to this test. This examination involves your walk with the Lord.

The first part of this test is found in **1 John 1:6-7**,
"If we say that we have fellowship with him, and walk in darkness, we lie, and do not the truth; But if we walk in the light, as he is in the light, we have fellowship one with another, and the blood of Jesus Christ his Son cleanseth us from all sin."

We must be walking in the light of Jesus Christ. If we are walking in this light, we will be His reflection to the world. As you can see, this light will deal with any sin in our life.

Ephesians 5:8-11 states,
"For ye were sometimes darkness, but now are ye light in the Lord: walk as children of light: (For the fruit of the Spirit is in all goodness and righteousness and truth;) Proving what is acceptable unto the Lord. And have no fellowship with the unfruitful works of darkness, but rather reprove them."

The second examination is found in **1 John 2:3-6**,
"And hereby we do know that we know him, if we keep his commandments. He that saith, I know him, and keepeth not his commandments, is a liar, and the truth is not in him. But whoso keepeth his word, in him verily is the love of God perfected: hereby know we that we are in him."

Obedience to the Word of God is evidence of love and that you are abiding in Christ. (See **John 14:15 & 15:7-10**.)

The third part of this test is found in **1 John 2:15**,
"Love not the world, neither the things that are in the world. If any man love the world, the love of the Father is not in him."

We are in this world, but we are not a part of it. We must separate ourselves from it in order to avoid entanglement with it. Our relationship with the world will determine what kind of relationship we have with God.

1 John 2:17 tells us this about the world,
"And the world passeth away, and the lust thereof; but he that doeth the will of God abideth for ever."

The final part of this test can be found in **1 John 3:10**,
"In this the children of God are manifest, and the children of the devil: whosoever doeth not righteousness is not of God, neither he that loveth not his brother."

Believers are being called into an intimate relationship with God. He desires them to be His children, but this relationship expresses itself in obedience and love.

Personal Notes: ____

____

The Fruit Test

The fruit test is the examination, which will tell on you. You can talk the talk, walk the walk, and dress the dress of a self-righteous individual, but you cannot fake the fruit of the Spirit on a consistent basis. There are four parts to this test.

The first one is found in **1 John 3:14-15**,
"We know that we have passed from death unto life, because we love the brethren. He that loveth not his brother abideth in death. Whosoever hateth his brother is a murderer: and ye know that no murderer hath eternal life abiding in him."

Love is the big test in Christianity. In fact, you cannot make it to heaven without it. Love is defined as Christianity in action. It is a commitment to be right before God and do right by others. It will stand when all else fails. Remember, you can find all the fruit of the Spirit listed in **Galatians 5:22-23** in the definition of love found in **1 Corinthians 13**.

The second examination in this area is found in **1 John 1:3-4**,
"That which we have seen and heard declare we unto you, that ye also may have fellowship with us: and truly our fellowship is with the Father, and with his Son Jesus Christ. And these things write we unto you, that your joy may be full."

If we have fellowship with God, we will know joy. We will delight in what we know, see, and learn about our beloved Lord. This joy will become complete as we share it with others.

The third test can be found in **1 John 2:29**,
"If ye know that he is righteous, ye know that every one that doeth righteousness is born of him."

Peace with God is a product of an upright life.

James 3:18 states,
"And the fruit of righteousness is sown in peace of them that make peace."

The final part of this test is found in **1 John 5:4-5**,
"For whatsoever is born of God overcometh the world: and this is the victory that overcometh the world, even our faith. Who is he that overcometh the world, but he that believeth that Jesus is the Son of God?

If Christ is in your life, you will be an overcomer. Overcoming is not an option, but a manifestation of the Christian life.

Revelation 21:7 confirms this,
"He that overcometh shall inherit all things; and I will be his God, and he shall be my son."

Consider your fruit. Does it verify that you have a relationship with God?

Personal Notes: ____

____

In Conclusion

There are many enemies ready to rob us of our faith in God. It is an ongoing battle to maintain a pure faith that will stand in all persecution and trials. The battle for faith can involve fighting for others as well.

Jude 20-23 tells us,
"But ye, beloved, building up yourselves on your most holy faith, praying in the Holy Ghost, Keep yourselves in the love of God, looking for the mercy of our Lord Jesus Christ unto eternal life. And of some have compassion, making a difference. And others save with fear, pulling them out of the fire; hating even the garments spotted by the flesh."

Like Paul in **2 Timothy 1:12,** we must,
"...know whom (we) believed,..." (Parenthesis added.)

It is the knowledge of our precious Lord that gives us confidence and authority to overcome all of our enemies and endure to the end.

In conclusion, I want to leave you with Paul's words found in **2 Timothy 4:7-8**,
"I have fought a good fight, I have finished my course, I have kept the faith: Henceforth there is laid up for me a crown of righteousness, which the Lord, the righteous judge, shall give me at that day: and not to me only, but unto all them also that love his appearing."

May you have the same declaration as the Apostle Paul had at the end of your earthly journey. May you fight the battle, finish the course, and keep your faith pure. In so doing, you know there is a crown of righteousness waiting for you. But, like those in **Revelation 4:10** you will end up casting your crown or crowns at the feet of the One who made you heir of salvation with His blood.

The only fitting declaration to end this course is found in **Revelation 22:20**,
"Amen. Even so, come, Lord Jesus."

Personal Notes: ____

____

____

Supplements:
(For the purpose of understanding true ministry.)
Read the following books, and do the following Bible Studies.

The Christian life will produce effective ministry. Sadly, the foundation and the true Gospel has been eroded away by the many watered-down versions or counterfeit versions of the Bible that are invading the Church. The following books and Bible Studies will help sincere Christians understand what true ministry is all about, and keep it in perspective.

Volume 7, Books 3, 4, & 5:
Rose of Light, Thorn of Darkness
(Fictional book based on actual happenings.)
From Prisons and Dots to Christianity
So You Want to be in Ministry?

Bible Studies:
How to Serve God, **Sup. 2**
What True Ministry Is All About, **Sup. 1**

GENTLE SHEPHERD MINISTRIES SUPPLEMENTATION

Course Two

INTRODUCTION

Gentle Shepherd Ministries Supplementation is a combination of Bible Studies, articles, and sermons that have been presented over the past 17 years by Jeannette and me. They are meant to challenge people to gain insight into the Word. The problem with much of Christianity is that Christians are not firmly established in the Word of God. Without the foundation of the Word, the Holy Spirit does not have the means by which to bring revelation and growth to a person's life. In fact, people without a scriptural foundation become tossed to and fro with every wind of doctrine that comes their way **(Ephesians 4:14)**.

This manual was comprised in relationship to the *Gentle Shepherd Ministries Discipleship Course* that had been written for overseas missionaries. As we considered the Bible Studies, along with sermons and other materials that have been presented throughout the years, we realized that we could enhance the *Discipleship Course* by instituting these different sources within the course. Hence, we established this supplementary manual.

The first section of this supplementation is comprised of the Bible Studies written by Jeannette, and the second section is a collection of Bible Studies that I have written over the years. The last section is a conglomeration of sermons and articles by both of us.

It is our goal to give those seeking saints an opportunity to establish a firm, scriptural foundation that will enable them to stand, discern, and overcome with the Word of God. As the Apostle John pointed out in his first epistle, there are three levels of the spiritual life. There are the children who have been born again and know their sins are forgiven. There are the young people who have overcome Satan because the Word of God abides in them. Then, you have the fathers and mothers who know God in a personal intimate way **(1 John 12-14)**. Notice how the Word of God bridges the spiritual gap between immaturity and maturity in the kingdom of God.

The student will find a lot of repetition throughout the study, but he or she must remember that God commanded that the Law be read on a regular basis. In fact, <u>Deuteronomy</u> means "repetition of the Law." Since God's truths are eternal, they can be approached from various angles in order to bring dimension to the Christian foundation, the Person of Jesus Christ.

Needless to say, the supplementation is optional and would require time and energy, but my hope is that those who accept the challenge of discipleship, will take up pen and pad, and allow the material in this supplementation to challenge, enlarge, and bring them to a greater spiritual maturity in their walk with God.

❖ Distinguishes some of the questions from the rest of the text.

Supplementation
One

By

Jeannette Haley

This Supplement Features the Following Studies:

FOUNDATION OF OUR FAITH

IN PREPARATION

PRAYER: Dear Heavenly Father, In the name of Jesus I humbly beseech You to teach me Your Word. Help me to understand that which You have revealed in it concerning the Godhead, Jesus, the Holy Spirit, sin, and salvation, and the many other things it is Your desire for me to know. Open up my heart and mind to the truth. May Your Holy Spirit come and guide and teach me Your ways. Lord, help me to be teachable and submissive to Your perfect will.

Lord, I thank and praise You for Your salvation and for the great love You have for me. Grant that I may always walk in the ways of Your truth and love to bring glory to Your most Holy Name. Amen.

LESSON ONE

THE GODHEAD

Genesis 1:1 "In the beginning God..." God-Elohim, (plural...Gods)

Genesis 3:22 and **11:7** prove plurality of the Godhead.

There is one God. See **Isa. 43:10-13, 44:6, 8, 45:5, 14, 21-23, 46:9; Ja. 2:19; Mark 12:29-31; 1 Cor. 8:4; 1 Tim. 2:5. Read Ex. 20:23; Jer. 10:10, 11; 2 Cor. 4:3, 4.**

❖ What types of gods are there?

The word one means one in unity as well as one in number. In **1 John 5:7; John 17:11** and **21-26** "one" means unity. Yet, there is one God the Father, one Lord Jesus Christ, and one Holy Ghost. See **1 Cor. 8:6** and **Eph. 4:3-6**. There are three separate persons in divine individuality and divine plurality. The Father is called God (**1 Cor. 8:6**), the Son is called God (**Isa. 9:6-7; Heb. 1:8; John 1:1, 2; 20:28**), and the Holy Sprit is called God (**Acts 5:3, 4**).

❖ Does the Bible definitely teach one God with three distinct persons in the Godhead?

❖ Who are they?

GOD THE FATHER:

Col. 1:12-15
John 3:16
John 4:24
Eph. 1:19, 20, 21
Psalm 91
Psalm 147

GOD THE SON:

Isa. 9:6, 7
John 8:42, 10:30, 52-59
Rev. 1:8, 2:8, 22:13
Phil. 2:5-11
1 John 1:1-3
Micah 5:2
Col. 1:15-19
Eph. 3:9
John 1:1-3, 14
1 Tim. 3:16
Heb. 1:8

GOD THE HOLY SPIRIT:

Gen. 1:1, 2
Matt. 4:1
Isa. 11:2, 59:19, 61:1-3
Study: Matt. 3:16, 17.
Eph. 6:18
Rom. 8:14-17
Hebrews 10:29
1 John 5:6; 4:4-6; 2:27
John 14:16-18, 15:26, 16:13

MEMORY VERSES:

Genesis 1:1
John 4:24
John 1:1
John 10:30
Genesis 1:2
Acts 1:8

1. How many gods are there? See **Isa. 43-46.** Back up your answer with Scripture.
2. Who makes up the Godhead?
   a) Which one is God in the flesh? **(See John 1:14.)**
   b) Which one is the Creator? **(See Col. 1:16.)**
   c) Which one leads into all truth? **(See John 16.)**
   d) Who did Ananias and Sapphira lie to? **(See Acts 5:1-11.)**
   e) Who calls us? **(See John 10:27.)**
   f) Who is the one that has given Jesus His disciples? **(See John 10:29.)**
   g) Who is the author and finisher of our faith? **(See Heb. 12:1, 2.)**
   h) Who seals us until the day of redemption? **(See Eph. 4:30.)**
   i) Who holds the title of Melchizedek? **(See Heb. 6:20-7:1-28.)**
   j) Who resides in man? **(See 1 Cor. 3:16, 17.)**
   k) According to **1 Cor. 6:20** who do we need to glorify?

LESSON TWO
GOD THE FATHER

1. BIBLICAL DESCRIPTIONS OF GOD:

a) God - The word God means deity or divinity.
b) Godhead – This term means that which is divine. It is used of Jesus in **Col. 2:8,9** as having all the qualities of divinity in His manifestation of God to man. It is also used of all three persons in the Godhead. **See Rom. 1:19, 20; Acts 17:29.**
c) God is a real person – Personal names are given Him in **Gen. 1:1; Ex. 3:13-15; 6:3; Ps. 68:4** and His names are found over 19,000 times in Scripture. Some names are:

- I AM THAT I AM – **Ex. 3:14**
- Jehovah-Adonai – The Lord our Sovereign; Master Jehovah – **Gen. 15:2,8**
- Jehovah-Jireh – The Lord will see or provide – **Gen. 22:8-14**
- Jehovah-Nissi – The Lord our banner – **Ex. 17:15**
- Jehovah-Ropheka – The Lord our healer – **Ex. 15:26**
- Jehovah-Shalom – The Lord our peace – **Judg. 6:24**
- Jehovah-Tsidkeenu – The Lord our righteousness – **Jer. 23:6; 33:16**
- Jehovah-Mekaddishkem – The Lord our sanctifier – **Ex. 31:13; Lev. 20:8**
- Jehovah-Saboath – The Lord of hosts – **1 Sam. 1:3** (Occurs 281 times)
- Jehovah-Shammah – The Lord is present – **Ezek. 48:35**
- Jehovah-Elyon – The Lord most high – **Ps. 7:17; 47:2; 97:9**
- Jehovah-Rohi – The Lord my shepherd – **Ps. 23:1**
- Jehovah-Hoseenu – The Lord our maker – **Ps. 95:6**
- Jehovah-Eloheenu – The Lord our God – **Ps. 99:5, 8, 9**
- Jehovah-Eloheka – The Lord thy God – **Ex. 20:2, 5, 7**
- Jehovah-Elohay – The Lord my God – **Zech. 14:5**

d) God is Omnipresent (present everywhere at once). Omni means all. **(1 Kings 8:27; Ps. 139:7-10; Isa. 66:1,2; Jer. 23:23, 24; Ps. 46:1; Matt. 28:20)**
e) God is Omniscient (God is infinite knowledge). **(Ps. 139:1-10; Prov. 15:3; Isa. 46:9, 10; Ps. 147:5; Heb. 4:13; Matt. 10:29-31)**
f) God is Omnipotent (God is all-powerful). **(Gen. 17:1, 2; Rev. 4:8, 11, 19:6; Job 26:6-14, 42:2; Matt. 19:26)**
g) God is Immutable (God is unchangeable in His essence, attributes, consciousness, and will). **(James 1:17; Ps. 102:25-27; Mal. 3:6; Heb. 1:12, 13:8).**

2. MORAL ATTRIBUTES OF GOD:

a) HOLINESS: **1 Sam. 6:20; Ps. 99:9; Isa. 6:3; Rev. 15:4.**
b) RIGHTEOUSNESS & JUSTICE: **2 Chron. 12:6; Ezra 9:15; Ps. 48:10, 97:2, 119:137, 145:17.** (Believers are secure in the righteousness of Christ...**1 Cor. 1:30; 2 Cor. 5:21.** (The obedience of the believer will not go unnoticed)...**Prov. 19:17; Heb. 6:10.**
c) GOODNESS OF GOD:
1) Love of God: **Isa. 63:9; John 3:16; 2 Cor. 13:11; 1 John 4:8, 10, 16.**
2) Benevolence of God: **Ps. 145:9, 15; Gen. 1:31; Job 14:15; Matt. 6:25-34, 5:45.**
3) Mercy of God: **Eph. 2:4; Ps. 103:17, 108:4; Joel 2:13; Titus 3:5.**

4) Grace of God: **Eph. 1:4-7; 2:7-10; 1 Pet. 1:13; Rom. 5:21; 2 Cor. 12:9, 10.**

d) GOD IS TRUTH: **De. 32:4; 1 John 5:20; Jer. 10:10; Rom. 3:4; Rev. 3:7, 6:10.**

1. What does the word God mean?
2. Does God have personal names? List ten of them and give the meaning:
3. According to **John 14:6**, who is the truth?
4. Give definitions for the following words: grace, mercy, love, and benevolence
5. Match the letter to the correct meaning:

OMNIPOTENT ______________________	A-God is present everywhere at once
OMNIPRESENT ______________________	B-God is all-powerful
OMNISCIENT ______________________	C-God is unchangeable
IMMUTABLE ______________________	D- God is infinite knowledge

6. List seven attributes of God and give three Scriptures to prove each attribute.

LESSON THREE

CREATION AND FALL OF MAN

1. BIBLICAL DESCRIPTION OF MAN

a) MAN IS CREATED IN GOD'S IMAGE: **Genesis 1:26, 27, 5:1, 2; James 3:9.** (Image in Hebrew means resemblance; representative figure). Man was created to be, as it were, a 'mirror' to reflect the divinity, glory, and holiness of God. We were not created to be 'gods', but to reflect the ONE TRUE GOD.

b) For Further Study:
--Mental likeness: (reason, conscience, and will). A spirit is a rational, moral, and therefore also free agent: **Col. 3:10**
--Moral likeness: **Eccl. 7:29; Gen. 1:31; Ps. 100:3.**

2. TEMPTATION AND FALL OF MAN: Genesis Chapter 3

a) Physical consequence of sin: **James 1:14, 15; Jer. 17:9; Isa. 64:6, 7; Gal. 5:19-21; Rom. 5:12; 3:2, 6:23; Eph. 2:1-3; 1 Cor. 15:47.**

b) Spiritual consequence of sin: **Gen. 3:8-14, 3:22-24.**

c) Other effects of fall upon mankind:
1) Relationships with each other – **Gen. 4:8.**
2) On our bodies – **Gen. 2:17, 3:19; 1 Cor. 15:22; Rom. 5:12, 8:23.**
3) On our nature – **Gen. 3:7, 2:17; Rom. 5:12, 19.**
4) On our environment – **Gen. 3:17-19; Rom. 8:21, 22.**

3. THE NATURE OF SIN:

a) Violation of God's Law: **James 2:10; 1 John 3:4; Rom. 3:23, 5:19-21.**

b) Sins of omission as well as commission: **James 2:9-10, 4:17; Matt. 23:23, 25:45.**

c) Sin is a principle or disposition (inclination and tendency) as well as an act: **Matt. 15:19; James 1:14, 15; 1 John 1:8, 2:1, 2.**

d) Sin includes pollution as well as guilt: **Isa. 1:5; Jer. 17:9; Luke 6:45; 1 Cor. 2:14; Eph. 4:18, 19; Titus 1:15, 16.**

e) Sin is essentially selfish: **Isa. 53:6; Rom. 13:10; 2 Cor. 5:14, 15; 2 Tim. 3:2-5.**

4. How has the fall affected your life in each of the following areas: 1) spiritual, 2) emotional, and 3) physical.
5. In whose image was man created?
6. In your own words write out what "image" means.
7. In what ways is man created in the image of God?
8. Who tempted man to sin?
9. What is sin?
10. What are some of the consequences of sin?
11. What is the nature of sin?
12. What does God say about sin?
13. Why do you think Satan tempted Eve?
14. How did Adam react to God's call after he sinned?
15. What did God do to make a covering for Adam and Eve?
16. What do you think the shedding of innocent blood represented?

17. When Adam sinned, in what respect did he die?

True or False:

True	False	
_____	_____	Eve wanted to be as a god, knowing good and evil.
_____	_____	Adam wasn't responsible to inform Eve of God's commandments.
_____	_____	God knew Adam and Eve would choose to do before He created them.
_____	_____	Gen. 3:15 is the first promise God made to man of a Redeemer.
_____	_____	The serpent wasn't very smart and neither was he crafty.
_____	_____	Before the fall, God and man had fellowship together.

LESSON FOUR

GOD THE SON

1. **THE REASONS FOR THE INCARNATION:**

   a) To confirm God's promises: **Rom. 15:8-12; Isa. 9:6, 7:14; Micah 5:2.**
   b) To reveal the Father: **Matt. 6:9, 5:45; John 1:18, 14:9, 16:27, 3:3, 5.**
   c) To become a faithful High Priest: **Heb. 2:10, 17, 4:15, 16.**
   d) To put away sin: **Heb. 9:26, 2:9; Mark 10:45; 1 John 3:5; John 1:29; Isa. 53:6; 2 Cor. 5:21.**
   e) To destroy the works of the devil: **1 John 3:8; John 10:10, 12:31, Acts 10:38; Heb. 2:14, 15.**
   f) To give us an example of a holy life: **Matt. 11:29; 1 Pet. 2:21-25; 1 John 2:6.**
   g) To prepare for the Second Advent: **Heb. 9:28; Rom. 8:18-25.**

2. **THE NATURE OF THE INCARNATION:**

   a) He emptied Himself (by giving up the *independent* exercise of his relative attributes): **Phil. 2:7; John 1:14, 5:20, 36, 8:28, 38, 10:17, 18, 17:5; 2 Cor. 8:9.**
   b) He was made in the likeness of men: **John 1:14; 1 John 4:2; 2 John 7; Heb. 2:14, 15, 10:5; Col. 2:9; Rom. 8:3, 1:3; 1 Tim. 3:16.**

3. What does the word incarnate mean?
4. What type of relationship did Christ come to establish? **(John 1:12, 14:6)**
5. What kind of example did Christ leave us with? **(John 13)**
6. What brings us near to God? **(Eph. 2:13)**
7. Where does Christ sit now? **(Col. 3:1)**
8. What form did Christ take on? **(Phil. 2:7)**
9. In your own words explain **Phil. 2:5-8:**
10. How do we avoid the wrath of God?
11. From what do we need to be dead with Christ? **(Col. 2:20)**
12. What does **Heb. 13:8** declare about Jesus Christ?
13. In your own words explain **Heb. 4:14-16.**
14. What do these scriptures say about Christ?

John 1:1	**John 4:13, 14**	**John 10:11**
John 1:8	**John 6:35**	**John 11:25, 26**
John 1:29	**John 10:9**	**John 15:1**

15. Explain **John 3:14-18** (refer to **Numbers 21:5-9**).

LESSON FIVE

GOD THE HOLY SPIRIT

1. HIS RELATIONSHIP TO THE WORLD:

a) IN CREATION AND PRESERVATION:
Gen. 1:2; Job 33:4, 26:13; Ps. 33:6, 95:5, 104:30.

b) IN THE AFFAIRS OF NON-BELIEVERS:
Mark 3:28, 29; Gen. 6:3; Acts 7:51, 6:10.

2. HIS RELATIONSHIP TO SCRIPTURE AND TO CHRIST:

a) TO SCRIPTURE:
2 Pet. 1:21; John 16:13, 14; Eph. 3:5, 1:17; 1 Cor. 2:10-16.

b) TO CHRIST:
Luke 1:35, 4:16-19; Matt. 3:16, 17, 4:1.

3. HIS RELATIONSHIP TO THE BELIEVER:

a) THE WORK OF THE HOLY SPIRIT AT SALVATION:
   1) He Regenerates: **John 3:3-8, 6:63; Titus 3:5, 6.**
   2) He Indwells: **Rom. 8:9-11; 1 Cor. 3:16; Gal. 4:6, 7.**
   3) He Baptizes Believers into the Body of Christ: **Matt. 3:11; John 1:33; Acts 1:5, 11:16.**
   (The rite of water baptism symbolizes Spirit baptism)
   Rom. 6:3; Eph. 4:4, 5; Col. 2:12

b) THE CONTINUING WORK OF THE HOLY SPIRIT IN THE LIFE OF THE BELIEVER:
   1) He fills: **Acts 2:3, 4, 8:17, 10:44, 19:6; Eph. 5:18.**
   2) He Guides: **Acts 8:29, 13:2, 15:28, 29, 16:6; Gal. 5:16-26.**
   3) He Empowers: **Acts 1:8, 4:33, 19:11, 12; Mi. 3:8; Zec. 4:6; Lu. 4:14.**
   4) He Teaches: **John 14:26, 16:13; Ne. 9:20; Lu. 12:12; 1 Cor. 2:13; 1 Jn. 2:27.**

c) BAPTISM OF THE HOLY SPIRIT:
Acts 2:1-18, 37-39, 10:38, 11:16, 19:6.

d) GIFTS OF THE HOLY SPIRIT:
Rom. 12:1-8; 1 Cor. 12:1-11, 14:1-40.

4. How has the work of the Holy Spirit affected your life?
5. Is the Holy Spirit a force, energy, or Person?
6. Who is the living water? **(John 4:10)**
7. See **Matt. 25:1-13; Ja. 5:14; Rev. 3:18.** Who is the oil?
8. What kind of relationship does the Holy Spirit have to the following: The World,
9. Scripture, Christ, the believer, and non-believers. (Use Scriptural proof.)
10. List the fruit of the Spirit.
11. What is the baptism of the Holy Spirit?
12. Who is the Baptizer?
13. What is the purpose of Holy Spirit baptism? **(Acts 1:8)**
14. Does He fill believers today?
15. List some of the gifts of the Holy Spirit.

LESSON SIX

DOCTRINE OF ANGELS, SATAN AND DEMONS

1. FACTS ABOUT ANGELS (Messengers)

a) Angels, (including Lucifer), were created before the earth: **Ps. 148:2-5; Col. 1:16.**
b) Angels are not to be worshipped: **Col. 2:18.** When the specific title of the "Angel of the Lord" is used in the Old Testament, it is a "Christophany" (or appearance of Jesus in the Old Testament and worship was accepted.)
c) Archangels (arch means chief): **Jude 9; Rev. 12:7-9; Luke 1:19, 26; Book of Daniel.**
d) Common Angels, (the words angel and angels are used 294 times in Scripture): **Matt. 1:20, 24, 2:13, 19, 24:29-31, 28:2-7; Luke 1:11-38, 2:9-21; Acts 5:19, 10:3-8, 12:7-11.**
e) There are two classes of fallen angels:
   1) Those bound: **2 Pet. 2:4; Jude 6, 7.**
   2) Those still loose along with Satan: **Rev. 12:7-12; Eph. 6:12.**

2. LUCIFER/SATAN

a) Prince of demons: **Ezek. 28:11-17; Isa. 14:12-17.**
b) Satan is a real being: **1 Chron. 21:1; Job 1:6-12, 2:1-7; Rev. 12:7-12; Zech. 3:1, 2; 1 Pet. 5:8, 9; Ps. 109:6; Luke 10:18.**
c) Jesus was tempted by Satan: **Matt. 4:1-11; Luke 4:1-13.**
d) Jesus Christ waged war on Satan: **1 John 3:8; Acts 10:38; Luke 13:16.**
e) Satan wars with the saints: **Eph. 4:27, 6:10-18; 1 Thes. 2:18, 19; 1 Pet. 5:8, 9; James 4:7; 2 Cor. 11:14, 15.**
f) Satan's activities during the last days: **Rev. 12:3-17, 13:1-7, 16:13-16; Matt. 24:15-31.**
g) Doom of Satan: **Gen. 3:15; Isa. 24:21-23, 25:12; Rev. 20:1-10.**

3. DEMONS (evil spirit or devil):

a) Some demonic works: **Matt. 9:32, 33, 12:22, 15:22; Luke 4:36; John 10:10, 8:44; Eph. 2:1-3; 1 Tim. 4:1; 2 Tim. 1:7.**
b) Duty of Saints:
   1) Armor of God: **Eph. 6:11-18**
   2) Know devices of enemy: **2 Cor. 2:11**
   3) Resist the enemy: **James 4:7; 1 Pet. 5:8, 9.**
   4) Overcome enemy by Word of God: **Matt. 4:1-11; 1 John 2:14; Rev. 12:11.**

4. Are angels created beings or are they eternal?
5. Can we worship angels?
6. What are the names of two archangels?
7. What are the two classes of fallen angels?
8. Who is the prince of demons?
9. What Scripture proves Satan is a real being?
10. Why did Satan tempt Jesus?
11. How did Jesus resist Satan?

12. Who wars with Satan?
13. In your own words tell what Satan's activities are in these last days.
14. What will happen to Satan?
15. What happens to those who serve Satan rather than God?
16. List some demonic works.
17. What is the armor of God?
18. Why is it important?
19. How do Christians defeat Satan?

LESSON SEVEN

DOCTRINES OF DEATH, HELL, HEAVEN, RESURRECTION AND THE RETURN OF CHRIST

1. **DEATH** – "The word death as applied to man in Scripture means *separating* or a cutting off from realizing God's purpose for which he was created. One can logically substitute the word *separation* for *death* in every scripture where it is used." - Dake's Annotated Bible
   a) Cause of death: **Gen. 2:17; Rom. 5:12, 6:23.**
   b) Physical death: Physical *death* is the separation of the inner man from the outer man; the soul and spirit from the body: **Ja. 2:26; Heb. 9:27.**
   c) Spiritual death (eternal separation from God because man chooses to remain separated from God in sin): **Matt. 10:28, 25:41, 46; Rev. 2:11, 14:9-11, 20:11-15, 21:8.**
   (The second death is the second separation from God).

2. **HELL** – (The English word hell is defined in our dictionaries as, "The abode of evil spirits; infernal regions; place of eternal punishment or extreme torment; in ancient times, the place of departed spirits.") *Sheol* is a Hebrew word for *hell* and *Hades* is the Greek equivalent.
   a) The unsaved go to hell at time of death: **Luke 16:19-31; Acts 2:27; 2 Sam. 22:6; Ps. 9:17, 55:15, 86:13; Prov. 9:18, 24, 23:14; Isa. 5:14, 14:9.**
   b) Hell is a literal, eternal place of torment: **Matt. 25:46; Rev. 14:9-14, 19:20, 20:10-15.**

3. **HEAVEN** – "The abode of God, the angels, and the souls of those who are granted salvation." -- The American Heritage Dictionary.
   a) Heaven is a place: **Gen. 1:1, 2:1; John 14:1-3; Acts 7:55.**
   Heaven is a better country: **Heb. 11:10-16.**
   Heaven is the highest part of creation: **Eph. 1:20-23, 4;10; Luke 2:15; Job 22:12.**
   Heaven is a paradise: **2 Cor. 12:1-4: Rev. 2:7.**
   Heaven is God's dwelling place: **Deut. 26:15; 1 Ki. 8:30, 39, 43, 49; Is. 66:1; Lu. 11:2.**
   c) The saved enter heaven upon physical death: **2 Cor. 5:8; Phil. 1:21-24; 1 Thes. 5:10; Rev. 6:9-11; Heb. 12:22, 23.**

4. **THE RESURRECTIONS:**
   a) The resurrection of Jesus Christ: **Matt. 28; Mark 16; Luke 24; John 20, 21; Acts 1:1-11; 1 Cor. 15:1-23; Rev. 1:18.**
   b) The resurrection of the saints: **Job 14:14, 15; Dan. 12:2; John 5:28-29; 1 Cor. 15:35-38; 1 Thes. 4:13-18; Rev. 20:4-6; Matt. 22:29-32.**
   c) The resurrection of the wicked dead: **Ps. 9:17; Isa. 14:9; Rev. 20:11-15, 21:8.**

5. **RETURN OF JESUS CHRIST:**

a) The second coming of Jesus Christ: **Matt. 24:29-31, 25:31-46, 26:64; Mark 14:62; Acts 1:11; 1 Cor. 15:23-28; Heb. 9:28; Rev. 19:11-21.**

b) Millennium Reign of Christ: **Jer. 30, 31, 32:36-44; Isa. 11, 65:18-25; Acts 3:20, 21; 2 Tim. 4:1; Rev. 11:15.**

6. What is "death"?
7. What is the cause of death?
8. What is hell and who goes there? (Give at least five scriptures to prove your answer).
9. What is heaven and who goes there? (Give at least three Scriptures)
10. What happens to a Christian when they die?

True or False:

True	False	
_____	_____	Jesus Christ was resurrected from the dead.
_____	_____	The resurrection of Jesus isn't really important to Christianity.
_____	_____	The saints will be resurrected at the end of the millennium.
_____	_____	Christians will be resurrected in an immortal, incorruptible body.
_____	_____	Eventually the wicked dead will be converted and not sent to hell.
_____	_____	Hell is a place of eternal torment.
_____	_____	Heaven isn't really a literal place.

LESSON EIGHT

DOCTRINE OF SIN AND SALVATION

1. **SIN** – "A condition of estrangement from God as a result of breaking God's Law"; disobedience; rebellion; offense, etc.
   a) How did sin enter the world? **Gen. 3:1-8.**
   b) Who has sinned against God? **Romans 3:23; 6:23.**
   c) What is the consequence of sin? **Ezek. 18:4; Rom. 5:12.**

2. **SALVATION** – "The deliverance of man or his soul from the power or penalty of sin; redemption."
   a) JESUS CHRIST as savior:
   Definition of savior: "A person who rescues someone or something from dire circumstances."
   John 3:16, 14:6; Acts 2:21, 4:12; 1 Pet. 3:18; Rom. 6:23.
   b) JESUS OFFERS SALVATION TO <u>ALL</u> MEN:
   Isa. 60:3, 4; Dan. 7:14; Hos. 2:23; Acts 17:30; Rom. 5:6, 10:9-13; 1 Tim. 2:4-6.
   c) SALVATION IS BY GRACE AND NOT EARNED BY WORKS:
   Rom. 3:12, 5:1, 2, 8:31-39; Gal. 2:16; Eph. 2:8, 9; Titus 3:5-7, 2:11.
3. Is there really any such thing nowadays as "sin"?
4. Who has sinned?
5. Why did God send Jesus to die?
6. Who can be saved?
7. Is everybody going to eventually go to heaven?
8. Is it necessary to ask Jesus Christ to be your Savior and Lord to be saved?
9. Can good works save you?

PRAYER: Dear Lord, thank You for sending Jesus Christ to die in my place on the cross. I believe with all my heart that He took my place, and that I, as a sinner, need to ask Your forgiveness for all my sins. Lord, I invite You to come into my heart and cleanse me of all my unrighteousness. Please help me to be all that You want me to be, and use my life for Your glory. I praise You and exalt You for loving me and saving me. In Jesus' Name. AMEN.

DISCIPLESHIP BIBLE STUDY

CHAPTER ONE

DISCOVERING THE MEANING OF DISCIPLESHIP

Disciple – Means A Student

1. **Luke 14:26-33:** What did Jesus say a person must be willing to do in order to be His disciple?
2. According to **John 6:69** what must a true disciple of Christ believe?
3. Complete the following sentence **(John 8:31):** "Then said Jesus to those Jews which believed on Him, If ye ________________________, then are ye my disciples indeed."
4. **John 15:8:** Why did Jesus tell His disciples that they should bear much fruit?
5. **Matt. 16:24-26:** In these verses, explain in your own words what Jesus meant.
6. Read: **Rom. 8:1-18.** List some of the contrasts between living in the flesh and living in the Spirit:
7. Read: **Gal. 5:24 and Col. 3:1-10.** According to these verses, what are some of the things God requires of a disciple? What are some of the benefits?

MEMORY VERSES: Rom. 12:1, 2

8. **Matt. 10:24:** According to Jesus what is the position of a disciple?

   This is the highest position in power and in life for a disciple **(John 13:16, 14:12-15; 17:18; 20:21)**.

9. Look at **Acts 9:16.** Why do you think Jesus forewarned Paul what he must suffer?
10. Name other people who suffered in the Old and New Testaments because of their faith:

(Gen. 37) ____________________________ **(Psalm 3)** __________________________
(Job 13:15) ____________________________ **(Jer. 38)** __________________________
(Dan. 3) ____________________________ **(Dan. 6)** __________________________

Phil. 3:10: "That I may know Him, and the power of His resurrection, and the fellowship of His sufferings; being made conformable unto His death."

"KNOW HIM" – Spiritual knowledge builds faith, hope, and love. See: **Jer. 9:24; Ho. 6:3, John 8:31, 32**

"POWER OF HIS RESURRECTION" – Spiritual resurrection builds faith, hope, and love. See: **Ezek. 37:10; Luke 15:24; Rom. 8:11; Eph. 2:1; Col. 3:1**

"FELLOWSHIP OF HIS SUFFERINGS" – Suffering for Christ builds faith, hope, and love. See: **Rom. 8:17, 8:35-39; 2 Cor. 1:7, 11:23-33; 2 Tim. 2:12; Heb. 11:24-29; 1 Pe. 1:7, 2:20, 3:14, 4:16, 5:10; John 16:33; Ja. 5:10-11**

"CONFORMABLE UNTO HIS DEATH" – See: **Rom. 6:6; 2 Cor. 4:11; Ga. 2:20; Col. 2:20; 2 Tim. 2:11**

Fellowship in suffering with Christ causes our spirit to understand His love for us in His sufferings. We respond to His love because "He first loved us." **1 John 4:19**

11. See: **Rev. 12:11.** How do the saints overcome the devil?

    Personal: As you search your own heart and allow the Holy Spirit to shine His light deep inside your spirit, are you able to truthfully say you are willing to enter into His sufferings and lay down your life if He asks you to?

12. We will discuss the Scriptures given in the following list of fourteen ways we are to be like Jesus: (Please prayerfully consider each attribute and verse).
    a. Righteousness – **1 John 3:7; John 15:10-14; 1 Cor. 1:30; Eph. 1:4, 5:27.**
    b. Freedom from the world – **John 17:14-16; Rom. 12:1; Ja. 4:4; 1 John 2:15.**
    c. Self crucifixion – **Rom. 6; Gal. 2:20.**
    d. Walking in newness of life – **Rom. 6; Gal. 5:16-26; Eph. 4:1-24.**
    e. Enduring persecutions – **Matt. 10:28; John 15:18-20; Mark 10:30; Acts 9:16.**
    f. Works – **John 14:12; Mark 16:17-18, 9:23; Matt. 17:20-21.**
    g. Fruit of the Spirit – **Gal. 5:22, 23; John 13:34, 15:11-13.**
    h. Total setting apart for God's work – **John 10:36, 17:17-19, 20:21.**
    i. Walking in the light – **1 John 1:7.**
    j. Unity with God – **John 17:11, 21-23.**
    k. Suffering for others – **1 Pet. 2:21-23, 4:1; Phil. 3:10.**
    l. Life and conduct – **1 John 2:6, 4:17.**
    m. Enduring temptations – **Heb. 2:18, 4:14-16; Jam. 1:2, 12; 1 Cor. 10:13.**
    n. Manifesting the fullness of God – **John 3:34, 7:37-39, 14:12; Eph. 3:19.**

13. Define the following words: Righteousness, Freedom, World, Self, Newness, Endure, Sanctification, Light, and Suffering. (In relationship to the above 14 points).

CHAPTER TWO

BLESSINGS PROMISED TO DISCIPLES

BLESSINGS PROMISED TO FOLLOWERS:

1. **SPIRITUAL KNOWLEDGE - Col. 1:9; Jer. 9:24.** What is the condition in **John 7:16, 17** for receiving spiritual knowledge?
   a) In **John 8:31, 32** what does knowledge of the truth do?
   b) According to **John 17:3** what does spiritual knowledge lead to?
   We also see in **Ho. 6:3** that spiritual knowledge is acquired by acquaintanceship with God.

2. **SPIRITUAL LIGHT – Isa. 9:2.** Who is the prophet talking about?
   a) Fill in the blanks: **(John 8:12)** "Then said Jesus unto them, I am the____________of the world; he that followeth me shall not walk in ____________________________but shall have the _________________________ of life."
   b) Look up **John 1:4, 9; John 12:35; 2 Cor. 4:6; Rev. 21:23.** Explain **Eph. 5:14** in your own words.
   c) Read **Col. 2:13.**

3. **GUIDANCE OF THE STILL SMALL VOICE – John 10:27, 18:37.**
   a) How do YOU hear God's voice?
   b) Can you think of examples in the Old and New Testaments of how other men and women heard God's voice?

4. **HEAVENLY HONOR – John 12:26** and **Ps. 91: 14, 15.** Look up the word "honor" in a dictionary. What does it mean?
   a) Whom does the Bible say God honors?

5. **A DIVINE EXAMPLE – 1 Pet. 2:21; Matt. 11:29, 16:24; John 13:15; Heb. 3:1; Heb. 12:2; Rom. 15:5; 2 Cor. 10:1; Phil. 2:5; Col. 3:13.** What Divine example does the Bible give us in each of these verses? (For example: **1 Pet. 2:21** – "suffering")
   a) **John 3:16** is called the "Greatest Verse." If you have not already done so, definitely commit it to memory. Many souls have been won for Christ from just this one verse.
   b) Read **John 11:25, 26.** Meditate on this great promise from our Lord. Read **John 14:1-3.** Can any other offer what Christ does for those who love Him?
   c) Read the books of **John** and **Revelation** and underline, or write in a notebook, the Lord's promises to you!

CHAPTER THREE

TEMPTATION, THE ENEMY, AND THE DISCIPLE'S ARMOUR

As we commit our lives to the Lord and begin to apply His word to our hearts and lives, the enemy (Satan) pushes harder against us causing us to be tempted to sin. One of the greatest Divine examples in Scripture is the account of Jesus' temptation in the wilderness.

1. Read **Luke 4:1-13.** In what ways did Satan tempt Jesus? How did Jesus resist the devil?
2. How is this an example of how believers can defeat Satan when he tempts them?

Memorize 1 Cor. 10:13.

4. Read **Gen. 3.** This is the record of the first temptation of mankind. Is temptation itself a sin?
5. In **Gen. 39** how did Joseph respond to temptation in **vs. 9?**
6. What were the results? **(vs. 20-23)**
7. **James 1:2, 3.** What is the Biblical definition of temptation?
8. What good comes out of it?
9. According to **James 1:12** who will receive a crown of life?
10. **Heb. 2:18.** Why is Jesus able to help us in our temptations?
11. **1 John 2:16.** Explain in your own words what these different areas of temptation are:

    Read **Eph. 6:10-18.** Putting on the armor of God is not incidental to the Christian's life…it is a command and absolutely necessary to enable the disciple to stand victorious. We are told in **2 Tim. 2:3**, "Thou therefore endure hardness, as a good soldier of Jesus Christ." A soldier would never think of going into battle without first putting on his armor. When a person believes on the Lord Jesus Christ and commits his life to the Lord, he is automatically involved in the greatest battle that ever was or will be… and that is the war between God and Satan, light and darkness, good and evil.

12. In **John 10:10,** what did Jesus say the Devil came to do?
13. What did Jesus say that He came to do?
14. What do you think Jesus meant by the words "abundant life?"
15. Read **James 4:7.** What must we do before we resist the devil?
16. What do you think it means to "submit to God?"
17. Read **Eph. 4:26, 27.** What is the Holy Spirit warning us about?

    2 Cor. 10:3-5. In these verses we see that we do not fight in the natural, but in the spiritual. Many times we meet people whose behavior causes us to react with dislike, anger, resentment, etc. What we need to remember is that it's not the person who is the problem, but the spirits that influence, manipulate, and even sometimes control that individual. This allows us to be able to understand, love, and pray for them. These verses are powerful weapons of warfare against the enemy when used in intercessory prayer and prayed back to God. Try to memorize them and use them when doing "warfare"!

Fear is one of the greatest weapons of the enemy, but in **2 Tim. 1:7** we read, "For God hath not given us the spirit of fear; but of power, and of love, and of a sound mind." This is another powerful verse that can be used against the enemy and should be committed to memory.

18. Look in a Concordance and find at least six other verses of Scripture showing God's help in times of fear:
19. **SATAN – WHAT HE IS:** (A study for your information).
    1. Satan is a real person – **1 Chr. 21:1; Job 1:6-12, 2:1-7; Ps. 109:6; Zech. 3:1,2; 1 Pet. 5:8, 9; Rev. 12:7-12.**
    2. Jesus Christ dealt with him as a person – **Matt. 4:1-11 and Luke 4:1-13.**
    3. Jesus Christ waged war on Satan as a person – **Luke 13:16; 1 John 3:8; Acts 10:38.**
    4. Christ taught that Satan was a real person – **Luke 10:18; Rev. 12:7-12; Rev. 13:1-4; 20:1-10.**
    5. The apostles fought with Satan as with a real person – **Eph. 6:10-18; 1 Thes. 2:18; 1 Pet. 5:8, 9.**
    6. The apostles warned men against a personal devil – **Eph. 4:27, 6:11; Jas. 4:7; 1 Pet. 5:8, 9.**
    7. Personal singular pronouns are used of Satan – **Matt. 4:7-11, 12:26; Luke 11:18.**
    8. Personal statements are made to him – **Isa. 14:12-14; Ezek. 28:11-17; Zech. 3:1,2; Job 1:6-12, 2:1-7; Matt. 4:1-10; Jude 9.**
    9. Personal conversation is carried on with him – **Job 1:6-12, 2:1-7; Isa. 14:12-14; Matt. 4:1-10; Jude 9.**
    10. Personal descriptions are given of him – **Isa. 14:12-14; Ezek. 28:11-17.**
    11. Personal names and titles are given to him:
        - **(a)** Lucifer – **Isa. 14:12-14**
        - **(b)** Devil and Satan – **Rev. 12:9**
        - **(c)** Beelzebub – **Matt. 10:25, 12:24**
        - **(d)** Belial – **2 Cor. 6:15**
        - **(e)** Adversary – **1 Pet. 5:8, 9**
        - **(f)** Dragon – **Rev. 12:3-12, 13:1-4, 20:1-3**
        - **(g)** Serpent – **2 Cor. 11:3; Rev. 12:9**
        - **(h)** God of this world – **2 Cor. 4:4**
        - **(i)** The prince of this world – **John 12:31**
        - **(j)** Prince of the power of the air – **Eph. 2:1-3**
        - **(k)** Accuser of our brethren – **Rev. 12:10**
        - **(l)** Enemy – **Matt. 13:39**
        - **(m)** Temptor – **Matt. 4:3**
        - **(n)** The wicked one – **Matt. 13:19, 38** (That wicked one – **1 John 5:18)**
20. He is an angel with a body, soul, and spirit like all other angels – **Ezek. 28:11-17; Rev. 12:7-11.** (But is now fallen through pride).
21. He is described as a most beautiful creature who fell through personal pride over his own beauty – **Ezek. 28:11-17; 1 Tim. 3:6.**
22. He has been seen with a body – **1 Chron. 21:1; Job 1:6-12, 2:1-7; Ps. 109:6; Zech. 3:1-2; Matt. 4:1-11; Rev. 20:1-3.**

23. He will be bound bodily with a chain and cast into prison – **Rev. 20:1-3.**
24. He has a heart – **Isa. 14:12-14;** pride – **Ezek. 28:1-7; 1 Tim. 3:6;** speech – **Job 1:6-12, 2:1-7; Matt. 4:1-11** and knowledge; power – verses in **Job, Acts 10:38; 2 Thes. 2:8-12; Acts 26:18; Rev. 13:1-4;** desires – **Luke 22:31;** lusts – **John 8:44; Eph. 2:1-3;** and many other bodily parts, soul passions, and spirit faculties.
25. He goes from place to place in a body like anyone else – **Job 1:6-12, 12:1-7; Matt. 4:10, 11; Mark 4:15.**
26. He has a kingdom – **Mark 3:22, 26.**
27. He has access to heaven – **Job 1:6-12, 2:1-6; Rev. 12:9-12.**
28. He is a great celestial and terrestrial ruler – **Eph. 2:2, 6:10-18; 2 Cor. 4:4; John 12:31.**
29. He rules the business, political, social, and the religious activities of the majority of mankind.
30. His realm is divided into organized principalities and powers in the heavenlies – **Dan. 10:12-21; Matt. 12:24-30; Eph. 6:10-12.**
31. His subjects are fallen angels, fallen men, and demons of various kinds – **Matt. 25:41; Rev. 12:7-12; John 8:44; 1 John 3:8-10; Jas. 2:19.**
32. He is head of some religions and is a leader in religious affairs – **2 Cor. 11:14; Rev. 2:9, 3:9.**

The above study on Satan is by no means exhaustive, although much of the Scripture is repetitive. Christians need to understand who Satan is, why, and how he attacks believers and what the truth is concerning him. We also need to know how to do warfare against him and his hordes of demons. Today there is much error rampant in the church, as well as in the world concerning Satan. The devil has never ceased to try through the centuries to convince men that he doesn't really exist, that he is only an "error in thinking," or he doesn't really have any ability to attack, influencing, or manipulating a Christian. Some actually believe that he is the "good guy". We know from the Word of God that all of these assumptions are not true. You may ask, "Why does God allow Satan to continue?" That is a very good question and as we look at the following Scriptures, we shall see some of the reasons for God allowing him, for the time being, to operate in the world. Read **Jas. 1:12; 1 Pet. 1:7-13, 5:8-9; 2 Pet. 1:4-9; Jude 20-24.**

From these verses we see that God wants to develop faith and character in the believer. God also allows Satan to keep the believer humble – **2 Cor. 12:7.** God has told us that He will reward the overcomer; but if there is nothing to overcome, then what reward could there possibly be? See **1 John 2:13, 4:1-6; Rev. 2:7, 11, 17, 26-28, 3:5, 12, 21.** God also wants to demonstrate His power over the power of Satan – **Mark 16:17-20, 1 Cor. 4:9, Eph. 2:7, 3:10.** Unfortunately, many times God knows certain individuals would never repent if He did not allow Satan to afflict them – **1 Cor. 5:1-6; 2 Cor. 2:5-11; Job 33:14-30.** In **Rev. 21** we see that God utilizes Satan to purge man of all possibility of falling in the eternal future.

Once a person is truly born again, he cannot be literally POSSESSED by demons; BUT Satan can, and does, attack the physical and the soulish areas in man. The soul is that part of us where our mind, will, and emotions are. When we succumb to lust, fear, anger, jealousy, envy, worry, etc. we can actually open a door for the enemy to come in and occupy that "territory" in our soul. Unforgiveness is one of the most devastating attitudes that any person can entertain. God has much to say in His Word about forgiveness, and in the following chapter we will see what the Bible has to say about this important subject.

CHAPTER FOUR

THE NECESSITY OF FORGIVENESS IN THE DISCIPLE'S LIFE

The entire Holy Bible from **Genesis** to **Revelation** is the story of God's love for His creation, and reveals His grace and forgiveness through Jesus Christ. Once we have committed our lives to Him and have become one of His disciples, we learn that our Heavenly Father begins to work in our lives by the Holy Spirit to restore that broken fellowship that man once had with Him before Adam fell into sin. Our example to follow is Jesus Himself, and He has much to say to us about forgiveness. We can never truly enter into genuine fellowship with God if there is any unforgiveness toward another person in our hearts. God in His grace and mercy has forgiven us; and He in turn commands us to forgive others.

When feelings of unworthiness and sin overwhelm you, turn to **Psalm 51** and read how David prayed to the Lord for forgiveness. Look up **1 John 1:9** and **Romans 8:1.** When we truly repent with our whole heart, then God forgives us and forgets it. When the enemy tempts you to despise yourself because of sins that you have already confessed, quote the Word of God to him and command him to flee in the Name of Jesus. As long as all known sins are confessed to the Lord, the Christian has the power and authority to defeat Satan!

1. Read **Matt. 6:14, 15.** If we forgive others, what will God do?
2. If we refuse to forgive others, what will God do?
3. Read **Matt. 18:21-35.** Explain in your own words what Jesus is saying to you personally in this parable.
4. Read **Matt. 5:43-48.** Why do you think Jesus emphasized forgiveness in these verses?
5. According to **Eph. 2:8, 9** does God forgive us because of any good works that we may have done?
6. Why not? **(See Isaiah 64:6, 7.)**

Read **Eph. 4.** The Holy Spirit, writing through the Apostle Paul to the church at Ephesus, is calling Christians to unity, understanding, wisdom, maturity, spiritual growth, and genuine love.

7. According to **vs. 32** how are we to treat others?
8. According to **Heb. 12:15** who suffers when we allow a "root of bitterness" to spring up in our hearts?
9. Read **1 Thes. 5:15 and 1 Pet. 3:9.** When someone wounds, mistreats, or abuses us in any way, what does God's word tell us to do?

Notice, however, that the Lord is talking specifically about people in the world, in the Church, in our families, neighborhoods, communities, friends, etc. We are to love FROM OUR HEARTS all mankind as God loves them, BUT THIS DOES NOT MEAN THAT IN THE EVENT OF A VIOLENT ACT TOWARDS US OR A MEMBER OF OUR FAMILY THAT WE SHOULD STAND BY HELPLESSLY. Yes, we love and pray for all men that they should be saved; and we live in peace as much as possible!
However, there are times when we are called upon to defend ourselves, our family, or our country from enemies, and the Bible, especially in the Old Testament, is full of

historical examples of God's people doing just that under the leadership of the Lord. Many times, God's chosen people, Israel, were commanded to destroy immoral and perverse people. God has given all men the opportunity to seek Him and find Him **(Deut. 4:29).** But, once they have totally rejected and despised Him, judgment and destruction are sure to come. **(See Heb. 9:27, 10:29-31; Rev. 20:11-15; Gen. 18:16-19:29.)**

It is very difficult, to be sure, to forgive every time we are wronged...it is not easy to recall events of the past, or even in childhood, and choose to forgive with all our hearts...but IT IS possible with God's help! If you are having difficulty in this area, pray and ask God to make you willing to be forgiving...tell Him how hurt you are and how you feel. Tell Him you want to obey Him and be pleasing in His sight. (See **Rom. 7:18-25.**) Remember, once you have received Jesus as your Savior by putting your trust in Him, **(Rom. 10:9, 10)**, your spirit is born again and the Holy Spirit indwells your body **(1 Cor. 6:19, 20)**. He begins to change you into the likeness of Jesus **(2 Cor. 5:17; Col. 3:10 and Titus 3:5)**, and He gives you power to be God's son or daughter by adoption **(John 1:12; Rom. 8:14-17)**. PRAISE THE LORD FOR HIS LOVE, MERCY, GRACE, AND FORGIVENESS!! OH TO BE LIKE HIM!! "Forgive, and you shall be forgiven."
God is able to change the foulest sinner into the purist saint.

Some examples of God's transforming power in men's lives are as follows:

Peter, the profane fisherman, **Matt. 26:74**, becomes a man whose every shadow heals, **Acts 5:15.**

The restless demoniac, **Mk. 5:5,** becomes a quiet disciple, **Mk. 5:15**.

John, the vindictive Jew, **Lu. 9:53, 54**, becomes the apostle of love, **1 John 4:7.**

The woman of Samaria of unsavory reputation**, John 4:17, 18** becomes an evangel of truth, **John 4:29.**

Saul, the bloodthirsty persecutor, **Acts 9:1**, becomes Paul, the tenderhearted brother, **Acts 21:13.**

The cold-hearted Philippian jailer, **Acts. 16:24**, becomes a sympathetic friend, **Acts 16:33.**

No matter how difficult the road may be that you are traveling on, remember that "...we know that all things work together for good to them that love God, to them who are the called according to His purpose" (**Rom. 8:28**).

"Blessed are they that do His commandments, that they may have right to the tree of life, and may enter in through the gates into the city." **Rev. 22:14.** See **1 Pet. 1:4-8.**

Prayer: "Dear Father in Heaven, I praise You and thank You for all You have done for me. Thank You for sending Your only begotten Son to die for my sins. I believe in Him and I believe that by faith I can lay hold of the eternal life He provided for me by dying on the cross and shedding His precious blood. Thank You for raising Jesus from the dead and for the promise that He will return and take me to live with Him forever in the home He is preparing for me. Lord, help me to be open to the searchlight of the Holy Spirit, and forgive me for all my sins...for rebellion, selfishness, hatred, anger, resentment, self-centeredness...help me to genuinely love others and to forgive them as You love and have forgiven me. Teach me Your ways and impart to me the Spirit and Truth always. In Jesus' Name, Amen."

PRAYER BIBLE STUDY

CHAPTER ONE

LEARNING ABOUT PRAYER

PRAYER is conversing with God. It is the contact of the soul with God, *not in meditation or contemplation, but in direct access to Him.* Prayer may be silent (in the heart); or expressed verbally. Hannah prayed in her heart and only her lips moved **(1 Sam. 1:13)**, and God heard and answered her request. David, to illustrate the other extreme, said "I cried unto the Lord with my voice, and he heard me out of his holy hill." **(Ps. 3:4)**

Prayer is beseeching the Lord **(Ex. 32:11)**; pouring out the soul before the Lord **(1 Sam. 1:15)**; praying and crying to heaven **(2 Chron. 32:20)**; seeking unto God and making supplication **(Job 8:5)**; drawing near to God **(Ps. 73:28)**; and bowing the knees **(Eph. 3:14)**.

Heb. 11:6 says, "But without faith it is impossible to please Him: for he that cometh to God must believe that He is, and that He is a rewarder of them that diligently seek Him." According to the above verse, what are the prerequisites to approaching God in prayer?

1. Read **Ps. 66:18.** What kind of a heart condition will keep God from hearing prayer?

2. Is there an exception to this verse? See **Ps. 51:17; Ho. 14:2; Joel 2:12,13; Acts 8:22.** See also **Luke 18:13.**

   This man was a sinner but Jesus said God honored his prayer. Why do you think this was so?

   Ps. 34:18: "The Lord is nigh unto them that are of a broken heart; and saveth such as be of a contrite spirit." God searches the heart and knows when we come with sincerity and true repentance or if we are still clinging to some vestige of rebellion. Surrender to Him! He knows our every secret and hidden thought! Praise Him for His longsuffering, love and mercy.

   Prayer can be (1) secret, private; (2) social, as in family prayers; and (3) public, in gatherings of believers, church, etc.

3. **1 Cor. 14:14, 15:** What does it mean to "pray with the spirit?" (See **Acts 2.**)

4. According to **vs.14** praying in an unknown tongue edifies the believer. What does it mean to "pray with the understanding?"

6. Read **Rom. 8:26**. Who helps our infirmities?

7. Why do we need help?

8. Jesus is the Great High Priest Who intercedes for us. Look up the following verses and note the different things Jesus prays for. **(Rom. 8:34; Isa. 53:12; Luke 22:32; Luke 23:34; John 14:16; John 17:9; Heb. 7:25)**

Jesus is our Example. In the next chapter we shall examine the model prayer that Jesus gave to His disciples when they asked Him to teach them how to pray. They knew that He was a great Man of prayer and that God, through the Holy Spirit, honored Him and always answered His prayers. How they must have longed to have that special relationship with the Father that Jesus did! Should not we, as God's children, desire to know how to fellowship with Him in prayer?

CHAPTER TWO

THE MODEL PRAYER

Read **Matt. 6:1-13.** Jesus is telling His disciples to pray in secret. God knows our innermost needs and is willing to meet with us in secret. Those who love to make loud and long public prayers for the purpose of gaining recognition and applause do not pray with the sincerity to God. They are looking for the praise of men rather than the praise of God! It is in private times with the Lord that we can share our deepest, heartfelt feelings; and it's there in secret that He talks to us and reveals His will for our lives. When we love someone, we desire to have special times of privacy with him or her. We long for the quiet times of sharing and oneness that can only be achieved in private. The Father yearns to have our undivided attention and fellowship; He is worthy of our adoration and praise. Let us remember each day to set aside a time alone with the One who loves each of us with a special and personal love. (Read **Psalm 139**)

1. What does **Psalm 139** mean to you?

   Vs. 7, 8. In these two verses in **Matt. 6** we read that God is not pleased with "vain repetitions". Since God already knows what we need before we ask Him, we do not need to resort to chanting, long boring dialogues, or "formulas" to attract God's attention. Remember, God is looking at our hearts! To monotonously reiterate the same words or phrases to God indicates a lack of faith and true knowledge of the God whom we serve. Intercession and supplication to God means that we are "standing in the gap" and "praying without ceasing" from the heart and with the help of the Spirit to make our petitions known to God. Jesus told us to "ask, seek, and knock."

2. Read **Psalm 34.** What does this Psalm say about those who "cry" to the Lord?

   Vs. 9. The beginning of what is known as "The Lord's Prayer" but should be more accurately labeled "The Disciple's Prayer." This prayer serves as a model because in any prayer we pray we can utilize the meanings of this prayer and know that we are pleasing to the Lord.

3. To whom is the prayer addressed?

   Directly to God in Heaven! Right at the start, when we pray in this manner, we are specifically directing our prayer to "Our Father", thus establishing who God is in relationship to us and also confirming that we are His children, (which gives us the right to approach Him). We are also acknowledging His holiness and giving Him due recognition and praise. Our approach is to be one of adoration and worship; submission and trust. Read **Psalm 100**. How are we to approach God according to this Psalm?

   Vs. 10. In this verse Jesus is showing us that we are to pray in accordance with God's Divine will. We are to bring our own wills into submission to God and enter in as a co-laborer with Christ to execute God's perfect will on earth and in our own lives as well. This verse reminds us to pray for those men and women who are laboring around the world to bring about God's will. Also remember to pray for Israel and the peace of Jerusalem, as this is definitely part of God's will on earth. 4. Read **Psalm 37.** What does this Psalm say about God's will on earth? **Vs. 11.** This verse shows us that it is acceptable to our Father to ask for what we need for each day. We have the privilege of expecting God to meet our needs, not only physically, but also spiritually. Remember that Jesus is the "Living Bread". Asking God to supply our spiritual needs also means that we acknowledge that He knows better than we do exactly what those spiritual needs are.

5. Read **Psalm 23.** Rewrite in your own words what needs the Good Shepherd meets.

Vs. 12. Anytime we approach the throne of God in prayer He expects us to be as forgiving to others as He is to us. God knows that there can be no true communion with Him in the Spirit when we are clinging to some specific sin in our lives. It is God's will that our relationship with Him be restored completely. Originally, man lost his relationship with God because of sin. Once the tie was broken, fear overtook man. With the advent of fear man lost his confidence, trust, faith in God. God offered forgiveness first to us so we could fellowship once again with Him and come to Him in faith. God expects us to also forgive others as He has forgiven us. We are adopted into His family...we are His children; and as His children we are to be like Him. It is impossible for us to fellowship with our Heavenly Father and to become like Him if we have any bitterness or unforgiveness in our hearts. We limit God and bind our own blessings by harboring such attitudes.

6. Read **Psalm 51.** If you were a reporter and had just interviewed David, (the author of this Psalm), how would you describe his spiritual condition?

Vs. 13. God does not tempt us! The evil one is Satan who desires our souls! We are to pray for God's protection against him, thus stating our position against the enemy and for God. We have perfectly aligned ourselves up with Almighty God, and are committed to godliness and opposed to evil. As we pray, we are to be willing to be totally set free from all sin and ask God for help to live a holy life for Him and for His glory.

7. Read **Psalms 91** and **121.** What do these Psalms tell us about God's protection from the evil one?

Vs. 13b. The Kingdom is God's and all the power and glory forever. Pray in acknowledgement that God has supreme authority, power, and glory...that we do have the victory in Him!

8. Read **Psalms 46, 47,** and **48.** List the verses in these **Psalms** that have to do with God's eternal reign:

There are **150 Psalms** and reading through them carefully and often will bless and strengthen the Christian because of the wonderful lessons on how to praise the Lord, worship Him, trust Him, please Him, and know Him. Read them faithfully.

Exercise: Write a prayer, in your own words, using the Disciples' Prayer as an outline.

CHAPTER THREE

IMPORTANCE OF PRAYER

1. **I Chron. 16:11** states, "Seek the Lord and His strength, seek His face continually." Which word is repeated twice and emphasized in the above verse?
2. Read **Matt. 7:7-11**. According to these verses would you say that God encourages us to approach Him with our needs as a child approaches his earthly father?

   Notice the action verbs: "Seek", "ask", and "knock". Would it be wise to seek for that which could never be found; or to ask for that which never would be given; or to knock when there would be no opening?

3. If it is God's desire to give us good things, why do you suppose He tells us to come to Him "seeking, asking, and knocking?"
4. Read **Luke 18:1-8**. What does this parable mean to you?

   John 16:24 says, "Hitherto have ye asked nothing in my name: ask, and ye shall receive, that your joy may be full." Read **John 17**. This chapter is truly the Lord's Prayer. Notice **verse 13**.

5. According to **John 16:24** and **17:13** what does the Lord desire for His disciples?
6. Would this be possible if the Christian never prayed? Why?
7. Read **Eph. 6:18**. What are some of the things we are commanded to do in this verse?
8. Read **Phil. 4:6**. Why is this important? (See **verse 7**).
9. Look up **Col. 4:2** and fill in the blanks: "____________________ in ______________, and ____________________ in the same with ______________________________."
10. According to **James 5:13-16**, what are we to do when we are sick?

Our Heavenly Father wants us to understand that He is the One who answers our prayers, and that it is He who is our Savior, Provider, Defender, Deliverer, Comforter, Redeemer, Lover of our souls, Nurturer, Hiding Place, Fortress, Rock, Advocate, Author and Finisher of our faith, Righteousness, Door, Hope, Light, Master, Protector, Physician, Peace, Resurrection, Sure Foundation, Teacher, and King. How can we truly know Him if we neglect to converse with Him daily?

Commune with Him in your heart...sing to Him with your lips...praise Him with uplifted hands...adore Him, revere Him, appreciate Him, extol Him...love Him.

CHAPTER FOUR

ADMONITIONS CONCERNING PRAYER

1. "Pray without ceasing." **I Thes. 5:17**. The Holy Spirit, through the Apostle Paul, is telling us to pray continually. What do you think this means?
2. Since God is looking at our hearts, and prayer is conversing with God, do you think this could mean that we are to be communicating with God in our hearts continually?

   Remember, the Holy Spirit indwells the born-again believer and He is interceding for us. It is possible to be praying in the spirit while the mind is occupied with other thoughts. See **I Cor. 14:14, 15**. God wants our hearts to be upright at all times before Him and in communion with the Holy Spirit within us. Read **Ps. 28:2, 63:4, 134:2, 143:6; I Tim. 2:8.**

   God's word is telling us to lift up our hands in worship to Him. Most of us are inhibited and self-conscious and therefore find it difficult to abandon ourselves, especially publicly, and freely worship the Lord. However, we are admonished in Scripture to raise our hands to the Lord in prayer and praise. Pray and ask the Holy Spirit to set you free to worship God. Ask Him to remove all fear of man, all bondages of the flesh, all pride, and to make you an instrument of praise. Once you experience freedom in worship, your relationship with God will take on new meaning and depth. Joy, peace, and love will fill your heart as you love and adore your Creator. Let the Holy Spirit praise God through you...lift your hands in surrender to His Majesty and open your lips in joyful praise to the One who created all things for His pleasure. The only gift we can possibly bring to the One who is the Possessor of all things is our sacrifice of praise! See **Psalm 107:22, 116:17; Jer. 33:11; Jonah 2:9; Heb. 13:15.**

   Matt. 26:41 says, "Watch and pray, that ye enter not into temptation: the spirit indeed is willing, but the flesh is week."

3. What do you think it means that "the spirit indeed is willing, but the flesh is weak?"
4. Is it always easy to pray?
5. Why do you think it is so hard to pray sometimes?
6. See **1 Pet. 5:8**. Who is seeking to destroy us if we are not watchful?
7. Why is prayer important in resisting the adversary?

   (See **Ps. 39:1**) If we are not "confessed up" and "prayed up", then we lose our confidence (faith) before God. Then, like Adam who hid from God because of his sin, we try to ignore the Lord and try to "hide" from Him by keeping busy and not getting into prayer. God is our Defender and Protector. He wants us to remain in fellowship with Him, to submit to Him, so that in times of trouble we will be able to resist the devil.

   James 4:7. If we are "out of touch" with the Lord, so to speak, the enemy has the advantage because he is able to attack us with lies, fear, temptation, and so on. Overcoming the lazy tendencies of the flesh is not always easy, but with the help of the Lord all things are possible to those who believe. Ask God to cause you to come to Him, to give you strength. See **Ps. 143:8**.

8. Jesus is our Great Example. Look up the following verses and note where and/or when Jesus prayed: (**Mark 1:35** (Example: Early in the morning); **Mark 6:46, 47; Luke 5:15, 16; Luke 6:12; Luke 9:18; Luke 22:41, 42**)

CHAPTER FIVE

FASTING AND PRAYER

Matt. 17:14-21 is the account of the healing of the demoniac son. Jesus mentions to His disciples the necessity of fasting and prayer in **verse 21**. Faith needs prayer for its development and full growth, and prayer needs fasting for the same reason. To fast means to abstain from food (that which caused the fall of man). Fasting humbles the soul before God **(Ps. 35:13)**; chastens the soul, **(Ps. 69:10)**; and crucifies the appetites, as well as denies them so as to give entire time for prayer, **(2 Sam. 12:16-23; Matt. 4:1-11)**; it manifests earnestness before God to the exclusion of all else **(1 Cor. 7:5)**; shows obedience, and gives the digestive system a rest, **(Matt. 6:16-18, 9:15; Luke 5:33-35)**.

1. Look up the words "fasted", "fasting" and "fastings" in the Concordance for just a few examples in Scripture of fasting.

2. There are 23 things that constitute a true fast in **Isa. 58:6-14**. There are also 20 blessings from a true fast mentioned in these verses. List below some of these facts and blessings:

3. Read **Joel 1:14** and **2:12**. How important do you think fasting is in these two Scriptures? Why?

4. Read **Matt. 6:17, 18**. What instructions does Jesus give for us today about fasting?

   All believers are supposed to fast, but no regulations or set rules are given as to how long or how often. That is determined by individual desire and needs. See **Matt. 9:14, 15; 2 Cor. 6:5; Acts 13:1-5**. Men should fast when under chastening, **(2 Sam. 12:16-23)**; under judgment, **(I Kings 21:27)**; in need, **(Ezra 8:21)**; in danger, **(Esther 4)**; when worried, **(Dan. 6:18)**; in trouble, **(Acts 27:9, 33);** in spiritual conflict**, (Matt. 4:1-11)**; and when desperate in **prayer (Acts 9:1-9, 10:30)**.

   In the following chapter we will look at a few verses on true prayer and the assurance that they are heard by God.

CHAPTER SIX

TRUE PRAYER IS HEARD

1. **Job 34:28**. God hears the prayers of whom?

2. **Ps. 4:3**. Why was David so confident that the Lord would hear when he called to Him?

3. Fill in the blanks **(Ps. 34:17)**, "The ____________________cry, and the Lord heareth, and ____________________ them __________ of __________ their ______________."

4. Read **verse 18**. Who is the Lord close to?

5. See **Ps. 18:6**. How was David feeling when he prayed to the Lord in this instance? What happened? (Read the whole **Psalm**)

6. Read **Prov. 15:29**. Who is the Lord far from? Whose prayers are heard?

   Read **Micah 7:7**. What are the two things that Micah said he would do? Was he sure that God would hear him? Why do you think he was so certain that his prayers would be answered?

7. How can we know that God will answer our prayers? (See **I John 5:12-15**.)

8. **Ps. 91:15** tells us that "He shall call upon me, and I will answer him: I will be with him in trouble; I will deliver him, and honour him." Look up the following words in a dictionary and write out a brief definition of each: "answer," "deliver," "honor."

9. Look up **Isa. 65:24** and **Jer. 33:3**. How soon does God answer?

10. Read **Dan. 10:10-14**. Was Daniel's prayer heard immediately? Why was there a delay in answer?

11. See **John 15:7**. What are the two conditions of answered prayer in this verse?

12. Read **Matt. 21:22**. What did Jesus say one had to do in order to receive an answer to prayer? Below are listed some verses which show God's promises to answer prayer:

    Ps. 91:15; Isa. 58:9, 65:24; Zec. 13:9; Luke 11:9; John 15:7; I John 3:22

    In the Bible itself there are 221 actual prayers recording (not to mention references to prayers). There are 176 in the Old Testament and 45 in the New Testament.

    In the next chapter we will discuss why some prayers are refused.

CHAPTER SEVEN

WHY SOME PRAYERS ARE REFUSED

Throughout Scripture there are many instances when God did not answer prayer. That does not mean that He did not hear those prayers, but there were certain reasons why He did not answer them. Let us consider some of these examples for our learning! Read the **first chapter** of **Deuteronomy**. Notice **verse 45**:

1. Explain in your own words why the Lord would not answer the children of Israel.

   See **I Sam. 14:37** and **28:6**. King Saul was living in disobedience to the Lord. God is not obligated to answer our prayers when we are living in willful disobedience! See **Ps. 66:18**. While some may be living in obvious sin, others harbor secret sins in their heart. This, too, is a hindrance to answered prayer!

2. Read **Prov. 1:24-33**. In your own words tell why prayer is refused.

3. According to **Prov. 21:13** what will happen if we ignore the needs of the poor?

   Other reasons for unanswered prayer are the following: Turning away from the truth – **Prov. 28:9**; Blood-guiltiness – **Isa. 1:15**; iniquity – **Isa. 59:2** and **Micah 3:4**; stubbornness – **Zec. 7:13**; instability – **Ja. 1:6, 7**; self-indulgence – **Ja. 4:3**; refusing to humble self – **2 Chron. 7:14**; forsaking God – **2 Chron. 15:2**; provoking God – **Deut. 3:26**; dishonor of companion – **I Pet. 3:7**; unbelief – **Matt. 17:20, 21, 21:22**; sin – **John 9:31**; **James 4:1-5**; parading prayer life – **Matt. 6:7**; unforgiveness – **Matt. 6:14, 15**; **Mark 11:25, 26**; hypocrisy – **Luke 18:9-14**; worry and anxiety – **Phil. 4:6**

   In **Ezek. 20** we read about the iniquity of Israel. In **vs. 3** we see God's response.

4. List some of the reasons God was angry with His people:

5. Read **2 Cor. 12:7-10**. What was Paul's attitude about his request to God and God's response?

6. Read **Matt. 26:36-46**. Why was Jesus in such agony?

7. How did He pray to the Father? **(vs. 39)**

   Have you ever been in a stressful situation and yet prayed, "Not my will, but Yours be done?" Are you willing to lay your life on the altar as a living sacrifice and allow the Lord to use you in any way He chooses? Have you come to a place in your Christian walk where you can honestly commit everything into His hands and leave it there? Ask the Lord to search your heart and show you any areas which may not be pleasing to Him.

Pray that He will increase your faith as the father of the demoniac child did when he said, "Lord, I believe; help thou mine unbelief." In the following chapter we will look at conditions of successful prayer.

CHAPTER EIGHT

CONDITIONS OF SUCCESSFUL PRAYER

1. Read **2 Chron. 7:14**. What is the condition in this verse for answered prayer?

   God also promised in **Ps. 34:18, 51:17; Isa. 66:2; Joel 2:13, and 2 Cor. 7:10** to be nigh, save, not despise, look at, be gracious, merciful, slow to anger, kind, and save those that be of a contrite heart. So, we see in these verses that contrition is acceptable to the Lord.

   Then in **Jer. 29:13** we read, "And ye shall seek me, and find me, when ye shall search for me with all your heart." See also **Joel 2:12 and Matt. 22:37.** Thus, we learn that whole-heartedness is required by the Lord. God does not approve of "half-way" commitments.

2. Read **Rev. 3:15, 16.** What does God think of being "lukewarm"?

3. Read **Mark 11:24.** What is the key to answered prayer in this verse?

4. Read **Luke 7:1-10.** How did Jesus know that the Centurion had faith?

   As we already studied, without faith it is impossible to please God. **(Heb. 11:6).**

   Righteousness is the other pre-requisite to answered prayer. Remember **Jam. 5:16** which states, "Confess your faults to one another, and pray one for another, that ye may be healed. The effectual fervent prayer of a righteous man availeth much."

   ❖ See **I John 3:22.** According to this verse, why do we receive what we ask of God?

5. Read **Matt. 18:19.** How many people need to be in agreement in order for God to answer their prayers?

6. Read **Luke 1:1-17**. What great thing happened while all the people were praying outside the temple?

7. What did the people do after Jesus' ascension? **(Acts 1:14)**

Look at **Acts 4:24; 12:12,** and **21:5** for other examples when the believers were of one mind in prayer. Remember, there is power in agreement!

At the conclusion of this study on prayer, may we suggest you try to memorize as much of God's Word as possible; especially those verses which give God's instruction and promises regarding prayer. When the tempter comes and tries to undermine your faith, use the Sword of the Spirit, which is the Word of God against him. Commune with the Lord in your heart; praise Him with your voice; and pray without ceasing. Review this study from time to time and add other verses that are helpful to you. Share with others what the Lord is doing in your life. This will not only help them, but will build your own faith as well. May the Lord bless and guide you as you seek His face!

WHAT IS THE CHURCH

IN PREPARATION

PRAYER: "Most gracious Heavenly Father, help me to want the truth of Your Word with my whole heart, soul, and mind. May Your Holy Spirit guide, direct, and teach me as I search the Scriptures in this Bible study, and grant that I may learn what You would have me to know. I pray that in thought, word, and deed, I may be pleasing and acceptable in Your sight. And, Lord, with all my learning, help me to gain understanding - - understanding of Who You are; understanding of Your ways; understanding of Your will for my life; and a greater understanding of Your Holy Word. I pray in the Name of Jesus. Amen."

* * * * * * * * * * * * * *

Read **Psalm 111:1** in the King James Version. Notice the words "assembly" and "congregation".

Definitions:

Assembly – A session; company of persons (in close deliberation); intimacy; consultation.
Congregation – Assemblage – a family or crowd; company, multitude of people.

1. Where was Jesus preaching and teaching in each of the following verses?
   Matt. 5:1-2; 13:1-2; 14:15-21; Mark 1:21, 39; Luke 5:17-20; John 2:19-21

Read **Matt. 16:18.** This is the first time the word "church" occurs in Scripture.

Definition:

Church – ekklesia – A calling out; a popular meeting;
community of members on earth or saints in heaven; assembly.

The above definition applies every time the word church or churches occurs in the New Testament except in one verse, **Acts 19:37**, where the emphasis is on the despoiler (person who robs). In this verse "churches" refers to the pagan sanctuary of the goddess Diana at Ephesus. So, we see that the word "church" does not in any way whatsoever mean "building" or "denomination".

2. Since "church" means assembly of believers, read the following verses and write down the different places they met: **Acts 1:13-14; 16:13; Col. 4:15**
3. Read **Matt. 18:20.** How many people did Jesus say were necessary in order for Him to be in their midst?

According to the Book of Knowledge, Volume 3, pages 281 and 282, after the apostles died, leadership passed to the local pastors known as bishops. Under them were ministers of lower rank, presbyters and deacons. For the first three centuries, Christians assembled for their weekly worship in private houses. At that time only people baptized as Christians could join in Christian worship. After the Roman Emperor Constantine set himself up as ruler of the whole-civilized world in about 324 AD, he began to erect church buildings. The Roman Catholic Church has always maintained that the Apostle Peter was the first "pope". However, according to the very thorough and excellent book, *The Two Babylons or the Papal Worship* by the late Rev. Alexander Hislop, it was about 378 AD when the bishops of Rome fell heir to the keys that were the symbols of two well-known pagan divinities at Rome. For intensive study, please refer to *The Two Babylons*. The point we wish to make here is that the early church did not meet in designated buildings set aside for the sole purpose of "having church" at specified times as we practice today in our "modern" society.

4. What are Elders and Deacons? A good comparison of these two positions is found in **Acts 6:1-7.**
5. Who would be similar to the elders?
6. Who would be similar to the deacons?

Let's consider each of these positions. Elders means, bishop, overseer, and spiritual superintendent. **(1 Tim. 3:1-7; Tit. 1:5-9)**

7. What are the qualifications of an Elder?
8. What are their responsibilities? **(1 Peter 5:2; 1 Timothy 3:2; Titus 1:8- 9; James 5:14)**
9. Summarize the right attitude of an elder according to **1 Peter 5:2-3.**

Deacons/Deaconess means "Servant, Minister, Helper, and Assistant". **(Acts 6:3; 1 Timothy 3:8-13)**

10. What are the qualifications of a Deacon?
11. What are their responsibilities? **(Acts 6:2)**
12. What qualities must the wives/women uphold?

When Paul wrote "Unto the church of God which is at Corinth, to them that are sanctified in Christ Jesus, called to be saints, with all that in every place", he was writing to all the believers in that particular area and also to all believers everywhere and not just to a particular group who met on a regular basis in a certain building on certain days of the week!

Read: **Ro. 8:15-18; 12:5; 1 Cor. 6:15; 12:27; Ephesians; 1 Tim. 3:15; Col. 1:18.**

13. Who is the Body of Christ?
14. Are there many different bodies or just one?
15. Who is the Head?
16. Does every Christian have a part in this body?
17. Is church membership necessary for salvation? Explain: (Use scripture for the basis of your answer)
18. Read **Eph. 4:11, 12.** What do apostles, prophets, evangelists, pastors, and teachers do according to these two verses?

Definitions:

Apostle – "to send out on a mission; a delegate;
an ambassador of the gospel; officially a commissioner of Christ
["apostle"] (with miraculous powers); apostle, messenger, he that is sent."

Prophet – "a foreteller; an inspired speaker."

<u>Evangelist</u> – "a preacher of the Gospel; to announce good news, ("evangelize") especially the Gospel: - - declare, bring (declare, show) glad (good) tidings, preach (the Gospel)."

<u>Pastor</u> – "shepherd"

<u>Teacher</u> – "an instructor, master."

19. Read **1 Cor. 9:1-16.** Are apostles, prophets, evangelists, pastors, and teachers entitled to support by other members of the Body of Christ?

In **<u>verse 13 of 1 Cor. 9</u>** Paul is referring to the priests' dues in the Old Testament. God set it up that way. For further study, read: **Lev. 2:3; 10:13; 27:21; Nu. 3:48; 5:9; 18:9, 12, 21; De. 18:3; 2 Ki. 12:16**. Paul is applying these principles to the body of Christ. In **Mal. 3:10** the word "meat" means just that - - "meat" for God's priests.

Read **Gal. 6:6** and **Heb. 13:15-17.**

Definition:

<u>Communicate</u> – "to share with others: distribute, be partakers."

20. How does God expect His people to treat those who teach them and watch over their souls?
21. Read **2 Cor. 8 and 9**. In your own words summarize Paul's teachings concerning benevolence.
22. Are you a "cheerful" giver?

Read **Acts 20:35.**

23. What does **James 4:17** mean?
24. What does **1 Tim. 6:6-12** say about riches and the Christian life?
25. What is "covetousness"? (Look in the Concordance)
26. Read **Ex. 20:17; Col. 3:5; Luke 12:15**. Why do you suppose God included the commandment concerning covetousness in the Ten Commandments?
27. Read **Jer. 6:13**. Does this resemble today's church in America and other parts of the world? In what ways?
28. Read **1 John 3:16, 17.** How are we to treat our brethren in Christ? **(Gal. 6:10)**
29. How are we to treat those outside of the household of faith?
30. Read: **1 Cor. 3:16; 6:19, 20; 1 Pet. 2:5**. What is our body called if we are a Christian?
31. Why should Christians glorify God in both body and spirit?
32. How does God expect His people to live? **(2 Cor. 6:14-18)** (Tell in your own words.)
33. If you are a "born again believer", what are you a part of? **(Eph. 2:19-22)**
34. What do you think "spiritual sacrifices" are? **(1 Pet. 2:5-10)**
35. According to the following verses, how should we live as members of Christ's body? **Phil. 4:2: 1 Thes. 4:9b, 11, 12; 1 Pet. 3:10-14; 1 John**.
36. List some of the problems of the early Church. Do we have these same problems today? **(1 Cor. 3:3; 6:6; 2 Cor. 12:20)**
37. Read **1 Cor. 12, 13** and **14.** Does God want us to be ignorant concerning spiritual gifts? List some of God's spiritual gifts:
38. Re-read chapter **12 verse 28** and also **Ro. 12:5-8**. Write what you think each of these gifts are and how they can be used in today's assembly.
39. Which gift (s) do you think God has given to you?

40. According to chapter **13** of **1 Corinthians**, which is more important, tongues, prophecy, knowledge, good works, self-sacrifice, or love?
41. Re-read **chapter 14**. According to **verse 1**, with love as our motivation, then what are we to desire?
42. See **14:4.** What does prophecy do?
43. Is there supposed to be an interpretation of tongues when a prophecy is given in the church?
44. Concerning our private, personal prayer language given to us by the Holy Spirit when we are baptized by the Spirit, what does Paul mean in **verses 14** and **15** of **chapter 14**?
45. What will the unlearned say if they hear all the people in the church speaking in tongues at the same time?
46. See **verse 39**. Are we to forbid speaking in tongues?
47. See **verse 33.** What is God the author of?
48. See **verse 40.** How are all things to be done?
49. Have you been filled with the Holy Spirit? Study **Matt. 3:11; Luke 3:16; John 1:33; Luke 11:13; Acts 2:1-21; 4:31; 10:44-48; 19:6.**

    If you have not been baptized by Jesus in the Holy Spirit...simply ask Him in faith believing, and you shall receive.

50. Read **Acts 2:41-47** and **Acts 4:32-37.** At this time, in the early church, how were the finances handled?
51. How do you feel this compares with today's modern church system in America?
52. Can you think of any specific examples?
53. Look up the words "tithe", "tithes", and "tithing" in your concordance. Find how many times Jesus admonished His followers to tithe.
54. Read **Matt. 6:19-21.** What does Jesus mean by "...lay up for yourselves treasures in heaven?"
55. Read **Matt. 19:16-26; 7:12; 25:31-46; Mark 12:41-44; Luke 10:30-35; 16:19-31; 18:18-27.**

    - How does Jesus expect us to give?

    See **Matt. 6:1-4; Luke 11:41; 12:33; Acts 10:2-4, 31**. Alms are not mentioned in the Old Testament.

Definition:

Alms – "compassionateness, i.e. (as exercised towards the poor); beneficence; tender mercy."

However, God instructed Israel to care for the poor, widows, fatherless, strangers, etc.

56. Read **1 Cor. 16:1-3**. "Collection" means contribution. Who was it for?
57. Read **Rev. 1-3**. Below is a list of the seven churches in these three chapters. Beside their names are two columns...one for Jesus' commendations and one for His rebukes. List the correct answers in each column. (Briefly)

CHURCH	COMMENDATIONS	REBUKES
Ephesus	______________________	
	______________________	

Smyrna ____

____

Pergamos ____

____

Thyatira ____

____

Sardis ____

____

Philadelphia ____

____

Laodicea ____

58. Read **Eph. 5:25-27.** What kind of a church is Jesus returning for?

Jesus said, "And, behold, I come quickly; and my reward is with me, to give every man according as his work shall be. I am Alpha and Omega, the beginning and the end, the first and the last. I Jesus have sent mine angel to testify unto you these things in the churches. I am the root and the offspring of David, and the bright and morning star. Surely I come quickly." **(Rev. 22:12, 13, 16, 20.)**

Prayer: "Dear Lord, help me to understand that I am a part of Your body, and that You died to purchase me. Help me to honor You in word and deed all the days of my life; and may I bring glory to Your Holy Name, so that in that great day when I shall stand before You face to face, I will hear the words, 'Well done, thou good and faithful servant'." AMEN.

WHAT TRUE MINISTRY IS ALL ABOUT

INTRODUCTION

The Bible study you now hold in your hands is the result of our desire to bring the Christian worker into a balanced understanding of what true ministry is. So many today view "the ministry" as something glamorous with Hollywood style trappings. Not so! We advise dedicated Christians to read the works of A.W. Tozer, Oswald Chambers, Fox's Book of Martyrs, and other classical works about the great men and women of time past whose lives exemplified the heart of true Christianity.

We are building a holy habitation for the Holy God who has declared in His word that our bodies are the temple of the Holy Spirit. As with any successful building, the foundation is of utmost importance. If the foundation is off even one degree, the entire structure will be out of line. Therefore, it is our sincere desire that each Christian seriously consider their foundation. All that is needed for the construction of this holy temple is given in the word of God. Therein we find the blueprint, instructions, tools, and source of strength for this task.

God's goal is to mature us in Christ, raising us up to be the light and the salt of the world. This cannot be accomplished if any part of us remains attached to the things of this world. There must be a complete separation. We are to be a separate, holy, undefiled people. If we are to experience the presence of our Holy God within our midst and partake of His anointing and miracles, we must be vessels of honor.

Each of us is responsible for the welfare and future state of our own soul. No one can make the necessary daily decisions for us. It is up to us. Our prayer is that God will so form his character within your heart that your only goal in this life and the next will be for Him. Remember, character is formed through the purifying fire. There is no other way. There is a price to pay, but we must first be willing to pay that price. God will never force us into His presence or kingdom. The choice is ours.

Time is short, the harvest is ripe, and the night is coming when no man can work. May you hear the Shepherd's call to feed His sheep, and may you diligently study to show yourself approved, a workman that need not be ashamed. For we shall all stand before the judgment seat of Christ where our works shall be revealed for all time and eternity. As Oswald Chambers wrote in *My Utmost For His Highest*, "The conditions of discipleship laid down by Our Lord in **Luke 14:26, 27** and **33** mean that men and women He is going to use in His mighty building enterprises are those in whom He has done everything. 'If any man come to Me, and hate not . . ., he cannot be my disciple.' Our Lord implies that the only men and women he will use in His building enterprises are those who love Him personally, passionately, and devotedly beyond any of the closest ties on earth. The conditions are stern, but they are glorious.

All that we build is going to be inspected by God. Is God going to detect in His searching fire that we have built on the foundation of Jesus some enterprise of our own? These are days of tremendous enterprises, days when we are trying to work for God, and therein is the snare. Profoundly speaking, we can never work for God. Jesus takes us over for His enterprises, His building schemes entirely, and no soul has any right to claim where he or she shall be put."

LESSON ONE

THE COMMISSION

"And Jesus came and spake unto them, saying, All power is given unto me in heaven and in earth. Go ye therefore, and teach all nations, baptizing them in the name of the Father, and of the Son and of the Holy Ghost: Teaching them to observe all things whatsoever I have commanded you: and, lo, I am with you alway, even unto the end of the world. Amen" **(Matt. 28:18-20)**. It is generally understood that as Jesus gave this commission to the eleven disciples, they represent all disciples of Christ down through the ages. Therefore, this great commandment is as much in effect today as it was nearly 2,000 years ago.

The Greek word for <u>disciple</u> is "mathetes," which means a learner and/or pupil. Jesus told His disciples to teach to <u>observe</u> all things that He had commanded His disciples. In this context, <u>teach</u> means to learn. <u>Observe</u> means to guard by keeping the eye upon; hold fast; keep; serve, and watch. This is where we extract the message of these verses "to make disciples" with the understanding that a disciple is not equivalent with a convert.

<u>Convert</u> means one who has been converted from one religion or belief to another. To be converted means to persuade or induce, to adopt a particular religion, faith, or belief. In other words, people who are converted have been persuaded to change their mind. But true Christianity involves far more than a changed way of thinking! It is a whole new way of living, which are the results of spiritual rebirth and a total yielding of the self to Christ.

Notice these action words in "The Great Commission": Go; teach; baptizing; teaching to observe. This is our part. God's part is outlined in the opening statement of Christ's dialog and in His final statement. In other words, He promised," All power is given unto me in heaven and in earth. . . . lo, I am with you always, even unto the end of the world." This reminds me of a sandwich; the Bread of Life surrounding and protecting the "meat" of the Gospel message.

Mark 13:10 tells us, "And the gospel must first be published among all nations."

1. What is the definition of the gospel? (See **1 Cor. 15:3, 4; Lk. 24:46-48**.)
2. What is the definition of "witness"? (Look it up in your Concordance.)

If you have never written out your testimony, please do so now. Your testimony is a powerful means of witnessing to others. It is also a weapon against Satan. (See **Rev. 12:11**.)

The Bible tells us, "Therefore if any man be in Christ, he is a new creature: old things are passed away; behold, all things are become new" **(2 Cor. 5:17)**.

3. Look up **verses 18** and **19**. What ministry has God given to us?
4. What does the word "ambassador" mean?

Being a representative of Christ is a grave responsibility.

5. How does one attain the position of ambassador for Christ?

6. Look up the following scriptures and write the key to being Christ's representative. (**2 Cor. 6:1, 3, 4-10)**
7. Would you conclude from the above scriptures that true ministry is glamorous?
8. What does the word "minister" mean? (Look in your Concordance #1249 in the Greek Dictionary section.)

   Many people today want to be in the ministry. The same was true in Bible times.

9. Following is a list of some Bible characters. Write your opinion as to why God could or could not use them as His ministers and/or witnesses. (Note their characteristics). John The Baptist **(Matt. 3:4, 7; 3:15; 11:11; 14:4, 10; Mk. 1:5,7; 6:20; Lk. 7:24-27; Jn. 1:19-23; 5:35; 10:41)**
10. (Note: Are miracles necessarily a sign of greatness in the Kingdom of God?) Why?
11. (What constitutes greatness in the Kingdom of God? See **Jn. 13:1-17**.)

Abel **(Gen. 4:4; Heb. 11:4)**
Enoch **(Gen. 5:22; Heb. 11:5)**
Noah **(Gen. 7:1, 5; 8:20; Heb. 11:7)**
Abraham **(Gen.18:17-33; Gen. 22:18; Heb. 11:8-10)**
Sarah **(Heb. 11:11)**
Joseph **(Gen. 39:7-9; 41:38, 39)**
Moses **(Heb. 11:24-29)**
Joshua **(Ex. 33:11; Josh. 24:15)**
Caleb **(Josh. 14:8, 9)**
Ruth **(Ruth 1:16; 2:12; 3:11)**
Samuel **(1 Sam. 3:19)**
King Saul **(1 Sam. 13:12, 13; 28:5-10)**
David **(1 Sam. 16:7; 17:45-47)**
Job **(Job 1:1, 8, 20-22; 2:3; Ja. 5:11)**
Isaiah **(Is. 6:5-8)**
Daniel **(Da. 1:8; 5:12; 6:4, 10, 11)**
Peter & Andrew **(Matt. 4:18-20)**
John & James **(Matt. 4:21, 22)**
Nathanael **(Jn. 1:47)**
A Ruler **(Lk. 18:18-27)**
Explain **Lk. 9:57-62**
Saul (Paul) **(Acts 9:6, 16, 20)**
Stephen **(Acts 6:5, 8, 10)**
Phebe **(Ro. 16:1, 2)**

12. What kind of people does God call? (See **1 Cor. 1:26-28**) Why? **(1 Cor. 1:29-31)** Read **James 3:1** and look up, in your Concordance, the word master.
13. What does this word mean and what warning is in this verse and why?
33. Describe the call of God on your life.
34. What is the power of God? **(1 Cor 1:18; Ro. 1:16)**
17. What does **Galatians 6:14** mean to you?
18. What was Paul's desire? **(1 Cor. 2:2)**
35. What kind of people does God give grace to? **(Ja. 4:6)**
36. Do you believe people who are "in the ministry" are somehow superior to others? Explain.

LESSON TWO

WHAT TRUE MINISTRY IS *NOT*

One of the most important lessons we as disciples can learn is what ministry is *not*! This lesson will deal with important issues that Christians must be aware of if they are to represent Christ. These topics are alphabetically listed below and then discussed in more detail in the following pages of this chapter.

Arguing	Assuming	Bragging
Bigoted	Competitive	Causes
Defensive	Demanding	Expectations
Entertainment	Financial gain	Fame
Glamorous	Guaranteed "success"	Harshness
Here to serve self	Ignorance	Immunity from problems
Joining unequally	Knit picking	Knowing it all
Leaning on flesh	Legalism	Mostly being up front
Man-pleasing	"Noo-noo land"	Obnoxious/Out of order
Puffed up	Predictable	Quick results
Religious	Rude	Self-serving/striving
Talking too much	Trying in own strength	Understood by others
Undisciplined behavior	Validated by man	Walking by sight
Worshipping your work	Yielding to flesh	"Zoning out"

1. Concerning arguing, what does Jesus' warning in **Matt. 5:25** mean to you?

   Look up **2 Tim. 2:14; 23-25**.

2. Why did Paul advise young Timothy to warn the believers against arguing?
3. What kind of questions cause strife among people?
4. What must the servant of the Lord do?

   All of us make assumptions, but assuming things about others is especially dangerous in Christianity. How many times have you heard someone say, "I'm a Christian," and later on it turned out they were far from it? Because someone goes to church and "talks the talk" doesn't mean they are born again. The other assumption that can get us into is trouble is assuming others think and believe the way we do. It pays to be a good listener before exposing our own viewpoints. Of course, the most dangerous assumption is when we assume we are "A-okay" with the Lord, while ignoring admonitions from the Word; rebukes by the Holy Spirit, or others who may be lovingly trying to get our attention.

5. Read **Ex. 32:1**. What did the Israelites assume?
6. What was King Saul's assumption and what was the result according to **2 Sam. 21:1-14**?
7. In **1 Ki. 13:11-34**, what did the prophet assume?
8. What was John's assumption in **John 9:38**?

9. What did the apostles assume Jesus was going to do according to their comment as recorded in **Acts 1:6**?
10. What was the terrible assumption Jesus spoke of to His disciples in **John 16:2**?
11. What did Saul of Tarsus assume in **Acts 9:1, 2**?
12. According to the account in **Rev. 3:14-22**, what did the Laodicean church assume?
13. What does **Prov. 14:12** mean to you? (**Memorize this verse**.)

The next word on our list, <u>bragging</u>, is the same as boasting. The focus is on self rather than Christ. Boasting is not only displeasing to the Lord, (because it is pride and a form of idolatry), but it causes people to turn away from us.

14. Read **1 Cor. 1**. Write what you learned in this chapter about the kind of people God chooses to use and why.
15. What does **Prov. 27:1, 2** tell us about boasting and self-praise?
16. What does **James 3:5** and **4:16** say about the tongue?

A <u>bigot</u> is a person who is rigidly devoted to his own group, religion, race, or politics and is intolerant of those who differ. As Christians, we know the Way, the Truth, and the Life, and those who disagree with us concerning Christ do not threaten our position in Christ. As His servants, we are called to be "made all things to all men, that we might by all means save some." (See **1 Cor. 9:22**.) Our goal is to win the lost to Jesus, not impose upon them our own ideas and causes! Bigoted people do much harm to the cause of the Gospel of Jesus Christ because of their unyielding and judgmental attitudes.

17. Read **Acts 10** and explain what Peter learned.
18. Who was bigoted in **Luke 19:7**?
19. What is the result of prejudice? **(Mark 6:3)**

Concerning competition in the Christian realm, the disciples were just as human as the rest of us. Jesus addressed their competitive spirit more than once.

20. What example did the Lord give of true ministry in **John 13:3-17**?
21. What was Christ's admonition to Peter in **John 21:18-22**?

Phil. 2:14 says, "Do all things without murmurings and disputings."

22. What does competition lead to? (See **Gen. 37:4; 1 Sam. 18:8; Matt. 20:12; Lu. 15:28**.)

Phil. 2:3, 4 tells us, "Let nothing be done through strife or vainglory; but in lowliness of mind let each esteem other better than themselves. Look not every man on his own things, but every man also on the things of others."

Gal. 6:1-5 says,

> Brethren, if a man be overtaken in a fault, ye which are spiritual, restore such an one in the spirit of meekness; considering thyself, lest thou also be tempted. Bear ye one another's burdens, and so fulfil the law of Christ. For if a man think himself to be something, when he is nothing, he deceiveth himself. But let every man prove his own work, and then shall he have rejoicing in himself alone, and not in another. For every man shall bear his own burden.

In **verse one** we see to whom is committed the ministry of reconciliation; those who are spiritual and who have the spirit of meekness. The reason for this is if we confront one who has gone astray with a spirit of pride or self-righteousness, then that very temptation will trip us up. This is because *pride goes before a fall* and by confronting another with a spirit of pride, we have just opened the door to the enemy. Then we will discover the truth of Jesus' words when He said,

> Judge not, that ye be not judged. For with what judgment ye judge, ye shall be judged: and with what measure ye mete, it shall be measured to you again. And why beholdest thou the mote that is in thy brother's eye, but considerest not the beam that is in thine own eye? Or how wilt thou say to thy brother, let me pull out the mote out of thine eye; and, behold, a beam is in thine own eye? Thou hypocrite, first cast out the beam out of thine own eye; and then shalt thou see clearly to cast out the mote out of thy brother's eye. **(Matt. 7:1-5)**

As Christians, all confrontation must be for the sake of the other person and for the glory of God. Personal causes should never be the motivation behind confrontation. Rather, than being in competition with one another, we need to obey verse **two** of **Galatians 6** which means to help lift up what is weighing down (or bringing down) another person. This is true ministry; that is, having compassion which literally means, "entering into and suffering with."

Lest there be confusion concerning **verse six** of this same chapter where we are told to bear our own burden, burden here means our service, work, or responsibility. Not only are we to be faithful with what the Lord has called us to, but we are also accountable where our flesh is concerned. Each of us must carry our own cross, or, crucifying the flesh and allowing the Holy Spirit to regenerate us.

Personal causes have done much to discredit true Christian service. Some areas where the Christian worker may be tempted to take up causes are politics, the abortion issue, religious works, building churches, etc. These may be "good" things, but they take the place of the best, which is Christ.

23. What did the Apostle Paul tell the believers at Corinth according to **1 Cor. 2:2**?

Satan prefers we become entangled in "causes" rather than preach Christ. He knows very well causes usually take God's people on detours, wasting precious time, energy, and resources. Causes can give a false sense of "doing something for God" which also appeals to our vanity and pride. Realistically, if we wish to see our government change, society change, and the church change, we need to pray that God's people everywhere humble themselves and repent. **1 Chron. 7:14** says, "If my people, which are called by my name, shall humble themselves, and pray, and seek my face, and turn from their wicked ways; then will I hear from heaven, and will forgive their sin, and will heal their land."

When we minister our causes, we minister in our own strength for our own ends. Some people may outwardly conform to a cause, but God is not interested in *conformation*—He is interested in *transformation*!

24. Read **John 12:1-7**. What was Judas' cause?
25. What did Paul charge the elders and why in **Acts 20:17-38**?
26. What did Paul tell the Corinthians in **2 Cor. 4:5**?
27. Is it possible to be caught up with another Jesus, spirit, or gospel? See **2 Cor. 11:3, 4**.

Causes can also cause us to be *defensive.* We want everybody to line up to our way of thinking. However, in true ministry, we must always line up to Jesus. Christ was never defensive, for He is the truth. Truth does not need to be defended because regardless of what people think or do, the truth will always remain! In **1 Peter 3:15, 16** we read, "But sanctify the Lord God in your hearts: and be ready always to give an answer to every man that asketh you a reason of the hope that is in you with meekness and fear. Having a good conscience; that, whereas they speak evil of you, as of evildoers, they may be ashamed that falsely accuse your good conversation in Christ."

28. What does **2 Tim. 4:2** mean?

Unfortunately, many people enter the ministry with a demanding attitude. No Christian has the right to make demands! Our Lord certainly did not, and if anyone had the right to, it was Christ! We see an increasing number of Christian "stars" today who hold prominent positions because of their Hollywood-type TV success. Behind the scenes, many of these people are arrogant and demanding. This attitude has to be brought to the cross and crucified. Ministry means service. We are here to follow Christ's example of servitude.

29. What is the opposite of pride and arrogance according to **Prov. 8:13**?
30. Read **Nu. 11:4-6.** Would you say that the people were a demanding people?
31. Explain **Prov. 21:10.**
32. What did the Apostle Paul command believers according to **Eph. 5:21**?

All of us have expectations! When we become engaged, we have great expectations for the forthcoming marriage. When we begin a new career, we hold to expectations of success and prosperity. Vacation planning brings with it certain expectations also. We find this is true for those aspiring to become ministers of the Gospel. Unfortunately, most expectations of ministry for the inexperienced are based upon false images erected by today's TV and radio personalities along with unrealistic printed material.

Hope in the promises of God is not the same thing as having expectations based upon pre-conceived notions and concepts. Often our expectations are based upon personal desires and agendas. It takes a great deal of integrity and time before the Lord to sort out fact from fiction. The Christian worker must receive a love for the truth so deception will not take root. (See **2 Thes. 2:10**.)

33. What did the Lord Jesus tell Saul of Tarsus in **Acts 9:16**?
34. What did Jesus mean when he prophesied Peter's future in **John 21:18**?
35. What did Jesus say were the requirements for discipleship in **Luke 14:26-27**?

What about entertainment? Entertainment means, to hold the attention of; to amuse. Let's get right to the point on this one. In the majority of modern churches today we see entertainment at an all time high. It's almost as if there is a kind of competition going on to see who can come up with the latest, the biggest, and the most outlandish form of amusement. The idea seems to be that since the world holds the interest of the masses through entertainment, then the Church must somehow compete to gain people's interest.

Aside from truly evangelistic and/or biblically based plays, musicals, and such, this concept is right from the pit. Bottom line, entertainment is a *thief.* It steals valuable time, energy, and resources. It competes with the truth, the power, and the anointing of the Word of God and the Holy Spirit. Entertainment lulls people's reasoning powers to sleep, and causes a sort of mental lethargy. Basically, it can become an addictive idol, appealing to the flesh and resulting in spiritual dullness.

Let's face it, much of the Church today would rather play than pray! How can I be so sure about that? Easy! Just look at the mess our country is in and tell me how entertainment has influenced it for good (and for God, for that matter.)

36. What did the Israelites do when they were waiting for Moses in **Ex. 32:6**?
37. Who enjoyed sports and entertainment, and who was the one to provide it according to **Judges 16:23-25**?
38. Who held a great feast in his house and what kind of a man was he according to **1 Sam. 25:3, 26**?
39. Who had a birthday party and what was the tragic result according to **Matt. 14:1-12**?
40. What did God say about the pre-flood world in **Gen. 6:5, 6**?
41. Read **Col. 3:17, Phil. 4:8, Luke 21:34, Ro. 12:2, Col. 3:2, Tit. 2:12-15, 1 Pet. 1:13, Eph. 5:4, 16-20.**

By using the above texts and other cross references, explain how God's people are to think, act, and speak. You may make this in sermon form, as an article, topical teaching, or however you feel led.

Do a study on the joy of the Lord and show the difference between worldly entertainment and true celebration of life in Christ. A study of the feasts and celebrations of the traditional Jewish people will greatly enhance your understanding of the true meaning of rejoicing and life without the emptiness and meaninglessness of worldly entertainment, which is Satan's powerful counterfeit.

42. What was Christ's mission? (Look up **Lk. 4:43; 12:49; 19:10; Jn. 3:17; 9:39; 10:10**.)
43. How did Jesus say all men would be drawn to Him? **(John 12:32)**
44. Did Christ at any time teach or train His disciples to "entertain" people into the Kingdom? (Yes ________ No _______)
45. What did Paul say about the gospel? **(Ro. 1:16) Memorize this verse**.
46. What does **Dt. 4:29-31** promise and to whom?
47. Describe the wicked according to **Ps. 10:4; 36:1-4**.
48. Read **Psalm 27**. What should the believer be seeking and how should he spend his days?
49. According to **2 Tim. 2:15**, what should the disciple be doing and why?
50. What did Jesus say about the Christian life according to **Matt. 7:13, 14**?

It is with the wrong motivation that some enter the ministry as a profession rather than in obedience to the commands of Christ. Many are standing behind pulpits today that have neither the heart nor the call of the Holy Spirit. To serve the King of kings and the Lord of lords is the highest calling. One's own purpose, plans, policies, and programs must be laid aside in order for the higher calling in Christ to be realized. It is a holy calling with great responsibilities and grave consequences. (See **Ja. 3:1, 2**.) The Bible is explicit concerning covetousness, greed, and riches.

51. Look up the following scriptures and match the thought with the correct verse:

Pr. 22:16 ______________________	A. Iniquity of covetousness
Job 31:24______________________	B. A man's life
Ecc. 5:10 ______________________	C. Erred from the faith
Isa. 57:17 ______________________	D. Giveth to the rich
Matt. 6:19, 20 __________________	E. Gain is godliness
Matt. 16:26 ____________________	F. Added unto you
Eph. 5:3 _______________________	G. Love not the world

1 Tim. 6:5 ______________________	H. Earthly treasures
1 Tim. 6:6 ______________________	I. High minded
1 Tim. 6:8 ______________________	J. Vanity
1 Tim. 6:9 ______________________	K. Great gain
1 Tim. 6:10 ______________________	L. Rejoicing in wealth
1 Tim. 6:17 ______________________	M. Gain the world
1 Jn. 2:15 ______________________	N. Drown men
Matt. 6:33 ______________________	O. Covetousness
Lk. 12:15 ______________________	P. Content

52. What is better than rubies according to **Prov. 8:11**?
53. What do the righteous do? **(Prov. 21:26b)**
54. What did the Israelites do in **Ex. 35:22?**
55. How does **Acts 4:34, 35** compare with the mindset of the American church today?
56. What was the purpose of working according to **Eph. 4:28**?
57. What did Jesus say to do in **Matt. 6:19**?
58. What does **Prov. 22:1** say about a good name and loving favor?

Fame means, great reputation and recognition; renown; public esteem.

59. What motivates our desire to be famous?
60. What did John the Baptist say in **Mark 1:7** and **John 3:30**?
61. What did the Apostle Paul say about himself in **1 Cor. 15:9**?
62. What is promised to those who are prideful and those who are humble according to **Prov. 29:23**?
63. Who does God Almighty dwell with according to **Is. 57:15**?
64. Who is the greatest in the kingdom of heaven according to Jesus in **Matt. 18:4**?
65. What is good? **(Mi. 6:8)**
66. What did Paul write in **Ro. 12:3**?
67. What will happen to the one who chooses the place of honor according to Jesus in **Luke 14:8-11**?
68. Our Lord was free from all worldly pride. Look up the following scriptures and ask yourself if you are willing to do likewise in your walk with Him: Appearance ---- **Is. 53:2**; Worldly success----**Is. 53:3**; Reputation----**Matt. 2:23**; Riches----**Matt. 8:20**; Rank----**Matt. 13:55**; Kingship----**Jn. 13:5.**
69. According to **Prov. 11:2**, what is the result of pride?
70. List the three things that are of this world according to **1 Jn. 2:16**.

Glamour means, an air of compelling charm, romance, and excitement, esp. when delusively alluring; magic; enchantment. And, how many people today view the ministry as glamorous? The truth is, there is nothing glamorous about it, and especially so in light of the definition of glamorous. Nevertheless, there are still many zealous people, lacking in knowledge, who jump into "the ministry", per se, with the delusive idea that somehow it is all going to be romantic and enchanting. For those who begin their service with this false notion, the end is tragic.

71. What did the Apostle Paul write about his brethren, Israel, in **Ro. 10:1-3**?

In this passage of scripture, we see unwise zeal, legalism, spiritual ignorance, self-righteousness, stubbornness, and trust in works. These are the kinds of things which result from lack of knowledge of the truth. Can you see why discipling is so important?

72. What are the things which, if they be in you and abound, will make certain you are neither barren nor unfruitful in the knowledge of our Lord Jesus Christ? (Study **2 Pet. 1:1-7**.)
73. What is the condition of that person who lacks these things? **(vs. 9)**
74. Does entering the ministry guarantee "success"?
75. What is success to you?
76. According to **Matt. 6:24-34**, what does Jesus guarantee us if we obey His admonition?
77. What is success to God? **(Matt. 25:21)**

There is a large movement within the Church today that basically claims all Christians are supposed to be wealthy. These aberrant teachings have been widely accepted because of their appeal to the flesh. Christian beware! We are living in the last of the last days, which Christ warned us about, and, at the top of the list are false Christs and false prophets. (Read **Matt. 24**.) This doctrine of covetousness is contrary to Paul's warnings as recorded in **1 Cor. 6:9,10** which reads, "Know ye not that the unrighteous shall not inherit the kingdom of God? Be not deceived: neither fornicators, nor idolaters, nor adulterers, nor effeminate, nor abusers of themselves with mankind (homosexuals), nor thieves, nor **covetous**, nor drunkards, nor revilers, nor extortioners, shall inherit the kingdom of God."

At the core of this movement is the belief that we are all "little god's," or "little Christ's". This is pure occult and New Age belief. Nowhere in scripture are we told we are "god's" in the sense of having the same nature and attributes of the One True God. In **Psalm 82:6** where it is written, "I have said, ye are gods; and all of you are children of the most High." The word "gods" in this text means "judges".

78. What does God say will happen to "The gods that have not made the heavens and the earth," according to **Jer. 10:10, 11**?

To understand success according to God, we need to turn to the word in it's entirety and study the lives of His servants.

79. According to **Matt. 6:2, 5,** and **16**, who was to be rewarded and where do you think that was?
80. Read **Is. 1:23**. What did the princes love and what did they neglect to do?
81. What opportunity did Daniel pass up? **(Dan. 5:17)**.
82. What did the Apostle Paul say about those who preached another gospel than the one which was preached by him and the other disciples? **(Gal. 1:8, 9)**
83. How do Satan and his ministers appear? **(2 Cor. 11:12-15)**

- ❖ Do you see the fulfillment of **2 Peter 2** within the church today? Explain.

How far better is it to labor for that reward which will not pass away! **Isaiah 40:10, 11** says, "Behold, the Lord God will come with strong hand, and his arm shall rule for him: behold, his reward is with him, and his work before him. He shall feed his flock like a shepherd: he shall gather the lambs with his arm, and carry them in his bosom, and shall gently lead those that are with young."

84. Look up **Rev. 22:12** and write it out:

Within this "prosperity" movement one finds, among other things, an attitude of harshness. It stems from a heart of pride and superiority that often expresses itself in mockery to the traditional and biblical ways of God. Of course, the intent is to discredit the truth and establish a "new revelation". Jesus said we would know them by their fruits **(Matt. 7:16-20)**.

85. According to **Gal. 5:22, 23**, what is the fruit of the Spirit?
86. What have those who are Christ's done? **(vs. 24)**
87. How are we to live according to **verse 25**?
88. What three things are we told not to do in **verse 26**?
89. Are we called into ministry to serve self? Yes _______ No _______
90. What does **Ro. 12:1** mean?
91. According to **Eph. 6:6, 7** how are we to serve Christ?
92. How can Paul's advice to Timothy in **2 Ti. 4:5** apply to you?
93. Preparation for ministry is threefold: mind, spirit, and body. Why did Paul advise Timothy in **2 Tim. 2:15** to study?

Ignorance can cause much embarrassment and shame! Diligent study of the Word of God is foundational to, not only having the ability to live a victorious Christian life, but to be used by God as His minister.

94. What did Paul say about being an able minister in **2 Cor. 3:6**?
95. What did Paul say about being ignorant in **1 Cor. 12:1**?
96. Study chapters **12** and **14** of **1 Corinthians.** What do you believe your spiritual gifts are?
97. What did Paul warn about knowledge in **1 Cor. 8:1**?
98. Study **1 Cor. 13** and write an explanation of love.
99. What did Paul mean in **Gal. 2:20**?
100. What is crucified and destroyed according to **Ro. 6:6**?
101. What are we to put on? **(Ro. 13:14)**
102. What does **Col. 3:5** tell us to mortify?
103. What did Peter say fleshly lusts do? **(1 Pe. 2:11)**

We see the balance in Paul's writings between knowledge, (the mind), the spirit, (gifts of the Spirit for ministry) and the flesh.

True ministry does not mean we will have immunity from problems! It goes without saying if we are following Christ, then we will have our own cross to bear and our own "Golgotha" to climb. The idea that we can positively think our way clear of problems, persecutions, and perplexities is not Christianity, but occult mind science religions. A study of the Bible will readily reveal the fallacy of such unrealistic notions.

As we all know, Christ chose His twelve disciples and then sent them out in two's to preach the good news of the kingdom. Today He still calls and leads His people into the ministries He has chosen for them. Tragically, sometimes people will join themselves to different areas of service to which Christ has not called them; or sometimes they allow others to join alongside them whom God has not chosen for that particular service. This is being "unequally yoked". It pays to pray and let God, who knows the hearts of all men, build individual ministries.

104. How was Judas Iscariot's position filled according to **Acts 1:15-26**?
105. How did the early believers determine who should minister together? **(Acts 13:1-3)**
106. How were seven deacons chosen in **Acts 6:3-6**?

107. What does **Jer. 33:3** promise?
108. What does **Is. 5:21** mean to you?
109. What is the difference between the way the Lord sees and the way man sees? **(1 Sam. 16:7b)**

Sometimes we meet Christians who have the "ministry" of "knit picking". They thrive on picking everybody and everything apart in the name of "ministry" because they feel contempt or disdain toward that which they consider inferior. This person is a <u>scorner</u>.

110. What does **Prov. 22:10** tell us about scorners?
111. Look up **Psalm 1.** This is a good Psalm to commit to memory!

There is a subtle temptation for Christian workers to begin to think they know it all once they have successfully completed certain Bible courses and/or have been used in a powerful way by the Holy Spirit.

112. What are we according to **2 Cor. 4:7**?
113. Who enables us to do all things? **(Phil.4:13)**
114. What does **Ja. 4:6** tell us?

Today we see people running to and fro, chasing the latest movement and following the latest Christian "guru". In **2 Timothy 4:3, 4** we read, "For the time will come when they will not endure sound doctrine; but after their own lusts shall they heap to themselves teachers, having itching ears; And they shall turn away their ears from the truth, and shall be turned unto fables."

God wants us to lean on Him, not on the "arm of flesh". This means we cannot place our dependence on our own abilities or that of others.

115. What does **Psalm 44:3** say?
116. According to **Jer. 17:5**, who is cursed?
117. What did the man in **Psalm 52:7** trust in?
118. Who are we not to put our trust in according to **Psalm 146:3**?
119. What does **Prov. 28:26** say?
120. Read **Is. 47:7-15**. Do you see America in these verses? Yes ______ No ______
121. Explain what these people trusted in.

When the Lord begins to separate us out to Himself, first He allows us to study and learn from certain teachers and ministers of the Gospel. Along with this time of preparation, He also uses people to teach us what not to do! We call it the "school of the Holy Spirit", for the lessons learned and the insights gained can never be taught in Bible school.

God may allow us to spend *years* undergoing our process in order to prepare us for the ministry He has called us to. The Lord never sends unseasoned and untrained soldiers into the front lines alone. If we push past Him and insist we're ready when, in fact, we are not, He will let us experience the wounding and hardness in order to show us just where we are!

The Lord leads us through stages of learning and preparation, using different instructors and examples. When we have gone as far as we can in certain situations, (i.e. churches, classes, fellowships, etc.), then it's not unusual for Him to bring a separation so we will continue to grow in dependence upon Him, rather than upon another person.

One of the things true ministry is not is legalism, because legalism goes hand in hand with religiosity, pride, and the flesh. Sometimes people embrace legalism because it can give a false appearance of holiness to others. Religion and legalism boils down to man's self-righteous efforts to outwardly conform.

122. What does **Prov. 12:15** say?
123. What do most men proclaim according to **Prov. 20:6**?
124. What is the mindset of the generation in **Prov. 30:12**?
125. Who is not wise according to **2 Cor. 10:12**?

Do a Bible study on the difference between being <u>conformed vs. transformed</u>, or, <u>true righteousness vs. religiosity</u>. Write what you discover. You may make this a message, teaching, article, or testimony. Tell how you would minister to someone who is deluded by their own outward "righteousness". Be prepared to share this with the class.

Many Christians view "ministry" as being mostly "up front", under the lights, in center stage. This misconception is far from the truth! Since ministry means service, true ministry takes place in the ho hum drudgery of daily living. (We will go into what true service is in subsequent chapters of this study). *What people do not realize is the actual preparation time for up front preaching and teaching is about 95 percent, while actual up front time is about 5 percent!*

Consider Abraham, who waited about 14 years for God's promise to be fulfilled concerning the birth of Isaac. Moses spent 40 years in Pharaoh's courts and another 40 years in the backside of the desert before God called Him for service. Joseph spent at least two years in an Egyptian prison before he was set free to become a great leader in that country. It is believed David could have possibly spent about 14 years in the wilderness, hiding from Saul before he became King of Israel. All of the prophets had years of preparation before God used them publicly. Jesus, Himself, was around 30 years old when His public ministry began, and it is believed the Apostle Paul spent about three years in Arabia where he received his revelation of Christ before he began his ministry.

Being "up front" is a grave responsibility. Before any of us are ready to be publicly used by the Lord, we must have self out of the way first. It is a dangerous thing to touch God's glory!

126. What does **Is. 42:8** and **48:10, 11** say?

It is a natural tendency to want to please people, but this tendency has to go if we are to serve God unreservedly.

127. What did the Apostle Paul say about this problem in **Gal. 1:10**?
128. Read **Jer. 1:8, 17**. What did the Lord God command Jeremiah?
129. What did Peter and the other apostles say to the high priest and the council in **Acts 5:29**?

Now we will discuss "space cadet" Christians and those whom we refer to as being in "noo noo" land. This may cause us to smile, but basically these are the people who hold to unrealistic ideas concerning God, Christ, the Holy Spirit, the Word of God, and the Christian life. Because they have never been discipled, these unstable and often times self-righteous souls delude themselves where the truth is concerned. This is the type of person who is in love with their own perception of Jesus, rather than the real Christ. Having formed a theological mindset based on ideas and false notions which appeal to their flesh and pride, these individuals are nearly impossible to reach with the truths of scripture. Usually, they equate truth with negativity.

130. What does Jesus warn us about in **Matt. 7:21-27**?
131. What does **Is. 44:20** say about a deceived heart?
132. What does **Ja. 1:22** say about self-deception?
133. Write out **1 Jn. 1:8**.
134. What does **Rev. 3:17** say about spiritual poverty?
135. What does **2 Cor. 13:5** tell us to do?

One of the most displeasing things to God is being out of order, or obnoxious. Because we are to exemplify Christ at all times, we need to examine ourselves before expressing ourselves! Beware of your own causes and fleshly impulses! Make sure you are being led by the Holy Spirit!

136. What does **1 Cor. 14:33** say about God?
137. How are things to be done in the church, concerning the different gifts of the Spirit? (See **1 Cor. 14:40**.)
138. What does knowledge do according to **1 Cor. 8:1**?
139. What does a man know if he thinks he knows any thing according to **verse 2**?
140. What is more important according to **1 Cor. 13:2, 8** love or knowledge?
141. What does God say about pride in **Prov. 8:13**?
142. What does **Prov. 16:18** say? (**Memorize this verse**).

As God's servants, we have no reason to boast. Remember, God can use a jackass!

One of the things people quickly discover about true ministry is that it is not predictable! We cannot control or engineer circumstances, people, situations, responses, devils, or angels in this Christian walk. Christian workers must not allow interruptions, irritations, and irregularities to throw them off track. For the person who must have a schedule, control, or plans for the day, this fact can be a real source of unpleasantness. One quickly discovers how yielded he or she is to the Holy Spirit when there are sudden changes of direction or plans. Following Jesus means just that; He is leading and we are following. He rarely gives us His blueprint ahead of time. Remember, *the just shall live by faith.*

143. What did Jesus tell Peter to do and what was Peter's response? **(Lk. 5:1-11)**.

If you study the ministry of Christ in the gospels, you will discover the disciples were continually surprised and amazed at the things that He said and did. In fact, they did not understand the crucifixion until after the resurrection. Because God is sovereign, and we are not, do not expect "predictability" to be the norm in the ministry.

Most of us want quick results. We are used to living in a fast-paced society where we have instant meals, fast cars, conveniences, and computers. And when it comes to serving the Lord, we want instant results.

As we have already studied, God allows us to go through years of process. These years may involve many trials and tests designed to develop spiritual maturity in us.

144. What does Jesus say in **Lk. 8:15** about those who have patience?
145. Who is better than the proud in spirit according to **Ec. 7:8**?
146. What are we commanded in **Lu. 21:19**?
147. What does **Ro. 12:12** tell us?

148. What is needed according to **He. 10:36** and for what purpose?
149. What kind of work does patience have? **(Ja. 1:4)**
150. What did the Lord do in **Ps. 40:1** and why?

Religion is the greatest enemy to reality and truth. Religion is man's solution to man's problem by doing things man's way. On the side of truth and reality, however, is the absence of flesh depending on flesh. Our sufficiency, strength, and substance depend upon the Living God who holds our breath in His hands. Never forget it.

It's a natural tendency of our fallen human condition to be religious. Before the fall, Adam and Eve had fellowship with their Creator. After the fall, however, this relationship was lost and fallen man substituted religion for relationship. Adam and Eve sewed fig leaves together to form a covering for their nakedness. Ever since that time, down through the centuries, people have naturally depended upon their own "coverings" and works of righteousness.

151. Since religion signifies man's efforts to reach God through his own efforts, what is the difference between religion and Jesus' words in **John 14:6**?
152. Read **Ro. 3:10, 11; 5:8; 6:23; 9:9, 10**. Do any of these scriptures conclude we must be religious to be saved? What do they tell us?
153. Who continually sought to lay hands on Jesus and silence Him?

Now we come to the subject of rudeness. Simply put, we need to mind our manners! Many times through the years we have witnessed such rudeness among God's people that it is embarrassing. Sometimes we are so busy chasing the "big" things that we fail Christ in the small, everyday things. For example, years ago we were sitting in a restaurant in Seattle with other Christian friends. One of the ladies who was an evangelist talked quite boisterously at the table. But what really shamed us was the sharp, demanding way she spoke to the waitress! When her lunch arrived, she screwed up her face in disgust and made the waitress take it back to the kitchen to make changes. Her whole attitude was one of superiority without a second thought as to what kind of witness she was to the waitress and others within earshot. It doesn't matter how many people you may preach to here or abroad if you don't care about the souls around you, you're missing it!

Let's try to remember the little things that really go a long way, such as, "please", "thank you", and other courtesies.

154. What did Jesus promise in **Mk. 9:41**?
155. What did Jesus tell us in **Matt. 25:40**?
156. Who will be rewarded according to **Matt. 10:42**?
157. God's people are **not** here to serve self. What did Jesus tell his disciples in **Matt. 16:24**?
158. What is the requirement for discipleship? **(Lu. 14:26, 27)**
159. What have those who belong to Christ done? **(Gal. 5:24)**
160. What does **Ro. 15:1** tell us to do?
161. What does **2 Tim. 2:24** tell the servant of the Lord?
162. What is the one thing man cannot tame? **(Ja. 3:8)**

One of the things which we have learned not to do is talk too much! This is especially true with people whom we scarcely know. Wisdom dictates that we hold our peace and listen to what others have to say. One of the fastest ways to discredit the Lord, the ministry, and yourself is to "spill your guts" to everybody. This is a hard lesson to learn, but we can ask the Lord to put a watch on our lips and help us! (See **Ps. 141:3**.) Let's look at some admonitions from scripture concerning the tongue.

163. What does **Prov. 18:4-8** tell us about the tongue?
164. What will a person who has knowledge do according to **Prov. 17:27**?
165. Who is counted wise and is esteemed a man of understanding? **(Prov. 17:28)**
166. How does one keep his soul from troubles according to **Prov. 21:23**?
167. What does **1 Pet. 3:10** tell us about a good life?
168. What is to be put away from us according to **Eph. 4:31**?
169. How does **Ja. 3:6** describe the tongue?

We all have a tendency sometimes to feel like it's up to us to make things happen. After all, there are three kinds of people in the world, aren't there? You know the old saying, there are those who want things to happen, those who watch things happen, and then there are the ones who make things happen.

However, in ministry, it's another story! We who are Christ's are led by the Spirit. This means, we must seek the Lord's direction before we go running off on our own. God engineers our circumstances even when we think He is not aware of where we are.

Once we have received the vision of where God is bringing us, then it is our responsibility to pray for His leading. It is much harder to wait than it is to walk. God is the only One who can open the right doors. Sometimes He allows us to push our way forward, but we soon discover we've botched things up, which forces us to fall on our face and ask for forgiveness. It's called, "getting ahead of God."

The leading of the Lord may come in the following ways:

- The Word of God
- Messages or sermons
- Word of knowledge
- Prophecy
- Visions
- Dreams
- Prayer (by His Spirit)
- Through others (always a confirmation)
- Strong impression; sense; feelings; an inner "knowing"
- Circumstances

170. What does **Prov. 3:5, 6** say about trusting in the Lord?
171. What is God's word according to **Ps. 119:105**?
172. Look up **Ps. 119:130**. What does God's word do?
173. Who is cursed according to **Jer. 17:5**?
174. Read **Jer. 17:7, 8** and describe the man who trusts in the Lord.
175. Fill in the blanks of this verse from **Nahum1:7**: The _________is good, a __________ _____________in the ________of _________________; and he _________________ them that __________________in ________________. (Use King James Version).
176. Read **Acts 16:6, 7**. Who forbade Paul and Timothy to preach in Asia and Bithynia?
177. Read **verses 9-15**. What did Paul see in his vision?
178. Is this the person whom he met in Macedonia? Yes ______ No______
179. Who did Paul meet in Macedonia?

God works in mysterious ways. Our part is to be obedient, not relying on our own abilities and perceptions.

You can be sure that as you follow the Lord closely, many people will not understand you. Even Jesus was misunderstood by his friends. (See **Mk. 3:21**.)

180. What did Jeremiah proclaim in **La. 3:14**?
181. What did King David write in **Ps. 69:12?**
182. Who did the Pharisees deride according to **Lk. 16:14?**
183. What did Jesus warn believers of in **Lk. 21:16.17**? (List the different people).

Our behavior in the ministry must be disciplined!

184. What kind of behavior does Peter warn against in **1 Pet. 4:2, 3, 15**?
185. How does he tell believers to live? **(1 Pet. 4:1, 7-14)**
186. Why should we be sober and vigilant? **(1 Pet. 5:8)**
187. What should we be clothed with and why? **(1 Pet. 5:5, 6)**

True ministry is not necessarily validated by man!

188. Who confirmed the preaching of the Word, and how, according to **Mark 16:10**?
189. Who was approved of God in **Acts 2:22**?
190. Read **Ro. 14:17-19**. How does a believer become acceptable to God and approved of men?
191. What did Jesus say about the approval of the world in **John 15:18-21**?
192. How are we to walk? **(1 Jn. 1:6)**
193. Read **Ro. 8:1, 4**. How are we not to walk?
194. Who are we to walk after?
195. What does **Hab. 2:4; Ro. 1:17; Ga. 3:11; Heb. 10:38** tell us about the just?
196. What is faith? **(Heb. 11:1)**
197. How can a believer live by faith? Explain.

One of the greatest temptations the Christian worker faces is "worshipping their work". The following excerpt is from Oswald Chamber's, *My Utmost for His Highest*, pg. 114: "Beware of any work for God which enables you to evade concentration on Him. A great many Christian workers worship their work. The one concern of a worker should be concentration on God, and this will mean that all the other margins of life, mental, moral and spiritual, are free with the freedom of a child. A worker without this solemn dominant note of concentration on God is apt to get his work on his neck; there is no margin of body, mind or spirit free, consequently he becomes spent out and crushed. There is no freedom, no delight in life; nerves, mind and heart are so crushingly burdened that God's blessing cannot rest. But the other side is just as true—when once the concentration is on God, all margins of life are free and under the dominance of God alone. There is no responsibility on you for the work; the only responsibility you have is to keep in living constant touch with God, and to see that you allow nothing to hinder your cooperation with Him. The freedom after sanctification is the freedom of a child, the things that used to keep the life pinned down are gone. But be careful to remember that you are freed for one thing only—to be absolutely devoted to your co-Worker.

"We have no right to judge where we should be put, or to have preconceived notions as to what God is fitting us for. God engineers everything; where He puts us our one great aim is to pour out a whole-hearted devotion to Him in that particular work. 'Whatsoever thy hand findeth to do, do it with thy might.'"

Our flesh continually wars against the spirit. Satan also knows our weaknesses and uses them to tempt us.

198. What was Paul's battle recorded in **Romans chapter 7**?
199. Rather than yielding to the flesh, what are we to yield to? (Read **Ro. 6:19**.)
200. Look up **Ro. 6:13** and fill in the blanks. *(King James Version).* Neither ________ ye your ______________ as instruments of ___________________unto ______: but ____________ yourselves unto ________, as those that are ______ from the ____________, and your _____________ as instruments of ______________ unto ________.
201. How are we enabled to stand? (See **Eph. 6:10-18**.) ____________________________

Remember, yielding to the flesh in ministry usually involves "good" ideas or plans. This doesn't necessarily mean, however, that these things are of God, but rather for the edification of the flesh. **Isaiah 55:8, 9** declares, "For my thoughts are not your thoughts, neither are your ways my ways, saith the LORD. For as the heavens are higher than the earth, so are my ways higher than your ways, and my thoughts than your thoughts."

The greatest temptation for Christian workers is to yield to the tendency to become "religious", "super spiritual" or to adapt a "holier than thou" attitude.

202. Read **Ps. 51:16, 17**. What does God desire?
203. According to **Is. 57:15**, who does God dwell with?
204. Who does God look to according to **Isa. 66:2b**?
205. Describe the Lord God from **Joel 2:13**.
206. Write out **Ps. 37:23** and **memorize** it.

Prov. 11:14 declares, "Where no counsel is, the people fall: but in the multitude of counsellors there is safety." This is very important to remember in the ministry when it comes to making decisions. Satan likes to push us into impulsive decisions which end in disaster.

207. What does **Prov. 15:22** tell us about plans without counsel? With counsel?
208. Who is the great Counselor in **Isa. 9:6**?
209. What other names are given to Him?
210. Who is the teacher of **1 Jn. 2:27**?
211. Who did God give to the body of Christ according to **Eph. 4:11**?
212. What was the reason according to **verse 12**?

You may ask, "why do we need teachers when the Bible says in **1 John** that we need no man to teach us if we have the Holy Ghost?" You need to understand that God gifts people, *through the Holy Spirit*, to teach His Word; but it is only *by* the Holy Spirit that God's Word becomes *living* because of the anointing (of the Holy Spirit). In other words, teachers break the bread of the Word of life to our minds, but it is by the *quickening* of the Holy Spirit that this bread becomes *living* in our *hearts*!

The last subject in this chapter about what true ministry is not, is "zoning out". This is a popular term for turning off your mind; or checking out from reality. God wants His church to come to terms with truth and reality. We are to be vigilant, sober, watching, and praying. This takes an effort. It means stirring up the flesh.

213. Why does Peter tell us to be vigilant according to **1 Pet. 5:8**?
214. What did Jesus command in **Matt. 25:13**?
215. What is the wonderful reward promised to the vigilant in **Luke 12:37**?
216. What are we the children of according to **1 Th. 5:5, 6**?
217. How is Jesus coming according to **Rev. 3:11** and **Rev. 16:15**?

218. Why are we told to watch and pray in **Matt. 26:41**?
219. What does **1 Co. 16:13** warn us about?
220. Write out **1 Co. 16:13**.
221. What are we to continue in according to **Col. 4:2**?
222. Why should we memorize the Word of God? **(Ps. 119:11)**

Isaiah 60:1, 2 declares, "Arise, shine; for thy light is come, and the glory of the Lord is risen upon thee. For, behold, the darkness shall cover the earth, and gross darkness the people: but the Lord shall arise upon thee, and his glory shall be seen upon thee."

What a promise to those who are His faithful servants! May your heart and spirit be stirred up to reach ever higher for His glory!

LESSON THREE

WHAT TRUE MINISTRY IS

Now that we have discussed what true ministry is not, in this chapter we will study what true ministry is according to the Word of God.

Our greatest example of true ministry is the Lord Jesus Christ Himself. Read **Matt. 20:28**.

1. What did Jesus say he did not come to do?
2. What two things did He come to do?
3. What does ministry mean?
4. Briefly tell why you want to be in Christian ministry.

As Christian workers, we need to check our motivation.

5. What was Christ's motivation? **(Jn. 5:30; Heb. 10:7, 9)**
6. How did Jesus abide in God's love? **(Jn. 15:10)**
7. What is the result of Jesus' obedience according to **Ro. 5:19**?
8. Who did Jesus say was wise in **Matt. 7:24**?
9. What is the key to spiritual knowledge according to **Jn. 7:17**?
10. What secures the blessing of divine fellowship? **(Jn. 14:23)**
11. How does the will of God come forth in our lives according to **Ro. 12:2, 3**?
12. What is not God's will? **(2 Pet. 3:9)**
13. Read **2 Cor. 9**. What is the reason for our labor?

Oswald Chambers writes in *My Utmost for His Highest*, pg. 77, "My worth to God in public is what I am in private. Is my master ambition to please Him and be acceptable to Him, or is it something less, no matter how noble?"

Study the **gospel of Mark**. The main theme of this gospel is "Christ, the Tireless Servant of God and Man." Write, which aspects of His ministry you want to see in your own life and service.

14. What did Paul emphasize in **1 Cor. 9:16**?
15. What service did Jesus call Peter to? **(Jn. 21:16, 17, 19)**
16. Who did Mary minister to in **Jn. 12:3**?
17. How did Paul serve the Lord according to **Acts 20:18, 19**?
18. What did Jesus say about a servant in **Luke 16:13**?
19. How did our Lord minister according to **Lk. 22:27; Jn. 13:4, 5; Ph. 2:7**?

Our motivation for ministry must be (1) to minister to the Lord Jesus, (2) to bring glory to God, (3) to be obedient, and (4) it is because we love Him. Commitment to service because of a moment of emotional response to human need is the wrong motivation. Wanting to be in the ministry because of personal causes and agendas is also the wrong motivation. Check your heart.

To step out in ministry with any other motivation is courting disaster.

20. What did Paul say about those who did not preach out of sincerity in **2 Cor. 2:17**?
21. Explain what Paul meant in **2 Cor. 4:1, 2**.
22. What ministry did Paul say God had given to him in **2 Cor. 5:18-21**?
23. Read Matt. **25:31-40**. List the ways we can minister to the Lord Jesus Christ.
24. What are some of the offices God has set in the Church according to **1 Cor. 12:28**?
25. Let's examine the important, but often overlooked, little word "helps". What did Jesus call the helper in **Lk. 10:30-37**?
26. Did this kind and righteous man have anything to gain (in this life) by what he did? Yes or no.
27. What is the Great Commandment? **(Mk. 12:33)**.
28. What is pure religion according to **Ja. 1:27**?
29. What does God desire according to **Ho. 6:6**?
30. What has God showed us? **(Mi. 6:8)**
31. What helpful deeds were done as recorded in **2 Chr. 28:15**?
32. What did Job proclaim in **Jb. 29:15, 16**?
33. How did the woman in **Prov. 31:20** minister helps?
34. What does **Is. 50:4** express about helping?
35. What did Paul ask be done for the women who ministered with him in **Ph. 4:3**?
36. What are we to do for the poor and fatherless, afflicted, and needy? **(Ps. 82:3)**
37. What is the warning to those who refuse to hear the cries of the poor? **(Prov. 21:13)**
38. What causes us to know the Lord? **(Jer. 22:16)**
39. Who will God deliver in time of trouble? **(Ps. 41:1)**
40. How can we lend to the Lord? **(Prov. 19:17)**
41. What did Jesus say to the rich ruler which would make him perfect? **(Matt. 19:21)**
42. What did Paul write to the **Romans** in **12:13**?
43. List the virtues of **Tit. 1:8**.
44. What should we be not forgetful of according to **Heb. 13:2**, and why?
45. What attitude did Peter warn against concerning hospitality in **1 Pet. 4:9**?
46. List some ways you can offer hospitality:
47. Let's examine some special teachings concerning brotherly love. True love of God is impartial. Read **De. 10:19**. Who are we to love?
48. Unselfishness is the true mark of a child of God. What does **Matt. 22:39** command?

In recent years the New Age teaching of self-esteem and self-love has permeated the church. This particular verse has been twisted to mean we must have great love for ourselves. The correct meaning of this verse is we are to love others and care for their daily welfare the same way we take care of ourselves. This verse concerns practical, every day living. **1 Jn. 3:16-18** gives tell us how we are to treat our neighbor:

> Hereby perceive we the love of God, because he laid down his life for us: and we ought to lay down our lives for the brethren. But whoso hath this world's good, and seeth his brother have need, and shutteth up his bowels of compassion from him, how dwelleth the love of God in him? My little children, let us not love in word, neither in tongue; but in deed and in truth.

49. What is the proof of discipleship? **(Jn. 13:35)**
50. How much are we to love one another according to Jesus' words in **Jn. 15:12**?
51. What does **Ro. 12:9** say about sincere love?
52. What is to abound according to **1 Th. 3:12**?
53. What are we to be fervent about? **(1 Pe. 1:22)**
54. How is helpfulness carried out in **Ac. 20:35**?
55. What types of helpfulness and caring do we see in **Is. 58:7**?

56. According to **Ro. 15:1** we that are strong ought to bear the infirmities of the weak, and not to please ourselves. (True or false)
57. What disciple did good works and alms deeds? **(Ac. 9:36)**
58. Read the following scriptures regarding blessings to those who give. (**Prov. 11:25; 22:9; Is. 58:10; Mal. 3:10; Lu. 6:38; 2 Cor. 9:6)**
59. What is the purpose of good works? **(Matt. 5:16)**
60. List some of the ways you can let your light shine.
61. Besides good works, what does Paul write in **Tit. 2:7** about doctrine?
62. What are we supposed to provoke one another to according to **He. 10:24**?
63. When is faith dead? **(Ja. 2:17,18)**
64. What are we to pursue? **(Ps. 34:14)**
65. According to **Lk. 6:35** who are we to love?
66. Explain **Ja. 4:17**.

We have studied at great length the ministry of "helps" in this chapter because servanthood and helps *are* the heart of God; for His heart is people. When we minister His love to people, then we are ministering to Him. The offices of apostle, prophet, evangelist, pastor, and teacher are to be motivated by the love of God. If at any time individuals in one of these categories fail to be motivated by the love of God, it matters not how "famous", "successful", "popular" or "great" they may appear—they have failed the highest calling of all; that is, to be a servant in the Kingdom of God.

Remember, it's not always the spectacular things we do in front of others that makes us great in God's Kingdom; but rather, greatness is often the small things we do in secret for God's glory.

> But when thou doest alms, let not thy left hand know what thy right hand doeth: That thine alms may be in secret: and thy Father which seeth in secret himself shall reward thee openly. But thou, when thou prayest, enter into thy closet, and when thou hast shut thy door, pray to thy Father which is in secret; and thy Father which seeth in secret shall reward thee openly. **(Matt. 6:3, 4, 6)**

LESSON FOUR

WHO AND HOW

Years ago, after about four or five years of intensive Bible study, I became convinced I had finally become educated enough and smart enough to be "in ministry". Then one day I read **1 Corinthians chapter one**. Much to my dismay it informed me that God chooses the foolish, the weak, the base, and the despised so no flesh should glory in his presence.

Looking back on that time, I have to laugh at myself. Because I actually was foolish, (but nevertheless totally willing and available), God has taken me through the furnace of affliction as part of the preparation process to be a vessel for Him. The mistake so many of us make is we begin to dictate to God who, where, and how He is going to use others and us. Believe me, it's not worth it, because the Lord will quickly turn your plans, and world, upside down!

1. What does **1 Cor. 1:25** say about the foolishness of God?
2. Why has God chosen the foolish things of the world? **(vs. 27)**
3. Why has God chosen the weak things of the world? **(vs. 27b)**
4. Explain **verses 28-31**.
5. According to **Eph. 1:4**, when and why does He choose us?
6. Who has God chosen according to **Ja. 2:5**?
7. Read **Jn. 15:16**. Who chooses, ordains and sends forth, and for what reason?
8. According to **2 Cor. 3:4, 5**, who is our sufficiency, and who makes us able ministers?
9. What kills and what gives life?
10. What must a minister of the gospel renounce and what are some of the things we see in the world and the church today which fit in this category? **(2 Cor. 4:1, 2)**.
11. Read **vs. 5**. What are we to preach, and what are we to consider ourselves?
12. How do we labor and why? **(2 Cor. 5:7-9)**.

Every Christian needs to minister as a witness, not just "special" believers.

13. Read **2 Cor. 5:10-12**. Write out who will appear before the judgment seat of Christ and why; why we persuade men; who we are not to commend and what we are and are not to glory in.
14. What is the message all of us are to proclaim according to **2 Cor. 5:14, 15**?
15. Read **2 Cor. 6:1**. Who is our co-worker?
16. What does **verse 3** mean?

The prevailing attitude of a worker for Christ must be <u>genuine humility</u>. Humility is a combination of the fear of the Lord and holiness. Many people today desire to be in the ministry whose motivation is not pure. Match the following scriptures with the correct definition:

2 Pet. 2:1	______________________	cunning craftiness
1 Tim. 1:7	______________________	profane
Tit. 1:11	______________________	vain talkers
Mi. 3:11	______________________	sorceries

Ph. 1:15	______________________	proud
2 Tim. 4:3	______________________	blind; ignorant; dumb
1 Tim. 6:3	______________________	envy and strife
Matt. 5:19	______________________	covetous
Ez. 33:6	______________________	destitute of the truth
Rev. 18:23	______________________	antichrist
Ro. 16:18	______________________	deceiving
Matt. 15:9	______________________	damnable heresies
1 Tim. 4:2	______________________	consent not to wholesome words
2 Jn. 7	______________________	vain and foolish
La. 2:14	______________________	people be not warned
1 Tim. 6:5	______________________	least in the kingdom
Isa. 56:10	______________________	their own lusts
1 Tim. 6:4	______________________	commandments of men
Jer. 6:13	______________________	understanding neither what they say
2 Tim. 3:13	______________________	false apostles, deceitful workers
2 Cor. 11:13	______________________	hire and money
Eph. 4:14	______________________	deceive the hearts of the simple
Ti. 1:10	______________________	hypocrisy
Jer. 23:11	______________________	for filthy lucre's sake

17. God uses those who are humble. Explain **Matt. 18:4**.
18. According to **Mi. 6:8**, what is good?
19. What did Jesus tell his disciples in **Lk. 22:26** and how does that apply to you?
20. How are we to think? **(Ro. 12:3)**.
21. What should we do in God's sight and what will the result be? **(Ja. 4:10)**
22. What does Peter admonish in **1 Pe. 5:5**?
23. Let's examine some of the great people of the Bible and their attitudes. Look up **Ge. 32:10**. What was Jacob's attitude?
24. What did King Saul say in **2 Sam. 9:21**?
25. What did King David do and say in **2 Sam. 7:18**?
26. What did King Solomon say about himself in **1 Ki. 3:7**?
27. What did John the Baptist say to Christ in **Matt. 3:14**?
28. What did the Centurion say to Jesus in **Matt. 8:8**?
29. What was the Syrophenician woman's response to Jesus in **Matt. 15:27**?
30. What did the Apostle Paul say about himself in **1 Ti. 1:15**?
31. What was Mary's attitude in **Lk. 1:38**?
32. What are we to submit to God according to **Ro. 6:13**?
33. What did Abraham say about himself in **Ge. 18:27**?
34. What did Moses say about himself in **Ex. 3:11** and **4:10**?
35. What does **Pr. 30:2** say?
36. What did Isaiah declare in **Is. 6:5**?
37. What did Job conclude about himself in **Job 40:4**?
38. What did Paul confess in **1 Cor. 15:9**?

Remember, Jesus said, "Blessed are the poor in spirit: for their's is the kingdom of heaven" **(Matt. 5:3)**. God is looking for people who are poor in spirit and humble, to use for His glory! The second virtue in the Beatitudes is contrition. "Blessed are they that mourn: for they shall be comforted."

39. Who ministers comfort according to **2 Cor. 1:4**?

40. How did God use Titus according to **2 Cor. 7:6**?
41. What ministry does God require in **Is. 40:1**?
42. How are we to minister to a believer who has truly repented of his sin? **(2 Cor. 2:7)**
43. Read **1 Th. 5:11, 14**. List the ministries named in these two verses.

God uses people who are meek. **Matt. 5:5** says, "Blessed are the meek: for they shall inherit the earth. "

44. What is commanded and promised in **Zep. 2:3**?
45. What behavior should come forth from meekness? **(Lu. 6:29)**
46. What does the Lord want to see in the lives of His servants who minister in His name according to **Ga. 5:22, 23**?
47. What is essential if one is to teach according to **2 Ti. 2:25**?
48. What are God's people to lay aside and what are they to receive? **(Ja. 1:21)**
49. What is of great price in the sight of God according to **1 Pet. 3:4**?

Matt. 5:6 states, "Blessed are they which do hunger and thirst after righteousness: for they shall be filled." God is looking for people who have a genuine hunger and thirst after righteousness.

50. Does this describe you?

Before people can pour out to others they must first be filled themselves.

51. What did Jesus say in **Jn. 4:14**?
52. Explain **Jn. 6:35**.
53. What did Daniel tell the king in **Da. 4:27**?
54. What does **Ho. 10:12** admonish God's people to do?
55. What was Paul's rebuke in **1 Cor. 15:34**?
56. What part of the Christian's armor is righteousness? **(Eph. 6:14)**
57. Explain the three-fold meaning of **Ph. 1:11**.

Mercy is the natural result of God's great love. **Matt. 5:7** says, "Blessed are the merciful: for they shall obtain mercy."

58. Study **Lu. 6:27-38** and list the different ministries contained within these verses.
59. What accompanies mercy according to **Pr. 3:3**?
60. What benefit does the merciful have according to **Pr. 11:17**?

God's ministers must be pure in heart. **Matt. 5:8** declares, "Blessed are the pure in heart: for they shall see God."

61. According to **1 Ti. 1:5** what is the "end of the commandment"?
62. Read **1 Ti. 5:22**. What three things does this verse command Christian workers?
63. Look up **1 Pet. 1:22** and fill in the blanks: (King James Version) Seeing ye have ________________ your souls in ______________ *the* ________ through the ____________ unto _________________love of the _____________, see that ye ____________ one another with a ________heart ________________.
64. Would it be possible to be a servant of God, working in ministry, if **1 Jn. 4:7** was ignored? Yes ______ No ______ Explain your answer.
65. In scripture, who was "a man after God's own heart"?

66. What did Jesus say about His heart in **Matt. 11:29**?
67. Explain **Matt. 15:8**.
68. What is the Great Commandment? **(Matt. 22:37)**
69. What does **Prov. 4:23** say about the heart?

Using your Concordance, look up and meditate on every scripture regarding the heart in the Book of Proverbs. Write what the Holy Spirit impresses upon your heart. Come before the Lord and humbly ask Him to show you your heart.

Matt. 5:9 says, "Blessed are the peacemakers: for they shall be called the children of God." God's servants are called to be peacemakers. This does not mean, however, that we are to be tolerant of sin, false doctrines, and the like. The Apostle Paul, writing to the Church, exhorted the brethren to live in peace with one another.

Romans 14:17-19 wrote: "For the kingdom of God is not meat and drink; but righteousness and peace, and joy in the Holy Ghost. For he that in these things serveth Christ is acceptable to God, and approved of men. Let us therefore follow after the things which make for peace, and things wherewith one may edify another." We see peace is in between righteousness and joy. There can be no real peace without righteousness, for it is through the blood of Christ we are made righteous before God. Therefore, guilt and condemnation has been done away with, we've been reconciled to God, and enter into His peace. This produces the fruit of joy, as we experience the indwelling presence of the Holy Ghost. We are commanded to follow after the things which make for peace. What do you think some of those things might be?

Paul also wrote we are to follow after the things wherewith one may edify another. What are some of the ways you can edify another in the body of Christ?

The servant of the Lord must always labor to point people to Christ. We are not here to convert people to our opinions!

70. What does **Ph. 2:3** tell us?
71. **Memorize 2 Ti. 2:24**.

Matt. 5:10 states, "Blessed are they which are persecuted for righteousness' sake: for their's is the kingdom of heaven." The Christian worker will be persecuted for righteousness' sake: but woe to that worker who is persecuted because of wrong doing in the flesh.

Read **1 Pet. 4**. Note especially **verse 15** which says, "But let none of you suffer as a murderer, or as a thief, or as an evildoer, or as a busybody in other men's matters." (Emphasis added.) Most of us read the word "murderer" and become so stunned we tend to skip the rest of the verse. Let's take a closer look. While murderer does refer to intentional homicide, remember this action, (along with the three other condemned behavioral practices in this verse), stems from a wicked heart. A person with an evil heart not only has the potential to commit literal murder, but will also murder people with his or her tongue. Hate is hate!

Jesus said in **Matt. 5:22**, "But I say unto you, That whosoever is angry with his brother without a cause shall be in danger of the judgment: and whosoever shall say to his brother, Raca, shall be in danger of the council: but whosoever shall say, Thou fool, shall be in danger of hell fire."

72. What does **Eph. 4:31** say about evil speaking?
73. Look up **Tit. 3:1,2; Ja. 3:6; Ja. 4:11; 1 Pet. 2:1**. Write a short summary of what all of these verses admonish.

Concerning "thief". There are many ways a person can qualify as a thief! We need to examine our hearts to ensure we are not stealing people's time, energy, and resources for our own ends. We must have integrity (truth) in the inward parts. (See **Ps. 51:6** and write it out.)

Concerning "evildoer". This is any action contrary to the righteousness of God.

74. Look up evildoers in **Ps. 37:1, 9**. What are we told concerning them?

Now we come to the fourth behavior, that is, "busybody." Perhaps most of us can sail through "murderer", "thief", and "evildoer" but, if we're honest with ourselves, this thing called "busybody" hits too close to home. If this is a major temptation in your life, I pray the Lord will stir you up to hate this evil and give you strength to overcome it! If we fall into this trap, Satan gets two advantages: (1) he gains access to torment and persecute others who are the object of our gossip, and (2) he brings judgment on our own head for participating in it. Remember, as a servant of Christ, we are to set aside our own personal causes, agendas, opinions, prejudices, and goals. These things are of the flesh and if allowed to reign will bring a reproach on the gospel, a breach between brethren, (sowing discord among brethren), give advantage to the enemy, destroy our testimony, and discredit the ministry.

75. What is another description for busybodies according to **2 Th. 3:11**?
76. What does **Le. 19:16** warn?
77. Who has a faithful spirit according to **Pr. 11:13**?
78. How does one lose good friends according to **Pr. 17:9**?
79. What does **Pr. 18:8** say about the words of a talebearer?
80. Explain **Pr. 20:19**.
81. How does strife cease according to **Pr. 26:20**?

All who minister in the name of the Lord must control their tongue. Not only must the Christian worker never show shock or dismay at what is confidentially disclosed by another, but he or she must never, ever betray to anyone what was told in confidence. Review the following verses: **Ps. 34:13; Pr. 13:3; Pr. 21:23; Ja. 1:26; 1 Pe. 3:10**.

Matt. 11:11, 12: "Blessed are ye, when men shall revile you, and persecute you, and shall say all manner of evil against you falsely, for my sake. Rejoice, and be exceeding glad: for great is your reward in heaven: for so persecuted they the prophets which were before you." It is impossible to follow Christ and not experience reviling, persecution, and slander.

82. According to **Matt. 27:12**, what did Jesus do when he was accused of the chief priests and elders?
83. What did Peter teach in **1 Pet. 3:15-18**?
84. What godly person was falsely accused in **1 Sam. 1:14**?
85. What was she doing? **(vs. 13)**
86. What is the situation in **Ne. 6:9**?
87. Who did Satan accuse to God in **Jb. 2:5**?
88. What is one of Satan's names? **(Rev. 12:10)**
89. Who falsely accused Job in **Jb. 22:6** and what was the accusation?
90. What was Jeremiah, God's faithful prophet, accused of in **Jer. 37:13**?

Tragically, not only are Christians slandered, but all too often they participate in it themselves! Such activity immediately takes us out of God's will and puts us in Satan's camp. Remember, we shall be judged by every idle word we speak. **(Matt. 12:36)**

91. What is the result of slander according to **Ps. 31:13**?
92. What is the judgment pronounced on those who slander in **Ps. 101:5**?
93. Who is a fool according to **Pr. 10:18**?
94. How does a hypocrite destroy his neighbor and how shall the just be delivered according to **Pr. 11:9**?
95. What was the slander the Pharisees brought against Jesus in **Matt. 9:34**?
96. What did they accuse Him of in **Matt. 11:19**?
97. What was Christ accused of in **Lu. 23:2**?
98. What were the disciples accused of in **Acts 2:13**?
99. What slander was brought against Stephen in **Acts 6:13**?
100. What was Paul falsely accused of in **Acts 24:5**?
101. What did slander do to King David's messengers in **2 Sam. 10** and what was the drastic result?
102. What was Satan's confidence and lie in **Jb. 1:11**?
103. Who was slandered and by whom in **Amos 7:10**?

We have studied in this chapter who God chooses to serve Him. To summarize what we have learned thus far, God chooses the weak, base, foolish, and despised. He looks for those who are poor in spirit; mourn (because of their lost condition without Him); who are meek; those who hunger and thirst after righteousness; who are merciful; pure in heart and peacemakers. The Lord calls people who are available.

104. Read **Matt. 4:18-22**. What did these men do when Jesus called them?
105. What did Peter say they had left to follow Christ in **Mk. 10:28**?
106. What did Matthew leave so as to follow Jesus in **Lu. 5:27**?
107. Who cannot be Jesus' disciple according to **Lu. 14:33**?
108. What does **Lu. 18:29, 30** tell us?
109. Fill in the blanks. **(Ph. 3:8)**. "Yea doubtless, and I count _________ things but __________ for the excellency of the ____________________ of Christ Jesus my Lord: for whom I have _______________the __________ of _______ things, and do count them but ____________, that I may_____________ Christ."

God is looking for those who will surrender their lives to Him. This means totally yielded to His Lordship, 24 hours a day, every day for the rest of your life. It means you have no more personal, "private", life apart from the Lordship of Christ. It means you no longer have any rights to call the shots in your life. Indeed, it means you are a bond slave to the Lord Jesus Christ. Let's look at some scriptures depicting the surrendered life.

110. Read **Ro. 6:2, 11**. What are we to be dead to?
111. What have those who are Christ's crucified? **(Ga. 5:24)**

Many Christians do not step out in ministry for Christ because they feel inadequate, or because they have never been equipped for the ministry by the church. Part of the problem is God's people don't understand just what true ministry is! As stated before in this study, it is not necessarily being up in front of a lot of people. Ministry for Christ is first ministry *to* Christ. It begins by sitting at His feet and learning who He is. It means sitting at His table and partaking of the daily food He gives. It means being faithful to

Him, first, at all times so that as His life begins to be formed in us, then we in turn, are enabled to share that life with others.

Every believer can minister the life of Christ, and indeed, is called to do so. Read **Matt. 5:13-16**. Here we see we are the salt and the light. We are to make people thirsty for Jesus and to shine His light into a dark world.

Here are some very practical ways that can be accomplished based on **Matt. 25:35-36**:

Feed the hungry and give drink to the thirsty (both physically and spiritually)
Take in strangers (both physically and spiritually - "strangers" to the gospel)
Clothe the naked (both physically and spiritually - "robe of righteousness")
Visit the sick (both physically and those who are sick spiritually)
Visit those in prison (both physically and spiritually - sin puts us in prison)

Each of the above areas can be elaborated upon. Christianity is practical, not mystical! People have needs, and it is through those needs we can provide love and comfort and share the Gospel. Many are starved for acceptance and love. Many are thirsting for a word of encouragement and honest praise. (Never flattery.) Many are lonely and have no family ties, no one to care. Many are full of shame and guilt and need to be ministered to. Many are sick, both physically and spiritually. Some are sick of this world and are suicidal. Some are sick of religion and dead works. People without Christ are in a prison of hopelessness. Some are prisoners of Satan and his demons and need deliverance. Think about it. I am sure you can add many more examples of areas of ministry. **Memorize Luke 4:18, 19**.

How do you minister? First, you begin with the person closest to you! If you fail with that which is in front of you, you will never be given more. And you can be sure, God will test you on this. "His lord said unto him, Well done, good and faithful servant; thou hast been faithful over a few things, I will make thee ruler over many things: enter thou into the joy of thy Lord" **(Matt. 25:23)**. **Ec. 9:10** says, "Whatsoever thy hand findeth to do, do it with thy might; for there is no work, nor device, nor knowledge, nor wisdom, in the grave, whither thou goest." Therefore, whatever is in front of you do, no matter how small or insignificant it may seem. Read **Matt. 10:42** and note the reward. You will be surprised to find the presence of the Almighty in the simple and seemingly unimportant, small, every day things!

LESSON FIVE

THE MATURE WORKER

In the ministry, the greater the maturity of the Christian worker, the greater will be their responsibilities. In the last chapter we studied at length who God chooses to serve Him. In this chapter we will consider the progression and seasoning of those in ministry.

Paul's admonition to Timothy concerning an overseer of the church included the statement in **1 Timothy 3:6**, "Not a novice, lest being lifted up with pride he fall into the condemnation of the devil." We can conclude from this warning that those who desire to be in a position of leadership in ministry, but who are novices, will fall victim to pride. Remember, pride is of Satan and pride condemns! Furthermore, anyone who is puffed up with pride will (1) have a wrong motivation for ministry, and (2) is immature and unseasoned. Novices have the potential of causing much damage to the Body of Christ, those who are without and themselves.

1. Read **Heb. 5:11-14**. Who are those to whom "strong meat" belongs?
2. Spiritual growth is evidenced by fruitfulness in your life. Explain **2 Co. 9:10**.
3. What does **Ep. 4:15** say about growing up?
4. What are we to increase and abound in and how is this accomplished? **(1 Th. 3:12)**
5. What does **Heb. 6:1** say about perfection?
6. What causes us to grow according to **1 Pe. 2:2**?
7. List the progression of **2 Pe. 1-6** and define each word.
8. What does **2 Pe. 3:18** admonish?
9. The scriptures tell us what we must do to attain spiritual maturity. What does **1 Co. 13:11** reveal?
10. What are some childish things in your life?
11. What does **1 Co. 14:20** tell us we must cultivate?
12. Explain **Ep. 4:13** (keep it in context).
13. Read **Heb. 5:14** again and explain how we are to exercise our senses, (judgment).
14. Read **1 Jn. 2:14** and give the key word to spiritual maturity.
15. All believers should be on the path of spiritual progress. What does **Jb. 17:9** proclaim?
16. What does **Pr. 4:18** say about the path of the just?
17. What admonition did Paul give to Timothy in **1 Ti. 4:15**?
18. Who gives us the larger life according to **2 Sam. 22:37**?
19. What did God give Solomon? **(1 Ki. 4:29)**
20. What was Jabez's prayer? **(1 Chr. 4:10)**
21. What does **Ps. 18:36** declare?
22. What is the fullness of God according to **Ep. 3:17-19**?
23. What is a sure sign of spiritual immaturity? **(Ep. 4:14)**
24. According to **1 Tim. 3,** if a man desire the office of a bishop, that is, overseer, he desires a good work.

However, there are strict qualifications attached to this type of leadership. Let's examine these.

25. List the qualifications from verses **2-12**:
26. According to **Titus 1:6-9**, what are the qualifications of ministers?
27. What is the Christian leader to speak? **(Ti. 2:1)**.
28. **Titus 2:7-15** gives many exhortations for those who would be spiritually mature. List these admonitions.
29. Read **Acts 6**. What was the responsibility of the disciples?
30. Why did they ask for help serving at the tables? Was it "beneath" them?
31. What kind of men did they select for this task?
32. Describe Stephen.
33. Was this an important task? Why? (Note **vs. 6**).
34. Consider **verse 8**. If you were Stephen, would you feel belittled by being asked to serve tables? Be honest! Explain your answer.
35. What was the result according to **verse 7**?
36. Why must God's servants have knowledge and understanding? (See **Je. 3:15**.)
37. Read **Ne. 12:43; Ps. 40:8; 126:5, 6; Lu. 10:17; Jn. 4:36**. What should a worker's attitude be?

MATURITY COMES FROM KNOWING AND OBEYING GOD!

LESSON SIX

EXERCISING THE GIFTS

In order to serve God, there must be a time of preparation. Just as soldiers are thoroughly trained before being sent to the front lines, so too the Christian worker must be equipped and prepared before being placed into "cutting edge" ministry.

God sent the Holy Spirit to enable His Body, the Church, to carry on the work of the Lord. **Acts 1:8** gives us the purpose for the infilling of the Holy Ghost: "But ye shall receive power, after that the Holy Ghost is come upon you: and ye shall be witnesses unto me both in Jerusalem, and in all Judaea, and in Samaria, and unto the uttermost part of the earth."

1. What kind of vessel must we be if we are to be filled with the Holy Ghost? **(2 Chr. 5:5)**
2. What is a prerequisite for the Christian life and service according to **Ro. 12:1, 2**?
3. What did Paul say to every member in **Ro. 12:3**? Why? (**verses 4, 5**)
4. Read **verse 6a**. Do we all have the same gift? Yes ______ No ______.
5. Read **verse 6b**. If we have the gift of prophecy, how are we to prophesy?

This gift is that of speaking to men to edify and exhort them. Turn to **1 Cor. 14:3-6**. Prophecy, according to **verse 3**, is spoken to teach men, and will be spoken in their language. Prophecy is to build up, encourage, comfort, and entreat. The tongues mentioned in these verses refer to one's private prayer language to God. This should not be employed audibly in public for tongues are spoken to God; prophecy is spoken to teach men. Tongues, (prayer language), edifies the speaker; prophecy edifies the speaker and others.

Romans 12:5 compares the Body of Christ to a human body. Study **1 Cor. 12:12-31**. Do you know your place in the body of Christ? Are you content, or are you envious of another's office?

6. What does **verse 25** say?

Ro. 12:7a says, "Or ministry, let us wait on our ministering." The Greek word for ministry in this verse is diakonia, service rendered by a diakonos, a deacon, (overseer). Jesus said, . . . "whosoever will be great among you, let him be your minister; And whosoever will be chief among you, let him be your servant: Even as the Son of man came not to be ministered unto, but to minister, and to give his life a ransom for many" **(Matt. 20:26b-28)**.

This commandment of our Lord is the "bottom line" of all true ministry. The second part of this verse says, ". . . he that teacheth, on teaching;" (instructing others). **Verse 8a**, "Or he that exhorteth on exhortation," which means, to call aside; make an appeal to by way of exhortation, entreaty, comfort, or instruction. This includes preaching. The next part of this verse reads: "he that giveth, let him do it with simplicity;" refers to the rich that give to help others. "Simplicity" means not to give with an outward show or pride. The words, "he that ruleth, with diligence," refers to the leader, pastor, superintendent, or the one over any business of the church. Diligence in the Greek is spoude, haste **(Mk. 6:25)**; diligent **(Heb. 6:11; 2 Pe. 1:5, 10; Jude 3)**; earnest, **(2 Cor.**

8:16); carefulness **(2 Cor. 7:11)**. Finally, the last part of this packed little verse says, "...he that sheweth mercy, with cheerfulness." **(Pr. 15:13; 17:22; Jn. 16:33; Acts 27:25, 36)**

7. Study **verses 9-16**. List the twenty commands regulating Christian brotherhood.
8. Read **verses 17-21**. List seven commands regulating Christian conduct to the world.
9. Read **2 Cor. 12** and read **verse 1**. What did Paul say concerning spiritual gifts?
10. Read **verses 2-7**.

We see in **verse 7** that the, "manifestation of the Spirit is given to every man to profit withal." Manifestation in Greek is phanerosis, making visible. The visible manifestations are the visible healings, miracles, manifest prophecies, tongues, interpretations, and even the giving forth of wisdom, knowledge, and discernments of various kinds. **Verses 8-10** read: "For to one is given by the Spirit the word of wisdom; to another the word of knowledge by the same Spirit; To another faith by the same Spirit; to another the gifts of healing by the same Spirit; To another the working of miracles; to another prophecy to another discerning of spirits; to another divers kinds of tongues; to another the interpretation of tongues."

The gifts fall into three natural divisions as follows:

GIFTS OF REVELATION - THE MIND GIFTS

1. The word of wisdom. This is supernatural revelation, or insight into the divine will and purpose, showing how to solve any problem that may arise. **(1 Ki. 3:16-28; Matt. 2:20; Lu. 22:10-12; Jn. 2:22-24; 4:16-19; Acts 26:16; 27:21-25; 1 Cor. 5)**
2. The word of knowledge. This is supernatural revelation of divine knowledge, or insight in the divine will, or plan; and also the plans of others that man could now know of himself. **(1 Sam. 3:7-15; 2 Ki. 6:8-12; Acts 9:11, 12; Matt. 16:16; Acts. 5:3-4; 21:11; Eph. 3)**
3. Discerning of spirits. This is supernatural revelation, or insight into the realm of spirits to detect them and their plans and to sometimes "know" what are in the minds of men. **(Matt. 9:4; Lu. 13:16; Jn. 2:25; Acts 13:9-11; 16:16; 1 Tim. 4:1-4; 1 Jn. 4:1-6)**

GIFTS OF INSPIRATION - VOCAL GIFTS

1. Prophecy. This is supernatural utterance in the native tongue **(1 Cor. 14:3)**. It is a miracle of divine utterance, not conceived by human thought or reasoning **(Acts 3:21; 11:28; 21:11; 2 Pet. 1:21; 1 Cor. 14:23-32)**. It includes speaking unto men to edification, exhortation, and comfort **(1 Cor. 14:3)**.
2. Divers kinds of tongues. This is supernatural utterance in other languages which are not known to the speaker **(Isa. 28:11; Mk. 16:17; Acts 2:4; 10:44-48; 19:1-7; 1 Cor. 12:10, 28-31; 13:1-3; 14:2, 4-22, 26, 27-32)**.
3. The interpretation of tongues. This is simply supernatural ability to interpret in the native tongue what is uttered in other languages not known by the one who interprets by the Spirit. **(1 Cor. 12:10; 14:5, 13-15, 26-28)**

GIFTS OF POWER - WORKING GIFTS

1. Faith. This is supernatural ability to believe God without human doubt, unbelief, and reasoning **(Ro. 4:17; Ja. 1:5-8; Matt. 17:20; 21:22; Mk. 9:23; 11:22-24; Heb. 11:6; 12:1-3)**.

2. The gifts of healing. This is supernatural power to heal all manner of sickness without human aid or medicine **(Mk. 16:18; Jn. 14:12; 1 Cor. 12:9)**.
3. The working of miracles. This is supernatural power to intervene in the ordinary course of nature and to counteract natural laws if necessary **(Heb. 2:3,4; Ps. 107; Ex. 7:10-14, 21; 2 Ki. 4:1-44; 6:1-7; Matt. 17:20; Mk. 9:23; 11:22; Jn. 14:12)**.

11. Read **1 Cor. 12:27-31**. Who is the Body of Christ?
12. What is the Church? (Look up the word church in your Concordance.)
13. Is it a building? Yes _____No ____
14. Who has God set in the church?

Apostle means one sent forth. According to *Smith's Bible Dictionary*, "(1) The original qualification of an apostle, as stated by Peter on the occasion of electing a successor to the traitor Judas, was that he should be personally acquainted with the whole ministerial course of our Lord, from his baptism by John till the day when he was taken up into heaven. (2) They were chosen by Christ himself. (3) They had the power of working miracles. (4) They were inspired **(John 16:13)**. (5) Their work seems to have been pre-eminently that of founding the churches and upholding them by supernatural power specially bestowed for that purpose. (6) The office ceased, as a matter of course, with its first holders; all continuation of it, from the very conditions of its existence **(1 Cor. 9:1)**, being impossible."

Many today are claiming to be apostles.

15. According to the above definition, do you believe there are apostles in the church today? (Yes or no.)

This is a difficult question! Let us consider the office of "missionary" at this point. The word missionary is nowhere to be found in scripture, yet the ministry of the true missionary fits closely with the office of apostle. Through careful and prayerful study of the word, a missionary is acquainted with our Lord and His work. Secondly, missionary work is a special call from the Lord through the work of the Holy Spirit. Third, missionaries often do have miracle-working power. Fourth, they are definitely inspired, and fifth, missionaries found and establish churches around the world. Consider the work of a dedicated missionary. They are "sent forth" (apostle) to evangelize (evangelist); establish churches (pastor); preach (prophet); and teach (teacher) (including training up nationals). This is the five-fold ministry as depicted in **Eph. 4:11**! (And, I might add, the greatest percentage of this work done around the world is by women.)

The second group God has set in the Church **(1 Cor. 12:28)**, are prophets. The definition of prophet from the Hebrew means to bubble forth like a fountain; hence the word means one who announces or pours forth the declarations of God. The English word comes from the Greek "prophetess", which signifies in classical Greek one who speaks for a god, and so interprets his will to man; hence its essential meaning is "an interpreter." Prophecy is basically foretelling and forthtelling. Therefore, preaching falls under this category. The office of prophet is active in Christ's body today, (including many false prophets as scripture foretold).

16. Read **Ro. 10:14-15**. What three questions does Paul ask in **verse 14** and what are we to preach according to verse **15**? Also, what is beautiful and why?
17. What did Philip do according to **Acts 8:26-38** and what was the result?

The third office is that of teacher, *didaskalos* in the Greek which has been translated "Master" 48 times in the Gospels, except **(Lu. 2:46)**. Teaching is the bedrock of discipleship. Read **Acts 11:25, 26; 13:1; 15:35; 18:24-28.**

18. How did Jesus say man was to live according to **Matt. 4:4**?

God has set miracles in the church. Miracles in the Greek is *semeion* which means a sign or token by which something is known; a token of confirmation of a divine work or call.

19. Read **Jn. 2:11**. What was the purpose of this miracle?
20. Read **Heb. 2:3, 4**. Who is this written to, believers or non-believers?
21. What was the purpose of the miracles?
22. Read the book of Acts, making note of all the miracles and their purpose. Do you believe miracles are for today? (Yes or no.)
23. Next we come to gifts of healing. What did Jesus do in **Matt. 10:1**?
24. What did Jesus tell His disciples in **Mk. 16:18** about the sick?
25. What did Jesus do according to **Lu. 4:40**?
26. What happened in **Lu. 13:10-13**?
27. Tell what happened in **Acts 28:8**.
28. What does **Ja. 5:14-16** say about sickness?

The ministry of helps has been set by God in the Church. This little word, helps carries with it tremendous importance, meaning and benefit for the Body of Christ. In the Greek this word is *antilepsis*, a support; help; succourer; an aid. To be a help in the church you must be sensitive to the needs of those around you. Helping can range from cleaning toilets, to sharpening pencils, to organizing supplies, to tuning cars, to running errands, to assisting anybody who needs aid in doing anything *ad infinitum*! The possibilities are limitless! In other words, whatever needs to be done, if you see it and can do it, **DO IT!**

The next office in **verse 28** of **1 Cor.** is governments. The Greek is *kubernesis*, a steering; pilotage; a guiding. Used only here and refers to all the means of guidance God has set in the church. It has no reference to power to rule, but to men of extraordinary wisdom, knowledge, and discernment to guide the Church in all its problems. The gifts of wisdom, knowledge, and discernment of spirits are all involved in this ability of guidance.

Now we conclude the study of this verse with diversities of tongues. This takes us back to **verse 10** where we read that one is given, "divers kinds of tongues." The study of tongues in **1 Cor. 14** reveals that there are two purposes for tongues. One is the heavenly prayer language where men pray and sing to God in the spirit, **(verses 2, 4, 5, 14, 15, 18,)** and the second type of tongue is that which is used when God speaks through the Spirit, in a tongue, to the Church, which must be interpreted. (See **verses 5,13, 21, 22 ,26-28, 39**.)

Read **Acts 3:1-8**. Pray about this passage of scripture, asking the Lord if you are prepared to have Him put within your heart that which Peter had.

29. What did he have that was so much better than silver or gold?
30. Do you believe **Jn. 16:23**? (Yes or no.)
31. What are the qualifications a believer must have before he can pray this way? (Use scripture for your answer.)

Some people have trouble believing the gifts of the Spirit are for today. Quoting **1 Cor. 13:8-10**, they point out that when that which is perfect is come, then that which is in part shall be done away. The problem with this argument is, three-fold. (1) That which is perfect, Jesus Christ, has not returned to set up His kingdom, and (2) God sent the Holy Spirit for the purpose of continuing the wonderful works of Christ until His return and (3) knowledge **(vs. 8)** has not yet passed away. The point is, when we are gathered together unto Him, we will no longer need the specific offices God has set in the Church. But, the one thing that will last for all time and eternity is LOVE!

LESSON SEVEN

DISCERNMENT AND DELIVERANCE

In our last lesson we learned that the manifestation of the Spirit is given to every man for his profit, and that one of the gifts of the Spirit is discerning of spirits. Every Christian worker needs to ask God for the gift of discernment!

In **Hosea 4:6a** we read, "My people are destroyed for lack of knowledge." The Lord is explicitly <u>not</u> speaking of those who are unbelievers; but rather, He is addressing His own people. Knowledge of God is gained through discipleship, (teaching, preaching, etc.); study, and meditation upon His word; faith and obedience along with a relationship with the Lord through prayer.

1. What does **Je. 4:22** and **8:7** say about God's people?
2. What did Jesus say the world would do to those who belong to Him and why? **(Jn. 15:21)**
3. Look up **Is. 11:3** and fill in the blanks: "And shall make him of quick ______________________ in the ___________ of the ____________: and he shall not _____________ after the _____________ of his ____________, neither _______________ after the __________________ of his ____________."
4. What does **1 Cor. 1:14** say about the natural man and discernment?
5. Discernment can also be written as perception. What did David perceive in **2 Sam. 5:12**?
6. What did the Shunammite woman perceive in **2 Ki. 4:9**?
7. What did Nehemiah perceive in **Ne. 6:12**?
8. What did Jesus perceive in **Lu. 5:22**?
9. What did the Samaritan woman perceive in **Jn. 4:19**?
10. What did Peter perceive in **Ac. 10:34**?
11. What does **1 Jn. 4:1** admonish and why?
37. Read **1 Cor. 2** and note especially those verses that apply to the wisdom of God, revelations and spiritual discernment and knowledge.
38. What does **1 K. 3:9** reveal?
14. Read **Mark 6:7**. How did Jesus send His disciples and what did He tell them to do?
15. What does **Matt. 18:20** say about two or three together in His name?
16. Read **Ec. 4:9, 10**. Why do you think Jesus sent His disciples out in two's?
17. What is another reason Christian workers should work in two's or more according to **Matt. 18:16**?
18. What are we to do in Christ's name? **(Mk. 16:17)**
19. **Memorize Lu. 10:19**.

    This verse is frequently employed when casting devils out of people.

20. What does **2 Cor. 10:3-6** tell us about our walk, war, and weapons and what are we able to destroy through God?
21. Turn to **Eph. 6**, the famous chapter about the Christian soldier's armor. What two things does **verse 10** admonish?

22. What do we wrestle with according to **verse 12**?
23. What is Satan called in **Jn. 16:11, 2 Cor. 4:4, 1 Pe. 5:7**?
24. What four things are we to do according to **Eph. 4:13**?
25. Describe the armor. **(Verses 14-17)**
26. Who has provided the armor for us?
27. Using your Bible, define truth, righteousness, the gospel of peace, faith, salvation, and the Word of God. Show how this armor represents Christ in the believer's life.
28. What does **Verse 18** tell us to do?
29. What was Jesus anointed with according to **Acts 10:38** and what did He do?

This verse confirms that Satan oppresses. Oppressed in this verse means exercise dominion against. There are many scriptures dealing with oppression that can be located in your Concordance.

Read **Matt. 8:28-34**. In this passage of scripture, we learn that demon possession can cause people to be fierce. In my experience in the ministry, I have witnessed people who possessed supernatural physical strength and who were very aggressive. As Christians we must know our Lord, His Word, who we are in Him, and our authority to be able to withstand and overcome such demons. We must be free of all sin and in a humble position before the Lord. We cannot harbor any bitterness, hate, pride, unforgiveness, lust, greed, covetousness, lack of faith, and the like. We can have no secret sins, for Satan knows such and he will have an advantage. In other words, the Christian worker cannot afford to have any area of his or her life that is not submitted to the Lordship of Christ.

Look at their proclamation in **verse 29**. Demons manifest, (react and expose themselves), in the presence of God. There are different kinds of manifestations besides crying out, such as uncontrollable shaking, twitching, growling, foaming at the mouth, nausea, burping, spitting up, uncontrollable laughter, eyes rolling up in the head, falling to the floor, slithering, striking as if to bite, strange physical contortions, different voices, eyes changing color, moaning, loud unnatural crying, "religious" chatter, screaming, profanity, lewd gestures, sounding like an animal to name a few.

Naturally, with such obvious manifestations, one doesn't need a lot of discernment! (We will discuss discernment later in this lesson.)

We also notice from **verse 29** that demons recognize the Son of God. Believe me, if He dwells in you, they will also recognize you! Demons can inhabit animals, as we see in **verse 31** and **32**. In this instance, they were so unclean they wanted to go into an unclean animal.

30. What one word did Jesus say to them?
31. Look up **Matt. 9:32, 33**. The devil that possessed this man was a deaf and dumb spirit.
32. Go to **chapter 12:22**. What did the demon do to this person?
33. Read **Matt. 15:22**. What did the woman of Canaan say a demon did to her daughter?
34. What did she have that Christ honored?
35. Go to **chapter 17:14-21**. What did the demon do to the man's son?
36. What did Jesus say about their faith, and what did He say was required?
37. What did Jesus do to the devil and what happened?
38. Turn to **Mark 1:23-27**. What kind of spirit did the man in the synagogue have?
39. How did it manifest?
40. What did Jesus say and do?
41. What did the unclean spirit do?
42. What did Jesus have according to **verse 27**?
43. What did Jesus say to the unclean spirit in **Mark 5:8, 9**?

44. Is it possible for a person to have many demons at the same time?
45. What were the two things the women were healed of according to **Lu. 8:2**?
    (Note: Nowhere in scripture does it indicate Mary Magdalene was a prostitute or any such thing. This is another example of traditions of men and false doctrine.)
46. What did Jesus teach in **Lu. 11:21-26**?
47. Read **Lu.22:3**. Using your Bible write what you think the open door was for Satan to enter into Judas Iscariot.
48. What is the prerequisite for true worship according to Jesus in **Jn. 4:23, 24**?
49. Why do you think these two things are necessary in deliverance ministry?
50. **Memorize Jn. 14:6.**
51. Read **Matt. 4:1-11**. In what three areas did the devil tempt Jesus? (See **1 Jn. 2:16**.)
52. These are the same areas Satan tempts us. How do we overcome him? **(Rev. 12:11)**
53. Who is of the devil? See **1 Jn. 3:8-10**.
54. What did Jesus promise in **Jn. 8:32** and **38**?

People who need deliverance need to *hear the truth, receive the truth, believe the truth, and obey the truth.* This is a very important principle to remember! They also need the *right* Spirit. (Remember, **Jn. 4:23.24**, Spirit and Truth). The Bible tell us in four places how the just shall live.

55. What is it and where are these verses?
56. What part of the Christian armor is faith?
57. How powerful is the word of God? (See **Heb. 4:12**.)
58. Read **Ps. 149:6-9**. What do these marvelous verses reveal about spiritual warfare?
59. What does **Is. 11:4** say about the Word of the Lord?
60. Who shall be consumed with the spirit of his (the Lord's) mouth? **(2 Th. 2:8)**
61. Describe Jesus according to **Re. 1:16**.
62. Is it possible to defeat Satan if you do not know God's word? Yes ______ No _______
63. Explain your answer.
64. What is the authority and power behind God's Word?
65. What lie did Satan give to Eve in **Ge. 3:5**?
66. What does Satan do with scripture? **(Matt. 4:6)**
67. What kind of plans does Satan have? **(2 Cor. 2:11)**
68. How does Satan appear according to **2 Cor. 11:14**?
69. What does **Ja. 2:19** say about devils?

Remember, Satan, fallen angels, and demons believe in God! Remember, too, that they are very "religious". According to *The American Heritage Dictionary*, religious means of, pertaining to, or teaching religion. Adhering to or manifesting religion; pious. Extremely faithful; conscientious; religious devotion to duty. Religion is basically opposite of true faith and could be considered its counterfeit. Satan and demons are very religious because they are completely devoted to counterfeiting true spirituality, *for they desire above else to be worshipped in God's stead.*

People who are involved in deliverance need to understand Satan wants attention and be careful not to be subtly drawn into an unnecessary, exhausting, and time-consuming battle. This takes discernment! (And experience, the best teacher.)

Both minister and the oppressed person seeking liberty must submit to God in humility, repenting of all pride before resisting Satan **(Ja. 4:6, 7)**. We must also be sober and vigilant, steadfastly resisting Satan in faith **(1 Pe. 5:8, 9)**. We must never be flippant with Satan or his demons **(Jude 9)**. The Christian worker must know and believe that the Spirit of God within him is greater than that which is in the world (the devil) **(1 Jn. 4:4)**.

Satan operates in the realm of fear. He cannot stand the love of God however, for, "there is no fear in love; but perfect love casteth out fear: because fear hath torment. He that feareth is not made perfect in love" **(1 Jn. 4:18)**. "For whatsoever is born of God overcometh the world: and this is the victory that overcometh the world, even our faith. Who is he that overcometh the world, but he that believeth that Jesus is the Son of God?" **(1 Jn. 5:4, 5)**. Satan cannot and will not confess that Jesus is God Incarnate, or God in the flesh. You will always experience a violent manifestation if you try to get a demon to admit who Jesus Christ is. **1 Jn. 4:2, 3** tells us, "Hereby know ye the Spirit of God: Every spirit that confesseth that Jesus Christ is come in the flesh is of God: And every spirit that confesseth not that Jesus Christ is come in the flesh is not of God: and this is that spirit of antichrist, whereof ye have heard that it should come;l and even now already is it in the world."

Concerning the spirit of fear, all believers need to **memorize 2 Tim. 1:7**. Without an exception, every person we have met in need of deliverance had a spirit of fear! The second part of this verse tells what God has given, that is, "...power, love, and a sound mind." Satan brings just the opposite; weakness and bondage, fear, and a spirit of insanity. This is a powerful verse to use in deliverance against Satan.

70. Using your Concordance, look up the scriptures on <u>overcoming</u> and write your findings using scriptural references.
71. What does **Matt. 16:18** and **18:18** promise?

The study of demonology is extensive and this is by no means an exhaustive teaching on the subject. Some reference works we suggest for you to study are: *The Bondage Breaker* by Neil T. Anderson; information contained within *Dake's Annotated Reference Bible*. (We do not necessarily agree with everything in these works, but much beneficial information can be gleaned.) Recommended is Rayola Kelley's book and workbook on the subject, *Battle for the Soul.*

In the beginning of this lesson we touched on perception, or perceiving. Often we come into contact with someone or something that has an evil spirit, and our spirit reacts in different ways. Some of the ways a person can perceive unclean or evil spirits are as follows:

You may experience:

Unusual, uncontrollable nervousness
Irrational fear
Nausea
Inability to concentrate (i.e., if reading something the Holy Spirit forbids)
Feeling unclean
Inability to look that person in the eyes (the eyes are the mirror of the soul)
A desire to "escape"
A feeling something is covering your head/mind

<u>Never forget, a person must want to be set free in order to surrender to Christ!!!</u>

We are to always test both the fruit of a person's life as well as his or her spirit. The Holy Spirit will give discernment if we ask for it! Satan will accuse you of being judgmental, unloving, and unjust. Don't listen to his lies, but go with your "gut" feelings. If your heart is upright before God, you will not be out to "see" something in other people. Sometimes we can actually "see" spirits with our spiritual eyes and "hear" what is demonic with our spiritual ears. Remember, every experience we have adds to our understanding and knowledge, and it must always line up with scripture, in context. Our work is to help liberate Satan's captives so they may receive all God has for them.

A person can be technically right and spiritually wrong. That is why we must worship God and live *in spirit and in truth.* Truth without spirit is merciless, harsh, cruel, religious, and legalistic. Spirit without truth has no stability or foundation, and has no way to test anything. The Christian worker must daily examine him or herself, allowing the Holy Spirit to search his or her heart; guard against pride, conceit, selfishness, and fake nobility; "die daily" to the flesh; submit to the Lordship of Christ, and follow where He leads! Praise be to God who always gives us the victory in Christ Jesus!

ADDITIONAL INFORMATION

Psalm 106:37 says, "yea, they sacrificed their sons and their daughters unto devils." The word "devil" appears only four times in the Old Testament, **(Ps. 106:37; Lev. 17:7; Dt. 32:17, 2 Chr. 11:15)**, but 51 times in the New Testament. There are many devils, but only one chief devil. Two Hebrew words are translated devils: shed, a spoiler; destroyer; a malignant, and evil spirit **(Dt. 32:17; Ps. 106:37)** and sair, shaggy, hairy one; kid; goat; satyr; devil **(Lev. 17:7; 2 Chr. 11:15.)** Devils are the familiar spirits of the Old Testament **(Lev. 19:31; 20:6; Dt. 18:11; 1 Sam. 28:3, 9; 2 Ki. 21:6, 23:24; Isa. 8:19; 19:3)**; and the supernatural spirits back of witchcraft.

There are 12 forbidden heathen practices that you can look up using your Concordance:

1. Enchantments -practice of magical arts.
2. Witchcraft - practice of dealing with evil spirits.
3. Sorcery - same as witchcraft.
4. Sooth-saying - same as witchcraft.
5. Divination - the art of mystic insight or fortune-telling.
6. Wizardry - same as witchcraft. A wizard is a male and a witch is a female who practices witchcraft. Both were to be destroyed in Israel.
7. Necromancy - divination by means of pretended communication with the dead.
8. Magic - any pretended supernatural art or practice.
9. Charm - to put a spell upon. Same as enchantment.
10. Prognostication - to foretell by indications, omens, signs, etc.
11. Observing times - same as prognostication.
12. Astrology and star gazing - divination by stars.

All the above practices were and still are carried on in connection with demons, called familiar spirits. All who forsook God and sought help from these demons were to be destroyed.

The word demon is not found in Scripture; but it means evil spirit or devil. The word devil is used of Satan, the prince of demons. The Greek word for devil used in connection with Satan is diabolos, meaning adversary, false accuser, slanderer, devil. According to Finis Jennings Dake, (*Dake's Annotated Reference Bible*), "There is only one prince of devils but many demons. He has an angelic body and cannot enter bodily into anyone; but demons are disembodied spirits, and do not seem to be able to operate in the material world except through possession of the bodies of men or beasts."

It is important to distinguish what is the *flesh* and what is *spirit*. To quote from "Steps in Deliverance by Ralph and Liz Brown on this subject, "The minute one mentions "deliverance," someone usually counters with "those are works of the flesh" –

---Galatians 5:19. Let's get our terms straight. You "cast out" demons, but you "crucify" the flesh. One cannot "cast out" problems of a fleshly nature any more than he can "crucify" demonic spirits! They are two distinctly different problems with two distinctly different remedies in Scripture. There are remedies for both deliverance from demonic problems and crucifying the fleshly problems in Scripture. If it's *always* a problem of the flesh, why does God give us a remedy for demon oppression and possession? If it is indeed a fleshly problem, one needs to fully commit his life to Christ and proceed to crucify the flesh, as one is commanded to do in **Galatians 5:24**. On the other hand, if it is "flesh out of control" and all attempts to crucify it have failed, then it most likely has become a demonic problem, and the Scriptural remedy for that is to cast out the demons as in **Mark 5:8, 16:17; Acts 8:7;** etc. The word possessed is incorrectly translated from the Greek word *"daimonizomai."* A more correct translation would be: "under the influence of a demon spirit, acting under the control of a demon, or demonized."
It is also extremely important when ministering to people to know their nature; that is, if they are submissive, stubborn, self-assured, or strong-willed. Understanding their nature will help you determine what is natural, or normal, for them and what is extreme, or unnatural. Remember, Satan pushes us to extremes. To study this important subject, read Chapter 19, "Identifying Satan's Tactics For Each Nature" in *Hidden Manna*, by Rayola Kelley and Jeannette Haley.

There is an on-going argument among Christians about whether or not a believer can "have demons". Let's examine this subject from scripture. Paul warned Christians in **1 Corinthians 10:9, 10** that we could be destroyed by serpents or the destroyer if we do certain things not pleasing to God. In **Revelation 3:5** we are told, "He that overcometh, the same shall be clothed in white raiment; and I will not blot out his name out of the book of life, but I will confess his name before my Father, and before his angels." Did you notice the words "overcometh and blot out?" Remember, no one can snatch you from Jesus' hand, but you can leave the protection of His hand by your own free will.

The Word of God gives many examples and warnings about Satan, our adversary. Peter was rebuked by Jesus when he momentarily gave place to Satan in his mind. (See **Mark 8:33**.) Jesus said in **Luke 22:32-32a**, "Satan hath desired to have you, that he may sift you as wheat: but I have prayed for thee that thy faith fail not." Peter was a believer; he knew Jesus was God in the flesh; he loved the Lord and was committed to Him; but, a lying spirit drove him to deny Christ. Satan attacked him in his thought life, and he gave in to those thoughts.

To further quote from "Steps in Deliverance", "Paul warned the church at Corinth about Satan getting an advantage over them in **2 Corinthians 2:11**. From what we read, the Corinthian church was made up of spirit-filled, tongue-talking Christians. He even warned them about the possibility of receiving another spirit – **2 Corinthians 11:3:4**. He was fearful of their minds being corrupted by Satan – just as Eve's was. He must be warning Christians about evil spirits here, as "another spirit" and "corruption," are contrary to God's teachings. And in **1 Peter 5:8**, Peter warns Christians to "be sober, be vigilant; because your adversary the devil, as a roaring lion, walketh about seeking whom he may devour." If Christians were not vulnerable, I don't believe God would be warning us to be vigilant.

He also warns us in **1 Timothy 4:1**, " that in the latter times some shall depart from the faith, giving heed to seducing spirits, and doctrines of devils (demons)". One cannot depart from Christianity unless one is first a Christian.
Acts 5:3 tells us Satan filled the hearts of both Ananias and his wife, Sapphira. Paul, in **Ephesians 4:27**, admonished the Christians not to give place to the devil. We conclude Christians were not immune to the adversary's harassment, even in the early church.

Consider Jesus, our example. He was not automatically immune to Satan's temptations and He was the Son of God. If Satan was allowed to tempt Him, why not us? Consider what the Bible has to tell us about our armor and "overcoming". We are to overcome three things; namely, the world, the flesh, and the devil.
Following is a brief list of signs of demonic activity:

Hindrances to spiritual growth – Inability to concentrate on Scripture reading and/or no desire for the Word of God. Feeling drowsy when it comes to Bible reading and/or prayer. Mental confusion, scattered thoughts, inability to concentrate, frustration, agitation, and nervousness around spirit filled people and gatherings.

Feelings of guilt, worthlessness, inferiority, rejection, and heaviness – Person thinks his sin is far too great to be forgiven (which is a lie from Satan, not true conviction by the Holy Spirit); a sense of rejection, utter despair, hopelessness, sorrow, sadness, self-pity, depression, suicide, and insomnia prevails.

Strong, uncontrollable urges, actions, or attitudes – Anger, hatred, bitterness, unforgiveness, often much cursing in conversations and actions.

E.S.P., deja vu, clairvoyance, and premonitions – People that have been into Eastern religions, meditation, drugs, etc., sometimes have spiritual abilities that are not of God. This usually indicates a familiar spirit or spirit guide is present.

Unrelenting fears, doubts, and worries – Phobias, strong fears and torments, wild and frequent nightmares, and distrust of people closest to them.

Medical problems that cannot be diagnosed or helped by medication, such as: some forms of arthritis, nervous disorders, digestive disorders, fatigue, breathing difficulties, unusual and unidentified chest pains, numbness, some forms of seizures, etc.

Bizarre, compulsive, or unusual behavior – The person prefers to be a loner, thinks people can read his thoughts, fears people and crowds, laughs or talks when no one is present (may be a familiar spirit or spirit guide), seems restless, is nervous, has uncontrollable tics and/or muscular twitches, has a wild imagination, fantasizes, avoids eye contact, does not want to be hugged or touched (not able to love others), has uncontrollable laughter, anger, or rage, gossips, is double-minded (has dual personalities), is constantly lying and exaggerating, is extremely haughty, has a wild look in his eyes, hardly speaks, is arrogant, brags and is full of pride, talks excessively, babbles a lot, flatters others, is extremely rebellious, is contentious, stubborn, has radical changes in moods and personality, and is mocking, lewdness, etc.

Excessive Idolatrous Practices – Any activity or past-time that becomes obsessive. "Obsession leads to possession." Anything that occupies a person's entire thought life, focus, time, energy, finances, etc. Inordinate affection.

Unteachableness – Extremely argumentative, defensive, twists sound doctrine to suit self, denies deity of Christ and existence of Satan and hell; feels he is a god, humanistic, defends evolution, existence of UFOs, etc.

Mental problems – Insanity, epilepsy, foaming at the mouth, gnashing of teeth, pining, crying, suicidal tendencies, constant whining, prostration, hallucinations, paranoia, etc.

Addictions – Alcohol, drugs, nicotine, gluttony, perverted sex, etc.

(Note: Always take into account the person's physical condition. It is possible for people to have hormone imbalances, blood sugar problems, thyroid imbalances, malnutrition, exhaustion, congested liver, food allergies, parasites etc. It helps to have some education and experience in the area of natural health and remedies, which are not linked with the New Age).

Following is a list of how demons enter humans:

- Sins and compromise
- Inherited factors (curses)
- Soul ties
- Uncontrolled fleshly appetites
- Shock, trauma, and grief as in:
  - Molestation
  - Rape
  - Incest
  - Accidents
  - Death of a loved one
  - Viewing violence (fights, murders, etc.)
  - Marriage breakdown
  - Transference of spirits from wrong laying on of hands
  - Transference of spirits from heavy petting and/or sexual intercourse
  - Touching of people at death
  - Hypnosis
  - Abortion
  - Altered state of consciousness through drugs, (any kind), trances, etc.
  - Anesthesia (general)
  - Giving way to anger, hatred and unforgiveness
  - Going into Satanic places where he is venerated
  - Horror movies (fear)
  - Invitation (inviting in a spirit guide or any other spirit being or demon)
  - Initiation into any secret order or lodge
  - Meditation (As in Eastern Religions)
  - Occult involvement (including mind science religions and cults)
  - Rock and Roll

About soul ties: Soul ties are formed when two people are bonded together, in the spirit. Soul ties make you feel like you're attached to a bungee cord which pulls you back every time you try to move forward. Some words used to describe soul ties in the Bible are as follows:

Knit - to draw together, closely and firmly, to unite in agreement – **1 Sam. 18:1**
Bound - confined by binding, closely connected - **1 Sam. 25:29; Nu. 30:4**
Clave - (archaic past tense of cleave) – to Adhere, akin to, to cling, to be faithful, to stick – ***Gen. 34:3***

Ungodly soul ties are sometimes called unholy, counterfeit, perverse, or evil. They are formed with people who have controlling spirits (spouses, relatives, friends, leaders, etc.). Control is the same as witchcraft. Fear, perversion, lust, inordinate affection, inability to function apart from the other person, inability to think or make decisions independently, complacency, and confusion can all be indications of a soul tie. Soul ties are formed when ungodly oaths, or ungodly binding agreements with others are made; by all sexual sins committed outside of marriage, by occult connections such as Satanism, witchcraft, fortune-telling etc.

Soul ties will be formed by the following:

Fornication and harlotry - (sex between unmarried partners) **(1 Cor. 6:16, 17, Gen. 34:2-3a)**

Adultery - (when a married person has sex outside of marriage) **(Prov. 6:32)**

Sodomy - Any abnormal sexual relationships, such as: lesbianism, homosexuality, or bestiality **Ro. 1:26-27; 2 Ki. 23:7; Lev. 18:23; 20:15)**

Incest - (sex between family members. It can also be considered as fornication or adultery.) **(1 Cor. 5:1, 2; Matt. 14:3, 4; Mark 6:17, 18; Lu. 3:19; Lev. 18).**

Through ungodly oaths, ungodly vows, and ungodly agreements - This can create an ungodly soul tie with the other party, or with members of an entire group: Masonry, witchcraft, Satanist groups, etc. **(Ja. 5:12)**

With those in idolatry and occultism - Astrology, divination, hypnotism, fortune-telling, tarot card reading, etc. are forbidden throughout the Bible. This can also be termed spiritual adultery. **(Pr. 22:5; 1 Cor. 10:14; 10:21; Ja. 3:15)**

Christians need to be aware of the reality of spoken word curses. Spoken word curses are any negative or evil words spoken by our enemies, or those with malice in their hearts toward us, which hold power when they speak them forth. Some scriptures relating to the power of the spoken word are: **Matt. 21:19-22; 12:37; Lu. 4:38, 39; 8:24; Prov. 6:2; 18:21; Job 5:21; Ps. 57:4; Jer. 18:18; Ja. 3:8, 10.**

Generation curses are very common. When there is a predisposition to certain mental and physical diseases in families, addictions, psychic tendencies, abnormal sex drives, poverty, divorce, etc. we find the roots can often be the direct result of sin in the ancestral line. Sin can open the door for a generation or inheritance curse to follow a family line. Sin always creates a crack in the spiritual armor, giving Satan a legal right or an open door to come into a person. Involvement in the occult opens the door for generation curses also. See **Ex. 20:5b; Ps. 109:14; Jer. 11:9-11; 32:18; 1 Sam. 15:23; Lev. 26:3-15; Deut. 30; 2 Sam. 12:10-12.** According to "Steps in Deliverance," there were over seventy sins listed in the Old Testament that generated generation curses. In **Deut. 27:14-28:68** there are 124 curses.

After fifteen years of active ministry, I can attest to the fact that, yes, Christians often *do need deliverance from soul ties, generation curses, bondages, and oppressions.* As Christians, while we have been redeemed from the *curse of the law,* nevertheless, to be free from *word curses or witchcraft*, deliverance is often necessary.

We must believe in our heart, and repent and confess with our mouth, our own sins and those of our ancestors **(Lev. 26:40)**, and break the power over all curses in our family line in the name of Jesus Christ. Because these curses are empowered by Satan, we must also command all demons that came into the family line with the curses to leave. They no longer have a legal right to remain.

Consider **Matt. 27:25**, "Then answered all the people, and said, His blood be on us, and on our children." Subsequently, the Jews were visited with the same kind of punishment and worse, for the Romans crucified them in such numbers that there were no more crosses or place for them. As many as 500 a day were scourged and crucified. Their children for ages have gone through untold sufferings in all lands. What a curse!

Following are some helpful hints for deliverance ministry:

1. Never work in the enemy's camp, especially the home of the counselee. If you purposely go to places controlled by Satan, you can be attacked.
2. It's wise to pray at least a day prior to deliverance, and fast if possible. (The Holy Spirit will direct here). Some spirits only come out with fasting and prayer **(Matt. 17:21; Mark 9:29)**.
3. Have counselee assist by fighting Satan verbally, ordering him out of his or her territory. It is important for him or her to sincerely praise and worship the Lord, also.
4. If in a stalemate, ask the Lord if there are still curses, soul ties, or sins that have not been dealt with. Also, sometimes it is a good idea to stop and have everyone sing songs emphasizing the Blood of Jesus, pray, praise, and sing in the Spirit and with your understanding. **(1 Cor. 14:14, 15)**.
5. Be sure to praise and thank the Lord Jesus for every obvious release of a demon.
6. Never let the demons rest or keep the person on the floor. Keep the commands and Scriptures going constantly. (Always work in not less than two, preferably three or four, so you can switch off as you tire.)
7. Never minister alone! (Especially with one of the opposite gender).
8. Remember, all sin is idolatry and comes from pride and rebellion.
9. **Never converse with demons**. We are not to have conversations with demons, but rather lean into the Spirit for the discernment, wisdom, guidance, and knowledge we need. Demons often wail, moan, shriek, yell, curse, cry, or sob. They sometimes contradict when commanded out by screaming "No" or "they're mine" and the like. Take authority over them and cast them out. Beware of spirits of self-pity, slumbering, complacency. (The latter usually holds down the spirits of lust and fear).
10. All involved in deliverance must be free of known sin and in agreement. Satan loves to divide and conquer! Don't allow this to happen.
11. To test the spirit, make it verbally confess, "Jesus Christ is God Incarnate; God in the flesh". No demon will confess this, but the counselee must be able to do so without manifestations. Never forget, religious spirits are good at quoting scripture.
12. Be sensitive to the Holy Spirit at all times, and He will guide you into all truth **(John 16:13)**.
13. Always have tissues and a plastic container available as sometimes people expel foam and/or vomit up mucus. Other signs of deliverance are burping, coughing, and loud sighs. You may smell sulfur. (Demons stink and smell like Hell).
14. If the counselee has a fit of laughter, smirks, or assumes a mocking expression, bind the mocking spirit. Sometimes it can be present because the counselee has mocked God. If this is the case, he needs to truly repent of it, and ask for forgiveness. Sometimes demons try to be "funny" or "entertaining". Don't give in. Remember, Satan and his demons want attention and worship.
15. Be aware that demons can cause a person to become violent, enduing them with supernatural physical strength. The Christian worker must know God, His Word, and his or her authority in God. Pray for warring and restraining angels to assist.
16. It is wisdom not to lay hands on the opposite sex, (or one of the same sex if the counselee is a lesbian or homosexual) especially when dealing with areas of sexual lusts, etc.
17. **Do not let** the counselee bring along friends, relatives, or children. It usually hinders progress and isn't necessary. If the spouse or friend of the counselee insists on being present, do not let them sit close to one another or hold hands. We find that demons gain strength from one another if they both happen to have the same ones.
18. Witches, Satanists, schizophrenics, and people with "MPD" are difficult to work with. Don't even mess with them until you are very experienced and knowledgeable!

19. Mind altering strong drugs, especially anti-depressants or painkillers can surround and protect demons, making it more difficult for their release. Deliverance of people on medication of this nature is very difficult, and not advisable. However, counselors can do the preparatory steps of working on forgiveness, breaking ungodly soul ties, and curses, etc., until such a time that the counselee can be free of the drugs. People in this category need to learn how to bind the spirits in Jesus' Name that are harassing them during this waiting period.
20. Stay scriptural! Don't try methods and ideas used by people that have no scriptural backing. Command demons to go into a "dry place" and not return **(Matt. 12:43).**
21. To avoid confusion, it is best if one person at a time, under the leading of the Holy Spirit, takes the lead and has the attention of the counselee with eye contact. Workers can change off as the Lord leads or as they tire. Others can also command, pray, or read Scripture in a quieter voice at the same time.
22. People occupying houses indwelt by demon spirits can become ill and/or suffer from insomnia, irrational fears while in their house, have nightmares, become nervous, etc. Make sure the counselee understands spiritual housecleaning and help him or her rid oneself of both articles that attract demons and the spirits themselves. Houses can be anointed and sanctified for the Lord. (Educate people! It's amazing how many Christians unwittingly invite Satan into their homes through their television sets, videos, Satanic children's games, cartoons, rock and roll music, (and other forms of fleshly music), unholy books, magazines, certain decorations, art, nick knacks, jewelry, and Indian woven rugs and artifacts, etc.)
23. Remember, not everything a Christian sees or hears during deliverance is always from God. There are **two** "stations" broadcasting!
24. Read **Mark 9:26, 27**. Sometimes the evil spirit feigns death in the host. In Jesus' Name, rebuke the spirit of death. If he falls, take him by the hand, commanding him to get up as you help to lift him.
25. Usually during deliverance, we command demons to leave in the name of the "Lord Jesus Christ of Nazareth who is God come in the flesh" because it is possible for a spirit guide, familiar spirit, or religious spirit to go by the name of "Jesus".
26. Intercession can be powerful - proxy deliverance in scripture. **Job 22:30** - Amplified – "He will even deliver the one (for whom you intercede) who is not innocent; yes, he will be delivered through the cleanness of your hands." **(Matt. 15:22-28)** – The Canaanite woman came to Jesus saying her daughter was grievously vexed with a devil, etc., and Jesus healed her. One need not be there physically to be delivered. **Acts 19:11, 12** – "And God wrought special miracles by the hands of Paul: so that from his body were brought unto the sick handkerchiefs or aprons, and the diseases departed from them, and the evil spirits went out of them."
27. Watch the eyes. As already mentioned in this study, "the eyes are the mirror of the soul." Sometimes a demonized person's eyes will change color. We have seen eyes change from blue to swamp green; or even to clear, almost white. It is not unusual for the eyes to become protruding and/or roll up into the person's head. Demons look through people's eyes. With experience, you will soon learn how to recognize them. Following are some tips on how to recognize spirits:

    Eyelids half shut/ glazed eyes/intense - Lust/seducing spirit (beguiling)
    "Fish eyes" - Delusion or possession
    Bright/piercing - Religious spirit/fanatical/delusion
    Habitually eyeing you from the corners of the eye - Control/witchcraft
    Wide, staring - Deluded/hypnotism/trance states
    Black/sinister - Satanic/familiar spirit

Pale/penetrating/cold - Familiar spirit/anti-Christ
White entirely surrounding the pupil - Possession/New Age involvement
Muddy eyes - perversion
Shifty eyes, usually blue (brown eyes are hard to "read") - lying spirit also blue eyes which veer off to green
Bright, blazing blue (brown hard to "read") - alcoholic spirit
Very pale eyes, blue - spirit of fear

Always pray over the people involved, the building and pets, pleading the blood of Jesus and His protection.

Some reasons deliverance fails:

1. Insincerity
2. Unbelief
3. No true forgiveness
4. Unconfessed sins
5. No true repentance of sins
6. Failure to break or come clean with some aspect of the occult.
7. Not truly saved – no born again experience. (These people just want "relief", not the true Jesus.)
8. Pride (The Bible tells us that pride goes before a fall. It's an open door!)
   (All persons desiring deliverance through GSM are required to complete certain questionnaires prior to their appointment.)

LESSON EIGHT

COUNTING THE COST

This final lesson is a summarization of what we have studied thus far and presents a challenge for those seeking ministry. The cost of discipleship and Christian work is high. It cost God His best, His all, to provide for our redemption and adoption. The question is, are we willing to give our lives as a living sacrifice, which is our reasonable service? It may be easy to say "yes", but living it out on a day-to-day basis takes everything you have, and then some. Only by the indwelling presence of the Holy Spirit are we able to overcome. And even then, the Bible tells us the "righteous are scarcely saved" **(1 Pe. 4:18).**

Therefore, we have no cause to boast or glory in ourselves. All that we are, all that we accomplish is done by the enabling of the Lord. Our duty lies in total and complete surrender, living daily in faith; that is, total dependence upon Him. We are nothing in ourselves and cannot succeed in anything by ourselves **(Jn. 15:5)**. Truly, our sufficiency is of God **(2 Cor. 3:5)**.

As God entrusts us with the least, (ministry), we need to humbly embrace His choice and wisdom for our lives. Anything less than this, and we give ourselves away; namely, we are still in the flesh, living for our own causes, agendas, desires, and ideas. "Therefore seeing we have this ministry, as we have received mercy, we faint not; But have renounced the hidden things of dishonesty, not walking in craftiness, nor handling the word of God deceitfully; but by manifestation of the truth commending ourselves to every man's conscience in the sight of God" **(2 Cor. 4:1, 2)**. Fainting, dear believer, is more apt to occur in the valleys of daily drudgery than on the pinnacles of public performance. The real test of our faith will always be in the dark valleys where we cannot perceive God's presence. It is there we question our calling, our capabilities, and our commitment. Remember, God's purposes are only fulfilled as we allow Him to press us through *process* and *preparation.* It is through the pressing, the crushing, that the anointing and the fragrance comes forth. The olive must be pressed before the precious anointing oil can come forth. Likewise with the grape, for there will be no new wine unless the pressing process is applied. Fragrances also come forth from bruising and crushing.

All of these things point to the suffering and death of the Lord Jesus Christ, who was sacrificed for us **(Is. 53:5)**. If we are to walk as He walked, **(1 Jn. 2:6)**, then our hearts must willingly follow Him along the dusty roads of suffering humanity; through the valleys of humiliation and persecution; up the steep, barren, and rocky slopes of temptation; across stormy seas of loneliness and frustration; into the hypocrisy and judgmentalism of the religious systems; into the bizarre world of the demon-possessed; up mountain heights of fleeting moments of ecstasy and revelation; through the dark night of the soul in the Garden of Gethsemane; into the tormenting hands of lost men, and finally up a hill called Calvary. But, remember, the promise is eternal life!

"In righteousness shalt thou be established: thou shalt be far from oppression; for thou shalt not fear: and from terror; for it shall not come near thee **(Is. 54:14)**.

1. According to **Col. 2:7**, what things must the Christian worker be?
2. Look at **verse 8**. What are we to beware of?
3. Why? **(vs. 9, 10)**

4. Fill in the blanks. **(2 Th. 2:15)** "Therefore, brethren, ______________ fast, and __________ the ________________which ye have been _______________, whether by ________ or our _____________."
5. According to **1 Pe. 2:9** what are the believers?
6. Is it possible for the believer to fall? (See **2 Pe. 3:17**.) Yes _______ No _______
7. What are we to do according to **verse 18**?
8. What two things are we to hold? **(1 Ti. 1:19)**
9. What does the Spirit expressly speak? **(1 Ti. 4:1)**
10. Read **2 Ti. 4:5.** What will the Lord Jesus Christ do at his appearing and his kingdom?
11. What does **verse 2** say and how does this verse relate to you?
12. Are **verses 3** and **4** being fulfilled today? Yes ______ No ______ Explain your answer. (Give examples)
13. What does **verse 5** admonish the Christian minister?
14. Look up **Acts 20:27**. What did Paul declare and can we do less?
15. What did he command in **verse 28**?
16. What did he know and warn them about? **(vs. 29)**
17. Where will some of these men come from, what will they speak, and why? **(vs. 30)**.
18. What did he tell them to do? **(vs. 31)**. Does this apply to us today? Why?
19. Read **2 Cor. 11:3, 4, 14, 15**. What was Paul's fear for the church?

Satan comes in a beguiling and subtle way. His attack is against our mind, trying to corrupt our simple faith in the uncomplicated Gospel of Christ. People who need deliverance have usually always opened a door to Satan by a *decision* that excludes *faith* in the word of God (*truth*). Remember, Satan gains entrance through deception built on a lie. This decision is based upon their perception of events, happenings, trauma, etc. in their lives. Satan appears as an angel of light (*religious and good*), (but not truth), to set the person up. His input appears so *logical* to our human way of thinking. It appeals to our flesh, to our emotions. According to these verses in **2 Corinthians 11**, "it is possible for people to receive another Christ, another gospel, and another spirit" **(vs. 4)**.

If this Bible study does nothing else but force you to get into the Word of God for yourself and to become established in the truth and sound doctrine, it has succeeded in its intent and purpose. The believer cannot be warned enough of all the false doctrines, false teachers, and damnable heresies **(2 Pe. 2:1)** in the world *and in the church and Christendom today.* This is why discipleship is a must! We are living in the last of the last days when, "all who will not receive the love of the truth will be sent strong delusion that they should believe a lie" **(2 Th. 2:11)**. And, who will be able to deliver from this delusion?

As a Christian leader in ministry, you have a tremendous responsibility to oversee the flock of God with all diligence, righteousness, truth, love, and holiness. God will hold you responsible for feeding His sheep His Word, rightly divided. "But though we, or an angel from heaven, preach any other gospel unto you than that which we have preached unto you, let him be accursed. As we said before, so say I now again, If any man preach any other gospel unto you than that ye have received, let him be accursed" **(Ga. 1:8, 9)**. "My brethren, be not many masters, (teachers), knowing that we shall receive the greater condemnation" **(Ja. 3:1)**.

We are called to, "earnestly contend for the faith which was once delivered unto the saints" **(Jude 3b)**. Because of the perilous times in which we live, every Christian must be made aware of the devices of the devil. Just because someone says he or she is a Christian, or that this person believes in God, doesn't mean the he or she knows the Lord Jesus! Oh, how we need discernment in the body of Christ!

Finally, there is the call to holiness. This is not an option, nor is it for the select few. God is holy. (See **Ex. 15:11; 1 Sam. 6:20; Ps. 99:9; Is. 6:3; Eze. 39:7; Hab. 1:13; Re. 4:8; 15:4**.)

20. What did God command in **Le. 11:45**?
21. What does **2 Co. 7:1** enjoin?
22. Fill in the blanks: **(Heb. 12:14)**. "Follow __________________ with all ____________, and ______________________without which ______ man shall __________ the Lord."
23. Write out **1 Pe. 1:16**.
24. Explain **2 Pe. 3:11**.
25. Read **Lu. 14:26, 27**. What does Jesus mean in these verses? (Do cross reference.)
26. What does it mean to hate your own life? Find supportive scriptures.
27. What is the three-fold commitment in Jesus words in **Matt. 16:24**?

And whosoever doth not bear his cross, and come after me, cannot be my disciple.

We began this study with the "A, B, C's" of what true ministry is *not*. Following are the "A, B, C's" of what true ministry *is*:

Always bearing about in the body the dying of the Lord Jesus, that the life also of Jesus might be made manifest in our body **(2 Cor. 4:10)**.
Believing all things which are written in the law and in the prophets **(Acts 24:14b).**
Cleaving to that which is good **(Ro. 12:9b)**.
Denying ungodliness and worldly lusts **(Tit. 2:12)**.
Enduring (to the end) **(Matt. 10:22)**.
Faithful unto death **(Rev. 2:10)**.
Going the extra mile **(Matt. 5:41)**.
Holding forth the word of life **(Ph. 2:16)**.
Interceding **(Isa. 59:16)**.
Judging righteous judgment **(Jn. 7:24)**.
Knowing this, that the trying of your faith worketh patience **(Ja. 1:3)**.
Loving the Lord our God with all our heart, soul, and mind **(Matt. 22:37)**.
Making melody in our hearts to the Lord **(Eph. 5:19)**.
Never showing respect of persons **(Ja. 2:1-10)**.
Opening the door of faith to the lost **(Ac. 14:27)**.
Praying and singing with the spirit **(1 Cor. 14:15)**.
Quickly agreeing with our adversaries **(Matt. 5:25)**.
Reproving unfruitful works of darkness **(Eph. 5:11)**.
Sacrifice and service **(Ph. 2:17)**.
Taming the tongue **(Ja. 3)**.
Understanding what the will of the Lord is **(Eph. 5:17)**.
Valiantly overcoming through the Lord **(Ps. 108:13)**.
Wisely winning souls **(Pr. 11:30)**.
Yielding to the Lordship of Christ **(Col. 1:18)**.
Zealous of good works **(Ti. 2:14)**.

Supplementation
Two

By

Rayola Kelley

This Supplementation Features the Following Studies:

What Must I do to be Saved?: Copyrighted © 1991
What are you doing with Jesus?: Copyrighted © 1990
Evangelism: Copyrighted © 1998
The Call to Holiness: Copyrighted © 1991
How to Serve God: Copyrighted © 1991

WHAT MUST I DO TO BE SAVED?

INTRODUCTION

There is only one question an individual can ask when he or she truthfully considers life and death in light of God and eternity, *"What must I do to be saved?"*

It is important we do not consider this subject lightly. Today, there is much assumption made about man's spiritual condition. If we hear someone talk about Jesus, or see someone go to church, we assume that this individual is on his or her way to heaven. I wonder how many people the church has literally assumed into hell?

I have tried to cease from assuming. I have learned some people in the church assumed they are saved, but do not even know Jesus Christ. I have encountered people who talk the talk, but cannot give an account of the hope in them **(1 Peter 3:15)**. I have watched people play the religious games, but lack commitment towards God and spiritual fruits. As I have taught basic Christian principles, people have come forward with tears in their eyes confessing that until the sincere teaching of the Word of God challenged them, they assumed they were saved even though they could not really explain salvation.

The Church is in an identity crisis. The preaching of a watered-down gospel has produced this crisis. This watered-down gospel has no power to convict and bring people to a real knowledge of their need for the only Savior of their sin-laden soul, Jesus Christ. The tragedy is that such an error catches unsuspecting and doomed souls off guard. They are not ready in life or death to meet their God, and ultimately, some in the Church will be held accountable for the destruction of these souls.

This study answers this question by presenting the simple ABCs of salvation, *acknowledgment, believing* and *confessing*. It upholds Paul's main desire in declaring salvation to others, "And my speech and my preaching (teaching) was not with enticing words of man's wisdom, but in demonstration of the Spirit and of power...For I am not ashamed of the gospel of Christ; for it is the power of God unto salvation" **(1 Corinthians 2:4; Romans 1:16)**.

Let me ask you a question. Are you assuming you are saved or are you really saved? Do not take this question or study lightly. Instead, challenge yourself and settle the question as to whether you are standing condemned because of a false assumption or saved by the blood of Jesus Christ.

ACKNOWLEDGMENT:

RECOGNIZING OUR CONDITION

1. What does it mean to be saved?
2. According to the following scriptures what does man need to be delivered from? **Galatians 3:10-13; Romans 3:23, 25; 5:12; 6:23 1 Thessalonians 5:9**
3. Define death in your own words.

As you study these three questions, you realize that salvation implies deliverance. We need to be delivered from the curse of the Law. Death means separation. For instance, physical death means the separation of our spirit and soul from our physical body. Death in the spiritual sense simply means separation from God who is life.

Genesis 1:26 and **27** states that God created man in His image. In **Genesis 2:7** we are told God breathed into man's nostrils and he became a living soul. This shows man is in essence an eternal being just as his Creator.

When man physically dies, his spirit and soul remain alive.

4. According to the following scriptures where can the spirit of man go for all eternity? **2 Corinthians 5:6-9; Philippians 3:20 Matthew 10:28; Luke 9:25; Revelation 20:10-15**

Note the word destroy in **Matthew 10:28** does not mean extinction. According to the *Vine's Expository Dictionary of Biblical Words*, it implies ruin or loss of spiritual well-being. (See **Luke 16:19-31**.)

Obviously, man is in need of deliverance from spiritual death. God is the only hope for man's deliverance.

Why does death plagued man? Let us examine this subject in greater detail.

4. Look up **Isaiah 64:6; Romans 3:10, 23** and **5:6-15**. Explain the hopeless condition of man according to these scriptures.

All men have a sin problem. This sin came through Adam in the Garden of Eden. This spiritual disease of the soul separated man from fellowshipping with his Creator.

It is important to note if man does not recognize and acknowledge this sinful condition, he will not see the need for deliverance. This is why man must acknowledge that he is a sinner in need of salvation from sin and the consequence of death. It is only by recognizing this spiritual condition that an individual will see a need for God's intervention in his or her life.

5. Look up **1 John 1:8** and **10**. If you deny you have a problem with sin, what are you lacking in your life, and in essence calling God?

If you are denying the condition of sin in your life, the truth is not in you.

6. Based on **John 14:6** who is the truth?
7. If Christ is missing in your life, what else are you missing according to **1 John 5:11**, **12**?

God is not a liar **(Titus 1:2, 3; Hebrews 6:17-19)**.

8. What does **Romans 3:4** say about this subject? (Read **Romans 3:1-8**.)
9. Look up **Hebrews 9:27**. Once an individual physically dies, is there any second chance available to him or her to make it right with God if he or she has rejected God's salvation? (Yes or no?)

Man needs God to deliver him from the consequences of his sinful condition. There is no second chance for man to change his eternal destination once he dies physically. If his sin has not been dealt with on earth, he will be separated from his Creator, God, who is the giver of spiritual well-being for eternity.

Once an individual acknowledges his or her need for deliverance, then he or she can take the next step, which is to *believe* in the salvation provided for him or her by God.

BELIEVING:

CHILDLIKE FAITH

There are many words, which describe the word *"believe."* The problem is the word has been watered down in today's society. According to *Vine's Expository Dictionary of Biblical Words*, believe means to place confidence in and to trust. It implies faith and assurance.

The main word we will consider is the word faith. Faith implies a trust that is a result of persuasion.

1. According to the following scriptures, why would we be persuaded to trust God for our salvation? **1 John 4:19** refer to **John 3:16-19**

   God so loved us He gave His only begotten Son to die on the cross for each of us.

2. What significance did Christ's death on the cross play in the salvation of man based on the following scriptures? **Ephesians 1:3-7; Colossians 1:12-14; Romans 5:8-11**
3. What does the word redeem mean?
   Jesus died on the cross to redeem us. The blood of Christ serves as the necessary tender for man's sins. (See **1 Corinthians 6:20 and 7:22-24**.)
4. How do **Hebrews 9:11-15, 22** and **10:11-18** confirm this truth?

   Remission means to release or to forgive. As we see scripturally, there is no release from the consequence of sins without first the shedding of blood.

5. What did John the Baptist say about Jesus in **John 1:29**?
6. According to **Romans 10:17** how does faith come?
7. What kind of trust must exist in order for true conversion to take place in the heart of an individual? **Matthew 18:2-4**

   We must *believe* or have faith in the salvation God has so freely offered us. We must accept the truth of our sinful condition and the provision of eternal life in Christ Jesus by faith.

   Faith comes as we hear the Word of God. The Word of God shows us our need for salvation. As we begin to *acknowledge* our sin, we than can trust in the provision God has made through His Son, Jesus Christ.

   A "childlike trust" is necessary to receive the salvation of Christ. For adults this means regression of intellectualism, preconceived notions, and ideas to receive what God has freely provided.

   It is important to note a person's intelligence has often kept him or her from receiving God's offer of salvation. The reason for this is because God's ways are higher than man and will not fit into his limited, fleshly concepts, yet they are simple enough that a child can embrace them as being so. (See **Isaiah 55:8-9**.)

8. What did Paul say about the wisdom of man in **1 Corinthians 1:19-29**?
9. Define justify.
10. What does **Ephesians 2:8-10** say about grace?

It is by faith in Christ we are justified **(Romans 5:1)**. Justification points to being acquitted. To be acquitted spiritually involves an act of grace on the part of God. Grace means undeserved favor. We can clearly see man can't work his way to heaven by good works or religious affiliations. God's salvation has nothing to do with man's best attempts.

11. What does **Isaiah 64:6** say about man's best?

The gospel or good news is the death, burial, and resurrection of Christ **(1 Corinthians 15:1-4).** The fact that Christ died on the cross is part of the message of hope, but the other part is He rose from the grave three days later.

12. What significance does the resurrection of Christ play in the salvation of man according to the following Scriptures? **(1 Corinthians 15:12-26, 49-57)**

Many men died on the cross during the time of Christ. The real hope of man rests in the fact that Christ did not remain in the grave. The real message of salvation is that death no longer has victory over us because Christ rose from the grave. This is why Christ alone is man's only hope. I must point out many great men have died for great causes, but not one of them has risen from the grave!

This is why Paul tells us in **Roman 10:9** that we must *believe* that God has raised Christ from the dead.

13. Where must such belief take place in man according to this scripture?

We must believe this message of hope in our hearts. In other words, it is not really an intellectual or emotional realization; it is simply a heart response of receiving and knowing this truth based on who God is and the declaration of His Word.

Our salvation rests totally on God. Our understanding of it must consist of the simplest form of belief and trust. In the end, our only conclusion is that we can only glory in what our Lord has done for us via the cross.

14. Look up **1 Corinthians 1:29, 30**. Write out these scriptures.

CONFESSION:

AGREEING WITH GOD

For review purpose, here are the first two steps of salvation: 1) we must *acknowledge* we are sinners in need of salvation; and 2) we must *believe* in our heart that Christ died on the cross for our sins and rose from the grave three days later to prove victory over death.

Now let us consider the third step necessary for man to come to terms with the salvation God is offering.

1. This third step is found in the first part of **Romans 10:9**. Write down this step.

   It is necessary for an individual to realize the significance of *receiving* Jesus into his or her life. Jesus is not just anyone. He is the King of kings and the Lord of lords **(1 Timothy 6:15)**.

   As King, Jesus is royalty and by *confessing* Jesus as Lord, you are in a sense recognizing the significance of His title, rights, and position He has in regard to the believer's life. Although this position is not fully realized by a new believer, it is *acknowledged* and declared, setting forth an attitude and response that will set the pace for the future relationship such a position requires.

   It is very important we each understand what the term *Lord* means. It implies ownership, and it has the same authority as a king or emperor.

2. Look up the following scriptures. Examine the title of Lord in relationship to the position Christ should have in your life. Write your findings. **Ephesians 4:4-6; Acts 2:36,** refer to **Luke 4:18-19; 1 John 2:22-23; Psalm 100:3** refer to **John 1:1 Isaiah 45:21 Psalm 23:1**

   First, there is only *one Lord* in which we serve or pay homage to. He owns our life and has total say over it. As His devoted servants, we give up our rights, our private goals, and our life to serve the King of kings and the Lord of lords.

3. What does **Romans 12:1** say about a life which has been set apart for service to God?

   Our Lord is The Christ or the Messiah. Christ means the "Anointed One." He came to set the captive free from all bondage, to bring healing to the broken hearted, and to give sight to the blind. This spiritual liberty, healing, and sight are available to those who are poor in spirit **(Matthew 5:3)**.

4. What is the warning found in **Matthew 24:23-24**? Our Lord Jesus is also God!
5. How many gods are there according to **Isaiah 45:5, 14, 21; 46:9; 1 Corinthians 8:4-6;** and **James 2:19?**

   There is only one God by nature **(Galatians 4:8)**. Within the unchanging nature of God are three persons, the Father, the Son, and the Holy Spirit. The Word refers to all three as the Godhead **(Romans 1:20).** There are two Hebrews words that describe the Godhead's oneness. There is **yachid** which means absolutely and indivisibly ONE in nature. The other one is **echad,** which is a compound unity (Godhead) (one made up of parts.) And there is also **echod** which points to unity composed of two persons: The Father and the Son are one (**John 10:30**).

1 John 4:2-3 and **2 John 7** declares we must *believe* Jesus is God in the flesh or God Incarnate. Jesus is divine by nature, and He came to this world in the flesh. He was completely God and completely man. This union between two distinct and diverse natures is referred to the **hypostatic union.** Jesus was seen, touched, and beheld by man. He represented the fullness of the Godhead in bodily form **(Colossians 2:9)**.

Because Jesus is divine, He was able to pay the price for sin, thereby, saving man to the uttermost **(Hebrews 7:11-25)**.

6. Summarize what Paul declared about Jesus in **Colossians 1:14-20**.

Jesus is our <u>*Savior*</u> as well. His name, <u>Jesus</u>, means **Jehovah saves**.

7. What does **Acts 4:12** declare about the very name of Jesus?
8. What does **1 John 4:14** say about Jesus?

There is no other name by which man can be saved; therefore, there is no other Savior except Jesus. He is the only one who can save or deliver man from the consequence of sin. He alone is the only way to heaven **(Matthew 7:13, 14; Hebrews 5:5-10; 1 John 5:10-13; Romans 10:13)**.

9. The word *"Savior"* also denotes one who sustains spiritual life. Look up the following scriptures. Identify how Jesus maintains one's spiritual life (**John 6:32-35; John 7:37-39; John 8:31-36 John 15:1-14)**.

Jesus as Lord is our <u>*Shepherd*</u> as well.

10. What qualifies Him as the Good Shepherd? **John 10:11**

The picture of Jesus as our Shepherd shows us His gentleness and love. He has purchased us by His blood. His desire is to bring us to a full, complete life. As both Lord and Shepherd of our life, He has our best in mind at all times. He is capable of managing our lives. He protects us from our enemies and leads us in the right paths of righteousness into a valid relationship with the Father.

11. Identify the positions He holds between God and man. **1 Timothy 2:4-6; Hebrews 8:1-6; 12:24; 1 John 2:1-2**

Jesus is everything to us. He is the only One who can claim the right of a Lord or owner in our lives. We must confess Jesus <u>*is*</u> Lord. Note the present tense.

12. What does the word <u>confess</u> mean to you?

If you look on the word "confess" in relationship to its Greek meaning, you will find it is considered a contract. To confess Jesus as Lord is actually entering into a contract with Him as His servant. He has all say over you and you do nothing apart from Him.

13. What did Paul declare about the final response of all towards Jesus in **Philippians 2:9-11**?

To embrace salvation, we must come to an understanding of the Lordship of Jesus and agree with God, that He is indeed Lord. This will lead us into a relationship inspired by love, service, and commitment to Him. In obedience, servitude, and humility, we will respond correctly to His wonderful leadership.

IN CONCLUSION

When we consider the story of the jailer in **Acts 16:25-34**, we see the simplicity of salvation. The jailer caught a glimpse of God's power and cried out, "What must I do to be saved?" Paul's reply was, "Believe on the Lord Jesus Christ, and thou shalt be **saved**, and thy house." (Emphasis added.)

As you consider this incident, you will once again see all three ingredients of salvation coming together: the jailer's *acknowledgement* for the need of salvation, Paul's declaration for him to *believe* on the Lord Jesus, and his personal *confession* to his family resulting in their salvation.

The beauty of this message is that once you do *believe,* you are born again into a spiritual family and kingdom **(John 1:12; 3:5-8; Romans 8:14-17)**. A new life will come forth, which will reveal a new creation being transformed into the image of Jesus Christ **(2 Corinthians 5:17; Romans 12:2; 8:29)**.

Salvation is free and the requirements to obtain it are within the reach of everyone. In fact, salvation is easy for a sincere heart to understand.

If you desire to know how to be saved, take heart. Just *acknowledge* your need for salvation due to your ungodly state, sinful ways, and your opposition to God's reign in your life. (See **Romans 5:6-10**.) *Believe* in your heart that God raised Christ from the dead to secure salvation for you. *Confess* Him as Lord and receive Him into your heart as your God, the Christ, Shepherd, and your Lord.

Then rejoice, for you can be assured that you have become an heir to eternal life in Christ Jesus.

14. What does **Luke 15:3-7** say about heaven's reaction to the sinner who turns from sin to life in Jesus Christ?

DETERMINATION:

A RESPONSIBILITY

1. What is one's responsibility towards his or her salvation according to Paul in the last part of **Philippians 2:12**?
2. What does it mean to work out our salvation?

Hebrews 2:3 gives us insight into working out our salvation, "How shall we escape, if we neglect so great salvation, which at the first began to be spoken by the Lord and was confirmed unto us by them that heard Him." Remember it entails a relationship with the living God. As we all know every relationship must mature to ensure its existence.

The Word calls us to maturity or perfection in this relationship. It also shows us how we can grow. Let us now examine some Biblical instructions for spiritual growth in this relationship.

3. Look up the following scriptures. Identify the ingredients, which promote maturity. **Daniel 1:8** refer to **Psalm 34:18 & 51:17; 2 Timothy 2:15** refer to **Psalm 119:105; 1 Thessalonians 5:16-18** refer to **Hebrews 13:15-16; James 5:15-16; John 4:24**.

A RIGHT HEART

We must have a right heart condition. A right heart entails a fixed or determined heart towards God. Such a heart must be seeking God.

4. What does **1 Chronicles 28:9; Psalm 69:32,** and **Hebrews 11:6** say about seeking God?

One must have a broken heart and a contrite (repentant) spirit. A broken heart implies an open heart before God. To have an open heart denotes a willingness to be changed by God.

5. What did King David ask God to do with his heart and spirit? **(Psalm 51:10)**.

A repentant spirit is a spirit that desires to line up with God. Repentance is an about face from doing it our way to doing it God's way. It is God's will that we have such repentance working in our lives **(2 Peter 3:9).**

6. Look up **Psalms 37:3-11**. Summarize in what way one needs to respond to God.

Repentance also includes *confession*. This keeps the channels open to God.

7. What does **1 John 1:9** declare about confession? (Refer to **1 John 1:5-7**.)

The truest and most acceptable forms of sacrifice involve a right heart.

8. What does **Psalm 97:10, 11** say about the upright heart?

THE WORD OF GOD

Hosea 4:6 states that God's people (Israel) were destroyed for lack of knowledge.

9. What knowledge should we be seeking after according to **Philippians 3:7-14; 2 Peter 1:3-8, and Romans 16:24-26**?

The written Word becomes the dead letter of the Law without the revelation of the Living Word, Jesus Christ **(Romans 7:6; 2 Corinthians 3:6; John 1:1, 14)**. The whole purpose of the Word of God is to bring us to the knowledge of Jesus Christ.

It is not enough to know *of* Christ or to know *about* Him, we must *know* Him. In order to know Him we will have to study the Word of God. To study the Word of God involves meditating on it, and allowing our spiritual teacher to penetrate our spirit with its practical truths.

10. Who is our spiritual teacher? **(John 14:26; 16:13)**
11. What is the goal of our teacher when it comes to establishing the Word of God in our lives? **(2 Corinthians 3:2-5)** (Epistle means a letter of formal instruction.)

The Word of God will lead you into the full knowledge of Christ. Such knowledge will bring needed changes in your life. This is the ultimate goal and purpose for its inspiration **(2 Timothy 3:16, 17; 2 Peter 1:19-21)**.

PRAYER

Prayer is simply having a conversation with God. We all know there must be communication in a relationship in order for it to survive and grow. The Word of God tells us to, "pray without ceasing" **(1 Thessalonians 5:17***)*. In other words, keep the channel open at all times to God.

Part of effective prayer involves praise and worship. Praise is a sacrifice to God. It is simply recognizing and exalting Him for who He is and what He has done for us.

12. What does **Psalm 22:3** say about the results of praise?

God will meet with and honor His people in the praises directed towards Him. Thanksgiving is also a part of powerful praise. To be thankful implies contentment before God.

13. What does Paul say about being content in **Philippians 4:11-13**?

Prayer can result in true worship. Worship is paying homage to God. You can only worship in spirit and truth (**John 4:24**).

14. Can you have fellowship with God if you don't have His Holy Spirit in you? (Yes or No.) *(***2 Corinthians 6:14-18)** (Fellowship means communion, agreement or sharing.)
15. What is the summary of all absolute truth according to **John 1:14** and **14:6**?
16. What serves as the Christian's only foundation according to **1 Corinthians 3:11**?

We can only have effective prayer, praise, and worship when we have the Holy Spirit in us, and Christ as our only foundation and truth **(Matthew 7:24-27)**.

It is important to note genuine worship results in the person entering into the presence of God. To be in the presence of God is the ultimate in having a growing relationship with Him.

IN CONCLUSION

Salvation is a beautiful gift from God. It offers eternal benefits, but we must maintain it through a growing relationship with God **(Philippians 2:12)**. We need to keep in mind at all times it is a gift that has been offered because of love, and we need to receive it in like fashion.

God's salvation not only provides us with eternal life, but also offers us an abundant, fruitful life, which produces a right relationship with God **(John 15:1-17)**.

The key to having such a life begins with each of us determining in our hearts to seek Him in order to know Him. We need to set our faces heavenward as Abraham did when he realized the city he was really seeking after was made by God and not by man **(Hebrews 11:8-10)**. We need to know the gift of salvation is part of our eternal inheritance and reward, which can be summarized in four words: The *LORD JESUS CHRIST*.

WHAT ARE YOU DOING WITH JESUS?

INTRODUCTION

This study scripturally challenges an individual to consider what he or she is doing with the One who is truth personified, as well as is the only way to an abundant and eternal life. Unbelievers will have to recognize hell awaits those who refuse to acknowledge God's provision of Jesus Christ. Christians must consider that they will not pass through the door of eternal glory without first facing the reality of their life in Christ. They will either stand in shame, realizing all works were burned up, or they will stand with a lasting reward **(1 Corinthians 3:11-15).**

Those who stand ashamed will have to face the awesome truth that service to Jesus and service for Jesus are distinctly different. Service to Jesus means one is actually serving Him because he or she has a relationship with Him. Service for Jesus is often based on an individual's perception of religious duty.

What are you doing with Jesus? The question is vital. Our Lord's response to each of us on judgment day will hinge on our response to Him on a daily basis.

Each believer can avoid future shame and sorrow by opening him or herself up to the Holy Spirit. The Holy Spirit desires to lead each of us into all truth: truth about the Lord we are called to serve, and truth about our response to His call.

I pray each participant of this study will take up the challenge and allow the Holy Spirit the freedom to answer this question. The truth may appear harsh at first, but it has the ability to set an individual free to change the course of his or her life, as well as Christ's final response to him or her.

Section 1

TYPES OF RESPONSE IN SERVICE TO JESUS

TESTIMONY

"But, what have you done with me?" Have you walked with me, sat with me, communed with me? What have you done with me?" His questions penetrated my heart.

I had been a Christian for seven years. I had done things in the name of my Lord, Jesus Christ. However, I realized in light of the cross of Christ all my deeds were feeble. All accomplishments fell short of the high-minded image of my life of service to the King of kings and Lord of lords.

It occurred to me there had to be more to serving Christ than in name or deed only. The scriptures in **Matthew 7:21-23** came to mind.

1. Summarize the verses in **Matthew 7:21-21** in your own words.

In this portion of scripture, we see people who declared Jesus to be Lord. They had done good deeds, some involving power beyond mere man. Yet, they were rejected. We see reference made to disobedient workers of iniquity.

Christians often try to serve Christ without first understanding His will. To know someone's will, or desires, means one has to establish a relationship. This relationship enables the individual to see the heart of a person and learn his or her likes and dislikes.

We consider these factors in relationships with people, but often neglect to do so in our relationship with Christ. Somehow if we do something religious and good, we feel our Lord will accept it.

In **Matthew 11:29** we are commanded to, "learn of Christ." A command is not an option, but a requirement. We actually see the Apostle Paul describe those who had not learned of Jesus and were Gentiles that still walk according to the vanity of their darkened mind in **Ephesians 4:17-20**.

2. What does **1 John 5:3** say about obeying God's commandments?

My Lord's words from **Revelation 3:20** came to light, "I stand at the door (of your heart) knocking." Christianity is not a matter of being saved from hell. Rather, it is a means of being saved or delivered to something. This something is the right to enter a complete relationship with the living God.

This relationship implies *intimacy* with God. It means we have the opportunity of knowing God in a personal way. By knowing God, we will know what is acceptable to Him. As this knowledge of our Lord grows, we will know how to serve Him. Acceptable service to God declares Christ is Lord of our life.

It is hard for Christians in America to understand the implication of Lordship. It is easy to say the word, Lord, but <u>Lordship</u> means total ownership. A Christian belongs to

Jesus. He or she does not have any personal rights. A believer's only focus should be obedience to the Lord.

3. What does **1 Corinthians 7:21-24** say about this subject?

Martha and Mary

In considering my life of service I was given scriptural examples. My attention was drawn to Martha and Mary in **Luke 10:38-41**. I saw a distinction in both attitude and response to Jesus from these women.

4. What attitude did Martha display towards Jesus in **Luke 10:40**?
5. Who was Martha looking at in these verses?

Martha was serving Jesus. Her service would appear to be acceptable to any onlooker. However, Jesus accused Martha of being anxious and troubled about many things. We know that the cares of the world can take our eyes off of what is spiritually important (**Matthew 13:7, 22**). Obviously, Martha's motive for serving was not about solely honoring Jesus, but like Peter in his case of wanting to know what was going to happen to John in **John 21:14-23**, Martha intruded into an area that was not her concern. If Martha's focus was to serve Jesus to honor Him, she would not be concerned about what Mary was doing or not doing.

Service is between the individual and the one he or she is serving. It is important to note Martha's service was practical and obvious, but we must always examine our motive because others' response to their particular call of service may not be the same as ours, and it may reveal points of jealousy, spots of judgmentalism towards others, and prideful competition.

6. What does Jesus say about this condition in **Matthew 6:25-34**? (Note **verse 31**.)
7. According to **Matthew 6:33** what is the solution to Martha's anxious and troubled heart?
8. What was Mary doing in **Luke 10:39**?
9. Can you see similarities in Mary's response to Christ and the instruction found in **Matthew 6:33**? (Yes or No) Explain your answer.

Mary was sitting at the feet of Jesus in preparation for upcoming ministry of anointing Him for His burial. According to Christ, she had chosen the *necessary* and *good part* of a matter, while Martha's service was needful and important, but it was her ministry to carry out and not Mary's. This brings us down to whether her service was a religious act inspired by duty, or a response of the heart. Once again, Martha's concern about Mary's actions reveals that it was a matter of duty and not a response of the heart.

We also see diversity in these two women's approach to Christ in the death of their brother Lazarus in **John 11:1-44**.

10. What were the different responses of Martha and Mary when they heard that Jesus was near? **(John 11:20, 28, 32)**

Both Martha and Mary recognized Christ could have healed their brother **(John 11:21, 22, 32)**. Both fell short in understanding that His power could reach beyond the grave.

Failure to understand Christ in greater ways is not unusual in any Christian's life, and will only diminish as one grows in the knowledge of Jesus Christ.

One of the differences between Martha and Mary is their approach to Jesus Christ. Martha casually came near to Christ. Granted there was a close relationship present between this servant and her Master. That became clear when Martha confessed she believed and testified that Jeus was the resurrection and the life, but she did not come in need of intervention. Mary came upon request from Jesus, and then fell at His feet.

Falling at the feet of someone implies homage. Mary was at the feet of Jesus, seeking answers, mercy, and comfort from the One she honored with all of her heart.

In **John 12**, we can once again observe these two women.

10. What was Martha doing? **(John 12:2)**

This feast took place six days before Christ's crucifixion. These sisters were in Bethany at Simon the leper's house **(Matthew 26:6-13** & **Mark 14:3-9)**. Being a person of action, Martha was still faithfully serving, unaware that the most historical event of all time was about to take place, Christ's crucifixion! However, Martha was not the one called and prepared to become identified with this event.

12. What was Mary's part in the feast? **(John 12:3)**

Once again, we see Mary at the feet of Jesus. She was anointing Him for His burial. This action was exemplary of true service to the Lord who was about to lay down His life. There are other reactions we must note.

13. What was Judas Iscariot's response in **John 12:4-6**?

It is not unusual for those who appear righteous, but fall short of real servitude to point fingers at those who are serving Christ. Finger pointing is a feeble attempt to direct attention away from self by pointing to those whose lives silently convict through example.

14. What was Lazarus doing? **(John 12:2)**

Jesus had raised Lazarus from the dead. He was sitting at a place of honor with the Lord.

15. According to the Apostle Paul, who sits at a place of honor with Jesus in **Ephesians 2:6**?
16. Who is considered the chief in the kingdom of God? **(Matthew 20:25-28)**

Like Lazarus, we have been endued with resurrection power. We have entered from death to life. Although we are positionally sitting in a place of honor, we need to be serving Jesus (See **Ephesians 2:6**). Lazarus' example should challenge us. Are we sitting around waiting to be served, or are we being prepare to serve. We do not know if Lazarus proved to be a real servant or not, but we need to recognize there are two distinct responses to serving Jesus. The opportunities to serve our Lord vary according to the situation. This is why every Christian stands at the crossroad of decision as to whether they are going to serve, or whether they are going to prove to be indifferent to the opportunity.

Today many Christians appear content to simply enjoy their position in Christ, without fulfilling their scriptural responsibility of service.

17. What is every Christian's responsibility? **(Mark 16:15, 16; Matthew 28:18-20)**.

There are different responses to service to Christ. The type of reaction to service is motivated by the type of relationship we have with our Lord. A right relationship renders acceptable service.

When we consider the actions of these people, we distinguish four categories:

Judas Iscariot stood in the midst of God's presence, but fail to honor Jesus.

Lazarus benefited from God's power, but did not appear to serve Jesus.

Martha witnessed God's greatness, but was not called to be part of Jesus burial.

Mary partook of God's glory by honoring Jesus Christ.

The consequences of these distinctions are clearly defined by scriptural examples. For example, Judas Iscariot actually *missed* God. Even though people may benefit from God's power like Lazarus, it actually makes them more accountable to respond to the Lordship of Jesus.

18. How does **Numbers 14:20-24** confirm the previous statement?

To be bystanders of God's greatness like Martha, does not ensure salvation for a person. Many followed Jesus, but few knew Him in an intimate way. In fact, the closer He got to the cross, the greater the test became for those following Him to remain near to Him.

19. Why did the multitudes follow Jesus **(John 6:2)**?

Salvation comes to the individual who is seeking Christ alone. The personal encounter with Christ brings deliverance to the lost and hurting soul.

Mary became a part of the death, burial, and resurrection of Jesus Christ. Although Mary spent her time at the feet of Jesus in humility, submission, and servitude, she was exalted for the whole kingdom of heaven to observe. Her example was preserved for eternity in the pages of God's Word **(Mark 14:6-9)**. In Mary's life we see an individual who never settled for less, but desired the best part of the kingdom of heaven, as well as having knowledge and an intimacy with the Lord Jesus Christ.

20. Summarize **2 Peter 1:2-8**.

To be partakers implies we will become like Jesus in attitude, lifestyle, and service. It means His glory will be evident in our lives.

21. What does **2 Corinthians 3:18** say about this subject?

What category do you fit in? Are you a Judas or a Lazarus? Maybe you are a Martha who at times lack the right heart and perspective in service and must be reminded that everyone has their place? Hopefully you are a Mary who heeds to both the calling and preparation. If you are, your life will show it.

Section 2

JESUS AS THE WAY

INTRODUCTION

Jesus Christ summarized His ministry on earth in **John 14:6**.

1. What is His ministry to us?

   Jesus is the way, the truth, and the life. In Him we can find the direction, substance, and purpose for our very existence. He is the only way to a relationship with the Father.

   Our responses to Jesus as the way, the truth, and the life can be found in **Matthew 7:7, 8**.

2. What needs to be our responses to Jesus?

   We need to *ask* Christ to have His *way* in our life. We need to be *seeking* His *truth*. We must *knock* on all doors to find the *life* He has provided for each of us.

   It is important Christians understand how Christ's ministry and their response to Him intertwine and complement each other. The correct combination will result in a right relationship with God and a powerful life of service.

The Way

The word <u>way</u> has many meanings. It can mean a thoroughfare or a passageway such as a door. The *Vine's Expository Dictionary of Biblical Words* tells us metaphorically it can mean "a course of conduct," or "a way of thinking."

<u>Way</u> also implies there is a journey involved. Christianity is a journey.

3. How does **1 Peter 2:11** confirm this statement?
4. What serves as our door in this journey? **(John 10:9)**
5. What will we find in this journey according to **John 10:9**?

   Jesus serves as man's door.

6. How does **Matthew 7:14** describe the way we must travel?

   According to the *King James Version* of the Bible, the way to heaven is narrow and strait. The *Vine's Expository Dictionary of Biblical Words* tells us narrow and strait implies being hemmed in or pressed for room.

   We must understand the differences between God's ways and man's ways. To grasp these differences is to understand why the path to heaven is narrow and strait.

7. Look up the following scriptures. Identify God's ways verse man's ways. **(Psalm 18:30; Proverbs 21:8 Psalm 145:17; Proverbs 16:2; Isaiah 55:8, 9; Proverbs 2:13-15)**

God's ways are higher. Man's ways are perverse and unacceptable to God. Man's ways may appear clean, but God considers the heart.

8. What do **Proverbs 14:12** and **16:25** say about this subject?

When man does it his way, he is in rebellion against God. God's ways are summarized in two words, *Jesus Christ*. He is man's only door to an eternal inheritance. He is man's example as to what is acceptable. He is the only pathway to an intimate relationship with the Father.

Christ-The Passageway to Life

9. Summarize **1 John 5:10-12**.

Contrary to popular and acceptable belief, there is only one way to heaven, *Jesus Christ*. He is the passageway to life.

10. What kind of life can we find in Jesus? **(1 John 5:13; John 10:10)**

Death means separation. In the case of humanity this death is the separation from the life found in Christ. This life is everlasting and complete. It is for now and for eternity.

11. What has created the separation that can exist between man and his God **(Romans 3:23)**?

Man is hopelessly lost because of his fallen, sinful condition. The wages of sin is death **(Romans 6:23)**.

12. How did Christ close the gap between man and his Creator? **(Ephesians 2:16; 2 Corinthians 5:18-21)**

According to *Vine's Expository Dictionary of Biblical Words,* reconciliation means to change in relationship. Because of Christ, man can experience friendship with God.

By death on the cross, Christ provided the means by which man can be delivered from the consequences of his sin. This deliverance is known as *salvation*.

13. What do **Romans 6:23** and **Ephesians 2:8-10** say about salvation?

Salvation is a free gift and comes by way of God's grace. Christ not only saved us from eternal separation from God, but He saved us to enjoy a relationship with Him. This relationship is the real key behind the gift we have been given. Remember what the last part of **John 14:6** says, "No one comes to the Father but by (Christ)." (Parenthesis added.)

Christianity is a relationship with God. We can go through religious motions, belong to a church, and do good deeds and still miss God. Religion without a relationship with God is only man's futile attempt to get to heaven on his own merits. This path is attractive to man's pride, but it is a broad way that leads to destruction.

14. What does this destruction imply? **(Matthew 5:21, 22; 10:28)**

Hell is a real place. The suffering and torment are described in the Bible. It is not God's will for anyone to end up in hell. Hell is the choice rebellious man makes when he neglects or rejects God and His plan of salvation.

15. What is God's will for man? **(2 Peter 3:9)**

It is God's will that all come to repentance. Repentance is a change of heart and mind about sin; and a change in direction from doing it our way to doing it God's way.

By allowing the life of Christ to be worked in us, we will experience the abundant life. This life denotes a complete and fruitful life.

16. What kind of virtues will be evident in the abundant life? **(Galatians 5:22, 23)**
17. In order to possess this life, what must we be doing according to **John 15:4-6**?
18. Explain what it means to abide in Christ? (You may need to look up the word "abide" to gain a picture of its implications.)

All spiritual life and well-being come from abiding in Christ. It is allowing the life of Christ to be established in every fiber of our heart and mind.

Do you have life? Christ is standing at the door of your heart, waiting for admission. Allow Him to come in. The life available through Him is indeed complete and fulfilling.

The Purpose

Many people are searching for the reason behind their existence. They desire to understand their purpose for being here. Their search often leads them to disillusionment and hopelessness.

To reach a conclusion about the purpose of life, we must begin with the One who created us. All creation is designed with a function in mind. We must consider what was in the mind of our Creator when He formed man out of the dust.

Genesis 1:27 clearly tells us God created man. **Jeremiah 18:1-6** describes God as the Potter.

19. What does **2 Corinthians 4:7** say about man in relationship to the Potter?

The Word declares man to be no more than a clay vessel. For clay to take on a form, it first must lose its identity. In order for it to lose its identity it must go through a rigorous process. The final product will not only serve a purpose, but it will bring honor to the potter.

20. According to the following verses, what is the purpose of man's existence? **(1 John 1:3; Matthew 5:16)**

God created us to have fellowship with Him. By having an intimacy with God, we can bring glory to His name. This honor is established by a life of service to Him.

There are four types of vessels we can observe not only in our home, but also in Christianity. The type of vessel stipulates the value and purpose behind its existence.

The Closed Vessel

The *closed vessel* is full, but useless. Such a vessel must be opened and the contents poured out before it can serve any purpose to God, our Potter. A closed vessel in Christianity symbolizes an individual who is full of self.

21. What does **Romans 7:15-25** say about self?

Romans 7:18 tells us, there is no good thing in the flesh. In other words, there is nothing beneficial in the flesh. Flesh points to the self-man or the old man. Self is comprised of pride. Pride is an image of self. Self is always subject to the dictates of the flesh.

22. What are the works of the flesh? **(Galatians 5:19-21)**
23. Will those who display the works of the flesh inherit the kingdom of God? (Yes or No)

A person's life must become open. They must become empty of self in order for the life of Christ to be imparted. This implies death to self.

The Empty Vessel

The second vessel is the *empty vessel.* These vessels are mainly for decoration. They may be valuable, but serve no purpose. They will only require much attention.

There are Christians who decorate the church pews with their presence, but offer nothing to further the kingdom of heaven. They may have a form of righteousness, but in appearance only.

24. What does **2 Timothy 3:5** say about such an individual?

To have God's Spirit implies a life of power. This life will produce fruit. It is not a life of show, but a life of action. It is not a life where one is served, but where one serves others. It is not a life where one has a form of righteousness, but has the righteousness of Christ being manifested through him or her.

The Broken Vessel

The third type of vessel we can come in contact with is the *broken vessel.* These vessels cannot serve any purpose; therefore, they are discarded.

The human race is full of broken lives and hearts. We see these broken vessels in the Church that Jesus also died for. People who come to the cross of Christ do so because they are broken by their life, or they will find themselves broken by the reality of their sin.

25. What does **Psalm 34:18** and **51:17** say about brokenness?

Brokenness can occur in times of tribulation and tragedy. It can occur in times of great loss and hopelessness.

26. According to **Luke 4:18** who is able to make broken hearts and lives complete?

Brokenness is a certainty in life. It is a necessary ingredient in salvation. According to the Word of God, spiritual brokenness comes in two different forms. One form is worldly remorse. The other one is referred to as repentance. These diverse reactions determine the final destination of the vessel.

27. What will be the final destination of both of these types of broken vessels according to **2 Corinthians 7:10**?

The Open Vessel

The fourth vessel is the *open vessel*. This vessel is ready for use. It has purpose and is used accordingly.

28. What does **2 Timothy 2:21** say about the vessel used by the Lord?

Our holy God must prepare vessels that will be used by Him. The vessels He will use must be open and available. The Living Water must cleanse them.

29. Who is the Christian's Living Water? **(John 7:37-39)**

By allowing the Living Water to flow freely through our lives we will be made fit for God's use. Cleansing purges us from unrighteousness, and the fruit of the Spirit is the product of such separation. In the end, we will attract others to the kingdom of heaven.

What kind of vessel are you? Is your life reflecting Jesus Christ or are you full of self? Do you have a religious form without the power, commitment, or life? Maybe you are broken, displaying an inconsistent life? Jesus Christ is in the business of making lives complete. Turn to Him. Like the father in the parable of the prodigal son, He will meet you **(Luke 15:11-32)**.

The Map

In order to go on a journey, we must first have a destination.

30. What is our destination? **(Philippians 3:20; Hebrews 11:8-10)**

To find the way to our destination, we must have a map.

31. What gives us direction according to **Psalm 119:105**?

The Word of God is our spiritual map. According to the verse in **Psalm 119**, it will be a lamp unto our feet.

32. What kind of walk will it involve? **(2 Corinthians 5:7)**
33. Define faith in your own words.

Faith is knowing and trusting God. It allows you to walk towards God in assurance because of what He has said. Faith comes from hearing, and by hearing the Word of God **(Romans 10:17)**. You know it is so because of who He is **(Hebrews 11:6)**. He never lies for He means what He says and says what He means. However, one cannot develop a strong trust towards God until he or she knows Him. Once an individual has confidence in God, he or she can take Him at His Word. Standing on the promises of the Word serves as the immovable rock in every situation.

34. What is the ultimate destination reached by following the directions of the spiritual map? **(John 5:39; 1 Peter 1:9)**

Both the map and walk of faith will lead us to Jesus Christ and His salvation. We must understand, "knowledge of the Word without the revelation of the Living Word (Jesus) makes the Bible dead letter." The goal of the Bible is to lead us to the knowledge of Jesus Christ. Christ is our only sure foundation.

35. How does **Matthew 7:24-27** confirm this statement?

There are three main commands found in the Bible that summarize man's necessary response to a life of service.

36. What are these commands? **(1 Samuel 15:22; 1 John 2:3-11; Romans 8:29; Philippians 2:5 Matthew 28:18-20; Mark 16:15-18)**

True faith results in obedience. Obedience will give us confidence in our relationship with God. This creates openness so the life of Christ can be worked in us. Such a life motivates us to share the Gospel with others.

37. What is the Gospel? **(1 Corinthians 15:1-4)**

It is hard to share a message unless it has been validated. The Gospel becomes validated when people see Christ in us. Sharing Christ with others makes us obedient to the Word of God.

The Route

38. There is a route Christians must travel. What is this route? **(Matthew 10:38; 16:24)**

The way a Christian must travel is the way of the cross. The <u>cross</u> means death and suffering. A Christian must die to self in order to have the life of Christ imparted in and through him or her **(Galatians 2:20)**. A Christian must suffer in order to see His glory **(Romans 8:17, 18)**.

39. What does **2 Timothy 2:11-12** say about this subject in the *KJV*?
40. What is the purpose of suffering according to the following scriptures? (**2 Corinthians 1:3-7; 2 Corinthians 4:7-10; 1 Peter 1:6-10)**

When we consider the way of the cross, we begin to understand why the way to heaven is narrow and hard. The way of the cross will hem or press in on those who travel it. As it becomes narrow, more of self will be left to the wayside. As it becomes harder, Christ-like characteristics will be worked in hearts.

By applying the three main commands of the map *(Bible)* to the route of the *cross*, we gain a decisive picture. Let's consider the following illustration. The *vertical* part of the cross represents man's correct response to God. The *horizontal* part of the cross symbolizes man's response and responsibility to others.

Obedience is the longest part of the cross. It puts our life in perspective with God.

Without this, our relationship with others will bring burdens we cannot carry.

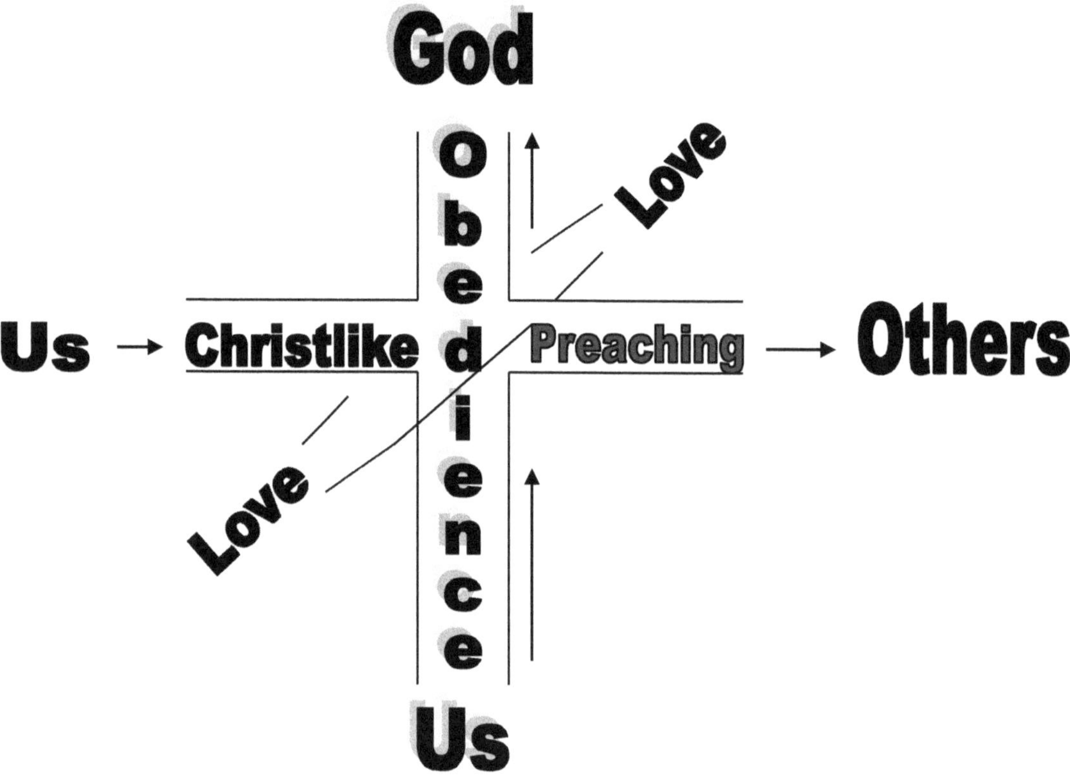

The ingredient that ties this cross together is the love of God.

41. What does **2 Corinthians 5:14** say about it?

The love of God will give us a level of commitment. This commitment will create a desire in us to be right before God and to do right by others. Without the motivation of God's love all will be in vain.

42. How does **1 Corinthians 13:1-3** confirm the last statement?

Are you carrying your cross? Remember, the way to heaven is narrow and few will find it. It is a life you must search for on a daily basis.

Section 3

JESUS AS THE TRUTH

The Truth

In our world today, there is a growing consensus that there is no absolute truth. Without a standard of truth to guide our lives, we reside in confusion. It is no wonder chaos is prevalent everywhere.

Jesus said He is the truth. If this is so, Jesus is the summary of all truth. In Him we can find a standard upon which we can base every decision. We can be assured of standing on the right foundation for now and eternity.

The Word of God shows us how Christ represents absolute truth in three areas. The first area of truth, which is summarized by Christ, can be found in **John 14:7-9**.

1. What reality is personified in Jesus Christ?

   Jesus is God in the flesh. He represented God's love, mercy, and judgment (righteousness) to mankind. These three attributes were brought together and made real by His death on the cross.

   The second area of truth Jesus represented can be found in **John 1:29, 2 Corinthians 5:21,** and **Hebrews 4:15.**

2. What does Christ symbolize in these verses?

   Christ is the truth about man's spiritual condition. He was tempted in all areas. He became sin for man in order to pay the price for its destruction.

3. What does **Philippians 2:6-8** say about this subject?
4. The final area of verity can be found in **John 13:15** and **1 Peter 2:21**. What truth does Jesus represent in these scriptures?

   Jesus is the example of true Christianity. The Christian walk is a life of service and suffering. It entails allowing His characteristics to be worked into our lives.

   John 1:1 tells us Christ is the Living Word. He is God's communication to man. We can clearly see this communication in the truth Christ represented in His humanity.

5. What can truth accomplish in our life? **(John 8:32)**

   Christ is also the light. Light exposes the condition of our spiritual life.

6. What can we be assured of it we are walking in the light? **(1 John 1:5-7)**
7. What virtues will be displayed if we are children of the light? **(Ephesians 5:8-9)**
8. What is man's preference according to **John 3:19**?

   Men love darkness. Darkness implies deception. The ruler of darkness is Satan. Is Jesus, or Satan, determining your standard of truth?

Attitudes Towards the Truth

There are three attitudes people display towards truth. The first attitude is based on a *false premise of self.* Self is influence by the standards and images of the world. These rulers or concepts include the latest fads or ideas which either society or the church are promoting. People who adopt this approach are like corks on the ocean; tossed about by every wave.

9. What does Paul say about this attitude in **Ephesians 4:13-16**?

The second approach is based on a *pseudo premise of religion or personal righteousness* or *goodness.* Such a premise involves those who establish their own standard of truth. These people prove to be motivated by pride and are unteachable. Their standards can be comprised of both truth and deception which can include both a type of veil over the mind, a wrong spirit or both. The combination is destructive. The religious leaders of Jesus' day fit this category.

10. What did Jesus say about the religious leaders in **Matthew 15:1-9**?

The third group are comprised of the *truth seekers.* These individuals desire truth and will not accept anything less. Once truth is found, they will discard any beliefs that run contrary to it.

Truth seekers are the exception and not the rule. The reason is because the route of truth will lead to the Person of Jesus Christ rather than a philosophy, doctrine or theology. It will be Jesus in His glory and power and through His Spirit who will establish the truth in the lives of those seeking it. To know Jesus in this capacity will entail a relationship.

11. What promise does the truth seeker have in **2 Corinthians 13:8**?

The truth will stand when all else fails. What a promise for those seeking it out!

Responses to the Truth

Truth in our midst will create a response. Jesus warned that He did not bring peace, but a sword that would divide families **(Matthew 10:34-36)**. **Hebrews 4:12** tells us the Word of God is the sword.

There are four responses to Christ standing in man's midst as the absolute truth. The first group and their response to consider are the religious leaders.

12. What did Jesus say about these religious people in **Matthew 15:7-9**?

Christ came to call the sinner to repentance **(Matthew 9:12-13)**. If the sinner responds, he finds spiritual healing. **Luke 5:17** tells us the power of the Lord was present to heal the religious leaders, but they did not respond. Their self-righteousness or religious pride kept them from receiving. In fact, they became *threatened* by the presence of Jesus.

13. What did these people finally do with the truth? **(Matthew 27:20-24)**

Today there are people in our churches who feel threatened by the truth. They prefer to hold onto their religious pride and traditions. Their unwillingness to submit to the truth will result in them crucifying it.

The second response can be found in **Luke 4:16-30**. Jesus was in His hometown, Nazareth. He was in the synagogue. He read out of the book of **Isaiah**.

14. What did the scriptures say? **(Luke 4:18-19)**

Jesus, truth personified, was offering the people healing, freedom, and life. They became *insulted.* How could the son of Joseph, a mere carpenter, make such claims?

15. What was their response? **(Luke 4:29)**

Luke 4:21 states these promises were fulfilled in their ears and not in their lives. We can see the same pathetic situation in churches. There are people who are comfortable with Jesus as a Savior, but reject His Lordship. They are very secure in His love, but do not bother them with His righteousness, which will require judgment. Challenging such people will insult them, resulting in wrath.

16. What was Jesus' reaction to the people of His hometown? **(Luke 4:30)**

Jesus passed through their midst. The result was no one was saved, healed, or delivered. What a tragedy. Today we see this same tragedy in churches and in the lives of some Christians. Jesus is passing through their midst because they refuse to know Him in greater ways.

This refusal of the people of Nazareth stems from an attitude that wants to remain comfortable. This comfortable state can be described by one word, complacency.

17. What did Jesus say about complacency in **Revelation 3:15-16**?

The third response can be found within the Gadarenes. Christ's encounter with these people started with a deliverance. A man tormented by demons came across Jesus' path. The demons recognized Jesus. They addressed Him.

18. What was their statement to Him? (**Matthew 8:29** refer to **2 Peter 2:4.**)

Christ delivered the man of his tormentors. He sent the demons into a herd of swine. The swine rushed into a body of water. All drowned. Those who attended the swine went to town and told the residents.

19. What was the residents' reaction to Jesus when they met Him? **(Mark 5:17)**

As Jesus stands in the midst, man finds himself at a crossroad. This crossroad can bring either deliverance or fear.

In the case of the Gadarenes, it brought conviction and fear. Conviction can materialize when a person gets a glimpse of the cost involved in having Christ in his or her midst. Such individuals become reluctant to lose, in order to gain it all. They end up convicted as they go the opposite direction from Jesus. Such is the case of the rich young ruler in **Matthew 19:16-25**.

Occasionally people see something they cannot understand or control. This will create fear. This fear is a form of unbelief. Unbelief will cause the Lord to withdraw His presence. This especially is true in the area of the moving of the Holy Spirit. Ignorance of the Holy Spirit is what causes this fear. It ultimately produces confusion and rejection.

The fourth response comes from those who are hungry and thirsty. These individuals are personally seeking out Jesus. They may be in the crowd, but they are not a part of it. Their goal is to encounter Jesus in a personal way. They seek Him out in faith, and receive in abundance. They stand in His midst, receptive of the truth about His greatness and their need. They walked away changed. Some experienced His forgiveness and salvation. Other left healed or set free.

20. Look up the following verses. Identify what each individual received after his or her encounter with Christ. **(Luke 19:1-10 Matthew 9:20-22 Mark 7:24-30 John 4:5-38 Matthew 8:5-13)**

The people who had an encounter with Jesus were often considered unacceptable to those of the world and the religious realm.

21. What does the Apostle Paul say about this subject in **1 Corinthians 1:26-28**?

Remember, Jesus is calling the sinner to repentance. **Luke 15:3-7** tells us He is looking for the one lost sheep. His search started when Adam sinned in the Garden of Eden. **(Genesis 3:8-9)**

What is your response to Jesus as the truth? Lets review both the attitudes and responses towards the truth:

Attitudes	Responses
Unteachable	Offended-crucified the truth
Comfortable	Complacency-wrath
Fearful/Convicted	Fearful-asks the truth to leave.
Truth Seekers	Encounters the truth-change.

Ask the Lord to show you which category you fall in. No one can afford to have Jesus pass through their midst. Everyone needs to encounter Him in a personal way.

Section 4

JESUS AS THE LIFE

JESUS AS THE LIFE

We have already discussed Jesus as the summary of the eternal and abundant life. He is the only door to this complete life. This life is found in an abiding relationship with the Living God.

It is in this relationship we find substance and purpose. We recognize our substance comes from fellowshipping with God, and our purpose is realized when we begin to bring glory to our Lord.

As the only door to life, Jesus serves as the Good Shepherd. He calls us to follow Him into this relationship.

1. What does **John 10:3-5** say about this subject?

   If we belong to the Good Shepherd, we will hear His voice and follow Him. There are no in-betweens in the kingdom of God. In fact, we see four distinct reactions to the Shepherd's call.

   The first reaction to the Shepherd's voice can be compared to that of a *wolf.* A wolf is a sneaky animal. Wolves are predators and prefer weak and wounded animals. Their actions are solely for survival purposes; therefore, they show no mercy to their victim.

2. In **Matthew 7**, Jesus warned us of such an individual. What kind of position do such individuals fill in the churches? **(Matthew 7:15)**

   The wolves who infiltrate the churches usually operate within respected positions. They can be cleverly disguised behind titles and degrees. They go after Christians who are new or weak. They have no regard for the spiritual destruction brought into innocent lives. Their actions are prideful and selfish. Their goal is to survive.

3. Summarize what **Jeremiah 23** says about the false shepherds (pastors) and prophets.

   The second response to Jesus can be related to the swine.

4. What did Jesus say about these animals? **(Matthew 7:6)**

   Swine are considered unclean animals in the Jewish culture **(Leviticus 11:7; Isaiah 65:4; 66:3, 17)**. These animals live in unacceptable conditions. They eat leftovers and garbage. They actually prefer mud due to their exposed, sensitive skin. They appear complacent until you invade their space. It is at such an intrusion that they then can prove to be aggressive.

   There are Christians who want both worlds. They refuse to separate themselves from that which is unholy. They want just enough of Christianity to avoid hell, while preferring the benefits of the world. They appear complacent until their comfort zone is challenged or exposed. They are thin-skinned due to pride and once challenged, they can become insulted.

5. What did **James 4:4** make clear about an individual's association with the world? **(1 John 2:15-17; 5:4-5)**

The Apostle Paul gave decisive instructions about the type of reaction believers must exhibit towards that which has not been sanctified.

6. What needs to be the Christian's response to the unholy? **(2 Corinthians 6:14-18)**

Jesus' attitude towards the swine was to leave them alone. To the complacent individual it simply means Christ will pass through their midst.

The third reaction can be equated with a goat. Goats will follow but can easily be sidetracked by small patches of grass, garbage, weeds etc. By becoming focused on insignificant things, they end up missing the best. They like to stand on small hills or piles of rocks like some king of the mountain. They may look upon other goats, but it is from some small mound of independence that actually amounts to nothing.

There are Christians who have responded to the Shepherd's call, but become caught up with other causes. These causes may include good deeds, moral issues, or religious activities, which can even make them feel elevated above others, but they have nothing to do with doing the will of God.

7. What did Jesus say about this issue in **Matthew 25:31-46**?

Jesus' goal is to lead Christians into a life of effective service. To serve Jesus means investing Christ into the lives of others. Many Christians make assumptions about serving Christ, which causes them to miss the mark of real servitude giving them a faulty religious foundation.

8. What will happen to the individual who does not follow the Shepherd into true service? **(John 10:3-5, 16)**

Sheep are an investment. The shepherd purchases the sheep. He then invests time and energy to ensure the welfare of the animal. The investment as a whole requires an exemplary commitment. Our Good Shepherd has purchased us with the shedding of His blood. He leads us to green pastures and still waters where we can be filled. He protects us so we can know rest. He brings us to the place where we can forever dwell in the house of Lord **(Psalm 23)**.

9. How does **John 10:10, 11, 27** and **28** confirm the picture of Jesus as the Good Shepherd?

Jesus is calling those who belong to Him. Do you hear His voice? Are you responding? The Word shows us He only had to call the disciples once. Adhere to His call before He leaves you behind.

Section 5

THE HEART

AN EMERGING PICTURE

There is a clear picture coming into focus for us. As we study the responses and reactions of people towards Jesus Christ, we can see the connection between all of these examples. Examine the following table.

Response To Service	**The Way** *(Ask)* **Vessels** **(Attitudes)**	**The Truth** *(Seek)* **Responses**	**The Life** *(Knock)* **Reactions**
Judas Iscariot **(John 12:3-8)**	Closed Vessel **(Romans 7:15-25)**	Self-Righteous **(Matthew 25:1-20)**	Wolf **(Matthew 7:15-20)**
Lazarus **(John 12:1-2, 9)**	Empty Vessel **(2 Timothy 3:1-5)**	Complacent **(Luke 4:16-30)**	Swine **(Matthew 7:1-6)**
Martha **(Luke 10:38-42)**	Broken Vessel **(Psalm 34:18)**	Fearful **(Matthew 8:23-34)**	Goat **(Matthew 25:31-46)**
Mary **(John 12:3-8)**	Open Vessel **(2 Timothy 2:21)**	Hungry/Thirsty **(John 10:1-18)**	Sheep **(Matthew 25:31-46; John 10:1-18)**

By studying the diagram one can see how Judas Iscariot's response can be related to a self-righteous, closed vessel. This type of response is similar to that of a wolf.

Although one cannot come to a definite conclusion about Lazarus in **John 12**, his lack of response in these scriptures could be an example of complacency. Complacency reigning in the heart can be compared to the empty vessel. These vessels respond like the hometown group at Nazareth, and react like the swine.

Martha's response can be compared to that of the goat. These responses imply inconsistency in focus and the result is often brokenness that produces fear and conviction. It will lead to a decision.

Mary is the example of being hungry and thirsty. She is an open vessel, following her Shepherd into a relationship, and a life of true service.

Remember, the people above serve as examples in their responses. We know the end of Judas and the exaltation of Mary, but the Bible does not mention Lazarus or Martha again.

The question you must ask yourself is what is my response to Jesus Christ? What does your life of service say about you? Can it be compared to the wolf, swine, goat, or sheep? Is Jesus truly your Shepherd or are you closed to His voice? Does your life seem empty or broken?

The truth is, the type of life that comes forth is determined by our heart condition.

1. How does **Proverbs 4:23** confirm the previous statement?

Jesus reiterated this scriptural truth in **Matthew 15:17-20**. He stated it is in the heart where all perversion begins. The prophet, Jeremiah, summarized the condition of the heart.

2. What did Jeremiah say about this subject? **(Jeremiah 17:9, 10)**

Man's heart will always condemn him, but hope is found in Jesus Christ. He is in the business of changing hearts.

3. What is the promise found in **2 Corinthians 5:17**?

Jesus is always calling individuals to Himself. Scriptures show us Pharisees such as Nicodemus and Joseph of Arimathea became believers. They both assisted in the Lord's burial **(John 19:38-42)**. In the case of the Gadarenes, He sent the man he had delivered from the legions of demons, back to his people so that he could testify of His greatness.

Jesus will go great lengths to find the one lost sheep, but we must not test His patience. According to notes taken from Schofield's study Bible, Jesus' visit to Nazareth in **Luke four** was His last appearance there. (This notation can be found above **Matthew 13:53-58**; *The New Scofield Reference Bible*, 1967.)

4. What warning do we find in **Genesis 6:3**?

Jesus is busy looking for the lost. The secret to being found rests in the lonely, broken heart longing to be set free by God's love, mercy, and grace. Oh, how we need to be set free from our misery. How we need to know love, peace, and joy. How we need to follow our true Shepherd to such a life.

Maybe the Holy Spirit has revealed to you that your response is not that of the sheep. You recognize the lack in your life. You need to know Jesus is in the business of making men into new creations. He can change your disposition from a self-serving wolf, self-centered swine, or self-absorbed goat into a receptive sheep. He will do it by giving you a new heart for Him.

The Heart Condition

The Word of God says much about the heart. We have already established a foundation on this subject. God is in the business of changing hearts. Look up the following verses.

5. Explain how God changed the heart condition of each individual. *(***1 Samuel 10:9** (Saul); **1 Kings 4:29***;* (Solomon) **Job 23:16***)*

In **Psalm 51:10** we see how King David recognized the importance of a right heart.

6. What was his request to God?

David asked God to create a new heart. When you study the character of David, much is said about his heart.

7. What other responses do we see coming from the heart of David? *(***Psalm 139:23, 24; 11:1; 51:17***)*

David had an <u>open</u> heart to God. He desired it to be <u>searched</u> by the Creator of the Universe. He recognized that God is interested in the heart of man, and searches it to find who is sincere in his or her desire for Him **(1 Chronicles 28:9; Jeremiah 17:10)**.

The second quality of David's heart is that it was <u>trusting</u>. He displayed the obedient, child-like response that is necessary if God is to reign.

The third characteristic about David's heart was <u>brokenness</u>. He was willing to be broken when sin was revealed in his life. He acknowledged the type of devastation it wrought. He humbled himself and repented.

1 Kings 11:4 summarized the virtues of David's heart by referring to it as perfect. Let us now examine the different heart conditions. The type of life that is coming forth can identify each heart condition.

Recognizing our Heart Condition

In **Matthew 13:3-23** we find the parable of the sower and the seed. This parable shows us four heart conditions.

8. Explain each heart condition found in this parable.

When a lawyer asked Jesus what was the greatest commandment, He said to love the Lord, your God with all your heart, soul, and mind. A right heart is one that is sold out to God. We see four decisive heart conditions.

The first heart condition represents those who hear the good news, but the news never takes root because the heart is *hard* due to unbelief. This allows the enemy to come along and rob the individual of the seed of life.

The second condition symbolizes those who receive the good news, but it never gets very deep in the soil of their heart because of the stones of *self* being in the way. When tough times come along, the weeds of despair will take over.

The third heart condition in this parable describes a *worldly* heart. The things of the world choke out the word of God.

9. What action must we take to ensure our hearts do not fit in the first three categories? **(Jeremiah 4:3, 4; Joel 2:12-14)**

Daniel purposed in his heart to do what was pleasing to God **(Daniel 1:8)**. We must decide to love God with all of our heart. We must become open so the things of God may take root. We have to separate ourselves from the world. Humility, submission, and repentance need to be our constant companions.

The idea of an acceptable heart is out of the reach of man. The secret of such a heart comes back to Jesus Christ. Remember, Christ is in the business of changing

hearts.
Let us now examine each heart condition with the four different responses and reactions to Jesus Christ in the following table.

Response To Service	The Way (*Ask*) Vessels (Attitudes)	The Truth (*Seek*) Responses	The Life (*Knock*) Reactions	Heart Conditions
Judas Iscariot **(John 12:3-8)**	Closed Vessel **(Romans 7:15-25)**	Self-Righteous **(Matthew 25:1-20)**	Wolf **(Matthew 7:15-20)**	Hard Heart **(Matthew 13: 4, 9)**
Lazarus **(John 12:1-2, 9)**	Empty Vessel **(2 Timothy 3:1-5)**	Complacent **(Luke 4:16-30)**	Swine **(Matthew 7:1-6)**	Stony Heart **(Matthew 13:5-6; 20-21)**
Martha **(Luke 10:38-42)**	Broken Vessel **(Psalm 34:18)**	Fearful **(Matthew 8:23-34)**	Goat **(Matthew 25:31-46)**	Worldly Heart **(Matthew 13:7, 22)**
Mary **(John 12:3-8)**	Open Vessel **(2 Timothy 2:21)**	Hungry/Thirsty **(John 10:1-18)**	Sheep **(Matthew 25:31-46; John 10:1-18)**	Receptive Heart **(Matthew 13:8, 23)**

What does your life say about you heart condition? What truths does it reveal about your relationship with Christ? In the end, it will expose what you have been doing with Jesus.

Ask the Lord to create a right heart within you. Repent of attitudes and ways that are not pleasing to God. Make a determination to be a Mary. Seek out God's truths and knock on all doors. In doing so you will not only find Christ, but the doors of heaven will open unto you.

Take this opportunity to write a short summary of your testimony in relationship to Jesus being your only Way, Truth, and Life.

EVANGELISM

INTRODUCTION

Evangelism along with discipleship constitutes the two-pronged commission of the Church. The Church, from all appearances, has risen to obey this commission. Many different programs have been devised or implemented to teach believers how to evangelize the lost, but in time most of these attempts fizzle out allowing Christians to slip back into their nominal lives.

Is something of vital importance missing out of all of these programs and attempts? We can conclude there must be. What is lacking, the programs or the people? Maybe what is lacking in both: is the heart that fails to see something through to the end, which entails true discipleship.

At the heart of evangelism is the person of Jesus Christ. Jesus told how the Church of Ephesus did all the right things, but this body of believers had left their first love behind, meaning they had left Him behind. Their light was in jeopardy of being snuffed out by the One who had brought real meaning and purpose to their lives in the beginning **(Revelation 2:1-7).**

Another reason for the lack of evangelism is the existence of sin. Sin can come in many forms such as complacency, fear, doubts, and excuses. We humans can always find justification for not complying with the Great Commission, but it is a command and not an option.

The time is short and we need to redeem it. It is important that we are found faithful and obedient when our Lord comes for His Church. We need to be working with urgency in the harvest field. We need to be reaching out to the lost and hurting. It is the least we can do for our Savior and Lord.

Hopefully this study will do away with myths concerning evangelism and put it in the right perspective. I pray it will challenge wrong attitudes and inspire right actions. I trust it will give you insight into God's design for the commission He purchased with His blood and entrusted to His disciples before He ascended.

His last instructions have not changed. His words have not lost their power or their clarity. They continue to reverberate in the ears of all those who claim to be His disciples. Are you His disciple? If so, then you need to adhere to the Great Commission. Deny self, take up your cross, and become the next torchbearer who dares to let your light and the message of Jesus and Him crucified, shine with brightness, authority, and power.

1

OUR COMMISSION

Turning the World Upside Down

What comes to your mind when you hear the word, "evangelism?" Many people envision great crusades where people hear a call to come to Christ and many respond. You feel the chills and excitement run down every nerve as you watch hundreds of people flock towards the front. Perhaps in your heart you are dreaming of being the one preaching the message that will impact many lives.

Is this really evangelism? Yes, but only one aspect of it. There are different ways to present evangelism. Evangelism does have one main message and goal. It has the power to change lives and eternal destinations of people.

Some see evangelism as a means to change individuals so the world will believe. Others strive to change the world in order for people to believe. However, evangelism is viewed, the message of God is able to change lives.

1. What claim was made about Paul and Silas in **Acts 17:6**?

   Paul and Silas were two men who were changed by the message of God. In turn, they turned the world upside down with the same message which caused others to believe. I believe the life-changing message of God is able to change both the lives of men and the world around us.

2. What message is able to cause such an overwhelming response according to **Romans 1:16**?

   The Greek word for <u>evangelism</u> means good messenger or good news. This is translated to "preach the Gospel".

3. What is the Gospel? **(1 Corinthians 15:1-4)**

   The good news is the power of God unto salvation. Christ dying for sins reveals the terrible truth about man's hopeless spiritual condition. We have all sinned and come short of the glory of God **(Romans 3:23)**. The wages of sin is death, (separation from God), but the gift of God is eternal life through Jesus our Lord **(Romans 6:23)**.

   This gift of life came through the death, burial, and resurrection of Jesus Christ.

4. What is the significance of Jesus' resurrection? **(1 Corinthians 15:11-14)**
5. What is the command in **Mark 16:15**?
6. What is the command in **Matthew 28:19**?

   Evangelism is not an option but a responsibility, a command from our Lord.

7. What does **John 15:9, 10** and **I John 2:5** tell us about obedience?

Excuses

Our commission of evangelism is not just about lost souls or even the reality of the love of God as giving the ultimate sacrifice. Rather, it is about obedience to God, which is motivated by a love for Him. It is a desire to do that which is pleasing.

8. Do you really love God? (Yes or No.)
9. If you love Him, are you involved in evangelizing? (Yes or No.)
10. If you are not evangelizing, then how can you say you love God?

You might say to me, "Rayola, I am not smart enough to evangelize. I am an unprepared Christian because I am not well versed in the Word of God."

11. What do **1 Corinthians 1:25** and **8:1** say about man's intelligence?

You may say to me, "I would make a fool out of my testimony of Christ and myself if I evangelize. I'm not equipped."

12. What does **1 Corinthians 1:27** say about human weakness?
13. What did Paul say about such weakness in **1 Corinthians 1:25** and **2 Corinthians 12:9**?
14. Did Christ send the disciples out in their own power? (Yes or No.)
15. What did Jesus say to His disciples in **Matthew 28:18**?

Jesus told them all power had been given to Him. He has the authority to send us out, which means He also has the ability to send us forth with the necessary power to carry out His commands.

16. What did Jesus give us to carry out our commission? **(Luke 24:49; Acts 1:8)**
17. How does **Zechariah 4:6** confirm the previous question?
18. What position do Christians officially hold according to **2 Corinthians 5:20**?

Jesus did not send us forth without the power and authority to carry out this commission. We simply need to do it.

Your next excuse could be, "I am insignificant. I have nothing to offer. How could I be effective in evangelism?"

19. What does **1 Corinthians 1:28** say about this subject?
20. What does the Apostle Paul tell us in **2 Corinthians 4:7**?
21. Where are your excuses now?

Evangelism is an act of obedience. We are given the authority to carry out this commission in the power of the Holy Spirit. Through our foolishness, weakness, and insignificance, God has the greatest opportunity to be glorified.

Evangelism is about sharing the message that is the power of God unto salvation. As worthless vessels, we are not only good candidates for the job, but we have been entrusted to carry this priceless message everywhere we go. We, therefore, cannot afford to be casual or irresponsible with our commission. Time is short and we must take up the challenge.

2

WHAT EVANGELISM IS NOT

A Message with a Purpose

Spreading good news is not an unusual event for most people. It is easy for people to talk about the latest diet, movie, new wonder drug, or a happy event or occasion.

Sharing any good news is a form of evangelizing. This understanding should make one aware of how generalized evangelism can be in our society. We must, therefore, ask ourselves as Christians, what sets our message apart from other proclamations. It is simple. The good news we are commanded to share with others has the potential to save a person from eternal damnation.

The idea of possessing something, which could forever change a person's eternal destiny, should make us stand in awe. But, even in the Christian realm there are different messages being shared. We must always ask ourselves if we are sharing the most important message, the Gospel of Jesus Christ.

It is not unusual for Christians to share about various aspects of their Christian life. These things may be good, but can they change a person's destination?

Let us consider some of the various "good news" Christians proclaim.

1. Let me ask you can a church save a person?
2. Will promoting a certain doctrinal belief save a person?
3. Can changing the moral and political views of a person save an individual?
4. Does promoting God's love save people?

It is not unusual to hear people talk about their church and pastor. Here is a challenge. Show me in scripture where Jesus and the apostles invited someone to their religious establishment to get saved.

Many Christians are apt to invite people to church without ever mentioning the name of Jesus. What kind of good news are we proclaiming when we point a person to a church rather than Jesus? Maybe our good news is that since I don't really know Jesus like I should, come to my church and hear my pastor. It is his job to know Jesus and share the Gospel.

The Word of God is clear that as believers it is our responsibility to know Jesus and share the good news. Our conversation should be centered on Jesus. We should be excited about Him, not a doctrine, building, or a religious leader.

Some people will never enter a church building, and the only opportunity we have to share Christ with them is at that moment. Church buildings have never saved anyone, but the loving attitudes, actions, and commitments of Christians have drawn many to the Lord.

It is not unusual to find Christians harping on different doctrinal beliefs. Some of these religious dogmas will not determine a person's eternal course; however, certain wrong doctrines will send a person to hell. Such dogma is often a matter of religious pride.

5. What does **Titus 3:9** tell us?

Arguing over religious issues is unprofitable. The good news in such cases is not about Christ who saves, but about how right we are and how wrong someone else is.

Even though we may be technically right, we may still be wrong. Arguments and contention lack the right spirit. Without the right spirit, arrogance always gets the best of any zealous person when he or she sets out to prove his or her particular point of view. Some people will quickly be persuaded, but you will find these people will flow with any new belief or challenge.

In the cases where people are strong in their beliefs, they come out with the same opinion they had before the discussion. Unless there is a conviction of the Holy Spirit, most people will hold onto their religious beliefs. So why argue over such matters? Lift up Jesus, He is every believer's common ground. Fellowship and agreement need to be based on Him.

How about the political forums Christians get involved with such issues as abortion and immorality? I can speak from personal experience on this subject.

I was involved in getting Scientific Creationism into the schools. The battle was hard and long. Disappointments escalated as people who claimed to be believers of God and the Bible became our biggest foe.

New Age teachers watched with quiet glee as Christian teachers refuted our attempt to apparently tell them what to teach. I became aware that something was missing.

After my political pursuits came to an end, the Lord asked me a couple of questions. "Was anyone saved during your crusade?"

"No Lord."

"How many people were insulted and mad?"

"Everyone, Lord!"

He then reminded me of my real commission, to preach the Gospel.

6. What did Jesus say about His kingdom? **(John 18:36; Matthew 22:21)**
7. What does the Word of God say about our part in the Lord's kingdom? **(Philippians 3:20)**
8. What is our official position? **(2 Corinthians 5:20)**
9. What is our responsibility as an ambassador of Christ?

Don't get me wrong. As citizens we need to be alert and vote, but we must never substitute or confuse our moral and political pursuits with our commission to preach the Gospel. Ask yourself, has anyone ever been saved by your involvement in such matters? If not, maybe you need to ask God if you are in His will.

Diluting the Gospel

It is easy to add false ideas to the Gospel such as Christ plus church saves you. Christ plus anything is an addition to the Gospel, demeans the sacrifice of Christ. The Bible presents only one Christ in the Gospel. As a result, it is so easy to take away from the Gospel. We compromise the Gospel when trying to make it attractive to those who seem squeamish about sin, and mocking towards the death, burial, and resurrection of Jesus Christ.

Let us consider some possible additions or subtractions that some Christians are falling into concerning salvation. In fact, some of these different religious emphases are causing confusion and a false security.

10. Does knowing about God's love save us?
11. Will encountering signs and wonders save us?
12. Can we be saved by believing Jesus lived?

13. Will water baptism save us?
14. Will going to church on a particular day such as Saturday or Sunday save us?

Knowing that God loves us does not save us. His love may make us feel special, but we need to go further and understand what His love provided. Christ's death on the cross was not just about the love of God, but it was also about man's sinful condition and God's provision to redeem his soul. The cross was not only an expression of God's love but also a revelation of His holiness.

15. What does **Hebrews 12:14, 28, 29** and **2 Peter 3:9-18** say about the subject of God's holiness?
16. What does the Word say about signs and wonders? **(Matthew 12:39; 24:23, 24; Mark 16:16, 17; Hebrews 2:2-4)**

Many Christians are running to and fro to experience signs and wonders. Jesus declared that only a wicked generation seeks after signs. Signs and wonders will follow and confirm the message of Christ. They will ultimately glorify God. However, Christians are put in a precarious position of being set up for delusion when they seek after signs and wonders to fulfill their own spiritual pursuits.

17. What did Jesus say to Peter in **Matthew 16:15**?

There are many different types of "Jesus" being presented today. It is not enough to believe in a historical Jesus. You must know the Jesus who became our Savior by dying on the cross, and who now sits on the right hand of God. You must know Him as God Incarnate, the Messiah, and the Son of God.

18. Who revealed the truth to Peter about Jesus? **(Matthew 16:17)**

A revelation of who Christ is and who He must be in our lives comes only from God. We cannot intellectually or emotionally come to the right conclusion without God first taking the blinders off of our eyes **(2 Corinthians 3:13-16; 4:3-6)**.

The Gospel is not about a historical Jesus who did a good deed, but it is about a resurrected Jesus who, "is able to save us to the uttermost...seeing he ever lives to make intercession for us" **(Hebrews 7:25)**. Make sure you and others know the real Jesus.

19. What does **Mark 16:16** tell us about baptism?

Note, those who do not believe will be condemned. Baptism is a response to salvation not part of salvation. Baptism is our way of identifying with the One who saves us. The water represents the grave and the washing away of our sins. Raising a person out of the water is symbolic of the resurrection of new life.

20. What does Paul say about the Sabbaths in **Colossians 2:16, 17**?

Everything in the Old Testament from the lives of men, the temple, and sacrifices were fore-shadows of Christ. They point to His nature, life, and sacrifice. Christ was the fulfillment of the Law including the Sabbath. He fulfilled hundreds of prophecies. We must not accept the shadow in lieu of embracing the real essence of what they represented, the Person of Jesus Christ.

No wonder Paul stated, “For I determined not to know any thing among you save Jesus Christ, and him crucified” **(2 Corinthians 2:2).**

Take note followers of Christ. We need to adhere to what Paul said and not proclaim any other Jesus than the one who has been revealed in the Word of God.

3

PROCLAIMING THE CORRECT GOSPEL

A Call to Repentance

1. What does **Luke 24:47** say?

The first order of the Gospel for the evangelist is to preach about repentance and remission of sin. The first response of the hearer needs to be repentance. There is no need for repentance unless there is an understanding of the terminal disease of the soul, SIN.

All men have the problem of sin. The fallen condition of man was passed down to us from Adam and its consequences of death. This inherent disposition results in the "old man" wanting to reign with a vengeance. It reigns by encouraging us to give way to personal sins. Paul understood the battle and merry-go-round created by sin, and yet there was solution. In fact, the first part of the Gospel tells us we can overcome by believing, declaring that Jesus died for our sins **(Romans 3:10-23; 5; 7:15-25)**.

There is a tendency in the human thinking to water down sin and make it sound non-threatening and more acceptable. Sin is sin. It is rebellion against God. A person in rebellion often displays an, independent, stubborn and fearful heart. Such a person has an attitude that is contrary to the nature and will of God.

Sin brings devastation to people. This spiritual disease is destroying lives, relationships, and souls. Many people's lives are empty. They feel destitute, lost, and lonely. As the great spiritual Physician, the Lord Jesus Christ came to address the destruction of sin.

2. How does Jesus bring restitution to the areas affected by sin? **(John 6:35; 2 Corinthians 8:9; John 8:12; John 10:9, 11, 14)**

We are instructed in **Luke 24:47** to preach repentance and remission of sins. We need to be honest with people about their spiritual condition. Many live in condemnation because of sin, but if they can see their sins in light of how Jesus came to remit those sins, they will have hope.

3. What does <u>remission</u> mean?

Once individuals understand their sin, they can repent. <u>Repentance</u> means to change your mind with the intent of changing direction. People usually need to change their mind in a couple of ways about sin. Some individuals need to simply agree with God about their spiritual condition so they can take on His attitude towards it. These individuals are in darkness, which leads to delusion. Many are deluded about their sin; therefore; they refuse to change their mind about their condition and receive God's intervention.

4. What do the following scriptures say about this subject? **(John 1:5; John 3:19-21; Ephesians 4:17-19; 2 Corinthians 4:2-4)**

The second group of people are those who believe they have gone too far for God to save them.

5. There are those who may regret their actions, but where will such worldly sorrow lead them? **(2 Corinthians 7:10)**

D. L. Moody made this statement, "The inquirer is not to seek sorrow, but the Savior." Sorrow can keep us from seeing Jesus. This individual needs to change his or her mind about how far God's mercy and grace can extend.

6. What do the following scriptures state about the attributes of God? **(Psalm 100:5; 103:17; Romans 5:20)**
7. What promise do we have in **1 John 1:9**?

Repentance is simply changing your mind or belief, but a change of mind should result in a change of heart and lifestyle.

8. What do the following verses say about this subject? **(Luke 3:8; Acts 26:20)**

Repentance is invisible, but there should be fruits that bear witness of this change. True repentance is an act of faith. Faith is choosing to believe what God has said. A repentant person goes from a state of unbelief to a state of belief.

9. How does the event in **Acts 11:17-18** confirm this?

Faith is the only requirement for salvation. Repentance ends in salvation because it walks hand in hand with faith.

10. What does **Romans 3:22-25** and **Ephesians 2:8** say about faith?

True faith makes up three important ingredients. It consists of knowledge, mental assent, and reliance. Faith is based on knowledge, which comes from the Word of God.

11. How does **Romans 10:17** confirm this truth?

We must know the person of Jesus Christ based on His Word. He is fully God and fully man. He died for our sins and rose from the dead. If a person does not understand and know the Person of Christ in this manner, how can he or she have faith in Him? If such an individual does not believe Him, how can He save him or her?

12. What does **1 John 5:10-13** say about this subject?

There must be a mental ascension. This is where repentance comes in. It is a change of mind because a person has been persuaded or convinced something is true because there is evidence. If there is knowledge and acceptance, there is belief.

13. How did the incident with Thomas prove this point? **(John 20:24-29)**

The next step of faith is reliance. Reliance is trust and trust believes. Believing produces response and action.

14. What kind of action will real faith produce? **(James 2:17-26)**

As you can see, preaching repentance and remission of sins come first. If a person sees his or her need for Christ and believes Him for salvation, you can take him or her to the next step.

Baptism, Signs, and Wonders

15. What does **Mark 16:15-18** state?

Once again, we see the first part of our commission is to preach the Gospel to everyone. But, note the second part of the command. Upon believing we are commanded to baptize them. Baptism is not part of salvation, but a product of salvation. It is identification with Jesus.

16. What do the following scriptures say about this subject? **(Romans 6:2-5; 1 Corinthians 12:13, 14; Galatians 3:27; Colossians 2:12)**

Believing the Gospel is the inward commitment, but water baptism is the outward declaration that a person has chosen a new Lord and a new life.

17. Why is it so important to have a personal, public declaration about Jesus Christ? **(Matthew 10:32, 33)**
18. What is the procedure for Baptism? **(Matthew 28:19)**

There is a debate about how to baptize someone. Some believe a person should only be baptized in the name of Jesus **(Acts 8:16)**. There are different explanations for this instruction. First of all, to baptize in the name of Jesus is to baptize a person in line of Jesus' character. It is also important to realize people knew of the Father and the Spirit, while the Person of Jesus was often missing from their understanding. In spite of the debates, Jesus is the One who gave us the instruction in **Matthew 28:19** as to how to baptize; therefore, we must conclude there is no contradiction in **Acts**.

Colossians 2:9 tells us, "For in him dwelleth all the fullness of the Godhead bodily." Jesus was the physical representation of God. To be baptized in Jesus is simply acknowledging our need to be identified with God. All three persons of the Godhead were present during Jesus' baptism in **Matthew 3**, all three are involved in the work of salvation, and all were involved with the resurrection of Jesus. Since baptism is a product of salvation, it only makes sense that we are baptized in the name of each Person of the Godhead. It is not unusual for a person to get caught up with one or two scriptures and make a doctrine out of it. When in doubt about the subject of baptism, consider Jesus' last instructions to His disciples in **Matthew 28:19**. There will be no room for debate for He has the final say in all matters.

19. What will follow those who believe? **(Mark 16:17-18)**
20. What does **Hebrews 2:3-4** say about signs and wonders?

Some people believe miracles have ceased because of what was stated by **1 Corinthians 13:8**. Paul said the gifts and miracles would be done away with when that which is perfect has come. The perfect One they are referring to is Jesus Christ. He has not yet come (to set up His kingdom on earth) and since we know in part, God continues to step on the scene in supernatural ways.

Miracles are very prevalent in many foreign countries today. It is God's way of confirming the message of His Gospel. He has not changed His mode of operation.

On the other hand, there has been an abuse of signs and wonders in America. It is amazing that instead of miracles following believers, Christians are pursuing them. Signs and wonders have a purpose. They were used to confirm what Christ was saying about Himself twenty centuries ago. It is vital we keep our focus right by seeking Christ for ourselves, and preaching the Gospel. Obedience and faithfulness to our Lord and His commission should be our main concern. We need to let Him worry about the miracles.

Have you become identified with Christ? Does your life display authority and power? How can you be effective in your Christian life and testimony if you have not followed Him into baptism or purposed in your heart to preach the Gospel?

Making Disciples

21. What is our final instruction? **(Matthew 28:20)**

Effective evangelism must be immediately followed by instruction. Conversion is just the beginning. Conversion costs nothing, but discipleship costs everything.

22. How did Jesus bring this out in **Luke 9:57-62**?

You will not be popular if you decide to count the cost and follow Jesus.

23. How did Jesus confirm this truth in **Matthew 10:34-36**?

Discipling includes evangelism, baptizing, and teaching. To be a disciple of Christ you must submit your will to His will. You must choose to die to self up front.

The problem with many followers of Christ is they put off dying to self. Many believe when the time comes, they will graciously die, but when they come to a place that requires self-denial they end up in a wrestling match. They lack the fortitude because they avoided the initial decision, while choosing to hold on to a corner of self.

24. What does <u>observe</u> mean?

Many new converts are left to define Christianity on their own. Their conclusions are often devastating. They must be taught to obey and guard all of Jesus' commands for their own protection.

25. What does **Hebrews 5:11-6:6** say concerning this subject?

New believers must be fed the pure milk of the Word (doctrine), so they can move on to milk toast by partaking of the Bread of Life (identification with Christ) in order to graduate to partaking of the meat of the Word (Doing His will).

26. What does the meat of the Word do for Christians? **(Hebrews 5:14)**

Discipling equips the saints for ministry.

27. What does **Ephesians 4:11-16** say about this subject?

28. What did Jesus say about obedience to His Word in **Matthew 5:19, 20** and **Matthew 7:24-27**?

Christians are being tossed to and fro because they have not been established on the Rock of Jesus. They are not being equipped for ministry, and many are losing heart. They find themselves serving church and man, but not Jesus.

29. What was Paul's concern in **2 Corinthians 11:2-4?**

Many converts are left vulnerable. They are becoming victims to wolves. Doctrines of demons and vain philosophies of man are leading them astray.

It is obvious that many Christians have dropped the ball when it comes to true discipleship. I remember a story about an evangelist who witnessed many coming to Christ in his meetings. One day He met another minister. This minister had led only a few people to Christ, but he was taking the time to disciple them. The dynamic evangelist realized many of his converts probably fell to the wayside, and the rest most likely remained nominal in their Christian life. However, this minister was equipping a few to carry on in an effective powerful work for Jesus. Their work would be an ongoing work for the glory of God.

I have never been happy with just converting people. It has always been my heart to disciple new converts. Conversion to righteousness is an ongoing work that comes from exhorting people to first seek the kingdom of God and His righteousness in all matters. It requires us to set forth the examples of what it means to walk as Jesus walked. There are times I did not have the time or resources to disciple new converts, so I left them in God's hands.

30. What does the Apostle Paul say about working in the harvest field? **(1 Corinthians 3:5-8)**

One person cannot do all the work in the harvest field. This is why it is important that each individual in the kingdom of God does his or her part.

31. What are the promises to those who are discipling others? **(Matthew 5:19b; 28:20)**

Are you doing your part in the harvest field? Allow the Lord to show you the answer to the question.

4

OBEYING THE COMMISSION

Putting Our Shoulder to the Plow

1. What did Jesus say in **Luke 9:62**?

What will it take to obey our commission properly? It comes down to not looking back. There is a job to do. We need to put our hand to the plow, and begin to make ourselves available to work in the harvest field. We need to adhere to our commission.

Evangelism is more than just proclaiming the Gospel. It lies at the heart of God's plan for man. Its purpose is to bring about conversion in order to bring the person into the kingdom of God. Its simple intention is to bring reconciliation between man and his Creator.

2. What did the Apostle Paul say about reconciliation in **2 Corinthians 5:18-20?**

Evangelism is not an act of nobility to keep a person from hell or a show of spiritual superiority when there appears to be success. It is not a great religious feat that earns us rewards. It is simply an act of obedience, which is our reasonable service in the kingdom of God **(Romans 12:1)**.

We need to get rid of our foolish ideas of grandeur when it comes to our part in man's salvation. Saving souls is neither your business nor my business.

3. Whose responsibility is it to save souls? **(Hebrews 5:8, 9)**

It is not up to me to persuade individuals about their need for salvation.

4. What did Paul say about this matter in **1 Corinthians 2:1-5**?
5. Who really brings conviction to a person's life? **(John 16:7-11)**

It is not up to me to bring the lost souls to the cross of Christ, it is up to God.

6. How did Paul confirm this truth in **1 Corinthians 3:6-9**?

I have worked in potato fields. I never had to worry about bringing in the harvest. My part was to do my particular job during the process. As a result, I did not worry about the outcome of the harvest. Neither did I fret over whether the owner would receive ample payment for his product. My main focus was to see it through to the end, regardless of how cold, hot, or overwhelming it became.

The Apostle Paul talked about the different responsibilities of being involved in the harvest of souls. He stated some plant and others water, but God brings in the harvest. Why then, do we Christians avoid being part of the harvest?

John R. Scot made this statement about the Great Commission, "The church in other words, is fundamentally a mission society, commissioned and committed to the whole.

The greatest single reason for the church's evangelistic disobedience is centered in the church's doubts."

There you have it. The biggest obstacle to evangelism is nothing more than the culprit of unbelief that finds its basis in selfism. As soon as we consider how evangelism will affect me, myself, and I, we lose sight of whom is really responsible for bringing in the harvest. We see ourselves small, ineffective, and possessing the potential of being the greatest flop in the kingdom of God. We sense the awful responsibility for someone's eternal destination, and are stopped in our tracks by fear and complacency.

We see the disciples stopped by fear in **John 20**.

7. What was Jesus first statement to His disciples? **(John 20:19)**

Jesus comes on the scene and His first order of the day was to calm their fears. He stated twice, "Peace be unto you." He knew that once they focused on Him, they would have peace.

8. How do **Isaiah 26:3** and **Philippians 4:7** confirm this statement?

The next thing the Lord tries to do was to confirm to them that everything He ever told them was true. He showed them his hands and side.

9. How did His disciples respond? **(John 20:20)**

Finally, Jesus once again commissioned them.

10. What did He say to them in **John 20:21**?

The Father did not send Jesus out in His own power. Likewise, Jesus would not send the disciples out in their own power.

11. What did He do in **John 20:22**?
12. What does **Luke 24:49** and **Acts 1:8** tells us?

We are being sent out with authority and in power.

13. Once again what is our official position? **(2 Corinthians 5:20)**

We have all heaven before us, and yet we are afraid, uncertain, and full of doubts. I can remember my zealous days of evangelism. I was fairly new in my Christian walk. I shared Christ every time I got a chance. I don't know how many times I overstepped the line and caused people to avoid me like the plague. My concern for the possible damage I caused compelled me to take it to God. I told Him it was a miracle He could get anything accomplished through my blunders. I will never forget what He said, "Your evangelistic mistakes will never make me fall off the throne." Years later I looked back and realized how He actually used some of those mistakes to bring people to Himself.

The only limitation God has when it comes to His work is you and me. It is important we get past self and unbelief, and trust God with the harvest.

God does all of the work. We are just mouthpieces.

14. What promise did He give us in **Matthew 10:18-20**?

We have nothing to worry about except failing to obey the commission our Lord gave us over two thousand years ago.

Have you put your shoulder to the plow of the Gospel? If you have, have you looked back? Lot's wife became a pillar of salt because she looked back. Will you end up being a pillar of salt or the salt of the earth? It is your choice.

The Method

15. What is God's method for evangelism?
16. Does He have one?

God does have a method and it is simple. God's method is people.

17. What did Jesus say in **Matthew 4:19**?

Jesus invested in a few men for over three years. He walked with them, supped with them, slept with them, and traveled with them. He served as their patient, anointed teacher and their constant companion, example, and leader. He was a leader in authority, attitude, and conduct. He was as big as the outdoors, yet He was meek and humble. He was powerful, yet obedient and disciplined. He was great, but as a servant to all, He became the least among men. He was God, but became man.

His purpose was to save people out of this world for Himself and build a Church that could not be moved by hell, but only by the Spirit of the Living God.

18. What did Jesus tell His disciples in **Acts 1:8**?
19. What does the word "witness" mean?

Note, where Jesus first sent His disciples: to Jerusalem. They were to start right where they were located. They were to be witnesses or martyrs. It took persecution of the Church to get those of the early Church to become witnesses elsewhere.

Did these men have a method? From all appearances, they had the Word of God, the Holy Spirit, and their testimonies about Jesus.

20. What does **Revelation 12:11** say about the power of our testimony?

Is it wrong to have a method? Even though God is not looking for methods, I don't think it is wrong for you and me to have a method as long as we are flexible and sensitive to the Holy Spirit. Having some method can give a person enough confidence to move forward in obedience. For instance, I ask questions to find out where the person is coming from in order to relate to them personally.

21. What did Paul say about this in **1 Corinthians 9:18-23**?

As Christians, we must meet and serve people where they are in their lives. Jesus made a distinction between people. He asked Peter to feed both His lambs and sheep **(John 21:15-17)**. G. Michael Cocoris in his book about evangelism divided Christians into four groups. He noted that John distinguished three of them in **1 John 2:12-14**. They are the babes who are noisy and defenseless, the children who are noisy and busy, the young men who have energy and ambition, and the fathers who have much wisdom.

You must respond to each person based on his or her spiritual maturity. The babes need the pure milk of the Word **(1 Peter 2:2)**. The children need to be trained which takes much investment **(Proverbs 22:6)**. The young men need to be instructed and learn to be disciplined and sober **(1 Peter 5:5-8)**. The fathers need to be encouraged.

In evangelism we see many faces. Some people preach like Billy Graham who holds an office of an evangelist. Other people are busy edifying the Body so that people can go out and evangelize. Some people make opportunities to evangelize in spontaneous ways. They may ask one question such as, "When you stand before God and He asks you to give Him one reason why He should allow you in His kingdom, what would you say?" This can open a person up. I have asked this question and the answers often reveal people's ignorance about God.

I know of people who hand out tracks. Others use their gift to share the message such as writing and singing. God uses it all because He is not limited. But, no matter how you approach a person about his or her soul and eternal destination, indirectly or directly, this person must sense a genuine concern for his or her welfare. If it is just a duty or religious exercise, most people will see through it and be turned off.

I usually pray about recognizing an opportunity to share Christ. When the opportunity arises, I have used the famous **Roman's Road** in leading a person to a scriptural understanding of his or her sin, its consequences, and God's provision of Jesus. If you do not know the **Roman's Road**, here it is in Scriptural sequence.

Romans 3:10
Romans 3:23
Romans 5:12
Romans 5:8
Romans 6:23
Romans 10:13
Romans 10:9, 10

You need to understand this simple presentation, maybe even memorize it. It is a handy tool in evangelism. But, note in **Romans 10:9, 10** a person must believe the Gospel in the heart as a matter of truth. **John 1:12** tells us we must receive Jesus. Most people use the term "accept Jesus." To "accept" Jesus is a mental acknowledgment, but not necessarily a heart revelation.

In our presentation we tell people that they must *receive* Jesus. Receiving and believing work hand in hand. Believing involves me receiving something as truth. Believing is taking God at His word and agreeing with Him. Receiving is the same as receiving a valuable gift in an honorable way. In other words, believing the Gospel and receiving Jesus by faith entails me valuing and honoring Him and His redemption. This is how salvation comes by faith.

You need to keep in mind at all times that the Holy Spirit is the One who convicts, Jesus is the One who invites and saves, and God, the Father is the One who draws and will preserve that person according to His plan until the day of Jesus. It is important now that you understand what it will take for you to personally fulfill this commission.

Steps in Becoming an Effective Evangelist

To fulfill your commission or to be a good evangelist, you must first learn to be a good follower of Jesus. You cannot lead a person any further than you are in your relationship with God, nor can you offer something you do not truly possess.

Like many Christians, you cannot just get by and expect to make a real difference. If you decide to make a difference, then you must choose to make the necessary commitment. You must seek to know the Person of Jesus. He is the One who lies at the heart of the Gospel.

God wants to translate people out of the kingdom of darkness into the kingdom of light. He establishes these people into a priesthood and a powerful Body. It is in His design that this Body or Church would be an extension of Jesus, who is the head, in spirit and truth.

22. What two ingredients are necessary for me to be a good follower of Jesus? **(John 13:34, 35; 15:12-14)**

Obedience comes out of sacrificial love. Jesus spent precious time with His disciples. In doing so their love grew. It inspired commitment and obedience. This obedience brought them into line with His will.

Jesus had to teach these men in such a way that His instructions went from theory to application in their lives. He reinforced His instructions by His unwavering example.

23. What does **2 Corinthians 3:2, 3** tells us?

Our lives must serve as an object lesson because people will read our responses and actions to see if our claims are more than a theory.

I have learned people want to see the real thing. They might not agree with you, but they will respect you. They may not receive your message, but they will not be able to bring legitimate accusations against you.

According to G. Michael Cocoris in his book about evangelism, there are three types of people you will encounter in sharing the Gospel. There are the religious people, those who are plagued by hurts, and the intellectual wolves. The religious people have some concept or foundation of God like Nicodemus in **John 3**. They may know about God, but they have never come to terms with the salvation of Christ. These people think they are in line with God but are missing the boat.

24. What does **1 Peter 3:15** tell us?

God needs to be set apart in our hearts. We do this through knowing Him, His will and Word. We must be able to give a scriptural account of this hope in order to present the real truth to effectively challenge the religious man's concepts.

25. What is the hope we possess? **(Colossians 1:27)**

The people who are plagued are the ones who are hurting and wounded. It does not take long to discover these individuals. I must admit, such people can be fickle. They are not always looking for a healing. Sometimes they are looking for someone who will simply listen and feel sorry for them.

Jesus looked for those who were hurting and wounded **(Luke 14:13)**. He knew if they were really hungry and thirsty like the Samaritan woman in **John 4**, they would respond to His invitation.

26. What is Jesus' invitation to these people? **(Matthew 11:28-30; John 6:35, 37-39)**

All you need to do is enter in with these people by relating to them directly or indirectly.

27. What do the following scriptures say about this subject? **(Romans 12:15; 2 Corinthians 1:3-7)**

Be careful that you do not put yourself in a position of being an all-wise counselor. People in this condition rarely need your advice. You will appear cold and turn them off. What they need is a solution. We know the solution and His name is Jesus.

28. What promise do we find in **John 12:32**?

The intellectual wolves will intimidate you. They give the appearance of being quite wise. These wolves represent the people who are educated or motivated by the ways of the world. This intimidation is often a bluff. Their intellectual questions never reach beyond the most basic question like, "If there is a God why are all of these terrible things happening?" Most of these individuals are not looking for answers; rather, they want to land on their excuses for not believing there is a God. You don't have to outsmart them and you will never suffice their questions. Don't try to bluff your way, argue with them, or shrink from them. If you don't know how to answer the question, admit it up front and stick with your testimony and the facts you do know that are true about God.

29. What did Paul say about these people? **(1 Corinthians 1:25)**

You need to realize you are the one with the facts. Your belief is based on the truth. Unbelievers have absolutely no basis to argue with you. They have opinions and educated theories, and hearsay, but they lack scriptural foundation. You need to keep in mind that you have nothing to lose and they have everything to lose. Even if you are wrong, your life has been enriched by your faith in Christ. If you are right, they are on their way to hell; therefore, the greater proof of burden is on their shoulders. Such understanding will bring confidence to you, and will put them on the defense instead of the other way around. I have also learned I do not need to defend God; He is able to do it without my limited interference. We cannot go wrong by what we believe if it is based on who God is and His Word. Trust Him!

The Lord has put everything we need at our disposal to be effective in evangelism. This does not mean we will meet with success every time because people still must make a choice. But what it does mean is that I can obey the commission set before me in confidence. This confidence will not have anything to do with personal ability, but with God's power to accomplish what He has ordained.

30. What does **Isaiah 55:11** tell us?

Take heart. If God is for you, who can be against you? Know your place and your part in the Kingdom of God, let God be God, and He will take care of the rest. Just be faithful and obedient to your commission.

Fighting the Good Fight

Paul made this statement at the close of his life on earth in **2 Timothy 4:7**, "I have fought a good fight." Here was a man whose whole life was centered on preaching the Gospel. He made it quite clear it was a battle.

Jesus told His disciples to "...be wise as serpents, and harmless as doves" **(Matthew 10:16)**. He told this in light of them being sent among wolves. A serpent is under everyone's feet and a dove has no power in light of its gentleness.

It is important you understand your enemy because Christians will be pitted against the forces of darkness.

31. What do the following scriptures say about our enemy? **(John 8:44; 10:10; 2 Corinthians 4:3, 4; 11:3, 4, 13-15; Ephesians 2:2, 3; 1 Peter 5:8)**

Our enemy is powerful. He blinds the minds of men to keep them in darkness, unable to see the Gospel. His goal is to rob, kill, and destroy. He does not play fair. But Jesus knew that by being wise as a serpent and harmless as a dove, Satan will not be able to entice you or me in his many snares.

Even though these qualities of a serpent and dove appear to cause us to have the disadvantage, they possess qualities of greatness and strength. Like a serpent, servants of Jesus are beneath the authority of others, but we, as believers need to be wise servants. Wisdom walks hand in hand with the fear of the Lord, righteousness, and sensitivity towards the Spirit of God.

32. What does Jesus say about servants in **Matthew 20:26-28**?

There is greatness in servitude that can never be undermined even by Satan. A dove is meek and gentle.

33. What does **Matthew 5:5, 2 Samuel 22:36** and **Galatians 5:22, 23** say about these two virtues?

A serpent and a dove will balance each other out. Being wise as a serpent can make you aggressive without the gentleness. You can be argumentative and unreasonable. On the other hand, a dove needs the alertness of the serpent to avoid traps, pitfalls, and destructive detours.

Some Christians go to the extreme. Some are so gentle that much is robbed from them. Some are so aggressive and hard, that they end up destroying people they are called to uphold and lead.

Jesus has shown us the necessary balance in our life and attitude. He let us know we were being sent out among the lion (Satan) and the wolves. The purpose for this is not to make us victims, but victors. There is a dying out process, which evolves into a training process. The Lord is trying to separate us from attachments, entanglements, and enslavement to self, the world, and Satan. Such separation comes by death to self. Out of the death comes a resurrected soldier, ready to live totally for Christ and fight a good fight.

34. What has Jesus made available to us according to **Ephesians 6:10-18**?

We have armor to protect, a sword to fight, and access to our Commander by prayer. Satan may be powerful, but in light of our armor and the God we serve, he has already lost the war.

35. What does the sword do? **(Hebrews 4:12)**

The Word of God can cut through darkness and expose man's condition. Satan responds to people who know how to effectively use this weapon. He actually mocks at ignorance, toys with religion, and laughs at creeds and doctrines. But he respects those who confront him with the authority of Jesus Christ, in the power of the Spirit, and with the anointing of the Word. Satan is silenced, defeated, and forced to flee when encountering these spiritual tools.

Another powerful tool is prayer. It is in prayer both power and strategy are provided. No person should evangelize or minister without prayer first.

36. What should we pray about according to the following scriptures? **(Ephesians 6:18-20; 1 Timothy 2:1, 2; Luke 10:2)**

We need to pray for each other. It is important we pray for the missionaries, our spiritual leaders, and ministers in the harvest field. The battle is great and exhausting. They need our prayers to survive.

Paul also asked people to pray for boldness to testify of his Lord. Take note, even the great Apostle Paul requested Christians to pray for his boldness. This man's voice could not be silenced, yet he recognized it could never be accomplished in his own power. He knew prayer needed to occur before the Holy Spirit could make him a powerful, bold mouthpiece. Pray for boldness not only for others, but also for yourself.

We need to pray for more laborers in the harvest field. The problem with this is that God may answer the prayer by sending you!

We need to pray for the leaders of our country. The reason behind such prayers is for the purpose of peace. Peace is a wonderful backdrop for evangelism to take place.

There is debate whether we should pray for the unsaved. Paul confessed how he prayed for the salvation of Israel.

37. What does **2 Peter 3:9** tell us?

I do not think anything is done without prayer including the salvation of a person's soul. Christians need to accept the responsibility of their commission. Like John the Baptist, we are forerunners to Jesus Christ's Second Advent. The call to repentance for the remission of sins must be urgent and loud. Time is short and there is no room for irresponsibility. We must begin to be an active part of the harvest before Jesus comes for His Church.

When He comes, will He find you complacent or working in the harvest field? Will He find you watching or sleeping? Will He find you ready to go or comfortable to stay? It is your commission, your life, and your choice.

CHRISTIAN CONDUCT

INTRODUCTION

1 John 2:6 tells us, "He that saith he abideth in him ought himself also so to walk, even as he walked." What does it mean to act and walk like a Christian? The answer is simple; we need to walk as Jesus walked on earth.

Jesus came from the glories of heaven, took on the disposition of a servant, the form of a man, and set His face towards Calvary. His walk was self-denying, and it resulted in His death on the cross.

As we examine Jesus' walk, we begin to understand our walk. Christianity is not a religious belief, but a way of life. It is not based on righteous acts, but on sacrificial love. It is not a glamorous walk, but a walk that leads to suffering and death. All of these responses are contrary to the world and much of what the American Church is presenting today.

Christian conduct should manifest the heart, attitude, and life of Christ. The actions of many in American Christendom fall short of reflecting Jesus. From all appearances, scores of Christians are imitating religious leaders or are defining their own Christian conduct. The results are devastating as the light of their testimony becomes dimmer.

Many believers are losing heart because discrepancies plague them. They are powerless to change their life or circumstances. Some are giving up in despair and walking away from what appears to be an unobtainable life.

This study is about understanding and obtaining this life. Our Christian conduct must express the heart and attitude of our Lord if we are to be the salt of the earth and the light of the world. It must reflect a life that silences all accusation from a suspicious, accusing world. It must be humble in response, sacrificial in caring, sincere in loving, godly in compassion, and distinct from the world.

You may be saying about now, "Rayola, you are asking for the impossible. You are asking me to be like Christ." Yes I am. We are told to be like Him. He left us with an example to follow, but first it helps to understand the man, Jesus.

Jesus was fully God and fully man. It was as man that Jesus walked this world twenty centuries ago. He was tempted like we are, and yet He passed the test. He suffered and died as a man, but as God, He rose from the grave. Jesus as God, went one step beyond humanity and the grave to lead us to a life of hope, power, and victory.

Won't you now follow the Son of Man in His humanity and find out the secret behind His conduct?

Section One

THE HEART

Tearing Away the Mask

Jesus gave us our first rules to acceptable Christian conduct during the Sermon on the Mount.

1. What must we exceed to ensure acceptable righteous conduct? **(Matthew 5:20)**
2. What can we learn about the scribes and Pharisees? **(Matthew 6:1-7, 16-18; 15:19; 23:13, 14, 23, 25-29)**

We see the righteousness of the religious leaders of Jesus day was simply an outward show of religiosity.

3. What is God testing? **Psalm 7:9**
4. Why? **(Proverbs 4:23; Matthew 15:17-20)**
5. When your life lacks heart, what will it be void of according to **2 Timothy 3:5**?

Jesus died for our sins, but as the Great Physician He came to address our fallen condition. This fallen condition confirms the claims of **Romans 7:18** and **Isaiah 64:6**, "there is no good thing in us," and, "our best is as filthy rags"

6. What does **Jeremiah 17:9, 10** say about the heart?
7. What promise do we find in **2 Corinthians 5:17**?

Christians must ask themselves, "How can God make me into a new creation?" It is obvious there is nothing a person could offer God that is of any worth. It is not enough to put on a religious veneer. God rejects such hypocrisy. This walk is not just about reading the Bible or praying, it goes farther and deeper. It goes right to the heart.

A Right Heart

8. What does God desire to do for His people? **(Ezekiel 18:31; 36:26)**

When a person finally comes to Christ seeking salvation, Jesus will come into his or her life and give him or her a new heart.

9. Who received a new heart? **(1 Samuel 10:1-10)**

It is a new heart that makes us a new creation. This new heart has the capacity for the love of God to be shed abroad in our lives. What are the three commandments that Jesus pointed out to His disciples? **(Mark 12:29-31; John 13:34, 35)**

If we love God with all of our hearts, we will obey His commandments **(John 14:15)**.

10. What does **John 15:9-14** and **1 John 2:3-6** say about this subject?

If we are obedient because we love God, we will be upright in heart as to our motives.

11. What does upright mean?
12. How does God view those who are upright in heart? **(1 Chronicles 29:17)**
13. What characteristics do the upright display according to the following scriptures? **(Psalm 37:21, 30; 140:13; Proverbs 10:11; 11:23; 12:10; 13:5; 15:28; 21:26; 28:1; 29:7)**
14. What are the promises for the upright? **(Psalm 1:6; 5:12; 7:9; 11:7; 34:15, 17; 37:17; 55:22; 64:10; 97:11; 118:20; 146:8; Proverbs 3:32; 10:2, 24; 11:8, 28)**

Since we have been given a new heart after our saving encounter with Christ, what is next? There is more. A new heart is an enlarged heart that enables us to reach our potential in God.

15. What do the following scriptures say about these new hearts? **(1 Kings 4:29-30; Psalm 119:32; Isaiah 60:5)**

We see in the case of King Saul and King Solomon that a new and enlarged heart did not keep them upright before God.

16. What happened to Saul **(1 Samuel 15:20-28)**
17. What happened to Solomon? **(1 Kings 11:4-14)**

Our heart is often referred to as soil.

18. What does **Jeremiah 4:3** say about this subject?

Our hearts can become hard, stony, or full of thorns and weeds. We must keep our hearts cultivated to ensure maturity in our relationship with God. According to the following Scriptures, what must we do to keep our heart open and right before God?

I Kings 3:6; 9:4
2 Kings 20:3; 23:25
Psalm 34:18; 51:17; 69:32; 119:2, 10
Jeremiah 4:4; Acts 7:51; Romans 2:29; 6:17; Ephesians 6:5
Joshua 24:23; Psalm 119:112
Psalm 4:4
Joshua 22:5
Psalm 66:18; 119:11; 141:4; Ezekiel 14:3-4
James 1:26
1 Peter 1:22; 1 John 3:14-20
Ephesians 4:24; Colossians 3:1-17

We are told in **Numbers 32:11** that most of the people did not enter the Promised Land because they did not wholly follow the Lord. This is why our heart must be totally committed to God. To be half-hearted can bring devastating consequences.

19. What happened to the following people because they did not wholly follow God with their whole heart? Rehoboam **(2 Chronicles 12:14)**; Abijam **(I Kings 15:1-4)**; Jehu **(2 Kings 10:31)**; Israelites **(2 Chronicles 20:33)**; Amaziah **(2 Chronicles 25:2, 14, 15)**

Being half-hearted will result in idolatry and disobedience. Some may serve God out of duty, but not out of love. Eventually, the fruits coming out of their lives will expose their hearts.

What does the fruit in your life reveal about your heart? Is your heart in line with Jesus Christ? If your heart falls short, so will your Christian walk. Let your cry be as David's in **Psalm 139:23, 24** and **51:10,**

Search me, O God, and know my heart;
try me, and know my thoughts:
And see if there be any wicked way in me,
and lead me in the way everlasting.
...Create in me a clean heart,
O God: and renew a right spirit within me.

Section Two

RIGHT ATTITUDE

Becoming Void

1. Define attitude.

   Oswald Chambers often referred to attitude as a person's disposition. According to Webster's New Collegiate Dictionary, disposition is a prevailing tendency, mood, or inclination. Clearly, disposition is a state, while attitude is a manifestation of the state that is present.

2. What does **Philippians 2:5** say?

   Attitude is used in the place of mind in the *New International Version* of the Bible. We are instructed to have the mind, attitude, or disposition of Christ.

   Philippians 2:6-8 gives us an insight into the mind of Christ. We begin to see Christ's prevailing tendency, mood, or inclination unfold in an incredible way. First of all, let us consider Jesus' tendency.

3. Define tendency.
4. What was Christ's tendency according to **Philippians 2:6, 7**?
5. What does **2 Corinthians 8:9** tell us about Jesus?

   Christ gave up the glories of heaven and made himself of no reputation. According to *Strong's Exhaustive Concordance*, Jesus made Himself of none effect. As God, He simply became void of His sovereign rule in order to take on the form of a servant.

   A true servant's tendency is to serve, not rule

6. How does Jesus confirm this in **John 13:5-17**?

   Jesus as servant humbled Himself and exalted man. He left us an example. Therefore, to have His mind we must become void of self or our vainglory.

7. What must we do to bring ourselves to a place of servitude? **(Matthew 16:24)**

   Servitude is contrary to the arrogant disposition of man. The cross is the only instrument that is capable of dealing with man's pride effectively. As self is nailed to the cross, it will decrease in authority and power.

8. Why must man decrease? **(John 3:30)**

   Romans 12:1-2 tells us our next step in bringing the rule of self down.

9. What must we do according to **Romans 12:1-2**?

Emptying self involves a sacrifice. Once the sacrifice is made, a transformation in the mind can take place.

Once the mind has become transformed, a person can begin to think like a servant. According to the following scriptures, what will an individual's tendency be when it comes to his or her attitude and response towards others?

Romans 12:3, 10, 13-15, 20, 21
Romans 15:1
Galatians 6:1, 2, 9, 10
1 Peter 4:8

Servitude is contrary to the arrogant disposition of man, just like Jesus becoming a servant was contrary to His disposition as God. Yet, Jesus humbled Himself and became a servant so you and I could have life.

Giving up self is the secret of changing our tendency to rule, enabling us to come into subjection to the Lordship of Christ.

Ask the Lord to show you your tendency right now. Are you still calling the shots or have you come into a place of real submission as a servant of your God?

Prevailing Mood

Webster's Dictionary defines mood as a conscious state of mind or predominate emotions, a prevailing attitude.

10. What was Jesus' prevailing attitude in **Philippians 2:8a**?

Here we see the Creator of the universe, the I AM of the Old Testament taking on the form of a man.

11. What does **Psalm 103:14-16** and **James 4:14** say about the frame of man?

Jesus, who is eternal, took on the form of a temporary entity. He allowed Himself to be limited in every possible way. We must ask ourselves why did Jesus allow this limitation to take place.

12. What does **Hebrews 2:16, 17** and **4:15** say about Jesus becoming man?

In the form of man, Jesus went one step further, He humbled or abased Himself. Here is that word again. We cannot seem to get around Christian maturity or victory without the virtue of humility.

13. What principle do we find in **Luke 18:10-14**?
14. Did Jesus' humility end in exaltation? (Yes or No.) **(Philippians 2:9-11; Hebrews 2:6-9)**

God resists the proud and gives grace to the humble. Humility closes down all avenues forcing the enemy to flee. **(James 4:6-10)**

Humility is teachable, compassionate, and kind. It does not demand its own way, and serves as a peacemaker. It is meek and displays a sweet temperance. We see this same prevailing mood in Jesus in **Matthew 11:28-30**.

15. What does this set of scriptures tell us about the humility of Christ?

What is your spiritual mood? Is it one of humility, upheld by grace, or is it of pride giving way to the enemy?

To have the mind of Christ means humility is the predominate attitude of response. If humility is lacking, you need to examine why. Be quick to respond as **James 4:8, 9** instructs.

Draw nigh to God, and he will draw nigh to you.
Cleanse your hands, you sinners; and purify your
hearts, you doubleminded. Be afflicted, and mourn,
and weep: let your laughter be turned to mourning,
and your joy to heaviness.

Inclination

According to the *Webster Dictionary*, inclination means natural disposition, character, to lean, or to become drawn toward an opinion or course or conduct.

16. What was Jesus' inclination according to **Philippians 2:8b**?

Christ's natural disposition was that of obedience to the Father. This natural disposition of obedience cannot exist in a person until he or she first becomes empty of self and develop a predominate response of humility. When we have a mind of Christ, we are inclined to obey in spirit and truth.

17. What must we incline towards God and His commandments to ensure obedience? **(Joshua 24:23; Psalm 119:36)**

Even your attitude will come back to your heart attitude or condition. Notice where Jesus' obedience led Him **(Philippians 2:8c)**.

18. Where will our obedience lead us? **(Matthew 10:38, 39; Romans 6:8, 11; 2 Timothy 2:11, 12)**

Once again, we are brought to the cross in denial of self and obedience to God. There is no way around the cross. Avoidance to it simply means we lack the mind of Christ. As you can see our attitude is based on our decisions. Jesus chose to die, so must we.

We are commanded to have the mind of Christ. Our disposition must be that of a servant. Our predominate mood must be humility, and our natural character must display obedience to our Lord.

Do you have the mind of Christ?

Section Three

LIFESTYLE

Walking in the Light

Jesus Christ lived a life beyond reproach. His adversaries could only falsely accuse Him of wrongdoing. We need to keep in mind, the world can only promote a lifestyle that is based on pagan cultural influences and will prove to be empty and temporary, but Jesus brings life that is eternal.

1. What do the following scriptures say about this issue? **(2 Corinthians 5:21; Hebrews 4:15; 7:26; 1 Peter 1:19-22)**
2. If Jesus walked a life beyond reproach, should we walk in like manner? (Yes or No.)
3. What kind of lifestyle should Christians be living?
4. Are you living a right lifestyle before God? (Yes or No.) Explain your answer.
5. What did God command Abraham to do in **Genesis 17:1**?

According to *Strong's Concordance*, the word perfect has different meanings to it. In the Old Testament, this word can mean unspotted, upright, or undefiled. In the New Testament it implies greater growth (maturity), completeness, mental, and moral character, and consecrated.

6. What brings about perfection in our life? **(2 Timothy 3:16, 17; 1 Peter 5:10)**
7. How does the Word maintain uprightness? **(Psalm 119:11)**
8. What does it mean for us to be perfect?

The answer is simple; we must follow the example Jesus gave us.

9. What do the following scriptures say about Jesus? **(John 1:4, 5; 1 John 1:5-7)**
10. What is our responsibility according to **Ephesians 5:8**?
11. What does it mean to you to walk in the light?

Light results in different reactions on the part of God's people. Our walk will be exposed in every area. There are some very important ingredients to make sure we walk in the light of Jesus Christ.

12. What is the first ingredient we must walk in to ensure we are in the light? **(1 Kings 2:4; Isaiah 2:5; Romans 13:13; 3 John 2-4)**
13. What promise do we have if we walk in this first virtue? **(John 8:32)**

Jesus is truth. If you walk in His light, you will be walking in truth and you will have honesty.

14. What does **1 Thessalonians 4:11, 12** say about this honesty?

We must be the reflection of the light of Jesus and His truth. If we are walking in light and truth, we will be obedient to the Lord's commands.

15. What do the following verses say about this subject? **(1 Kings 3:14; 2 John 4-6)**

We must be obedient to God. If we are obedient then we will be walking in His ways.

16. What do the following verses say about walking in His ways? **(Deuteronomy 8:6; 10:12; 11:22)**

It is interesting to note that the <u>fear of the Lord</u> is associated with walking in God's ways.

17. What is the fear of the Lord?
18. Why is it so important that we walk in the fear of God? Back up your answer with scripture.

The fear of the Lord is the beginning of wisdom.

19. What are we commanded to do in **Colossians 4:5**?
20. Do you have the fear of the Lord? (Yes or No.)
21. Why do Christians need to walk in the ways of God? **(Isaiah 55: 8, 9)**
22. Are you walking in the ways of God? (Yes or No.)
23. What does **Romans 4:12; 2 Corinthians 5:7** and **Colossians 2:6, 7** tell us to walk in?
24. Why is this ingredient important to our walk? **(Hebrews 11:6)**
25. What ingredients do **Micah 6:8** and **Ephesians 4:1, 2** add to our walk?
26. How can I walk this walk? **(Romans 8:1-2; Galatians 5:16, 18, 25)**

You cannot walk this life without the intervention of the Holy Spirit. Striving to walk in the light, truth, obedience, faith, and humility gives way to the Holy Spirit. The Holy Spirit then empowers us to live this life in greater ways.

Romans 12:9-21 gives us a vivid picture of the type of life that will be produced from an upright walk before God.

27. Summarize the picture presented in **Romans 12** about what our Christian life should look like.

This is what the godly walk looks like. It is done in the spirit of God's love, always maintaining the truth about our Precious Lord. It is pure and humble. It does not tolerate evil. It is a life of hope, patience, and prayer.

Are you displaying such a life right now? If not, you are walking in darkness and need to repent.

We have seen what it means to walk in the light, but what does it mean to walk in darkness?

Walking in Darkness

28. What one word associates a person with darkness? **(Romans 8:1; 13:14; Galatians 5:16, 17)**
29. What are the works of darkness? **(Galatians 5:19-21; Ephesians 5:3-5; 2 Peter 2:10; Jude 18)** (Be sure you know what each word means.)

30. Another word for <u>flesh</u> is carnal. What do **Romans 7:14; 8:6, 7,** and **1 Corinthians 3:3** say about the fruits of carnality?

It is amazing to see how many Christians are fleshly in their lifestyles. It is not unusual to hear about all kinds of works of darkness operating among Christians. Sexual immorality, pornography, abortions, and sensual pursuits of every imaginable kind are often bragged about or condoned by Christians. Either the world has come so much into the Church there is no discernment between what is clean and unclean, or we are spiritually dull because of compromise and pride. If the world has come in, then Christians' lifestyles are being determined by the world, and not by the Word of God and the example of Christ.

I remember hearing a story about a young Christian girl. Her mother admitted the daughter had two abortions after praying about it. They felt God approved of her actions. It was apparent that neither the girl nor her mother knew the real character of God.

The Church is in trouble. It is lukewarm on all fronts, from the preaching of the Gospel to Christians' attitude towards sin. Like the Laodicean Church, we think we are rich and have need of nothing, when we are really wretched, miserable, poor, blind, and naked. We have nothing to offer our Lord, and He is about ready to spew us out. Will we wake up to late? **(Revelation 3:15-17)**

31. What should be our attitude towards all works of darkness? **(Ephesians 5:3-14)**

The Apostle Paul instructed us that we need to reprove works of darkness instead of partaking of them. We need to awake, and rise up from the dead and Christ will give us light once more.

32. What was Paul's command in **Ephesians 5:16, 17**?
33. What should our response be towards evilness, fornication, idolatry, iniquity, love of money, and youthful lusts? **(Proverbs 4:14; 1 Corinthians 5:1-9; 10:14; 1 Timothy 6:6-11; 2 Timothy 2:19-22)**
34. What should we pursue after according to **1 Timothy 6:11, 12**?

The problem with many Christians is that they are not fleeing from sins; rather they are toying with them. They feel they can handle the temptation.

35. What does Paul say about this matter in **2 Corinthians 6:14**?

Jesus Christ was the only One who could overcome darkness. Christians are simply reflectors of the light of Christ. Darkness will overtake any Christian who submits to its enticements. Therefore, we must come out and be separate if we want God to be our Father and us his children. **(2 Corinthians 6:17, 18)**

36. How do we put the flesh down? **(Romans 13:14; Galatians 5:16-18)**
37. How do we overcome the world? **(Romans 12:2; Galatians 6:14; 2 Thessalonians 3:6; 1 John 2:15; 5:4, 5)**
38. How do we overcome Satan? **(James 4:7-10; Revelation 12:11)**

The purpose of the flesh is to entice, the world to entangle, and Satan to enslave people. The main goal of all three of the enemies of our soul is to destroy us.

Christ overcame all three of these enemies. Likewise, we must overcome all three if we are going to walk a victorious walk in Christ.

39. What are the promises awaiting those who are obedient to the instructions of God and overcome the three enemies of the soul according to the following scriptures? **(1 Kings 3:14; 6:12, 13; Psalm 119:45; 1 Thessalonians 4:1; Revelation 2:7, 11, 17, 26-29; 3:5, 12, 21; 21:7)**

Overcoming is not an option. We must overcome, as you will see in the following section! We can overcome because God has given us everything we need to be victorious in our walk.

The Consequence of Walking Amiss

40. What does **Matthew 7:13, 14** tell us about the choice of paths we have to choose from?

It is easy to get on the broad path to destruction. All you have to do is adjust your Christian walk to satisfy the flesh, appease the pride, conform to the world, and submit to Satan.

41. What will happen to an individual who gives into enticement of the flesh? **(James 1:14, 15)**
42. What do **Deuteronomy 29:19-21** and **Zephaniah 1:17, 18** tell us about the consequences of sin?

Galatians 5:19-21 warns us that those who do the works of the flesh will not inherit the kingdom of God. You can claim you are a Christian but if you live like the devil, you will be faced with the same judgment as Satan.

43. How do **Ezekiel 18:20-26, Hebrews 10:26-31** and **2 Peter 2:10-22** confirm this truth?
44. What does **1 John 2:15-17** tell us about the world?

The world is passing away along with those who put value in it.

47. What does Jesus tell us about Satan in **John 8:44** and **10:10**?

It is obvious Satan is out to destroy us. He uses the flesh and the world to entrap us into his snares. It is amazing how many Christians are doing all they can to feed the flesh, pursue the world, and bow down to Satan.

48. What exhortation do we find in **2 Peter 3:9-18**?

Which path are you on? Are you on the broad path or the narrow path? If you are on the broad path, stop, repent, and allow Jesus and His Word to put you on the correct path. Eternity is on the line.

Section Four

THE TONGUE

The Wicked Tongue

1. What do **Proverbs 18:21** and **James 1:26** say about the tongue?

   The tongue is the most dangerous and destructive member of the body. Both scriptures are quite clear about the credibility and power of this object. It has the power to destroy and the ability to unmask any hypocrisy in our lives.

2. What do **Romans 3:13, 14** and **James 3** tell us about the tongue?

   The tongue is the last member to be tamed. It is so powerful that at times it takes an intervention of God to bring it under control. Even though you may say the right thing, your tongue will prove how fickle or deceitful you are by revealing your actual heart condition.

   This was true for the Pharisees. They said all the right things, but eventually their tongue revealed their real heart attitude towards God when they yelled those famous words concerning Jesus, "Crucify him, crucify him." **(Matthew 15:8-20)**

3. What kind of qualities does a wicked tongue possess? **(Psalm 10:7; 50:19; 52:2-4; 73:9; Proverbs 21:6; 26:28)**

   There is much lying and deceit that follows a wicked man.

4. What would be God's attitude towards a lying tongue?

   Wicked tongues also sow seeds of discord among the brethren, which God hates **(Proverbs 6:14, 16, 19)**. This discord usually comes from such practices as slander, gossip, or innuendoes.

5. What does God consider a person who slanders? **(Proverbs 10:18)**
6. What does **Proverbs 17:9b** and **14** say about gossip?

   Paul and Peter called people who meddle in people's lives and shared their findings with others, "busybodies".

7. What did these two men say about this subject? **(2 Thessalonians 3:11, 12; 1 Peter 4:15)**

   Unruly tongues cause many problems such as suspicion, false accusation, and contention. In fact, the most vicious attacks on this ministry have come from the tongues of people who call themselves Christians. The damage has been incredible. It has brought a reproach on the Gospel, and poisoned the souls of those who needed help for they often shied away from this ministry.

Like Paul before his conversion, these religious people believe they are doing God's work by "warning" others. The truth is, it has nothing to do with heretical doctrine but a personal vendetta, a board in their eye that it is so large they cannot see because of the pride and wickedness in their own heart.

8. What are the consequences according to **Proverbs 6:15**?

Righteous crusaders, beware! No one has the right to be the judge, jury, and executor. Even a person who may be right in his or her conclusions about an individual must be careful to check out his or her motives and check in with God. Such an individual might be surprised at His perspective. It could be, *"Keep your mouth shut and pray!"*

God does not give any of us permission to purposely set out to destroy a person's character or life. Even David refrained from killing King Saul.

9. What principle do we find in **Romans 12:19**?
10. What was David's request in **Psalm 120:2, 3**?

You cannot trust a person with a froward mouth. Froward means perverse or perverted. This type of individual devises mischief and will ultimately sow discord.

11. What else will an evil person do? **(Proverbs 6:12-14)**

I heard of a businessman (who was an unbeliever), use **Proverbs 6:13** in determining whether he would hire someone. He admitted that he was able to develop a work force of reliable people based on this simple test.

The Apostle Paul gave instructions about the tongue.

12. What else must be removed from our conversation? **(Ephesians 5:4)**

I remember when I became a new Christian, I continued to tease my mother as I did before my conversion. I never thought about how it appeared to be disrespectful until one day at church. As everyone was coming out of the church, I called out to my mother in my usual teasing manner and the lady right in front of me thought I was talking to her. She turned around in such a manner I thought she was actually going to hit me. It struck me at that moment how my foolish teasing was really unacceptable in my new life. I immediately stopped.

13. What should come from our lips? **(Ephesians 5:4; Hebrews 13:15)**
14. What did the Apostle Paul warn us about in **Titus 1:9-12**?
15. How should we respond to those with unruly tongues according to **Titus 1:13, 14**?

The Apostle Paul even takes us one step further.

16. What is his instruction in **Ephesians 5:12**?

The conversations I hear Christians participate in appall me at times. They are talking about subjects in a casual or familiar manner that should never be mentioned.

We need to regard with sobriety our conversation. It must be beyond reproach. We must be careful about what we talk about. Everything in our life, including our tongue, must bring glory to God.

17. What judgments await those who have wicked tongues **(Psalm 12:2-4; 52:2-5; 64:7, 8; Proverb 6:14, 15; 10:31)**

What does your tongue tell you about your Christian life? If you consider our example of Jesus, there was no guile in His tongue.

The Tongue of the Righteous

18. What command do we have in regards to the tongue? **(Psalm 34:13)**

My greatest battle has been my tongue. There are times I have allowed it to expound when I should have been quiet. It has often been a point of major pride as I discreetly boasted of different accomplishments. It has been used to display power games as I toyed with other people's lives in the form of gossip. It has fearfully remained quiet in the proclamation of the Gospel. It has cut down vulnerable victims. In recent years it has been to warn, instruct, encourage, and edify.

I realize that over the years my tongue has set forth both sweet and bitter water. I have come to recognize that this member is very unruly. In fact, it only appeared to have one gear, and once the opportunity was right, it would begin a habitual momentum that often left me with great regret.

19. What did David say about his tongue in **Psalm 39:1**?

Disciplining the tongue has been a hard task. It continues to this day. One slip of it can cause such a destructive momentum. You actually have to learn to put your mind in gear before engaging the mouth.

20. What did Job request in **Job 6:24**?
21. What are the qualities of the tongue of the righteous and wise? (**Psalm 15:2-3; Proverbs 10:10, 20, 31, 32; 12:18; 15:2, 4; 25:15)**

We can see the tongue of the righteous can bring life.

22. What should motivate our speech? **(1 Corinthians 13:1; 1 John 3:18)**
23. What promises were given to those who keep their tongue? **(Proverbs 21:23; 1 Peter 3:10)**

It is vital our tongue lines up to our Lord, upholds our claims, and verifies our life.

24. What does **2 Corinthians 3:2-6** tell us?

We are living, walking letters. People will not give us a second thought if our life contradicts itself. One day, every tongue will make the same declaration.

25. What will it be? **(Romans 14:11; Philippians 2:10, 11)**

I am thankful that I have already confessed with my mouth the Lord Jesus **(Romans 10:9, 10)**. This declaration should set the pace for the rest of our conversations, which should be pleasing to our Lord and bring honor and glory to Him.

We are a blessed people. Not only should our lives show it, but also our tongues should confirm it. Our tongues should be used to simply agree with God and His Word.

The tongue needs to challenge people to consider Christ, teach people to grow in the knowledge of Him, and exhort others to become responsible to His Lordship. It needs to be God's vehicle to be used for His glory.

What about your tongue? Is it unruly or being tamed daily? Would it reveal a wicked heart or an upright heart? Would it make you a hypocrite or confirm a strong devotion to the Lord. Ask the Lord to show you. Let your heart prayer express the same thoughts as King David requested in **Psalm 141:3**.

Set a watch, O LORD, before my
mouth; keep the door of my lips.

Section Five

GODLY CONDUCT TOWARDS OTHERS

Caring Enough to Get Involved

The area most Christians miserably fail at in their conduct involves how they respond and treat other people, especially those of the household of faith.

1. How should we treat those of the household of faith? **(John 13: 34-35; Romans 12:15; Galatians 6:2, 9; 1 Peter 1:22; 1 John 3:14-18)**

We have a greater responsibility to help our brothers and sisters in the faith. Today many Christians look past the real needs of those of the Body of Christ to what they consider to be more worthy programs. This is their way of excusing themselves from getting involved with others. In fact, Christians are quicker to help people they do not know, rather than the ones they are personally involved with.

Being a single woman in full-time ministry has given me the taste of American Christian charity. It can be quite a bitter pill to swallow.

My very motive for serving God has been tested in extreme fires. If you are not serving Him out of love, you will walk away from Him. I want you to know I am a Christian in spite of Christians.

Christians are to be an extension of Jesus on this earth. Many Christians in America are so into self, living for self, they cannot see the forest for the trees.

2. What did Paul say in **2 Corinthians 1:4-7**?

Our whole purpose on this earth is to serve others, yet here is where many Christians fail. Those who show sacrificial service are usually those who cannot afford to. These people are the poor and often considered insignificant, but like so many other saints of old, out of a love for their Lord, they have concluded that they cannot afford not to give a 100 percent.

3. What did Jesus say about the widow in **Mark 12:41-44**?

People do not know what sacrifice really is until they have lost it all, and then they begin to give out of whatever is left.

The same principle applies to God. We can say we want all of God, but we will not possess Him until He is all we have filling our lives up with His reality.

People have their reasons for not helping those in need. Judgment day will expose every erroneous, selfish motive behind people's lack of giving, which is usually nothing more than a lack of love.

Many people have not helped us because they figure we could work to support ourselves regardless of being in full-time ministry. If you admit you have a need, they look at you as a spiritual sluggard! Others snub your ministry's validity because they compare you with the big glitter of mega-churches and the Christian TV.

4. What do the following scriptures say about some of these subjects?

James 1:27 refer to **Deuteronomy 26**

(Note: widows include single women. God pronounced judgment upon His people when they ignored the widows, the fatherless, and the stranger. Beware Church, we could be facing judgment. Our highest calling requires us to consider those of the lowest estate.)

Proverbs 22:16

(Note: how many Christians are oppressing the poor by giving to rich organizations? We have a tendency to let our churches or ministries worry about the poor, yet the Word is clear. You are personally responsible for the poor around you, especially to those of the household of faith.)

Deuteronomy 15:7-11; Psalm 41:1; Proverbs 19:17

(Note: How many Christians are looking for happiness? It is clear that if we could get past ourselves and help those in real need, we could begin to experience happiness. The more self-serving individuals are even in their giving, the more miserable they become.)

Proverbs 3:27, 28

(Let me ask you a question. Is the church, (or ministries), you support building greater personal kingdoms to serve their own lusts, or percentage wise are they actively working for the kingdom of God by serving others such as missionaries, the widows, the fatherless, the stranger, those in need etc.? Be honest.)

If you do find people who will actually help you, many of them have unspoken conditions you must live up to. We had a friend who believes ministers of the Gospel should not have decent clothes or waste money to go out to eat. Yet, she wasted her money on an unbecoming habit.

Another time a young couple helped us around the house. One day we had an emergency. We called them. We sensed they were perturbed. We unknowingly stepped over the invisible line, where we were previously considered as servants in need, but felt we had suddenly become inconvenient leaches.

I realize helping brothers and sisters in Christ does not seem as important or noble as helping an unbelieving, troubled soul. Once again there is a self-serving motive. In such instances a person is often trying to bring attention to him or herself and not God.

5. What does **1 Corinthians 1:31** say about this subject?

We really need to test our motive and attitude with the Word. We have invested a lot of time into people. Some of the beneficiaries thanked us and happily skip on their way without any thought to our personal needs.

6. What does Paul say about this subject in **2 Corinthians 1:11, 14** and **1 Timothy 5:17, 18**?

How many true servants of God have been muzzled by the Church? God did not intend His true servants to work to earn money and serve His people at the same time. It is hard to serve two masters. Of course, you have to make sure people are the true servants of God. God will show you if you ask.

How many Christians have invested in your life? Have you given anything back to them or the kingdom of God?

If Christians invested as much resources into the kingdom of God as they do in their fleshly pursuits, the results would be incredible. I was shocked recently to discover that even though America was the major source of financial donations to missionary organizations, they only gave 2% of their gross income. How can we expect God to bless this nation financially? In our present situation you would argue with me unless you understand economics.

Our economy is nothing more than a house of cards. The national debt and the fact that all success hinges on nothing more than paper (stocks, bonds etc.) should give us a reality check. Instead, many are deluding themselves, even Christians.

7. What did Paul tell us in **2 Corinthians 9:6**?

It is easy for some people to give money, but nothing else. It is sort of a payoff off or a bribe. Ministry involves getting involved with people, and finding out what they really need. Money is not the answer to every need or challenge. Sometimes people are in distress for other reasons. It is our responsibility to find out and avail ourselves to help them. After all, we are an extension of Jesus. Jesus rarely used money to solve the problems of people; rather, He multiplied what people supplied such as the boy with two fish and some bread that ended up feeding over 5,000 people. We are looking for blessings rather than seeking to bless. We hold onto our crumbs until God can provide us with endless manna from heaven, while God is waiting for us to offer Him all our crumbs so that He can bless not only us with abundance, but many others as well.

Confronting Sin in the Camp

Sin in the camp will bring a body of believers down and subject them to the judgment of God. Today there are two types of extremes that can be found in churches concerning sin in the camp. There are those Christians who maintain we need to love those who are in sin, and in due time they will come around. Then there are others who become judge, jury, and executor. Both of these attitudes are wrong. One lacks truth and the other lacks a correct spirit.

8. What does **1 Corinthians 13:6** tell us about love?

Real love will not ignore sin.

9. What insight does **James 5:19, 20** and **Jude 20-23** say about a person who is in error or sin?

Love may cover a multitude of sins, but it does not do away with the consequences of sin.

10. How did Paul confirm this fact in **1 Corinthians 5**?

The Apostle Paul told the Corinthians their attitude towards the blatant sin of this man in **1 Corinthians 5** was not love but pride. It is amazing how Christians give the impression that they actually have more grace than God. Why do I say this? Because, God will not ignore sin. His attitude has nothing to do with "mushy love" or "grace" that believers often attempt to display, but rather holiness and judgment. The love or grace we think we are showing a Christian in sin is nothing more than tolerance and compromise. As Paul declared a little leaven will leaven the whole lump, and God has called us to be separate from such actions and people.

Then there is the other extreme. These people are the crusaders. It is not that righteousness is a major issue with them even though they put forth such piousness. These people are usually motivated because they or their religious standards have been offended. They lack the right spirit.

11. What does offense mean?

According to *Strong's Concordance*, it means a snare, cause of displeasure, or sin, a stumblingblock.

12. What does trespass mean?

<u>Trespass</u> means to err or to sin which occurs when one trespasses some area that would prove questionable or offensive. This definition is according to *Strong's Concordance*. Paul tells us we must not be an offense or a stumblingblock to others in **1 Corinthians 8, 9**. To actually cause an offense, I would cause someone else to sin, such as a weaker brother by my fleshly actions in regards to a religious matter. Offense does not include differences that offend me because I do not like how someone else responds or does something. If such differences would lead me to sin through anger and bitterness it is not because of an offense on another person's part, but because of my own pride.

13. What does Paul say about this attitude of superiority? **(Romans 12:3, 16; Galatians 6:3; 1 Corinthians 10:24, 33; 1 Timothy 5:21)**

Trespass is actually a sin against God's Law or covenant, or an error such as the man who had to be confronted in the Corinthian Church.

14. What instructions did Jesus give us concerning a brother or sister who is found in a trespass? **(Matthew 18:15-17)**

Jesus established this procedure in **Matthew 18** in relationship to confronting someone in sin to stop gossip, petty complaints, and personal causes. If you must go to a brother or sister about real sin, it will be motivated by a legitimate concern for his or her soul, not because you have some personal cause or complaint. Note, you are to first go to him or her personally, then with a brother, after that the church. If obeyed, this procedure will prevent speculation, complaining, and gossiping that usually take place in this type of situation.

15. How should you go to someone who is in sin? **(Galatians 6:1; 2 Timothy 2:24-26)**
16. Why must we approach a brother in this manner? **(Galatians 6:1c)**

We are so arrogant that we can be like sharks who smell fresh blood in the water towards a brother in sin. There can be superiority, fake nobility, or piousness to such a person. We must approach him or her with an understanding that, except by grace, we could be in his or her same situation.

If Christians would only obey the Word, so much strife and confusion would stop. People who are in blatant sin could be restored and reconciled once they have truly repented and turned back to God.

17. How must we confront a leader in sin? **(1 Timothy 5:1, 19, 20)**

You never confront a leader of the church by yourself. Other leaders such as elders must be informed of the pastor's indiscretion, and they must initially confront the pastor in the hope of bringing them to repentance in order to properly maintain their witness and restore them. I remember a pastor who was in blatant sin. A new convert went to him personally. Even though he was in the wrong, he tore her up one side and down the other. As a result, she became discouraged and left the church.

Unrepentant sin on the part of Christians must be brought before the whole body. Separation must occur for the sake of the person in sin as well as the church. We must be a holy body.

18. How will such procedures affect other members of the body?

It will bring a fear, a respect to others. People will discipline themselves when they consider there could be consequences that will not be pleasant.

This study only highlighted this extensive subject. The truth is, godly conduct cannot be faked. I must have a right heart and attitude. I will have neither if Christ is not the center of my heart or serving as a standard to what I expose my mind to and the way in which I conduct my life.

19. How does **Philippians 4:8** confirm this truth?
20. What does **Titus 1:15** tell us?

We cannot fake humility, be obedient to the complete Word, sincerely care about people, and hate sin without loving God with all of our heart and fearing Him. We cannot be the salt of the earth or the light of the world until we are dead to self and alive to Christ. We may be able to play the religious games to console our struggling conscience and fool others, but we cannot fool the One who sees our heart. We can talk the talk, but the world will ignore and mock it until we back it up with an upright lifestyle.

This study was written so Christians can no longer claim ignorance about their responsibilities. It is time to adhere to the call, deny self, and take up the cross. The discipline of being a true disciple will lead us into the complete life in Christ through identification with His death, burial, and resurrection. It is the resurrected life of Christ that will make our lives, claims, and testimonies valid and powerful.

Won't you accept the call today?

THE CALL TO HOLINESS

INTRODUCTION

You are about to embark on a journey, a journey that begins with Jesus Christ and ends with Jesus Christ. But, like all adventures, before the mountaintop is reached, the long road through the valleys, canyon lands, and deserts of life must be traveled. For it is in the valleys one must come to grips with the impoverishment of one's own heart and soul. This condition motivates the seeker of truth and righteousness to cry out to the Savior. It is there, in the valleys of life, that the Lord comes in all His glory and power to rescue us.

Regardless of the challenges, we must always continue our journey through the deep canyons of repentance and commitment to God. Deeper and deeper the light of the Holy Spirit will search out every last vestige of selfishness and sin.

The narrow path climbs ever closer to the goal. However, first come the lonely, scorching trials in the desert. Faith is refined like fine gold. The soul is strengthened for the mountainous ascent to holiness.

At last, the mountain is reached. However, the high calling of holiness is at the summit. The way appears to be impossible, and yet the call to holiness persists. Eager but reluctant, we respond to the call. We are looking up now. The ongoing work of forgiveness, sanctification, and regeneration enables us to press forward and upward. As we near the apex of our Christian journey, the Spirit of God, the Living Water, continues to wash away every sin and weight that would hinder our progress into His presence.

A pure heart and submissive spirit give us sure footing on the narrow path. Faith in God and His Word propels us onward. Praise and worship ushers us in. At last! We are in the Holy of Holies. His presence, His glory, His majesty, and His holiness are our reward!

This is the goal of this Bible Study, *The Call to Holiness*. It is my sincere prayer that through each section, step by step, you will discover the secret to a life of holiness.

Section One

BEING SET APART

"But just as he who called you is holy, so be holy in all you do; for it is written: 'Be holy, because I am holy.'" (**1 Peter 1:15, 16** NIV)

Because they serve a holy God, Christians are called to a life of holiness. Words such as divine perfection, righteousness, and sacred can be used to describe God's attributes of holiness. To us, holiness means to be set apart or sanctified for God's use and glory, and our attitude towards God should be one of reverence.

1. According to **Romans 6:19** and **1 Thessalonians 4:7** what is the opposite of holiness?

Christians today need to be trained, challenged, and encouraged to live holy lives before the Lord. Sadly, all too often holiness has been reduced to man's causes, extreme viewpoints, or burdensome relationships. For example, some believe man cannot be holy. We know this cannot be correct because **1 Peter 1:15, 16** contradicts this concept. Others believe man can be holy but such holiness rests totally on the shoulders of the person. This belief results in people taking up causes and "swatting at a gnat while swallowing a camel." Such a belief misses the whole point of holiness and proves to be burdensome to both those who promote it, and those who labor under its demands.

2. What should the true message of the Church be according to Paul in **Romans 1:15-17** and **1 Corinthians 1:17-31**?

The subject of holiness will not bring salvation, *but rather true salvation will result in the work of holiness.*

3. Read the following scriptures: **1 Corinthians 1:30; Ephesians 5:9; Philippians 1:11; 2 Thessalonians 2:13; and 1 Thessalonians 3:13**. According to these verses who works holiness into our life? (Note: Remember righteousness is synonymous with holiness.)

Holiness, which is established by God in our lives, is His holiness.

4. According to **Isaiah 64:6** and **Romans 7:18** does man have any holiness in which he can boast about? (Yes or No)

5. The truth is God does the work of holiness (sanctification). Based on **1 Corinthians 1:30** and **1 Peter 1:2**, match the particular work of sanctification to the Person of the Godhead.

Places the believer in the place of sanctification: __________________________
Is the place of sanctification: __________________________
Does the work of sanctification: __________________________

God cannot look upon us as long as we are in sin; therefore, upon salvation He places us in His Son. It is then that the Holy Spirit begins the work of sanctification.

Although holiness comes from and is instituted by God Almighty, man does have the responsibility in the establishment of it in his own life. It involves consecration. God's work of sanctification is sandwiched between the work of consecration. For example, man must consecrate of separate from the unholy to ensure sanctification. Once he begins to respond to the work of sanctification, man will consecrate himself unto the work of God. Although we will discuss both of these works of holiness, it is important to point out that man must come to a place of holiness. In other words, holiness becomes an environment in which man will operate in accordance to the character of God and His Word.

Believers need to submit to God's requirement of holiness. There is a route involved which man must travel. This route, depending on whether one is saved or not, intertwines in a simple but profound way. If one is unsaved, his or her route involves the three "S's": sin, salvation, and sanctification. The route of a believer who has failed to adhere to the work of holiness after his or her born again experience, entails the three "R's": repentance, regeneration, and revival. These routes involve acknowledgment, responsibility, and response to the work of holiness by God in one's life.

Christians need to realize without the work of holiness they will never be able to make a difference in the world. In the next section we will begin to examine these routes to holiness. In so doing, we will catch a greater glimpse of the holy God we are called to serve.

Section Two

SIN AND REPENTANCE

"Sin" is a term we whitewash today. Because the word "sin" provokes a response, many avoid using it altogether! Instead, other terms such as *problems* or *mistakes* are substituted. Sin has been excused, condoned, pardoned, and justified. Often it is explained away as being *hereditary* or categorized as a *mental disorder* or *imbalance*. The humanistic mindset of our complex society has all too often pressured and molded the Biblical definition of sin into socially acceptable psychological jargon.

Sin is the one subject the American Church desperately needs to reconsider. If there is one distinct problem in the Church today that must be dealt with in order to reach the goal of true holiness, it is the reality of sin. In other words, the Church needs to come into agreement to the Biblical definition of sin. <u>Sin</u> means rebellion against God. It means missing the mark, or the unwillingness or inability to line up with God's righteousness. The attitude and goal of sin is to demand its own way, which is contrary to God's ways.

1. Read the following scriptures and write what each has to say about God's ways: **(John 14:6; Isaiah 55:8, 9; 2 Samuel 22:31; Nahum 1:2-8; Matthew 7:13, 14)**

God's ways are not obtainable through our own human efforts. Because of this, God in His great mercy and love has prepared the way for us to travel. It is a narrow way, but a glorious way. This way leads to the person of Jesus Christ.

Christ in our lives is the essence of eternal life. The fact that all mankind is affected by sin is part of the foundation that true Christianity rests upon. It is man's recognition of sin in his life, which brings him to the realization of his need for a savior. Therefore, man's awareness for his need of salvation to avoid hell, compels him to seek out the only One who can ever offer forgiveness and hope of eternal life.

Because of what Christ did on our behalf, we have been redeemed and have forgiveness of sin.

2. What does <u>redemption</u> mean?
3. According to **Ephesians 1:7**, what do we have redemption through?

Christ's blood was used to pay the price for our sin. As a result of the price being paid, we now have been set free to choose between liberty in Christ or remain in bondage under sin. The latter choice results in spiritual death or separation from God **(Romans 5, 6:23; Galatians 4:19-5:1)**.

Today there are those who would deny the power of the blood of Jesus.

4. According to **Hebrews 10:11-19** did the blood of Christ pay the full price for sin? (Yes or No)
5. We can have boldness to enter into what place because of the blood of Christ?
6. According to **Revelation 12:7-11** who will we overcome by the blood of the Lamb and our testimony?

Sin restrains us from spiritually and morally lining up with God. It separates us from the life God originally intended for man—a life lived in right relationship with God, full of beauty and truth. Sin is a terminal disease of the human soul. It masquerades itself as sensual pleasures, while ensnaring us much like a spider web does to its helpless victims. Yes, the horrible result of sin in man's life is as infinite as God's mercy, grace, and love in the life of the believer. The choice is ours. (Read **Luke 16:19-31; Psalm 51:3-5 and Romans 5:17-21**.)

If Christians are to travel the route to holiness, they not only need to understand sin, but they need to agree with God about this subject. There can no longer be a casual, complacent, or compromising approach to it. Sin is the opposite of holiness, and recognition of this fact will bring us to a place where we can respond to God properly. As we begin to respond to the call of God, our lives will commence to reflect His glory.

Prayer: "Lord, open my eyes that I may see as You see. Give me the courage to ask You to show me my own heart! Forgive me, oh God, for falling so short of your holiness, and create within me a new desire and hunger for You. Cleanse me by the power of Your shed blood. Help me, Lord, to walk so close to You that my life may truly be a reflection of Your holiness to others. In Your precious Name, Amen."

The Disposition of Sin

Disposition is a word that points to the inward state of man. We know the ways of sin is contrary to holiness, and that it does not line up with the very nature of God.

7. Read **Ephesians 5:3-7** and **Colossians 3:5-7**. What are some of the results of sin that works in the children of disobedience?

It is important to note how God judges sin in our lives. Many imagine God's judgment as a lightning bolt blazing out of the sky and striking one dead. His judgment, on the other hand, is usually carried out in a more subtle way. God who is full of grace, simply gives one over to his or her sin to pay some unpleasant circumstances and to taste the bitterness of it. God will draw, convict, and chasten, *but He will never overstep a person's will.* If any of us insist on our ways of sin, He will turn us over to the consequences of them. The boundaries of His grace will be lifted as we drift deeper and deeper into the cycle of sin.

In the book of **Romans** there is a route one travels in this cycle of sin.

8. What are the three stages, or cycle of sin the Apostle Paul wrote about in **Romans 1:24, 26,** and **28**?

In the above scriptures we see that God first gives us up to the desires of our heart. It is in the heart that seeds of disobedience take root. Once we submit to the desires of our heart, God then begins to turn us over to the passions of our flesh. This results in outward sin. As we begin to justify (or make right our actions in denial of guilt and conviction), He gives us over to the final stage—a reprobate mind.

A reprobate mind is a mind that is perverted and beclouded with its own speculation. God will reject such a mind. Note in **Romans 1:28** such a mind will be turned over to do those things which ought not to be done.

9. Look up the following verses and write out the attitudes and responses of those who were turned over to deception. **(Isaiah 5:20; Jeremiah 9:14; 16:10; 18:12)**

If we continually insist upon and demand our own way, God will eventually turn us over to it. Sadly, the consequence of this judgment is separation from fellowship with the Lord. The idea that I could place myself outside the boundaries of God's grace, protection, and intervention scares me. The key to God overseeing and being in control of our lives is found in **Romans 8:28**.

10. What is the key?

Many people quote **Romans 8:28** as a means of hope in difficult times. This special verse serves as a promise from God, but almost all promises have conditions. For God to be in control of our lives, we first must have a love for Him that will result in obedience. (See **John 14:15**.)

11. What is love's response towards sin? **(1 Corinthians 13:6)**

Today there is a strong tendency in many Christian circles to blame Satan for every adverse situation. This is not always true. We must take into consideration other factors. For one thing, God, in His faithfulness, chastens us. Also, His Word tells us that we reap what we sow.

12. Read **1 Peter 3:17-18** and **4:14-19** and write what Peter had to say concerning true suffering among believers.

Sometimes Christians suffer as a result of their own sin and count it as suffering for Christ's sake. We need to test and examine our heart condition, motivation, attitudes, and response according to the Word of God. We all too often do things in the name of Christianity, which do not line up with God's Word. We need to test our motives and actions to see if they are in the spirit of truth. Unhappily, Christians can and do become a reproach, not <u>for</u> the sake of Christ, but rather a reproach <u>to</u> Christ. We must examine our heart condition before God!

As we walk humbly with our loving God, let us refrain from the ever-present temptation to mercilessly judge our Christian brothers and sisters.

13. What do the following scriptures tell us about such acts of judgment? **(Matthew 7:1-5; Romans 14:10-13; 1 Corinthians 4:5; James 4:12)**

The workings of sin, which reigns in our lives, has great capacity to justify personal wrongs. The hypocrisy of sin disguises itself by pointing the finger of judgment at others. Sin, clothed in personal self-righteousness, convinces an individual that he or she is either persecuted for Christ's sake or under attack from Satan. This delusion blinds a person to the fact that he or she may be reaping what he or she has sown. The bottom-line root of the workings of sin in our midst is *DECEPTION*.

14. What does **Hebrews 3:13** say about this subject?

Deception must first take place if sin is to take root and reign. In other words, man must first become deceived to accept sin on any level. This truth should not surprise us when we consider what Jesus called the enemy of God, (Satan).

15. What did Jesus say about Satan in **John 8:44**?

16. Tell how the following individuals deceived themselves concerning their sinful actions:

Abraham **(Genesis 12:10-20)**
Isaac **(Genesis 26:6-16)**
The brothers of Joseph **(Genesis 37)**
Saul **(1 Samuel 13:1-14)**
King David **(2 Samuel 11, 12)**
King Herod **(Mark 6:14-29)**

17. What did Jesus say would be one of the great signs of the end days in **Matthew 24:4, 5**?
18. Men can always declare they did not know about sin and separation from God, but according to **Romans 1:17-20** will this declaration stand in the end? (Yes or No.)

Sin's tendency is to *release* man from his wrongdoings. We all need to understand and define the work of sin within our own disposition. We need to get real with who God is and who we really are before Him. We must be totally honest with ourselves about the deception of sin.

Prayer: "Gracious Heavenly Father, thank You for Your Word which gives me understanding of the real workings of sin! Lord, help me to recognize in my own life if I am undergoing an outright attack of the enemy or if I am being chastened by Your hand. Help me to know, oh Lord, if I am indeed reaping what I have sown. If that is so, please forgive me Father. Help me to have a clean and upright heart at all times. Give me Your love for those around me so I will not be judgmental or condemning. Thank You, Lord for the victory in Your precious Name! Amen."

Sin and Humanity

It is important for us to understand human nature.

19. According to **1 Thessalonians 5:23** what is man made up of?

Our body includes the flesh; the soul represents our mind or emotional makeup and personality, and our spirit is the heart of the spiritual part of man's invisible being. Our flesh is tangible. We can see and touch it. The flesh responds according to the five senses.

20. What are the characteristics of man's flesh according to the following scriptures? **(Romans 8:1-5, 8; 1 Corinthians 15:50)**

Another word, which signifies flesh or fleshly response, is carnal. Carnal means sensual, controlled by animal appetites, or governed by lust. It means becoming submissive to the desires of flesh.

21. What other part of man does the Bible refer to as being carnal? **(Romans 8:6, 7)**
22. What does it mean to you to be carnally minded?

Modern man spends most of his time in a vain pursuit of carnal pleasures. Outward works of darkness originate from an inward carnal heart or mind.

23. Is there anything good in the flesh? (Yes or No.) **(Romans 7:18)**

In the Word of God *"soul"* and *"spirit* are often used interchangeably. Both soul and spirit specify the invisible part of man. In both the soul and spirit, man perceives, reflects, feels, and desires. The difference between soul and spirit is the spirit of man is considered the higher state of man, while the soul is considered the lower state. *(See Vine's Expository Dictionary of Biblical Words.) Spirit* implies *"the wind"* or *"breath",* and is the life principle bestowed on man by God. It is in the spirit that revival takes place. Soul represents the emotional makeup and consciousness of man. It is in the *soul* that regeneration takes place.

24. Where must spiritual birth take place according to Jesus in **John 3:1-8**?

We must be born again in the spirit to see the kingdom of Heaven. Recognition of sin is the beginning of this new birth in the life of an unbeliever. Once we receive Jesus Christ into our lives, the Holy Spirit, (symbolized by wind), comes into our spirits to reside.

25. What does Paul say about the relationship of the Spirit of God and man in **1 Corinthians 3:16**?

Before God can have His way in our lives we must come to terms with our own miserable state. If we have not experienced the spiritual birth, then we are spiritually dead; or in more explicit terms, separated from God.

26. Read **Romans 1:28; Colossians 1:21,** and **Titus 1:15**. Since our soul is representative of our mind, what kind of mind, other than the carnal, reflects sin in our lives?

Both mind and body can become submissive to carnal animal appetites. Man was not created to respond as an animal. God created man in His image and gave him dominion over the animals **(Genesis 1:26-28)**. God must be Lord over both our minds and our flesh.

27. Read **Romans 8:6, 13; Philippians 2:3-5** and **Galatians 2:20**. What must happen to our minds and flesh for God to have His way?

28. All sin falls under three categories. What are they according to **1 John 2:16**?

It has been an interesting observation on my part to see how the different types of sin affect the different areas of man. Just for fun, match the letters of the types of sin to the area of man that they would most likely affect.

A. Lust of the flesh	_____Soul or mind
B. Lust of the eyes	_____Spirit or heart
C. Pride of life	_____Body

In order to have a clear understanding of the lust of the flesh and the lust of the eyes, we need to comprehend the word <u>lust</u>.

29. Define lust.

Not all lust is considered evil unless it is inconsistent with the will of God. (See **Luke 22:15; Philippians 1:23** and **1 Thessalonians 2:17**.) The type of lust that is evil involves ungodly desires that are ready to be expressed in lustful, bodily activity.

30. What kinds of sin are associated with the works of the flesh? **(Galatians 5:19-21)**

<u>Lust</u> is also translated as passions, (inordinate affections), covetousness, and pleasures. There are two channels by which all things enter our minds, through our eyes and ears. The eyes are considered the main avenue of temptation. (See **Matthew 6:23** and **Luke 11:34**.)

31. What are some of the sins that have been grouped with an evil eye? **(Mark 7:21-22)**
32. According to *Vine's Expository* there is one sin that is translated as falling under the lust of the eye. What is the sin? **(Matthew 5:27-29)**

It is obvious that there is no good thing in man's flesh. Sin enters by way of the eyes and, as stated before, materializes in our flesh.

33. Where does all sin originate? **(Matthew 15:16-20)**
34. What sin is associated with the heart according to **Proverbs 16:5** and **21:24**?
35. Give a definition of pride.

Descriptive words for <u>pride</u> include: boastful, haughty, arrogant, high-minded, puffed up, and vainglory. It can also be summarized as an excessively high opinion of self.

Today, pride is one of the major problems in Christianity. It is rarely recognized for what it is because it has been exalted through concepts such as self-esteem, self-acceptance, self-awareness, self-confidence, self-importance, and dozens of other *"selfisms"*.

36. What are some evidences of pride according to the following scriptures? **(Proverbs 10:17; 11:2; 13:10; 16:19; 25:14; 28:25; 30:12; Mark 12:38, 39 Luke 11:43; Luke 14:8, 9 Romans 1:22; 11:17-25; 12:3, 16; 1 Corinthians 3:18-21; 5:2; 8:1, 2; 10:12; 13:4; Galatians 6:3-5)**

The Word is replete with admonitions concerning pride and its devastating results. People who submit to the pride of life basically submit to self-importance. People who are self-righteous, self-exalting, self-sufficient, all-knowing, unteachable, unloving, and contentious are full of pride.

37. What is the opposite of pride? (See **Proverbs 11:2; 16:19; 29:23; Matthew 23:11** and **Philippians 2:3-11**.)

<u>Humility</u> means being of low degree or of low estate. Saying the "right" things or "looking" the part does not determine humility. It comes from a disposition that manifests itself in genuine submission.

Even though pride may be clothed in self-righteousness, stand behind a pulpit, and expound Bible verses, it is still sin.

38. Who must be exalted at all times? **(1 Corinthians 1:31)**
39. Who will exalt and reward us? **(1 Samuel 2:7; Psalm 75:7; Luke 18:9-14; 2 Timothy 4:7, 8)**

Pride is totally contrary to holiness! Each of us must allow and desire God to reveal any type of pride in our lives. Pride is not pleasant for us to look at from God's perspective, but it is necessary if we are to be right before Him.

Now that we have a picture of man's makeup, and how sin works within it, we need to know how to recognize and overcome it.

Prayer: "Father in Heaven, thank You for allowing me to see as You see. Thank You for Your precious Word. Thank You for Jesus' sacrifice for me. Help me, oh Lord, to walk humbly before You as You lead me in paths of righteousness for Your Name's sake. Help me to be holy! In Jesus' Name. Amen."

Repentance

The key to overcoming sin in our lives lies within one word, repentance.

40. Explain what repentance means to you.

Repentance means to make a change, not only in actions, but also in mind and purpose. In the military the command of "about face", which is a 180-degree turn, is a descriptive illustration of repentance.

41. What does Peter say about repentance in **2 Peter 3:9**?

Repentance is necessary if God's salvation and will is to be instituted and worked out in our lives. It is important to note the word *all* in **2 Peter 3:9**.

Today there is a growing belief among some Christians that once they have received Christ they no longer have need of repentance. Examples such as Job and King David do not agree with such a conclusion **(Job 42:6; Psalm 51)**. I have always been taught there are two types of people in the world; they are sinners and sinners. The difference between the two types is that one group of sinners have been saved by the grace of God, and are being made into saints, while the second group are walking in condemnation **(Ephesians 2:8-10)**.

We need to re-examine the teachings of Jesus Christ and the Apostle Paul. Christ told us to pick up our cross daily. The cross, scripturally speaking, is symbolic of death. In our case, it is death to self. Self is representative of the flesh, sin, and association with the world. Paul talked about dying daily, and detailed the war between his flesh and the spirit. He wrote about being crucified with Christ so the life of Christ could be worked in him. What Christians need to understand is *because of Adam we are in a fallen condition or disposition.*

42. What does Paul say about this subject in **Romans 5:12-21**?

(Note: Christ's work on the cross delivered us from the consequences of sin and spiritual death, but not from our fleshly influences.)

It is for this reason the Bible tells us to mortify or put to death our flesh **(Romans 8:13; Colossians 3:5)**. Just because we have a problem with a wrong disposition does not mean we are excused from being responsible to overcome such a state. We must face this disposition and allow the Holy Spirit to regenerate our soul area.

John put a strong warning forth to people who claim they did not have to contend with the problem of sin.

43. What did John state about such a declaration in **1 John 1:8-10**?

We have been given a promise concerning sin in **1 John 1:9**, "If we confess our sins, he is faithful and just and will forgive us our sins and purify us from all unrighteousness?" Why put the promise there if it we do not have to contend with sin? Granted, if we are saved, we should not be walking in sin. However, we will occasionally fall into sin. And if we do, we have an Advocate that will intercede on our behalf **(1 John 2:1-2)**. The truth is, we will contend with the flesh and sin as long as we are in these mortal bodies. But, the key to victory is first recognizing sin, and then quickly repenting of it.

If we deceive ourselves about sin in our life, we will fail to see the need for repentance. Remember, for sin to take root and grow we must first buy a lie about its existence in our lives. The call and need for repentance are ongoing for all of us.

44. According to **2 Corinthians 7:10** does all repentance lead to salvation? (Yes or No.) Explain your answer.

There are many people who despise their lifestyle, but rather than swallow pride and come to God for forgiveness, they make "resolutions" and try to "pull themselves up by their own bootstraps." The truth is everything within the human disposition resists godly repentance. Rather, than truly repenting, many resort to a "confession". But merely giving verbal lip service to God is a far cry from a true heart response. *One may confess without repentance, but true repentance will include confession.* Confession to God is the first step, but it must lead to another important step that is necessary in true repentance.

45. Read **Matthew 5:23-24**. What is this step?

To come clean of the results of sin we must not only go to God, but also to those we have wronged. Sin damages our relationship with both God and others. The goal of true repentance is to rebuild "relationship bridges" after they have been shattered by our own wrong doings. Note: It is much easier to go to a loving, Heavenly Father for forgiveness than to an individual where we may end up "eating crow"!

The result of godly repentance is reconciliation and healing of relationships. When relationships are healed, burdens are lifted and we experience a new liberty in our life before God. If healing does not take place, we find ourselves carrying burdens of guilt. Obviously, worldly sorrow weighs us down.

46. What does **Hebrews 12:1, 2** tell us to do with the weight that besets us?

Worldly sorrow always falls short of true reconciliation with God and others. We need to understand how both types of sorrow and our disposition interact in our response to God and people.

Prayer: "Oh Lord Jesus, search my heart. Help me to truly repent of all that is not of You. Restore my relationship with You and others. Lord, I want to know You in greater ways and walk with You in truth and righteousness. Thank You for the sword of Your Word which sets me free and cuts asunder the weights I need not carry! In Your Holy Name I pray. Amen."

Repentance and Human Nature

To summarize the result of sin in our lives, we must begin with *deception* that is born out of a wrong heart condition. Once it takes root, it comes forth as works of darkness.

47. Read **1 Corinthians 10:13**. What does this verse say about temptation?
48. Does God ever tempt us to do evil? (Yes or No.) **(James 1:12-13)**
49. What is the reward for enduring temptation? **(James 1:2-4)**

Temptation is not sin in itself. Sin is produced when we submit to it! God does not tempt us to do evil, but rather, He provides a way out of temptation. In your own words explain how we can overcome temptation based on the following scriptures:

1 John 5:4, 5; John 16:33; Revelation 12:11
James 1:13-21
Romans 12:17-21
Ephesians 4:22-32
James 4:7-10

Some of us, like Eve, "fall" into sin while others, like Adam, commit it fully aware of their actions, but later blame others when faced with consequences **(Genesis 3)**. We need to be sober-minded watchmen over our spiritual lives. Regardless of the cost, we need to hate and avoid sin. If we find ourselves in sin, we can confess it and look to Jesus Christ, our Advocate and High Priest, to deliver us and cleanse us from all unrighteousness **(Hebrews 6:20-7, 28; 1 John 2:1, 2)**.

The big challenge for most of us is that our pride convinces us that we are capable of contending with our own sins and problems. This attitude of self-sufficiency is based on total deception. We even become deceived about our motives.

Why do we do the things we do? Christians who desire to serve God must question and properly discern their motives. As God's servant are we serving Him to receive recognition for ourselves or to bring glory and honor to Him? If our motives are wrong, then it does not matter what we do in the name of Christ. There are two distinct results from wrong motives.

50. Read **Matthew 7:21-24** and **1 Corinthians 3:11-15** and identify the two different motives.

The love of God serves as the only motivation that brings honor and glory to Him. God's love in us is the heartbeat of an effective Christian life, and is the cord that binds our life in Christ together.

In summary, we have learned there is no good thing in our flesh. We need to be honest about sin in our lives, repent and allow God to take care of it. Repentance is the key to unlocking closed doors in our relationship with God.

At this time lay your life before God. Ask Him to expose any rebellion in your way of thinking and doing. As He shows you your rebellion and sin, come to Him in repentance and start the process of learning to die to self daily through submission to God. It is in this process of dying to self that we begin to catch a glimpse of God and His work of salvation and regeneration that must be worked in our lives by His Spirit.

Prayer: "Lord, I praise and worship You! Thank You for Your great salvation! Father, show me the motives of my heart and cleanse me by the blood of Your Son. Thank You for Your overcoming power and victory over all sin. I want to serve You, love You, and walk with You forever. Grant my requests O' Lord. In Jesus' Name, Amen."

Section Three

SALVATION AND REGENERATION

One of the terms I have heard was "good saved". I have often thought about this statement. I considered all the people I've met through the years who claimed to be Christians to be such. Yet, some of these same people, by their lifestyle, as well as their understanding of God and Jesus fall short of scriptural definitions of true Christianity. Is there truly a difference between a "good saved Christian" and those who appear to be missing the mark?

1. What does it mean to you to possess God's salvation?
2. What are we being delivered from through the salvation offered to us? **(Romans 5:8, 9)**
3. What must one do to receive God's salvation? **(Romans 10:9, 10)**
4. Based on **Acts 4:12** is there any other way we can obtain salvation outside of Jesus Christ? (Yes or No)

   We must believe upon the Lord Jesus Christ. We must believe He is who He is, and that through belief, confession, and reality of His death, burial, and resurrection we can receive eternal life.

5. What does the word <u>believe</u> mean to you in conjunction with God's plan of salvation?
6. What kind of role does faith play in our relationship with God according to **Romans 5:1** and **Galatians 3:6**?
7. Read **Hebrews 11:6**. Can we please God without faith? (Yes or No)
8. What proves our faith is alive? **(James 2:14-26)**
9. Finish the following sentence, "...whatsoever is not of faith is __________." **(Romans 14:23**, KJV*)*

   To have faith in God's plan indicates we believe God concerning our salvation. **Hebrews 11:1** gives us a definition of faith.

10. In your own words explain the definition of faith.

    One of the simplest definitions of faith is found in **Hebrews 11:6**, "And without faith it is impossible to please God, because anyone who comes to him must believe that he exists and that he rewards those who earnestly seek him." Your faith is determined by your perception of God. You either believe God is God or you don't. When people talk about great faith, they are simply referring to a child-like trust in a great God. People who have little faith lack vision and a growing relationship with God.

    Real faith is alive! It demonstrates itself in the life of a believer by unwavering confidence and assurance. Good works will abound out of a heart of faith, love, and obedience. Faith in God is not "blind faith"; rather, it is sincere confidence that trusts God's sovereignty.

    In this generation there is an ever increasing number of people who seek signs, wonders, and prophecy as a means of direction and "faith building" in their lives. On the contrary, we need to diligently seek out *God* for who He is and should be in our lives. Unfeigned faith believes that no matter what happens it is for the glory of God and for our spiritual benefit.

Salvation carries with it certain requirements and responsibilities. The condition and results of faith prove this alone. There is more to salvation than verbal confession and head knowledge. It is not enough to casually believe; one must know. True belief carries authority and power that leads to a greater relationship with God.

At this point, carefully consider the following question.

11. Are you truly saved? (Yes or No)

If you are in doubt, or your answer is no, let me at this time encourage you to open your heart to Jesus Christ. Recognize you are a sinner in need of salvation. Confess your condition to God and ask Jesus into your heart to save you for eternity. If you truly confess to the Lord your hopeless condition, seeking His forgiveness for your sins, and open your heart to Him, He will come in through the Holy Spirit and begin the work of salvation in your life.

Prayer: "Oh Precious Savior! Thank You for the priceless gift of salvation. Help me to never take it for granted, oh Lord, but to rejoice in You and Your love every day of my life. Lord Jesus, I want to be like You! Increase my faith and help me to walk in authority and power as Your child. I ask this in Your wonderful Name. Amen."

Responsibilities of Salvation

Salvation is a free gift from God, but so are children. Although children may be gifts, tremendous responsibilities accompany them **(Romans 6:23; Psalm 127)**. Likewise, there are responsibilities surrounding salvation.

When we invite Christ into our life, we are actually giving Him permission to save us. Jesus comes into our heart through the Holy Spirit. He then begins to do an eternal work in us **(Philippians 1:6)**.

12. What does Paul say about God's work in our lives according to **Philippians 2:13**?
13. What does **Hebrews 12:2** say about Jesus and the salvation He gives us?

Scripture definitely shows there is a work of salvation that goes on in our lives.

14. According to **Philippians 2:12** what should our response be to our salvation?

In the introduction I mentioned the attitude that represents holiness. It is *reverence*. Holy fear or the "fear of the Lord" is the act of reverence towards God. Another word, which expresses this attitude, is *marvel*.

15. What did Solomon say about the "fear of the Lord" or "fearing God" in **Ecclesiastes 12:13**?

The fear of the Lord expresses itself in an attitude of wholesome awe and respect of God, obedience, reliance on Him, and avoidance of evil. This fear also possesses a dread of meeting God outside of what is considered acceptable, upright, and holy before Him. It does not want to face Him in sin, disobedience, or indifference.

True wisdom and real life begin with the fear of the Lord. Paul exhorts us in the last sentence of **Philippians 2:12** to, "work out our salvation in the fear of the Lord." Within the boundaries of the fear of the Lord our response to salvation will be right.

16. What are some of these responses according to the following scriptures?

Matthew 3:2; Luke 3:8; Acts 2:38; 3:19
John 3:3-18
John 5:24; 6:28, 29, 47
Luke 14:25-33

True salvation produces upright responses from the heart and obedience to the Word. Our salvation begins with simple faith in Jesus Christ as Savior. As we grow in revelation and knowledge of Christ, reverence will be established in our attitudes. It will manifest itself in godly works. Since attitude is part of the mind, or soul, we need to understand how to protect and maintain a right attitude towards God.

The Helmet of Salvation

1 Corinthians 3:16-17 declare we are the temples of God. We need to be holy in order for God to reside in us. We can see that like man, the Old Testament Tabernacle and Temple were made up of three main parts. There were the Holy of Holies where God resided; the Holy Place where the things of God were kept as a reminder of His promises, provision, and intercession for His people; and the Outer Court where sacrifices were made on behalf of the people's sins (**Exodus 36-40; Leviticus 16**). Our spirit represents the Holy of Holies, our mind the Holy Place, and our body the Outer Court.

As believers, **1 Peter 2:5** and **9** tells us we make up a lively priesthood. In the outer court, the priests would enter through the sole *gate* of the tabernacle to minister on *behalf* of others, and then they would enter through the *door* of the Holy Place to minister *before* the Lord. Finally, the High Priest would enter once a year through the *veil* into the Most Holy Place to minister *to* the Lord. The design of the tabernacle and the practices of the priests leave us valuable examples as to what it means to be both the temple and part of a lively priesthood.

However, our temple can easily be defiled by what we expose ourselves to. Subsequently, our mind or the area of our souls is the major area under attack by Satan. Notice in **Ephesians 6:10-18**, where the piece of armor that was designated to protect our salvation was located. Our salvation represents the head, or our mind, and the helmet protects it. The base of the mind represents conscience. If the Holy Spirit is not influencing our conscience, we will be inclined to walk according to how something affects us. The physical brain is responsible for our bodily functions. Likewise, all spiritual functions of our soul will influence our salvation.

Our mind needs to be the Holy Place where there is a continual awareness of who God is and who He must be in our lives.

17. Whose mind should be in us according to **Philippians 2:5-8**?
18. According to **Philippians 2:1-5** what would be the result of the mind of Christ being placed in us?

The Word of God stresses a right attitude towards God. In the above verses we see the attitude of humility.

19. What needs to take place if we are to have the mind of Christ according to the following scriptures? **(Isaiah 26:3, 4; Romans 12:1-3; 1 Corinthians 2:14-16; Philippians 4:8; Ephesians 4:22-27)**

20. What does transformed mean?

    How do the things you watch on TV, the music you listen to, and the things you read survive the test found in **Philippians 4:8**? How much time do you spend meditating upon the Word of God so that the Holy Spirit may instruct you in the ways of God and renew your mind? Satan knows if he can defile our minds by using the things of this world, he will defile us!

21. What does **Titus 1:15-16** say about this subject?

    We need to be serious about protecting our minds with the helmet of salvation. We need to press forward towards a holy life by eliminating the garbage in our lives and in our minds.

Being Double-Minded

Double-mindedness means "two-souled". The results are confusion, uncertainty, insecurity, and lack of purpose or direction. Remember, it is within our soul that we perceive, reflect, feel, and desire due to the influence of our conscience.

22. What does **James 1:8** say about this subject?

    Christians who suffer from such a mind can experience a paradox in their lives before God. True Christianity does not come from knowledge alone; it must be worked out in practical everyday living. Double-mindedness may allow you the knowledge of real Christianity; but it will deny you the power and ability to apply it in practical living, thus creating a paradox in your life.

    Man's mind is a popular subject today. There is an increasing awareness in our society of emotional instability and "mental disorders". Christians are also contending with such problems, and are turning to worldly solutions. Although some disorders are caused by physical problems, many are associated with spiritual problems. The answer to all spiritual problems can only be found in Jesus Christ and His unchanging, living Word.

    There is not one mention of *"mental disorders"* or *"mental illness"* in the Bible. Disorders, which were clearly visible, were dealt with as spiritual oppression. Jesus came to deliver and set the captives free **(Luke 4:18)**. As we begin to discuss this subject, it will become apparent that Satan is the author of mental disorders or oppression that are spiritual in nature. This type of spiritual oppression is often the result of fear, guilt, erroneous doctrine, and sin.

23. Look up the following scriptures and describe the condition of each individual Christ set free: **(Mark 1:23-28; 5:1-20; Luke 9:38-43)**

    A major cause of double-mindedness among Christians is found in **2 Timothy 1:7**.

24. What is this cause?
25. Based on this scripture, where does such fear come from?
26. What other two areas are affected by a spirit of fear besides one's ability to think?

    Fear is opposite of faith and results in idolatry because it becomes a form of worship as the person begins to focus on it rather than God. Other products of fear are depression, anxiety, paranoia, confusion, and doubt. This fear is from Satan and classified as coming from a spirit.

27. What must we do to put this fear in perspective? **(Hebrews 10:19-23)**

Demonic fear stifles the power and authority we have in God. It is with God's power, and not our own, we overcome our enemy.

28. How do **1 John 4:4** and **1 Peter 5:5-9** confirm the previous statement?

Another area affected by fear is our ability to allow God's love to become a reality in our lives. We often fear God or others will reject us if we admit we have a sin or problem.

29. What does **1 John 4:17-19** says about this matter?

When fear is a part of our lives, we cannot trust God's love and acceptance. As a result, we fail to enter into His rest. God's love must be a reality in our lives so we may come to Him with confidence and boldness.

30. What other capability does God's love have according to **1 Peter 4:8**?

Guilt is another problem produced by double-mindedness. The meaning of guilt is to be liable, or deserving of punishment because of the violation of a law or a breach of conduct. Guilt puts us under judgment and makes us a debtor. Such judgment brings condemnation.

31. Look up **Romans 8:1-4**. Is there any condemnation to those who are in Christ Jesus, who walk according to the Spirit? (Yes or No)
32. What is the only spiritual debt we can, and are required to pay? **(Romans 13:8-10)**

God will convict us through the Holy Spirit, but He will not put a "guilt trip" on us. We could never pay the necessary price for our sins in order to be released from their consequences.

Satan is our accuser and brings condemnation on us. This condemnation can only take root when we agree with his lies. Once a Christian agrees with Satan, he or she begins to tolerate guilt. There are four reasons for this tolerance: 1) fear of rejection, 2) lack of faith and trust in God, 3) inability to receive forgiveness, and 4) pride.

We need to know we can find total acceptance, forgiveness, and victory by coming to God in trust and repentance. God will never turn any of us away if we will only draw near to Him on His terms in good faith. Sadly, many Christians are wounded and guilty. Guilt forces a person to look back at situations he or she cannot change. Lot's wife is an example of a person who looked back and never experienced spiritual deliverance and healing in her life **(Genesis 19)**.

We need to look to Christ and follow Him. He will lead us to a new and complete life. We need to remember, if God forgives us, who are we to not receive forgiveness? Believe me, it is not wise for us to hold ourselves wholly responsible, nobly spurning the healing God offers to us in abundance. Too often the motivating factor to such guilt is pride. Christians need to lay their past and guilt on the altar and trust God with both.

(Commit to memory Isaiah 26:3.)

Guilt brings uncertainty and hopelessness.

33. Where does our only hope rest? **(Ephesians 2:12-18)**
34. What promise do we have in **1 John 1:9** if we have committed sin?

Another problem which results from double-mindedness is found in **Ephesians 4:14**.

35. What is the problem?

False doctrine will cause us to be double-minded. There is only **ONE** God, **ONE** Spirit, **ONE** foundation, **ONE** body, **ONE** baptism and **ONE** faith **(1 Corinthians 3:11; James 2:19; Ephesians 4:4-6)**. Today another Christ, another doctrine, and another spirit are carrying multitudes away to spiritual destruction **(2 Corinthians 11:2-4)**. Paul warned us about what would happen to sound doctrine in **2 Timothy 4:2-5** in the end days.

36. What will happen to those who will not endure sound doctrine?
37. What is Paul's warning in **Ephesians 5:6, 7**?
38. What is Paul's exhortation to us in **2 Timothy 1:13**?

Jude 3 tells us to contend for the faith. Contend is the same as wrestling for our faith. Satan wants to rob us of sound doctrine. He entices us to believe in a form of "watered-down" Christianity that allows for worldly compromise. With religious acts and games, Satan lulls us into a spiritual sleep. He affords us the false luxury of believing we are on the correct path, when in fact, we have not even begun to pay the necessary price to know God **(Luke 14:28-33)**.

Our faith and life in Christ are something we must contend for. Sound doctrine will uphold and maintain both our faith and life in Christ; however, we must love the truth!

39. What does **2 Thessalonians 2:8-10** say about what will happen to those who do not love the truth?

If we are to be the light of the world and the salt of the earth, we must allow God to separate us from the world. We need to be willing to pay the price, even if it means sacrificing "comfortable, convenient Christianity". We are soldiers in the army of God, called to overcome the world, the flesh, and the devil. Overcoming requires contending, pressing forward, running the race, and fighting the battle **(1 John 2:12-14; Jude 3; Philippians 3:14; Hebrews 12:1, 2 Timothy 4:7, 8)**.

40. What must we do to withstand the storms of life and the attacks of the enemy based on the following scriptures? **(Matthew 7:24-27; Ephesians 6:11-18; James 4:7-10)**

Another root cause of double-mindedness is sin. Christians who try to strike a balance between serving Christ and serving the world are miserable and unhappy people. The most frustrated Christian is the one who recognizes sin in his life, but cannot overcome it and is afraid to seek out help. The most defeated Christians are those who are spiritually asleep, motivated by self, unteachable, and deluded.

Thus far, this has been an extensive overview of sin and how it operates. As previously discussed, sin is an endless cycle. There is one other simple, but profound, fact concerning sin that we must carefully examine. That fact is: *all sin comes from the sin of idolatry.*

41. What does idolatry mean to you?

The evidence of sin in our lives simply states we have submitted ourselves to another god. Anything can be a *god* to us, but there is *only one God by nature!* **(Galatians 4:8)**

42. What does **Isaiah 45:5-23** and **46:9-12** say about this subject?

God will not tolerate nor take a "backseat" to any other god in our lives.

43. What does **Joshua 24:18-21** say about God in conjunction with the previous statement?

Our God is a jealous God. He has every right to be because of who He is. The real decision in our lives will always be who we are going to submit to.

44. Look up **Matthew 4:3-11** and summarize what transpired between Jesus and the devil.

Hebrews 4:15 tells us Christ was touched with the feeling of our infirmities and in all points tempted like us, yet without sin. The real temptation being presented to Jesus was whether He was going to submit to the will of the Father or the temptation of the devil. Satan used all three types of sin as a means of enticement.

Once again, match the temptation presented to Christ to the three types of sin found in **1 John 2:16**.

A. The bread **(Matthew 4:3)** ____The lust of the flesh
B. Proving who He was **(Matthew 4:5, 6)** ____The lust of the eyes
C. The worldly kingdoms **(Matthew 4:8, 9)** ____The pride of life

We need to understand Satan was using the desires and weaknesses of the flesh to tempt Christ so that He would submit to him. Christ was hungry after 40 days and nights of fasting. Seemingly, it would not appear to be important if Christ submitted to His fleshly needs. However, there was something far greater than Christ's need for physical bread. All of humanity was on the line. If Jesus had submitted to Satan's temptations, He would have allowed His flesh to *become a god.*

Christ was the Son of God. What would have been wrong if He had simply proven it? Christ identity was a fact that would not change. Submitting to this temptation would have been an act of pride. Pride always exalts self on the throne, *making self a god.*

Satan had every right to offer Jesus the kingdoms of the world for they belong to him **(Ephesians 6:12; Daniel 10:10-14; 2 Corinthians 4:4; Ephesians 2:2; John 8:44)**. Christ one day will come and take His rightful position as King of kings and Lord of lords over all, but He knew His Father's plan and timing was of greater importance. He had to go first to the cross as a suffering servant and sacrifice. If Christ had submitted to this test, He would have *made something else god.*

Satan uses our fleshly desires to entice us into bowing before him.

45. Summarize **James 1:14-16** in light of Satan using our fleshly desires to entice us.

When we submit to anything other than God and His ways, we are submitting to another god. Such a submission also reveals that we are walking in unbelief towards the God of heaven. Consider what has been presented to you concerning idolatry.

Who are you submitted to? Jesus recognized there was far more at stake than His own needs and position. We need to realize living outside of God's Word and plan entails far more than what we may assume or observe in the natural. We need to be like Abraham in purpose and vision.

46. What was Abraham really looking for? **(Hebrews 11:8-10)**

We are simply pilgrims and sojourners passing through this world. We hold the position of ambassador. Our citizenship is in heaven. Our focus must take us beyond this world to that which is eternal. Yet, even though we look forward to that day when we see Jesus face to face, we are to redeem the time we have here **(Matthew 5:13-16; 1 Peter 2:11; 2 Corinthians 5:20; Philippians 3:20)**.

Through this study you may have seen that your life has fallen short of true salvation. You recognize you are caught in a cycle of sin and submission to Satan. You are dissatisfied with your life and long for more of Christ. Hopelessness overwhelms you because you feel you cannot overcome. If this is true in your life, or in the life of someone you love, here are three steps to follow which will set you free:

1) *Confession:*
   You must owe up to your sins and confess them to God. You also need to be willing to confess your faults to others **(James 5:16)**. Sharing with others brings healing and release. Having wise counselors also provides a "check and balance" system which becomes a source of protection. (Beware of who you do confess your faults to. Ask the Holy Spirit to bring godly Christians into your life in whom you can trust.)
2) *Repentance:*
   Turn from what you are doing. Purpose in your heart to become right before God and remain so **(Daniel 1:8)**. Ask God to help change your heart, attitude, and direction, and to put all things in perspective. Avoid those people, places, and activities that may be a source of temptation. Surround yourself with good Christian fellowship. Fill your life with God by reading His Word and seeking His face daily in prayer.
3) *Submit:*
   Submit your life totally to God on a daily basis. Yielding to God allows Him to have His way in your life and causes Satan to flee **(James 4:7)**. Present your life as a living sacrifice, willing to be separated from those things which are not pleasing to your Lord. Draw nigh to God and He will draw nigh to you. Allow the searchlight of the Holy Spirit to expose sin. Be willing for Him to cleanse you for His glory and purpose.

If you find it difficult to pray a prayer of confession to the Lord, turn to **Psalm 51** and use it as your guideline. Pray it with all your heart.

Once you become "real" with God, He will begin the work of regeneration in your life.

Regeneration

Regeneration in our lives can be compared to the freshness and life of springtime after winter.

47. What does **2 Corinthians 5:17** mean to you in the light of regeneration?

Regeneration stresses the beginning of new life.

48. Which person of the Godhead does the work of regeneration in our lives? **(Titus 3:5)**

John 3:5, 6 talk about the washing of the Word. In the work of regeneration, a cleansing takes place. Areas that have not been regenerated are not cleansed. An unregenerate man is one who has not been cleansed by the presence of a new life, heart, and spirit.

49. Read **Luke 5:36-39** and describe what would happen if new life was to be put into an unregenerate man?

As Christians, we need to allow the Holy Spirit to come in and regenerate our entire being. All too often we stubbornly hold on to attitudes, thoughts, or lifestyles that need to be changed. Our Heavenly Father is certainly aware of these things in our lives. Remember, we are the temples of God. We either belong to Him or we don't.

50. Look up **Ezekiel 8:5-18**. Give an explanation of these scenes and how they could relate to us as temples of God.

We must give the Lord every area of our lives.

51. Based on the following scriptures what must we turn over to God? **(Psalm 51:10; Romans 12:1, 2)**

Note: Every part of the Christian will be regenerated---spirit, soul, and body. Our responsibility is to present our bodies as a living sacrifice.

52. Read **1 Corinthians 15:31** and **2 Corinthians 10:5**. According to **Romans 8:29** what is the final result of this new life in us?

A regenerated life means the life of Christ will be flowing forth through and from us. We are to be vessels through which the Living Water of the Holy Spirit freely flows. Our lives are to be renewed, refreshed, and filled with godly fruit. The mind of Christ will be formed in us so that our attitudes and thoughts line up with Him. We will be vessels of honor, bringing glory to the Potter. And in the process of regeneration and sanctification, revival will occur.

Prayer: "Oh Lord, I come in the Name of Jesus and repent of those things in my life that are not pleasing to You. Forgive me Lord, and help me to present myself a living sacrifice. I want You to cleanse me, fill me, and use me for Your glory and honor. It is my heart's desire to have You shine through my life. Oh God, thank You for the miraculous and wonderful work of regeneration You are doing in my life. Cause me to walk in singleness of heart and mind before You. I praise You and thank You. In Jesus' Name, Amen."

Section Four

SANCTIFICATION AND REVIVAL

As previously mentioned, both sanctification and consecration are works of holiness. Sanctification is the actual work of being set apart for holiness. Only God can actually sanctify something for His use and glory. **Consecration** is the act of setting something apart for the purpose of holiness.

Circumcision is a good example of consecration. In Israel, circumcision represented being set apart to be God's people. This act involved the cooperation of both God and man. God sets the standards for the act of consecration and man carries it out. We see this in the case of the priests in the Old Testament. God set forth the rules that would govern every area of their lives. They complied with their God-given responsibilities. God accepted them as priests, and sanctified them for His use and glory.

While consecration results in some kind of outward acknowledgment on our part, sanctification is an inward work of the Holy Spirit **(2 Thessalonians 2:13; Romans 15:16; 1 Peter 1:2)**. The result of sanctification is a transformed life. A life that has been transformed is set apart for God's purpose.

1. What did God sanctify according to the following scriptures? **(Exodus 29:43, 44; 31:13; Jeremiah 1:5)**

   Note: God's presence sanctified the temple and all that was in it.

2. As Christians, what are we to God? **(1 Corinthians 3:16, 17 Romans 12:1; Galatians 4:5-7; 2 Timothy 2:20, 21; 1 Peter 2:5, 9; Revelation 1:6)**

   As you can see, we are set apart in position, relationship, and purpose.

3. Describe how God sanctifies us through spiritual means based on the following scriptures. **(John 17:17, 19; Acts 26:18; 1 Corinthians 6:11; Ephesians 5:25-27; Hebrews 10:10; Hebrews 12:10)**

   Christians who fail to experience the fullness of Christ have not been fully sanctified. This can happen if we insist on maintaining a convenient form of Christianity that limits our Christian life to a "comfort zone". Judgment and chastisement are the results. If sanctification is to occur, we must adhere to the Scriptural established standard of righteousness based on who Jesus Christ is!

4. Who is Jesus Christ according to the following scriptures? *(***John 1:1-29; 4:1-26; 6:35 John 11:25, 26; 14:6; 14:27; 15:1-14; Colossians 2:9; Hebrews 1:3-11; 1 John 2:22; 4:2, 3; 4:14, 15)**
5. Who is our example according to **John 13:12-17** and **1 Peter 2:21**?

   Rather than looking to churches, religious leaders, and others for a standard to live up to, we must keep our eyes upon Jesus. We need to avoid establishing Christian standards for others to adhere to. Such a practice leads to self-righteousness and judgmentalism. Neither should we allow ourselves to be put in bondage to other's standards of righteousness!

Mature Christians are aware of the greatness of God and their own pathetic condition before Him. This awareness results in submission and a sacrificial life of service—all the result of outward consecration and inward sanctification.

The Goal of Sanctification

What God has not sanctified, does not belong to Him. Sanctification involves the work of regeneration by the washing of the Word of God **(Ephesians 5:26)**. Our faith will be tried as by fire to produce precious gold **(1 Peter 1:7)**. The finished product results in us becoming a sanctified vessel.

1. What will such a vessel be fit for? **(2 Timothy 2:21)**

In order to be set apart we must be separated from the origin of that which promotes a life contrary to holiness.

2. What are some of the things we need to be separated from? **(2 Peter 1:4; 1 John 2:16; James 4:4)**
3. What does **James 4:4** tell us about a relationship with the world?
4. Why does an association with the world put us at odds with God? **(John 15:18-27)**

We must be purged from the things of the world. This means a complete transformation of one's life.

5. What does it mean to you to be transformed?

<u>Transformation</u> means to change into another form or fashion. The spiritual implication means the change takes place in the inward part of man. The Holy Spirit rearranges priorities, attitudes, desires, and thoughts. These changes line up with the attributes and desires of God. Next, we will examine how holiness is worked into our lives as we submit to it.

Being Temples and Priests of God

Holiness is the work of the Holy Spirit as we submit to God. Our responsibility is to turn from our old ways and yield to the new life God has called us to. This response is not in itself holiness, but rather repentance. We need to beware of falsely thinking we establish holiness in our lives by living a disciplined lifestyle.

6. What does **Romans 10:1-12** say about this attitude?

Self-righteousness develops as we begin to take credit for the work of holiness. Such "holiness" manifests itself in attitudes that are religious, overbearing, dogmatic, and unrealistic. This is not attractive to a dying world already enslaved to an unbending and unloving religious leader known as Satan.

We are called to be temples and priests of our Holy God **(1 Corinthians 3:16, 17; 6:19, 20; 1 Peter 2: 5, 9; Revelation 1:6)**. The temple was the center of the spiritual life of Israel. The priests served as the religious leaders and intercessors between God and

His people. God designed the temple, the clothing, and the procedures of the priests. (See **Exodus** & **Leviticus**)

As New Testament temples and priests we serve in a similar capacity in the kingdom of God.

7. What was the purpose of the temple? **(Exodus 29:42-46)**
8. What sanctifies the temple of God? **(Exodus 29:43)**
9. What is the significance of Christians being God's temple today? **(Acts 7:44-50; 17:24, 25)**

As temples, God meets with us and establishes an intimate relationship with us as His dwelling place. We commune with Him, learning His will and desire for our lives.

As priests, we must ensure that the temple of God remains holy.

10. How must we respond to sin in our lives? **(1 Corinthians 6:15-18; 2 Corinthians 6:14-18; Acts 15:20**, **29; 1 Thessalonians 4:3; 5:22; 1 Peter 2:11).**
11. As New Testament priests, what do we need to be spiritually clothed in according to **1 Peter 5:5**?
12. Look up **Exodus 30:10** and **Leviticus 4**. What was one of the major responsibilities of the priests of the Old Testament?
13. As New Testament priests, what should be our sacrifices to the Lord?

Hebrews 13:15-16
Romans 12:1
Philippians 4:18
1 Peter 2:5

As priests we have a high calling. It is high because we serve a Holy God. As temples we need to be a place in which God can reside. His presence will set us apart in this present world, and our lives will bear good fruit. If we fail to maintain both of these holy positions in God, our lives will be ineffective. Our fellowship will become uncertain and our direction confused. If we discover ourselves in this condition, there is one solution. It is *revival.*

True Revival

Preachers today are calling for revival. True, the Church desperately needs a refilling of the Holy Spirit and revival! True revival means to be brought back to life or consciousness. It brings hope of renewed health, excitement, and spirit. Effectiveness springs from a revived life that cannot be counterfeited.

14. What would revival mean to you and the Church today?

As I sought the Lord concerning revival, He revealed to me that true revival begins in the heart. If the Church as a whole is to experience revival, it must begin in each individual's heart. Large numbers of people who give lip service to revival does not necessarily give evidence of it, *but rather, evidence of revival is changed lives.*

15. Look up the following scriptures and explain what needs to take place for revival to occur. *(***2 Chronicles 7:14; Psalm 80:17-19; 119:24-40; Proverbs 29:18)**

Note: the word <u>quicken</u> is another word for revive.

Revival starts with repentance. It is God who meets us in our brokenness and revives us. As He leads us through death to self, new life springs forth. His Word cleanses us in preparation for sanctification. We gain a vision of who God is and His purpose for us in His kingdom.

16. Is it possible for an entire Body of believers to experience revival?

Yes, it is possible! It happened to Nineveh in the Book of Jonah, and it happened to Israel.

17. Turn to **2 Kings 18:1-6** and **2 Chronicles 29-31**. Explain what took place for revival to occur in Israel.

In the case of Hezekiah, much of what happened was a reformation, but reformation often comes out of a revival of leadership. If America is going to survive, there must be true revival of God's people. Christians need spiritual awakening, and must be open to the scrutiny of the Holy Spirit. They need to repent and eliminate every trace of idolatry. As believers, each of us must get serious about our high calling, spiritual condition, and responsibility towards our Holy God.

True revival is ongoing. Christians need to be revived on a continuing basis by the Living Water of God. This is necessary if we are to be a sanctified vessel, consecrated and fit for the Master's use **(2 Corinthians 4:16).**

A Consecrated Life

As previously stated, <u>consecrated</u> means the act of setting something apart. It is God who establishes the acts of consecration, and it is man's responsibility to comply. Such consecration results in a life that is set apart for God's use and glory. This life is our reasonable service and not something we take credit for. Our consecrated and obedient lifestyle opens the way for and reveals the work of sanctification.

18. Read **Exodus 29** and explain the acts that took place for the consecration of the priests.

The water represents regeneration or cleansing. The clothing physically set the priests apart, and was representative of a holy calling. The oil represented anointing or being designated for a specific purpose. The sacrifice served as the means to cover the priests' sins in order for God to accept their service.

As priests who make up a living priesthood, we are already accepted as such because of the shed blood of Christ. We have the Holy Spirit who revives, regenerates, and anoints us with authority and power. In the midst of such work, we become sanctified vessels fit for the master's use. The result is a life set apart from the world, and ultimately exalts God Almighty.

Something else to be considered is the salt used in the Old Testament that was sprinkled over the meat to be sacrificed. It served as a covenant **(Leviticus 2:12-16)**. We are called to be the salt of the world **(Matthew 5:13)**. We are part of a new covenant because of the blood of Christ **(1 Corinthians 11:23-32)**. Note: the word <u>testament</u> means covenant. If we fail to respond to the call of holiness, we have failed to keep our part of the new covenant. In other words, our salt (life) will lose its savor.

The call today needs to go beyond mere revival or holiness...it needs to be an urgent call of warning. If I were to make such a call it would be, *"People of God arise! Arise from your sleep, your complacency and your lack of love. Arise from religious works and games. Arise to the call of God, to holiness, to serve, and to overcome!"*

Section Five

SAINTS ALIVE!

Since the Holy Spirit is the mighty source behind the work of holiness, we need to know who He is and His purpose in our lives. First of all, He is part of the Godhead **(1 John 5:7)**. He is a person—not a force or power.

We read in chapter **five** of the Book of **Acts** of Ananias and Sapphira's lying to the Holy Spirit. You can only lie to a *person*, not a power or force!

The work of the Holy Spirit can be symbolized by various elements of nature.

1. In the following scriptures describe the elements symbolic of the Holy Spirit and how such work relates to our spiritual lives.

   John 7:37-39
   Isaiah 4:4; Revelation 4:4, 5
   John 3:8; Acts 2:2
   Psalm 72:6; Isaiah 18:4

   Oil, a dove, a voice, and a seal are also representative of the work of the Holy Spirit in our lives **(Psalm 45:7; Matthew 25:1-13; 1 John 2:27; Matthew 3:14; 10:20; Hebrews 3:7-11; Ephesians 1:13, 14)**. He anoints, comforts, directs, and seals us as special possessions of God. He equips us with authority and power to overcome.

2. According to the following scriptures, what are some of the responsibilities of the Holy Spirit in the lives of believers? **(Matthew 3:11** (Refer to **Acts 2:1-13**); **John 16:7-15; Romans 8:26, 27; 1 Corinthians 12; Matthew 10:19, 20)**
3. What is the main purpose for the gifts of the Holy Spirit? **(1 Corinthians 14:26)**

   God is a God of harmony and order. His purpose for the gifts of the Spirit is to edify the Body of believers.

4. What does edify mean?

   Godly edification results in spiritual growth of the Body. To ensure edification all conduct within the Body must line up with God's Word.

   It is the responsibility of each of us to test each gift to ensure all things are done according to scripture. Abuse of these gifts has turned many people off to the work of the Holy Spirit. We need to be responsible for what transpires in our local churches.

   Today, there are many Christians who seek after personal prophecies, signs, and wonders. Some live from personal prophecy to personal prophecy. This is a dangerous practice.

5. What did Jesus say about false prophets, signs, and wonders occurring in the end days? **(Matthew 24:4, 5, 11, 23, 24)**
6. What are Christians to seek after? **(Psalm 27:8; Proverbs 8:17; Matthew 6:33; Colossians 3:1, 2)**

Scripture reveals the multitudes were more interested in their stomachs than in the Person of Jesus. On the contrary, we also see that those who sought out Jesus, experienced His greatness. They became part of His plan for man, rather than simply bystanders in the crowd. Today, many Christians have become bystanders to the life Jesus is calling them to. Real commitment and dedication cannot be established in our lives by miracles, but rather by faith in God. We are not called to a life of ongoing prophecies and miracles, but to a life of service and self-sacrifice. Once Jesus is in His rightful position as Lord of our lives, we will begin to experience the abundant life. This life is lived in the power of the Holy Spirit.

7. Look up **Romans 8:14** and **Galatians 5:18**. Who must be leading us if we are to be a child of God?

Being led by the Holy Spirit is a walk of faith and obedience. This walk enables us to enter into an abundant, powerful, and fruitful life for the glory of our Lord.

The Walk of Faith

8. What does it mean to you to walk by faith and not by sight? **(2 Corinthians 5:7)**

We talk a lot about faith and the people who displayed great faith such as those in **Hebrews 11**.

9. What was faith able to do? **(Hebrews 11:33-35)**
10. What were the consequences that confronted these heroes of faith? **(Hebrews 11:36, 37)**
11. What compliment does **Hebrews 11:38** pay to those who walked by great faith?

Jesus told us faith could move mountains **(Matthew 21:21)**. Remember, it is not our faith that moves the mountain, but rather our great God who moves them. Faith allows God to be God. Faith trusts God to the point of total confidence that whatever happens is for His glory and our benefit. Such trust is not blind for it rests on the Solid Rock, Jesus Christ.

12. What is another virtue of faith? **(1 Corinthians 13:13)**
13. What does real faith protect in our Christian lives? **(Ephesians 6:16)**

According to historians, the ancient shield could protect every bodily part. Men could kneel behind their shields for both protection and advancement. Faith protects the whole of our spiritual lives. It is not only necessary for salvation and to please God, but also for the work of holiness *(***2 Thessalonians 2:13)**.

Contrary to popular belief, Christianity is not a life free of problems and challenges. Jesus' words dispel this "candy store fantasy". (See **Acts 14:22**.)

14. What did He say in **John 16:33**?

Tribulation is part of the process necessary for sanctification. It is in tribulation our faith is tested.

15. In what way is our faith tested according to **1 Peter 1:7**?

The fiery tests of our faith produce maturity. Our faith is established and refined by testing and trial **(Colossians 1:20-23)**.

16. Look up **Malachi 3:1-3** and **1 Corinthians 3:11-15**. What does it say in regard to the test of fire?

Remember, worthy vessels go through the fire. The key to overcoming the trials of life rests in our faith being founded in Jesus alone. By withstanding we become more valuable to our Maker.

Naturally, most of us want to avoid the fires of tribulation. Our flesh desires the promises without the price; however, if the Spirit leads us, there will be fiery trials on the "sanctification road". May we follow where He leads in complete faith and trust.

17. What qualities come forth in our lives due to different trials? **(2 Corinthians 4:7-10; James 1:2-4)**
18. What promise can we be assured of if we keep our eyes on Jesus? **(Romans 8:35-39)**

Maturity in Christ is brought forth through the fiery trials of life. Maturity is also another word for perfection. Such perfection is not divine perfection, but instead represents ongoing growth in our relationship with Christ.

Because there are varied responses to the walk of faith, we need to consider our own reply to the call to holiness.

The Responses

The Lord showed me there are four different responses to the walk of faith. Jesus Christ's command to all Christians is, *"Follow Me."* Following Jesus requires love, commitment, and faith. Many well-meaning Christians fall to the wayside, take detours, or cease to hear His call. It is in every day living that our walk of faith is put to the test. Falling to the wayside, taking detours, and failure to hear Jesus' voice does not happen suddenly, but day by day, decision by decision.

In helping me to understand these four responses, the Lord showed me a fence. On one side of the fence was the world. On the other side was a mountain with a narrow path whose route and destination could not be seen. Surrounding the fence were four distinct groups of people. The first group represented the world. This worldly group was distinctly on the worldly side of the fence. The second group of people stood on the fence. They were trying to strike a balance between the world and Christianity. The third group held onto the fence and simply faced the mountain. They were aware of their need to let go of the fence in order to have a life in God, but fear prevented them. The fourth group of people were individuals who by faith were beginning to embark upon the unknown path.

19. Which of these groups do you think you fit in? Is it the fourth group walking by faith? Explain your answer.

Christians in America spend much time talking about faith, but few understand what walking by faith really means. This is because of our affluent society. Walking by faith costs. Jesus told the rich young ruler to sell all he had and give it to the poor. The worldly cost was too high for the young man to consider. How many of us would respond in like manner? If we were to suddenly face great loss or persecution because of our faith, how many of us could stand?

There are certain requirements given in scripture for us to walk the walk of faith in Jesus Christ.

20. Based on the following scriptures what are the requirements?

Luke 14:25-33
Galatians 2:20
Matthew 22:36-40
Romans 8:4-14
1 John 2:3-6

If we are to walk by faith, we must be willing to forsake all, including self and the world. We must be in obedience, totally motivated by the love of God.

Walking by faith involves a battle.

21. Look up the following scriptures and explain them in conjunction with the previous statement. **(1 Timothy 1:4, 5, 19; 6:12; Hebrews 4:1-11; 1 John 5:4; Jude 3)**

The walk of faith totally rests in God. It does not balance between the world and Christianity. It is a walk determined by a sold-out life to Christ. It is a walk that goes forward. Those walking it are confident in their God.

22. Are you walking by faith? (Yes or No)

If your walk depends on sight or understanding a matter before you act, you are holding onto something that will not stand in the end. Religious positions, recognition, and relationships will also fail. All these things are the wrong foundation.

23. Are you the type who wants both the world and Christianity?

If so, remember you cannot serve two masters. Are you playing religious games? You need to know God is not impressed; He is still looking at your heart.

Those who have paid the price and are walking by faith will tell you it is well worth it. They are the people whose transformed lives are making a difference. They not only know how to rest in God, they know Him in a personal and intimate way.

If you are not walking by faith, now is a good time to repent. **Romans 14:23** tells us whatever is not of faith is sin. Let us examine our lives to see whether or not we are in the true faith **(2 Corinthians 13:5)**.

The Living Water

Jesus said, "come unto...learn of me" in **Matthew 11:28-30**. In **John 15** He describes His relationship with the believer as the vine to the branch. His command and desire for us is to abide in Him. This is the only way our lives will bear fruit for God's glory.

John the Baptist stated in **Matthew 3:11** that Jesus Christ would baptize us with the Holy Ghost.

24. What did Jesus compare the Holy Spirit to in **John 7:37-39**?

The Holy Spirit is the Living Water. Without water life cannot exist. Without water productive land becomes a desert. Without water there is no hope for life and beauty.

As the spiritual living water, the Holy Spirit, produces life, beauty, and spiritual fruit in the Christian. If our spiritual lives are to be productive, the Holy Spirit must immerse us. The dams of self must come down so the river of life can flow freely into every area of our life. This immersion is known as the baptism of the Holy Spirit. This baptism is not the same as the born again experience anymore than our water baptism is the same as salvation.

When we receive Jesus into our lives, we receive eternal life as a result of the new birth. John the Baptist distinctly stipulated that Jesus is the one who baptizes the believer with the Holy Spirit **(Matthew 3:11)**.

Jesus, as our Vine or life source, brings forth the Living Water throughout our lives. This Living Water enables us to produce fruit.

The purpose of the baptism of the Holy Spirit is for preparation and power. The preparation involves the responsibility of proclaiming the Gospel of Jesus Christ. The power entails the authority that is necessary to establish the validity of the Gospel.

The Gospel of **Mark** deals with this authority or power.

25. What does it say in **Mark 16:15-18** about this subject?

God does not make this power available to the believer without reason or cause. We need the power from above to be both effective in the kingdom of heaven and to endure to the end in these last days.

26. According to **Galatians 5:22-23** what is the fruit of the Spirit?

The manifestation of the fruit of the Spirit is a transformed life. This life displays conformity to the very image of Jesus. Such a life is set apart to produce results for the kingdom of heaven. When those who are lost and who are seeking God come in contact with such a life, they will be drawn to the One who made it possible.

We need to be Spirit filled and Spirit led. We need to walk by faith with a desire to have and be all that God intends for us. We must ask, seek, and knock to enter into such a life **(Matthew 7:7, 8)**.

The key to holy living is found in the Holy Spirit. As we allow Him to move in our lives, He will lead us into the very presence of God. We need to carefully guard the freedom of the Spirit in our lives, and not allow anyone or anything to rob us of it. Our life before God is our sole responsibility. Pray to be sensitive to the Holy Spirit, and learn the Scriptures as they are the Christian's final authority. When we stand before God, we will not be able to hide behind any other person or religious system.

If we are to be holy, then we must establish an intimate relationship with our holy God. The reality of His holiness becomes evident and life changing as we abide in His presence.

The Presence of God

We are the temples of the Holy Spirit. As a result, we have the very presence of God in us. As we learn to walk by faith, His presence becomes evident, and we experience love, joy, and peace. In His presence we become conformed to the image of Christ. We find rest, assurance, and strength. There is a way in which to enter into the very presence of God.

27. What is this way in which we can enter the presence of God? **(John 14:6)**

28. Who is the High Priest who leads us to the very throne room of God? **(Hebrews 4:15, 16)**
29. Explain in what other ways we can be brought into the presence of God. **(Isaiah 6; 2 Corinthians 12:1-10)**
30. What kind of heart condition will we need to see God? **(Matthew 5:8)**
31. What type of relationship must we have with God? **(Romans 8:14-17)**

God wants to be our Father, but we must desire to be His children. All relationships are two-fold in response and responsibility. Our response should be one of love, awe, and respect. Our responsibility is that of obedience.

32. What did our holy God tell Moses in **Exodus 3:1-5**?
33. What did God almost do to His servant Moses in **Exodus 4:18-26**?

We serve a holy, mighty God.

34. What do **1 John 1:6, 7** and **3:22** say about obedience and walking in the light?

As we become responsible to our position as God's children, we realize we must have a right heart condition. Our attitudes reflect reverence and fear of the Lord. Our entrance into His presence reflects knowledge of His holiness. Such an approach comes from preparation of our soul (the mind) and our spirit (the heart). This preparation occurs through praise and worship.

Praise and Worship

35. Look up the words praise and worship. Write the definition of each.

Praise and worship are a vital part of a Christian's life. Praise prepares the soul to enter into the presence of God. David showed examples of true praise.

36. Look up **2 Samuel 6:1-9** and explain how praising God benefited the people of Israel.
37. What does **Hebrews 13:15** say about praise?

Giving praise to God means exalting God by recognizing who He is. Recognition of who God is prepares the mind. Praise can be offered to God individually or in a group. Through praise the Holy Spirit will manifest Himself for the purpose of ministering to us.

Worship prepares our hearts to enter into the presence of God. Worship denotes an act of homage. It indicates service. Through worship we subject ourselves to God in adoration and respect.

38. What did Jesus say about true worship? **(John 4:24)**

Worship is between God and the individual. The places of worship, religious acts, or traditions have nothing to do with true worship. Worship must be done with the heart.

If you have never experienced God's presence, why not seek Him in brokenness and sincerity right now. God will meet you in the midst of your failures and shortcomings. God desires your fellowship. Remember, Jesus died to provide a way for you to enter this intimate fellowship with the Father.

39. What are the promises to those who seek God? **(Psalm 69:32; Lamentations 3:25; Hebrews 11:6)**

In Conclusion

To justly explore the subject of holiness would take many more pages! What we need to understand is that God wants to wholly sanctify spirit, soul, and body to preserve us blameless unto the coming of our Lord **(1 Thessalonians 5:23)**.

The reality of holiness comes as we realize the holiness of our God. This reality can only be realized in Jesus. After all, we must have His mind to see God in His majesty, we must possess His Spirit to hear His voice, and we must have a consecrated life to walk out the life He has called us to. Clearly, Jesus must become our all in all. We must have a right relationship with Him to understand our position of holiness in Him, the work of holiness in us by the Spirit of God, and the reality of holiness because of His life in us.

Fill out the following chart. This shows our position in Christ. For instance, the first example shows Jesus as the Word, and we are His epistles. Consider how the work of God is completed in every Christian who comes to Jesus, as he or she gives way to the Spirit, and enters into communion with the Father.

POSITIONAL RELATIONSHIP OF MAN TO CHRIST

MAN	CHRIST
1. ____________ **2 Corinthians 3:2-3**	1. Word **John 1:1**
2. ____________ **Ephesians 4:12**	2. God **John 1:1**
____________ **2 Corinthians 3:6**	
____________ **Revelation 1:6**	
____________ **1 Corinthians 3:16**	
3. R____________ **Ephesians 1:7**	3. Lamb of God **John 1:29**
4. Reflectors **Matthew 5:15**	4. Light **John 1:4, 9**
5. ____________ **John 10:11**	5. Good Shepherd **John 10:11**
6. ____________ **Matthew 5:13**	6. Bread of Life **John 6:35**
7. ____________ **2 Timothy 2:20 & 21**	7. Giver of Living Water **John 4:13, 14**

8. ____________________
1 Peter 2:11

9. S____________________
Matthew 7:7

10. ____________________
John 15:2

11. ____________________
John 15:14

12. ____________________
Matthew 5:9

13. ____________________
1 Corinthians 12

14. ____________________
1 Peter 2:5 & 9

15. ____________________
2 Corinthians 5:1

____
1 Corinthians 3:16

16. Defendant
1 John 2:1-2

17. ____________________
Luke 16:1-13

Special People
1 Peter 2:9

18. ____________________
2 Timothy 2:3

____
2 Corinthians 5:20

____
Philippians 3:20

8. The Way
John 14:6

9. The Truth
John 14:6

10. The Vine
John 15:1

11. Friend
John 15:13

12. Prince of Peace
Isaiah 9:6

13. The Head
Colossians 1:18

14. High Priest
Hebrews 7:24-26

15. Foundation
1 Corinthians 3:11

16. ____________________
1 John 2:1 & 2

____
Hebrews 8:6

Intercessor
Hebrews 7:25

17. Lord
Matthew 7:21-23

18. King

19. ______________________________
2 Corinthians 5:17

20. ______________________________
Ephesians 2:10

Finished Product
Philippians 1:6

19. Creator
Colossians 1:16

20. Author & Finisher of our Faith
Hebrews 12:2

Is Christ your all in all? I pray God will raise a standard of His holiness in your life and in the Church that no one can deny. Time is short. As God's people, we His saints, need to stir ourselves up and allow the Holy Spirit to prepare us to meet our Bridegroom, Jesus Christ!

HOW TO SERVE GOD

INTRODUCTION

How to serve God should be a question each Christian must prayerfully examine and pursue. There are so many assumptions, false images, and unrealistic standards surrounding the Christian realm about this subject, that confusion and failure seem to plague those who truly want to serve God.

What does it mean to serve God according to His perception? This Bible study will hopefully tear down all misconceptions about service and establish the right attitudes and understanding. It is our desire to break the conventional modes and present the scriptural truth that will set the servant of God free to pursue his or her calling.

We pray this study will prove to be a valuable guide as you begin to seek the answer to this vital question. We trust that our faithful teacher, the Holy Spirit, will personally unveil the answer to this important question in your search.

God bless you.

Chapter One

DEFINING SERVICE

1. Define what it means to you to serve God.

   One of the most misunderstood plights of a Christian comes in the area of true service. Some view service as a series of religious deeds. Others have images of grandeur that never materialize. Both perceptions often create frustration, jealousy, anxiety, anger, and judgmentalism. Such service becomes a great burden, rather than a means of expressing love to the Lord of lords. As joy eludes the believer, Christian service becomes a millstone around his or her neck resulting in skepticism.

2 Look up the following examples of service: Cain, **Genesis 4:2-13**; King Saul, **1 Samuel 18:10-12** refer to **1 Samuel 28:6-20**; the Pharisees, **Matthew 12:1-11** and Martha, **Luke 10:38-42**. What one common denominator is missing in each example of service?

   People who desire to serve God often begin with the wrong perspective of acceptable service. The question of true service to God does not begin with who we are, but with who God is.

   We need to intimately know the God we serve. Although Cain, King Saul, and the Pharisees, had a *form of service*, they failed *to do acceptable service.* They did not understand the God they were serving. As a result, their deeds became stumbling blocks and ended in disobedience. God rejected some of their overtures.

   In **2 Timothy 1:12**, the Apostle Paul stated, "...for I know whom I have believed,..." God's ways are higher than man's ways **(Isaiah 55:8, 9)**. Acceptable service must be in compliance with the nature of God.

3. What are some of God attributes? **(1 John 2:29; 4:7, 8; 1 Peter 1:15, 16; Titus 3:5; Psalm 25:8; 1 Corinthians 1:9; 2 Corinthians 8:9; Romans 9:22, 23; Job 26:14)**
4. Explain how God's characteristics would influence a life of service.

   A servant is no greater than his master, but likewise, he or she must be a representative of his Lord.

5. How does **2 Corinthians 3:18** confirm this truth?

   In order to serve Jesus, we must catch a vision of Him in glory. Oswald Chambers made this comment in *Still Higher for His Highest*, "You never know Jesus Christ, and Him crucified, unless you have seen Him transfigured in all His transcendent majesty and glory; the cross to you is nothing but the cross of a martyr."

   The cross may arouse us emotionally, but the revelation of Him in glory will help us grasp the reality of our sin. Christ gave up the glories of heaven to die on the cross for our sin. The cross was the judgment of God upon sin, but the sacrifice of Jesus was the reality of God's love, grace, mercy, and holiness extended to man. We must know Christ in His majesty to gain insight into the extent of God's service to mankind. Our service to Him will never exceed His commitment to man, but it must reach beyond mere man's ways and perception to become acceptable and honorable.

We must therefore, sit at Jesus' table and learn of Him. We must seek after Him in spirit and truth. We must desire to know Him in greater ways in order to ensure pleasing service.

6. What lesson can we learn from **Matthew 7:21-27**?

Chapter Two

PRECONCEIVED NOTIONS

True service can only begin when preconceived notions about ministry are discarded. For instance, the word, minister or ministry, means a servant, deacon, or to do service. The popular consensus about these two words is associated with "great ministries" which are seen and known by many. The simplicity of these words is therefore lost. Many who sense a call early in their Christian lives become discouraged. Their zeal is turned into discouragement, and their newfound love ends in spiritual complacency because of unrealistic notions about ministry.

The problem with looking at ministry from a worldly perspective is that we miss the reality of the One who calls us. Jesus calls every believer into ministry.

1. What did Christ say about this call in relationship to sheep in **John 10:26, 27**?
2. What did Paul say about the body of believers in **Romans 12:4-8** and **1 Corinthians 12:1-31?**

Much of the conception about ministry has been inspired by worldly standards. These standards are based on education, positions, titles, and numbers.

3. What does **1 Corinthians 1:25-28** say about God's choices?

The Apostle Paul and Luke the writer of the Gospel of **Luke** and **Acts** were educated men, but how about the other disciples? Peter, John, Andrew, and James were fishermen. Matthew was a tax collector. Most of them would fit the qualifications found in **1 Corinthians**, but would they be considered acceptable servants today to the visible Church?

There was one common denominator found in the lives of these men. They were busy working. Peter and Andrew were casting nets into the sea, James and John were mending nets, and Matthew was busy in his profession when Jesus called each of them to follow Him (**Matthew 4:18-22, 9:9; Mark 1:16-20; Luke 5:1-11; John 1:35-51)**.

4. Look up the following scriptures and explain what each of these men were doing when God called them.

Moses **(Exodus 3)**
Gideon **(Judges 6:11-15)**
King David **(1 Samuel 16:10-13)**
Elisha **(1 Kings 19:19-21)**
Amos **(Amos 1:1)**

God calls servants from personal obligations into service to Him. Some were reluctant, but others saw great rewards beyond their personal responsibilities.

5. What did Paul say about laziness among believers in **2 Thessalonians 3:6-10**?
6. What did Paul say about those who do labor in the harvest field? **(1 Thessalonians 5:12, 13)**

Another preconceived notion involves what God requires from His servants.

7. Look up the Scriptures and explain how each individual's idea of service turned out to be wrong in God's eyes.

Cain **(Genesis 4:2-8)**
Sarah **(Genesis 16; 17:15-19; 21:1-10)**
Aaron's sons-Nadab and Abihu **(Leviticus 10:1-3)**
Judas Iscariot **(John 12:2-8** refer to **John 18:1-9)**
The Pharisees **(Matthew 15:1-9** refer to **Matthew 23)**
Peter **(Matthew 16:13-23; 17:1-7)**
Ananias & Sapphira **(Acts 5:1-11)**
Saul (Apostle Paul) **(Acts 7:58-60; 9:1-9)**
Simon the Sorcerer **(Acts 8:9-24)**

Three of these men offered wrong sacrifices to God.

8. What are acceptable sacrifices Christians can offer to God? **(Psalms 51:17; 116:17; Romans 12:1, 2 Philippians 4:15-18)**

If you take the example of Sarah, you find a woman taking matters into her own hands. She tried to fulfill the promises of God in her own way.

9. What does **Genesis 18:14** say about God's ability to fulfill His plan and promises?

King David waited many years before he took his rightful place as king *(***1 Samuel 16** refer to **2 Samuel 5***)*. Waiting on the Lord is necessary. Acceptable service to God is based on His plan and timing. Often servants find themselves waiting.

10. What promise do we have in **Isaiah 40:31**?
11. What promise was fulfilled in the life of Simeon after he had waited for it? **(Luke 2:22-32)**

It is important Christians learn to wait upon the Lord. Christians who receive prophecies or dreams concerning ministries need to put such revelations on the shelf until God fulfills them. Many servants have made the mistake of trying to fulfill God's plans in their own power according to their own take on it. They get ahead of God and are met with disaster.

It is important for ministers of God to keep ministry in perspective. Acceptable ministry involves serving others. This type of service comes out in practical ways. It has sensitivity to the plight of others. It concludes with action to minister to hurting or needy individuals.

12. What does **James 4:17** say about those who know what is right, but will not do it?

Judas Iscariot and the Pharisees' means of service were comprised of religious acts.

13. What did Jesus say to the Pharisees in **Matthew 15:8-9**?

Man's religion and its acts are like a seashell on the shore. It may echo the ocean, but it is not the ocean. It does not contain the power, the beauty, or the life the ocean contains.

Christianity is a relationship with God. This relationship can be compared to the ocean, for it inspires life, beauty, and power. The heartbeat of this relationship is not religious deeds, but godly love.

The real problem of Ananias and Sapphira was not the issue of money; but lying about the content of their service to God. They were trying to give an impression of service to others without paying the necessary price.

14. What did Jesus say in **Luke 14:26-35** about counting the cost?
15. What example was given to us concerning true giving in **Mark 12:41-44**?

The widow gave it all to God. Jesus said of her that she had cast in more than all who gave. It was not the quantity of the widow's giving, but the quality. She gave it all, and her giving came out of a heart response of faith towards God.

16. What should the real motivation be behind giving to the Lord? **(2 Corinthians 9:7)**
17. Read **Acts 2:45; 4:31-37; 6:1** refer to **Philippians 4:15-18; James 1:27** and **Matthew 25:32-46**. Explain how true giving is a part of our life of service.

Simon, the Sorcerer was a man supposedly saved out of witchcraft under the ministry of Philip. He continued on with Philip in service. Simon saw the power of the Holy Spirit and offered money for it.

18. What was Peter's response to the money proposition? **Acts 8:20-24**

God gives us His life and power because of His love and grace **(John 3:16; Ephesians 2:8-9)**. This life and power cannot be bought, earned, or obtained by our own attempts. Church attendance, Bible reading, praying, and good works do not guarantee entrance into heaven.

19. What ensures a person's entrance into heaven? **(Romans 8:1; 10:9, 10; 1 John 5:10-13)**

When we study the disciples' lives, we see a mixture of attitudes toward physical force.

20. What was Jesus' attitude about this concept? **(Matthew 26:52-55; Luke 9:51-56)**

There is a growing belief that Christians must set up an earthly kingdom before Christ's return.

21. Who will set up Christ's kingdom when He comes back? **(Revelation 19:11-20:6)**

Peter and Paul displayed zeal to serve God. Zeal means eager and ardent interest in the pursuit of something.

22. What does Paul say about a wrong type of zeal in **Romans 10:2-4**?
23. What was the end result of Peter's zeal towards Christ? **(Matthew 26:30-34)**
24. What did Paul's zeal towards God result in according to **Acts 9:1-9** and **Philippians 3:4-6**?

People can be zealous and sincere about serving God, but be totally wrong. Zeal without knowledge and understanding is dangerous.

Like Peter on the Mount Transfiguration, we can put our "foot in our mouth." If we lack understanding in spiritual matters, we can easily miss the eternal purpose behind events.

25. How can we ensure a right perspective in ministry? **(Matthew 17:8)**

The right perspective of ministry is Jesus Christ. As God in the flesh, we sense His majesty that calls us higher in a life of service. As the Son of Man, we have an example of acceptable ministry on earth. As the Son of God, we have before us the life we must possess and the image we must conform to in order to validate all service. As our sacrifice on the cross, we sense the sacrificial service that must come from a heart of love.

Any service that does not express Jesus Christ is not acceptable ministry. Christian ministry is always minimized when Jesus is not expressed or seen in a life.

Acceptable ministry is born out of a relationship with God through Jesus Christ. Ministry that is void of this relationship will be void of the life of Christ. Ministry without the life is nothing but an empty shell that has a form of righteousness, but lacks the power **(2 Timothy 3:5)**.

What does your life of service say about your relationship with God? Do you have a valid relationship with the Creator of the Universe? If you do, you will know how to serve Him based on who He is, and not according to preconceived, self-serving, worldly notions.

Chapter Three

THE RELATIONSHIP

1. Who is the greatest in the kingdom of God? **(Matthew 20:25-28)**

    The opposite of servant is Lord. Lordship means He owns us and we must be available to do service on any ground.

    Servant signifies bondage. Words such as minister, attendant, deacon, and bondman are synonyms. Servitude to Jesus means subjection without bondage. It implies a true freedom that enables one to be all that God intends him or her to be.

2. What does **Galatians 5:1** tell us?

    A life of Christian service can also be compared to the duties of a soldier. Soldiers endure hardships and the rigors of war **(2 Timothy 2:3, 4)**.

3. What are we fighting against? **(Ephesians 6:12; 1 Peter 5:8; 2 Corinthians 10:3-5)**

    Like servants, soldiers have no rights except what has been bestowed on them by those in authority. Both the servant's and soldier's needs are all provided for.

4. What kind of provision does Christ offer to His servants and soldiers? (**John 1:4; 6:35; 10:10; 14:1, 2; Romans 8:17; Ephesians 6:14-18; Philippians 4:19 Luke 10:19)**

    Servants in the Old Testament were considered possessions **(Deuteronomy 15)**. **Titus 2:14** and **1 Peter 2:9** refer to believers as peculiar people. Peculiar in Greek means special possessions. This shows us Christians are possessions of Jesus Christ.

    Some servants were in their position because of debt or captivity due to war.

5. With this in mind, relate how this is applicable to position of servitude for a Christian. **(Romans 5:6-21; 6:11-23; 1 Corinthians 6:20; 7:23)**

    Man is enslaved to someone. Either he or she is serving Satan or the person is serving Christ. Like the servants and saints of the Old Testament, believers must choose who they are going to serve.

6. How does **Joshua 24:14, 15, 19, 20** confirmed this truth?

    We will never exceed our Lord in service, but can our response of ministry be any less than our Master's?

Excuses

Like Moses, some Christians convince themselves that others are more capable of serving than they are.

7. According to Scripture, what kind of service is acceptable to Christ? **(Matthew 25:43-45; Galatians 6:1-5-9; James 1:26, 27; 2:1-9; 5:13-16)**
8. With the previous Scriptures in mind can any one person serve Christ? (Yes or No)

When it comes to reasons for not responding to Christ's salvation or to Christian ministry, human beings never run out of excuses.

9. Look up the following scriptures and identify the excuses found in each response. *(***Exodus 4:10;**
Judges 6:15; Proverbs 22:13; Jeremiah 1:6, 7; Matthew 25:24, 25, 41-46; Luke 14:18-20)

<u>Excuse</u> means to justify a wrong. Our reasons for not serving are excuses because God is the One who does the work. The Father draws, Jesus invites and saves, while the Holy Spirit convicts of sin, regenerates, and sanctifies **(John 6:44; 7:27-39; 14:26; 16:7-14; Ephesians 1:13, 14; Romans 15:16; Titus 3:5)**. An individual is simply an available clay vessel who must be open, separated, submissive, and obedient to the Potter's work in and through them **(Romans 9:18-23; 2 Corinthians 4:6, 7; 2 Timothy 2:19-22)**.

10. Since God does all the work, what excuse will stand justified in His presence?
11. What was the end result of those who did not repent of their excuses? **(Matthew 25:26-30, 40-46; Luke 14:16-24 refer to Revelation 19:1-9.)**

Acceptable service comes out of a correct foundation. This foundation is comprised of a right motivation, attitude, and response.

12. What should our motivation be? **(1 Corinthians 13)**
13. What kind of attitude ensures pleasing service? **(Ephesians 6:5-7)**
14. What should our response be towards others? **(Ephesians 5:21; Romans 12:1-21)**
15. What response should we want to hear from our Lord? **(Luke 19:17)**

It is important we examine each area. Any service that does not have these three ingredients will not be honored. Let us now examine these areas.

Chapter Four

A RIGHT MOTIVATION

1. What did Paul say in **2 Corinthians 5:14**?

   Paul's motivation in ministry was the love of God. The cross of Christ inspired this love. Christ's cross revealed both God's love and righteousness.

   In the light of God's righteousness, Paul became aware of his sin. In his letter to Timothy, he referred to himself as a chief of sinners. He shared with others how he had zealously persecuted believers before his conversion **(Acts 21:39-22:10)**. He knew he deserved hell. His keen awareness of God's righteousness and wrath made him acknowledge the extent of God's grace and mercy that was made available at the cross **(1 Timothy 1:12-16)**.

2. How does **Romans 5:20** confirm the above statement?

   Paul knew he could obtain forgiveness through Jesus Christ. He loved Jesus because he knew Christ first loved him. He was sold out to the knowledge and message of Christ crucified.

   The love of and for Christ compelled Paul to share Jesus with others. He desired to see people make it to heaven. He overlooked human frailties and became all things to all men in hope of winning a few **(1 Corinthians 9:19-23)**.

   1 Corinthians 13 shows us that without love we have nothing. Love is not only the heartbeat of Christianity, but it is the heartbeat behind all godly service.

3. Look up the scriptures and explain the part God's love plays in a life of service. **(John 13:35; 14:21-25; 15:9-17; Romans 13:8-10; 1 John 3:14, 17-24)**

   Without God's love there will be no power to minister to the unlovable, the lost, or the enemy. Our love for God is not an emotion, but a commitment to do right by Him and others. This commitment looks beyond faults, status, and problems in order to see individuals in light of God's commitment to them.

4. How does **1 Peter 4:8** confirm this truth?

   God's love is sacrificial. Mankind may be in a pathetic condition. People may appear worthless and hopeless, but God has paid a high price for everyone. Once someone redeems something, it ceases to be a piece of worthless junk.

   Man has value at the foot of the cross. This value is totally found in the love of Christ. Investment in man must be done in the shadow of Christ's cross. After all, it is at the cross love abounds, forgiveness is offered, and purpose is revealed.

5. What happens if love ceases to be a motivating factor in ministry? **(Revelations 2:2-5** refer to **Matthew 15:9-15; 1 John 3:18)**

Heartless religion becomes the product of Christianity when love is missing. Remember, love is the heartbeat in our relationship with God. If the heartbeat ceases, it means death. We may have a form of godliness, but deny the power there of.

6. What ingredient is able to nullify the love of God in our life? **(2 Timothy 1:7; 1 John 4:17, 18)**

   God desires to pour out His love and forgiveness. Demonic fear brings guilt and condemnation.

7. What promise do we have in **Romans 8:1**?

   The key of being free from demonic fear is that we walk after the Spirit.

8. What will be present in our life if we walk after the Spirit? **(2 Corinthians 3:17)**

   Satan's main goal is to rob us of liberty and put us in bondage. The fear Satan produces results in oppression. The fear of the Lord serves as boundaries in a Christian's life. It will produce a right response that will result in our conscience being free of condemnation.

Right Attitude

God has put within man a certain amount of fear. This fear can be positive in potentially dangerous situations, serving as a protection. For instance, we will not jump off of a cliff for fear of injury or death. We will not play in traffic out of fear of being hit by a car. And in most incidents, people will avoid doing dangerous stunts.

The fear of the Lord serves a Christian in a similar way.

9. How does **Proverbs 10:27** confirm this truth?

   The fear of the Lord is necessary.

10. What does **Ecclesiastes 12:13** say about the fear of the Lord?

    The most popular definition for <u>fear of the Lord</u> is awesome or reverent respect for God. Many stop short of referring to it as actual fear. But the truth is, fear of the Lord is just exactly that, <u>fear</u> of standing before a righteous and just God who is not pleased with us.

    Of all the accounts I have read where individuals actually witnessed hell, their reaction was that of fear towards a God who has the power to send them there. Those who have caught a glimpse of God's holiness experienced fear of a God, whose righteousness demands eternal judgment of those who reject Him and His commandments. When you consider that the demons' reaction towards God is that of fear and trembling, how can man stop short of anything less **(James 2:19)**? He must dread meeting God on any other bases but that which is pleasing and acceptable to Him.

11. In whom should we fear? **(Isaiah 8:13)**
12. With this in mind, what must we work out in fear and trembling according to **Philippians 2:12**?

Psalm 111:10 tells us the fear of the Lord is the beginning of wisdom. In **Luke 12:42**, Jesus describes the profitable servant as wise. Wisdom implies knowledge that is being applied in obedience. A wise servant knows his master's wishes and complies.

13. Based on the following scriptures, explain why the fear of the Lord is the beginning of wisdom. **(Psalm 19:9; 34:9; Proverbs 3:7; 8:13; 1 Peter 1:17)**

Fear of the Lord means one has distinction between what is acceptable and what is unacceptable. This distinction serves as spiritual boundaries that result in service.

14. How does **Ephesians 6:5** confirm this truth?

Fear of the Lord causes singleness of heart. This singleness of heart means total commitment to the Lord. It implies lowliness that is expressed in an attitude of meekness.

15. What does **Romans 11:17-22** say about this subject?

Finally, the fear of the Lord produces the right responses, which are submission and faithfulness.

Right Responses

Jesus is our example of ministry. His ministry to man can be summarized by **Philippians 2:7, 8**, "...taking the very nature of a servant,...he humbled himself and became obedient to death—even the death on a cross!"

Christian servitude comes from a heart of love that results in submission. Christ submitted Himself to the cross for our sake.

Godly submission inspires sensitivity towards the needs of others. It gives way to that which is worthy of consideration for the benefit of those it is serving. Christ became associated with the unlovable, the downtrodden, and the lost. He showed these people consideration, kindness, truth, and compassion. As a result, many sinners were saved, healed, and set free.

16. In the following scriptural examples, explain in your own words what ways Christ was submissive to the needs of the sinners He encountered. **(Luke 7:11-16, 36-50; 9:43-49; 13:10-13; 19:1-10; John 3:1-21; 4:1-39; 8:1-11)**
17. What does **Ephesians 5:15-21** say about submission and the Christian?
18. What attitudes produce an opposite response to submission? **(Luke 14:7-35; 18:9-14; Romans 12:3; James 2:5-13)**

God does not show favoritism. Therefore His servants have no right to display elitism, self-righteousness, or self-importance towards others. These attitudes make us the judge of others because self has been exalted. All of these contradict the Lordship of Jesus.

Jesus gave up His identity as God when He gave up the glories of heaven and took on the likeness of man. His goal was to be submissive to the Father's will, and to find the lost.

Christians must give up all rights to self in order to be conformed to the image of Christ. As servants of Christ, they have no personal rights. The only right they have is to become a living sacrifice for God's glory.

19. What are the believers' relationship to God according to **Romans 6:12, 13; 2 Corinthians 4:7** and **2 Timothy 2:20, 21**?

    Christians must be available at all times for their Master's use. They are to be on duty 24 hours a day, seven days a week. There is only one response that will assure this availability.

20. What is it? **(Luke 19:17; 1 Corinthians 4:2)**

    Faithfulness implies both trustworthiness and dependability. According to **Luke 19:17**, if we cannot be trusted with little, our Master will not entrust us with greater responsibilities. For instance, if you cannot love your neighbor, how can God trust you with others? If you cannot be content in the undesirable places in ministry, how can you be entrusted with places of honor?

21. How does **Zechariah 4:10a** confirm this truth?

    There are no short cuts to acceptable ministry. Those who are exalted have learned the secret of servitude in the closets of intercessory prayer, as well as in what is often considered dishonorable positions among the Body and in the service to the hurting.

22. Identify the other qualities of a faithful servant according to **Luke 12:41-48**.
23. Read **Matthew 25:14-30**. What other area does the Lord want to find Christians faithful in?

    Talents can represent abilities, spiritual gifts, and even our own testimony. If Christ is Lord, then all talents should be under His guidance and control. His precious blood bought our testimony of Him; therefore, it should bring glory to His name.

24. What does **1 Peter 4:10** say about this subject?

    Growth will come when a servant learns to give away his or her talents for the glory of God. As a servant gives out of sacrifice, the Lord will provide him or her with more from His unlimited resources.

25. According to the parable in **Matthew 21:28-33**, are we always going to like the responsibility our Lord may give us? (Yes or No)

    God is more concerned about each Christian's relationship to Him than his or her life of service. A life of service that does not come from a growing relationship with God will run out of power.

    A believer who is keeping his or her relationship with God in proper focus will find ministry is more of an avenue of preparation for God's greatness to be manifested, rather than the ultimate goal of Christian living.

Chapter Five

THE PROCESS

Christians are referred to as soldiers and ambassadors (**Ephesians 6:10-13; 2 Timothy 2:3; 2 Corinthians 5:20)**. Both positions require training. For the soldier it means attending boot camp where he or she will go through intensive training that will challenge every facet of his or her life.

In the case of ambassadors, diplomacy is often acquired through example. It becomes more defined as the individual learns the goal of his or her leaders, the rules of his or her government, and about the people among whom he or she must live.

With this training comes one main instructor.

1. Who is He? **(John 16:13-15)**

   The Holy Spirit will change priorities and lifestyles to make Christians powerful soldiers and godly representatives. As effective soldiers, believers will become the salt of the earth. As salt they will preserve God's kingdom by the correct use of His Word. As the light of the world, they will serve as ambassadors of Christ to a lost and dying world **(Matthew 5:13-16)**.

2. What will the final results of this change be? **(2 Corinthians 5:17)**

   We can gain an understanding of this training by observing the lives of men such as Jacob, Joseph, Moses, and Peter.

   When a new believer first begins to realize he or she has a call, pride usually escalates. This self assurance brings such an individual close to disaster.

3. In what way did these four men's over confidence get them in trouble?

   Jacob **(Genesis 27)**
   Joseph **(Genesis 37:5-28)**
   Moses **(Exodus 2:11-15)**
   Peter **(Matthew 16:13-23)**

   New believers have a zeal, but lack the boundaries of wisdom to guide them. God must take this untapped zeal and refine it with His wisdom.

4. How does **James 3:13-17** described God's wisdom?

   The process God takes His followers through to obtain this wisdom is what I call the wilderness experience. The wilderness the Israelites found themselves in symbolized the harshness of this experience in the lives of God's servants. This place is where man comes face to face with the barrenness of his own soul. He recognizes he is not <u>self-sufficient</u> and he has <u>nothing</u> to offer his God.

5. What served as a wilderness experience to these four servants of God?

   Jacob **(Genesis 31:36-48)**
   Joseph **(Genesis 39, 40)**
   Moses **(Exodus 2:17-3:1)**
   Peter **(Luke 22:54-62)**

It is in the spiritual wilderness that the inner man crumbles. Insecurities replace self-importance and worth. Dreams, illusions of grandeur, and promises lay broken in the midst of spiritual poverty. But it is in the midst of this depravity and harshness that the great Potter begins to mold and shape lives into vessels fit for His purpose.

After the wilderness, God begins to move His servant to a life of service. Part of the route the servant must take will lead him or her back to the place where he or she first received his or her call or vision.

6. In what way did these four men find themselves at this place?

Jacob **(Genesis 28:10-19** refer to **Genesis 35:1-15)**
Joseph **(Genesis 37:5-11** refer to **Genesis 42:5-7)**
Moses **(Exodus 2:15** refer to **Exodus 4:20-23)**
Peter **(Luke 5:1-11** refer to **John 21:5-22)**

Jacob met God at Bethel twice. The first time was when he left home after Esau plotted to kill him. The second time was after he came home after 20 years of service to his uncle, and found himself a stench to those at Succoth because of the actions of his two sons Levi and Simeon. It was at Bethel, he told his family to put away all idols—they were going to begin to serve God Almighty, fulfilling the oath he made to God over 20 years earlier.

Joseph's plight as a slave and prisoner in Egypt proved to be part of a plan to save his brethren. God had given Joseph dreams when he was young. These dreams created jealousy among his brothers. His brothers were stirred up to wrath resulting in them selling him as a slave. Years after he was sold into slavery, his brothers stood before him in homage. God miraculously fulfilled Joseph's dreams and reunited him back to his father.

Moses spent 40 years in the wilderness. He came from the high estate of being the son of Pharaoh's sister down to a shepherd, a position considered an abomination to the Egyptians. When called by God to lead His people out of Egypt, he declared that he did not even have the capability of speaking properly. Moses had left Egypt out of fear for his life only to return to Egypt, chosen, called, and prepared by God to be one of the greatest leaders of Israel **(Exodus 2:10, 11, 15; Genesis 46:34; Exodus 4:10)**.

The best idea Peter could come up with after the death of Jesus was to go fishing. Although, Christ had appeared to the disciples, they still had no real direction. Christ first called Peter while He was working at his profession. Once again, the fisherman hears the voice of the Creator. He forsakes all by jumping into the water and swimming to shore to meet with Him. He had denied Christ three times. Now, before his companions, he declares his love and commitment to Him three times. Peter, a man with zeal, but lacking wisdom, now stood before his Lord with sobriety and wisdom. In a short time, he would be endued with power from on high. In the power of the Holy Spirit, he would preach a sermon that would bring salvation to 3,000 souls. Peter at Pentecost became Cephas, a stone upon which other stones would be added to build the Church. This Church would be the very means by which Christ would be glorified. It would be the very Body that one day He would come back for in power and glory.

Processes are never easy, but they are necessary. Without the necessary preparation, mere man cannot receive from God. A man must first accept the truth about his own unworthiness before he can receive from God. It is only after self is put down that an individual gains worth in God.

Once a vessel is void of self, God becomes the potter in the life of the individual. Each vessel is designed with a purpose in mind. Each will be entrusted with distinct responsibilities in His kingdom.

Are you allowing the Potter access to your life or are you holding on to self? God will not be able to have His way in your life if you insist on holding on to your right to self.

Chapter Six

THE SERVANT'S RESPONSIBILITIES

In one person's attempt to discover the will of God, she stated, "The will of God is whatever we do in the name of Christ." **Matthew 7:21-23** disputes such a concept.

God does have a will, and it is clearly lined out in His Word. His main concern is with our relationship with Him.

1. What is His will for us? **(John 6:40; 1 Thessalonians 4:2-6; 5:18; 1 Peter 2:11-16; 2 Peter 3:9)**
2. What does **Romans 12:1, 2** tell us needs to happen in our lives in order for us to know what is the acceptable will of God?

   As Christians, we must become responsible to God's great commission.

3. What is our commission? **(Matthew 28:18-20; Mark 16:15, 16)**

   As you can see, our commission is two-fold.

4. What is the Gospel? **(1 Corinthians 15:1-4)**
5. Break down the different parts of the Gospel and explain how each part is significant to our salvation.

   The good news we share with others is not about man's hopeless condition. Rather, it is about the provision God made through the Person of Jesus Christ. This good news of Jesus is for all men. It is expressed through our testimony. <u>Testimony</u> means to bear witness to a fact. What each Christian bears witness to is the revelation of Jesus Christ in his or her life.

6. What does <u>revelation</u> mean?

   It is the reality and work of Christ that sums up this life-changing message. It brings hope to hopeless man from spiritual bondage, and is a means of salvation from the consequences of death through Him.

   It is amazing how people, in their excitement of something new such as a recipe, a joke, the latest diet or fashion, can readily share it. Yet, to share the solution to all man's problems, Jesus Christ, is another story.

   Fear binds us up making us focus on self rather than God. Fear is opposite of faith.

7. What does **2 Timothy 1:7** say about fear?

   It is the Holy Spirit in us who will give us knowledge of what to share with others if we are open to it. If people reject what is said, they are rejecting Christ and not us.

   Proclaiming the good news is the responsibility of all of us. There are three facts we need to understand about the value of sharing our testimony. First of all, our testimony, or life in Christ is not ours. It is His life and we have it because of Jesus Christ dying on the cross for us.

8. Who does our testimony belong to? **(Romans 14:8; 1 Corinthians 6:19, 20)**

The second reason for giving our testimony away is to establish spiritual growth.

9. For example, what happened to the two servants who gave their talents away in **Matthew 25:14-30**?

God will entrust us with a greater testimony as we are faithful to give it away. A growth in our testimony means a greater revelation of Jesus Christ. As we are faithful to study the Word, share our testimony, and continue to enter into an intimate relationship with God, we will grow in love and in faith.

A testimony that does not grow can most likely be accredited to a lack of fellowship with God and the lack of a poured-out life of Christ into others.

The third reason our testimony is so important to the kingdom of God and ourselves is found in **Revelation 12:11**.

10. What is the reason?

Our testimony of Jesus gives us power to overcome Satan.

11. What promise do we find in **1 John 4:4** concerning our victory?
12. What was the warning to Ezekiel in **Ezekiel 3:16-21** that Christians should take heed to?

The message we are claiming is one with eternal consequences. Our testimony of how we overcome through Christ is valuable to those who are lost and seeking God. We must share our testimony or we will participate in the destruction of the lost whom we have neglected with the silence of indifference.

13. What signs will follow as long as the Church is lined up and following the commands and responsibilities of God? **(Mark 16:17, 18)**

If these signs are not happening, I can assure you it is not because God has changed, but because of disobedience and loss of vision.

14. What does **Proverbs 29:18** say about a lack of vision in the *King James Version*?
15. What does it mean to be a disciple of Jesus according to **Matthew 28:18-20**?

Disciple is a Greek word that means learner.

16. What does it mean to teach others to observe all things?

Jesus was called Rabbi or Master, which are the Greek counterparts to the word "teacher".

17. What instructions did Jesus give about being His followers? (**Luke 14:26-33; John 8:31; 13:13-16; 34, 35)**
18. What warning do we find in **Matthew 5:19** concerning teaching?

Being a teacher holds more responsibility than just standing in front of a group giving instructions. Jesus was an effective teacher because He served as an example.

There is a saying, "Your actions are speaking so loud, I cannot hear a word you are saying." An effective teacher must back up his or her verbal instruction in practical ways by living the Christian life.

19. Where must the Word of God be written? **(2 Corinthians 3:1-3)**
20. What is the fruit that shows we are truly Jesus' disciple? **(John 13:34, 35)**
21. Do you have this godly quality? (Yes or No)

Evangelism

Preaching the Gospel and teaching people to be followers of Christ comprises our commission. Both of these responsibilities point to evangelism.

There is a difference between the commission of evangelism and the position of an evangelist as found in **Ephesians 4:11**.

22. What is this difference?

The commission of evangelism is the responsibility of the whole Church to those who are lost and new converts. The position of an evangelist is a valuable function within the workings of the Body of Christ. Individuals with this office will not only preach the Gospel, but they will stir up and bring spiritual accountability and revival to the Church body. In fact, the great tragedy today is that the position of evangelist has been greatly limited or practically been pushed out of the Church.

I remember a pastor saying, "Why does my church need an evangelist? I have everything my people need." Today his church building stands empty as a silent reminder of his prideful attitude. It reveals his inability to be "everything" his sheep needed.

There are two extremes operating within evangelism among the believers. One of these groups can be found in **Romans 10:2**.

23. Explain this group.

The second group can be found in **Revelation 3:15-18**.

24. Summarize this group.

The first group has fire without wisdom, and the second group lacks the real fire and is basically ineffective and dead.

Zealous Christians are usually new converts. They must become flexible and teachable as God fine-tunes them. They must strive to never let their initial fire die out.

The second group I refer to as "spiritual nerds". This slang word simply means an "ineffective person" because they spend more time in their minds and accept the evaluation that comes out of religious notions that are void of reality. There are three types of nerds in the kingdom of heaven.

The first group of spiritual nerds are those who spiritualize Christianity. They are unrealistic and live in a fantasyland that often presents the kingdom of heaven as a candy store.

25. What did Christ promise us in **John 16:33**?

The second group are those who act like they are God's favorites. They come across with the attitude of having all the goods; just ask them. These people can appear to be apathetic because they feel they have fire insurance against hell. But on the other hand, they are disobedient towards the Word of God and stand on shifting sand. Like the people at Ephesus, they have left their first love **(Revelation 2:2-4)**.

Their attitude is pride clothed in self-righteous snobbery. It is unattractive to every onlooker.

26. What did Paul say about this type of spiritual nerd in **1 Corinthians 10:12** and **Galatians 6:3**?

The third group are those Christians who are out to find some kind of recognition in the kingdom of heaven. They want to appear zealous in their witnessing, but will come across as obnoxious, undesirable, and even insulting. Their greatest feat is not really salvation, but exaltation. Their attempts turn unbelievers off and embarrass believers.

27. What was Paul's instruction in **Romans 12:16**?

Spiritual nerds need to repent and ask God to give them a vision of who He is and an insight into their ungodly attitude about the lost.

28. What instructions did Paul and Peter give concerning Christians who are lukewarm or asleep in their spiritual lives? **(Ephesians 5:13, 14; 2 Peter 1:3-14)**

On-fire evangelists are opportunists at heart. They are always looking for openings to witness to others. In fact, every person they meet is a potential convert.

Evangelists can take detours. One of the ways is by relying on formulas rather than the Holy Spirit. As a Christian matures in his or her sensitivity to others, he or she realizes formulas cannot offer the personal element when sharing the Gospel. By putting too much emphasis on the verbal declaration of the Gospel, many have often ignored the most effective means of sharing which is personal ministry of one on one.

A second detour is that of assumptions. Because a person is affiliated with churches or religious activities does not mean that person is saved. We must seek to know if each person is an heir of salvation.

The Word of God instructs us to discern the spiritual condition of others.

29. How do the following scriptures confirm this responsibility? **(Matthew 7:15, 16; 2 Corinthians 6:14-18; 1 John 4:1)**

Jesus asked questions in order to reveal a person's motivation (spirit), frame of reference (belief/philosophy/foundation), and to expose their real attitudes about God. These questions brought self-examination, understanding, and ultimately challenged perspectives by breaking up religious foundations.

Another area Christians need to be careful about is using Christian slang. Christians have their own language that seems foreign or foolish to those on the outside. Christians often use terms or statements that serve as deterrents in sharing the Gospel.

30. What should our main message be? **(1 Corinthians 2:1-2)**

We must drop the Christian lingo ("Christianeze") and share the good news in the simplest terms. Below are some helpful questions that might help illuminate a person's spiritual condition.

1. Have you believed upon the Lord Jesus to ensure you are saved?
2. If you died tonight, where would you end up for eternity, heaven or hell?
3. If you died tonight and found yourself standing before God, what reason would you give as to why He should allow you into heaven?
4. Who do you say Jesus is?
5. Do you believe you are a sinner?
6. Tell me about the time you called upon the name of the Lord for salvation.
7. What are you doing with Jesus Christ?

Arguing is another detour we must avoid.

31. What did Paul say about arguments in **Titus 3:9**?

The different Jewish sects were known to argue much about genealogies and interpretation of the Law. Their arguments held no significance in light of spiritual truth. They majored in the minors and minored in the major things of God.

Today much of the Church appears to major in disagreements and minor in basic truths of Christianity. We see people making doctrinal statements based on denominational affiliation or schools of thought inspired by men, rather than on the Word of God. If you feel the need to argue to be right about something or prove a point, it is best to keep quiet. We cannot convince people unless the Holy Spirit brings the necessary conviction, instruction or truth to their spirit. We can stand on truth, because it will ultimately stand, but to argue a point is not profitable. (See **2 Corinthians 13:8**.)

It is not unusual to see people becoming identified with the latest Christian "guru" rather than *JESUS CHRIST*.

32. What is our hope of glory? **(Colossians 1:27)**

Spiritual agreement with God and one another comes by lifting up Jesus Christ and not through any other means.

33. What does **1 Peter 3:15** states?

To give a defense for the hope in you and to argue are two different things. To <u>defend</u> means to support something. Our pride, as an attempt to prove something, motivates us to argue.

We must cease to argue and learn to listen. The art of listening helps us get past ourselves and enter into another person's world. Often, people who are defensive are fearful and hurting. Arguing with them will reinforce walls, not open them up.

I can attest to every reader, evangelism is a process in itself. You will realize your best approaches can appear as dung when you come face to face with rejection. Your patience will be tested to breaking points as you reach out to unreceptive hearts. Your love will be tested. It will actually take on the heart of Christ or it will fail because it is carnal. Until you realize your sufficiency and victories are of God and not of yourself, your best attempt to reach out will fall short of the mark.

34. What does **2 Corinthians 3:5** say about this subject?

This lack of personal sufficiency to evangelize brings us to the realistic conclusion about our part in the kingdom of God. We cannot evangelize in our own power. It takes the power of God.

35. How does **Zechariah 4:6** confirm this truth?

Other Areas of Service

We need to preach and teach, but we must be faithful in other areas as well. An area of service is intercessory prayer. We need to be in intercessory prayer for others.

36. What does **James 5:15, 16** and **Matthew 5:44** say about this subject?
37. What was Christ doing in **John 17**?

Intercessory prayer is the most thankless job in a life of service, for only you and God know about it.

38. What does **Matthew 6:5, 6** say about the reward given in such a prayer life?

Positions and gifts are another part of service that are determined by the Holy Spirit.

39. Look up **Romans 12:4-8, Ephesians 4:11,** and **1 Corinthians 12:27-31** and name some of the positions and gifts within the body of believers which are available through the work of the Holy Spirit.

Positions carry leadership responsibilities and must not be taken lightly. All positions in the body demand a holy lifestyle, a meek attitude and a submissive way.

40. What kind of lifestyle must be upheld by leaders such as bishops (elders or overseers), deacons and teachers? **(1 Timothy 3:1-5, 8; 5:17; 6:3-5)**
41. Who must not be allowed to hold a leadership position? **(1 Timothy 3:6)**. Why?

Gifts are to edify the body. Edifying simply means the promotion of spiritual growth. It involves the building up of the Church. The Holy Spirit gives these gifts severally as He will.

42. What gift is not for the edification of the Church? **(1 Corinthians 14:1-5)**
43. What gifts should we covet? **(1 Corinthians 12:31)**

Our positions and gifts will not mean anything if we lack a certain godly fruit.

44. What fruit gives both clout and meaning to these avenues of service? **(Romans 12:9; 1 Corinthians 13:1-8)**

Christians need to desire the best gifts and then be faithful to use them correctly within scriptural boundaries.

Credentials and Problems

One should never look for a ministry. The Lord will place each of us in our positions and responsibilities as we prove faithful with what is in front of us. All too often people try to force God's hand in this matter.

We can cause problems for ourselves. I have seen people take their idea of ministry into their own hands and end up in left field. We think that God will be impressed with outrageous acts of religious commitment. These attempts often create religious monsters who either think themselves to be elite or they are totally frustrated with God's apparent lack of blessings and deliverance from situations.

45. What is the true evidence that will come forth from those who are really serving God according to **Romans 12**?

It is important to note most Christians want to know how God can serve them rather than how they can serve God. Christian maturity is determined by our understanding that God is the one who deserves service.

God is not here for us; rather, we are here for God. As new Christians, we are like new babies demanding everything. As we mature in Christ, we begin to recognize our responsibility to God.

46. What is the desired result of such maturity according to **Hebrews 5:14**?

It seems many Christians would rather put on their spiritual diapers of foolish expectation and suck on the pacifier of untested doctrine by standing on feelings and emotions instead of putting on their armor and standing on both the Rock (Jesus Christ) and the Word of God.

47. What is our spiritual armor comprised of? **(Ephesians 6:14-18)**

Another problem in the life of a servant is knowing the difference between causes and God's purposes. All too often we Christians get involved in causes. These goals may look moral, good, and right; however, we need to recognize causes should result in glorifying Christ. Many times, people close their hearts to God as a result of our causes.

We need to realize God's concern is for lost souls. Only the Gospel of Jesus Christ brings salvation. Personal causes that are political, spiritual, or moral can become crusades.

Crusades always leave victims. We are not called to crusades. We are called to war. God's battlefield entails the war we encounter over lost souls. Causes all too often strip people of their dignity, causing their hearts to harden toward the Gospel. When Jesus Christ is lifted up, it will not only allow people to maintain their dignity, it will bring forth salvation, deliverance, and healing to their lives.

48. Explain the following scriptures in conjunction with the previous paragraphs. **(Matthew 6:33; 9:36-38; 22:17-22)**

There will always be problems and challenges with every ministry. The key is to recognize the consequences of being in service to God.

People think being in the ministry is full of "peaches and cream." This is not true. Christ our example, was crucified. In the ministry one will be misunderstood, mocked, rejected, and slandered. **(Matthew 5:10-12)**

These attacks will often come from the very ones who call themselves Christians. If we do not have our eyes on Jesus and a correct perspective of service before God, we will end up being destroyed.

It is for this reason we must go through the process God takes us through in order to have a correct perspective of our life before Him. We must know who we serve and what really pleases Him. True credentials of a servant of God will be revealed in a right Biblical perspective and with a true commitment. This true commitment will result in faithfulness and endurance.

In Conclusion

The question now is, what is your idea of ministry? Is it the same as it was before you started this study? If not, explain what changes have been established.

Maybe at this time you would like to rededicate your life for service. If so, here is a prayer you might wish to follow.

Dear Lord Jesus:

Thank You for the gift of life. Right now, Lord, I want to give You my life, all of it. I present my life as a living sacrifice for Your glory. Reveal Yourself to me so that I might be able to serve. Help me to be a sanctified vessel fit for Your use. Create in me a new heart and change the motivation of self to Your love. Renew my mind and bring forth a submissive attitude. Help me to be faithful to whatever is set before me.

Lord, please use me, for I know it is an honor to be Your servant. Help me to have Your perspective which allows me to always focus on You and Your greatness. Help me to realize the less I am, the greater You will be, not only to me but to those around me. Please help me to regress in order for You to be lifted up; drawing all men to Yourself.

Thank You Lord for Your life. Thank You for choosing me to be Your vessel. Help me to pour the life You have established in me, out to others.

In Your Precious Name, Amen

We pray this study has challenged, encouraged, and blessed you.

SUPPLEMENTATION THREE

By

Rayola Kelley & Jeannette Haley

The Biggest Little Word
(Excerpts from a Sermon)
Rayola Kelley

In **Colossians 1:27-29**: "To whom God would make known what is the riches of the glory of this mystery among the Gentiles; which is Christ in you, the hope of glory. Whom we preach, warning every man and teaching every man in all wisdom; that we may present every man perfect in Christ Jesus. For this I also labor, striving according to his working which worketh in me mightily."

Last week I talked about what it means for Christ to be *in* us. I stated that only Christ can give us identity, be the light in our life, and be the essence of what we truly have need of. Only Christ can be all in all. Last week, I emphasized *Christ in us*, but this week I am going to talk about something else that's just a little bit different. I am going to talk about how *we are in Christ.*

We are in Christ; but sometimes we ignore the words or concepts of being in Christ or Christ in us. Now as I stated last week the word in means inclusion, location, or position within limits. And, of course, Christ **in us** shows us our identities, our rights, and our potential. But, what does it mean for **us to be in Christ**? The idea of us being in Christ actually shows us our position.

Position is very important because position shows you where you fit in a matter. In fact, if you study your position in Christ, you will realize that it is a heavenly position not an earthly position. **Ephesians 2:6** says, "And has raised us up together, and made us sit together in heavenly places in Christ Jesus." God has placed us in this position. We didn't do something to place ourselves in this position; it was God who placed us in this heavenly position.

This heavenly position determines how God the Father will view us. If you don't get this perspective right you will not understand the importance of what it means for us to be in Christ. Without this position of being in Christ, God would never be able to accept you or me into His kingdom. This is why He placed us in Christ to ensure that we would be brought to a place in our lives where we would experience this incredible position.

Now before you can be in Christ, you have to have Christ in you. If you have never received Jesus Christ into your life, God has never placed you in Him. Christ in you stipulates the inward work. When Christ is in you, He is working from the inward state through the Holy Spirit. Basically, what He is trying to do is to bring you to a place where you are an empty shell through death, consumed and possessed by His life in you. Obviously, such a life will cause you to be totally identified with Him, which will change how you view your present life and purpose.

As Christ becomes a greater reality within an individual, he or she will begin to be made perfect in Christ. What you now have is the inward and the outward coming together. The inward life of Christ meeting with the outward or heavenly position results in perfection.

Paul was stating here: *"whom we preach"* **(Colossians 1:28)**. He goes on to say we preach Christ whom we warn every man. Warning implies we must get real with God or pay the consequences. And, he goes on to say that they were teaching man in all wisdom that every man may be presented perfect in Christ Jesus. Whether or not you become perfect in Christ Jesus depends on how much you allow Christ to have His way in your life. And, if you are not allowing Christ to have His way through His Holy Spirit, you will not be brought to perfection in Christ.

What does it really mean to be in Christ? Now let's go one step farther to understand this. If you are in Christ you need to realize that your life is hid in Christ. **Colossians 3:3** says, "Your life is hidden with Christ in God." Why must we be hid in Christ? When you look at **Colossians 3:1-3**, you will see that there is a progression taking place where you become truly hidden in Christ. However, you first must seek Him out. As you seek Him out, you begin to set your affections on Him; and as you set your affections on Him you will begin to realize what it means to be in Christ, to be hid in Him.

Now the word hid means to conceal or keep secret. Why must you be concealed or be kept in secret? You can see we are actually concealed in Jesus. He is our hiding place. He is a place of peace and safety. But, why do we have to be concealed in Christ? Because when the Father looks down to consider His people, He must see His Son. He must not see us because we are subject to His wrath outside of Christ. Only in Christ can we be spared of God's wrath, and if He sees you instead of His Son, you stand condemned and subject to His wrath. He cannot accept you in your humanity, He can only accept His Son in you, and you in His Son. So, you must be hid in Christ to avoid the wrath of God. This is how important this position is.

What does the Father see when He looks at a person who is hidden in His Son? **1 Corinthians 1:30a** gives us a summary of what He sees. "But of him are you in Christ Jesus". Paul is saying because of God you are in Christ Jesus. Consider what Christ is made unto us: "...wisdom, and righteousness, and sanctification, and redemption." Do you know how important those four words are to our spiritual well-being? By Christ being in us, and us in Christ, He is made unto us these four virtues. So, when the Father considers the person hid in Christ, guess what He doesn't see: Our human wisdom.

Do you know what human wisdom looks like to God? According to **James 3:14-15** human wisdom is full of bitter envying. It's full of strife, as well as being earthly, it's sensual, and devilish, and yet it appears as if many Christians are pretty proud of their wisdom. If God sees such wisdom, you are going to be made out to be the biggest fool in the world.

However, when God looks down and sees Christ, He sees the wisdom from above **(James 3:17)**. He sees a wisdom that is at peace with Him. He sees a wisdom that's gentle in its responses, merciful, and easy to be entreated or instructed. Jesus is the one who is wisdom personified. Paul says this about Him, "In whom are hid all the treasures of wisdom and knowledge" **(Colossians 2:3)**.

Saints, if you want to be wise, know that heavenly wisdom can only be found in Christ. If you want to have knowledge, know that the knowledge you really need is only found in Christ.

When the Father sees a person concealed in Jesus, He sees righteousness. He doesn't see a struggling, fleshly heart. He doesn't see somebody trying to be righteous in his or her own attempts, which is considered nothing more than filthy rags to Him. Personal righteousness is an unacceptable stench to Him. Please begin to understand what it means to be hid in Christ. God doesn't see a person who covers his or her filthy rags with some form of personal righteousness. Rather, He sees the righteousness of His Son in us. He sees His Son who became sin for us. He sees His Son who satisfied judgment on the cross. He sees His Son who was willing to take on the depravity of man, so that you and I could be made in the righteousness of God **(2 Corinthians 5:21)**.

When the Father observes you and me in our secret place, He sees sanctification or holiness. In other words, He doesn't see holiness because some Christian or some person is trying to keep the Law. He doesn't see holiness because somebody is displaying pious actions. He doesn't see holiness, because there is no such thing in the flesh. We are totally defiled or profane. He doesn't see us; He only sees His Son who is holy.

Sanctification and holiness mean that you are set apart. Granted, we are responsible to set ourselves apart by presenting our lives totally to God. But on the other hand, if Christ is not in you and you are not in Christ, your will not be set apart at all. It is Christ in you that sets you apart. This is what the Father must see, the sweet, undefiled life of Christ in you. It is this reality that the Father accepts as holy.

When the Father looks on those who are in the hidden place of safety, He sees redemption. He does not see redemption because we have earned our salvation, for we cannot earn our salvation. He doesn't see redemption because we may have sacrificed much for God. Most sacrifices are our reasonable service. When God looks down, He doesn't see redemption because we have proven ourselves to be worthy, which is impossible to do. Rather, He sees redemption because He sees Jesus His Son, the One who shed His blood as the Lamb of God on the cross as a payment for our souls. Praise God, He sees Jesus and not you and me. Praise God His view is heavenly, via through His only begotten Son who sits on His right hand. Praise God that the Father goes through Jesus our High Priest, Mediator, and Advocate. He is the one who stands on our behalf, intercedes for us, and is able to save us to the uttermost.

We are the most blessed people because of the presence of Christ in us, and surrounding us. I am reminded of what **1 Corinthians 15:22** says, "For as in Adam all die, even so in Christ shall all be made alive". You are either in Adam today or you are in Christ. If you are in Adam, you are still dead in your sins. However, if you are in Christ today, you shall be made alive, because the Father sees Christ in you. As a result, you can be assured of reconciliation and fellowship with the Father.

When I ask people why Jesus came 20 centuries ago, most of them say to give us eternal life. This is not completely true, because eternal life is actually the byproduct of Jesus' purpose for coming. The reason Jesus came was to reconcile us back into a fellowship, an intimate relationship with the Father. It's all about reconciliation **(John 14:6; 2**

Corinthians 5:18). If you are really reconciled to the Father, you can be assured of salvation.

We cannot take credit for anything in our spiritual lives. Paul says, "...he that glorieth let him glory in the Lord." It's because everything has come from God, and has been accomplished through Jesus Christ. It's because He is in us, and we are in Him that we can walk in confidence in the life that God has prepared for us.

Are you hid in Christ? The problem with a lot of Christians today is that they are not hid in Christ because of sin, rebellion, and various other things. As soon as you decide to walk in any form of darkness, you are going to walk outside of Christ. And, if you are on the outside of Christ, you will open yourself up to every kind of major attack and defeat that you can imagine.

Maybe positionally these Christians are in Christ, but not spiritually. There is a difference between being positionally placed in Christ and being spiritually hid in Him. It is very easy to tell if you are hid in Christ because to hide in Christ actually means you are abiding in Him. Jesus said in **John 15:5**, *"I am the vine, you are the branches."* Consider how the very root and core of the branches is what is hidden in the Vine. All the consumption that causes life for the branches is because they are abiding in the vine. That is how you can tell today whether or not you are hid in Christ, whether you are abiding in Him or not.

People that are without Christ not only lack identity and purpose in life, but they cannot do anything outside of Jesus that is lasting. There are a lot of Christians out there that are doing things, but it's not as unto God.

Everything that is acceptable to God can only be done if we are abiding in Christ. If you are doing anything right now outside of Christ, I want you to know that whatever you are doing is all going to be in vain and rejected by God. You cannot please or serve Jesus outside of abiding in Him. Christ is the One who sustains a person in his or her spiritual life. Self-sufficiency will be missing. In other words, if you are looking to Christ, you are abiding in Christ for Him to sustain your very life. This is what will give you purpose and direction. And, if you are abiding in Christ, guess what is going to be missing in your life: Self-sufficiency. We will abide in Christ because we know that everything comes from Him that is necessary for life.

Your fruit will tell on you. If you have a nasty attitude you're not abiding in Christ. If you do not have any patience, love, and consideration for people around, you do not abide in Christ. If you are not truly spiritually in Christ, then you are abusing the position you have in Him. Your spiritual life depends on your abiding as the branch in the Vine. This is the only way you can be assured that you're not going to have any independence outside of Christ. Independence is the reason that so many Christians are miserable and unhappy. Abiding in Christ will make His words meat to your life. They will change your life.

If you can walk in your Christianity without really caring whether you grab a hold of the words of God, you are not abiding in Him. In fact, you are probably doing it your own way. And, your own way will always lead you outside of being in Christ. If we abide in Christ we will bring glory to the Father. Is your life really bringing glory to the Father? Or, are you bringing glory to yourself because you are such a wonderful, smart Christian? Think about it for a minute. Oh, aren't I smart, look at me. You are glorifying yourself, which makes you a fake. If you truly abide in Christ, you will bring glory to the Father, and you will bring it through love.

The Bible says if you abide in Jesus, His love will abide in you. You will be compelled by the love of God in your life. If you are abiding in the Vine, you will obey the words of God. You will obey the commandments. You will obey the principles. The obedience that Christ talks about is an obedience that can only come out of the right attitude. If you're not obeying, you are not abiding in Him. It is that simple.

You also will bring glory to the Father through godly sacrifice, sacrifice that brings Him honor, sacrifice that shows you are past yourself. If you're self-serving today you're not abiding in Christ. In fact, if you abide in Christ, He will be the one who will influence you the most.

Who is influencing you the most today? Is it Christ? If He's not, you are not abiding in Him. It is that simple. What is influencing you? Obviously, the reality of Christ should be consuming your life if He has become everything to you. If you are truly in Him, it's His reality; and it's His influence that is going to consume you. And in the end, you will be His disciple. Are you His disciple today? If you are not, you are not abiding in Him.

Are you beginning to get a small glimpse of what it means to be in Christ? The revelation of us being in Christ would just totally knock us on the floor. It is beyond our comprehension. It's something we receive by faith. It is important that we understand the reality that we gain by growing in the knowledge of Christ; therefore, causing us to understand the reality of what it means to be in Christ.

As I said, the word "in" is a small word, but it embraces one of the greatest realities of all, that we truly are in Christ and He is in us. Because it is on this basis that we have salvation; we have hope that we can walk in confidence that we will be spared from the wrath of God to come. Jesus is all we need, and He is all we are going to ever need. That is what you need today. It is because of Jesus being an inward reality that we will be perfected in Him, and in His life. Such a life is the type of life that the Father will accept and the world will marvel at.

In fact, if we truly are trying to grow in the knowledge of Christ and be consumed by that knowledge, then we will be rooted and built up in Him. Today, a lot of Christians do not have roots or "studs" in their life, as we would call them in a house, to hold them up. They have no real foundation because they are not in Christ. He is the one that builds us up. Christ in us is the one that gives us roots.

Let me ask you. Are you in Christ, or have you failed to allow Him to become all in all in you, to you, and through you? Does He possess your heart, mind, and will? Is He consuming your life?

Are you abiding in Christ or are you disconnected because of sin, independence, or personal rights? When the Father considers you, does He see His Son or does He see you? If He sees you, God have mercy on you. If He sees your stinking wisdom, God have mercy on you. If He sees your rotten pathetic righteousness, God have mercy on you. If He sees your worldly expression of holiness, God have mercy on you. If He sees that somehow you're trying to redeem yourself outside of Christ, God have mercy on you because you are still subject to His wrath.

PROGRESSION
Part 1
(Excerpts from Sermon)
Rayola Kelley

I have been talking about what it means to be in Christ, and I will continue along the same lines. But what we are going to look at is the fact that if you are in Christ, you should be living a victorious life. Today, I see Christians who live defeated lives, and I believe the Scripture verses in **Romans 6:6-13** will show us why Christians live defeated lives, why they are not victorious.

People often try to brainwash themselves in Christianity. They think that if they say a truth long enough that they are going to make it a reality in their lives, but that isn't how things come true in Christianity. You cannot brainwash yourself into believing something. You cannot go around and say I am in Christ, and then all of a sudden you start living like you are in Christ. Such a practice is nothing more than an attempt to indoctrinate.

The only way that we, in our finite pathetic little ways, can catch a glimpse that we are in Christ is through revelation; and I am not talking about the type of revelation that you try to conjure up. I am talking about revelation that comes from the Holy Spirit. He unveils to your spirit that you are in Christ, and from that point on it becomes more and more of a reality.

Such a revelation is not based on indoctrination. This type of revelation is inspired by what we call true faith. Faith is not some form of persuasion. This is what those in "Positive Confession" attempt to do. They think if they say something long enough that they will conjure up some faith. This is brainwashing, but it is not faith. Granted, real revelation is inspired by true faith that expresses itself in action. Since faith is active, you will begin to walk out revelation, which will enlarge you to receive more. It all starts out by you realizing you are in Christ.

Since you are in Christ, you choose to believe that by faith. Active faith will cause you to begin to walk the revelation out in your life. At the point of your active faith, the Holy Spirit brings life to the revelation. At this point, the revelation becomes real to you. But before revelation comes, there must be active faith. And, before active faith comes, you have to take something on the basis of it being truth, and begin to walk it out as truth.

I am going to talk more about this process later. At this time, I am going to also to talk about what it takes to realize victory in your life. In fact, there is a progression that is being presented here in **Romans chapter 6** that is very important for you and me to see. And, what we are going to see is that this progression leads you to a destination. It leads you to something called identification. Identification is important for us to understand. It only comes by revelation. You will never become identified with Christ unless you receive revelation from the Holy Spirit. This reality must be made real to your spirit. We know that revelation comes from active faith.

There are people out there who want to be identified to God, but they have no revelation; therefore, they stand on the outside of some spiritual vacuum always looking in. The key here is as Christ is revealed to you, He is revealed for the purpose of you becoming identified with Him. He is not being revealed so you can do your own thing or go your own way, but to actually become identified with Him.

Identification means the act of identifying, or the evidence that something is really going on in your life. Is there evidence of it in your life today? Think about it.

So what is this progression where I can really begin to become identified with Christ and encourage revelation in my life? Clearly, such progression is going to take place by faith. However, what is the beginning of that progression? There is only one way that you can enter to have revelation and truth, and that is by the door of death. Think about it, this progression starts with death. Look at **verse 6** in **Romans 6**. This is the first thing you have to come to terms with. "Knowing this", now notice he is using the word "know". <u>Knowing</u> means that you perceive, and the way that you spiritually perceive is by the revelation of the Holy Spirit. Paul says, "Knowing this that our old man is crucified with him." He is saying that you need to know that you are dead. And, if you are dead then sin has no reign over you." Sin cannot destroy you. The whole key here is that Christ died, and you are in Christ; therefore, you are dead. The idea of who you used to be has been crucified with Him on that cross.

We are told this in **verse 3** of **chapter 6**. Those who were baptized into Jesus Christ, were baptized into his death. If you have been baptized, you identified yourself with Christ in His death. And, if you are dead, you are dead in Christ, so that sin will not reign.

However, what has to die in you? The word talks about two types of sin. In **Romans 6**, it talks about sins. Sins are the product of your rebellious ways. Jesus Christ died on the cross and shed His blood so such sins could be taken far away. (See Psalm 103:12.) All you have to do is go to Jesus and receive the reality of what He did on the cross by faith, and your sins are cleansed. The issue is not your sins, for they are easily taken care of by the blood. But there is another sin that acts in your life and that is the sin of the fallen condition or the disposition of the old man. The old man reveals that sin is reigning in us.

Clearly, Jesus' shed blood does not do away with the defiant disposition in you. The blood takes away your sin, but it does not deal with the wrong disposition of the old man. So how did God deal with the old man in us? He dealt with it by the cross. He addressed it by crucifying the old man on the cross. That is how sin and rebellion are taken care of. The old man dies on the cross. Ultimately, the old man becomes totally identified with Jesus Christ on the cross.

We need to understand this because we have a wrong conception about Jesus. We think that His blood takes care of our foolish disposition. However, it is the cross that takes care of the disposition. Therefore, there must be a death on the cross. Paul states that such perception must be received as a revelation in your spirit. It is very important that you realize that you are dead to the influences of sin upon your disposition. This is why a lot of Christians live a defeated life. If you are dead, your enemies will have no power over you. Sin is an enemy, and it must lose its power over you. Likewise, the world and Satan will not have any power over you if you are dead. The disposition of the old man will not have any power over you if you have become identified in Christ's death.

I heard an example of this many years ago when I was a new Christian that I have never forgotten. The example had to do with Christians in Russia. The officials in Russia made this statement about the Christians, "How can you kill someone who is already dead?" Obviously, the Christians in Russia were so dead to their rights to their present life that they could not be threatened with death, torment, or imprisonment. These people have greater liberty than we do in America. Christians who are dead experience the greatest liberty of all. They experience the glory and the fullness of Christ because they are dead to the old life. The more that the old man is still alive, the more power your enemies are going to have in your life.

This is the reason Christians walk around in torment because they are not dead, they are still alive, and so the different enemies of their souls have a say over their lives. These enemies can drive them with torment. And, of course, the more you cling to the old life or this present life, the more Satan, the world, and sin will gain a foothold into your life. So the more the old man's disposition is alive, the more defeated you will be. The more you apply the cross to the old man, the greater the victory you will have over your enemies.

Based on your present life can people tell that you are dead? Are you still striving to survive? Are you still striving to keep the old man reigning? Now, once you perceive that you are dead to the reign of the old man in your life, then you can go to the next step, which is found in **verse 11**.

This verse says, "Likewise, reckon ye also yourselves to be dead indeed unto sin,..." Reckon means to count as true. Reckoning is an accounting term; and what it is saying is that when you reckon that you are dead, you are counting yourself as dead. For instance, if you say I know I am dead, then you reckon it as so. You are counting it as a truth. But, before you can count something to be true, you must first perceive it is true!

The problem is that a lot of Christians reckon they are dead, but they don't know it. And, when you reckon something without knowing it as true, it is going to come back and mock them. Christians can say that they are reckoning they are dead, but yet their lives declare them to be a hypocrite due to the fact that the old disposition in them is still alive and reigning in some way.

The reason a Christian is not dead is because he or she does not know it as a truth. Reckoning does not operate on fantasy, but according to truth. When you consider that Paul is using an accounting term, you realize he is saying you are indeed counting it as a truth, a fact.

Watchman Nee reinforced this concept by pointing out the only thing we can get right is accounting. For instance, one plus one equals two. If I go to Africa, and ask somebody who knows anything about math what is one plus one, he or she will always say two. Mathematics is a consistent fact, and Paul says that is the only thing we can get right. We occasionally may get stories right, and try to imitate the things of God, but the only thing we can get right on a consistent basis is accounting.

Knowing takes place in the spirit, but reckoning takes place in the will. To reckon something involves not only evaluation based on fact, but it's takes a determination to deem it as a truth. Reckoning is not just only based on evaluation of fact, but it is making a determination that it is a truth. It's an absolute truth, and this involves your will. Now this agreement of the will is an act of faith. Faith is a choice that takes place in your will. Real faith in God is not a blind faith.

Real faith is based on facts and principles that are clearly in operation. In fact, everything we agree to as fact is based on faith. Our most intellectual people think they have figured out everything because it is automatically known. This is not true. They are operating out of faith. Let me give you an example of what I am saying. One plus one equals two, but how do we know this is true? Well, so and so told me in class that one plus one equals two. Well, how does so and so know for sure? Well, it's called the principle of mathematics. Where did the principle of mathematics come from? Can you not see that we accept what we call truth and principles by faith? We have actually been told the truth about something, and so by faith we reckon or determine in our spirit that it is the truth.

It is amazing to me how many people claim they cannot believe what they do not see. Have you heard such a claim? And yet, these very same people believe things that they have no personal proof of, but they have accepted it on the basis of faith towards what they have been told or taught.

Everything that we believe today is based on faith. But the difference with Christianity is that is not just something that you believe by faith, it is something that activates your faith because you know it is true. You know that you are going to live according to that truth. Faith is a choice of the will to agree with the evaluation. And, the evaluation is that you're dead because Christ died and you are in Christ.

Reckoning takes you one step farther, and says it is a truth; therefore, I am going to act on it. I am dead, and when something comes along that entices the old man to rise, he is unable to respond. A good example of this is found in **Romans 10:17**. It says that faith comes by hearing. Hearing comes because there is knowledge or reality being presented to you. This hearing is strictly being influenced by the Word of God, which is considered infallible. That's how faith works. It is active because you have reckoned something as true, and you now walk according to that truth in your life.

Progression in our spiritual lives begins with knowing you are dead to the influence of the old man, and then counting it as a truth. What is the purpose of dying? Let us consider **Romans 6:4**,

> Therefore we are buried with him by baptism into death: that as Christ was raised up from the dead by the glory of the Father, even so we also should walk in newness of life. For if we have been planted together in the likeness of his death, (which if you are in Christ you have been planted with him in the likeness of his death) we shall be also in the likeness of his resurrection. (Parenthesis added.)

The reason we have to die is so that we can experience this new resurrected life. It is a resurrected life of Jesus Christ coming forth that will actually be manifested in our lives. However, you cannot experience this new life unless you know you are dead, and you reckon it as a fact. Because once you reckon that you are dead, consider what **verse 11** says: "Likewise reckon you also yourselves to be dead indeed unto sin, but alive unto God through Jesus Christ, our Lord." Once I reckon myself dead then I can reckon myself alive. I can count the reality that I am alive because I died in Christ. Since Jesus rose again in the newness of life, then I have also risen with Him in newness of life. This newness of life can only come by way of death. And, how we all avoid death to the self-life or life the way we think it should be!

Now that I reckon that I am dead and have been made alive unto God, then the next step is to present that life back to God. Consider this in **verse 13**. It says, "Neither yield…" Yield in this case means present. I am going to substitute the word "present" in the place of "yield" in the Scripture. "Neither "present" ye your members as instruments of unrighteousness unto sin." Paul is saying that now you have this new life, don't present it with the dictates of sin and unrighteousness still reigning. Rather, present this new life back to God.

You may wonder why should you present this new life back to God. God will not take anything unless it is presented to Him. Needless to say, He will never accept the old man in you. You can present the old man to Him all you want, but He will never accept it. He will only accept the new life of Christ in you. As you present this new life, He will take those characteristics that are part of that new life, and He will use your life as an instrument of righteousness for His glory.

Remember your old life is dead, but we have a tendency to think I will just present my abilities to God. No, you must not, for if it is a part of your old life, He is not going to accept it. I don't care how wonderful your abilities are. You have to kill that old life, and allow the new life to be established. It is the new life of Christ in you that must be presented to God for His purpose and glory.

What is the Scriptural principle behind presenting your life to God? It means you're consecrating your life. You are setting your life apart for God's use, and not for sin's use. This is what it means to present a consecrated life unto God. Just because you set your life apart doesn't mean you are holy. The key is that once you present the new, consecrated life to God, He is going to sanctify it. Such sanctification is what makes one holy before God. He has to actually sanctify the life of Christ in us. This should not surprise us when you consider what Jesus stated in **John 17:19**, "And for their sakes I sanctify myself, that they also might be sanctified through the truth."

Jesus sanctified Himself as our example. Sanctification in this text means it will belong to God. If you just consecrate yourself and He doesn't sanctify it, it still does not have His mark of ownership upon your life. He can only use those things that have been sanctified by Him.

Do not assume that the new life in you that is being established belongs to God. You must first present it to Him, and then He must sanctify it to ensure ownership. Such a presentation will make you servants of righteousness, establishing the fact that you are no longer servants of sin. If you have the new life working in you, but you have not consecrated it unto God, and He has not sanctified it, you will not confidently stand righteous and acceptable before Him. He has to sanctify it. Have you presented your new life of Christ in you to God or are you servants of sin today?

Now the final step of progression is walking after the Spirit. You will find this in **Romans 8:1**. "There is therefore now no condemnation to them, which are in Christ Jesus, who walk not after the flesh or the old man, but after the Spirit." Walking after the Spirit is a sermon in itself, and I am going to deal with that more next week. However, what I want you to understand is that you cannot walk after the Spirit until you first know and reckon that you are dead. People are trying to walk after the Spirit without going through this process of death. If you are not dead to self, you cannot walk after the Spirit. You may get glimpses of Him once in a while. He may direct you occasionally, but you will never walk after the Spirit since you always walk after the one that reigns in your life. If the old man is reigning in your life, you're going to walk after the flesh. The Bible tells us that the flesh wars against the Spirit. You must kill the old man so that you don't have that battle going on in your life.

Today many Christians are in a total battle because the old man has not died on the cross with Christ. Therefore, there is this war going on between the flesh and the Spirit. It is not unusual for such believers to say I don't know why I cannot get victory. I don't know why I live under so much condemnation.

If you're under condemnation it's because you're walking after the flesh. You have not died, you have not let death take care of the influence of the flesh. Once you reckon yourself dead, then you can reckon yourself alive unto God. Now that I am alive unto God, I have been raised with this newness of life, and He sanctifies me. It is in this state of sanctification that you will be able to walk after the Spirit, mortifying the deeds of the flesh **(Romans 8:13)**. The reason that we don't walk after the Spirit is because we don't have liberty. There are so many battles going on in our lives, and only by death through application of the cross to the old man in us, can we walk after the Spirit in liberty towards that which is righteous and acceptable to God.

The Spirit of God is the One that enables each of us to live a victorious life. He is the One that continues to reveal our life and our lot in Christ Jesus. He's the One that makes Christ Jesus real to us. And, as Christ becomes more real to us, it is His life in us that will rise up in newness and become alive. Such a life allows us to become more victorious. The greater the life of Christ in you the greater the victory, and only the Holy Spirit can make the life of Christ in you real. However, it comes by this progression of death when you reckon it as so, and by faith you present yourself to God so he can have His way in your life.

Are you living a victorious life today? If not, consider whether you have realized your life and position in Christ. The only way you are going to realize it, is to know and reckon that you are dead to the old man. Once you reckon that you are dead, then you can reckon yourself alive unto God for His purpose, His glory. And, then you present the new life back to God.

I want you to bow your heads and ask the Lord, "Where am I in this progression? Have I truly died by applying the cross to my life?" As you follow the progression of death, life, consecration, sanctification, and liberty in the Spirit, you can know that you will be victorious in your life before God. However, this progression must take place to ensure such victory.

PROGRESSION

Part 2

(Excerpts from Sermon)

Rayola Kelley

One of the books that people usually start out reading when they first become a Christian is the book of **Romans**. In a way it is an easy book to read, but there are many deep truths in this book. I don't know about you but I have always wanted to tap into its depth. In fact, I believe **Romans** is the hub for all of Paul's epistles. If you ever study all of Paul's epistles you will find that they lead you back to **Romans**, because this epistle maintains vital truths that we need to understand as Christians.

When you look at **Romans 8**, you get a sense that it serves as the hub in the epistle of **Romans**. It is like a dividing point where it brings the first section of **Romans (chapters 1-7)** together with the second section **(chapters 9-16)**. If you can study **Romans chapter 8** in light of the Spirit, the Holy Spirit will unveil the deeper truths of this chapter. Ultimately, He will give you tremendous insight. In this chapter, Paul will show you your life, hope, and responsibility. There are also tremendous promises in **Romans 8**.

Last week I talked about a path that we must walk to realize the victorious life that we have available in Christ. I am going to do a review of it because we are going to be referring back to last week's sermon.

The path started with **Romans 6**, and as you will see, it ends in **chapter 8**. First of all, it started in knowing that we are dead in Christ. We are dead because Jesus died, and we are in Him. We have died to self, the old man, our rights, and what we think we deserve in life. This realization that we are dead to self, and that it no longer reigns in our life lies at the core of real victory.

The reason that Christians do not experience victory is because they are not dead to the old way of life. The old man in them is still very much alive, calling the shots, and wanting to do things on its terms. As one gives way to the reality of Christ, he or she will see more victory. Now once you know that you are dead, you need to reckon or count it as true. When you encounter something that entices the old man in you, you must remind yourself that you are dead to it, thereby fleeing from it. The problem with many Christians today is that they toy with the enticements of the flesh. Suddenly, the old man rises up with a vengeance, causing defeat in their lives.

Once you count the old man dead, then you can count your self alive unto God. To be alive unto God means that the new life of Christ in you must belong to God. Everything you do will be as unto God.

We are no longer talking about Christ dying on the cross, we are talking about a risen Savior that sits on the right hand of God. And, it is His life that should be manifested in your life. Once you count yourself alive unto God, then you present that new life back to God. God can take that life of Christ in you and sanctify it for His use and glory. Once He sanctifies your life, then you can begin to walk after the Spirit. By walking after the Spirit, you will know what it means to be victorious in Christ. You will actually reach your potential in the kingdom of God.

What does it mean to walk after the Spirit? I am going to tell you right now what it means to walk after the Spirit. It will come down to who or what is reigning in your life. If you do not have the right source reigning in your life, you will never be able to walk after the Spirit.

The late H. A. Ironside in his commentary about **Romans** gives this insight into this book, He says there are two _heads_ that are revealed in the book of **Romans**. One head is Adam and the other head is Christ. There are two _masters_ presented in this book, one is sin and the other one is God. There are two _husbands_ exposed in this book, the Law and the risen Christ. You are bound to either the Law or you're bound to the risen Christ today. Whoever serves as your husband will determine who is actually influencing you the most. You are either being influenced by the disposition of Adam or you're being influenced by the mind of Christ. In fact, your head determines who you are in. You are either in Adam or you're in Christ. Your head will, in turn, determine your master. The master of your life will be based on whether you're walking after the flesh or after the Spirit. If you're walking after the flesh, it is obvious who or what the master of your life is going to be. If you're walking after the Spirit your master will be obvious. Your walk will determine your spiritual status. Today you are either walking in justification and liberty, or you're walking in bondage and condemnation.

Here is a very important truth. The husband we are spiritually bound to will determine the law that we are subject to. In **Romans 8:2** we read of two laws—the law of the Spirit of life in Christ Jesus or the law of sin and death.

One of the first things you need to understand is that all of us are subject to various laws in our life, but the laws we are going to look at today influence the spiritual realm. For instance, we are subject to gravity. You drop something and it falls to the ground. We are subject to the law of thermodynamics, which means that everything regresses to the state of practically nothingness. In other words, you can burn a piece of wood down to just a bunch of little ashes. But, speaking in regard to our spiritual lives, we are either subject to the law of the Spirit of life or the law of sin and death. A law simply means that something is working in you that is natural, and you will be responding according to a particular law, causing you to work within that law, making you subject and accountable to it.

For example, the law of sin and death has to do with the fact that you and I are sinners due to our disposition. Before we ever received Christ as Lord and Savior, this is the law that worked in you and me. This is the law that works in every unsaved individual. I don't care what the person's culture is or what his or her background is, the law of sin and death is working in each of us until we meet and receive Jesus Christ.

Now the reason that the law of sin and death is working in every person is because we each have a problem with sin. We are sinners due to the disposition that was passed through Adam. You see that a lot of people don't understand that they are either in Adam or in Christ. And, if you or I are in Adam, then the law of sin and death is working in us today. And, the reason the law of sin and death is working in us today is because Adam fell into a wrong disposition, and we inherited his fallen condition. Since we are subject to the law of sin, it is natural for us to sin. That is what the law of sin and death is all about.

If this law is working in us it means that death will be the result. I am talking about spiritual separation from God. We know that Jesus died on the cross to keep us from experiencing this type of death. But very few people have truly come to Christ so that this law of sin and death can cease to work within their lives. Now if the law of sin and death is working in you, I want you to know that it's natural for you to walk after the flesh. You will be bent towards the ways of sin and death. I don't care how religious you are, how pious you are, how many times you go to church, or how self-righteous you are, if you are walking according to the flesh, you still need to know that the law of sin and death is working in you.

There are a lot of Christians that are positionally in Christ, but their walk shows that they are still being influenced by Adam's disposition, and that there are parts of them still in Adam that are causing conflict and problems in their lives. We know that according to **Galatians**, the flesh wars against the Spirit. The more the law of sin and death is working in you, the more you are going to have a greater battle with the Spirit because your flesh is going to want life on its terms. You will also be operating according to the law of sin and death in that particular area.

This is very important to get down into our hearts today because one of these laws is affecting us. However, the more that we die to self, the less the flesh is influencing us, the less that this law of sin and death will have any power in our lives. Clearly, the flesh needs to lose all of its influence in our lives. We each need to give way to the Spirit instead of fighting against Him.

After all, the flesh does not mind the things of the Spirit. It doesn't care about the things of God. You might say that you are still walking in the flesh, but you care about the things of God. This cannot be true. God's heart is that you do not walk according to the law of sin and death, but according to His Spirit. Be careful that you are not deluding yourself. The flesh has no regard about the things of God. It will disguise this "so-called concern", it will change it and fit it into its own agenda, but it will never submit to the will of God. If you are fleshly in your walk, Adam is still your head, and his disposition is still determining your actions. The head always determines a person's actions.

Romans 8:7-8 says that the flesh is opposed to God. Since the flesh is opposed to God, it will never become subject to the law of God nor can it be. **Verse 8** tells us that if we are in the flesh, we cannot please God. Once again, it does not matter how religious you are, how wonderful you think you are, and that you doing things in His name, or going to church, if you are in the flesh, you are incapable of pleasing God.

There are a lot of Christians who have remained fleshly. As a result, they cannot truly please God. **Verse 13** warns us that if we live after the flesh, we shall die. We should be sober towards this warning. We must ensure separation from all our fleshly ways.

If we walk after the flesh, we need to keep in mind that we are also subject and bound to a husband. But, what husband? If you are walking according to the flesh, you are subject and bound to the husband of the Law. You might say, "Well, that's not so bad." You do not want to be bound to the Law. If you don't believe me read **chapter 7** of **Romans**.

Why do you think Paul felt the need to put **chapter 7**, the subject that we are about to consider between **6** and **8**? In **Romans 7** Paul is talking about the Law. He points out that if you are bound to the Law, you are subject to the law of sin and death. The Apostle Paul brings a powerful contrast between the Law and Christ. He also brings out the great conflict between the Law and the flesh. The flesh may be subject to the Law, but it is not natural for the flesh to please or obey the Law. Keep in mind the Law is spiritual, while people are fleshly. The natural cannot discern the spirit **(1 Corinthians 2:13, 14)**. Therefore, you cannot bring these two things together. The flesh is going to despise the Law, and the Law is going to condemn the flesh, as well as pronounce death and judgment on it.

Paul admitted that he had a real big battle raging because of the flesh and the Law. After all, there are two different laws in operation here. Now hear what Paul said because number one, Paul was a Pharisee and the Law that he is talking about is what: The Law of Moses. Paul candidly speaks of this conflict. He was a Pharisee who believed in adhering to the Law of Moses. However, in all honestly, no matter how much he wanted to keep the Law, he miserably failed to do so. He found himself to be wretched as he struggled with this issue. He compared the Law to a husband, that proved to be too burdensome to carry around. Eventually, this burdensome relationship will become a stench since there is no real life in it. However, since he was bound to this husband, he was hopeless. His only hope of being released from this harsh husband was through death. Since the Law is spiritual and eternal, Paul could only conclude that death had to occur on his part to be released from this unreasonable husband.

To be released from the husband of the Law, and removed from under the law of sin and death, we must die. This is why **chapter 6** speaks of every believer's death in Christ. Once you embrace the death experience in Christ, you are no longer bound to your first husband, the Law. In fact, your second husband is waiting to betroth you to Himself. The second husband's name is Jesus. Paul joyfully declared that Jesus was able to deliver him from his wretched condition.

Before you can embrace your second husband, you must die and be released from your first husband. Obviously, this is why Paul starts out in **Romans 6** calling us to die. Death will set you free to marry the ultimate husband, to come into union with Jesus Christ. This is why you must know, count, and reckon that you are dead to the old life. You must be set free from being haunted and tormented by your first husband.

There are Christians who are walking around tormented because they have not really reckoned that they're dead. If you are haunted and tormented by the first husband, the Law, you have never come to the point where you know you are dead. However, once you are dead, then you must be resurrected to embrace your new husband. In this new marriage you can present your brand new life back to God. As a result, you will be able to walk after the Spirit in liberty.

This new walk means you can now become subject to your second husband, Jesus Christ. Such a reality is vital to understand. Since Jesus fulfilled the Law and you are now in Him, the Law has been fulfilled in your life as well. In fact, in verse **4** of **Romans 8** it says, "That the righteousness of the law might be fulfilled in us, who walk not after the flesh, but after the Spirit." There are people who want to fulfill the Law, but they cannot. People can only fulfill the Law when they have come into union with Christ and are walking after the Spirit. And, if any one is trying to keep the Law in his or her own power, it will turn around and condemn him or her just as it did the Apostle Paul.

Now that you are in Christ, you are under a new law. Consider **Romans 8:2**, "For the law of the Spirit of life in Christ Jesus…" This law will make you free from the law of sin and death. It is a life that possesses the essence of righteousness. In fact, to experience the freedom that comes from within this new life means that a person is no longer under condemnation. If you are walking after the flesh today, you are under condemnation; but if you are walking after the Spirit, you are no longer under the condemnation of the Law because you are now under another law.

The law of the Spirit of life supersedes the law of sin and death. The only way a law can be superseded is that a greater or more worthy law is presented. If one law is less in its abilities, it can be superseded by another law that proves sufficient, complete, and satisfying. The law of the Spirit of life supersedes the law of sin and death because it is greater. Since the law of the Spirit is greater than the law of sin and death, you are no longer subject to the lesser law. The law of the Spirit of life supersedes all laws.

One day Jesus is going to come back and supersede the law of gravity. Right now, other laws may be affecting us. As a result, our outer man is dying, but the inner man is being renewed day after day. And, if we walk after the Spirit, we can be assured in the near future that our bodies will be quickened with the same resurrection power that raised Jesus from the grave.

Do you realize that you have the same resurrection power in your life because of the law of the Spirit of life? The Spirit reminds us that we possess resurrection power in us that is not only renewing and reviving, but it will raise us up on the last day. What an incredible revelation! Paul is trying to really get this into our spirits, but the key to experiencing this life will hinge on our demise.

Consider **Romans 8:13**, "For if ye live after the flesh, ye shall die: but if ye through the Spirit do mortify the deeds of the body, ye shall live." Mortify means to kill, to put down, or to crucify. You must mortify the deeds of the body in order to live. Real life hinges on our demise. Even the good things that are a part of our flesh must die to embrace the best. Granted, God may resurrect such things, sanctify them, and give them back to us, but all matters of the flesh must die. In fact, Oswald Chambers calls it a "white funeral." He says the biggest hindrance in the kingdom of God is the good things in our life. He stated that you must kill it, and attend the "white funeral" of it. You must get rid of it because it will keep you from the best.

The door of death is the most important door to a Christian. From personal experience, we have walked through a lot of doors of death and attended many "white funerals" along the way. However, each door of death allows us to walk after the Spirit to gain more and more of Christ. If Jesus tarries, we will all walk through the ultimate door of physical death. Needless to say, my greatest fear and concern is that no one walks through that door into a Christless eternity. The whole purpose of walking through doors of death to the old way of living is to gain Christ, so at the end of your life, you will walk through the final door with Him leading the way.

By walking after the Spirit, you will reach your potential in Christ. Now when I talk about potential, we think in terms of realizing our calling or discovering our gifts. However, I'm not talking about such matters. The potential that God desires you to reach is so simple that each believer can miss it. Our ultimate potential as Christians, is to please Him, and to become sons and daughters of God. I am not talking about in name only. There are a lot of Christians running around saying, "Oh, I am the son or daughter of God," when in reality they don't have any clue as to what it means to be child of God. We are talking about an intimate relationship with God. The heart of God is that you enter into an intimate relationship with Him, where you will discover emotionally and spiritually what it means to be His child. To actually walk after the Spirit means you are walking after Him to come into this intimate relationship.

Consider **Romans 8:14-15**. These Scriptures declare, "For as many as are led by the Spirit of God, they are the sons of God. For ye have not received the spirit of bondage again to fear; but ye have received the Spirit of adoption, whereby we cry, Abba, Father." Our potential is to become a child of God, but not in name only. Our place is on the lap of God close to His heart in fellowship, near His caring ears of compassion, and enjoying Him for who He is.

Progression in our spiritual lives will always lead us into a fuller relationship with God. This is the heart of God. I am not talking about ministries, callings, or gifts. I am talking about the heart of God towards you. He wants you to reach your potential as His child. It is as a child of God that you will have identity in Christ. This identity will allow you to understand your inheritance according to the Holy Spirit.

It is important for you to know who serves as your head today. Does Adam, or Christ, serve as your head? Who is your master? Are you a slave to sin or a servant to God? And, who is your husband, the Law or the risen Christ? If Adam is your head, then sin is your master, the Law is your husband, and you are walking after the flesh within the environment of death. If you are walking after the Spirit, Christ is your head, God is your Master, and the risen Savior your husband. What is the answer to this vital question? Are you walking after the flesh today or are you walking after the Spirit?

GOD'S OFFERING

(Article)

Part 1

Rayola Kelley

As a writer, I am aware of the power of the pen. I know that the presentation of a matter can change minds and influence worldviews. As a result, my goal has been to present the truth in the right spirit. After all, if you change the meaning of a word, you can change the spirit and intent behind it.

In my observation of how information is now being presented from the various platforms of religion and entertainment, I have noticed the power of these presentations influencing the point of view of many. This power does not necessarily lie in what is told to us, but what they fail to reveal. The problem is that when there is no balanced contrast between opposing views, information simply becomes propaganda, rather than the truth. This was made obvious by the Terri Schiavo's case. We received credible information that would have changed the present view of many people that never was released through the media. Obviously, the information coming out from the secular media was nothing more than a propaganda ploy to influence people's thinking, rather than to properly inform them, enabling them to draw wise conclusions.

As I listen to different presentations of Scriptural truths, I must admit I am concerned that most of it is nothing more than propaganda, designed to influence the thinking of others towards certain theologies or causes. Such propaganda is devoid of a right spirit; therefore, it is not the truth.

Christians must discern whether something is truth for the purpose of education or whether it is propaganda, a perverted attempt to influence and possibly change what is already perceived as truth. One such presentation that Christians need to consider is Jesus' sufferings. Today there is a lot of emphasis on this subject. But we must consider if it is true or nothing more than propaganda. After all, it is up to us to discern such matters, not based on preconceived notions or religious sentiment, but according to the Word of God.

The Bible clearly does not emphasize Jesus' sufferings. For example, the Gospel is that Jesus died for sin, was buried, and rose again. It is the blood of Jesus that redeems us. Obviously, Jesus suffered, but what importance do His sufferings play in our redemption? To come to terms with the concept of suffering, we have to understand its purpose.

There are four reasons people suffer. They are: 1) Consequences from wrong decisions and improper conduct, 2) getting caught up with causes, 3) suffering serves as part of the process, and 4) it is also a means of preparation. Let us consider each of these forms of suffering.

People who suffer because of consequences for wrong decisions or actions have no room to display self-pity. There are many people who are suffering because they refuse to take responsibility for their lives, and accountability for their ungodly ways. The Apostle Peter tells us not to think ourselves as suffering for the sake of Christ when we are paying consequences for our wrong conduct **(1 Peter 4:15)**. In such cases we need to repent, rather than act as if we are being noble about our unpleasant situations.

Some people suffer because of what is considered to be noble causes. Many individuals have suffered because of religious beliefs, political views, or moral causes. Some causes seemed quite noble, while others amount to nothing more than propaganda. However, falling into the traps of propaganda means that people are being led to the slaughter due to their ignorance. It is vital as believers that we understand the main spiritual battle involves our faith **(Hosea 4:6; Jude 3)**. We must know how to stand for truth, stand against delusion, and withstand the enemies of the soul. After all, faith can only find its basis in the faithfulness of God, who never changes nor does He lie. Faith believes what God says is true, will stand in the confidence of His character, and will respond in obedience because it will trust Him with the outcome.

Suffering for the Christian proves to be part of his or her process. This process is to establish the life of Jesus in each of us. Such suffering comes through tribulation and persecution **(Galatians 2:20)**. **Acts 14:22** tells us that Christians cannot enter the kingdom of God without many tribulations. Paul tells us that those who live godly in Christ Jesus will suffer persecution **(2 Timothy 3:12)**. However, those who suffer with Jesus will reign and be glorified with Him **(Romans 8:17; 2 Tim 2:11)**.

Finally, suffering is preparation for that which is greater. Once again, I am not talking about the suffering that we bring upon ourselves because of foolishness and rebellion. For the saints in **Hebrews 11**, suffering pointed to a greater resurrection **(Hebrews 11:35)**. These godly saints never did receive the promise in this present life, but their faith enabled them to obtain a good testimony in the present world, trusting that God would provide something far better in the next world.

For the patient Job, his reward was that at the end of his suffering and loss was a revelation of God. No doubt his suffering faded in light of his glorious God who proved to be beyond comprehension, and too wonderful to describe with words **(Job 42:5, 6; 2 Corinthians 4:16-18; James 5:11)**.

Now let us consider Jesus' suffering in light of the four reasons mentioned. As you consider the whole scenario around Jesus' journey to the cross, you realize He fell into all four categories of suffering. In the first case, Jesus was suffering due to consequences. However, the consequences had nothing to do with His attitude or actions, but with all of humanity. He would take the sins of each of us upon Himself so that we could be forgiven, and be redeemed back from the consequences of our sin.

Secondly, Jesus died for other's causes. The Pharisees wanted to keep their religious kingdom intact. Pilate wanted to keep peace with the Jewish leadership, the crowd was presented with what appeared to be a religious cause, and the Roman soldiers were simply carrying out the cause of those in leadership. As you can see, it is easy to get caught up with the emotional fervor of causes.

In the third area of suffering, Jesus was going through a process that entailed obedience. He was carrying out the will of the Father. In His process of suffering in obedience, He was being perfected as man. **Hebrews 5:8-9** confirms this, "Though He were a Son, yet learned he obedience by the things which he suffered. And being made perfect,

He became the author of eternal salvation unto all them that obey Him." It was in His suffering as man that He became the author of eternal salvation.

The final reason for suffering is preparation for something greater. Let us consider the first three reasons for suffering. Jesus was suffering on behalf of man, but it was out of obedience to the Father. Such obedience is one's reasonable service, which cannot be considered honorable or beyond the call of duty. Since He was suffering for the cause of others, there was nothing noble about His sufferings. It was accepted as a necessary step in the scheme of things. In fact, His suffering at the hands of man reveals more about the harsh reality of man and his sinful disposition, than Jesus' commitment to the Father's will. Since there was no real nobility in His suffering, He cannot be considered a martyr. In fact, He willingly gave up His life.

In the third situation His suffering was part of His process. He was being perfected as man. This brings us to the realization that Jesus was being prepared. The preparation He was going through entailed something of greater purpose and significance. What was Jesus being prepared for? It is simple. He was being prepared to be offered up as the sinless Lamb of God.

Jesus' sacrifice was about judgment. In fact, He faced three types of judgments. He faced the judgment before the religious system in the palace of the High Priest. The second judgment took place before the Roman authorities in the judgment hall called Gabbatha. God executed the final judgment on the altar of the cross at a place called Golgotha. In the palace of judgment, we are reminded that Jesus is indeed the King of kings. Gabbatha pointed to the fact that He is the ultimate ruler over all for all the governments. At Golgotha, there is no doubt that He served as the ultimate sacrifice.

In fact, if you study the three G's in Jesus journey to the cross, you will see that each one points to Him as this ultimate sacrifice. In Gethsemane, Jesus was being prepared as the ultimate sacrifice. At Gabbatha, He was declared to be without fault by Pilate. In other words, He was without sin, enabling Him to become the acceptable sacrifice. At Golgotha, He became the ultimate offering **(John 18:1; 19:13, 17)**.

Jesus came to be God's offering. His suffering prepared Him in every way to be offered upon the altar of the world, the cross. On the cross, God would judge all sin. As a result, Jesus would become the ultimate sacrifice for you and me. In fact, He would become a sacrifice in every possible way for each of us.

In next month's article, I will show how Jesus fulfilled every sacrifice in the Old Testament. As you will see, Jesus' journey to Calvary was not about His suffering, but the sacrifice He would present on behalf of every living soul. His suffering was simply the means by which to prepare Him to become God's ultimate offering.

GOD'S OFFERING

(Article)

Part 2

Rayola Kelley

The natural tendency for people when it comes to Jesus' death on the cross is to think of His great suffering. No one will debate that Jesus suffered, but His sufferings do not make up the Gospel, which is the power of God unto salvation. Jesus' suffering was a preparation for His death. Therefore, His suffering must be kept in that context, or Jesus will simply serve as a noble martyr who will be glorified in His suffering, rather than a victorious Savior who now sits on the right hand of the Father.

Jesus' main reason for coming was not to suffer, but to become a sacrifice. The problem with viewing Jesus in terms of His suffering is that we have a tendency to think that He suffered because we have value or worth. The Word of God is clear that man's best is filthy rags, and that there is no good thing in the flesh **(Isaiah 64:6; Romans 7:18)**. This reality is brought to the forefront if we view Jesus as the ultimate sacrifice. Such a sacrifice can only be understood in light of the Old Testament.

Jesus' sacrifice can only be realized when you examine the five major sacrifices found in **Leviticus 1-6**. Three of these sacrifices were voluntary, while the last two were involuntary, for they addressed sin. The first three sacrifices addressed what it would mean to have a relationship with God, while the last two types of offerings, the sin and trespass offerings, dealt with our sinful disposition and actions. However, all five sacrifices pointed to our need to be reconciled with God. Each offering brings us to a point of devotion and reconciliation for the purpose of restoration and service. Jesus actually allowed Himself to be clothed in flesh to fulfill all five offerings.

The first three offerings were the voluntary offerings. They were the burnt offering, meal offering, and peace offering. These offerings were consumed by fire. They would emit smoke or a fragrance that would be accepted by God. The burnt offering was an offering that represented total consecration or self dedication towards God **(Leviticus 1)**. The Apostle Paul points to this offering in regards to the Christian when he gave this instruction in **Romans 12:1**, "I beseech you therefore, brethren, by the mercies of God, that you present your bodies as a living sacrifice, holy, acceptable to God, which is your reasonable service."

In what way did Jesus present Himself as a burnt offering? As you study His life, He was an ongoing burnt offering as He submitted to the will of the Father. This was culminated in the Garden of Gethsemane. It was here that He once again submitted to the will of God in regards to Golgotha. It was also here that He submitted to those who came for Him. Like a Lamb, He was bound and led away to the slaughter **(John 18:12)**. In reference to Jesus' sacrifice, the prophet, Isaiah made this statement, "He was oppressed, and he was afflicted, yet he opened not his mouth: he is brought as a lamb to the slaughter, and as a sheep before the shearers is dumb, so he opened not his mouth" **(Isaiah 53:7)**.

The Apostle Paul summarizes the climax of Jesus' obedience as a burnt offering in **Philippians 2:8**, "And, being found in fashion as a man, he humbled himself and became obedient unto death, even the death of the cross."

The meal offering was considered the most holy of all offerings to God **(Leviticus 2)**. This offering had to do with the harvest, which included the first fruits of the harvest. Flour, along with oil and frankincense, were burned on the altar. This was the most holy offering because it represented a memorial to God as to His blessings and intervention on behalf of man. It was the fragrance from the frankincense that served as a sweet savor to God.

The Word of God describes Jesus as the Bread of Life who came down from heaven **(John 6:35)** We know that He not only was the meal offering as the bread from God, but He was the first fruits of the harvest of souls in regards to God's unseen kingdom. The Apostle Paul brings this out in his writings, "But now is Christ risen from the dead, and become the firstfruits of them that slept" **(1 Corinthians 15:20)**.

Every offering had to be brought to the priest for examination. As the first fruits and the offering of God, the priest examined Jesus after He was arrested. The priests determined that He was worthy of death. In fact, they would be willing to present Him as their scapegoat.

The term "scapegoat" came from **Leviticus 16**. Once a year, the High Priest would take two goats to offer up on behalf of the people of Israel for their atonement. One goat was offered up as a sin offering. The second goat was taken aside, and the priest would lay his hands on the goat's head and place all of the sins of Israel on the goat. The goat was then taken to the wilderness and left to wander in the wilderness, far from the people until its death.

When Jesus was standing before the Pharisees, John reminds us of what the High Priest, Caiaphas, said about Jesus in **John 18:14**, "Now Caiaphas was he, which gave counsel to the Jews, that it was expedient that one man should die for the people." Jesus would not just become the scapegoat for the Jews. All the sins of the world would be laid on Him, and they would be cast as far as the east is from the west **(Psalm 103:12**). He would be led to the cross, and upon His death, He would be taken to the barren wilderness of the grave. It is Jesus' death, burial, and resurrection that not only serve as our hope, but they are memorialized in our ordinance of communion. Once again, this points to Jesus being God's meal offering. It was during His examination before the priests and Pharisees that He was struck with hands. No doubt this was the beginning of Him being bruised. Isaiah reminds us that as our offering, "...he was bruised for our iniquities..." **(Isaiah 53:5)**.

For the Christian, the meal offering has a couple of representations to it. It points to a new life that can only come forth when a person is born again **(John 3:3, 5)**. This new life will be the life of Jesus. It is the life of Christ in us that will attract and produce fruits in the harvest field **(John 15:1-8)**. It is also the life of Christ that serves as a fragrance in the Christian's life. Such a fragrance is what serves as a sweet savour to God, an edifying fragrance in the Church, and a harsh reality to the unsaved **(2 Corinthians 2:15-16)**.

There is another aspect to the meal offering: that of salt **(Leviticus 2:13)**. This offering was seasoned with salt. Apparently, this salt pointed to the covenant. Because of Jesus' sacrifice, we have entered into a covenant with God. In this offering, Jesus serves as the flour and the first fruits, but the Christian is to be the salt of the earth **(Matthew 5:13)**. The only way Christians can be the salt is if Jesus' life is evident in them.

The third type of voluntary offering was the peace offering **(Leviticus 3)**. Apparently, the burnt offering was offered first. Commitment is the first step to ensuring the unveiling of the new life and peace with God. Therefore, it was only after the burnt offering was offered that the meal offering and the peace offering could be placed on top of the altar. In fact, these offerings were placed on top of the burnt offering as it was being consumed by fire.

The burnt offering pointed to self-dedication. As stated before, the meal offering was considered the most holy offering because it was void of man. The meal offering was without the shedding of blood, which always pointed to the harsh reality of sin. However, the peace offering was considered the bloody offering. Without the shedding of blood, there can be no remission of sin. Without pardon of sin, there can be no reconciliation with God. Reconciliation points to peace and restoration with God. The Apostle Paul brings this harsh reality out in his epistles:

> In whom we have redemption through his blood, the forgiveness of sins **(Ephesians 1:7a)**. But now in Christ Jesus ye who sometimes were far off are made nigh by the blood of Christ. For he is our peace...And that he might reconcile both in one body by the cross... and came and preached peace to you which were afar off, and them that were nigh **(Ephesians 2:13, 14a, 16:a, 17)**. And, having made peace through the blood of his cross, by him to reconcile all things unto himself I say, whether they be things in earth, or things in heaven **(Colossians 1:20)**.

How did Jesus become a peace offering? Amazingly enough, it was Pilate who offered Jesus as a peace offering. Pilate knew Jesus was without fault. He had no desire to see Jesus die, but he was afraid of the influence of the Jews. In his attempts to appease the Jews, as well as spare Jesus' life, he had the whip laid to Jesus' back.

Whipping was a form of chastisement. It is no wonder Isaiah declared this about Jesus' offering, "...the chastisement of our peace was upon him..." **(Isaiah 53:5)**. No doubt this whipping caused the blood to flow from Jesus stripes on His body. Jesus' body was torn open, so we could experience spiritual healing through peace and reconciliation with God. The words of Isaiah echo down through the years, "...and with his stripes we are healed" **(Isaiah 53:5)**.

The fat is what was burned on the altar in the peace offering. Fat points to anointing. Jesus was the Anointed One, the Messiah, who would be totally consumed as the sacrifice to bring about peace between man and God. We take this peace for granted because we do not understand what it meant for Jesus to be our peace offering. We cannot see the cost that it incurred for God.

The beauty about the peace offering is that believers can become peacemakers as the children of God **(Matthew 5:9)**. Possessing the peace of God is one of the greatest attractions to those who are afraid and uncertain about the world they live in. To see the peace of God, which passes all understanding, in operation during challenging times is a great witness of the faithfulness of our unseen God to keep His people.

This brings us to Jesus as the mandatory offering. He was God's sin offering for us. Man could not make himself acceptable to God. He was doomed in his present state. Only God could solve the problem. Since there is no remission of sin without the shedding of blood, God had to provide the appropriate offering. It was already established that the blood of bulls and of goats could not take away sins. Mere man could never become such an offering because he possesses a disposition that contaminates even his best. Therefore, God prepared and provided His Son to become the ultimate sacrifice **(Hebrews 10:4-12)**.

John the Baptist stated that Jesus was the Lamb of God who would take away the sin of the world **(John 1:29)**. The Prophet Isaiah clearly established that Jesus was God's offering on our behalf, "Surely he hath borne our griefs, and carried our sorrows; yet we did esteem him stricken, smitten of God and afflicted" **(Isaiah 53:4)**.

Jesus was a voluntary offering in the sense that He gave up His life as a sacrifice, but He was a required offering that would once and for all address the issue of sin. Where the Levitical priests once endeavored to keep up with the sacrifices on people's behalf, Jesus would offer the perfect sacrifice that would cease all such work, allowing Him to sit on the right hand of God **(Hebrews 10:10-14)**. In every way, Jesus was an offering that was complete. His offering addressed every aspect and area of man's disposition, actions, and relationship with God. As the Apostle Paul stated, Jesus became our sin offering, so that we could be made in the righteousness of God **(2 Corinthians 2:21)**.

As the sin offering, Jesus would die for our trespasses. The sin offering mainly addressed the selfish disposition that operates in unseen sins such as pride, fear, and opposition against God's authority, while the trespass offerings addressed outward sins that broke the Law or covenant of God. In fact, the breaking of the Law broke the tablets in the wilderness, and the result of man's disregard for God's heart towards him broke Jesus' heart on the cross. Jesus' broken heart was evident when the soldier pierced His side, and blood and water came forth **(John 19:34)**. Blood points to our New Testament covenant and water symbolizes the Word of God **(Ephesians 5:26; Hebrews 9:11-22; John 3:5** refer to **1 Peter 1:23)**. The blood and water coming from Jesus' side confirmed to the soldier that Jesus was who He said He was **(John 19:35)**. The Apostle John made reference to these elements along with the Holy Spirit. He stated that all three are what bear witness in earth: "And there are three that bear witness in earth, the Spirit, and the water, and the blood; and these three agree in one" **(1 John 5:8)**.

Jesus' blood is capable of cleansing us from all unrighteousness **(1 John 1:7, 9)**. The harsh reality is that His blood had to be shed to accomplish such a feat. He died for our trespasses. However, to give up His life for our sins, He had to be wounded to allow His blood to flow. As the prophet stated, "But he was wounded for our transgressions" **(Isaiah 53:5)**.

It is important to see that Jesus' suffering was a preparation for Him to be offered up as the ultimate sacrifice. Jesus' main reason for coming was not to be regarded in light of His sufferings, but in light of His offering **(John 10:18)**. His cry is not that of a suffering martyr, but as a victorious Redeemer: "It is finished" **(John 19:30b)**.

The next time you want to stop at Jesus' sufferings for sentimental reasons, push past it to the end of the Gospel. It is not one of sentimentality, but one of victory. For our Redeemer not only completed the task of redeeming us, but He rose from the grave to prove victory over death, and now resides in the courts of heaven where He serves as our High Priest who continues to make intercession for us. To me, that is something to rejoice in, knowing my expectation of His complete work on my behalf and in my life will be totally realized in glory.

SERVANT OR SLAVE?

(Excerpts from Sermon)

Rayola Kelley

Deuteronomy 15:16, 17, "And it shall be, if he say unto thee, I will not go away from thee, because he loveth thee and thine house, because he is well with thee, Then thou shalt take an aul, and thrust it through his ear unto the door, and he shall be thy servant forever. And also unto thy maidservant thou shalt do likewise."

To me one of the most beautiful chapters in the Bible about the subject that I am going to be speaking on today is **Deuteronomy 15**. I think it is an awesome chapter when you begin to realize what God wants you to understand.

The subject that I am going to be talking about today is a subject that I feel very few Christians really understand. As a result of this ignorance, we see an ineffective fruit coming out of the Church. The subject that I am going to be talking about is, "redemption".

I am going to make a statement: You cannot really understand your redemption unless you do so in light of the Old Testament." It is important to understand redemption. In fact, the New Testament book that might help you understand this subject is **Hebrews**. But the Old Testament really helps you develop a proper foundation on this subject. Therefore, I advise you to take personal time and study it yourself.

You might say why is redemption vital? I am going to ask you a question. Why did Jesus die on the cross? The usual answer I get is that he died to save me. However, salvation is the product of His death, but that is not why He died on the cross. He died to redeem each of us. His death is all about redemption. He said, "It is finished." He didn't say salvation was finished. He was talking about the fact that redemption was finished. Redemption is not the same as salvation. We have made a terrible mistake in thinking so.

I remember one time teaching Korean women, and I noticed they used the word "salvation" to describe such things as redemption. As I began to explain the difference between these words, I realized how precious our language is even though I have a terrible time with English. When you check out the meanings of redemption and salvation, you will find they have different definitions. Redeem means that something is being purchased or obtained or acquired. In other words, redemption is a monetary term. We are told in **1 Corinthians 7:23**, "Ye are bought with a price." Clearly, as believers, we have been redeemed, acquired, or obtained.

When you look at the word salvation it means you have been delivered from the restraint or oppression of something such as sin and death. Salvation is a product or fruit of redemption. The problem is many Christians think and act as if redemption is the work of deliverance. In other words, redemption comes out of salvation instead of the other way around. This is why I appreciate Oswald Chambers who always brings us back to the real issue of our salvation, which is redemption. He says salvation is always on the line of redemption. You might say to me well if redemption is not about salvation, then what is redemption all about? Redemption is not about salvation or deliverance; rather, it is about ownership that will end in deliverance.

Deuteronomy 15 gives us a clear picture of salvation or deliverance in light of redemption. It actually shows us how redemption works, and it is a beautiful illustration that you and I, as Christians, can grab a hold of to understand what Jesus truly did on the cross. This event that we are going to be looking at is called the Sabbatical year. Sabbath points to the concept of rest, or ceasing from activities. As we are about to see, the land was meant to rest, as well as Jewish servants.

The Sabbatical year occurred every seven years. God used this particular Sabbath to do something very important. We can begin to see it in **Deuteronomy 15:1-2**. He said, "At the end of every seven years thou shalt make a release. And this is the manner of the release: every creditor that lendeth ought unto his neighbor, shall release it; he shall not exact it of his neighbor, or of his brother; because it is called the LORD's release." So, every seven years at the end of the Sabbatical year the Jewish people were required to release their brethren or Jewish people from any kind of debt. This also included servitude brought on by some type of debt.

Occasionally, a Jewish brother could not pay his debts so he would offer his service as a servant to the one he was indebted to. It was during this event that such a servant would be released from his debt and his service. Sabbaths are important to understand, because many of the celebrations were signaled or concluded by recognizing the Sabbath. A Sabbatical year opened in what they called the Sabbatical month, and it was during this event that the Feast of Tabernacles took place.

If you know anything about the feasts of Israel there are about eight of them. You will realize that out of all the feasts that are celebrated, Jesus has in some way fulfilled or will fulfill all of them. The Feast of Tabernacles is the one feast that will continue to be celebrated even into the Millenium. It is during this time that Israel will be once again restored as a great nation, and Jesus will reign as its Promised Messiah.

As the Messiah, He will take His rightful place as King and will begin to reign over the people from Jerusalem. Once a year, during His reign, every nation will come to Jerusalem and pay homage to Jesus Christ, the Lord of lords and the King of kings. The Bible says that if a nation fails to honor Jesus, God is going to bring judgment on that nation through drought and wrath.

Clearly, the Sabbatical Year was a very important year, and we are going to see why in light of God's economy. During the days of the prophet Jeremiah, he prophesied against Judah. One of the great offenses that God had against Judah was that they did not observe the Sabbatical Year. As a result, God warned the Israelites that since they did not observe it, they would spend year for year in captivity that they had failed to let the land rest. Judah spent 70 years in captivity under Babylon. If you take seven times 70 it means that for over a 490-year period Judah did not recognize the Sabbatical Year. Apparently, their attitude about this matter became an intolerable offense to God.

The reason this year was important to observe is because it reminded the children of Israel that God had redeemed them from Egypt. In other words, He owned the children of Israel. We see this in **verse 15** of **Deuteronomy 15**, "Thou shalt remember that thou wast a bondman in the land of Egypt, and the Lord thy God redeemed thee: therefore I command thee this thing to day." He first redeemed or released Israel from the slavery of Egypt, and then He delivered them with a mighty hand from all their captivity.

Once God redeemed them, He deemed that the first fruits of the Jewish people, including their sons, belonged to Him **(Numbers 18:14-17)**. They were to be wholly dedicated and sacrificed for the glory and purpose of God. Since God doesn't require human sacrifice, He told the children of Israel that they had to redeem their first born with five shekels. The number five represents grace, and shekels were usually made of silver. Silver was symbolic of redemption.

When you study the Tabernacle, you see that the boards which held up the covering of the tent were established upon silver brackets. The boards represented the Church. Clearly, this shows us that believers are established in and by redemption that was acquired on the cross by Jesus Christ. Upon redeeming the firstborn son, God wanted the people of Israel to understand that they were redeemed because of His grace. He wanted to show them that by getting them the opportunity to buy back their oldest son, that His grace is a way of giving back to them something that they do not deserve.

Redemption serves as a seal of ownership and covenant. Jesus said that He was redeeming us. When we consider redemption in the New Testament, the covenant points to the reality that we now are sons and daughters of God Almighty. Since He had direct ownership over Israel, God had a right to lay the rules down. As our owner, Jesus has the right to lay the rules down, and He has done so in the Bible.

The Sabbatical Year did not apply to the Gentiles. There were Gentiles among the Jewish people, but they were not to be released. The reason God could not insist on their release is because He did not own them. Without ownership He didn't have any rights or say over them.

Every seventh year, Israelites were required to show the same level of grace to their brethren that God had shown them as a nation.

The Sabbatical Year was also an effective time of proving and testing the hearts of Israel. Consider what **Deuteronomy 15:7-9** says:

> If there be among you a poor man of one of thy brethren within any of thy gates in thy land which the Lord thy God giveth thee, thou shalt not harden thine heart, nor shut thine hand from thy poor brother. But thou shalt open thine hand wide unto him, and shalt surely lend him sufficient for his need, in that which he wanteth. Beware that there be not a thought in thy wicked heart, saying, The seventh year, the year of release, is at hand; and thine eye be evil against thy poor brother, and thou givest him nought; and he cry unto the LORD against thee, and it be sin unto thee.

The test that God had for the children of Israel is still the same test for the Church today. This simple test comes down to how we treat the poor. The poor will always be among us, but we need to understand what God's heart is toward the poor. Keep in mind we all start out spiritually poor before God. If your heart is open, your hands will be open, and you will ensure your brethren are released from that which enslaves them. However, if your heart is closed, your hands are closed, and you are going to ignore the fact your brethren are in captivity.

How many in the Church have a closed heart toward the poor? They may support missions, but they do not care about the poor among them. They can pay 10%, and still have closed hearts. And, some people who give do so as a means to soothe their religious conscience.

In redemption, God is actually pointing to sacrifice that comes out of true benevolence. He's talking about that which will cost on a personal level. In some cases, people perceive those who are poor as deserving their particular lot in life. Granted, some people are in their situations because of their attitudes and practices, but there are others that have been victims of circumstances. If you have a closed heart and hands, you will be indifferent to the plight of others, ultimately failing the test. Ask the Lord if your heart and hands are open.

God gave this promise to the Israelites if they had an open heart in **Deuteronomy 15:6**, "For the Lord thy God blesseth thee, as he promised thee: and thou shalt lend unto many nations, but thou shalt not borrow; and thou shalt reign over many nations, but they shall not reign over thee." God is saying that as long as His people keep an open heart and pass the test with the poor, they will never owe anybody anything. But, if His people closed their heart, they would still be indebted.

It is important to realize that due to God's heart toward the poor, believers have benefited. We all came to the cross recognizing our spiritual poverty. Some became broken by sin and others were in despair when they came to the cross. It is in poverty that God is able to meet us. "Blessed are the poor in spirit for theirs is the kingdom of God" **(Matthew 5:3)**. When we came to Christ on the cross, we were also indebted servants that needed to be redeemed from unbearable taskmasters such as sin, the flesh, and Satan.

God designated the seventh year so that the people of Israel could remember when He brought them out of Egypt. They came out as slaves **(Deuteronomy 15:15)**. He did not want them to forget their humble beginnings.

As Christians, do we have such a celebration when we remember we were poor? Yes, it is called communion. We came to Christ poor and wretched. Every time we have communion, it is to remember what Jesus did on the cross. We are reminded that we were poor, and that we needed the same consideration as the poor do around us. However, before you can partake of such a release, you must belong to Jesus. Has Jesus truly redeemed you or are you like the Gentiles on the outside of His release?

There is a beautiful thing about the Lord's release. It came to those who were in servitude. When the children of Israel were released as servants, they were not sent away empty-handed. Consider this beautiful picture in **Deuteronomy 15:13**, *"And when thou sendest him out free from thee, thou shalt not let him go away empty."*

When you went to the cross, did you leave it empty-handed? No, you came out with an eternal inheritance. The reason a servant is not sent away empty-handed is found in **verse 14**. "Thou shalt furnish him liberally (how stingy are we) out of thy flock and out of thy floor, and out of thy wine-press." (Parenthesis added.) Then, He goes down to the bottom line of why His people are be benevolent "of that wherewith the Lord thy God hath blessed thee thou shalt give unto him." God is saying I have blessed you so you could bless others. God reminded them of Egypt. They did not come out of their place of captivity empty handed. They brought so much out with them from this land that they were able to build the

Tabernacle. At one point, they were so enthused about giving that God had to turn some of their gifts away.

God's economy is not like ours. Before God, everybody has the same debt. However, Jesus Christ satisfied that debt on the cross, regardless of how great or small, just as God sufficed the debt when He brought Israel out of Egypt.

Why is it that if God has already redeemed these brethren, they need to be released? We cannot walk through this world without becoming indebted to something. Things happen that cause you or me to come into debt. God is asking the people of Israel that they show mercy and grace towards those who are indebted.

Why release these brethren now? Keep in mind God wants to release each of us from the debt of sin. He instructs us to pay all of our debts, but the one of love. However, there is a reason why God's people must be released. Freedom allows them to make a choice. When a servant was released in Israel during this time, he had to make a choice. We see this choice being brought out in **Deuteronomy 15:16**. The person could go back to his earthly inheritance, or he could choose to remain a servant. This would make him a bondservant.

To most people, there would be no choice in the matter. They would go back to their inheritance. This may be an easy decision, unless your master proved to be excellent in every way. By remaining under a fair, benevolent master, you would not have to worry about being indebted to anyone else. All your needs would be provided for by a caring, compassionate master. Therefore, the servant could choose to become a slave to a master who was excellent.

There is a difference between servants and slaves. It is important for us to understand that the main difference comes down to the person's attitude. A servant serves others out of duty. In some cases, they can actually choose which master they want to serve. The reality is that we are all servants to something. It is our choice as to what master we submit to.

A slave is someone who is totally dominated by something or someone. Such a person has no choice. Jesus made a reference to this difference in **Matthew 20:26, 27**. This is in relationship to pagan authority. "But it shall not be so among you: but whosoever will be great among you, let him be your minister; and whosoever will be chief among you, let him be your servant." The word <u>minister</u> means deacon or servant. When you consider the word <u>servant</u> it can be interchanged with the word "slave." What Jesus was saying is if you want to be great then become a servant to others, but if you want to be chief among others, become a slave. Jesus was a Servant of servants because He was a servant to man, but in total subjection to the Father, making Him a slave. In the end, Jesus was made chief or preeminent in all of creation.

You are either a servant or a slave. You could be a servant to God or Satan. Or, you could be a slave of God or Satan. There are three qualities that make a person a slave. The first quality is love. **Deuteronomy 15:16** says, "I will not go away from thee because I loveth thee." The servant loves his lord because of his kindness. Most likely this servant felt part of the household. He had found security, provision, and even greater liberty than he had as a freeman.

The second quality is abandonment. Consider **verse 17,** "...and he shall be thy servant for ever..." This individual decided to become a slave, requiring total abandonment on his part. To become a slave means the individual is becoming indebted to his lord for a lifetime. Such servitude means giving up your personal life in order to become dominated. As a slave, the servant will become an extension of his or her lord while sharing in His blessings.

The third quality of a slave is identification. Consider the beginning of **verse 17**, "Then thou shalt take an aul, and thrust it through his ear unto the door." This mark identified this servant to be the property of his lord. When you become the property of somebody else, you lose your personal identification, and become identified to the household of your lord.

If you are a Christian, you need to know that you have been redeemed. You do not belong to yourself. This may be a tough concept for Christians in America to understand. Consider **1 Corinthians 6:20**: "For you are bought with a price; therefore glorify God in your body, and in your spirit, which are God's." Notice it says the body and your spirit belong to God. They are His property. Are you going to glorify God? Your level of servitude will determine how much you glorify God. The more you serve God in abandonment, the greater you will glorify God. The more you choose the terms in which you serve Him the less you will glorify Him.

The key is that Jesus has redeemed you. You have been set free to choose your master. You can choose to remain a servant, and serve out of duty on your own terms. Your servitude might get you by until your ultimate release happens, that is when you meet Jesus face to face. God can use you to a point, but it also can mean that you are not totally sold out to Him. Your life of service will not make the type of impact it could. I'm sure you want your life to count in eternity as much as it can.

Perhaps, you are rethinking your attitude about servitude. Maybe, you want to be a slave or bondservant to Jesus. After all, there is no greater Lord to serve. Let me give you the qualifications to test your level of servitude as to whether you are His servant or His slave. Number one, as a slave you must love your Lord with all your heart, soul, might, and mind. You love Him because He first loved you.

Number two is that He died on the cross to redeem you. He owns you, and He has given all for your benefit. Therefore, can you do any less for Him? If you are a bondservant to Jesus, you have chosen to become indebted to Him the rest of your life, knowing He paid a debt for you that you could not pay. Since you are indebted to someone or something, why not commit to the Lord of lords?

Number three, you will not hold anything back as a slave. All that you have will be offered to your Lord. You have abandoned all to be dominated by Him, and to serve Him.

Number four you have the mark of the Master. The mark of Jesus Christ is the unhindered power and work of the Holy Spirit moving in and through you. That is the mark of a slave in the kingdom of heaven. It is the mark that identifies you to Jesus, and as you allow the Holy Spirit to come in and work in your life, you begin to take on His attitude. As a result, you will begin to look more and more like Him.

Number five, you have become a bondservant because nothing else makes sense. Nothing else holds significance in your life, but knowing, loving, and pleasing your Lord.

Number six, you have realized that in your Lord's household you have riches untold available to you. You have security and liberty because your Lord will take care of all the details. You don't have to worry about becoming indebted to anyone or anything.

Are you a servant or a slave, to the Lord Jesus Christ? Make sure that you are serving the one true Lord. Make sure that you are not serving Him according to your own terms. You have been redeemed; therefore, the only right decision is to choose to become a bondservant to the one who bought you back from the entanglements of sin and death.

Strange Fire and False Anointing

(Article)

Jeannette Haley

If someone were to ask you how to determine if we are in the last days, you might well answer, "The Bible tells us there will be wars and rumors of wars; earthquakes in different places; famines; diseases and plagues; divorce and remarriage; lawlessness and hideous crimes." All of these things are true. No one can deny we are most assuredly living in such times.

However, there is one vital sign of the end of the age missing in the above statement; that is, false prophets. Of all the topics Jesus warned His disciples about, this one thing, false prophets, was repeated three times in one discourse. **(Matthew 24:4, 5; 11; 24.)** Why do you suppose Jesus, Peter, John, Jude, and Paul placed such a great emphasis on end-time deceivers?

The answer lies in the fact that Jesus and the apostles knew nothing could deceive, devastate, and destroy the Body of Christ like the workings of false prophets. "Well, Jeannette," you may say, "there certainly are no false prophets in my church or circle of friends or life. Besides, I'd know one if I saw one." Are you sure about that? Jesus said in **Matthew 24:24**, "if possible, they shall deceive the very elect." If in the Greek language in this context is used to speak of things not merely probable but, rather certain and dependent on no condition (See Spiros Zodhiates, The Complete Word Study Dictionary, AMG Publishers, Chattanooga, TN, page 504).

Volumes could be written about false prophets, but at this time I feel strongly led to zero in on the Manifest Sons of God movement. Many of you have asked us about the Manifest Sons of God, so in this brief space, we will attempt to give you an overview of this occult presence in the Church today.

The MSG originated from the Latter Rain Movement of the 40's and 50's. In 1946 a major fasting and prayer daily revival center was established in San Diego, California under the leadership of Franklin Hall. Hall believed that the prayers of Christians would be hindered if they did not fast, and the prayers of pagans would be answered when they fasted. His insistence on fasting was not for the purpose of coming into God's presence in order to determine the will of God, but rather for the purpose of getting his way with God--a fanatical zeal for power.

Hall believed in "Christian astrology." He also taught that all those who applied his teachings would become immortal while living in their present flesh-and-blood bodies. He claimed there was such a thing as an "immortal substance" which was seen on those who attended his meetings as a fine gold or silver, sparkling material. He claimed this phenomenon was "Immortal Heavenly Objects" (IHO's), "Unusual Heavenly Objects" (UHO's), and "Unidentified Flying Objects" (UFO's). At this point, some of you may say, "Hey, this sounds familiar! Glory dust from heaven!" Really?

Nowhere in scripture do we find such a "manifestation." However, if you were to become involved in the occult, things such as "glory dust" would be no big deal. Think about it. Is

Jesus being lifted up? Are people being convicted of their sin and born again? Can Satan really produce visible, material "miracles?" You better believe it! Who do you think is the power behind lying signs and wonders? But rather than discuss this further, we need to learn about another "founding father" of the MSG.

William Branham was greatly influenced by Hall's teachings. Branham taught what he called "God's Seventh Church Age." Branham literally believed that he was the "angel" referred to in **Revelation 3:14** and **10:7**, the prophet to the Laodicean Age, the final era of time. Branham and his followers believed that the true evidence of possessing the Holy Spirit was whether or not you followed "God's prophet," which was Branham.

This false prophet brought forth many heretical beliefs including his "serpent's seed doctrine" that claimed that Cain was born of an adulterous affair between Satan and Eve. He denied the Godhead, and taught that the Word of God was given in three different forms: the Zodiac, the Egyptian pyramids, and the written scriptures. He claimed that his gift of healing was done by "his angel (and not the Holy Spirit).

To quote from Roger Oakland's excellent little book, *New Wine or Old Deception*, "A good indicator that a false doctrine in the church is underway is when a teaching projects that man can be big and powerful while God can be manipulated and made subject to man's plans and schemes. Clearly the 'Manifested Sons of God' idea fits into this category." "The Manifest Sons of God emphasize a 'Kingdom Message' by proclaiming the following:

The offices of prophet and apostle will be restored in the latter days. The prophets will call the Church to holiness and rejection of the world's influences found in the denominational churches. True sonship with God will come through stages of perfection: servant, friend, son, and, ultimately, godhood itself.

The apostles will rule the Church through the establishment of independent churches, unaffiliated with the corrupt denominations. The exception would be the denominational churches that leave their covering and join the movement.

Through signs and wonders wrought by the apostles and prophets, a world-wide revival will break out, and a majority of the world will be won to Christ. The signs and wonders will include blessings upon those whom the apostles and prophets bless, and curses upon whom they curse.

The revival will come as the result of the Church defeating demonic spirits through prayer, fasting, and spiritual warfare, conducted through intense worship and praise, and by rebuking demonic powers and territorial spirits. The restoration of praise and worship is known as the Tabernacle of David, and includes dancing, singing, and exuberant praise in tongues.

Those who achieve a certain degree of holiness under the direction of the apostles and prophets will overcome all enemies, including death, and will become immortal. They will complete the conquest of the nations before Christ returns. The conquering is done as Joel's army--an army of immortal beings--bringing judgment upon the ungodly and all who will not accept the authority of the apostles and prophets.

Some believe that the second coming of Jesus is in and through the Church. The Church will become the Christ on earth and rule the nations with a rod of iron. Others believe that after the Church has taken dominion over the nations, the Church, glorious and triumphant, will call Jesus back to the earth and hand the nations over to Him."

It is obvious that the majority of 'Latter Rain' theology cannot be supported by sound Biblical exegesis, and instead lines up with occultic ideas and methodology. It is a noble idea to live a sinless life without 'spot and wrinkle' but, every Bible believer who has an understanding of the grace of God, knows that our hope lies totally in the finished work of the cross and not in any goodness of ourselves.

This teaching seems to appeal to the human weakness of spiritual pride and the lust for power, which has always opened the door for false teachings connected with the occult.

Now, for your soul's sake, I am going to stick my neck out and name a scant few of the popular "apostles," "prophets;" and others who have their roots, and beliefs, in the "Latter Rain Movement" as well as other demonic end-time "movements." Here goes:

Paul Cain
Mike Bickle
Rick Joyner
The late John Wimber
Bob Jones
The Kansas City Prophets
The late Earl Paulk
Kenneth Hagin
Kenneth Copeland
Benny Hinn
Royal Cronquist
The late Oral Robers
The Hunters
Rodney Howard-Browne
John Arnott
Wallace Hickey
Morris Cerullo
The Crouchs

Along with nearly every entertainer on the TBN Network.

Some of the more familiar terms the MSG frequently uses are as follows:

Bride Company
Christ principle
People
Dominion
Elijah Company
Feast of Tabernacles
Five-fold ministries
Jezebel spirit
Kingdom principles
Kingdom theology
Many-membered man child
New Breed
New Order
New Wine
New Zion
Overcomers
Reconstruction
Serpent's Seed
Signs and Wonders
Sonship
Spoken Word
Tabernacles of David
Unity in Diversity

This heretical theology now being proclaimed in thousands of churches throughout the world today, concerning a great outpouring of power in the last days upon an elite group of believers, has no foundation in Scripture.

Jesus told us that the Gospel would be proclaimed as a witness to all the nations, and then the end would come. But, nowhere in scripture does it declare that there shall be a great revival over the majority of the world with people coming to Christ as their Savior. Rather, the Word of God warns us that there shall come a "falling away." We are definitely living in that time.

A "falling away" doesn't mean a departure from religion, but rather, a departure from the truth. That means a departure from the real Jesus (who is the Truth) and from the revealed, written Word of God. Remember that there will be a one-world religion, as prophesied in God's Word, but it will not be true Christianity.

Everywhere we turn we encounter the heretical teachings of the MSG. And what's even more tragic, we see multitudes of people within the Christian ranks swallow this poisonous heresy hook, line, and sinker. Many even fiercely defend it against clear Biblical instruction indicating they have been thoroughly brainwashed. The MSG is lacking in the fruit of the Spirit. Love is not a priority, neither is care for the poor and needy or giving to missions. Their goal is world domination at any cost.

The question is, how can a Christian be deceived? Answer: First of all, by not studying, knowing, understanding, and memorizing the Word of God (See **2 Tim. 2:15**). Christians need to be diligent, discerning, and not leave it up to others to teach them everything they believe. Like the Bereans, they need to check everything they see, read, and hear from Scripture **(Acts 17:11, Heb. 5:14)**.

We continually see believers falling into deception because they do not know the character of God! Rather, they usually define God according to their own frame of reference. This is the result of the shameful failure of the church to disciple new believers! People are left to flounder in the dark and figure everything out on their own. That's one reason why we must never assume that just because a person attends church or says he or she is a Christian that he or she understands what true Christianity is!

Christians need to know what a wolf looks like--a sheep! **(Matt. 7:15)**. A wolf appears to be a minister of righteousness! **(2 Cor. 11:15)**. A wolf also "talks" like a sheep **(Ro. 16:18)**.

Christian beware--pride, arrogance, self-importance, and a feeling of infallibility opens the door for major delusion.

Believers must have an intimate personal relationship with God the Father, the Lord Jesus Christ, and the Holy Spirit. This not only comes through a personal study of the Word, but through prayer. Most believers, sad to say, do not have an intimate relationship with the Holy Spirit. The Holy Spirit is a Person, not a "force" or an "it". He is not here to grant our every wish and whim, but rather to lift up Jesus, convict of sin, guide us to all truth, and lead us to righteousness **(John 16:8-11)**.

Learn how to test the spirit and the fruit. Who is being lifted up? Is it Jesus, or is it a person or doctrine, etc.? Is there liberty or bondage? Are you drawn closer to Jesus with a greater desire to live for Him and Him alone? Do you experience fear, uneasiness, or confusion? Ask the Lord to show you why.

Learn how to recognize a leader's ultimate goal. Is it to acquire a following? Gain income? Or is the leader's goal to exalt the Lord Jesus Christ alone? Some of the signs of true prophets are as follows:

Their prophecies come to pass **(John 1:29)**.

They lift up Jesus **(John 1:7)**.

They do not encourage a following **(John 3:30)**.

They make a straight way for the Lord, bearing witness that Jesus is the Son of God **(John 1:23)**.

Is the leader humble? True humility is one of the greatest tests of a true servant of God. Arrogance, vanity, and pride reveal a carnal, unregenerate heart.

Stick with "winners." If you find a church that still stands on the unadulterated Word of God, where the leaders love the truth and are teachable, stay with it. If you know of "good, old saints" who stand on the faith "once delivered to the saints," fellowship with them. Learn from their example. Toss out questionable books and treasure the "classics" such as those by Oswald Chambers, A.W. Tozer, C.H. Spurgeon, John Bunyon, Charles Finney, Andrew Murray and others who have left us a powerful testimony and witness through their example—a legacy of truth and Spirit. Purge your music collection of all hypnotic, repetitious choruses and words that do not line up with scripture. Study the lives of the old hymn writers, and study the hymns themselves. They were bought with a price!

Finally, ask the Lord to give you a love for the truth. Ask Him to give you a fixed heart. And pray you never, ever fall prey to any kind of delusion.

SUPERSTITION AND THE SUPERNATURAL WITHIN THE CHURCH

(Article)

Jeannette Haley

This is a tough subject to tackle, (because it is seemingly endless) but one that is necessary to address as we continue to hear of supernatural phenomena and "signs and wonders" occurring in both the world and the Church. It is no secret that in the past few decades major changes have occurred within Protestant Christianity—changes that pose a genuine threat to the "faith which was once delivered unto the saints" **(Jude 3b)**.

We need to ask ourselves what those changes are and if they are truly of God. We need to discover their origins, motivations (spirit behind them), and their goals. And most of all, we need to receive a love for the truth so that God will not send a strong delusion that we should believe a lie **(2 Thessalonians 2:10-12)**.

Most fundamental, Bible believing Christians know that weeping statutes, stigmata, apparitions, haunted houses, appearances of "Mary", automatic writing, channeling, witchcraft, psychic healing, incantations, hypnosis, magic, and séances, to name but a few, are not of God. However, an increasing number of Christians are becoming caught up in a "Christianized" version of the occult.

Why are people attracted to the supernatural? I believe the answer to that is simple—being made in the image of God we are more than mere physical beings, we are also spiritual beings. Our very disposition (fallen that it is) has a built-in curiosity and fascination with the supernatural. Fallen mankind also has an inclination toward religion (be it pagan or otherwise) in order to compensate for the loss of fellowship and communion with God. This may also include Christians, especially those who have never been properly discipled. All too often Christians are left to define Christianity on their own, which makes them prime targets for satanic delusions.

Sincere believers, who hunger and thirst for more of God and who have grown restless and dissatisfied with dead, dry, powerless churches are also at risk. Multitudes of Christians have crossed over denominational lines in recent years to join various charismatic groups in the hope of gaining new spiritual experiences and power.

The desire for spiritual power and supernatural experiences
is the common denominator between Christians and non-Christians alike.

Scripture makes it clear that in the last days there will be a great spiritual delusion and occult seduction prior to Christ's return. Jesus warned of false prophets who would perform "great signs and wonders" so convincing that "if it were possible, they shall deceive the very elect" **(Matthew 24:24)**. The apostle Paul also warned of a false "signs and wonders" movement in the last days **(2 Timothy 3:8)**.

To quote author and cult expert, Dave Hunt, "Today a growing "signs and wonders" movement in the Christian church is literally exploding and is involving not only charismatics and Pentecostals but even evangelicals who only a few years ago were opposed to what they would have characterized at that time as fraud. Today, in spite of the warnings by both Jesus and Paul, there is scarcely any thought that today's signs and wonders might be part of the very spiritual deception which the Bible foretells.

"We are also seeing, as a part of the "signs and wonders" movement, a burgeoning "church growth" movement, a "prayer and fasting for revival" movement, and a "spiritual warfare" movement, all working toward the same goal. Few are those who dare to see any connection between these movements within the church and the false "signs and wonders" which the Bible prophesies for the last-days apostate church. Those who call themselves Christians are just as reluctant to admit the possibility of any satanic involvement in the "miracles" as the secular world is to admit the possibility of such involvement in the human potential and psychic powers it seeks to develop.

It is the author's conviction, based upon more than 50 years of observation and research, that we are in the midst of an accelerating occult seduction of both the secular world and the church." (From *Occult Invasion*, Pgs. 15, 16)

People who want to be "spiritual" must be aware that not all "spirituality" is of God. New Agers, witches, fortunetellers, mediums, astrologers, shamans, psychic healers, and the like all claim to be "spiritual". The question is which spirit are they operating under? Why are so many Christians easily seduced into occult practices within the church? **2 Timothy 4:3** and **4** gives us one answer to this question. It reads, "For the time will come when they will not endure sound doctrine; but after their own lusts shall they heap to themselves teachers, having itching ears; And they shall turn away their ears from the truth, and shall be turned unto fables." (Emphasis added.) Today radio and satellite television exposes millions to an endless parade of "teachers".

Jesus said, "An evil and adulterous generation seeketh after a sign" **(Matthew 12:39a)**. Do we not live in an "evil and adulterous generation" today? **Matthew 16:1** records that the religious elite tempted Jesus to show them a "sign". When Jesus was asked by His disciples what the sign of His coming would be, He answered, *"Take heed that no man deceive you"* **Matthew 24:4**. Truly, one of the greatest "signs" that we are indeed in the end times is how many are being deceived by false "Christs" ("anointed ones"); false "prophets", and false "apostles"—all of whom curse those who dare to question their heretical doctrines.

Whether we like to admit it or not, Christians
can be just as superstitious as non-Christians.

According to Webster, <u>superstition</u> means "a belief or practice resulting from ignorance, fear of the unknown, or trust in magic or chance; an irrational abject attitude of mind toward the supernatural, nature, or God resulting from superstitious beliefs or fears."

While superstition among the unsaved can lead to ungodly beliefs and horrible practices among Christians, superstition is an open door for unscriptural attitudes, beliefs, practices (i.e. faith in faith, positive confession, "seed faith") and idolatry. Superstition can replace discernment, which results in a blind acceptance of anything supernatural regardless of the source.

Jesus' disciples exhibited superstition (ignorance) in the case of the man born blind. **(John 9:2.)** And when the disciples saw Jesus walking on the sea they "were troubled, saying, It is a spirit; and they cried out for fear" **(Matthew 14:26)**. In the Old Testament we read in **Judges 8:17** that Gideon "made an ephod thereof, and put it in his city, even in Ophrah: and all Israel went thither a whoring after it: which thing became a snare unto Gideon, and to his house."

In **Leviticus 19:26** God told the people that they were not to "observe times". This meant that they were not to practice magic or divine by the clouds or by flocks of birds that pass over. It refers to being superstitious regarding lucky and unlucky days, imagining omens in the skies, and other such practices by various means. Before we laugh at such superstitious practices let us remember that large numbers of people today who call themselves Christians are caught up in "seeing" angels in the clouds and other "supernatural omens".

Another practice God strictly forbade is that of tattooing. **Leviticus 19:28** says, "Ye shall not make any cuttings in your flesh for the dead, nor print any marks upon you: I am the LORD." (Emphasis added.) Tattooing was a practice of various pagan nations from the earliest times. They marked themselves with all kinds of paint and cuttings of the flesh. These were connected with superstition; therefore, any disfiguration of the body was an outrage to God and an insult to Him who originally designed the body.

We can read of other superstitious practices in **Genesis 30:14-16; 35:4**. In **Judges 21:18b** we read: "Cursed be he that giveth a wife to Benjamin." Dakes notes, "It seems that in those days men were so superstitious they believed if one bound himself to a curse with a vow, as here, the curse would come upon the one who vowed if he broke the vow. When men make vows that are not right the proper thing to do is to repent to God for them, making restitution wherever possible and doing only what is right from then on. All sin is to be repented of and put away, including vows that cause one to sin **(Mat. 12:31, 32; 1 Jn. 1:9).** (*Dakes Annotated Reference Bible*)

Superstitious Christians believe that if they vow to give tithes and offerings to God, then God is obligated to financially bless them. This is a triple tragedy because 1) almsgiving, not tithing, is taught by Jesus and the New Testament Church, 2) those who teach tithing as God's truth are usually always rich wolves in sheep's clothing (heretics), and, 3) "blessing" in God's economy has very little, if anything, to do with financial gain. In fact, Paul stated:

> But godliness with contentment is great gain. For we brought nothing into this world, and it is certain we can carry nothing out. And having food and raiment let us be therewith content. But they that will be rich fall into temptation and a snare, and into many foolish and hurtful lusts, which drown men in destruction and perdition. For the love of money is the root of all evil: which while some coveted after, they have erred from the faith, and pierced themselves through with many sorrows **(1 Timothy 6:6-10)**.

When a person gives to get, he or she reveals his or her ignorance of Scripture and God's character. "Give to get" is the mainstay "sales pitch" on "Christian" television today. This lie originated in the mind-science religions and lures superstitious Christians into a false

Gospel (faith in their faith). Money is given to the rich instead of to the poor, (which is sin to God). Authentic Christian ministries, missionaries, needy servants, and saints are oppressed as a result. Eventually the misled giver may completely turn from God when the desired results fail to materialize. We have witnessed this tragedy many times.

Vows and covenants with God must be kept within scriptural boundaries to ensure that one is not falling prey to the "devil's devices". Ignorance and superstition is a deadly combination because any person operating under both is automatically open to believe and receive anything as truth that he or she perceives as "spiritual" or "supernatural". Tragically, ignorant and superstitious Christians lack the necessary discernment to keep them from falling into the realm of darkness and delusion.

Superstitious Christians are wide open to occult powers that they assume are from God.

The Bible warns of "...another Jesus" and "another spirit" and "another gospel..." **(2 Corinthians 11:4)**. In the same chapter, **verses 13-15**, we are warned "For such are false apostles, deceitful workers, transforming themselves into the apostles of Christ. And no marvel; for Satan himself is transformed into an angel of light. Therefore it is no great thing if his ministers also be transformed as the ministers of righteousness; whose end shall be according to their works."

Acts 17:23 records Paul's statement to the superstitious Athenians, "For as I passed by, and beheld your devotions, I found an altar with this inscription, TO THE UNKNOWN GOD". While multitudes of Christians declare that they know whom they worship their attitudes, actions, and fruit reveals otherwise. Jesus said that His sheep know His voice and will not follow another. Today we see multitudes of people who call themselves Christians heeding the voice of others. These people swallow without question everything and anything that appears "supernatural" such as gold dust, gold fillings, uncontrollable laughter, splitting pulpits, strange lights, so-called angelic visitations, outlandish "visions" of Jesus, people en masse being "slain by the Spirit", false prophets and prophecies, etc.

People who claim to be Christian fall for and practice New Age Hinduism in such superstitious teachings as the following: "positive confession"; using Jesus' name as a "mantra"; believing that we are "little gods" and employing visualization techniques (psychic prayer). To such the Apostle Paul wrote:

> But evil men and seducers shall wax worse and worse, deceiving, and being deceived. But continue thou in the things which thou hast learned and hast been assured of, knowing of whom thou has learned them. For I know this, that after my departing shall grievous wolves enter in among you, not sparing the flock. Also of your own selves shall men arise, speaking perverse things, to draw away disciples after them. Therefore watch,... **(2 Timothy 3:13-14; Acts 20:30-31a)**.

ARE YOU WATCHING?

Kingdom Theology

(Article)

Jeannette Haley

There is somehow something magical about the captivating word "kingdom." This enchanting word can bring to mind mid-evil castles, kings, queens, princes, and princesses. Visions of grandeur flash across the screen of our mind's eye as we imagine knights in shining armor astride powerful war-horses. Ah, what lofty dreams can arise from the word "kingdom."

Within Christendom in the past few decades there has been a growing emphasis on the "kingdom." Mainstream Christianity has been flooded with a barrage of new, aggressive, militant, and doctrinally unsound "kingdom" choruses (music is a powerful medium for teaching doctrine, either false or true). The new "kingdom" songs are repetitiously and fervently sung to ear-splitting accompaniment. Needless to say, reverence, anointing, and true worship have been replaced with a sensuous, carnal sort of feel-good paganism.

"New revelations" about the "kingdom" are taught and preached throughout the land in churches and home fellowships. This revolutionary "reformation" doctrine has spread around the globe via television and radio programs, conferences, seminars, videos, books, and tapes.

What does all of this mean? What does the Bible tell us about God's kingdom? First, we need to understand these two terms can be used interchangeably. Jesus preached the "gospel of the kingdom" **(Matt. 24:14)**, which is the good news that through faith in Him we can be born of the Spirit and enjoy eternal life under God's undisputed rule **(John 3:1-18)**. The early apostles and disciples also preached the message of the kingdom **(Rom. 1:16, 17; 10:9, 10; 1 Cor. 15:4; etc. 8:12; 28:31)** in preaching faith in Christ as Lord and Savior.

Jesus Himself said, "Fear not little flock; for it is your Father's good pleasure to give you the kingdom" **(Luke 12:32)**.

It is important to remember that it is God who gives the true Christian the kingdom. We know that this is a spiritual kingdom, not an earthly one. Jesus declared that His kingdom was not of this world **(John 18:36)**.

For centuries the Church understood that the kingdom of God was not an earthly kingdom. However, we are living in the perilous times foretold by Jesus and the disciples when "kingdom shall rise against kingdom" **(Matt. 24:7)**. What did Christ mean by this statement?

To begin with, we must remember that Satan also has a spiritual kingdom over which he rules. His kingdom is made up of the fallen angels who participated in his rebellion against God and a myriad of demons. We all know that Satan has longed to be the visible ruler over the nations on planet earth ever since the Garden of Eden. He nearly succeeded at the tower of Babel, but the time was not right for Satan's short reign and God scattered the people across the world.

Down through the ages Satan has worked behind the scenes to set up his kingdom, or one-world religious system and one-world government. A more recent example of this is

Nazi Germany and Hitler (Satan has always tried to eliminate the Jewish people and Israel because they bear testimony of God and His promises concerning them). Jesus told us that at His Second Coming He will then, Himself (without our help), establish His kingdom on earth. He will rule and reign from Jerusalem for one thousand years. But prior to this event, the kingdom of darkness and the kingdom of light will "rise against each other."

Nothing is as destructive to the establishment of Satan's Kingdom as God's Word and the people who uphold that Word in Spirit and Truth.

Therefore, in order for Satan to be able to establish his visible kingdom in this world, which he will rule through the person known as the Antichrist, he must somehow deceive the Church into believing a lie. What is that lie? It is the deception that anything "spiritual," "religious," "supernatural," or "good" is from the God of the Bible.

One of the vehicles Satan is using today is called "Kingdom Theology," "Kingdom Dominion," "Restoration Theology," "Replacement Theology" or the "Manifestation of the Sons of God." It would take volumes to fully expose Satan's techniques to achieve global domination. Hopefully, this short article will shed light on one tributary to Satan's growing river of deception.

"Kingdom Dominion" is not a church or denomination, but rather a worldwide, Satanic leaven within Christendom. Deluded Christians are actually enabling Satan to set up his kingdom on earth through their generous donations and support.

This dangerous movement is an integral part of the "shepherding" (discipling) fellowships and house churches. It presents a New World view. Their basis is the false teaching that man must take dominion over the earth, subduing Christ's enemies (under the authority of the "apostles" and "prophets") for the purpose of presenting the newly-dominated world to Christ!

Kingdom Dominionists, in order to acquire a universal "Kingdom of God" on earth, must alter society and bring in biblical laws for the nations. This "reformation" is necessary in order to change man's habits of greed and violence (the Roman religio-political empire nearly achieved this in time gone by at the cost of thousands of lives of "dissenters" and so-called "heretics"). Today the "dissenters" and "heretics" would be, among others, those believers who refuse to accept these "doctrines of demons" and who refuse to come under the "covering" of the false "prophets" and "apostles."

The Apostle Peter wrote, "But there were false prophets also among the people, even as there shall be false teachers among you, who privily shall bring in damnable heresies, even denying the Lord that bought them, and bring upon themselves swift destruction" **(2 Peter 2:1)**. Concerning the kingdom dominion camp, they deny the Lord by their insistence that Jesus' sacrifice on the cross is not enough for our salvation; deny His Word by twisting it to conform to their heretical doctrines; deny prophesies of the end times, and deny that the Holy Spirit is sufficient to teach God's Word to God's people.

One of the ways these false teachers gain a foothold is through fair speeches and flattery! "Now I beseech you, brethren, mark them which cause divisions and offences contrary to the doctrine which ye have learned; and avoid them. For they that are such serve not our Lord Jesus Christ, but their own belly; and by good words and fair speeches deceive the hearts of the simple" **(Ro. 16:17)**. Daniel wrote that the Antichrist shall "obtain the kingdom by flatteries."

This kingdom system requires obedience to Law, and in this instance strict adherence to the Old Testament Law. However, the Bible clearly tells us that:

1) believers are saved by grace;

2) there is going to be a literal universal reign of terror through the Antichrist! It also tells us that before the Second Coming of Christ all nations will follow the satanic plans of the 'Beast' **(Rev. 13:3-4)**.

A careful study of the history, beliefs, and goals of the "Kingdom Theology" camp reveals a striking similarity to the Masons, Mormons, New Agers, Theosophists, Spiritualists, the Papacy, and other cults!

God's numerous promises to national Israel are one of the greatest obstacles to the objectives of both Satan and the kingdom dominion teachers. Therefore, in keeping with Satan's age-old animosity against Israel and his subtle ability to twist scripture, the Restoration leaders have to somehow convince their followers that God's promises recorded in the Old Testament to the nation of Israel now apply only to the Church (this is "Replacement Theology," see **Jer. 31:35-37**, etc.). The Word of God is clear that national Israel and the Church are two distinct entities! Israel has been promised an earthly kingdom; the Church looks for a heavenly kingdom.

Some of the other heretical and unbiblical teachings of the Restoration leaders are:

1) the removal (from believers) of awareness of the literal, visible, bodily return of the Lord with His saints to defeat the armies of the Antichrist at the battle of Armageddon, and set up His rule on earth;
2) denial of scriptural prophesies of the end-times;
3) denial of the sovereignty of the Godhead;
4) requirement of religious unity at the expense of truth and sound doctrine;
5) dependency on human ability and wisdom instead of the wisdom and power of the Holy Spirit;
6) the requirement of a structured church system based on human leadership which must be unquestionably submitted to (rather than Christ);
7) replacement of Jesus with the church who now has the power to kill all who do not bow down to her.

The "Kingdom Dominion" leaders have another agenda rather than obedience to Christ.

These false workers demand that their followers strictly obey God's laws, yet they themselves hypocritically ignore Jesus' command, "Go ye into all the world, and preach the gospel to every creature." **(Mark 16:15)**.

Oswald Chambers wrote, "The gospel is too profound for the lazy public; too positive for discursive thinkers. We have no right to preach unless we present the gospel; we have not to advocate a cause or a creed or an experience but to present the gospel, and we cannot do that unless we have a personal testimony based on the gospel. That is why so many preach what is merely the outcome of a higher form of culture. . . . Our obligation to the gospel is to preach it" (From *Approved Unto God*).

"Kingdom Theology" is intertwined with the other aforementioned "theologies" as well as current so-called revivals such as Brownsville and Toronto. The roots of these movements can be traced back through the twisted and musty corridors of time to Babylonian mysticism, illuminism, gnosticism, and esoteric mystery religions and lodges. And, through it all Satan has left his fingerprints.

To quote from a tract by Tricia Tillin of Banner Ministry:

> What we know today as restoration doctrine is a hybrid of Roman dominionism, liberal a-millennialism, post-millennial eschatology, and latter-rain doctrines. Many have discovered from bitter experience in restoration fellowships that behind the smiling faces, camaraderie, loving embraces and victorious praise, there lies a spirit of dominion that will wound and crush any who do not toe the line. An empire-building, self-seeking arrogance pervades much of the Restoration leadership, and they have proven themselves closed to correction.

Every false religion, belief, cult, "Christian guru" or leader must somehow ensure that their adherents check in their brains at the door. They must instill enough fear and guilt along with a substantial amount of brainwashing to guard against being questioned. What better way than to use scripture out of context to silence any opposition? After all, the Deceiver has used scripture for centuries, (along with half-truths and lies, of course) and it's always worked successfully for him.

The bottom line is, in order to establish this "kingdom" or "restore"`the church or the "old order" (meaning the "doctrine once delivered to the saints" **(Jude 3)**, must be undermined and destroyed.) Manifest Son of God leader Bill Hamon calls this "The Third Apostolic Reformation." He states, "We are being positioned to lay new foundations for a new era all together, foundations for the dawning of a new kingdom age. We are in the throes of the birthing of a whole new order--a whole new dispensation!"

This "new dispensation" will allow the church to exercise her "ministry of judgment" meaning the power to destroy (kill) all enemies (people who may hold to another view of Christianity!) They often cite the incident in **Acts 5** of Peter and Ananias and Sapphira, or Paul with Elymas the magician.

Those who dare question these "kingdom" leaders are accused of breaking God's commandment not to "touch God's anointed."

The scriptural admonition to "touch not God's anointed" has nothing whatsoever to do with exposing false prophets, heretics, and other opponents to the true Gospel! Rather, this Old Testament scripture simply warned the people that they were not to literally kill those who had been anointed with oil in any one of the three offices of priest, prophet, or king. This is why King David stayed his sword from King Saul.

To teach God's people that they are never to speak out against heretical teachers and/or or expose them is to go against scriptural examples and admonitions. We are commanded to test the spirit **(1 John 4:1)**; commanded to "earnestly contend for the faith once delivered unto the saints" **(Jude 3)**; commanded to "mark them which cause divisions and offences contrary to the doctrine which ye have learned; and avoid them" **(Ro. 16:17)**. The Apostle Paul publicly withstood Peter and he also named others (by name) that were contrary to the faith (see **2 Tim. 4:10, 14, 15; 2 Tim. 3:8**).

Christians need to wake up! What is taking place all over the world today is not God's "new thing," but rather, Satan's "old thing."

This danger is two-pronged:

1) delusion.

2) actual bloodshed.

Delusion is Satan's most powerful weapon. Because mankind has been given the power of free will, Satan knows he must delude people into choosing for him and against God through deception. Once a person has made a conscious decision to buy a lie, or half-truth, this gives place to the enemy to work undetected in destroying whatever foundations that person has in Christ. Scary, isn't it?

The danger is summed up in this verse, "There is a way that seemeth right to a man, but the end thereof are the ways of death" **(Proverbs 16:25)**. How can Christians avoid deception and/or delusion?

First of all, by recognizing that they can be deceived! Any person who thinks they cannot be deceived is deceived already.

Secondly, by asking the Holy Spirit to reveal the truth as you study God's Word. And, I mean STUDY.

Third, learn to recognize the difference between feeding your mind and feeding your spirit! If you study to feed your mind with facts, then remember "knowledge puffs up." Rather, study to nourish your spirit to receive a greater revelation of the living Christ.

Fourth, you must ask God to give you a love for the truth **(2 Thes. 2:10)**, regardless of the cost to your pride and conceit.

Fifth, do not be ignorant of Satan's devices; remember that whenever Satan is involved, there will be confusion, bondage, depression, strife, discontent, pride, fear, condemnation, and guilt.

Sixth, never allow another to think for you and/or make decisions for you. Go to God for yourself! Jesus must be your only Mediator and Great High Priest! (Read **Heb. 2:17, 18; 4:9-16; 8:6; 9:15; 12:24; 1 Tim. 2:5**).

In conclusion, be diligent, watchful, and alert. Compare scripture with scripture. Never assume that because someone tells you he or she is from God that he or she knows the real Jesus (be wise and ask for references!) "For there are certain men crept in unawares, who were before of old ordained to this condemnation, ungodly men, turning the grace of our God into lasciviousness, and denying the only Lord God, and our Lord Jesus Christ" **(Jude 4)**.

Be joyful in the hope of our Lord's returning to set up His kingdom knowing that, "God shall wipe away all tears from their eyes; and there shall be no more death, neither sorrow, nor crying, neither shall there be any more pain: for the former things are passed away" **(Rev. 21:4)**. Amen!

Has He Taken His Rightful Place?

(Excerpt from Sermon)

Rayola Kelley

Please turn to **Revelation 3:20-22**: "Behold, I stand at the door, and knock; and if any man hear my voice, and open the door, I will come into him, and will sup with him, and he with me. To him that overcometh will I grant to sit with me in my throne, even as I also overcame, and am set down with my Father in his throne. He that hath an ear, let him hear what the Spirit saith unto the churches."

Today we are celebrating Palm Sunday. I am sure that most of us know what Palm Sunday is all about. Jesus rode into Jerusalem on the back of a donkey as king. It not only confirmed He was the Messiah, but it was a fulfillment of prophecy found in **Zechariah 9:9**. While He was riding on this donkey the Jewish people honored him as their king. In fact, they were laying down Palm branches and their coats. In a way it would be like a red carpet treatment in our day. They were declaring Him to be the long awaited Messiah, who would be their king. They perceived that since He was the Messiah, He was the one who would deliver them from the oppression of the Roman Empire.

Acknowledging Him as king was wonderful, but down the line they would actually reject Him as king. This would happen a couple of days after He was honored as king. The question is why did they reject Him? One minute they acknowledged Him, and the next minute they were rejecting Him. They rejected Him because they expected an earthly king not a heavenly king. They expected a king that would immediately take possession of His earthly throne. They also rejected Him because they had their own agenda as to what they thought the Messiah would do for them.

The reason they had their own agenda is because they had roots that were attached to the world and not God. When we have a worldly agenda, we are going to define everything based on worldly concepts. Ultimately, such concepts will reject the spiritual. These individuals were also on the wrong foundation. They already rejected Jesus as king years before. You might ask how this was possible.

Consider what happened in **1 Samuel 8:7**. God is talking to Samuel, "...Hearken unto the voice of the people in all that they say unto thee; for they have not rejected thee, but they have rejected me, that I should not reign over them." The children of Israel had already rejected their true king years before Jesus walked on the scene as man. They rejected their king's reign in their life in preference of an earthly king.

The real issue is not whether Jesus was king for He was, but whether people would allow Him to reign as their personal king. That is the real issue today. Jesus came to Israel offering a different kingdom and a different type of reign. He did not come at that time to rule over a nation, but to rule over individual hearts. This is very important to understand. And, out of His reign would come salvation in people's lives.

The criteria that Jesus actually held caused the people of Israel to not only miss their Messiah, but they ended up crucifying Him. **John 1:11** says, "He came unto his own and his own received him not." To "not receive" in this scripture means the failure to associate with oneself in the familiar fashion. The people may have recognized Jesus as king, but they would not allow Him to take His rightful position in their personal lives.

It says in **John 19:15b**. "...Pilate said unto them, shall I crucify your King?..." Even Pilate recognized Jesus as king of the Jews. He also acknowledged Jesus' kingdom was not any threat to the Roman kingdom. Jesus had acknowledged so in **John 18:36**.

Consider the response from the religious leader, "Then, the chief priest answered, ...We have no king but Caesar" **(John 19:15c)**. The Jewish people still preferred an earthly king even if it was a king of a foreign government that was oppressive, rather than accept a heavenly king that would rule from the very throne of their hearts.

Christians are making the same mistake with Jesus as the Jews did centuries ago. We are also failing to let Jesus take His rightful place in our lives. And, this is why much of the Church is in the condition it is in today.

What position does Jesus hold in your life? Usually when I ask people about their life with Christ, they give me a testimony of their church. When I ask them, what position does Christ hold in their lives, they are quick to say, "He is my Savior." He's my Savior as well. In fact, I have acknowledged Him as such when I came to the cross of Christ to resolve the issue of sin and my eternal destination. It was then that I received Jesus as my personal Savior. Can you say that? Since Jesus is my personal Savior, you can conclude that I am saved. How many of you can agree with this evaluation?

Just because you consider Jesus as your Savior does not mean you are saved. Please hear my heart today because I have a very important message to the Church, its leaders, and those who call themselves Christians. Much of what the Church is preaching today is a watered-down gospel. As a result, many in the Christian realm do not really understand what it means to be saved. They don't understand the heart of the Gospel.

I have accepted this watered-down gospel. In fact, I preached it because I didn't know better. I am not saying that you are not saved today. You could have come this route, and very well be saved. However, it is important to make sure you understand the pure Gospel so that you can help others to understand what it means to truly experience salvation.

Over the years God has helped me realize what lies at the heart of salvation. What lies at the heart of salvation is not just deliverance. Now, remember what the Jews were looking for they were looking for deliverance. However, this is not why Jesus came. Deliverance is a product of salvation, but it does not lie at the heart of salvation.

Today many people are looking for deliverance. And, as a result they look amiss like the Jews did. The real issue with the people of Israel was not just acknowledging Jesus as King. Rather, would they allow Jesus to take His rightful place in their personal lives? That was the real issue then and it's a real issue today. When Jesus takes His rightful place in your life, you can then be assured of salvation.

The position of Savior is one of deliverance not one of authority. As Savior, Jesus has no say over our lives. This is why many people are comfortable with Jesus as Savior. As Savior He is simply going to deliver you and not bring you to points of decisions of self-denial. Granted, as Savior Jesus delivers us from the consequences of sin, but there is so much more to Him.

Let's consider the following popular scriptures. "For whosoever shall call upon the name of the Lord shall be saved" **(Romans 10:13)**. This declaration is also found in **Acts 16:30-31**. "And brought them out, and said, Sirs, what must I do to be saved? And they said, Believe on the Lord Jesus Christ, and thou shalt be saved, and thy house." This concept is found in **Romans 6:23** the last part of it. "But the gift of God is eternal life through Jesus Christ our Savior." Did I quote this correctly? If you were going along with me, you would have hit a sour note. What does **Romans 6:23** really say? It says, "...the gift of God is eternal life through Jesus Christ our Lord." The title or term here is not Savior, but Lord.

Romans 10:9 and **10** shows us the criteria of being saved. There are two requirements to be saved. We fail to explain them because we don't understand them. We skip over them. So here are the two criteria of what it means to be saved today. "That it thou shall confess with thy mouth the Lord Jesus", there is a confession that has to take place with the mouth. "And thou shall believe in thy heart that God has raised him from the dead." In other words, you believe in your heart the Gospel message, which is that you are a sinner, that Christ died for you, He was buried, and He rose again. Such a realization is not a mental assent; rather, it is a heart revelation. It is a heart that grasps the reality of Christ by faith. Once it becomes a reality, it will change your heart.

If you don't grasp the Gospel at the point of the heart, your heart will never change to reflect the salvation that has been wrought on the cross. Without a heart change, there will be no change in attitude or conduct. The Scripture in **Romans** states, "that thou shalt be saved." If you believe God raised Him from the dead, you shall be saved.

Paul explains why you will be saved, "For with the heart man believeth unto righteousness". If your heart is right before God, you are going to live and walk a life that is upright before him. It goes on to say, "and with the mouth confession is made unto salvation."

The heart has to do with your life, but confession has to do with assuring salvation. Did you note that the common factor in all these scriptures that I read besides the theme of salvation? It is the term "Lord". Clearly, Jesus is referred to not as Savior, but as Lord. Lord is a position of authority and rule. It is more than a matter of acknowledging that Jesus is Lord. How many of you are acknowledging this very fact today?

Philippians 2:10 tells us that every knee will bow. **Verse 11** goes on to say, "And that every tongue should confess that Jesus Christ is Lord, to the glory of God, the Father." Everyone is going to come to a point where he or she will acknowledge that Jesus is Lord. Every atheist, unbeliever, demon, and entity are going to bow their knees, and they are going to proclaim that Jesus is Lord.

Confession is different than acknowledging. Confession has to do with possessing a willful agreement, while acknowledgement can be noticing or recognizing something, but being able to remain indifferent to it on a personal level. In **Philippians 2:11** everyone will willfully agree that Jesus is Lord. However, this will not save them. Their confession will be for the glory of the Father. The real issue of salvation is that Jesus must become a person's personal Lord. It wasn't enough for the Jewish people to acknowledge that Jesus was king, he had to become their personal king.

There is a difference between the positions king and lord, which must be distinguished. Kings rule nations, but lords rule individuals. Kings have subjects and lords have servants.

Kings can put demands on their subjects, but lords have actual rights over their servants. Kings can demand and possess loyalty from subjects, but Lords actually own their servants.

There is more of an intimate relationship between Lord and servant than king and subject. Jesus was being presented to the Jews as their king, Messiah, and ruler of their nation. It is different for Christians. Jesus is strictly presented as Lord. Let us bring this down to layman's terms. **John 1:12** says, "But as many as received him, to them gave he power to become the sons of God, even to them that believe on his name." What name must we believe upon? You will constantly read it in Paul's epistles. The name we must constantly believe upon is the Lord Jesus Christ. We must receive him as Lord, not as Savior. Granted, we recognize or acknowledge Him as Savior. When you consider **Isaiah 45:21** you will see as Lord, Jesus is our Savior and King. If Jesus is just your Savior, He most likely is not reigning as your king and ruling over your life as Lord.

The greatest tragedy about mankind is not that we are bad, but that we fall short of the glory of God. **Romans 3:23** says, "For all have sinned and come short of the glory of God." It doesn't say we come short of not living right, of not doing it right, or of not feeling correctly about things. It says that we have come short of the glory of God. In other words, each of us falls short of our potential of the majesty and greatness of God in our lives.

When Adam was formed in the Garden, he was formed to serve as the reflection of God's glory. When he rebelled against God, sin marred that reflection, causing man to fall short of what he was designated for. We are now in a fallen condition of sin, hindered from reflecting God's glory.

The only thing that can bring us back to becoming a reflection of God's glory is the Lordship of Jesus. You cannot get yourself to the place where you will reflect God's glory. God can only be glorified when Jesus takes his rightful place as our personal Lord **(Philippians 2:11)**. It's vital to understand why Jesus must become Lord of our lives.

You are a servant of something. Receiving Jesus as Savior does not deal with what or whom you are serving. It may result in some type of deliverance, but it doesn't deal with the issue of your master. You can acknowledge Jesus as Savior, and still be serving the wrong masters of sin, self, Satan, and the world. If you are serving any of these wrong masters, you will make a mockery out of Jesus' death and deliverance.

Obviously, your master must change for salvation to be realized. If you serve the wrong lord and master, then you must repent and change your lord and master to be assured of salvation. Lordship means you do not belong to yourself, you belong to someone else. The lord you serve will determine the rights you have.

If you are under Satan today, you are also under the dictates of self and the world. If you are serving Satan, you may have freedom to live as you choose, but the only right you are securing for yourself in the future is the assurance of going to hell. If you are under the Lordship of Christ, you will serve God, giving you the right to become sons of God. In your walk, you will be prepared to go to heaven.

In Jesus' day people understood lordship. When they said, "lord" they knew what it meant. But, we in America have a limited understanding of this term. This is why the Lordship of Jesus is so often missing in our presentation of the Gospel. How do I explain lordship to self-centered arrogant people who basically want to do their own thing? How many of those self-centered people are going to say, "I don't want Christ because I want to be able to do my own thing and still get to heaven?" Clearly, this watered-down presentation is doing a grave disservice to people. It's easy for people to come to a loving Savior, but not a committed Lord. It's easy to come to Jesus as Savior for the benefits since there is no cost for it. After all, the Lordship of Jesus is going to cost you. You will have to die to your rights as you abandon the claims of the world.

If you fall in love with him enough, you will become a bondservant. A bondservant is someone who abandons everything for his or her master out of love. Obviously, we have done a grave disservice to the Gospel of Jesus Christ by not explaining that it is all about the Lordship of Christ in our lives. It's about changing masters so the heart can change. It's about changing our walk so that we can display the glory of God. That's what it is about, and it's missing today from the Gospel.

In **Revelation 3:20** Jesus is standing outside the door knocking. Is He knocking on the doors of the unsaved? No, he is knocking on the churches that have called upon His name. Do you know why? These churches had actually put Jesus outside of their church doors as Ruler. He is knocking at that door saying, "Hey, you have to let me back in as Lord, and allow me to call the shots." The Lordship of Jesus was replaced with pious works. Among the different bodies, His reign had been replaced with idols, His ways with paganism, His life with dead religion, and His light with delusion and darkness.

Read about the churches in **Revelation 2** and **3.** Clearly, His rule as Lord was replaced, neglected, or ignored. Sometimes Jesus is standing outside of the door, urgently knocking. At times He is wooing as He advises His people to hear what the Spirit is saying. He wants us to let Him come back in and take the preeminent place in our life. The reason Jesus stands outside of the door and knocks and contends with us is because He not only loves us, but He wants to avoid a certain conversation with us. We can find that conversation in **Matthew 7. Matthew 7:20** states, *"Wherefore by their fruits ye shall know them."*

The conversation follows the revelation about the fruit in **Matthew 7:21**. "Not everyone that saith unto me, Lord, Lord." Notice, these people didn't address Him as Savior, Savior, but they said Lord, Lord, "shall enter into the kingdom of heaven."

Our entering the kingdom of heaven hinges on the Lordship of Christ. If you are a Christian, your whole goal needs to be to make Jesus Lord of your life. The rest of **Matthew 7:21** states, "Not everyone that saith unto me Lord, Lord shall enter into the kingdom of heaven; but he that doeth the will of my Father, who is in heaven." What is the will of the Father? To make Jesus Lord. What does the Lordship of Jesus do? It will line you up to the will of the Father because Jesus did nothing outside the will of the Father.

Matthew 7:22 says, "Many will say to me in that day, Lord, Lord, have we not prophesied?" We see where people are arguing with Him about their spiritual status. It's hard to believe that people are going to be arguing with Him, but they are. How many people will end up arguing with Him because they missed coming to terms with Him on the basis of His Lordship?

This is the statement that He doesn't want to say to any of us. "And then will I profess unto them, I never knew you; depart from me, you that work iniquity" **(Matthew 7:23)**. Clearly, Jesus did not recognize these people because they were not truly serving Him. These people may have been doing great things in the name of the Lord Jesus Christ, but it was considered iniquity because they were doing it without any regard to His Lordship.

Are you making the same error as Israel did years ago? Oh, they acknowledged Jesus as king, but failed to let Him take His rightful place in their lives. Is He standing outside of your religious activities to gain entrance because you have left Him behind or put Him outside as Lord of your life? If He is not Lord of your life today, then rectify it beginning with repentance and confession. I don't want Jesus to have the conversation with you in **Matthew 7** that He did not know you. Is Jesus truly Lord of your life?

Prayer: Lord this is a simple message, but it is one that the Church has left behind in the midst of all of their entertainment, worship, and flag waving. How many of them really know You as Lord? How Your heart must be broken by the fact that the Church has watered down Your Gospel by leaving out people's need for You to be Lord of their lives. Lord, forgive us for presenting or buying a watered-down gospel. Stir up our hearts to present the pure gospel in such a powerful way that lives will be begin to change and bring glory to You. Thank You Lord. Thank You for your message. Thank You for Your Word. Thank You for Your truth, and I pray Lord that if somebody out there is playing the religious game, and You still are not Lord, that Your Spirit will contend and struggle with him or her until he or she opens the door and let You come in as Lord. We thank You, we praise You, and we say this in Your name. Amen.

Bibliography

Strong's Exhaustive Concordance of the Bible, World Bible Publishers

My Utmost for His Highest, Oswald Chambers, © 1935, Dodd, Mead & Company, Inc. Copyright renewed 1963 by Oswald Chambers Publications Association, Ltd.

Smith's Bible Dictionary, Thomas Nelson Publishers

Evangelism: A Biblical Approach, G. Michael Cocoris © 1984 by The Moody Bible Institute of Chicago

The Master Plan of Evangelism © 1993 by Robert E. Coleman

Webster's New Collegiate Dictionary © 1976 by G & C Merriam Co.

The American Heritage Dictionary, © 1982 by Houghton Mifflin Company

The New Scofield Reference Bible, © 1967 by Oxford University Press, Inc.

Still Higher for His Highest, Oswald Chambers, © D. W. Lambert 1970

Romans, H. A. Ironside, 25th Printing, November 1982

Vine's Expository Dictionary of Biblical Words; © 1985 by Thomas Nelson Inc., Publishers

Dake's Annotated Reference Bible; © 1963 by Finis Jennings Dake

The Complete Word Study Dictionary, AMG Publishers, Chattanooga, TN; Spiros Zodhiates

New Wine or Old Deception, Roger Oakland, © 1995 by The Word For Today

Occult Invasion, Dave Hunt, © 1998; Harvest House Publishers

Approved Unto God, Oswald Chambers, © 1997; Oswald Chambers Publications Association

Jewish Faith and the New Covenant, Ruth Specter Lascelle, © l980

A Gardener Looks at the Fruits; W. Phillip Keller; © l986

The Gifts of the Spirit; Harold Horton, 1934.

Other books by Rayola Kelley:

Hidden Manna (Original)
Battle for the Soul
Stories of the Heart
Transforming Love & Beyond
The Great Debate
Post to Post: (1) Establishing the Way
Post to Post: (2) Walking in the Way
Post to Post: (3) Meditations Along the Way

Volume One: Establishing Our Life in Christ
My Words are Spirit and Life
The Anatomy of Sin
The Principles of the Abundant Life
The Place of Covenant
Unmasking the Cult Mentality

Volume Two: Putting on the Life of Christ
He Actually Thought it Not Robbery
Revelation of the Cross
In Search of Real Faith
Think on These Things
Follow the Pattern

Volume Three: Developing a Godly Environment
Godly Discipline
Prayer and Worship
Don't Touch That Dial
Face of Thankfulness
ABC's of Christianity

Volume Four: Issues of the Heart
Hidden Manna (Revised)
Bring Down the Sacred Cows
The Manual for the Single Christian Life
Parents are People Too

Volume Five: Challenging the Christian Life
The Issues of Life
Presentation of the Gospel
For the Purpose of Edification
Whatever Happened to the Church?
Women's Place in the Kingdom of God

Volume Six: Developing Our Christian Life
The Many Faces of Christianity
Possessing Our Souls
Experiencing the Christian Life
The Power of Our Testimonies
The Victorious Journey

Volume Seven: Discovering True Ministry
From Prisons and Dots to Christianity
So You Want To Be In Ministry

Devotions
Devotions of the Heart: Books One and Two
Daily Food for the Soul: Books One and Two

Gentle Shepherd Ministries Devotion Series:
Being a Child of God
Disciplining the Strength of our Youth
Coming to Full Age

Nugget Books:
Nuggets From Heaven
More Nuggets From Heaven
Heavenly Gems
More Heavenly Gems
Heavenly Treasures

Gentle Shepherd Ministries Series:

The Christian Life Series
What Matter Is This?
The Challenge of It
The Reality of It
The Leadership Series
Overcoming
A Matter of Authority and Power
The Dynamics of True Leadership

Other Books By:
Jeannette Haley

Books co-authored with Rayola Kelley:
Hidden Manna (original)
The Many Faces of Christianity (Volume 6)
Post to Post 3: Meditations Along the Way

Other Books:
Interview In Hell (Volume 7)
Interview On Earth (Volume 7)
Rose of Light, Thorn of Darkness (Volume 7)
The Pig and I
Reflections of Wonder (Devotional)

Children's Books:
Little Stories for Little People
Traveler's Tales
The Adventures of Zack and Mira
The Adventures of Paul and Dana
(A House on the Beach)
The Monster of Mystery Valley

www.ingramcontent.com/pod-product-compliance
Lightning Source LLC
LaVergne TN
LVHW060635110826
845147LV00018B/989

* 9 7 8 1 7 3 4 7 5 0 3 9 3 *